S0-BCW-148

STUDIES IN CULTURE & COMMUNICATION

Martin S. Dworkin, General Editor

The series is devoted to education in its most comprehensive meaning, embracing the activities of formal instruction and learning carried on in schools, and all the forces of social influence upon the development and behavior of individuals and groups. Drawing upon a broad range of literatures, in many languages, the series presents new and rediscovered works, focusing closely on critical studies of the arts, educational implications of courses of thought and behavior, and tactics and instruments of profession and persuasion. No partiality of doctrine or expression is intended or imposed, the selections following a sovereign purpose to stimulate and inform the continuing critique of ideas, values, and modes of communication that is the growing tissue of education, and perennial flowering of culture.

MODERN AESTHETICS: AN HISTORICAL INTRODUCTION
The Earl of Listowel

JEFFERSONIANISM AND THE AMERICAN NOVEL
Howard Mumford Jones

THE RISE OF THE AMERICAN FILM: A CRITICAL HISTORY
With An Essay
EXPERIMENTAL CINEMA IN AMERICA 1921–1947
Lewis Jacobs

MAN AND HIS CIRCUMSTANCES: ORTEGA AS EDUCATOR
Robert McClintock

GRAHAM GREENE: THE FILMS OF HIS FICTION
Gene D. Phillips, S.J.

THE COMPOUND CINEMA:
THE FILM WRITINGS OF HARRY ALAN POTAMKIN
Selected, Arranged, and Introduced
by Lewis Jacobs

Harry Alan Potamkin
Photo: Irving Lerner

STUDIES IN CULTURE
& COMMUNICATION

THE COMPOUND CINEMA

THE FILM WRITINGS OF HARRY ALAN POTAMKIN

Selected, Arranged, and Introduced
by

LEWIS JACOBS

TEACHERS COLLEGE PRESS

Teachers College, Columbia University
New York and London

Grateful acknowledgment is made to the proprietors of the following publications for use of copyrighted material which appears in this book: *American Cinematographer, American Photography, The Arts, Billboard, The Boston Advertiser, The Boston Transcript, Cinema, Close Up, Creative Art, Experimental Cinema, Films, Film Weekly, Front, Hound and Horn, Liberator, Modern Thinker and Author's Review, Movie Makers, Musical Quarterly, The National Board of Review Magazine, New Freeman, New Masses, The New Republic, New Theater, New World Monthly, The New York Herald Tribune, Pagany, Révue du Cinéma, The Theater Guild Magazine, Transition, Vanity Fair, Workers' Theater, Behold America, International Pamphlets.*

Picture Credits: Museum of Modern Art Film Library; Irving Lerner; Artkino; Lewis Jacobs collection.

Library of Congress Cataloging in Publication Data

Potamkin, Harry Alan, 1900–1933.
The compound cinema.

(Studies in culture & communication)
Includes bibliographical references and indexes.
1. Moving-pictures—Collected works. I. Jacobs, Lewis. II. Title. III. Series.
PN1994.P657 1977 791.43 76-55401
ISBN 0-8077-1559-X

Manufactured in the United States of America

FOR
ELIZABETH

CONTENTS

ILLUSTRATIONS

Following page 274

23. Howard Hawks' *Scarface* (1932)
24. Michael Curtiz's *Cabin in the Cotton* (1932)
25. Cecil B. DeMille's *This Day and Age* (1933)
26. James Cruze's *Washington Merry-Go-Round* (1932)
27. Rowland Brown's *Blood Money* (1933)
28. William Wellman's *Wild Boys of the Road* (1933)
29. Cecil B. DeMille's *This Day and Age* (1933)

CRITICISM AND IDEOLOGY: A NOTE ON CINEMA

Partisan cultural criticism does not originate in the nineteenth or twentieth centuries, any more than does the idea that works of art must primarily serve purposes that are desirable, according to some canonic prescription. It is no surprise, then, that moralists – religious, educational, and political – are among the first to take seriously, pro and con, the "magic shadows" of the cinema, applying measures of intended meaning and potential consequence even prior to those of aesthetic value and merit as entertainment. Indeed, there are elements in the nature of cinema itself that from the outset compel such standards on the part of those so concerned. Here is something that seemed no more than a toy to its originators, that immediately developed such popular appeal, that society itself began to be transformed, from the secret depths of imagination of individuals to the innumerably complex structures of action wherein our lives are lived. There may be no clearer signal of awareness of what was happening than the response of the clergy, even before the turn of the century.

In the late 1890s, while some priests and ministers railed against the sinfulness, actual and possible, of what was beginning to go on in the movie theaters, on screen and off, others hailed the manifestly immense power of the new medium as a blessing, and carried films of Bible reënactments, moral uplift, and instruction on missionary forays into areas remote from the cultural advantages of cities. In the latter, it was even more apparent that motion pictures were particularly suited to the entertainment, and what social scientists would come to call the "socialization" of the urban population, which included ever growing numbers of people uprooted from their native institutions: migrants from the changing rural heartland of America, and immigrants from the towering Babel of nations and cultures of the world abroad.

While the intelligentsia – those worthies aware of their advanced education and superior literacy – except for a few educators largely disdained the new medium and all its works, there were clergymen who showed prescient understanding of what was recreating the spirit of the people, even as it altered their habits and occasions of communal living. In an early broadside – ignored by film historians and to this day inexcusably unknown – one minister of a Congregational church in Connecticut, Herbert A. Jump, proselytized for the incorporation of films in the liturgy, in order to confront the challenges to religion of the godless cities, and to make a new, powerful "appeal to the unchurched." Written in 1910, his language displays considerable sophistication about tactics of propaganda, shrewdly building on acceptance of the rhetorical and graphic arts by the faithful, won in recurring battles against the seductions of idolatry – and may be seen as authentically prophetic in other ways:

> We men and women who have ever shown interest in pictures, hanging them on the walls of our homes, seeking them in illustrated books and now in picture-postcards, should turn naturally to the motion picture sermon which puts the gospel in a pictorial form. Some of you who attend church love the doctrinal phraseology of St. Paul. There is many a hardheaded American working man, however, who confesses freely that to him St. Paul is only a prosy old theologian. Paul, however, was not a prosy theologian to the men of his day. Why not? Because his illustrations for the gospel were taken from the life of his contemporaries – the racing habits of his day, for example, and the boxing matches. We ministers of today may not quite dare follow Paul in illustrating spiritual truth from the trotting park or a recent famous prize fight in a western city, but we have a right to use stories taken from life in the shop and factory and on the street as illustrations of the gospel to the men of today. Because the motion picture carefully selected will tell to the eye moral truths with vigor of illustration and an eloquence of impression which the most enthusiastic orator cannot command, it has a proper place in the equipment of any church which is trying to reach the masses.[1]

[1] Herbert A. Jump, *The Religious Possibilities of the Motion Picture.* New Britain, Connecticut: Printed for private distribution, December, 1910; p. 8.

Not only the sense of the cinema as the "people's art," but as the modern rhetoric whereby to convey *the* (i.e., any correct) gospel, would be echoed by devout audio-visualists of all persuasions, religious, educational, and political, for the following sixty years and more – with appropriate emendations to acknowledge and promote the variant, yet related powers of television. Especially remarkable here, however, are the overtones of social and political awareness, hinting the ideological proselytization of the people, by the cinema, and for a new order, that was to come. With minimal alteration, the minister's language could be taken for pure Communist *prolet-kult* of a decade later – or, with suitable *Völkisch* and Nazi coloration, for good cheerleading of the *Reichsministerium für Volksaufklärung und Propaganda,* a few years later on.

The problems of critical thinking converging here are among the oldest, profoundest, and most persistently controversial in the history of ideas. In their educational phase, for only one, they involve the very definitions of intelligence, intellect, and their relationship to feelings and insight that divide teachers, and teachers of teachers, at least since Democritus and Socrates. For the latter, indeed, the persuasive powers of the arts in general and pictures in particular are so attuned to the emotions, and so implicated in what is later called "propaganda," that they must be brought under control of only those committed to and trained for the search for truth and the life of moral and political justice.

That pictures (and carvings) can falsify and mislead would probably have only corroborated the palaeolithic hunter-shamans of the Dordogne and Altamira, tens of thousands of years ago, in insisting on fidelity to the ritualized images and usages, which, it is a good guess, were held essential to the prosperity and even existence of the groups they served. To recognize that images can lie, and, if wrong or evil, actually harm the mind and spirit of man, is one way to acknowledge their potency, in moral and educational terms – an act of discrimination the more necessary whenever, as typically happens in periods of "enlightenment" and cultural change, there has been extravagation of the rhetoric of advocates of the image arts as persuasive force. It is with much wisdom, responsibility to the enterprise of teaching, and not inconsiderable wit, for example, that so famous a creator and theoretician of the art of film for education as Jean Benoît-Lévy recalls an earlier epoch of romantic claims for the graphic arts in furthering enlightenment, turning to one of Goethe's "domestic (table-talk?) epigrams" from *Zahme Xenien*:

> Many stupid things are often said,
> As well as written,

They do not kill the flesh or soul,
Nor any change effect.
But something stupid offered to the eye
Exerts a magic force:
Because it chains the senses
The mind remains a slave.[2]

For one who would think freely, enabled to give considered, arguable reasons for judgment, and who would encourage and inform the freedom of thought of others, here is the fundamental issue regarding the appeal and effects of the arts, particularly those of created images. Concern for purposes and outcomes haunts all discourse about the arts, since men first distinguished them, in thinking, from their actual pervasion of all human doing and making. Even to proclaim, as does Paul Valéry, that "the most evident characteristic of a *work of art* may be termed *uselessness* . . . ,"[3] becomes less an apology for Art-for-Art's-Sake extremism than a plea for validity of a notion of human sensibility beyond the demands of survival, of immediate utility carried to its ultimate requirement. The new media of industrial society, themselves expressing and furthering the immense social and political convulsions of the modern epoch, impose new meanings on critical terminology, however, restating purposive considerations of the arts in ways that intensify the difficulties for freedom of judgment.

So much and so deeply does cinema, for the sovereign example, involve individuals in collective imagining, so fully are the prepared and projected visions of motion pictures interiorized and assimilated into the mind and spirit, that it is no wonder that religionists take them seriously at once. And it is no wonder, too, that the criticism of the cinema, in the years of political, social, and economic cataclysm and depression, following the World War of 1914–18, should turn so fervently ideological, appropriating the language of earlier religious concern and converting it to new dogmatic purposes. Indeed, it is essential to ideologues – of the "Left" as of the "Right" – claiming any legitimacy as spokesmen for the forever rising "masses" of the modern world, to establish critical authority,

[2] Quoted in Jean Benoît-Lévy, *The Art of the Motion Picture*. Translated by Theodore R. Jaeckel. New York: Coward-McCann, Inc., 1946. Reprinted in *The Literature of Cinema* series, New York: Arno Press and The New York Times, 1970; pp. 140–141.

[3] "The Idea of Art," in Paul Valéry, *Aesthetics*. Translated by Ralph Manheim. The Collected Works of Paul Valéry, Volume Thirteen. Bollingen Series XLV. New York: Pantheon Books, 1964; p. 71.

at the very least, over the cinema, as the most glamorous exemplar of mass-oriented, technologically-produced media.

Not only is there conscious effort, in Soviet Russia and Nazi Germany, to transmogrify traditional religious institutions and practices via the communal experience of cinema — a process occurring in other countries without deliberate maneuver, in the dynamic development of cultural popularization. The new totalitarianisms demand complete indoctrination, and the rôle of all the arts, and especially of those so fully involved in and expressive of the transformations of modern society, is ideologically defined and institutionalized. Ideology is made the measure of art, and artist and audience are seen as integrated in an organism, the total state, in such ways as to define the former as no less than the articulated spirit of the latter — and nothing more, all contrary and manifestly decadent notions of individuality being suppressed or safely sublimated.

If one may speak at all of cultural *criticism* in the totalitarian state, its rôle is necessarily defined as inflexibly as is that of the arts, the critic primarily performing a recognizably sacerdotal function as guide to doctrinal orthodoxy and official approval. Only in *their* decadence, or in carefully managed deviations from established policy, do totalitarian societies allow open difference of judgment and creation, when, for example, the "one hundred flowers" (and no more?), encouraged briefly, by Mao Tse-tung in the 1960s, may bloom, before being cut down or uprooted by the omnipresent gardeners. Significantly (and hinting what promise, or what despair?), it is that most hopeful Marxist, Ernst Fischer, discussing "The Spirit of Criticism" in the context of a fundamental opposition of art and ideology, who writes:

> Every ruling system desires stability and hates criticism, unless it is "constructive," i.e. not criticism at all but affirmation. Criticism of any single point is often interpreted as denial of the entire system, because dogmatic creeds will only tolerate an unconditional Yea or Nay. Yet the spirit of criticism inherent in marxism (*sic*) demands that marxism, too, should incessantly criticize itself. "I am not a marxist," said Marx — meaning that marxism denies itself when it ceases to question itself. The spirit of marxism must, in constant contradiction to the system, continue to be dynamic and encourage freedom of criticism, doubt, renewal.[4]

[4] "Coexistence and Ideology," in Ernst Fischer, *Art Against Ideology* (*Kunst und Koexistenz,* 1966). Translated by Anna Bostock. New York: George Braziller, 1969; p. 71.

". . . in constant contradiction to the system . . . !" "Marx" as distinguished from "Marxism" is not a new notion. But what kind of "Marxism" is Fischer claiming to be in the true spirit of Marx? Whether the ideas of Marx (and Engels) must necessarily be organized as ideology, Marx*ism,* and must when put into practice require a totalitarian government, may be the most controversial question of modern political science. Historically, however, there is no question, since Lenin, Stalin, and the incarnation of the idea of the "dictatorship of the proletariat" in the Soviet state – and in all its epigones, imitators, and rivals in ideological purity. Fischer's "marxist" (*sic*) call for art versus ideology, and its explicit argument for freedom of criticism, cannot itself be taken out of its context of events, their interrelations and consequences. As another critic, the Canadian George Woodcock, who has written sympathetically of George Orwell as "the critic within the movement towards a libertarian socialist world,"[5] puts it:

> We come back . . . to the dilemma of the Marxist critics, who cannot face the fact that Marxist regimes have always in practice suppressed both the spirit of revolt and the creativity born of social discontent about which they write. It is not only capitalism that has – as Marx taught – its inherent contradictions, and until such critics have faced honestly the contradiction that Communism displays in actuality, its presence will flaw their writing and impair their credibility.[6]

In the totalitarian states we have come to know so well, the ideological limitations imposed on the enterprise of criticism are the essential complement to the circumscriptions of behavior that enforce authority, at the same time as they afford communal identity, political and social belonging, to all under their *kadaverdisziplin.* To approach critically the ideas of ideology, or those judgments imposed ideologically on works of art, requires suspension of the coercions, intellectual, physical, and social, which are of the very nature of ideology as ideology, and of ideology in power. This is so, *a fortiori,* in considering the cultural manifestations of ideology, and especially those arts, again best exemplified by cinema, that are themselves factors of mass communication and social change.

[5] See his article, "Orwell: Imperial Socialist," *Mother Jones,* I (June, 1976) 4; p. 60.

[6] George Woodcock, "Marxist Critics," *The Sewanee Review,* LXXXIII (April–June, 1975) 2; p. 334.

In fine, it is how disagreement is regarded and treated that distinguishes reasoning, the endless seeking of philosophy for wisdom rather than any fixation of "truth," from ideology — just as what is done with dissidence measures the free society and the authoritarian. An art open to untrammeled criticism, implying all the indeterminacies of man's reasoning for himself, is no longer invulnerable as ideologically orthodox and therefore sacrosanct. An ideology open to criticism, to disagreement, is no longer ideology; an ideologue who is "in constant contradiction to the system" is no longer an ideologue — or is an anomaly, in a way recalling the "monster" we are asked to "imagine" by Armand in Gide's *The Counterfeiters:* "an imbecile intelligent enough to know that he is stupid." [7]

Thus it is of the very nature of critical reasoning that there is acknowledgment of and provision for disagreement [8] — an essentiality that actually empowers and even requires the reasoner to contend with the most dogmatic positions. With these, of course, he would probably disagree — or, if he did agree, it would necessarily be for *reasons,* and not only in accordance with dogmatic authority. And thus, it is without fear (if there is any) of subverting criticism — albeit with all requisite caution— that we may read, consider, and even enjoy and benefit from the most ideological critics, writing about the most deeply and broadly persuasive of the arts of modern mass society, the cinema, during the terrible years of the 1920s and '30s (or thereafter).

To do so calls for understanding of the times, but without the automatic exculpation sometimes argued on behalf of those who were driven, then, to go one way or another. Many intellectuals, shaken by the immense, sustained horror of the war of 1914–18, and in aggravated anger and despair over what were seen in the Depression as final failures of modern industrial society, and its economic and political institutions, were attracted to the doctrinal security of ideological systems — of the Right, it needs to be remembered, as well as of the Left — and their promise of revolutionary action and ultimate utopia. But many were not, often enough at the risk of social, economic, and other persecutions by the ideologues, self-righteous in their causes, and self-corroborated in their commitment to what they were certain was true religion.

This latter attitude, we are well to be warned, does not ease the en-

[7] André Gide, *The Counterfeiters.* Translated by Dorothy Bussy. (New York: Alfred A. Knopf, 1927). Modern Library edition, n.d.; p. 271.

[8] Implications of this argument for philosophy were suggested (all-too briefly!) by the writer in "Disagreement: The Situation of Reason," *The Scientific Monthly,* LXXV (August, 1952) 2; pp. 117–119.

counter with many of the critics of those times, which Harold Clurman has aptly called the "Fervent Years." There is much sanctimoniousness, out of conviction of their vocation as prophets for all humanity. And there frequently is an overweening confidence – one in accord with the characteristic pretension of ideologies to being exact, true "science" – that only *they* were truly reasoning, in applying the interior consistencies of their systems to judgment of the world, and all the films therein. Dogmatic assurance is hardly conducive to humility, nor (usually) is consciousness of one's own brilliance – as is nicely revealed in a letter, written in 1927, by perhaps the best, but unquestionably the most influential, of American ideologue film critics, Harry Alan Potamkin.

Denying, in effect, that his was only another personal opinion (about films), that he was just one more of those "critics whose criticism is a rationalization of their prejudices," Potamkin went on to assert his credentials as properly scientific, as well as artistic:

> You see, I boast of an historical sense and a grasp of realities, and being something of a poet, I have a tendency to see things whole. I guess I am sounding conceited. This would be alien to my intention, but I'll chance it.[9]

This "historical sense and grasp of realities" Potamkin credited fully to his acceptance of "Marxist philosophy" and its practical manifestation in "Communist ideology." [10] This estimate is corroborated in his work, especially of his last years, as may be observed in the definitive collection, *The Compound Cinema: The Film Writings of Harry Alan Potamkin,* presented by Lewis Jacobs. But what also comes across strongly – and may be more exasperating today than it was when he flourished – is a sense that there was much, much more to him than ideological exegesis and propaganda – enough to raise doubts, tentative and hopeful, that he would end as but one more of the "party men," those – of the Right or Left – Ortega y Gasset called "walking suicides."

Had he lived longer, through the ideological – and physical – wars that split the Left over the "realities" of Stalinist totalitarianism, would not so dedicated a *critic* have had to come away from the sentimental Bolshevism coloring so much of his writing? And beyond his critical

[9] Unpublished letter (1927) to Herman G. Weinberg, who graciously made it available to the writer.

[10] Unpublished letter to Eric Knight, 28 January 1933, in the collection of Lewis Jacobs.

vocation — or, perhaps, so deeply within as to inform everything he wrote — was there not simply too much ego? Would not his own "cult of personality," which was so essential to his critical apparatus of sensitivity and passionate articulation, have brought him into final conflict with the ideological priests and hatchet-men, as the Party line twisted and frayed in the tergiversations of Soviet policy of the late 1930s and afterwards?

These are speculations, to be sure, out of feelings for what was admirable in Potamkin's writing, and recognition of so much that was positive in his influence. Even what Potamkin waved as red flags in his film criticism were often also banners for serious, critical understanding of the arts in general and the cinema in particular — that is, given time sufficient for critical consideration, and the necessary condition of liberty. And this only points again to the fundamental issue of critical thinking as opposed to ideology.

For Potamkin to write the way he did, and for us to be able to read him, in agreement or not, in his own time as now, calls for an openness for argument and the publication of ideas that was, and is, impossible — or accidental and very rare, apart from secret, *samizdat* efforts — in the kind of society and political system for which he thought he was working. What this has to do with his artistic judgments is a question we must ponder, one that brings up many of the most difficult problems of philosophy, religion, and politics, concerning the nature of the arts and their function in the formation of consciousness, of thought itself. But that we are able to think and decide, applying criticism to the judgment of criticism, may itself be one kind of answer, and a considerable one.

New York City
July, 1976

MARTIN S. DWORKIN

PREFACE

The majority of the essays and reviews assembled in this book are relatively unknown today. The articles originally appeared in the late 1920s and early '30s in many diverse and often specialized publications. A large number originated in fugitive, obscure, and out of print magazines no longer available, difficult to find, and in the main neglected by periodical indexes. With the addition of several unpublished manuscripts, they have been brought together here in a single volume for the first time.

The title of this collection has been borrowed from an essay included in the book because it seemed to best characterize the dual critical approaches of the author and also suggested an organizational principle that offered a satisfactory arrangement for the contents. Accordingly, the selections have been placed in a framework of two major divisions and a miscellany under whose nine categories the material is arranged to impose a design upon the gathering which tacitly supports the author's critical obsessions and that of the age in which the work was written.

The preparation of the book has been greatly facilitated by the cooperation of a number of individuals who, by direct interview or by letter, generously responded to personal questions about Potamkin, and in several instances made available to me tattered copies of old magazines containing his articles. My greatest debt is to Mrs. Elizabeth Goldman (formerly Mrs. Potamkin), whose influence on this project has been pervasive and to whom I dedicate the book in gratitude. I want especially to thank Jay Leyda, Irving Lerner, and Harold Leonard for their laborious work in compiling and making available the bibliography of Potamkin's film writings, and for copies of a number of the author's early essays and reviews. I also want to thank I. Klein, Joel Zucker, and Edward S. Perry, former Chairman of the Department of Cinema Studies, New York University, and now Director, Department of Film, the Museum of Modern Art, for additional help in obtaining material and for their critical comments. I am deeply grateful to Martin S. Dworkin, for providing me with stimulating occasions for testing ideas, and for his painstaking editorial labors on behalf of the book. Finally, I owe a great debt to my wife for her unfailing interest in the project and steadfast moral support.

New York City LEWIS JACOBS

INTRODUCTION

"No other American critic," said the *National Board of Review Magazine* at Harry Alan Potamkin's untimely death in 1933, "was his equal in technical knowledge, in sensitiveness to the fine qualities of cinematic art, or in a profound feeling for the social significance of the motion picture and had the literary power to express what he knew and felt with an analytic vigor and eloquence that put him into the lead of film criticism."

Equally impressed, *The Nation* eulogized, "Potamkin revealed in his reviews and articles a familiarity with the motion picture, past and present as complete as to inspire the same implicit confidence in his authority as a Bernard Berenson writing on Florentine paintings, or a T. S. Eliot writing on Elizabethan poetry."

Hound and Horn's tribute went further: "It is safe to say he knew more about the art of film than any one in this country, and except for the great Russian directors who were his friends and admirers, as much as anyone in the world."

Despite such distinguished acclaim from his contemporaries, Potamkin's fame and work disappeared quickly into obscurity after his death. What had once been received with distinction, became a vague item to another generation. To present-day film students and scholars, the writings of Potamkin have remained largely unknown. Hardly anyone interested in film culture before the current inundation of paperback anthologies and filmographies seems to have heard of or read Potamkin's critical articles. There were some references to him in *The Film Index,* published in 1941, in Kracauer's *From Caligari to Hitler* (1947), and a few articles were resurrected for anthologies by this author and Stanley Kaufmann in the 1960s and early '70s. But Potamkin's name does not appear in any of the film encyclopedias, annuals, or other contemporary reference works that include a "Who's Who" of the film world. The magazines – once so lively and provocative, which had published Potamkin – were small in circulation, often specialized, short-lived, difficult to find and for the most part were ignored by periodical indexes. According to Irving Lerner and Jay Leyda – then young documentary film makers – who saw Potamkin frequently in the thirties, he considered writing a history of the American film. But he never lived long enough to get to it. After his death, scattered notes and ideas for lectures, together with selected portions of published and unpublished articles and reviews, were collated, edited, and arranged by Irving Lerner into a pamphlet called *The Eyes of the Movie*. Published posthumously in 1934 in a small edition, it soon vanished into the dead files of motion picture memorabilia.

I met Harry Alan Potamkin on three different occasions. Our first meeting took place in 1925 in Philadelphia, where we were both living. At that time neither of us was involved with motion pictures. I was an art student; Potamkin, older than I, was writing poetry, contributing to "little" magazines, and was preparing to launch a magazine of his own. A mutual acquaintance had suggested that I might design a cover for it. We talked it over, but nothing came of it.

My second meeting with Potamkin took place four years later in New York, where he was now living. By this time, both of us were preoccupied with movies. He had become a film critic of some note in intellectual circles. His contributions ranged over a wide spectrum of topics, written in numerous styles and published in a variety of periodicals of diverse literary and aesthetic standards. I was making "experimental" movies in Philadelphia and was about to launch a magazine to be called *Experimental Cinema* devoted to the film as an art and social force. I had come to New York to ask Potamkin for an article for the first issue, and to invite him to become the New York correspondent. He granted both requests, even though there were no funds to pay the contributors.

What was to be our last meeting occurred in New York in July 1933. By this time, I was working in a motion picture laboratory and "optical house," producing "trailers" for coming attractions for theaters, and in my spare time making documentaries concerned with problems of the Depression. For his combination of Marxist approach and cinematic insight, Potamkin had become internationally recognized as a film critic – an original and vital force in the burgeoning sphere of motion picture criticism. He was very ill and had been operated on for stomach ulcers at Bellevue Hospital. A frantic call had gone out to friends and acquaintances for additional blood that was needed for an emergency operation. When I arrived, I learned that he had already received five transfusions in the preceding month. This was to be the sixth. Of the more than twenty volunteers who appeared with me, only three had the required type of blood. I was not one of them.

My last remembrance of Potamkin was the paleness of his face and his effort to smile as we awkwardly tried to make polite conversation. The next morning, at age 33, he was dead.

The facts of Potamkin's life were fairly typical of intellectuals of the "lost generation" who in response to the turbulence of the depressed thirties arrived at revolutionary conclusions. Born in Philadelphia in 1900, he was the fourth child of a poor family that had emigrated from Russia; two more children were born after him. His father was a learned man who earned a meager living by peddling fish in the ghetto in which he lived. The future film critic, early aware of the ephemeral nature of security, spent his childhod and adolescence doing odd jobs throughout his school years and dreaming of becoming a poet. At the University of Pennsylvania he worked for his tuition and contributed poems to school periodicals. In 1922 he earned a modest and short-lived fame by writing a diatribe in verse against President Wilson which appeared in the *Liberator,* the successor to the old *Masses.* Because he could not pass a swimming test in a course at the University, he was not given a passing grade, and moved to New York. He completed his studies at New York University, taking a degree in Liberal Arts.

After graduation, Potamkin returned to Philadelphia, where he worked as a part-time social worker at the Smith Memorial Playground. There he directed the "Children's Play Village," an experimental enterprise in educational play for ghetto children, and started a newspaper for young people, *The Village Gazette,* for which he also wrote poetry and plays.

At this time (1922–26), poetry was Potamkin's dominant creative interest. A number of his poems appeared in such "little," *avant-garde* literary magazines as *Tambur, SFN* (Stands For Nothing), and *Transition.* He also edited and published eight issues of his own literary magazine, *The Guardian.* During this period he met Elizabeth Kleiman, who like himself was a social worker, employed by The American Friends Service Committee. According to her, their "dates" nearly always consisted of going to the movies, because "it was the only pastime we could afford." In 1925, they were married and the following year, using her savings, the couple went off to Europe on a delayed honeymoon, a trip that was to change entirely the direction of Potamkin's artistic drive.

Potamkin's visit abroad had a more important purpose than to tour monuments and cathedrals. As a practicing poet and editor he looked forward to meeting some of the young writers whose work he admired, and hoped to bring back manuscripts for his journal, *The Guardian*. In Paris he met Blaise Cendrars, Jules Romains, Joseph Delteil, and other emerging literary figures who were concerning themselves with movies as a new, central force in modern life. Their discussions of literature were filled with a passionate admiration of motion pictures. Their high regard for screen devices as an influence on writing techniques conveyed an acute interest in the medium as a new art form. Delteil's pronouncement, "The cinema is the pink pill of literature; it gives it blood and color," was a judgment of the "silver screen" not commonly heard among intellectuals at the time. Other members of the circle, André Breton, Robert Desnos, and Marcel L'Herbier, had begun to publish mini "cinéarios" in *The Nouvelle Revue Française,* while the journalist René Clair and the painters Fernand Léger and Man Ray had already made short avant-garde films with an intensity and earnestness that must have appeared most impressive to Potamkin. The enthusiasm for movies of such older writers as Appollinaire, Aragon, and Auriol gave the screen a luster and dignity the American had not expected. His imagination touched, he set out to see for himself what had generated such fervor.

The process of conversion from poet to film critic began with Potamkin's reading the film articles of Ricciotto Canudo, Louis Delluc, Jean Epstein, Germaine Dulac, and Marcel L'Herbier. Under the umbrella of Louis Delluc's aesthetic doctrine, "The French Cinema must be *cinema,*" which gave importance to what was new and held out promise of what art the cinema was capable of, the young writers and film makers appearing in *Cinéa, Ciné-Club, Paris Midi,* and *Les Nouvelles* drew Potamkin's attention to the beginning of an independent movement aimed at shaking the screen free from the traditional grip of theater and literature. What made the speculations and promulgations convincing to Potamkin was the vitality and freshness of the films they wrote about and which he saw at the time in the *Théâtre du Vieux Colombier, Studio des Ursulines,* and the various mini Ciné Clubs – forerunners of the future "art houses" that were to spring up in Europe and America in the next years — where he encountered for the first time a preponderance of startling movies from all parts of the continent. Their fresh vigor, technical bravura, psychological intensity, and high imagination exemplified the new developmental impulses and aesthetic doctrines just taking hold in European artistic circles. Represented were such distinguished film makers from France as Abel Gance, René Clair, Jean Epstein, and Carl Dreyer; from Germany: Fred Murnau, Fritz Lang, Arthur von Gerlach, and Carl Mayer; from Sweden: Victor Seastrom and Maurice Stiller; from Soviet Russia: Lev Kuleshov, Sergei Eisenstein, V. I. Pudovkin, and Dziga Vertov. The impact of this concentrated intellectual and artistic encounter proved overpowering. Potamkin's pressing regard for poetry, challenged by the new and evolving art of the screen, was threatened. Since childhood he had committed himself to the formal practice of poetry; that concern had made him a poet. Now suddenly he found himself hovering between the two arts: exhilarated by the power and potentiality of the screen; disquieted by a faltering concern for poetry, weighing the earlier compelling lure of literature with the sweeping excitement of the motion picture.

On his return to the United States, the implications of his increasing attraction to movies became clear in his searching examination of American films and film literature. While trying to make a living from freelance journalism — writing verse, stories, plays, and songs for children's periodicals, and an occasional poem for "little" magazines — he made it a point to see as many movies as he could afford and to read all the books and articles on motion pictures he could find. One group of books — *The Theater of Science* (Robert Grau), *Motion Picture Work* (David S. Hulfish), *The Morals of the Movies* (Ellis P. Oberholtzer), *When the Movies Were Young* (Linda Griffith), *Behind the Screen* (Samuel Goldwyn), *A Million and One Nights* (Terry Ramsaye), *The House That Shadows Built* (Will Irwin), and others — had little interest in film art and were quite unaware of the aesthetic imperatives of the Europeans. However, what Potamkin learned from them about the movies' history, techniques, entrepreneurs, shaping forces, personalities, vogues, folklore, and economic and sociological ties, provided him with an encyclopedic overview of motion picture progress and influence. His mind became "a mental cross-index of thousands of pictures" of all types and periods, of hundreds of film companies, players, directors, writers, and technicians — all of which threw a strong light on the attitudes, development, and pervasiveness of the film medium and its culture.

A second group of books and some isolated essays boldly challenged popular standards and values. *The Dramatic Picture Versus the Pictorial Drama* (Horace Kallen), *The Kinematograph as Art* (Alexander Bakshy), *The Art of the Moving Picture* (Vachel Lindsay), *The Art of Cineplastics* (Élie Faure), *The Photoplay* (Hugo Münsterberg), *The Soul of the Motion Picture* (Walter S. Bloom), *The Mind and the Film* (Gerald Fort Buckle), *Let's Go to the Movies* (Iris Barry), *The Vivifying of Space* (Herman Scheffauer) and *The New Theatre and Cinema of Soviet Russia* (Huntly Carter) brought him face to face with a body of diverse, impassioned insights into the physical, psychological, and aesthetic characteristics of film art and helped set off and shape his own aesthetic thinking and seeking.

The combined European and American experience – upon which he would soon call with confidence and compelling exposition – concluded Potamkin's formative film education. In the last months of 1926–27 his feeling for poetry was more and more subordinated, until it was finally superseded by the more urgent compulsion and challenge of motion pictures. Thereafter he was to become a partisan for a new art in the process of discovering itself, with a dedication and commitment that was to last until the end of his life.

Potamkin began to write about the motion pictures in 1927. At that time American film criticism had not yet attracted much serious discussion. What passed for criticism was mostly a matter of journalism, divided among newspaper reviews of a general impressionistic nature, colorful reportage emphasizing anecdotes, legends, and myths, and publicity handouts – all directed to sustain the American family's weekly moviegoing habit. The occasional essay or review in the literary weeklies approached the motion picture in either an appreciative or patronizing manner. The most striking characteristics of film criticism were its narrowness and separation from general culture. The time was ripe for a vigorous, fearless approach to motion pictures by more knowledgeable standards, sound principles, and a concern for values that reflected the nature and tenor of the medium and the spirit of the times.

Potamkin brought the new quickening to film criticism. A freewheeling zealot who as yet belonged to no school of professionals, he provided criticism with a much needed injection of intellectual inquiry, staking out a claim for the importance of film art, and then developed that claim by elucidating the merits and faults of that art as it was practiced — elusive and in the process of discovering itself. Possessed of a sensibility that was both refined and pragmatic, he also concerned himself with the way the screen exercised its expressive and moral powers over subject matter and point of view. This demanding aesthetic led him to subject the medium to a fiercer scrutiny than it was accustomed to bear; thus along with what he thought and wrote about motion pictures, he struck at the very conscience of film culture and trivialized the criticism of more renowned contemporaries.

His brief career merged two aesthetic and ideological currents, developing from the aesthetic ferment of the '20s and the economic upheavals of the '30s. A small part of his criticism, that of the '20s, submerged all other considerations of film to a criterion that was formalistic. A considerably larger portion of his writing — that of the '30s — was generated by a social consciousness that responded to the crisis of the Depression with a critical approach that was sociological, tempered by a Marxist viewpoint. This compulsion "to change the world" linked Potamkin's aesthetic sensibility with political and economic insights into a synthesis that directed his criticism of the last years leftward, toward social reform.

The rationale of Potamkin's film writing during the '20s was greatly influenced by the aesthetic tenets of the "New Criticism." This literary movement had gained wide prominence after World War I. Its point of view was hostile to traditional criticism, which emphasized historical and biographical interpretations often at the expense of aesthetic considerations. The doctrine that "a poem must be regarded as a thing in itself and not another thing" and an emphasis upon the problems of style, language, and structure had contributed in large measure to Potamkin's own poetic practice. The posing of such formal questions as What goes on in a poem? How does its language work? What totality of meaning is achieved and in what way? had given Potamkin a special viewpoint and a critical approach that made it natural for him, on turning to the screen, to respond with immediacy to the formal aspects of the movie and scrutinize it "as a thing in itself and not another thing."

This regard for the motion picture as an autonomous and independent art form became the touchstone of his critical work. His first notable article, published in 1927, praising the esteemed Russian-English theorist Alexander Bakshy, clearly carried both the stamp of his debt to that pioneer and the firm emphasis in discriminations and evaluations the tenor of his own formal attitude toward the movie medium.

> No American has captured in the written word the qualities of cinema as well as Alexander Bakshy. . . . More than a decade ago (he) indicated the folly of the literary intrusion. . . . There is no quarrel between the mechanical and the non-mechanical, but between the artistic and non-artistic. . . . Bakshy saw in the ballet the rudiments of cinema rhythm. . . . Quite a few years later the Léger–Murphy *Ballet Mécanique* appeared. . . . Bakshy resolved the optical problems of the film into simple terms of camera — what director today knows that the camera and not the picture is the medium?

For the next three years, the majority of Potamkin's articles rested on an "internal" analysis of film structure. The quality of the film-maker's formal skill concerned him more than the picture's emotional effect on the viewer. He looked at movies closely, examining them as a special branch of art with a concrete body of materials, resources, and processes generic to their own structure. Thus any film that failed to register a fastidious craftsmanship, or lacked an essential independence of the theater or literature, lost for him its claims to artistic validity. He put it this way: "The film which does not dwell upon itself, does not realize itself." No practicing film critic in his day had seen the problem so clearly, or stated it so succinctly, or had yet made its assumptions the focal point of his critical thinking and seeking.

Whether written for the *avant-garde* readers of *Close Up* (he became New York correspondent in 1929, after a number of his essays had already appeared in the magazine) or for such trade and technical journals as the *National Board of Review Magazine, Theater Guild Magazine, American Cinematographer,* and *Billboard,* most of his articles yielded edifying insights of a mind and sensibility tuned to the screen medium's technical resources and formal processes. Arguing for the importance of the screen's own structural elements, he deplored "the shift of concern from the intrinsic qualities of film to what is fallaciously called communication." His high regard for "expressive form" made him downgrade the logic of characterization and the film's emotional effect on the viewer in favor of such camera devices as "an angle, a close-up, or a fade-out," on the grounds that these elements were the integral means of film structure and not merely isolated devices. Consequently they had to be seen as "an inevitable part of an inevitable pattern (where) the whole disciplines the detail and the detail disciplines the whole."

His grasp of the special formal qualities of film expression is still meaningful for film makers and viewers today. This comes through in his articles for mass circulation magazines such as *Vanity Fair* and *Cin-*

ema, the prestigious literary and art periodicals *New Freeman* and *Creative Art,* or the "amateur" *Movie Makers.* He did not seek out the off-beat or "experimental," but dealt with the so-called commercial productions, defining and analyzing excellence wherever he found it. "*The Front Page* . . . is the first American contribution to the sound–sight cinema. It puts forth the principle of pace set up by the verbal element." Or, "Eisenstein has called Griffith 'the Grand Old Man of us all,' though he is rather the Russian's stepfather than father. But D. W. did introduce effective tactics and a major strategy. Tactics and strategy have, lamentably, left flimsy tradition in their land of birth." Or, take his distinction between art and technique: "In America the close-up has remained a device for effect. . . . In Europe, it has evolved as a structural element, and has attained in *The Passion of Joan of Arc* the eminence of a structural principle. We must differentiate between his (Dreyer's) close-up method and the close-up as used – varied only in degree – with medium and long shots."

In analyzing the aesthetics of film expression, Potamkin was one of the first American critics to point out the nature of screen movement and the potentialities of sound, and to show how these elements could be made to function structurally with power and individuality. "The movement of a film is not cinematic unless it is plastic. There must be balance and contrasts. Repetitions in variations." Or: "We are passing from motion whose transmission is impact, to motion intensive . . . which is motion organized in the image and with the image . . . as against the literal-motion as recorded." His perceptive treatment of sound anticipated trends now current: "the development of a technique for fading, the use of sound inscribed directly on the track"; suggestions for multiple, dramatic, and aesthetic possibilities: "Years hence, a Joyce will not think of attempting his compounds with words. He will go into cinema, which unifies the verbal and aural with the visual and ultimately the spatial. . . ."

His assessment of the American film summed up a critical attitude of which we need to be constantly reminded, if only to reappraise it. "In both content and approach (it) is literal; that is why the American film is still rudimentary and why no one here has extended or even equalled the compositions of Griffith." Like that Old Master, Potamkin wanted meaning and value to be derived from the matter of content and the matter of form working not separately, but together. "An heroic form cannot be constructed on a frivolous content." Few native productions could satisfy that scrupulous demand. For never had the Hollywood Establishment been so successful and its serious film makers so frustrated.

Potamkin's formalistic evaluation of movies had not yet existed in film criticism in this country. Its application came to be recognized as his "signature" in the 1920s. At its best, it enabled him to probe the aesthetic imperatives of the still evolving art with an awareness that illuminated the differing qualities of film expression, and introduced a line of critical inquiry, of intensive formal analysis that never lost sight of its primary object: film art.

Until the economic depression of the '30s, Potamkin's assessments had given little attention to the influences of the forces and changes in the society from which movies sprang. But with the social and political upheavals of those years, and with large numbers of intellectuals, writers, and painters surging to the radical movement looking for answers to the malfunctioning social system, he began to have fresh thoughts about the human condition and the state of American culture. This induced a new examination of his aesthetic ideas and a change of critical direction, focusing more on an examination of the social matrix from and in which movies existed, toward what he called "the social idea as against populism, the highbrow inflation of the popular idiom: jazz, slang, movies. . . ." His former objective, the proselytizing for aesthetic values, began to tangle with sociological concerns. His social feelings, heretofore inactive in film criticism, took on a radical consciousness under the impact of accelerated unemployment, widespread shutdowns of industry, and mass disillusionment with the status quo; his political sympathies, as did those of many of his contemporaries, became more activated. He became the executive secretary of the John Reed Club in New York, attended the Revolutionary Literature Conference in Kharkov in 1930 as a "sympathetic" writer, and served on the advisory staff of the Film and Photo League – a group of young film makers organized in the early '30s to produce independent newsreels and documentaries that would foster a sense of class consciousness in the viewer. These commitments and activities branded him a Communist in the public's eye. One of the direct effects of this was the cancellation by *Vanity Fair* of a series of articles to follow his "Field Generals of the Film," because an irate Hollywod star, after reading that piece, called the editors and told them its author was a "Red."

There is no doubt that Potamkin thought of himself as a Communist. "Communism," he wrote to Eric Knight, then a film critic for the Philadelphia *Public Ledger,* "made me more thorough. . . . It does not trust to impulse or vagary, nor does it permit itself to evoke in the abstract, but refers its own tenets to the concrete truth." But whether Potamkin ever was a card-carrying Communist is doubtful. According to Daniel Aaron, author of the book *Writers on the Left* (1961), a very small percentage of Left Wing writers were actually members of the Party. A considerably larger number who were in "the movement" and sympathized "with the objectives of the Party, wrote for the Party press and knowingly affiliated with associations sponsored by the Party" were generally accepted by members as "fellow travellers." The true status of Potamkin's political commitment appeared in an obituary written by W. E. B. Dubois, editor of *The Crisis* (October 1933), a magazine devoted to the social betterment of Blacks. It stated that because "Potamkin upheld the Communist views on film and literature and had been a secretary of the John Reed Club in New York at the time of his death, he was the first non-Party member to be given a Red funeral."

Potamkin's association with the Communist cause led him in 1930 to become the regular movie critic of the *New Masses,* then the most influential left-wing cultural magazine in the United States. Here the *zeitgeist* had come into play. The concurrence of activated political conflicts and the acute perception and sensibility of a critic had come to impose upon film criticism a much weightier function than it had been accustomed to bear. Potamkin's critical engagement turned "political" in the deepest sense of the term. From that time until his sudden death three years later, he employed a Marxist view of society in his criticism, not only in his *New Masses* reviews, but in his articles for other magazines as well, judging every movie and a director's work in the light of the ubiquitous class struggle. With such an emphasis his judgments took on new and different standards of value. A movie was no longer an autonomous work to be evaluated as merely entertainment or work of art, but an ideological statement of the social group that produced it, serving a specific rôle in the cultural and political structure of society. He regarded content now as primary, as "informing the structure; and the conception as the expression of the social mind." Aesthetic values, while not ignored, became subservient, in favor of a socio-aesthetic coördinate of judgment which said, "The film as an art is a process; but to create a process requires an awareness of the processes of society."

This new aspect of Potamkin's critical philosophy wrenched film criticism out of narrow aesthetic habits of perception, exposed it to a deeper engagement of experience, and underlined the necessity of the film maker's responsibility to social and cultural forces. Evidence of this multiple view and enlarged vision can be found in almost everything he wrote during this period. Examining the problem of war films for example, he maintained:

> A war film cannot be evaluated simply as entertainment or an isolated production; it must be criticized for what it implies and what it omits. . . . The failure of *Journey's End* is that of the particular human relationships. The failure of *All Quiet on the Western Front* is that of the treatment. The film lacks the structure it deserves, the heroic structure. In none of these films of the continent or America has war been actually and inferentially presented for what it is: the peak of a competitive society.

Taking the same adversary stance, he deflated the popularly hailed "masterpiece," the all-Black film by King Vidor, *Hallelujah,* for its attitude "of the White American toward disparaged people (with) all the trappings of the legendary Negro as the white men like to see him."

Probing behind the moral façade of the gangster film, a most popular genre of the '30s, Potamkin uncovered hypocrisy, malice, cruelty, and ignorance. In *The Big House,* "society is accused by the warden who points to the over-crowded cells . . . by the genial guard who warns against putting the boy with hardened criminals . . . and by the machine-gun killer who revolts at the food . . . (but) we are not made to experience the accusations: the camera does not expose the filth . . . because there was no wish to construct it. The society that is callous in its cinema is callous in its attitude toward imprisoned men."

In other gangster films, Potamkin exposed the blind worship of the success syndrome and the supposedly "good-people" syndrome concealed behind "America's celebration of her corruption." In *Underworld,* "Ben Hecht's roseate picture of why gangsters kill, the burden of guilt is shifted and dissipated into a vindication of the American scoundrel and a benediction on the society that breeds him." *Streets of Chance* made the racketeer "Arnold Rothstein an altruist sacrificing himself for his brother's soul." In *Roadhouse Nights,* "not a word was whispered of the reporter's fraternal connection with his murderers. The slain newspaperman died for the glory of the Amalgamated Press and his immaculate conception — a servant of the people." *For the Defence* extolled "the late W. J. Fallon, criminal lawyer (for) his support of a murderer and thief, as love for the poor, a new Jesse James."

One of his strongest contentions was that the economic and political crisis in many countries was mirrored in the sociological assumptions of their films. "The film reflects the social mind that created it. It expresses the economy and politics of the land." Of *Washington Merry-Go-Round,* "The unemployed are panhandlers from among whom is distilled a nucleus for a fascist army, which fights the racketeers. . . ." *Gabriel Over the White House* "panders to the public desire for an expeditious solution to its plight. Hollywood and pander are one. But to what end is the audience's desire manipulated? Dictatorship, American style."

Foreign films: "*La Belle France* is a static economic nation, and a static social nation. The weight of a gold hoard burdens the energies of the land . . . in apathy, defeatism (and) in the making of foreign versions for American talkies. . . ."

Italy: "The grandiose Italian films influenced all other 'National' cinemas and now there is an Italian cinema writhing and steaming . . . sentimentalizing Italian imperialistic aspirations; the last utterance of Capitalistic hope."

Germany: "When you run away from society you hide in the four walls of the individual – irony and pity, etc. – into the cloistered walls of the studio. The Germans ran so completely into the studio that they sought to drag all art, all life and all emotions into the studio. . . ."

Japan: "The battle between the 'old drama' film and the 'new drama' film in Japan is a battle between the declining aristocratic society and the dominant bourgeoisie. The confusion in which the Japanese cinema finds itself, is the confusion of the class role, the aristocrat enacting the middleman."

Inevitably Potamkin's articles varied in their critical power. And it must be said there were a number of times when his tone and temper overrode his analytical vigor so that his criticism did not escape the influence of official dogma and personal vindictiveness. In particular the polemics of *The Eyes of the Movie,* the out-of-hand dismissal of *Un Chien Andalou, L'Age d'Or,* and a number of other films, seem overly strident and tendentious; while *Film Novitiates, Etc.* and the discussions of Gilbert Seldes and "H. W." offer other striking examples of an unfortunate tendency of Potamkin for bickering and name-calling. Such chiding and acerbated exercises in ideological and personal over-kill, however, were uncommon and generally inspired by some quick response to an acute feeling of violated sensibilities.

Despite such lapses of critical acumen and decorum, there is the immense intelligence and sensibility of a mind that could rise to the dazzling explications evidenced in his sweeping studies for *Hound and Horn* in 1932–33 of four internationally esteemed directors. Two were European, the humorist René Clair of France, and the humanist G. W. Pabst of Germany. Two were from the Soviet Union, V. I. Pudovkin and Sergei Eisenstein, both committed to the official doctrines which permeated Soviet life. All four were linked by a moral and intellectual kinship that transcended the commercial or political aspects of their work. Potamkin's regard for these directors was of the highest order. He respected them as among the most distinguished film makers of his day and in the forefront of the cinema of the world.

Writing at a time of open class warfare that was rapidly dividing the world into divergent political camps, Potamkin brought to bear in these essays a more rigorous political criterion than in any of his previous criticism. His deep faith was that the movies' relationship to the welfare of society was vitally important, and his conviction was that the social content and ideological allegiance of these directors was implicitly or explicitly engaged in their films. These views led him to give every aspect of their work – the sponsoring culture, the relevance to a crisis-bound world, aesthetic and philosophical speculations – comprehensive treatment. No one who had written before about motion picture directors had probed the aspirations and accomplishments of film makers so deeply, or put into sharper relief the nature and meaning of screen art. It was criticism as an act of revolutionary engagement, resplendent with challenging insights offering striking evidence of Potamkin's deepest concern for a film art primed toward ideological and determinant ends.

Applying his Marxist yardstick to *René Clair and Film Humor,* Potamkin drew incisive distinctions between the detailed, explicit, satirical achievements of the director's silent features – "where both subject and style" had functioned "in behalf of a (social) idea" – and his later musical extravaganzas, whose "abstract notions divorced from concrete social references" had blunted Clair's satirical intentions, "because there was no specific object to (their) thrust." Analyzing the erosion of Clair's comic vision with exceptionally vivid and illuminating observations about the personality and forces which shaped the confusions and lapses in the director's sensibility, Potamkin identified "the leitmotiv of (Clair's) humor (as) one of genial contempt for the social foible." His advice to "the directorial Playboy of the Western World" had a challenging immediacy: "Unless Clair is willing to identify himself with that portion of the society which can give him the instruments of criticism instead of platitudes" he will not "see more than extravaganza, where satire is wanted."

What intrigued Potamkin in his study of *Pabst and the Social Film* was the director's "humanistic" impulse which acted as an operational agent for the film maker's choice of subjects and themes "distilled from the war and the aftermath of inflation." Lauding the director for a social integrity "rare in bourgeois cinema," Potamkin centered his analysis on the interaction between Pabst's "perturbed" conscience and the social and political vicissitudes of German society, in an effort to show how the social stress exercised its expressive and moral powers on the film maker's ethical sense and artistic development. With an analytic power that never failed to observe the relation between Pabst's response to outward events and the growing "politicalization" of his films, Potamkin had many trenchant things to say about the social and political confusions, diversions, and oscillations of the director's early work, and about the "social suspicions" which "revived" his aesthetic sensitivity and motivated his later, more politically mature productions. Many of Potamkin's observations have retained a singular relevance: "The sharpening conflict in Germany, the polarizing of the social forces, would naturally touch a man like Pabst"; "He sought and found social material whose complexity the new compound of sound-sight could make articulate"; "Like Dreyer, he reaffirms the authenticity of the event by eliminating the obsessions of period curlycues, and historicism for the sake of propriety"; "From the war film (*Westfront* 1918), to *Die Dreigroschenoper,* thence to *Kameradschaft,* the progress of Pabst's conscience has been notable."

Few film makers however, including the Russian, wholly satisfied Potamkin's stringent criteria. When Soviet films were considered sacrosanct by radical critics and their criticism served a mostly political rôle, Potamkin's scruples acted against propaganda. Both Pudovkin and Eisenstein had created a body of classic films and artistic doctrines which had won world acclaim. Yet Potamkin's criticism of their films and ideas was neither hortatory nor evangelical; he neither overpraised them nor made them the object of personal glorification, but applied the same exacting reasoned analysis to the Soviet masters as he had to their Western European contemporaries. He saw their work in a fresh light and revealed important factors, both political and aesthetic, in their productions, with a keen sense of what revolutionary film art should be.

The relation between the Soviet film maker and the October Revolution demanded that the director "assume an active responsibility to the maintenance of that relation." Potamkin's essay *Pudovkin and the Revolutionary Film* strikingly proved that *that* relation was not "a fatalistic one." There could be ambiguity, errors of judgment, and a lack of diligence in practice.

The critic had highly praised Pudovkin's first feature *Mother* (1926), and rightly so, for its fusion of cinematic art and political astuteness in the delineation of the pivotal figure and her relationship to the mass, which was "sustained dialectically." Esteemed by Potamkin as the "archetype for a picture of revolutionary development," his exemplary critical consciousness was nevertheless strong enough to expose the negligence of that historical relationship in the director's subsequent films. With great skill and exactitude, and despite his political partisanship, he charted the disparity that had occurred between Pudovkin's vivid and explicit rendering of the revolutionary portrait in *Mother,* and the pronounced political "tentativeness" that had become evident in the characterizations of his revolutionary protagonists in the pictures which followed, where a failure of "diligence" had reduced pivotal figures to "inflated effigies."

A further aspect of Pudovkin's "errors of judgment" was revealed by Potamkin's keen scrutiny of the "overriding influence" of literary collaborators on the director's thought and films. A lucid explainer of ideas and techniques, the American critic tried to correct the confusion of method and the lapses in sensibility of the Russian director's outlook, caused by Pudovkin's admiration for "literary" effects. In Potamkin's conviction, the director's high regard for the "emotional, suggestive–non-technical literary scenario" had beguiled the film maker "into a demonstration of externals" and a "subjective, indeed passive . . . conception" that bore "no relation to the task of revealing the Soviet man and his way of life."

Although Potamkin paid tribute to the Soviet doctrine that demanded film makers be "alert in politics as in art," the subtle and strict standards of his criticism were very much his own. There could be no mistaking the power of his exacting concern to make clear that "the positive values of cinema" and the urge for self-expression should not be in conflict but must work to reinforce each other.

In the final essay of the series, *Eisenstein and the Theory of Cinema,* all of Potamkin's critical gifts – his exemplary intellectual outlook, his social and political consciousness, his general Marxist insight, and his sharp analytical powers – converged into criteria that approached his personal apogee. Impressive in many ways, not the least in its combination of erudition and lucidity in taking the measure of Eisenstein's exuberant personality and extraordinary productions, the essay was perhaps most remarkable in its forthright evaluation and denunciation of Eisenstein's montage prinicples. Undaunted by the director's reputation – who above all others at the time was "the pace setter in the world generally, and very particularly in the Soviet Union" – Potamkin without inhibition or restraint set out to prove that Eisenstein's intractable pursuit of montage precepts to an extreme in practice, had inflated their purpose "from an emphasis to a determinant." What had originally been worked out to achieve "a maximum of intensive editing," had in Potamkin's view become a system in its own right that stressed method and subordinated content "to a parallel, but not reciprocal rôle." Combining praise and derogation with a trenchant independence of mind, he argued eloquently that Eisenstein's "sympathy for objects," his predilection for "abstraction," his incontinent love for film as a problem to solve (forever qualifying, amending, reconstructing) – which stemmed from his education as an engineer – explained the disregard or reduction of "the socially inferential" values in the director's speculations and films, which could not be resolved aesthetically. Attacking Eisenstein's absolutism in theory and practice – which placed montage constructions above the human factor "as the material of experience" – Potamkin brilliantly balanced the director's virtues and faults, offering dazzling insights of the disproportions in Eisenstein's promulgations and methodology. "Eisenstein sees the physical container for the ideal. . . . His montage gives the weight of the physical, but not the meaning of the social, because the personality of the event is lacking. . . . The disproportion becomes an heroicism."

What was striking and surprising in Potamkin's analysis was not only his compelling persuasiveness, nor even the sharpness and vigor of his judgments that dared challenge "the greatest living master of construction." What was astonishing was the imprint of an uncompromising critical responsibility within the framework of Marxist thought, that never lapsed into rigid dogmatism or the strictures of official doctrine. Indeed Potamkin's superb assessment of Eisenstein's formal-aesthetic reached beyond its restrictive concepts to establish the point of intersection of aesthetic intensification and social content with a breadth and depth of vision that illuminated the art of film as no contemporary inquiry had.

Individually and collectively the *Hound and Horn* essays represented a critical engagement that summed up the extraordinary range and learning of Potamkin's socio-aesthetic philosophy and the dateline that shaped his principles and judgments. Here all the power and flexibility of his mind, the relativism of his point of view, and the unblinking fixity of his observation were revealed in an idiosyncratic style whose erudition and distinction gave American film criticism an extraordinary authority and the most profound extension it had yet received.

In the last months of his life, Potamkin completed two final assignments that underscored his concern that the vigor of film art should be used for socially valuable ends. This vision staked out the moral dimensions of a speech he gave at the annual conference of the National Board of Review, an organization sponsored by the movie industry to carry "on constructive programs having to do with community coöperation in the advancement of film art," and a plan for a school of the motion picture which he wrote at the request of a large eastern university. The talk was later published in the Board's journal in two separate articles under the titles *The Ritual of the Movies* and *The Child as Part of the Cinema Audience;* the school proposal, turned down "until better times," appeared in *Hound and Horn* several months after his death.

The speech was full of sharp observations and illuminating ideas. It dealt with a number of important matters that had generally been overlooked by those who concerned themselves with the social significance of movies. One was the inherent danger of turning movie-going into the "major contemporary ritual" where everything had been done by the industry to give their large theaters ("rightly called temples and cathedrals") an overpowering atmosphere of elegant surroundings and luxurious comfort in order to soften the audiences' objective attitude to what was on the screen. Another was the pressing need for the planning and organization of wide-spread film societies, film forums, and film clubs, to develop critical audiences and programs directed toward aesthetic and social ends. A third was the urgent necessity to "break down the wall of ambiguity and hypocrisy that exists between society and the child in relation to film" in order to prepare the child to relate "the fancies of film to the facts of his own experience."

On each of these topics, Potamkin offered considerable insights and sobering thoughts about the coercions, cynicism, and opportunism of an industry having a tacit tradition of conservatism and apathy toward any intellectual considerations of its medium and the interests of its diversified audiences, as he sought to make clear the connection between film culture and the class factor. Although much of the vigor of his views clearly derived from his radical beliefs and the urgency of the social and political climate of the times, they also reflected a deep concern for a socially relevant and humanistic cinema that would raise the sights and awareness of movie-makers and movie-goers.

It was this commitment to a screen used for bettering human understanding, and a consciousness of the need for widening areas of knowledge of film education, that motivated Potamkin's writing a tentative "Proposal for a School of the Motion Picture." Conceived in a period when nearly all other arts were amply represented in college and university curricula, while the pervasive presence of movies was still neglected, the plan attempted to integrate the study of film into the mainstream of the academic community, utilizing a program of courses that balanced historical, technical, aesthetic, and sociological subjects with a full-fledged training in film making and offered a degree in cinema studies equivalent to a Bachelor of Science from any established college. It was the first broad study of the motion picture, and sought to fill the gap in knowledge of screen art as a unique medium of creative expression, and as a vital force in contemporary society. Its devotion to ideas about the interplay between craft, sociology, and moral responsibility was without doubt — even in its speculative outline — the most systematized effort to give the film medium a sense of its profound intellectual rôle in education, and inaugurated the lines of inquiry along which a great deal of future film education in colleges and universities would proceed. At the same time the program's broad scope clearly suggested a philosophy of cinema that cogently underlined the extent of Potamkin's own searching sensibility and his militant occupation with the motion picture as a vital social artifact.

An erudite, brilliant critic, Potamkin's surveyal of the film scene spanning the critical transitional period of silent-to-sound pictures (1927–1933) was distinguished by an original vision and an arresting sensibility that had not been seen before in American film culture. Almost everything he wrote, although occasional in purpose, had an unusual authority. Sophisticated, demanding, he refused to compromise with mediocrity, agitating for artistic and social values that strikingly illuminated the distinction of a picture, the achievements of a director, or the significance of the screen medium. At his best, the challenging insights, highly charged prose, and idiosyncratic style provided an extraordinary and vigorous account of films and film makers during one of the most exciting periods of film history. Underlying the breadth and depth of his critical philosophy — even after almost half a century of neglect — there can be found a commitment, a sensation of ideas, and a moral imperative still blazingly alive, elevating film criticism to a height never reached before in this country and only seldom since.

"What is the Joycean method
if not a desire for the compound?"

—Harry Alan Potamkin

"The critic is committed, like everyone else to a particular stance, at a moment in time; he is governed by a point of view that method will not quite succeed in dispensing with."

ALLEN TATE

PART ONE: FILM AS ART (1920-1930)

1

FILM THEORY

THE COMPOUND CINEMA

Leon Moussinac, that excellent French critic, has called the film the first of the cinematic arts.

But the youngest critic establishes his viewpoint by exclusions.

The youngest critic says: "The film's idiom is silence. Silence is a cosmic virtue."

The youngest critic says: "The film's frame is the film's circumscription. The flat film in silence is the supreme film."

The youngest critic is absolute, but never exact.

The inference to be drawn from Moussinac's words is the complete answer: "There are a variety of possible forms in the cinema. The flat silent film is but one form."

The flat silent film without prismatic distortion is the first form of the cinema: Murnau has said as much. Within this category itself there are numerous subdivisions, according to content, sequence, harmonic organization, performance, attitude. There is the genre film, the poster film, the film of social commentary direct or comic . . . from these derive the films of various stylizations, of complex organization, and eventually the film of graphic or cinegraphic distortions. There is the film built on counterpoint, simultaneous or sequential counterpoint.

Counterpoint is an indicator to the compound cinema. In relation to the sonorous film this has been already stated in different terms by Kiesler*

* [Ed.]: The theatrical designer Frederick Kiesler had written a "Cinema Manifesto" as part of an article, "One Hundred Per-Cent Cinema," for *Close Up,* August, 1928, in which it was argued that films required theaters architecturally different from those for stage productions.

and the Russian directors. Kiesler did not fully or definitely state the contrapuntal or balance basis for the compound cinema, but he did suggest a union of various ingredients towards the end of an optophonetic art. He relegated speech to television. This was in August, 1928. On May 26th, 1928, there appeared in *The Billboard* an article by me on "Radio Entertainment," which said: "Television is the speech-sight medium. The medium of direct imparting and impermanence. The movie is the art of silent visual plastic fluidity. Speech is a monstrosity in the movie . . . Television is the sight medium which stresses speech." I wish to modify this. The present cinema, known as the *movie,* is the art of silent visual plastic fluidity. But I must also modify Mr. Kiesler. If speech may not be stylized for the cinema, utterance may. The explosive utterances: Oh, ah, or sounds like Te-te-te, which the remarkable Jewish Theatre of Moscow has used as a rhythmic detail in one play by contracting into T'T'T and expanding into Taa-Taa-Taa. I give these as instances. To utilize sound the principle of rhythmic fluidity must be exercised, or, as the Russians have expressed it tersely in the October *Close Up,* counterpoint. I have developed that viewpoint in two essays written some time ago, awaiting publication in two American journals: *The Arts* and *The Musical Quarterly*. As an hypothesis, consider a film so arranged: beginning in silence and a black screen it enters optically or visually into a graphic moving composition to which follows a counter composition of sound, unaccompanied by the screen (except perhaps by a linear equivalent to the music), to a simultaneity of sound and sight . . . This is a simple illustration which may indicate the new optophonic composition and scenario. It may suggest the utilization of the color-organ to create *fluid* color equivalents. This is making of the fault of the sonorous film, namely that it tends rather to separate sound and sight than to synchronize them, a virtue.

The objection to sound cannot be absolute. It can be only an objection to the compounding of it with a form intrinsically silent, the first form. In the typical confusion of the cinema entrepreneurs (a confusion typical of mankind), a not fully realized form is being thwarted, and a new form is being prevented. The new optophonic film needs another viewpoint than the optic film. Yet why are we just now raging about the imposition of the talking picture? Was not speech always present in the film, and is it not still present in the films of the very directors objecting to the talking picture? What logic was there ever in lip-movements imitating speech? If the movie needed or wanted naturalism, it had its instruments to obtain it. Every one has contributed to the confusion present in the movie, inventor, investor, impresario . . . actor, audience. . . .

Premature compoundings were attempted from the first, deliberately or in unawareness: in the musical accompaniment which attempts to render every point in the film, in the lecture-movie combination (Alexander Black thus introduced the motion picture), in the German kino-oper, in the American presentation, etc. Max Reinhardt has suggested that possibly the presentation indicates a compounding of stage and film. Why not, if the compounding is planned as a unit with one harmonious end in mind, a rhythmic pattern? The combination is hybrid now, because two separate units are being used. Such combination was used as a vaudeville act by Hobart Bosworth in "The Sea Wolf" years ago. American vaudeville has known it long as a "stunt." Piscator and Meyerhold have used it more pretentiously. The Russian Ballet has suggested the film's use in the dance. It is as yet only a possibility as a singular pattern of the cinema or stage.

The Russian directors expressed a disinterest in the stereopticon and color films, but is it not possible that depth and color (as differing from the present tone or color-value film) may create their own mountings? I cannot see how this can be opposed. It is like an objection to sculpture because it is not painting, or to a painting because it is not an etching. The depth film provides its own category, the color film its own. If the color film could achieve fluidity, it would be at once on its way to singularity. There are certain things that cannot be combined, harmonized or crossed. The confusion of the evolving silent movie with sound is an instance of this reciprocal hostility. But certain other things permit crossing—the abstract frieze, for instance, and the sculptural mask accept paint.

The handicap to the creation of independent forms in the cinema is largely literalness. It is evinced in a film like *The Crowd,* which demanded a less chronological and a more patterned production. It is evinced in speech-mimicry. Literalness is the absence of concept. It is matter-of-fact, cautious and fears organization on a plastic basis. It has kept the so-called epic film from being epic, and it is at the source of the inability of directors to incorporate the inferences of the subject-matter of films into the treatment. Alexander Bakshy has stated this well as the failure of *The Crowd.*

Literalness has kept the movie from utilizing its possible rhythms, to be found in the movements of the cinema, which, as Mr. Bakshy has said, are four: the film or pellicule, the camera, the player, the screen. Only now is the screen as an instrument beginning to be used, in the magnascope or phantom screen, in the triptych. Several years ago Mr. Bakshy offered a plan to use for symphonic, contrapuntal pictures of scope a screen within a screen, a multiple screen receiving its images from one camera, not three cameras, a screen subdividing and blending the action for dramatic and rhythmic effects. Nothing has come of it as yet. Nor is the enlarged screen being utilized for its dramatic and rhythmic effects. Eric Elliott calls it a close-up. That is its present use. But considered as a movement, not of the camera, but of the screen, it offers magnificent plastic opportunities in its gradual enlargement and diminishing, with the illusion of advancing and receding movements.

There are a few possible compoundings of cinema. There is the possibility also of color and animated cartoon for stylized ballet-like films. The projection of slides on the side-walls of the Studio 28 in Paris suggests a fanciful possibility: a film which will move not on one screen, but will utilize a moving projection-machine projecting the film in a rotating movement within the reach of eyes following the rotation. This may be a method for the stereopticon cinema.

CLOSE UP,
January, 1929.

THE COMPOUND CINEMA: FURTHER NOTES

I had been thinking long that the traditional Japanese theater of Kabuki and Noh could serve as a basis for sound filming, when two incidents confirmed my belief. One was the projection of a Japanese rice-paper cutout film at the Tribune Libre in Paris and the other an article in "Monde" by Eisenstein on the Kabuki theater. Says the Russian director: "If European painting owes the origins of impressionism to the Japanese, if modern sculpture stems from the Negro plastic, the phonetic cinema will be no less indebted to the Japanese. . . ." For Eisenstein not alone the Japanese theater, but the entire conceptional world of the Japanese, the alphabet and the lyric Tanka, are indicative of the sound-image mind of the Japanese; in other words, graphic sound—the key to the sonorous film. But the ultimate principle to be deduced from this establishment, Eisenstein has with singular accuracy and conciseness articulated: ". . . it is necessary to reduce to the same denominator the conceptions visual and phonetic." I leave the development of this tenet to whomever will exploit it. Even a casual reference to the Noh play, with its separation of the speaker from the enactor, the masks, the voices paralleling the gestures but issuing from behind masks, the musicians in the rear like a commentary, will indicate the relation between the Japanese theater and the stylized sound-film.

The rice-paper film certainly offers the opportunity for sound accompaniment, perhaps with mechanical music or shrill instruments. Similarly the silhouette film and the animated cartoon can be combined to loveliest effects. Universal in America, I understand, is sonorizing its animated cartoons, and the 'Orace films of England are being synchronized too. But from the reports of the latter venture, it seems that the producers are giving the creatures literal human voices. This would perhaps be interesting archaeology, if the films were lycanthropic. But since the entire structure of the animated cartoon is a flat one, and its origin is always manifest, it is a stupid confusion to vocalize the cartoons to give them human semblance. A film of personified creatures enacted by human performers is one thing, the animated cartoon another.

The pattern of the Japanese rice-papers are used in their films both for the characters and the background. The entire film is a rice-paper universe. The movements are rice-paper renditions of the Japanese sword-play and Japanese dance. The rice-paper patterns suggest the possibility of a combination of colour, cartoon and sound. The colours in this instance would not need to be fluid. In fact, fluidity would defeat the harmony, since the cartoon is best when it keeps within its limitation or its origin. I know that several people have been thinking of producing such films, with well-known literary works as the narratives. Any fanciful mind can discover ready-at-hand opportunities waiting to be converted into these compound animated cartoons.

Or the Starewitch puppets, do they not offer sound an opportunity? The artist himself has neither the present inclination to sonorize his films nor does he think his method allows of it. Starewitch frames each gesture, each grimace, each movement, each moment — photographs it; frames the next gesture, etc. — photographs it; and so on. The fluidity is not achieved by the puppets, they are planted and do not perform; the cutting or mounting accomplishes the *moving* picture. (Incidentally, does not this hint at a form of stylization available for human actors too?) Therefore Starewitch believes he cannot film sound because of the static nature of his method. But why not? It is my belief that the very separateness, the very staticness of the method permits for a film of stylized and rhythmically-intervalled instrumental sounds, noises and utterances.

It is in the detail of "interval" that one approach may be found to the sonorous film. André Levinson, a critic not always to be quoted, has said that *Jeanne d'Arc* was the film which offered the trial for sound or speech accompaniment. Charles Lapworth believes that Dreyer's technique is suitable for sound. Dreyer himself, I understand, is interested in the sonorous film. The emphatic employment of the actor, the timing of the lips and the time-intervals between the cine-portraits of the characters, suggest the opportunity for parallel utterance (even staccato speech) and contrapuntal sound.

May not sound bring in the poet? At present we hear about us in Paris talk of the cinegraphic poem. It has been applied to Kirsanoff's work, to Man Ray's and to others. In the case of Kirsanoff's *Brumes d'Automne* the term "poème" is an exaggeration applied to a sentimental succession of images, not singularly new in the history of the cinema. I reserve my hope for the future. I don't want the poet-commentator who may be used, upon Miss Iris Barry's advice, to write the film-captions, but the poet-creator. Not the poor maker of fragmentary images, nor even a Man Ray visualizing the figures of speech of Robert Desnos. But the epic poet, the dramatic poet; yes, can you not hear Shakespeare in the future sonorous film? The blank verse film! Dreyer's *Jeanne d'Arc* may ultimately lead to Marlowe's *Edward II* or Shakespeare's *Richard*. Am I fantastic? The principle of conversation will elucidate even the madman's vision.

To another compounding. I expressed in my notes on The Compound Cinema (*Close Up*, January 1929) the fanciful possibility of a film moving from the side-wall to the fore-screen to the side-wall. Almost simultaneously came the announcement that Film Arts Guild was building a "four-square" camera-plan cinema. One screen to receive the moving picture, the other to establish the "atmosphere" of the picture. I swore that this was a bombast, a perversion of the multiple screen conception of Alexander Bakshy, and a more highfalutin use of the fantastic, vulgarly ambitious "atmospheric" theater like the Roman garden Regal in London. I hear moreover that the theater built for Gould-Kiesler is hardly successful. A modest and attractive application of the camera-cinema is the Studio Diamant, where levelled rays issue from the projection booth to meet the levelled frame of the screen. Yet for so small a theater it is an error: because the screen is reduced, injuring its utilization as a receptive instrument and because the levelled or stair-like structure of the ceiling, close to the eyes of the spectator, distract the eyes from the screen or troubles the eyes with its sharp, progressive lines. The silver-toned Studio 28 is much the most satisfactory of the small houses. One can overstress architecture to the detriment of the film, or to the diversion of the limited funds from more immediate expenditures.

In relation to the compound cinema, the specialized cinema must remember that it is to be prepared for the experimental synchronized film as well as for the silent picture. There are not enough serious film-enthusiasts to patronize two kinds of cinemas, the visual and the optophonic. Mr. Kiesler's differentiation between the two is an academicism. Why can the visual kino not be an optophonic also? The specialized kino must, when it builds a pertinent hall, permit of the magnified screen and the multiple screen. This means increasing the height of the usual small house, and a modification of the early sagacious principle enunciated by Bakshy: that the blank square on the front wall of the picture-house determines the architecture of the ideal kino. This principle was developed into a set of principles by Seymour Stern in the *National Board of Review Magazine,* and I later commented upon them with immediate references in *The Billboard.* But they must be seriously altered to allow the new inventions their places. The magnascope makes the frame about the screen unavoidable, for it is the opening and shutting movements of the frame which makes the screen effective as an instrument in this application. Moreover, stereoscopic filming is not far away. The new cinema must be prepared for it, for films of three dimensions and for films which will burst into and climb upon the audience.

It must be remembered that whatever the future of these devices, the principle of the film remains dependent upon the inclusive concept of rhythm. The Gould kino in New York has sensationalized the idea of enveloping atmosphere. Many people in the movie-world think in terms of atmosphere. A London progressive exhibitor, after laughing at the atmospherical Regal as Jewish, told me that when he was showing "an Oriental film of deep meaning," he'd like to have incense subtly wafted to enhance the mood. And Robert Armstrong, the American actor, is happy to promise a "smellie" to follow the "talkie." All for realism and helping the poor image-film. How will one stylize odors, of hay, perfume, dung, cadaver, hair promade, cold cream, George Bancroft's sweat? And perhaps eventually we will taste with the fortunate or unfortunate actor Clara Bow's tears and lipstick. I know that Belasco is said to have played a reminiscent perfume upon Frances Starr to call forth an emotion. But why betray the spectator further? There are now tears and wistful grimaces (indexed and catalogued), music, light, misty photography (Fox Films). Spare us, O Potentates!

In my previous article on The Compound Cinema, I made mention of a relationship between the color-organ and the color-film, the key was *fluid colors.* Writing in the February *The Arts,* C. Adolphe Glassgold says: "Both the cinema and Lumina (color-organ) become aesthetic realities when, like music, they create perceptible rhythms which may be not only of two-dimensional shapes upon a flat surface but of illusory tactual forms moving in deep space. The motion picture and the Clavilux picture are subject alike to the dicta or static composition in the brief moment which is the flicker of an eye-lid; but the dynamic pattern in space, the inevitable movement and development of form, enlarge one's conception of comparison and make the structural organization of a painting pale by comparison. Movement, action, dynamism are the very life of these two mediums of aesthetic expression. Here the similarity ceases, for in the difference between the structure of the motion picture machine and the Clavilux lies a vast difference in accomplishment. The cinema is forever bound to the object; Lumina is foot-loose and free, with its elements as abstract as music . . . The cinema functions through the intermediary of solid realities . . . The cinema also is striving to attain color and . . . may eventually succeed in its efforts. At that time the Clavilux and the motion picture machine will approach identity with always the fundamental distinction in the use of objects."

Mr. Glassgold is speaking, apparently, of the only movie he knows, the concrete-movie, which includes the so-called abstract as well as narrative film. I can quote in reply from an article of mine in *The Film Weekly* of London: "He (Francis Bruguière, the American photographer living in London) understands that if a photograph is to have aesthetic virtue, it must make most use of its graphic medium, *light*. He understands that the object which is to be transformed by light must yield to the operations of light . . . This inter-relationship . . . means finally *design*." This would seem to abet Mr. Glassgold's contention, but in reality it signifies that there is another cinema not yet touched, the cinema of designed, *abstracted* light, utilizing not the play of light upon objects but the diffusion of light re-organized in the film. Glassgold concludes that when color-cinema is fully realized the film may be the agent for making the color-organ patterns permanent. Does this not suggest also a way to achieve fluid, mutating colors in the motion picture? It is not amiss to add that several American cinemas have installed color-organs. Perhaps pending the ideal color-movie, one may experiment with a coordination of movie and color-organ. Much may be discovered.

CLOSE UP,
April, 1929.

PHASES OF CINEMA UNITY: I

Anthony Asquith has recently written upon cinema unity with estimable pertinence. He is especially interesting in his observations upon camera devices. He says: "Roughly speaking, there seems to be three occasions where an unusual camera position is justified. First of all, where the point of view of one of the characters is represented. By imposing on the audience his physical point of view of the person, the director is putting it in touch with his mental state as well. . . . Secondly, it would be legitimate to use an unusual angle to intensify a dramatic moment even if the 'shot' represents no one's point of view . . . Lastly, the director may legitimately choose an unusual camera position to compose a good picture." It is in reference to this last rule that Mr. Asquith states the inclusive law: "But such occasions, unwarranted apparently by logic or drama, are more difficult to justify. A plea of aesthetic logic does not affect the resolutely common-sense critic of Cézanne's precarious apples. *And such 'shots' are only right in a film the whole texture of which is pictorial . . .*" The italics are mine.

This inclusiveness of viewpoint qualifies not only the last of Mr. Asquith's legitimate camera angles, but refers directly back to the first two as well. *The entire film must be preconceived in anticipation of each detail!* A curve or an angle, a close-up or face-out, must not be recognized as an isolated detail, but as an inevitable part of an inevitable pattern. The whole disciplines the detail, the detail disciplines the whole. There is a more demanding logic than the logic of the psychology of a character at any moment or the logic of the dramatic moment. There is the rhythmic structure of the unit determining the moment. No such thing as a "shot" exists in the aesthetic sense of the cinema, whatever one may call the immediate taking of a scene. Films are rhythms that commence and proceed, in which — ideally — every moment, every point, refer back to all that has proceeded and forward to all that follows. A stress or a deformation, an image or an absence of image, has validity only if it is justified by the pattern up to point, and if it leads again to the pattern from that point. In brief, one may not establish a camera angle unless the entire film contains the mind for *that* camera angle. When Dupont's *Variety* came to America, it hurtled all the Hollywood shopmen into angles. Critics like Gilbert Seldes greatly lamented the ignorant uses of the camera-viewpoint. But the confusion was only another instance of the typical confusion of mankind, of whose foibles Hollywood is so hilarious an epitome. Yet from the point of view of Mr. Asquith's rules, many of those angles were justified. Only, the literal American film had no mentality for those non-literal angles, and the justifications of a moment's psychology, drama and pictorial pattern could not surmount the terrific gainsaying of the integral film. Recently, however, there have appeared several instances of a more pertinent *incorporation* of the angle in the American film, always in association with another and inclusive treatment. In Clarence Brown's *Flesh and the Devil,* the angle is used in a decidedly non-American structure of setting and lighting, the first American instance, and only American instance I know of, where the environment envelops the characters: a pattern Swedish-German. The angles are never extreme and work into the patterned lines as part of the pattern. They are not planned in the method of *Variety,* where they determine the pattern, and all else submits to them. In Irving Cummings' film, *Dressed to Kill,* the angle is of the short-range view, a trifle under the characters, in front of them. It suits the entire muscular impact of the film, which qualifies it as an American device, since the American film is one of muscular impact. *The angle is justified always less by its point of origin in the camera than by the image at the other terminal.*

It is good to note that Mr. Asquith sees that the unit is paramount, even though his own film *Underground,* is replete with momentary reproaches not called for by the totality — in fact, *Underground* is hardly a film of a sustained unity. One director has always been aware that his form does not admit of the sophisticated devices of the French avant-garde or German virtuosos. F. W. Murnau has declared verbally that his cinema, which is the film's first realized form, is that of the reduced theme conveyed by simple movement. In *The Last Laugh* the character of the old doorkeeper and his fate determine the treatment of the environmnt. He is the demanding vertex towards which everything converges, the other persons, the rains, the swinging doors. *The Last Laugh* is the earliest fulfillment of intensive unity in the first form of the silent cinema. A more heroic extension of the same treatment is one that I believe will indicate the direction of two separate cinemas, silent and sonorous. I refer to Dreyer's *Jeanne d'Arc*. It is so emphatic an instance of the complete realization of the Germanic intensity (in the *"gros plan"*), reinforced by Russian uses of it, that many observers have failed to see it as the first traditional statement of cinema that has now been so firmly established as to be a source for the future. Dreyer's film is a unity throughout (save possibly in the captions); the bold image has been so completely realized as to ask for a background which will further set it in relief.

The law of unity, as I have expressed it in my second paragraph, clarifies the uses of the composite devices: the sectioned screen, the surface impression or multiple exposure, the triptych, etc. It is not enough to use such devices for effect, that is rather a smart intention than an aesthetic one. The smart intention of the double-exposure is apprehensible in Leni's *The Last Warning,* where the narrative is preceded by a composition of "the lights of Broadway," over which the legs and the thighs of a chorus descend diagonally. In itself this stunt is not bad, because Leni is a clever if questionable artisan, but does not belong to this film. A mystery film demands that the locale or the mystery shall be the sole universe for that enterprise. A recognition of this concept made Epstein's film of *The House of Usher,* despite the callow and fragmentary objections to it, about the only successful film of universe-torment.

American movies, because they are built usually on a single line, do not allow the composite structure, where the composite image should be intended as a gathering of the separate currents, expressed by separate sequences, into a cumulative pictorial or visual-motor arrangement. For this is needed a film built compositely, and it is such a film which ultimately asks for Gance's triptych and Bakshy's "screen-within-a-screen." The composite film waits to be fulfilled. It was first hinted in the grand and grandiose pictures of Griffith and Thomas Ince. It promises to be realized in Russia.

The reference to the background in *Jeanne d'Arc* suggests the place of the setting in the environment. With this, my reference to *The Last Laugh* and *Flesh and the Devil* indicate several relationships of setting to characters. These must be determined by the nature of the subject-matter and the nature of the treatment which the subject-matter has determined. In *Jeanne d'Arc* the setting brings forward the characters, while all the personalities and movements refer constantly to the Maid. In *The Last Laugh* the environment converges upon the man, who is determined by the environment. In *Flesh and the Devil* the environment envelops the persons. This latter natural immanence derives from the Swedish film. The Germans have made use of this enveloping environment in sombre and misty photography: *Joyless Street* and *The Tragedy of the Street.* In the latter, the entire treatment, as well as narrative, is rather the carbon copy of a formula lacking the informing principle or conception, than a complete work of singular justification. The effect is rancid.

In 1918 Mr. Victor Freeburg published his book on *The Art of Photoplay Making.* In it he classifies the settings thus: "a *neutral* setting, one which neither hinders nor helps the action . . . *informative,"* where the setting conveys "some element of the story which is not conveyed in any other way. The setting may be *sympathetic,* or harmonizing with the general mood or impression of the action. The setting may be *participating*; that is, it may enter integrally into the action of the story. And the setting may be *formative*; that is, it may actually exercise some power in moulding the characters or play." Despite a certain schoolmaster's tone, this subdivision is of import. I think the error lies in the inclusion of the first two kinds, neutral and informative. There can not be neutral setting. If a setting is not part of a film, if it does not *act,* it is not needed. Can one not conceive of a film without a setting? There have been instances of scenes without environments, where the screen itself is the background. But this is not neutrality, it *emboldens* the image. I can give a significant example of this: in *Secrets of a Soul,* when Werner Krauss narrates to the psychoanalyst his memory of the murder, the group of persons is recalled without the presence of place or objects. Freeburg's *informative* setting is in reality the extraneous decor. The other groupings have some general identity with my three instances, except that Freeburg is talking always about narration or exposition, whereas I am stressing always the unit-structure.

The Germans were the first to attempt to design the decor according to general mood and tempo. Instances are: *The Cabinet of Dr. Caligari, Torgus, Raskolnikov.* Despite the frequency of the failures of these attempts, due to heavy-handedness, palpable fantasy and over-concentration upon the decor, the principle these films articulated is a definite one and still waits to be fulfilled. *Torgus,* perhaps the most tedious and banal of these films, possesses two features of interest. Scrawls on the successive sets are intended to impart to the entire film a uniformity of tones and textures. The scene-openings and closings or fade-outs are designed, timed and alternated in the enclosing patterns (pod-shaped, elliptical, rectangular) moving toward or away from the center, horizontal to horizontal or diagonally. In Germaine Dulac's film of domestic pathos, *Mme. Beudet,* strands of the images — horizontal, vertical, diagonal — alternate with the full screen in an easy, dovetailing flow, which justifies their use. Contrast with this the multiple images, partial screen, figure in spotlight, silhouette — all strong *effects* in themselves — in Geza von Bolvary's clap-trap, *The Captive of Ling-Tchang* to understand the principle of suitability which has, in its execution, a thousand ramifications, all summed up in the phrase, the scruples of the author's intention.

The principle of unity elucidates the much-disputed matter of the caption. Eric Elliott in *Anatomy of Motion Picture Art* advances the very interesting defense that the caption is visual. But the fact it is read makes it pre-eminently verbal. The objection to the caption is not an absolute one, but an *ideal* one. The Aristotelian law of unity was not the absolute that academicians would have us believe, but a disciplinary ideal. D. W. Griffith reminds us that the first films were captionless, but that the title was decided upon to save footage. That, however, is a mercantile economy, not an aesthetic. Be sparing indeed, but not through makeshift. To afford visual caesuras and optic rest, which Elliott sees as purposes for the caption, there is a definite visual, non-verbal means hardly touched as yet, the bare screen itself, either black or white. There is the still photograph, suggested by the ciné-portraits of Man Ray, the stills in the *Camille* of Fred Niblo, and the comic use of it in René Clair's *Two Timid Souls.* But the unit-sense and unit-form, must determine what is to be the device used, and whether captions are needed or not. It will be found that most often better and more suitable means are available. Some films absolutely repudiate verbal legends. *Menilmontant* by Dmitri Kirsanoff is such a film, yet when it was released for general, commercial exhibition, titles with a moral intent were interpolated, reducing the film from a simple, sympathetic, human narration to an insolent, sentimental, ulterior preachment. A film like Germaine Dulac's *The Seashell and the Clergyman,* the only visual-motor film of a mental obsession, not the narration of a "case" like Pabst's Freudian film, would be killed by the insertion of captions, for there is no question of explaining the images, nor of referring them directly or precisely to the life of the obsessed minister. It does not concern us whether the images are exact from a psychoanalytic point of view, they are justified by their aesthetic, cinematic structure. The film does not ask for the oneirocritic, but for the ciné-critic. Recently I saw a film of 20 years ago featuring Mistinguett. A foreword said that the captions were deleted because they did not seem necessary to the telling. Indeed they were not, but 20 years ago captions were included, and I, two decades later, can suspect where they were inserted and what they said. I can suspect this because of my memory of the cinema — some ulterior intention was always thought necessary by the producers — and because the film contained an early and perpetuated contradition of cinema unity: the realistic lip-mimicry in a film of concentrated time and emotions.

The most casual reference to the law of cinema unity will indicate the confusion in the present practices of the sonorous film. Is it not obvious, from this vantage-point, that the producer knows or cares little about the categorical separateness of silent and sonorous film, when a motion picture is made as *both*? The whole matter of the creation of already created forms (novel and drama) into a cinema is a matter of changing one unity into another unity. From this conversion of unities as a principle may be studied the relative successes of the treatment of Zola in the films: *Nana,* by Jean Renoir, *Thérèse Raquin* by Jacques Feyder, *Money* by Marcel L'Herbier, *Fruitfulness* by Baroncelli, *Labor* by Pouctal. By it we are immediately informed that the enthusiasm for Brenon's *Sorrell and Son* is entirely sentimental. It distinguishes between the verbal cinema of a Lubitsch and the speculative cinema of an Epstein. The entire matter of social and philosophic inference in the movie may be ultimately explained by a development in reasoning from the principle of unity. The inference is determined entirely by the relationship of the parts within the unity and the constant reference of each part to that unity. Was that not present in the rigorous, unrelenting back and forth references in *Jeanne d'Arc?* Was it not absent from *Nana,* where Renoir accomplished an emphatic articulation of a principle of acting in the masklike ratio between the major characters, but beyond that immediate interplay was ineffectual? Was it not also absent from *Thérèse Raquin,* where Feyder concentrated on the characters within the walls, giving us a splendid film of a domestic tragedy, but not one of universal reference? This demands a deduction: the emprise of a unity is determined by the particularization of a theme.

By theme I mean the subject-matter. The particularization of a theme is the immediate story of the motion picture. The theme of Vidor's *The Crowd* was enormous: ineffectual man, doomed by prophecy, caught within the indifference or hostility of the mass. But the vast scope of such a theme is immediately reduced to a trite duplication of the irony-and-pity, human interest *feuilleton.* Not human experience, but human interest. Therefore the theme is not the determinant of the construction, but the particularization. Unlike *Jeanne d'Arc,* the particularization is not up to the theme.

It is the theme that would have justified the opening of the film with the colossal structures of New York (an introduction by now a banality). The particularization, in its pinched meagreness, does not meet with environment, nor can Vidor, being a chronologist rather than a synthetist, make a constant of the relationship between the environment and the individual. All through *The Crowd* one feels the whipping of the particularization to rise to theme. Or is it that any particularization, however mean and meagre, there is some trace of the theme, which man, looking for a generality, detects? If so, the director, King Vidor, is so much more incompetent for not having urged that trace of the theme to its fullness. This would have demanded the elimination of the "touches," the purposeful pre-established irony (verbal mostly). In short, it would have demanded the total elimination of the original scenarist, John V. A. Weaver.

When the daughter is killed, the father signs to a newsboy not to cry his wares. The newsboy signs to go to hell. That is realism. The father winds through the crowds trying to stem them, that they might not disturb his dead child. He wants all the world silent in grief. The crowd moves on oblivious of him. That certainly is symbolic. But—a policeman tells him to go back. The symbol is broken. Was his winding through the crowds *real*? In the light of the entire film, we are to assume it was real. But in itself it was surely not real. At least its sense was symbolic. Later in the film, there is the expressionistic symbol of the numbers twisting in his head. These two details, the symbolic counter-crowd walk and the numbers, suggest a level upon which Vidor might have attained to the theme, had he been aware. In this awareness is the secret to intelligence in the fashioning of the film. But the emprise of the particular unity of *The Crowd* did not permit of such non-literal details, which exist beyond its boundaries.

CLOSE UP,
May, 1929.

PHASES OF CINEMA UNITY: II

The entire matter of the Compound Cinema belongs to the concern of Cinema Unity. Unity differentiates between a hybrid and a compound. Chaplin, for instance, finds speech — and I add "all synchronized sound" — alien to his unity. His is the simple medium resisting compounding. In barest terminology, his medium is clowning, which refuses speech. To join speech to his form would create a hybrid. But Carl Dreyer sees speech as essential to his method. (Leon Poirier has called, in *Photo-Ciné,* the sonorous film a bluff. He finds sound sufficing for the informative documents, for "a spectacle not meant to move" the audience. He finds it, however, practically impossible for the expression of "the multiple and delicate nuances of the sentiments, the emotions, the impressions . . . The amelioration of the quality of sound will not change the situation. It is the conception itself of the sonorous films that must be modified." As to the talking film, well, has the colored photo dethroned painting? Movement is the principal essential of the cinema. The sonorous film will enrich the music, its veritable progress will be the improvement of the film's musical atmosphere. Poirier is talking here only of the simple film, "the film's musical atmosphere" indicates his attitude there is certainly a more serious error in this conception than in the sonorous film conceived as a unit. That is the sole justifiable conception of the sonorous film. I can but say to Poirier that if to him the sound-film is "a bluff," it means simply that he has not the mind for it, and let him staunchly stand by the silent film. That poor neglected will need its friends, and I am one of them and shall salute any director courageous enough not to be lured or browbeaten away from it.

There are altogether too many directors tampering with sound who have no sense of it. But there are as many tampering with sight who have no sense of it. Yes, movement is the prime essential of the cinema, but it is not all of it. And, moreover, just what is movement? What will M. Poirier say to the thought expressed in a letter to me by Francis Bruguière of a form of visual-oral cinema where the visual images *accompany the sound?* The music editor of the London *Times* has expressed a similar thought, although he has naïvely compared this accompaniment to the printed program notes). In short, it is not a matter of liking or disliking the talking film that will determine its survival. It is a matter of finding artists who will achieve their full expression through it. What is inevitable is—intrinsically and ultimately—good. What is the intrinsic talkie? By utilising it we will attain to the ultimate talkie. The aesthetic jargon of the last ten years of cinema limits nothing but itself. Mr. Betts calls the talkie not a film, but a "speech plus film." All right, it is a speech plus film. That is nothing more than saying the silent film is one kind of cinema (let us call it "film") and the talking film another kind (call it, if you will, "speech plus film"). If Mr. Betts intends to imply by that that speech is supplementary, I can only say he is thinking of the ideal silent film troubled by an instrusion. He cannot vision a compound unit of visual and spoken utterance.

For the entire key is "utterance." I am extending my heresy and at the same time contradicting Mr. Kiesler who said that speech cannot be stylized. I oppose also the Russian directors who accept the sonorous film but not the film of speech. Speech can be stylized, harmonized and unified into an entity with the visual image—and if it can, that settles the question. Personal preference is only personal preference, and to speak like a Frenchman that the cinema's aim is to "reveal the world of things" or that "the film is the art of the dream" is to speak only of the film that reveals the world of things or the film whose art is the dream. Everything in life belongs to the cinema, if the cinema can convert it into a functioning unity. To think otherwise is to restrict the cinema to a few simple forms and to confine it against its will. But the will of the cinema is stronger that the will of the opponents to the compound forms, as it is stronger than the will of the commercialists who would forever banish the simple forms.

Utterance. Stylization. Speech in the cinema differs from speech in the theater. The initial fact that we are dealing with indirect presentation rather than direct determines the difference. The film is a medium of projected images. It remains that even in the talking picture. We meet the image in closer intimacy than we do the image on the stage. It is, moreover, more concentrated, more condensed, always starker — if its nature is respected. The speaking film enhances this condensation and this intimacy. For the bolder, the more concentrated the image, the more exact is the synchronisation. That is one reason why Dreyer's method is ideal for the talking film.

If one has closely watched the lip-movements in *Jeanne d'Arc,* one will have observed that they are emphatic through concentration. It is not only a condensation of time — which is also one difference between theatre and cinema (yet not an absolute difference) — it is a concentration of movements. That is, the lips seem to hold an utterance longer than usual, because into that utterance is concentrated more than the word seemingly uttered. This concentration coincides with the total visual intensity, and relates to the time-intervals between the images and the duration of each image. It is a part of the rhythmic-unit and the time-unit. The captions in *Joan* (I speak now of the integral version originally Dreyer's) are never longer than the duration of an image. Timed to the total time-unit and intervalled to accord with the rhythmic-unit, they are justified. Here is another clue to the speaking film. I have spoken previously of the time-interval which affords counterpoint. The time-interval affords also harmony in that it permits of repetition of visual image timed to verbal image (speech or caption) and verbal image timed to visual image. Dreyer does this. He gives the visual image, succeeded by a caption carrying only a part of the words spoken, followed by a visual image, succeeded by the remainder of the words spoken. This very simple device contains everything the cinema pretends to offer, drama, suspense, visual emphasis, rhythm.

I have spoken in the previous paragraph only of the words not uttered simultaneously with the visual projection. The talking film is also one of simultaneous speech-and-sight. In fact, it is chiefly that. Non-simultaneous compounding refers more to those instances where sound does not issue from the visual image upon the screen. For, it must be remembered, it is not only the utterance of the visual image that will enter into the compound, but the off-screen utterance too. These off-screen utterances will be parts of the subject-matter and hence parts of the structure. They must not be *effects.* Effects contradict unity. The expedient sonorous film and film of sound-accentuations are counter-unit conceptions. The same objection applies to them as to the uses of the "close-up." Compare here Dreyer's "*gros plan*" with the Griffith close-up in *One Mysterious Night* or in the Gance film, *The Wheel.* These are effect concentrations, whereas Dreyer thinks the entire film as a *gros plan* unit, and no *gros plan* is inserted for its own pictorial quality or dramatic effect. Dreyer has made a principle of the *gros plan*.

Speech as utterance is stylized speech. Its basis lies in a variety of sources: explosive speech, uniform pitch, monotone, etc. Radio and phonographic articulation offer instructive analogies. In the *Nouvelle Revue Français* of March 28, Paul Deharme has outlined a "proposition for a radiophonic art," the study of which will prove valuable to all practicians of the speech-sound-sight film. Principles which can be utilized with profit in the cinema include: vocal masks (conventionalized voices; repetition of certain portions of phrases to reinforce the image and, I add, for rhythm; the noises of the action will not possess the character of reality; chronometry of the representation). . . . These will not apply to all kinds of the compound visual-oral film, for the character of Deharme's stipulations is dependent on the acceptation of the unreal as the intrinsic radio-form. But the conception of the conventionalized voice can afford, in its conversion into the integer of the particular film, the principle for a cinematic oration. The troughs and crests of an inflected phrase will be re-rendered by a mean concentrating the pitches to an *approximated* monotone, or reduction in the number of diverse tones.

Nothing is more important in the oral film than silence. The pause becomes valuable as accumulation of the oral image, as accentuation of the visual image. I dare to say that silence will find its completest power in the non-silent film. Again not the extraneous pause but the pause in the total pattern is the determinant of the uses of silence in the non-silent film. I have anticipated this declaration in an article written at the time of the latest advent of the sonorous film, but only just published in *The Musical Quarterly* for April, wherein I treat of the phenomenon of silence in the musical accompaniment. In the few instances where the pause has been allowed in the musical accompaniment, it has been for the purpose, not of a rhythmic construction, but of a momentary dramatic effect. Here in the non-unified accompaniment the effect is permissible to allow the visual image fullest physical transmission. But in the integrated compound-film, the moment counts only as the portion of an inclusive entity.

I must insert one exception here, and that is the film of broad comedy. The effect becomes rhetoric in a comic film, and rhetoric is the very nature of cinema comedy. The devices or effects in Clair's *Two Timid Souls* are justified by the nature of the film, and therefore satisfy its unity. That is why I prefer that film to *The Italian Straw Hat* in which effects or rhetoric is not employed. Facile fluidity is not a virtue in a farce-comedy, however virtuous it is in a film like *Vanina.*

Hardly had I suggested the possibility of Shakespeare in the compound cinema, when announcement was made of the Fairbanks-Pickford plan to film *The Taming of the Shrew.* Within the same period Glassgold quoted Griffith on the dialogue as hope of the movie. Euripides in the talkie, said Griffith, enthralled. And Glassgold scoffed. Dialogue indeed! His words of sarcasm are summed up in these words I quote from an article of mine: "Attach a phonograph to Mona Lisa?" I, however, was referring to the cinema's first form of non-oral images. The compound cinema is not phonograph to a flat film, it is a unity of independent structure. I do not know the nature of the Fairbanks-Pickford tentative, nor Griffith's conception. I suspect an error in the latter because of the use of the word "dialogue." Not a dialogue-film but a blank verse, recitative film, in which the verbal essence is extracted and refined to meet with the image projected. Only a great poet can re-render in the cinema the great poets of the drama. But may we not hope? Blank verse evolved a Shakespeare although it was born with a *Gorboduc.* Did Petrarch create the sonnet or did the sonnet create Petrarch? Later I hope to indicate (perhaps feebly) how a great poet may re-render a great poetic drama — or at least indicate a method. Again, it is a matter of the conversion of distinct, but related, unities. Yes, related, for the cinema is not so remote from the theater as dogmatists insist. The cinema has a source in the theater, the theater has a source in the cinema. No category is isolated.

Where does compounding cease? Where a unity is not creatable of the diversities. The "smellie," for instance. I have only frivolously referred to it before. Shortly after my reference to it, a writer in a French journal treated "the olfactory cinema" facetiously. But be assured, it will not end with offhand references. The "olfactory theater" has at least once been attempted. In the Théâtre d'Art in the Rimbaud-Mallarmé epoch, a production was mounted of J. Napoleon Roinard's *The Song of Songs* with an accompaniment of music and perfumes. This was the outgrowth of Rimbaud's sonnet of the vowels, of René Ghil's theory of instrumentation and of Chardin Hardancourt's *Book of the Orchestration of Perfumes.* It was an attempt to establish "a concordance between the tone of the music, the poem, and the decor, and the quality of the perfumes." (Leon Moussinac: *La Décoration Théâtrale*). I shall here but touch upon the physical difficulty in controlling the volume and diffusion and duration of the odors, and just hint at the physical discomfort of the audience, enveloped in fragrance. I accept the opportunity of commenting upon the question "where does compounding cease?" and its answer, "where unity is not creatable of the diversities." Stylization is possible only with defined and circumscribed forms. What cannot be stylized has no form. Odors are diffusive, not contained within limited areas. They cannot be set in counterpoint to the experiences of the sense of sight, as can be the experiences of the sense of sound. From past experience we are assured that odors will be seized upon to intensify visual sensations in the cinema, but this is again an enterprise of extraneous effects. The problem is: can odors enter the structural unit of the film? They cannot. Sounds can. In the terms of the task, it is the problem of "montage," as expressed by the Russian directors. Odors cannot be mounted because they cannot be kept within an area coinciding with the image upon the screen.

I leap at once to a phase of cinema unity which determines the entire philosophic nature of art as experience. I have stressed it in the May *Close Up,* 1929, in my words upon *The Crowd.* It is the matter of the theme, the subject-theme, in its relation to the treatment. The full theme may be expressed in various ways. It may be borne by the verbal legends, the sub-titles. There is the instance of Martin Berger's film, *Rasputin.* It is a grand, strong, voluptuous work. But its entity is disturbed by one thing. The visual film stresses the sensual conduct, the love-life of Rasputin. The verbal legends refer constantly to the spiritual debauchery of Russia by Rasputin. The level of the theme borne by these legends is other than the level of the experience borne by the visual progression. There is a space between these two that is not bridged, and one is disappointed by a film that would otherwise be, in its own category and on its own level, a masterpiece. The theme may be borne by the nature of the personal relationships. There is the instance of Pudovkin's *Storm Over Asia.* The personal relationships are indicative of a larger social relationship. The construction of the film, masterful as it is, is upon a level lower than the level of the experience which this social relationship, the ultimate theme, demands. Therefore the masterful construction, the construction in reality of the American physical film, does not satisfy the unity of the film, viewed from the principle vantage-point of theme, and the critical participating spectator feels himself cheated. I shall not here dwell upon the extremely low levels of social irony to which this same film often falls, although this indicates the same disregard for the theme as does the construction. We may contrast to this film Eisenstein's *Potemkin.* It is true that Eisenstein made no attempt to relate this episode to the entire revolutionary period of 1905. But that was his right, even though it probably kept his film from being more than a powerful film of surface-masses. (If I may seem presumptuous in my allowing *Potemkin* only the quality of surface masses, I may say that I expressed the same judgment in 1927 in the *National Board of Review Magazine*. Shortly after, Eisenstein said in *The Nation* (New York) that his film was a poster-film. This is exactly a synonym for my phrase, a synonym even less descriptive). The film stays within the boundaries of the theme, and for once experiences the pleasure of a decisive unity. Upon a higher level of experience (because of the wider reference of the theme), Dreyer achieved such a decisive unity in *Joan*. (The documentary film — *The Black Journey, The Trail of '98* — offers a brief opportunity to say something about levels of experience. It will be seen that that documentary most often succeeds where no narrative is attempted, for the narrative generally falls below the level of the experience of the document. Therefore, Poirier's *Black Journey* is a film of integrity, as is also the second part of his *Exotic Loves*; the first part of the latter fails in integrity because its narrative is of the level of simplism rather than simplicity. *The Trail of '98* is a very bad film entirely because of the intrusion of the narrative, which is of the level of the worst melodrama, whereas the document itself is man).

The consideration of unity necessitates at least a glance at the phenomenon of dissociation. Dissociation, as evinced today, received its first statement of creed with Remy de Gourmont. He was the prophet of dissociation. Its contemporary expression is mostly French in inspiration: dadaism and surrealism. I say this even though the propagandist of dadaism was not a Frenchman, Tristan Tzara. The cinema experienced the first deliberately dissociative film in Clair's *Entr'acte,* whose scenario was the work of Picabia, a dadaist. There have been many dissociative films since, mostly French and mostly the work of young men who have not taken the time to think through their intentions. For even a dissociative film must have an intention, if it is only to convey automatic ideas. *Entr'acte* has been called satire; that was its intention. But the nature of satire is entirely that of precise reference. And if anything demands a unit-direction it is satire. Dissociated images do not converge towards one reference. The implication in the characterization of *Entr'acte* as satire is: images are in themselves satirical. This is questionable. Precise reference implies a relationship which at once declares no image absolute and hence not in itself satirical. It is the reference that creates finally the satire.

But I oppose the entire principle of dissociation. One may even accept the theory of a multiverse, a cosmic pluralism, and oppose aesthetic dissociation. Remy de Gourmont scorned the endeavours of men to relate the separate categories, as he saw them, but each of his essays was a unity.

The task of the artist is to establish, or attempt to establish, the relationship between the dissociations. Baudelaire constantly transferred the categories and achieved a synthesis. He re-associated the dissociations.

One may forgive dissociation in the elder arts. Time may itself produce reduction, which is mistaken for purity, and disintegration. But if the dissociationists are faithful to their creed, they will admit that the cinema has its own character and upon it should not be imposed *all* the experience of aged arts. Isolations that do not re-establish their relationships thwart the cinema, which has been hindered entirely too long by accidents and non-accords. The cinema must go through a long experience of unity.

CLOSE UP,
September, 1929.

PHASES OF CINEMA UNITY: III

Very little, if any, attention has been paid to *light* as *unity*. The fact that the quality of lighting or filtering in a film is not uniform has generally called forth criticism of what people call technique. But uniformity can be judged only from the viewpoint of unity. Similarly, diversity of light-quality, of tone and pitch, is the concern of unity. Technique permits weaknesses that unity declares injurious. For instance, take the common practice of inserting frames from an old newsreel into a film, so generally employed in war-sequences. These portions are certainly authentic, but since they do not participate in the quality of light or the temper of the light arrangements, they are intrusive and *unreal*. The reality of the established light-unity has been contradicted. (Or refer to Epstein's *Six-and-a-Half x Eleven*. The inconsistencies of lighting seriously disturb the continuity of pattern and flow. Bad studio equipment may have produced this).

Of course, it is possible to incorporate different light-qualities — a variety of tones and pitches — into a single film. It is possible to *incorporate*, and the incorporation is the proof. But a film must be light-planned to achieve such incorporation and the alternations must be intervalled and timed in duration in the total rhythm of the picture. I have not seen many films that succeeded in doing this. Feyder's *Thérèse Raquin* was a contradiction — very delicate and to most eyes imperceptible perhaps — between the construction of two lightings not alternated nor balanced in the intention of a single organization: German studio lighting and the usual French interior light. In France, it is worth noting that unities of lighting are most often achieved by men who are originally painters:

Alberto Cavalcanti and Man Ray. (Another phase of light as unity is the relation of the lighting to the nature of the film. I include in the matter of light the tone of the raw-stock too. Frequently the use of a brown stock is antipathetic to the mood of the film. But in Clair's *The Italian Straw Hat* the stock provides just the period color-tone which coincides with the entire attitude of the film).

No one, so far as I am aware, has yet dwelt upon the unity of the absolute film. I shall here only record a few indications. They key to the unity of the absolute film is its *absoluteness*. The lesson of the films of Richter and Man Ray's first picture to the makers of films of machine sequences should be: the construction of a suitable material. Will not some absolutist construct the machine whose visual-motor rhythm he is to re-create on the pellicule for projection upon a screen? As it is, most machine films remain documents and not completely absolute rhythms. For while the screw and bolt of a machine are essential to its original function, they may not serve the film. We have by now documented enough machine movements to create an absolute machine as material for the absolute film. It will not, finally, be a working-machine, but may take the form of human semblance and find its source in those interesting sculptures of the German, Rudolf Belling, where human portraits are modelled upon machine-analogies. In the machine film, as in sculpture, spaces between solid parts are portions of the structural design. Belling is the sculptor who has best used actual hollows in the total design of his portrait.

Nothing so interferes with the unity of an absolute film as the presence of a human figure not arranged into the entire absolute structure. It may be true, as one critic has observed, that the appearance of a human figure into a film of non-human contents relieves the spectator's tension. But that very relief is intrusion. (In one of the most pleasing of the machine films, Deslav's *The March of the Machines,* at one point a man is visible behind the machinery. The austerity is broken for the moment and the mind needs to re-construct the absoluteness). The absolute film of all films makes no compromise with the spectator's prejudice and habit of mind. Its unity is its only determinant. (I have omitted certain major concerns of unity, especially important to the absolute film. They are the direction of a movement, the texture and the volume. I may take as an example of all three Mme. Dulac's *Arabesque*. The texture and the movement here are not sustained nor are they patterned exactly. The play upwards of the water-hose annoys the forward horizontal movement, and, because it is a concentrated slender force occupying only a portion of the screen interrupts the crystalline texture occupying a major part of the screen. The use of the woman as part of the *Arabesque* intrudes two distractions: one of a human subject not sufficiently impersonalized into an objective detail, and of a detail differing in volume or solidity. But this *Arabesque* was offered by Mme. Dulac as a tentative in design endeavoring to utilize a variety of details. It is most instructive).

In these days unity must pre-occupy itself mainly with the unity of compounds. Most objections to the sound film — though the objectors themselves seldom know it — are assertions that the sound or talking film contradicts unity. In the journal issued by Charles Dullin, *Correspondances,* a writer dwells upon the nature of this contradition. The article is not written with the film in mind, but the view expressed pertains to the cinema. The view is this: we are single-minded, and compounds of our senses achieve no singleness because one sense or another dominates. If this is true, then a movie can be seen only and not seen-heard simultaneously and equally. But I am not sure that the writer is correct. Indeed, I am sure that he is not. It may be true that we have not until now apprehended multiple articulations because these have not been aimed in harmonized concurrences. It may be true that one sensory medium has been so emphasized that it was predominant. But I think this is not absolute or unavoidable. To create an operative unity in the cinema certain cares will need to be taken.

If the writer referred to above is not entirely correct in his assertion, still within his statement there is discoverable the point of view for the compound film. The compound picture will need to be *preconceived* on the basis of one sense. That one sense will in itself be no simple sense. The film is not simply a visual medium: this needs to be said again and again. The film is visual-motor. The rhythmic pattern of the sound film will be conceived, as is the silent film (ideally), upon a visual-motor graph. Time and space are its structural elements. Upon these bases are imprinted the emphases of pitch (night sound), distribution (color-values, sonal tones), etc. Time and space, visual-motor fundaments, determine, however, the placements of these emphases. They comprise within themselves: scale, duration, alternation, counterpoint, simultaneity, climax . . . The film contains also elements that are visual-tactile (textural), as well as — in the sound film — those that are sonal; but these elements must be submissive to the visual-motor. In this way, may I call for Mr. Betts? The film remains a film — but that isn't really so very important. (Mr. Betts still waxes courageous against the sound film. What he still attacks is the stupid uses of the sound film to date and the unjustifiable suppression of the silent film. And shows thereby he condemns the compound film. When suddenly he says: "They [the Russians] are experimenting on different lines and putting sound in its proper place, as an adjunct to the film instead of the film being an adjunct to the sound." Then Mr. Betts is in favor of sound properly used? He goes on to entomology, with that cute irrelevance of English thinkers: "If the fly as it moved on, uttered a little squeak, do you imagine it would become more of a fly by consequence? No, it would become more of a nuisance." Is Mr. Betts implying that the silent film is nuisance enough?). What is a more important cosmic implication is that man *may* be on the verge of experiences that, though they are multiple in their origins, will be singular in their apprehension (by man).

Movement: that, we are told by the cinema critics, is the key to the nature of the film. Or it is visual drama. Another will say: dynamics. And still another: fluid rhythm. In brief, all of these characterizations are both too generic and too fragmentary. Movement yes, visual drama certainly, dynamics indeed, fluidity and rhythm positively. One contains the other and all are but terms until we re-associate them, separate the association into its several functioning parts (parts, that is, that are immediately usable). It is best, therefore, that we set down first several simple laws to clarify the nature of the terms.

The authentic perception of movement, to quote Jaques-Dalcroze, is not the visual order, but of the muscular order. (Visual-motor).

Movement is not succession of motions. In cinema movement no motion may actually take place, but an interval may occur, an interval of time, between two images and that is movement too. In other words, movements are two: the actual movement of a body, and the constructed movement attained through time and space-successions (in montage).

The movement of a film is not cinematic unless it is plastic. There must be balances and contrasts. Repetitions, repetitions in variation, "the progressive deformation of a theme": altogether rhythm, which practicably includes:

Time, space and pitch durations:

Of a scene, of a sequence.

Of an image, of a tone.

Mr. Matthew Josephson, an American writer and erstwhile film-enthusiast of the late *Broom,* saw in the American western film his ideal of film-movement. This was an enthusiasm generated by the French dadaists, and it is still being uttered in England—as yet, a decade behind in its film-judgments—by a writer in a weekly periodical. The movement of the American film has been movement, it is true, but the movement only of an object and not of the integral film. To clarify my meaning, I should like to refer again to Carl Dreyer and *Jeanne d'Arc.* Mr. Dreyer believes now that in the latter portion of his film he should have graded the bold images in first, second and third plans: the head first, then head and torso, then full body. This may have reduced the dramatic psychological attack upon the spectator which was so powerfully effected by the succession of first plans, but—and this is a first rule of a unity!—*the film and not the spectator determines the structure of the film.* The succession and alternation of first, second and third plans are part of the aesthetic organization of the film, its plastic, rhythmic movement. Dynamics is just another name for the climacteric construction and organization of these various elements. It refers to the accumulative forward march of the film. The drama refers to the narrative source (the literary experience) which the spectator receives in its final converted form through the repetitive, alternating, varying procession whose elements I have briefly considered above. There is no single kind of motion, no one sort of dynamics, no only form of rhythm, no one and only category of film.

I have thought it necessary to consider, if only for a moment, these inclusive film-terms to protect the film from the glib repeaters of old phrases who would circumscribe the cinema with these phrases. I say here that it is the creator of films who tells us how many kinds of films there are, and not the critic. Indeed, the studious and serious critic of the film will never say, on looking at *Jeanne d'Arc,* as did one young American journalist, that though the film moved him strongly, it was not cinema, which is, according to him, naught if not the movement of shadows. Again, you see, a rudimentary observation inflated to a final determinant.

The most casual observation of motion in the film should have indicated to the glib young commentators that the capture on the negative of a thing in motion is not the ultimate of cinema motion. A reference to the physical basis of cinema and to the final organization of the positive for projection should have elucidated the principle that the film is not merely a report but a construction. In the introduction to *Filmregie und Filmmanuskript,* Pudovkin attacks the viewpoint of the "turning" of a film, "the shooting." A film is *built,* he says. This building is *montage. Montage* is the construction of the unity. As such, it is no mere assembling of film-strips, but is pre-conceived in the initial conception of the theme. The montage is worked towards from the beginning, just as in the final act of montage, the entire film from its first definite expression in the film manuscript is included. Therefore, there is a montage of the manuscript. So long as montage is understood as an inclusive creative (constructing) unity, it is the valid vantage-point of film aesthetics, but the moment it shifts to the mere job of cutting or, as it frequently appears in the work and utterances of the Russians, a device for effecting the spectator, without regard to the level of the theme as experience, it is contradictory of unity.

The motion picture has been too occupied with the spectator. This shifting of the concern from the intrinsic film to what is fallaciously called communication has been one of the chief causes for the non-establishment of a film unity. It is true that a film is meant to be experienced by some one other than the creator of it. But experience — the systemic, ideational experience of art — is never a product of the intentional effect. That is a consideration *out of* the intrinsic work. But if the artist is faithful to the highest demands of his subject-theme, as articulated in the construction, experience is the result. That is purity. That is unity. That is the aesthetic as against the rudimentarily psychologic, which, in the film construction, is a physical attack. The film, on the whole, remains no more than a physical attack, and the talking film, as it is produced to-day, has further lowered the level of this physical attack. The view of film-making as effect makes for passive (even apathetic spectators), the view of film-making as the strict realization of the intrinsic makes for active, completely participating spectators.

The film, because it does not dwell upon itself, does not realize itself. In all lands it disdains idea. Therefore, it does not achieve complete conversion into a final form, therefore does not achieve unity — hence not the experience that is art. The entire mind of internationalism, whether it is the large sale of the American commercial viewpoint or the propagandistic reduction of the Russians, thwarts this penetration of the intrinsic theme and its re-making into the form of the film. The film to-day, only very, very seldom attains to more than a manner or a style — an aim discarded by every serious and earnest artist as spurious, specious and non-propagating — and almost never to form, which is the unity *informed* constantly by the thematic-philosophic intention. Without this intention, of course, there can be no form.

Unity, more than ever before in the history of the film and the history of mankind, challenges the consciousness of the artist. The film is alive at the very moment when the multiple-unit is being attempted in painting and in literature and in music (in the realm of the mecahnical), when artists are endeavouring to create entities of diverse utilities. Very little more than simplisms have been achieved through these endeavours, for an alien attitude prevails, an attitude which still is worried about effects, which thinks of purity as reduction, and the conglomerate as the inclusive. It is time a criterion was established, for without it the artist wallows in a morass. The experience of the artists in these mediums should prove most valuable to the artists working in the compound cinema. That literature, painting or drama is not the cinema does not mean that literature, painting or drama cannot by their experience clarify the intention and method and viewpoint (philosophy) of the cinematist. Not exclusiveness, but inclusiveness, is the valid mind for the artist. (I read that the olfactory film is an actuality, as is the tactile and the stereoscopic. The conglomerate mind is working. Confusion! Several months before the natural vision film was shown in America I heard from Spoor of the Essanay Company as to the depth film they would soon be urging on a public too easily persuaded. I saw, as I had already suspected, that those commercially interested in this three-dimensional movie would never recognize that it was a distinct form needing considerable study, and not another realistic effect. To take a hint from painting, perspective as a means of simulating reality has been a betrayal of painting. Perspective as a device for plastic organization is a major utility of painting).

To provide a basis for his film's unity, the film-maker must select his relevant sources and select from them. Is the French absolute film the source for the Dutch and Belgian artist? Compare the work of a Kirsanoff (a Russian, French-tutored) in *Mists of Autumn* with Joris Ivens' *Rain* (which I saw in Amsterdam, before its final mounting) and of which the idea and continuity are the work of M. Franken. *Rain* is the purer of the two because it is less troubled by effecting a mood upon the spectator, that is, it is less sentimental. Yet it creates a sense of the persistent melancholy. In *Rain* there is detectable a temper which, if it is perceived by the Dutch cinematists, can be further extended into a permanent Dutch cinema attitude. Contrast this temper with the *perpetrated* mood of the Kirsanoff film and you will detect in it the unsentimental perception of a uniform tone in a definite condition of nature. If this germ can be placed into the apprehended experience of the Dutch people (as the film will reveal), Holland will create an autochthonous and original cinema, contributing richly to the experience of the world. That the Dutch cinema-adventurers have felt the necessity for working with the indigenous life of Holland is whispered by the presence of the film made by Franken and Ivens, *The Breakers*. But strangely, what the phototechnician Ivens put into *Rain,* is not discoverable in *The Breakers*. And Franken, who directed the film, did not understand that the mere statement of a relationship is not the relationship. By simply stating the relationship of the three persons and the analogy with the dunes and sea — and not developing this relationship nor this analogy by insistence upon the evidences of sea-temper or the numerous other opportunities afforded, the subject lacked assertion, fullness and culmination. The analogy demanded the speculative mind, such as Epstein exercises upon phenomena, but so far as I was able to detect, this speculative metaphysical mind is not yet a portion of the Dutch film attitude, nor am I sure that the Dutch mind enjoys such effete practices as Epstein employs. *Finis Terrae,* I was told in Amsterdam, is a wretched film, and all that is good in it is here and there a *physical* device. Yet *Finis Terrae* should have meant something to the Dutch practicians as a study in the utilization of natural tempers and in the exploitation of native types. They might even avoid Epstein's speculative treatment to see his structural employment of bodily parts. I think it would be well for the Dutch cinematists to remain concerned with the physical evidences of *folk.* They have at hand a rich source in their graphic art. They should go, not necessarily to their greatest artists (though Rembrandt can teach every cinematist much about tones) but to those Flemish or German artists, who have remained most folkish: an Abel Grimmer, for instance. Or for grander employments of folk activities to the paintings of the Brueghels and to Bosch — these are full of the kinetic. The galleries in Antwerp, Brussels and Amsterdam are replete with sources. I refer this examination to the cinematists of Belgium too. In Antwerp, the Flemish Cinema Club has produced a film *Leentje van de Zee* (Peggy of the Sea), which I went to view thinking here might be the rudiments of a folk-film, if not a realized folk-film. The Dutch film *The Breakers* possessed a dignity and seriousness of effort. But this film of amateurs with its ancient story of childhood, love, the drunkard foe, the false accusation of murder, the crippled idiot's devotion and martyrdom was hilariously stupid. Nothing to redeem it, not even an honest intention. Yet for as little an expenditure these amateurs might have produced a document of some Flemish village which might have taught them just what material they possess. And by studying their graphic artists they might have learned something of tones and textures and stylizations. Carl Dreyer did not disdain the sources existent in graphic art. He found such sources in the medieval French miniatures, in Flemish art (the blood-letting scene), in Brueghel (the fair scene, the mob explosion, after the explosion the poignant prayer scene at the drawbridge), etc. (It is true that graphic knowledge may injure the cinegraphic, but such injury proves only the incapability of the injured. Murnau believes — if he has been quoted correctly — that the cinematist should leave other mediums out of one's ken, yet *Sunrise* is certainly enriched by paintings [the peasant and his wife at the table laid with heavy earthenware above which a lamp is tilted]. There is a difference between paintings being copied into film [De Mille's *King of Kings*] and the structure of paintings *incorporated* into a film. The latter is a fusion of basic attitudes, the former a confusion of false attitudes). The Dutch and the Belgian cinematists will do well if they study their folk-painters, look into their folk-writers, watch their folk-movements and remain folk for a while. Whereas in the lands of more ambitious cinemas of longer history, the fullest cinematic achievement will be attained if folk is utilized only as film-history. That is, Germany and America have done enough folk filming, now they must transcend folk. Germany has done this, for instance, in Hans Behrendt's film, *Die Hose*—the German comedy here leaves behind the redundant Harry Liedtke folk film, like *Wochenendezauber* (a jolly local picture), or the Fritz Kampers picture *Semkes sel Witwe. Die Hose* has left these behind but has its roots in it. America as yet has not extended beyond its folk-bases. These have accumulated for America a mythology which should, when the right artist comes, create a grand and gorgeous cinema. The western film remains a folk-myth. Had there been the mind for creation when Fred Thomson did *Jesse James,* there would have evolved a film as great as Quixote—or at least a film of broad and racy references. I shall, however, speak of these national cinemas later. My reason for bringing them into these paragraphs upon unity is summed up thus: in the unity that is the aesthetic problem of all film artists, there are the details of unity which in each land take on different necessities.

Close Up,
June, 1930.

THE PERSONALITY OF THE PLAYER: A PHASE OF UNITY

(I speak here in the main of the "egocentric" film, as contrasted with the film of mass-entities. Yet the former can be educated by the latter. If the individual performer should observe the integration of personalities—"types"—of a film like *Potemkin,* he would see exactly what is meant by submission to the unit-structure).

The actor or player cannot be viewed apart from the film. The "star" system exaggerates the performer above his place as human-instrument and thereby damns the film. The University of Washington Chapbooks, edited by Glenn Hughes, offers an example of this exaggeration in an essay by Edward Wagenknecht: "Lillian Gish, An Interpretation." It is an unqualified panegyric which I can epitomize in the following quotations:

"Miss Gish is not, in the ordinary sense, a versatile actress. Her temperament is not naturally and obviously dramatic, as that of Pola Negri, for instance, is dramatic; and she always claims the right to make her rôles over to suit Lillian Gish. Yet she has come to be accepted as the outstanding serious artist of the screen, the authentic, incomparable interpreter of the drama of the shadows. As far back as 1920, Mr. John Barrymore declared that Lillian Gish was an American artist worthy to rank with Duse and Bernhardt, a girl who had equalled if not surpassed the finest traditions of the theatre . . . each of her portraits is an individual achievement." Mr. Wagenknecht anticipates an objection: "he who feels or who pretends to feel that her Mimi and her Hester Prynne are the same person, or that her Angela Chiaromonte is not an essentially different girl from her Henriette Girard, is surely completely blind to any other than very elementary and wholly obvious distinctions: fine shadings in art are not for him. Versatility, in the usual sense, is comparatively easy for the character actor: he presents, one after the other, wholly different *types,* and he has all the resources of make-up to sustain the illusion."

What the author fails to recognize is that cinema performance is a detail of a structure, and the actor must become that detail. (Wagenknecht says that he is "not trying to absolve" the performer from fidelity to the play, he is — he explains — "simply suggesting that in acting itself there is a larger creative impulse than is commonly supposed." Before this he said: "If acting is in any sense among the arts, why should we not grant to the actor this same privilege — to re-character his material in terms of his own personality — which we impose upon the poet as a duty?" It is probable that when Shakespeare said, "The play's the thing," he was attacking this same presumption. Wagenknecht calls the characterization of acting as "interpretative," cant provoked by obtuseness. Well, I have avoided this epithet in the recognition of acting as an instrument and portion of a structure. When critics call for choreographic performance, this is what they mean or should mean: the unit-structure determines the stylization of the single performer. Stylization is not only fantastic playing à la *Caligari* or *Beggar on Horseback*: it is the structural conversion of the ordinary! This means much in the theatre, but a thousandfold more in the film where absolute histrionics are taboo. The clue is in "intensification," which even as casual an observer as George Bernard Shaw has recognized for an innate quality of the cinema). If, as Wagenknecht says, Gish's "Hester Prynne is not precisely Hawthorne's Hester, she is Lillian's Hester," he must answer the question: "Which of the Hesters belongs to the film by Seastrom?". Ostensibly, Hawthorne's. Lillian Gish's performance stood in the way of this realization of a structure which coincided with the director's temperament. This temperament would have created a film of strong indictments, whereas the result, because of Gish, was compromise. To say that the fault lies with Seastrom does not recognize the hindrances a director meets which should not be his problem. Murnau once said that between the pliable actor like George O'Brien and the assertive and more creative player like Jannings there can be no gradations. Gish lies between and what lies between is counter-cinema. Assigning, as the author of the chapbook does, poetry, "lyrical colouring," to Gish is a sentimentalism that agrees with the enthusiasms of Hergesheimer and George Jean Nathan. To this lyricism Wagenknecht adds, "dramatic intenseness." The lyricism and intenseness are nothing but mincing cuteness and mincing pathos. If, on rare moments, Lillian Gish seems to have achieved genuine condensation of power, that is simply because her habitual mincing acting has coincided with the necessities of these moments. There was such an instance in *The Enemy,* when she is informed of her husband's disappearance on the battlefield: her clipped movements, timed to the superimposition of the soldiers' march, appear ready to explode with compressed anguish.

The fault of Gish is traceable to the fallacious standard of performance set by David Wark Griffith in his Biograph days. Mr. Griffith's worst trait is sentimentality, expressed in the platitudes of social criticism that makes his compositions more grandiose than grand, and in his penchant for a spurious refinement or restraint. Samuel Goldwyn, in "Behind the Screen," says that Mary Pickford ran away from Griffith because she felt she was losing her individuality. She has never really run away from him. Nor has the American film. Movie acting in America, save with comiques like Langdon, has never sensed the meaning of structural stylization, which alone determines the validity of the particular condensation or restraint. And the particular stylization is determined by the structure of the particular film. The structure of the film is determined by the director.

Has the player a will of his own? Mr. Wagenknecht has this to say: "Without great personality, great art simply cannot exist, for it is in personality that the highest expression, the ultimate manifestation of life comes. This truth has long been recognized in connection with the other arts: it has been obscured only with regard to acting." To confuse the category of an art like acting with one like painting is an evidence of a failure to recognize the *submissive* character of the player: he is an instrument! Assuredly he is an instrument of greater importance than the mechanical instruments of the cinema, because, in a film of human content, he is also the content and the final experience. That is just where the will of the player enters. Either he must be pliable in his submissiveness or intelligently receptive. In the latter case receptivity becomes the expression of a conception of acting. In the expression of the conception lies the understanding of the structure of the experience of the character. The structure of the character is his place in the structure of the film.

John Grierson has said in an American newspaper that the most fitted player is the untrained person who moves through a film without self-consciousness. This sort of player makes the American film the cheerful entertainment it frequently is. It also works against the creation of a structural American film. Self-consciousness is essential to the understanding of the self, the character, in the unit of the film. Witness the playing of Werner Krauss, of Asta Nielsen, of Catherine Hessling, of Fritz Kortner. Each of these has a conception of performance very recognizable, as it should be, in each rôle enacted. Call this a personal idiom, or a personality, if you wish. But recognize it as highly versatile in its applications, which admittedly the idiom of Lillian Gish never is. Contrast the self-conscious idiom of Jacques Catelain with the self-conscious idiom of Harry Langdon. A flippant New York reviewer called Catelain's lovemaking Langdonish. This is not erring criticism. Catelain's idiom is restraint without reference to the structure of the character he is assuming: Langdon's always is.

Character acting does not satisfy this demand of versatility, since it is mimetic in its intention rather than structural. It may be put this way: cinema performance is the structural transfiguration of character acting. That describes this maligned but singular player, Catherine Hessling. Hessling's idiom of compressed and choreographic playing—the stylization of the quotidian—is permanent and defined. Her make-up is patently always the same, but the relation of her hair to her head, her head to her body, her body to her walk, re-articulates the idiom in each instance. Where she minces she constructs herself in the environment of the film. It is not idle mincing. Her refinement is a commentary upon the meaning of the character in the arrangement. Surpassing her in profundity, if not in agility, is Asta Nielsen: she is a monument that frequently builds the film. This is no condemnation of her, but of the failure of the director or the theme to attain to her. Of this I have spoken in my article, "Kino and Lichtspiel," in the November *Close Up*. We have often heard speak of "wasted acting." We know of the false theatrical standard which will let the actor "carry the play." Wagenknecht says: "The very great—*Hamlet,* for example, are never completed. *Hamlet* is no longer Shakespeare's exclusively, but the world's, and it will not really be finished until the last great actor has presented his conception of it." Again the vulgar persistent histrionic error: Hamlet the character is more important than *Hamlet* the play. Scholars as well as actors have argued the meaning of Prince Hamlet to the neglect of the significance of the poetic drama itself.

There are two poles of statement in performance: litotes and hyperbole. These are structural as well as critical (i.e., commentary). Elizabethan drama is a complete study in the sructural-critical uses of under and overstatement. Griffith and film directors in general, betrayed by a spurious restraint, avoid hyperbole. Yet hyperbole is the *test* of performance and the test of direction. The control of the hyperbolism of Jannings in *The Last Laugh* though the structure of the film accredits Murnau with directorial distinction, and the failure of Fleming and von Sternberg in *The Way of All Flesh* and *The Last Command,* respectively, is the complete criticism of their films.

Emerson and Loos in their popular manual, *Breaking Into the Movies,* assail a New York reviewer to whom there is no such thing as movie acting; to him it is posing before a camera. The authors find in film acting the most refined and intricate of mediums. The camera, being permanent and voracious, demands, so they believe, an intensely (read "restrainedly") realistic acting. And with it an ease of unawareness (of camera) which means freedom of all feeling of acting. This description agrees with Grierson's and the practice in America. Certainly it is preferable to the horrid pretense of mimicry indulged in by Dolores del Rio (griefs of the river!). But Emerson and Loos have not spoken of an ideal performance, they have merely interpreted, by recording usual practice. The camera is demanding. It acts as the immediate instrument of the director. The performer must be conscious of this instrument as he must be conscious of all the instruments – setting, etc. – including himself. But it is not of himself, the person off the set he must be conscious, but of himself, the personality, the form within the form. This means the loss of the non-theatric or non-cinematic personality – himself – for the theatric or cinematic personality, the rôle. With this as a critical viewpoint, the critic can reduce the value of a Maurice Chevalier or a Raquel Meller and fully appreciate the contribution of a Werner Krauss or an Yvette Guilbert. These are differences in self-consciousness which amount to opposite categories. Relevant self-consciousness brings intelligence into the performance of the player. For without intelligence there can be no structural modification, no control of one's self, for the needs of the unit, no appreciation of the directorial intention.

CLOSE UP,
April, 1930.

TENDENCIES IN THE CINEMA

Several positive tendencies are operating in the cinema: toward the compound, the reflective, and toward a new logic. The futile defense of the mute film evinces — or evinced, the defense being quite muted now — a failure to recognize the inevitable nature of the cinema as a form of evolution. Art has long been seeking to compound the simple. Twentieth century art records innumerable hybrids that could not survive nor propagate. The artists of Der Sturm, like Archipenko, sought to end the flat surface into space, sought, that is, to wed painting with sculpture. Dynamism was an attempt to add mobility to graphic and plastic. The theater of Europe, echoing *outre-mer,* has — in its more adventurous milieus — been attempting to multiply itself, indeed, to cinematize itself. What is the Joycean method if not a desire for the compound? Lance Sieveking, writer, and Francis Bruguière, photographer, have endeavored to compound the photograph with the word. These are aspirations against the medium and toward another form, the cinema. The cinema was born in the age of the multiple. Years hence a Joyce will not think of attempting his compounds with words. He will go into the cinema, which unifies the verbal and the oral with the visual, and ultimately the spatial. Color and tones with music, speech and typography — planes with solids, framed areas with images floating in space.

The cinema is, by nature of its potential structure, a compound form. The Russians have established montage, the arrangement of the images into a progressive structure, as the method of cinema unity. Montage enables, by its principle of organized motion (rhythm), the mounting of the verbal legend (caption) and the utterance (audible speech) into the unit of the film, so that the motion-picture becomes the justification of its diverse utilities. Having found a method for the compound, the cinema establishes the compound out of the hybrid.

Basically the film is a progressive medium like music, literature, the theatre, the dance. Progressive mediums are performing mediums, as contrasted to painting and sculpture and architecture—shall we call these "frozen" mediums, intensive mediums? But within the progressive there is also the intensive. That is why the cinema has not negated the suggestions of painting and sculpture. *The Passion of Joan of Arc* is a beautiful instance of the structural presence of the graphic and the plastic in the cinema. Having exploited the literal, muscular film to its ultimate—the Russian film has thus fulfilled the American—the seventh art finds it urgent, as Eisenstein has said, to utilize the "reflective processes." A number of causes are at work toward this intellectualization of the film. First, the natural development out of the immediate impact film; second, the insistence of criticism in the subject-matter of the film (the Russian influence at the moment); third, the increased sensitivity of the physical medium (panchromatic negative, light, etc.); fourth, the need for intensification to consolidate the components of the compound.

The film is the most intensifying of mediums. It concentrates hours into moments more resolutely than does the theatre or the novel. It concentrates the image *boldly*, bringing forth every particle to the apprehension of the experiencer. It can move facilely in space and back and forth in time with a minimum of burden. Intensification is physically the method of intensiveness. *The Passion of Joan of Arc* is the most intensive film yet realized, and every detail of it is a portion of and a contributant to that intensiveness. *Arsenal* is intensiveness expressed in the accumulation of forces in the stationary body. *The Old and the New* (*The General Line*) is intensiveness of this order cooled by Eisenstein's objectivity. The *idea* of intensiveness is reflection. The Russians have tried heroically, in the past failing momentarily but now succeeding consistently, to convey this idea in the symbol, which is the intensification of an extensive reference in an object of immediate reality. The failure was due to the employment of this reflective instrument in a non-reflective structure, the culmination of the film's first technique, the physical or American.

The establishment of a reflective structure is inevitable. The subject-matter of the Russian kino creates a form which will support the critical intention. The cinema, save in the brief instance of the Swedish, has never before dared criticism. It has been dramatic, whimsical, lively, has achieved pathos and even, as in Feyder's rendition of Zola's *Thérèse Raquin,* tragedy, but tragedy without extensive reference. The Russian film is propelled by criticism, and that explains its vitality. There can be no propagating art without the impulse of criticism. There can be isolations, as in France; there can be the momentarily effective, as in America; but for a cinema permanently great, strong and productive there must be criticism. The conversion of this criticism, the social theme, into its form is art, cinema. Form is the conception constantly *informing* the structure. The Russian film alone moves toward a permanent form. It is not likely that the American film, far removed from whatever critical center there is in the United States, will approximate, for some time to come, more than a style or a manner. And not until there is a release of the fuller, suppressed social energies of our land will there be realized a cinema of which the movie, rudimentary art, hints. We are yet, too long so, in the era of the legend and the myth. We come nearer to criticism, to art, than the symptom of the environment, and that environment at its lowest level of ideology and experience. I believe, however, that the years will bring them this change of production locale and the release of the social, meaning creative, energies.

The necessities of the critical subject-matter and the reflective processes have been evolving a new logic of cinema construction. The logic of film-construction is termed "continuity." The very word suggests the matter-of-fact, arithmetic or geometric, literal sequence of the American film progression. Griffith created the "flash-back," a diverting of the progression by means of a subtraction or fractional intrusion; but, since the American film, remaining muscular, literal and sentimental, could not see the structural significance of this device, it remained as merely a part of the practice of "cutting." Russia, re-studying the film at its source, developed the Griffith technique and established montage as cinema construction. The flash-back has become a paramount instrument within montage. In *Fragment of an Empire* it is the pivot of the rhythmic structure.

Beginning with this structural establishment of a device, the film could advance in its hunt for a language and get as far as the figure of the speech. The old logic of 1, 2, 3 or 2, 4, 8, the episode following episode like a child's tale or an elementary melodrama, was broken up. It is being broken up constantly. In *Arsenal* we find the new logic having attained to a non-logic — if we think in terms of sensible verbal cogitation — by means of juxtaposition of images not immediately leading out of one another, but producing a total conveying idea and form, fluidity. Elsewhere films have been made in a logic of images freeing itself from the logic of words (from which so many writers are struggling to free themselves, only bewildering themselves the more), but the practices are, for the most part, either documentary (as in the composite newsreel *Berlin*), or effetely fanciful, an *atelier* experiment, as in France. However, though they are not so vital or influential or mobile and generative as the Russian work, they support the tendency of the cinema away from literalism, bluntness, the non-structural, the insensitive: contradictions of the intrinsic evolving cinema. The new logic relates historically to the earliest modification of the literal in the "angle-shot" (a structural point of view), the multiple image and the impression of image upon image, and the magician's virtuosity of Georges Méliès in the '90s. But America, literal-minded, rudimentary-minded, which rejected these modifications of the literal or, as in the case of the angle, blundered with them, now accepts them in the new "virtuoso" film, the movie revue, as "stunts." The structure of the film is far from the mind of Hollywood and will be as long as the mind of Hollywood is composed of the non-critical mentalities of America. Indeed, Hollywood is bewildered by the evidences of the cinema's positive tendencies: toward the reflective, toward non-sequential logic. It has accepted the compound as fiscal salvation and as palpable technology. But the compound is an art, technology informed by philosophy. The philosophy, critical viewpoint, is absent. Russia alone is completely the land of the philosophic cinema; therefore we may hope for much from its compoundings. If the technology of the Russian film keeps up with its philosophy, a very great compound cinema will result.

AMERICAN CINEMATOGRAPHER,
June, 1930.

MOTION PICTURE CRITICISM

Before 1910, criticism of motion pictures in these States consisted of prejudice and diatribe. These were discharged from the pens of moralists and adherents of the theatre, who called the upstart expression "canned drama," "nickel madness," "moving-picture *ad nauseam*," etc. The motion picture was not conceded as a possible existence in its own right, but was called "the electrical theatre," "the silent stage," "the bi-dimensional theatre," etc. Most of these attacks were provoked by job-interest and class-interest; by resentment against a new and popular expression. None of these vengeful bourgeois gentlemen saw the film as a form of art, possible of high attainments. There were, however, a few, appearing about 1910, who recognized in the "nickelodeon" a distinct, if not distinctive, form of popular show. At least one, Horace Kallen, accepted it as "a totally new and unexpected force in the field of the theatre." But to Kallen it was a force not destined for an evolution toward the realized. He saw it academically as a rudimentary form, completed in 1910. He was not able to anticipate its development from the primitive to the intellectual – the evolution of all arts. Yet we may forgive this limitation as of 1910. The movie was then a gurgling infant, and the highbrow disdained it. This attitude is not yet extinct. I have had the pleasure of being told by a populist weekly of sober pretensions that I take the movie "too seriously. It is, after all, only a passing entertainment." It has "potentialities, of course." Yet this journal has never examined these potentialities – one needs, you know, to be serious for that.

Most of our film-criticism concerns itself, in the *cliché* of the seven fulfilled arts, with limitations. In 1910, Kallen saw the speechlessness and impact-nature of the new medium as barriers to the creation of an incisive film-comedy with social meaning. Chaplin came along in 1913. The late Professor Hugo Münsterberg, at the behest and by the subsidy of the film-industry, examined the movie to lend it scholastic sobriety and absolution as an art. In 1930, fourteen years later, a Hollywood movie crusader attacks the film-magnate for not studying this work by Dr. Münsterberg. "An understanding of Münsterberg's dicta," the manifesto reads, "would have saved the movie — from the dragon of the talkie." Which is nonsense. Münsterberg merely investigated the film for its contemporaneous character, rather than for its nature as a medium in evolution. He approached it in the capacity of a clinical psychologist drawing aesthetic conclusions which described the movie in 1916. His book gave the film its rights as an independent art, in the way that a psychologist grades an individual intelligence, and indicated its power over that of the theater to objectify "in our world of perception our mental act of attention."

Münsterberg stated the *initial* integrity of the moving picture as well as anyone following him. He was a modified absolutist. He recognized a possible argument for colors, tolerated certain captions, and accepted harmonious musical accompaniment. The purist forgets that films began without captions. Griffith says that captions were added as an economy. That this addition was an expedient does not alter the fact that the movie incorporated the expedient as a valid detail. Almost all innovations from the close-up to sound have been expedients. The film in its mobility has validated them as part of its structure. The absolutist does not recognize motion pictures as the organic process it is, giving validity to the elements composing it. The captionless movie is not a permanent absolute, but a disciplinary ideal. To force the movie constantly into its simplest form is to keep it forever simplistic, a lisping, spluttering idiot.

Purism becomes a cosmic law through the agency of a type of absolutist who resembles the megalomaniac. He strengthens his argument by inflating it to a cosmos — a juvenile metaphysical trick of self-defense. To attack the sound-film, "silence is the ultimate philosophy." This young man, an hysterical browbeater with no sense of intellectual responsibility, may pound his way into Hollywood, the home colony of the movie's vested interests. Here he is further frustrated, and his criticisms become the cry of his injured vertex. His intensity is the intensity of the thwarted articulation which explains much that filled the *Little Review,* and the painful attempts made by young artists to be at one with their environment: *populism.* The absolutist-purist-isolationist is a familiar figure in the history of art. Reduction is purity. The detail becomes the whole. Art is sustained by impoverishment and not by enrichment; by exclusion and not by inclusion; by the intensity of the irreducible and not by the intensity of a complete experience. Isolation — the separateness of the movie — is found to be the means whereby man attains to universal salvation in an organic unity with the entire cosmic realm. Actually this is evasion. The illusion of the film is, like the illusion of every other art, only its physical basis and not its final significance. Maturity demands not illusions, but realities.

II

The chief characteristic of the American movie and of its criticism is its immaturity. In this it reflects America. Immaturity is one of two things: a condition in the individual, or an impasse in the society. I believe it is the latter state which allows the immature individual — whose immaturity is by no means always a temporary thing — to exploit his own limitations as those of the art.

The enthusiasm, more quasi than real, for the lowly or "lively arts" has been the effort of young men who had been precocious and had missed the normal childhood intimacy with the popular amusements. These young prigs, of a disintegrating class and of an unstable group within that class, have sought to establish empathy between their antipathetic environment and themselves. Kallen anticipated this in 1910. Robert Coady, "the skyscraper primitive" of *The Soil,* 1917, and the *Broom* boys, followed by the literary weathercock, Gilbert Seldes, were reinforced in this nostalgia by the camphor of dada, which sensitized their aesthetic noses to the art of the serial, the Western, slapstick, the animated cartoon — the present populist passion. This agony reached its apex when the superior mind discovered Charlie Chaplin. The discovery was especially instigated by Frank Harris — to whom Chaplin was a great man because he liked Frank Harris — and by Chaplin's confession of a yearning for ideas and rebellion. The total of instigation and discovery has been a cult of Charlie Chaplin which has never allowed a decent study of a man of talent who has not realized the great work that might have been expected of him.

I should like to be hopeful of the younger men and women who have entered the *milieu* of film-criticism. The young women, taught in schools of journalism, looking for unsaturated fields of endeavor, become daily reviewers or possibly light essayists in criticism. These daughters of the less unfortunately situated are deflected from a natural genius for the typewriter by the fact of material advantages, and turn to the business of cinema or movie. That at least is one hope for criticism, since we already have enough of the decorative there. It does not promise so well for the film with its agonies of the social register, the Blue Book Blues.

The film-cosmogonists are a more insidious danger. By their undersigned, underline (in red ink) professions, these enthusiasts, feeding at their cores, are alone qualified to judge "the film as microcosmos." Each day, with its change of wind, brings its own irritation, and this becomes the philosophy of "the new World Cinema." Peripheries become experiences. Footnotes become categories. The danger is accentuated by the fact that these egomaniacs seize upon currencies and appropriate them. The hope for the film and for criticism, as for the society which includes them, is in a thorough inquiry into society. Dissociated aesthetics must today be re-associated with its source. The attempts at synthesis through literary materials must fail for lack of a precise and constant measure or instrument. Only a social ideology can supply the efficacious instrument. The motion picture does not escape this necessity. Criticism certainly does not; it is the instructor in the uses of the didactic instrument. The study of past American writings on the motion picture might reveal to these mad boys their own platitudes, the threadbare redundancies, the stagnation of ideas, the truncated efforts, the shallowness of criticism here. It might purge them of hysteria and the cosmos.

III

There will, however, arise in the motion picture, as there is rising in the other arts, a group of active critics, for whom the film is not the all-inclusive but a part of the inclusive. They will understand the form as the conception constantly *informing* the structure; and the conception as the expression of the social mind. And that is how they will examine the film — dialectically. To disparage criticism is a typical bourgeois self-defense. There are professed materialists guilty of this infantilism. Criticism is a part of creation; and creation is the culmination of criticism. Ultimately the artist creates the law, but not without the exercise of criticism. In the State school of the cinema in Moscow a knowledge of cinema theory in relation to general culture is one of the aims of the curriculum.

There is a definite connection between the greatness as artists of the Russians — Pudovkin and Eisenstein — and their important contributions to the theory of the cinema. Film criticism in Germany and France accords exactly with the film-practices in those lands. English motion pictures coincide with the plagiarisms and insincerities of English film-criticism. The stodginess of Italian criticism — in all the arts — is expressed in the

Fascist cinema. And to read Griffith upon the art of the movie is to understand the source — personal and national and class — of his platitudinous films and their childish social sentimentality. The impasse in American movie-criticism, its inability to advance, coincides with the failure of American film innovations to be accepted as structural principles, and with the failure to incorporate criticism in the content of the movie. The force that will set the film free to develop beyond its rudiments will not come from the film-industry itself. It will need to be an "outside force," the force of progressive antithesis to the *status quo,* the vested interests and closed circles of Hollywood. The young men, self-rationalizers, who go to "bore within" the compact monopoly of the film cosmopolis, will either succumb to the dominant bribe or be the more irascible in their cries. To read the hysterical letters of the frustrated emigrants, to meet the directors escaping from the morass of the West Coast, is to experience intimately enough the inimical relation between environment and artist in the motion picture.

Against these damned souls, against opportunists from depleted fields, young women seeking unique careers, bad dramatic reviewers, hoodlums of the daily press, circus advance-agents, middle-aged *émigrés* from life, "men of ideas," dilettantes, rich men's sons from patrician meadows, against all who tantalize the "ideal" motion picture with speculations in a vacuum, there will be gathered a unified force. Despite obstacles, a few splendid films have been produced. Art has always been a victory against odds. The odds now are more vicious than ever, as we move toward a qualitative change in society. The presence of the Soviet film has forced a reluctant attention to a fundamental method of cinema-production. The critics squirm — they attack what they pretend to see as machine-worship and barbarism. The squirming is important. A critic appears who does not squirm beneath the challenge of a basic idea. Another such critic appears. I believe that these appearances will become a co-ordinated movement at about the time when a definite social group begins to enact its social program in the motion picture. In the meantime, it is the critic's business to help force that movement.

THE NEW FREEMAN,
March 4, 1931.

THE FUTURE CINEMA: NOTES FOR A STUDY

Thomas Hardy, in his early novel, *A Laodicean,* describes a woman thus: ". . . her stillness suggested the stillness of motion imperceptible from its intensity." In this description the future cinema finds its characterization. We are passing from motion whose transmission is impact to motion intensive. Someone has called it "static motion." The development, and it is a development in the full sense of improvement, is inherent in the very nature of cinema motion, which is motion organized in the image and with the image. The French, always alert to the necessity of an apt terminology, have called this twofold organization, "exterior movement," and "interior movement." The former comprises, to quote the excellent young French director, M. René Clair, "the movement of the objects enregistered: the play of the actor, the mobility of the decor, etc."; the latter "the alternation of the scenes or motifs of the action." These two, with "the duration of each image," constitute rhythm, which is organized motion, as against the literal acceptation, typical of the American movie, of motion as recorded. Duration becomes more and more, in every cinema but the American, the paramount consideration of the cinematographer. In duration is an important means of accomplishing the cinema of the future, which will be philosophical or psychical as against physical or muscular, reflective as against the "emotional discharge," inferential as against literal. The quoted phrase, "emotional discharge," is from S. M. Eisenstein, the director of *Potemkin.* His commentary upon the necessities of the future is of great importance, in that the Russian cinema, which has been received with enthusiasm, recognizes that it has come to the end of the first epoch of the motion picture: the epoch of the muscular, physical, direct impact film. *Potemkin* is the conclusion of that epoch. The films of Pudovkin are a mingling of the first epoch with naïve attempts toward the second. In the Ukrainian film, *Arsenal,* the first articulation of the principle of the future Russian film is discoverable: symbolism and not the symbol is the determinant. The symbol is a representation detail which runs into the inflation of sentimentalism. Symbolism is inclusive, unified, structural. The symbolism however must be achieved with the plastic materials of the first epoch: concrete objects, human values — the human actor, the common experiences, social conditions. Another inferential cinema will be evolved: the abstract . . . which will be formed of the effects of light, fluid color and created materials — of paper, of draughtsmanship, of pigment, of puppets.

I seem to have gone afield, away from the theme of "motion" expressed at the beginning of this consideration. But, in truth, motion does not determine the form or forms of cinema as much as the development of the *interest* of the cinema as an experience or an art determines the character of motion in the cinema. Every sententious young aspirant to the rôle of film critic reiterates the platitude of motion as the key to the motion picture. Motion, however, is no such simple device as a key, it is a structure, a construction. To Matthew Josephson the literal record is motion: therefore the rudimentary American movie is ultimate cinema. Slater Brown, colleague of Mr. Josephson, apprehended the subtlety of film motion in his brief essay on "Sculptural Kinetics." In the epithet "sculptural" is contained the apprehension of movie kinetics as structure. Rhythm, Mr. Brown said, is "the progressive deformation of a theme." But the cinema is intensive as well as progressive. It is the intensive character that will be developed in the future. The most realized instance of intensive cinema is Dreyer's *The Passion and the Death of Joan of Arc.*

This film has indicated the importance of the composition and duration of the single image or picture. It has been, up until now, accepted that the fact of movement demands action, which, because of the domination of the American film, has been defined as antic and speed. The Russians have stressed the inclusiveness of the mounting of the individual image in the construction of the film and, although their realization of this *montage* is but an elaboration of the American impact film, this emphasis has turned the cinema to an examination of its basic vocabulary. With *Joan,* so consistent and complete in its intensiveness, as a statement of this vocabulary used for a non-physical intention, the cinema enters into its profounder era. *Arsenal* is the beginning of the profounder era for the Russian cinema returning to its nativity in the traditional intensive, introspective Russian, of whom Dostoievski was the transcendent flower. *Joan* would be the beginning of the introspective American cinema, if that national folk-utterance had realized itself; for *Joan* in its stark unmodified lighting *should* be near to American practice, which stupidly, at this late day, turns to German studio-light, French multiple exposure and all non-literal details that it arbitrarily rejected yesterday. It is impossible to find a logic in the American cinema, as one was able to find it in the Swedish cinema of the golden age of Seastrom and Stiller, as one is able to find it in the German kino and Russian kino, and, yes, in the fragmentary French cinema. The American film worries about nothing but expedience. Expedience does not cherish experience.

There was one national film of this first epoch that was even then already in the epoch of intensiveness of treatment for intensity of experience. That was the Swedish film, so soon at an end. At an end in Sweden, but the Russian film, in its frequent poignancy, certainly not in its occasional arrogance, is the perpetuation of the Swedish film. This is not surprising: Sweden and Russia have always been close culturally. Emotionally there is a close relationship between Selma Lagerlöf and Dostoievski. Between the Seastrom film, *The Phantom Chariot* (*The Soul Shall Bear Witness*) and the first of the post-Revolution Russian films, *Polikushka,* for instance, there is an identity. And the Russian film of the Wufku, which I take as suggestive of the truer Russia and future Russian film, grown mature out of vociferousness and braggadacio, is very much like the Swedish film of Stiller, *The Treasure of Arne.* The present Russian film, where its formula is rendered stolidly, I think of *The Village of Sin,* still contains a veracity of experience that was not absent from the Swedish film of its golden era, when that film was at its end, in Molander's *The Accursed.*

We may say the cinema is now fulfilling itself as an experience. Out of Griffith comes Russian *montage,* out of the Swedish film the reflective Russian, which returns to its source—what folk is nearer its source than the Russian or the Swedish? I expect the imminent new era to bring with it a re-examination of the art of the cinema's first great artist, Seastrom, just as the termination of the first epoch led to a re-examination of the first great composer (not artist) of films, D. W. Griffith. The interrelationship vindicates the cinema as an art with a tradition, the present instances of *Joan* and *Arsenal* assure it a future, in which it will attain to the heights of philosophic import and the depths of human experience. Intelligence will be contained in the intensive film structure, for concentration and organization are intelligence. Duration is sensitivity of the æsthetic intelligence. And duration is perhaps the most important single element in the rhythm of the future film. It is duration, contemplation and penetration of the image through the uses of time, which permits Jean Epstein, employing light and diagonal treatment of subject-matter, to rise above his puerilities and impurities to become the sole metaphysician of the cinema. Jean Epstein is an instance of the French cinematographer who has not yet realized his idiom, because he dwells in a confusion of an epoch whose mind is counter to his, which is the mind that will find a meaning for itself in the next epoch already developing. The French mind is pictorial, speculative, fond of stylization, sophisticated, intellectualized to the point of effeteness, reveling in irrelevances . . . *Arsenal* negates conventional continuity. This is a negation which achieved fluidity in the documentary montage-film, Vertov's *The Man With the Camera* [*sic*]. The French mind exploits dissociations: the cinema has fallaciously taken over the literary and graphic formulæ of dadaism. But lately this dissociationism has – in Germaine Dulac's *The Seashell and the Clergyman* – achieved unity (a first essential in the present cinema) through a central intention and a sustained flux of image-into-image upon a rhythmic scheme. Previously – *Entr'acte* by René Clair – the isolations were not re-established as a unity . . .

The question arises: Will the audible film, the optophonic film, survive into the speculative era? Certainly! There are two cinemas, as determined by the number of mediums employed: the simple and the compound. The simple cinema is the mute cinema, and it is subdivided into the linear and the composite. The compound cinema includes all compoundings of audibility, tacility, etc. with the visual (really the visual-motor). The compound cinema will exist in the second epoch and its form, sound-sight at the moment, will seek reflective utterance. It will find reflecttive utterance by dwelling upon two things: the integrated structure and speech-as-utterance. Speech is the visual-motor graph and speech as abstract sound . . . The duration of speech is of first importance in such organization, malleability and elasticity of utterance will be sought, and that search is a search for rhythm, "repetition in variation." Rhythm is always the answer, for, as William Carlos Williams once said, "rhythm is the poem."

What of dynamics in the future speculative, inferential cinema? Alexander Bakshy, who, more than all other critics, stresses the cinema as a dynamic art rejects films like *Chang* and *Joan* as being un-dynamic. To him dynamics is the physical "resultant of forces." *Chang* being a sequence upon a single line in a single direction would not be dynamic, lacking, as it does, plural play. But *Chang* is, nevertheless, cinema, rudimentary and forceful, of the linear simple form. *Joan* is certainly dynamic, it is plural:

but Bakshy evidently recognizes only the progressive in dynamics, not the intensive. What of the resultant of two forces: a progressive and intensive? In physics, perhaps, one may deny such possibility, but can one, in aesthetics, as an experience of the beholder?

PAGANY,
Spring, 1930.

2

FILM TECHNIQUE

CAMERA! SOME UNSUNG ARTISTS OF THE CINEMA

It is taken for granted among American film-makers that "cameramen rarely break into print." Although the photography and shots of a movie may be admired, the identity of the cinematographer excites no curiosity, save in the industry of the film and in the trade of the cameraman. What devotee of the American film will recall these names: Billy Bitzer, Alvin Wyckoff, Karl Brown, Charles Rosher, Gilbert Warrenton, George Folsey, Oliver Marsh, Bert Glennon, Karl Struss? The enthusiast may recognize two associated with direction, Karl Brown and Bert Glennon. But he would never remember that so many of the films which he enjoyed owed much of their merit to the camera work of either. Yet many a film has been given its outstanding quality by the cinematographer. Frequently the work at the camera has determined the film.

In a consideration of the cameraman (who is more truly the camera engineer), one naturally begins, in America, with George William (Billy) Bitzer. Indeed, before there was a movie, there was Billy Bitzer. About thirty-five years ago Bitzer turned to the camera from his trade of electrician, and American motion picture history wrote its first chapter. In 1896 Bitzer caught McKinley receiving the presidential nomination in Canton, Ohio. A few years later he recorded the Jeffries-Sharkey bout, inaugurating the practice of artificial lighting. This historical note is highly interesting, when we recall that Hollywood was founded in the search for natural sunlight. The movie began outdoors, but the Jeffries-Sharkey fight at the Coney Island Athletic Club on November 3, 1899, brought the film indoors. Some four hundred arc-lamps were clustered over the ring and the camera speeded to a night's mileage of seven-and-a-quarter of negative, then postal card size.* The American Mutoscope and Biograph Company was born into the studio world with that film and Bitzer was its dominant figure. The director was incidental.

With the new century, however, the film moved toward its creator, and that evolution was consummated in David Wark Griffith. D. W. was an actor. Bitzer was camera lord. One day the director of a film was absent, Griffith was called in to substitute. With that incident the famous AB (American Biograph) became a leader; the great Griffith-Bitzer team commenced.

This combination was responsible for the close-up. Of course, the bold image existed in the film before the Biograph days. The very first peep-show films were large scale. That, however, was an expedient to film a moment. The first use of the close-up in the movement of a narrative film was made in *The Mender of Nets,* in which Mary Pickford acted and which Griffith directed and Bitzer photographed. It is a victory such as this that I call camera engineering. The too superficially reasoning critic may condemn the close-up as a banality—its use has been banal; it is nevertheless, as a rhythmic component, intrinsic cinema. We may note here that in America the close-up has remained a device for effect. In Europe it has evolved as a structural element and has attained, in *The Passion of Joan of Arc,* the eminence of a structural principle. In this evolution we connect two great directors, Griffith and Carl Dreyer, who acknowledges the former as a pioneer; and we join as well two very great cinematographers, Billy Bitzer and Rudolph Maté.

Bitzer is responsible for certain controls of photographic quality. It was he who originated the soft focus, the elimination of the sharp corners of the film frame and the use of gauze to tone the film to a mist (as in *Broken Blossoms*). In America, again, we have not gone on with these modifications of the literal in film photography. It is in Europe we find their continuation and extension. Cavalcanti films *The Petite Lily* through gauze to depersonalize the characters, and Man Ray sees his characters through a mica sheet which grains the picture and renders it liquid in constituency. There is one European device we have borrowed and abused to death: the rising mist. This appeared in *Flesh and the Devil,* was used effectively in *Sunrise,* and then repeated in numerous Fox films. But otherwise our cinematographers have not learned the treatment that modifies the literal. The mind of the American film, regarding both content and approach, is literal; and that is why the American film is still rudimentary, and why no one here has extended or even equaled the compositions of Griffith or logically developed the innovations of Billy Bitzer.

For instance, let us refer to the camera angle, a major instance of camera engineering. In *Intolerance,* in 1915, Bitzer used the angle and the mobile camera to descend, in the Babylonian scene, from a view looking down upon three thousand persons to a close-up of the central personage. America quite forgot this powerful method until the German film, *Variety,* introduced the angle as the determining structure of a film and sent all Hollywood into a frenzy of angles from which it has only recently recovered. Nor has there yet been very much learned by director or cinematographer of Hollywood about the angle as a principle, rather than as an effect device. We have few camera engineers, or camera aestheticians; they are mostly cameramen.

Coupled with the name of Billy Bitzer is that of Alvin Wyckoff. Wyckoff is to the reputation of De Mille what Bitzer is to the realization of Griffith's ideas. There is no knowing what Wyckoff might have accomplished had he worked with the creator instead of the barker. Nevertheless, what remains with one after an early De Mille film is, besides the sense of claptrap content, a memory of photographic, cinematographic splendor. Wyckoff is especially noted for the invention of new lenses and for innovations in lighting. He is accredited with having first effected the reproduction in the film of the lighting of a cigar or cigarette. In 1928 the famous "originals" and old rivals, Bitzer and Wyckoff, joined together to film (at the behest of George Barnes, the Goldwyn cameraman) the movement of men through a marsh in *The Rescue.* This itself attests to the fact that the "originals" have not yet been duplicated.

These two men, Bitzer and Wyckoff, belong to the category of camera engineers. The camera aesthetician I term the cinematographer who is also an independent director. In America we may number among these, Schoedsack and Cooper, makers of *Chang*; Robert J. Flaherty, the great lyricist of the cinema who made *Nanook of the North* and *Moana of the South Seas;* and Karl Brown, who constructed and realized *Stark Love.* Brown is one of Billy Bitzer's boys, and his record in cinematography includes *The Covered Wagon* and *Beggar on Horseback.* Was not the cinematography of these films largely responsible for their success? Indeed, for me *The Covered Wagon* is a directorial failure and a cinematographic (camerman's) success. *Stark Love* is not a directorial success either, but it marks the passage of the cinematographer into control, a passage we find common in amateur film-making and in Europe. In *Stark Love,* however, Brown turned the camera operation over to James Murray.

Among the American amateur camera aestheticians I note Dr. John Watson, Ralph Steiner, Paul Strand and Charles Sheeler, Jo Gercon and Louis Hirshmann. Their films are personal declarations.

When we come to Europe we find the cameraman's contribution more generously credited. No one thinks of *The Passion of Joan of Arc* without remembering the work of Rudolph Maté: the intensive application upon the slow curve, the scrutiny of the physiognomy, the stark lighting, the composition in the lens, the resilient movement of the camera in the mob scene. When one mentions *The Armored Cruiser Potemkin,* immediately the name of Tisse follows for his terrific impact-filming. These are, of course, cardinal instances. But so are *Intolerance* and *The Birth of a Nation*—yet who recalls Bitzer as responsible for much of these? The point, however, has less to do with credit for the individual cameraman; the companies know of him. I am more concerned with a record of the work of these individual cameramen in the collective art of the cinema.

The most eminent of the Europeans in the contribution of camera engineering to the cinema is Karl Freund. Freund *established* the mobile camera in *The Last Laugh*; the camera angle in *Variety*. The numerous intermediate controls of the image, such as the multiplying and distorting prism, the haze-glass, the kaleidoscopic toy with its changing patterns in central balance, were introduced by Freund. He is responsible for the exciting edifices of *Metropolis,* all miniature models. We get here our milestones of cinematographic history: Bitzer, Freund, Maté. Bitzer uses the close-up for the first time in a film at varied arrangement; Freund first uses it revealingly in the structure in *The Last Laugh;* Maté, through Dreyer, makes it *the* structure, where it ceases to be a close-up and becomes a structure in relief. Bitzer uses the angle as a detail in *Intolerance*; Freund uses it as structure in *Variety;* Maté renders it rhythmic and poignant in *Joan*. At the present moment there is another comparison between Bitzer and Freund. The latter is today sponsoring in America a new color process; the former is active in the promotion of the wide film. These are logical terminals for camera engineers.

Freund made with Walter Ruttmann the composite document of *Berlin: the Symphony of a Great City*. In this he is the innovator of a new form of motion picture which stems from the simple newsreel and travelogue. In Russia, Dziga Vertov is broadening this form of objective, non-narrative film; and numerous young men in Paris are beginning their careers with such film arrangements. Among these are a number of young men who are cameramen as well as directors. The numbers include Vertov's youngest brother, Kauffmann. A third Kauffmann (this is Vertov's family name) is co-worker with Vertov, having made with him *The Man With a Movie Camera,* as yet the best example of what is called the montage-film. The montage-film is a film assembled of separate images which is not *immediately* related to a single thing or event, but which, when joined into sequences, becomes a unit organized in a definite rhythm.

Russian film-making is stimulated by a social idea, and hence its camerawork moves on toward new areas of greater magnitude. I have mentioned Eisenstein's cameraman, Edouard Tisse, who has worked under Eisenstein and Alexandrov (the latter must not be forgotten as a collaborator). But one cannot overlook the great work of Anatoli D. Golovnia, who realizes the imaginings of Pudovkin, the romantic of the Russian cinema. Golovnia's work in *The End of St. Petersburg* adds his name to the lists of the heroic in camera creation. Pudovkin's *Storm Over Asia,* which I saw intact in Amsterdam, will shortly be released here. The camera work is eminently structural, with its general perspectives, its hyperattentive eye, its intelligence. And certainly the most beautiful detail of *The New Babylon,* that film of sustained tones and stylization, is the camera as A. N. Moskvin employed it. To these names we must add those of Evgeny Shneyder for *Fragment of an Empire,* distinguished by such camera achievements as shooting as many as four levels or planes, and getting them tonally, structurally clear and outstanding. The American technique has not often achieved this multiple-level filming. A Bitzer could achieve it; not many more. Another name must surely be appended: D. Demutsky, cinematographer of *Arsenal.* The work of K. Kuznetsov in *The Village of Sin* actually transcends the directorial achievement itself.

It is in the Soviet cinema the camera engineer is recognized. His position in the collective scheme of film-making is equal to that of the director. He approaches his task not as one assigned to it after the plan is made and the scene set, but as one participating in the making of the plan. Tisse, for instance, studies the scenario first, then consults the scenewright, together with whom the relation of camera, lights, and decor are determined, proceeds thence to the mapping of the "light-scenario," which serves as a blueprint for his assistant, a sort of camera stage manager. Then, and only then, after the cameras and lights have been adjusted upon the basis of the camera chart does Tisse himself appear for the final relating of equipment to the thing filmed, to direct, that is, the camerawork just as the *régisseur* directs the players. The rank of cameraman as engineer is the basis and aim of the course in the State School of the Cinema, where the students receive not only practical training, from menial tasks to the command of the camera, but also theoretical, in the study of the literature and principles of cinematography as a medium. Chemistry is taught in the second year, but not solely as a laboratory science; rather in relation to the art of the cinema. The course concludes with a study of optics. The camera engineer coincides, in the Soviet cinema, with the camera aesthetician.

In France, as Mme. Germaine Dulac says, the successful film is found wherever the cameraman, director and cutter are one and the same. Such an identification we find among the American amateurs, but in Continental Europe the distinction between amateur and professional is not made. Most noted among the independents, the *avant-gardistes*, are Mme. Dulac, the American Man Ray, the Ukrainian Eugene Deslav, the Parisian André Sauvage, the Hungarian Moholy-Nagy, the American Francis Bruguière and the Dutchman Joris Ivens.

Germaine Dulac, recently named a Chevalier of the Legion of Honor, was among the first to introduce the screen-panel, where only a portion of the screen is used at a time. The effect is achieved by masking the lens to hide the portion that is not used. This is a simple instance of the treating of the initiating instruments, camera and negative, in relation to the screen. Dulac has also, in *The Seashell and the Clergyman,* effected the illusion of a body dividing in half. This simple device relates her to the father of film virtuosity, the Frenchman, Georges Méliès, the magician who used the movie in the 'nineties as an aid to his illusion-art. Dulac places a card down the center of a man's face. She moves the camera leftward from the card as the limit of the lens. The right half of the lens is masked to prevent light from striking that part of the negative which is not to be impressed. Then the other half is masked and the camera moved rightward from the limit of the card. The spectator sees the body as dividing away from the center. Mme. Dulac does not end with virtuosity. These devices are contained in the fluid rhythm of the film. The camera virtuoso becomes the camera aesthetician, the creative artist. Dulac was one of the first to use the prism, the distorting mirror, and similar devices as means to sensitive and descriptive detail.

Man Ray represents the entrance of the painter into the film. His entrance has come by way of photography, as is also the case with Moholy-Nagy. These men belong in the history of the absolute film, the film of organized, non-human components, which begins with the Norwegian Viking Eggeling and his disciple Hans Richter. The independent film includes other artists who have come by way of painting or photography. Francis Bruguière, an American resident in London, has made part of a projected film, *The Way,* which, by means of simultaneous images or multiple exposures, tells the story of the life of man, from birth to death. This is the work of a camera aesthetician. At present he is animating abstractions in paper, illumined and transfigured by light. The artist of the still camera and the light picture becomes the artist of the play of light. Eugene Deslav has turned his camera upon machines and electric lights and made them dramatic and compositionally significant. André Sauvage has turned his camera upon day-by-day Paris to study the movements about its subways, quais, and markets.

Joris Ivens of Amsterdam comes to film creation as a phototechnician. His first film was a documentation of the vertical opening and closing of the Rotterdam Steel Bridge. He then made a film of the oily Dutch rains. With his hand-and-eye camera poking under legs and between wheels, he has produced the most interesting objective study of somberness I have ever seen. This is a phototechnician's film, a film of filters and camera.

I have presented a summary of the diversified camera workers, the cinematographer. Inventors, engineers, aestheticians, creators are comprised in the term cameraman. Today the newsreel has begun to give recognition to the cameraman as a creator. The film actor knows how important to him or her is the cameraman, and Lillian Gish accordingly pays this tribute to one: "I have often been called a Griffith product. Well, in a way I am, of course. In a great many ways I am not. Nearly all my early pictures were directed by Tony Sullivan and Christy Cabanne, with the famous cameraman, Billy Bitzer, as valuable to the picture as the directors."

THEATRE GUILD MAGAZINE,
July, 1930.

* [Gen. Ed.]: Page 60 — Paper prints of selected frames for viewing in a Mutoscope machine.

THE CLOSEUP'S THE THING

The method of Carl Theodor Dreyer is as rigorous as it is simple. Its rigor and simplicity have been derived from a cinematic concept which has been Mr. Dreyer's since he began making films many years ago, for the plain but intensive and bold imagery of *Jeanne d'Arc* was anticipated in his first film, *Pages from the Book of Satan,* which he made for the old Great Northern Film Company. In *Jeanne d'Arc* Mr. Dreyer attained complete fulfillment of his concept through the use of continuous closeups. We must differentiate between his closeup method or *gros plan* and the closeup as ordinarily used. In *Jeanne d'Arc* the faces of the actors almost continuously fill the greater part of the screen. In other words, the closeup, varied only in degree, is used as the basis of motion picture technique rather than the usual medium shot, varied extensively by closeups and long-shots. The story is conveyed by the emotions of the characters displayed in the closeups of their faces rather than by action.

The steps in Dreyer's production of a film are broadly as follows:

1. The selection of subject matter or theme.
2. The construction of a detailed episodic synopsis.
3. The preparation of a general scheme of presentation.
4. Selection of the settings and players.
5. Writing the continuity (*decoupage*).
6. Photographing the production.
7. Cutting and arranging the final composition (*montage*).

The actors who are to interpret the theme are Dreyer's first consideration. As he said to me, no subtle idea or theme can reach the spectators unless the players presenting it possess an imaginative understanding of the theme. The players in *Jeanne d'Arc* were his personal selection and that he could see the Jeanne of his film in the lovely Falconetti of *Camille* attests his genius. Not until the settings and players are definitely known does Dreyer begin work upon the continuity. He must know the position of every door and window and the arrangement of the wall space before he arranges a scene and so he plans each day's work only the night before filming. The characteristics of each player are carefully studied, first, in relation to those of the other players and the structure of the story and, second, in relation to the most effective use of backgrounds.

Dreyer places extreme importance upon the literary manuscript, the scenario. He prepares it very much like an episodic narrative, thereby getting the subject matter completely unified before beginning the film. There is nothing in the manuscript that does not find a place in the film; there is nothing in the film that is not anticipated in the manuscript. Nothing is extraneous, nothing accidental. The scenario is the film's foundation, for it contains every scene, action and title. In *Jeanne d'Arc* (in its original form, as it came from Dreyer's hand, 2,400 meters long) there was not a scene nor a situation which had not been anticipated in the manuscript. In other words, the film is conceived in the manuscript. In other words, position of the camera in relation to the players and those interpretations which inspiration legitimately adds remains to be determined.

For inspiration is not an accident. Accident must not enter into a film that is continuously intense. Dreyer's method allows for the idea that may be born "on location" for his careful preparation of each day's work, only the night before filming, possesses flexibility. It permits careful following of the scenario and also gives inspiration its opportunity. But inspiration must be born of the body of the film. Dreyer allows no detail that will not enforce the dramatic construction. He is strict in his conception of unity and he will not have a closeup or *gros plan* that has no other justification than its own sentimental or visual appeal. He thinks of his *whole* film in enlarged images. Each image must add force to the whole and must be justified by it. There is no "ingratiating virtuosity" in Dreyer's work. His film is a life-experience and as such cannot play at being theatrical. He has not fallen into the error of the German virtuosos, although he has produced a film for Ufa.

Everything must yield to the unity of his conception. Hermann Warm, the architect, must see the importance of his sets minimized, for they must truly be but backgrounds. Rudolph Maté must photograph players without makeup. The actors must study the manuscript and assimilate the feeling of the character of the drama. The manuscript is always the guide for the performance. Dreyer wants no historical reconstruction. Therefore, he does not exactly follow the historical models in costuming, although he does present their general effect.

Once the film is under way there can be no experimenting. For three months prior to the commencement of the picture, Dreyer and Maté considered and quarreled over all possibilities of lighting and camera technique. The director presented his concepts as contained in the scenario. Research and experiment followed, for there must be no accident. Dreyer and Maté studied all possibly relevant treatments of the closeup. They found the final basis in the miniature art of medieval France. Therein was the source for the flat, moderated, stucco background which thrusts the fore-figures further into relief and constantly maintains relation between the large fore-figures and the minimized rear-figures.

Two elements are of particular interest in Dreyer's *Jeanne*. One is the use of portions of physiognomy and anatomy as a forceful graphic design. Here a segment of a head fits into the lower left corner of the screen, plastically harmonizing with the curve of a window frame. There half of a person, like a pillar, balances another vertical. This use of anatomy to complete a pattern has excited many painters and sculptors. These arrangements are not designed prior to filming. Dreyer does not use Fritz Lang's method of designing the groupings on paper before capturing them with the camera. Lang groups his players according to the sketched design and then sets them into motion. This accounts for the stolidity of Lang's work. It is an illustrator-architect's structure. The design is conceived as stationary and disintegrates into heavy components when it moves away from the preconceived position. Dreyer arranges the general grouping in the pre-plan, then looks through the camera, whose eye is his own. The camera's eye determines the final organization of the details. The camera designs the movements of the performers into curves and verticals that pass over the screen. The screen in Dreyer's film is a receptive canvas which enters into the design.

Another of the important elements in *Jeanne d'Arc* is time. Dreyer uses time rythmically by interweaving the images and controlling the duration of the various movements of lips and bodies. He does not, however, use the method that Murnau is said to use, in which the camera is set a given tempo. He trusts to his own sense of time, exactly as does the poet.

Thinking in terms of enlarged images, he leaves full consideration of composition until after the filming. Like the Russians, Dreyer places major stress upon this post-arrangement. It is the *montage*, or cutting, that the rhythm of the film as a whole is realized and the dramatic contrasts of the slow moving images and the staccato ones are introduced. For Dreyer believes in the motion picture as drama. He cuts for drama and the drama transcends the narrative. By a persistent back-and-forth cutting the images are in constant reference. In *Jeanne d'Arc,* her insistence upon God, the clerics' insistence upon the Church and Warwick's insistence upon State were emphasized in the editing.

MOVIE MAKERS,
September, 1929.

THE MONTAGE FILM

The French word, *montage,* is perhaps the most internationally accepted term for the film process which we call "cutting," or "editing." It refers to the arranging of images into a unified organic relationship. In Europe there has evolved, under the influence of the Russians, a special group of film creators whose work is known generically as "the *montage* film." The best-known of these workers is the Ukrainian, Dziga Vertov, who made *The Eleventh Year* and *The Man With a Movie Camera,* the latter known in America as *Living Russia.*

Actually, this type of picture has its ancestry in the newsreel and the travel picture. Before the advent of the organized *montage* film we had, as we still have, films assembled or faked from the celluloid clippings of film libraries. Frequently, excerpts of newsreels are inserted in feature films but, instead of giving authenticity to the whole, they often intrude disturbingly different light densities and movements.

An amateur might learn an enormous amount in film construction by assembling a film made up of diverse clippings, selected because of a relative unity of light, movement, imagery and theme. The *montage* film offers the amateur an independent opportunity. He takes his camera and does one of two things. He either collects a variety of unrelated shots which he may later join selectively into a film, or he decides upon a film and goes forth to discover the details which will comprise it. In the former instance, while there is no guiding intention of relationship, the amateur will probably find on looking through his library that he has enough shots which can be made into a short film. When he begins to "edit" this film he will be guided by the same method that controls the *montage* of the amateur who has chosen his theme prior to the shooting of the scene. However, the latter amateur will have acted more deliberately and wisely. He will first have prepared himself for the actual shooting by surveying his locale without his camera, recording in his mind's eye types of faces, categories of groups, settings, etc. Serge M. Eisenstein, the great Russian director of *Potemkin* and *Ten Days that Shook the World,* keeps a notebook in which he records types and their addresses so that he may reach them on need. Hollywood does the same with professional performers and the amateur can keep a similar notebook recording friends, scenes and other possible shots.

Three professional films may serve as a starting point for a consideration of the *montage* film. The first is Alberto Cavalcanti's *Only the Hours.* I choose this first because it preceded the others in production, because it expresses best the principle of rhythm which defines the good *montage* film and because it has deeply influenced many young Parisian amateurs. Cavalcanti has three motifs in his film, alternating progressively — a news vendor moving through the streets, a drunken hag drawing herself to the waterfront, the city about them. The interrelationship is fluid. One cannot separate the motifs while they are in progress. The amateurs who have been influenced by this film have often missed this principle of fluid interweaving. They have usually had a two-motif film — a simple undetailed story or episode with characters; the workaday city. But these two motifs are usually not dovetailed so that one feels they are inseparable. Moreover, the human episode is usually too insignificant for the proportions of the environment. This false scale of the motifs inflates the episode or crushes it.

The second film is *Berlin, a Symphony of a City,* by Walter Ruttman and Karl Freund. Here the sequences are more sharply delineated one from the other. There is no motif that tells a story as in *Only the Hours.* Not individual human episodes but the City is the pattern. *Only the Hours* is romance; *Berlin* is document. *Only the Hours* is subjective; *Berlin* is objective. Both, however, are more than matter-of-fact records; they are compositions. In *Berlin,* the city day is shown chronologically, the tempo increasing gradually to full speed, then closing abruptly. This is the city of human details but in the pattern, repeated at points, is a moving spiral, a store's ensign, which brings an abstract but moving detail into the human activity and provides an effective motif for the whole.

Vertov, in his *Man With a Movie Camera,* has produced, upon the objective principle of *Berlin,* a film of amazing fluidity with successive images which do not always connect directly with each other. He has, in the typical Russian way, sought to make the images symbolic of the land and has endeavored to include in the film all the various contrasts of the city's life, of human existence -- work and pleasure, birth and death. In films of no single continuous narrative the piling up of diversified scenes may increasingly obscure the underlying movement of the picture.

Amateurs frequently attempt to include too much in their films, too many images of too many different categories. Not only does this prolixity work against the memory of the spectator and, thereby, defeat the intention of the film itself but it is also very fatiguing. Mlle. Lucile Derain blundered thus in *Harmonies of Paris.* The very title indicates a too ambitious intention. Mlle. Derain attempted not one harmony but several, succeeding finally in getting less of harmony than of wearisomeness. Had she limited the film to one phase of Paris, the beautiful opening with the Montmartre byways, she would have produced a lyric of the cinema. Similarly the work of Lods and Kauffmann defeats its expert photography and rhythmic reiterations by going in for too many sequences. The final caption of the film, "Etc.," neatly characterizes its interminable succession of scenes.

For the amateur's first attempt in the film of *montage,* it would be wise for him to select a simple theme, a document. It might be a romantic document in which the details tell the story of the life of a particular people. Such is George Lacombe's film of the ragpickers of the Flea Market, the locale of *The Innocents of Paris.* In this film, *The Zone,* Lacombe follows the ragpickers from the early hours, when they hunt their wares, to the Sunday, when they sell them at the Clignancourt gate, recording as he goes the rare personalities of the quarter, the unusual sign-boards, the amusements, the incidents of family life, *etc.* It is a unified document in which the regular sequence of the actual details of the ragpickers' lives form a tale. This film, which will be shown in America, is a fine example of simple, sincere, direct documentation, an excellent model for the amateurs.

The American movie maker can find splendid ideas for films of documentation in the exceptional instances of American life or, better, in typical instances — an American lunch hour, American markets, an American Sunday. Every amateur ought to attempt to film his city or a part of it. It would be interesting to compare the data. Humor is possible in the documentary film. André Sauvage in his *Studies of Paris* couples his scenes so that the second comments on the first. A lay-figure in a shop window comments upon a preceding scene of a girl in the street. Often these are obvious but the principle is worth consulting.

The film of *montage* and document offers fundamental, manifold and independent opportunities. One need not trouble with human beings at all; there is subject matter in the natural elements. Franken and Ivens found such material in the oily rains of Holland; Blum in Europe and Steiner in America found it in the qualities of water, while Silka in France found it in the barnyard.

The movement of clouds, grasses, grain and treetops in the wind and the motion of machinery are all open to this treatment. There are many untried possibilities in the simplest relations of motion in familiar subjects. Your reel might not have any other purpose than the presentation of the beauty of motion as portrayed in varied patterns.

MOVIE MAKERS,
February, 1930.

THE MAGIC OF MACHINE FILMS

There is no more insistent experience in our lives than contact with the machine. It is with us from waking until sleeping, and, while we sleep, it is still at work. Of all the things that move, none is more assertive than the machine. It is most logical, therefore, that the machine should force itself upon the eye of another machine, whose function it is to record, construct and present motion. The machine is, for this reason, a basic subject-matter I recommend to the serious movie maker, whether he choose a press, derrick, steam shovel or locomotive.

One of the first films to be made was of the locomotive. The earliest serials were of the speed and force of locomotives and trains. Abel Gance, the French pioneer, made a film, *The Wheel,* whose interest was not only in the sentimental human tale but in the observation, analytical and synthetic, of the movements of a locomotive and its parts. From this film stemmed those made by other experimenting artists of the camera, films of the speed, structure and power of machines—machines that stand fixed while their arms move furiously, machines that rush through space. Among them have been the film, *Ballet Mécanique,* made by the French artist, Fernand Leger, aided by the American, Dudley Murphy; the film by Henri Chomette, *Of What are the Young Films Dreaming?* (called in France *Reflections and Speed*) and the film by the young Ukrainian, Eugene Deslav, *The March of the Machines,* all of which have been presented in America.

In filming a machine or machines, there are several things to aim for—the relation of the entire machine to its parts, the relation of the machine at rest to the machine in motion, the relations of the moving parts, the increase and decrease in speed, the texture or lustre, the sense of volume and sense of power. A machine film can be very dramatic!

The amateur movie maker will best know, by trial and error, or intuitively, how to arrange the continuity and where to place his camera, in order to attain the qualities mentioned above. But may I not describe a very elementary procedure, which may be made more intricate and fascinating after the movie maker has learned a few things about absolute composition?

Let us take a not too elaborate machine — one that possesses two movements, a horizontal piston arm and a vertical movement — like that of a simple steel-puncher used in shipyards. This is the sort of machine also seen in establishments where bottles are capped. The body of the machine, if I may call it that, is fixed. The movement is of the two parts. If I were beginning to film the machine, I would minutely examine it first. I would study it, both in motion and at rest, and again, in reverse order. I might begin by filming it at total rest and then follow as it worked into speed. That is the most obvious way, yet it has its difficulty. If you follow this procedure, you will have reached the highest pitch of movement before the film is long on its way. Perhaps you will prefer to wait a moment before diving into the motion of the machine. You may follow its parts at rest. That is, the camera will move, instead of the machine, which is the actor. The camera will examine the machine in one direction, then in another, or may alternate the examination in bits. The machine itself, its pattern, may decide for the movie maker the design upon which he will build the continuity of the film. A very simple machine with few parts and few contrasts in their forms may ask for nothing more than a sketching. Another machine, by its very volume, may ask for a slower, more observant and studious attention. A clever worker may be able to create, in his movement of the camera about the machine at rest, a sense of the machine growing from its parts into a whole. René Clair, the young French director, in his film, *The Eiffel Tower,* gave the sense of the tower's construction in actual progress by filming photographs of the Tower in successive stages of development. I am aware that this is not the same thing as filming a constructed machine — it belongs, rather, to the category of the animated cartoon. Still it indicates that one can use static things and get motion.

After this work of assembling the parts into a sense of progressive development, the next step is to film the machine actually moving. Perhaps the movement of one part will be taken before the whole machine at work is filmed, or *vice versa.* Perhaps an alternation of the whole and one part, the whole and another part, will be the scheme used. But you must be sure that your directions of movement are balanced and do not disturb the eye or the pattern of the entire film. Remember that no matter in what order you film the various sequences of your picture, they need to form a rhythmic continuity, or else — what's the sense of doing a machine film? It will be in the final cutting that a unified and moving design will be achieved from the film exposed. I recall in a film made by the French artist, Mme. Germaine Dulac — *An Arabesque* — how the movement, which was horizontal, was suddenly broken into by the vertical play of a fountain.

A machine film offers the opportunity for what may be called "controlled camera motion," that is, slow and fast motion and stoppages of movement. But all these should enter into the whole pattern of the film. To retard the actual motion for the sake of a moment's effect may mean to destroy the full progress of the picture. But if the slow motion contrasts with the motion filmed "as is," that is a contribution. Or if, by slowing the motion of a piston, you can convey a sense of elasticity or resilience of the movement of that part, that's a contribution. Perhaps an accelerated movement, ending in a sudden stop, will convey more sharply the terrific force of the machine. If the machine has a downward movement, you may find that alternating this with the same image reversed, moving upward, is very effective. You may discover that a richer arabesque of movement and form can be obtained by making a film, not of one machine only but of two or more. You may look for parallels in motion, for contrasts, or for both. A piston of a simple bottle-filling machine may fade into a piston of a locomotive in fierce motion, into parallels and contrasts of wheels, into cranes, steam shovels, etc.

As you become more skilled, you may try what Deslav did with multiple exposure — the movement of a steam shovel in central-balance with itself. The shovel moved away from the center leftward and rightward, giving a lovely dance effect.

I do not wish to go into more minute detail — that is the job of the movie maker himself. He will find a thousand combinations, but there are a number of generalities that might be suggested. Try to give a sense of the solidity and weight of the thing you are filming. Suppose, like René Clair, you are filming the elevator that climbs the Eiffel Tower. You discover that getting the machine at a certain angle carries just the force of weight you're after. Choose, therefore, the telling angle. Don't be too literal. The angle may foreshorten the image, but the foreshortening may coincide with what you want.

Be very careful in your camera work — you are after a unity of light, or texture, which helps, as much as anything, to make a machine film a thing of beauty.

Don't let human beings get into the picture, if it is absolutely a machine film and not a film that tells the trade-story of a machine. It's true that sometimes a human form relieves the starkness of a machine film, but it's a false relief. It injures the film by its intrusion. And if your film has succeeded in achieving grace of movement, as well as power, the relief will not be needed. Deslav's machine film was momentarily disturbed by a workman who was caught behind the machine. Fortunately it was only a moment's presence, and the variety and gracefulness of the film could surmount it.

Drawbridges are machinery inviting the camera. I think, at the moment, of *The Rotterdam Steel Bridge,* filmed by the young Dutch phototechnician, Joris Ivens. This bridge opens upward and closes downward. Ivens followed the languid pace of the opening and closing of the bridge, heeding, all the time, the nature of the structure. He was careful to capture only so much of the edifice as would convey its solidity. He understood that to take in too much of the bridge at a time would make the steel look webby rather than solid. That is a thing one learns with study. A machine-film is like a lyric; it must not be too long. Ivens carried his film beyond its logical point of duration, thereby weakening it. Still, it is a good film. At one point, the concrete base, or lock of the bridge, occupies the entire screen, making of the screen a concrete rectangle, and pleasing the tactile sense with its texture. Ivens also included the movements upon and about the bridge — trains, motor cars, wagons, boats — enlivening the languor of the bridge's pace and enriching the active pattern. I advise young amateurs, however, to avoid a too complex film until they have practised the cinematography of a simple scheme of machine motion.

MOVIE MAKERS,
November, 1929.

NEW IDEAS FOR ANIMATION

I need not go into detail concerning the making of the familiar animated cartoon. The method, of course, is based upon the physical principle of the movie — that a succession of static images conveys an illusion of motion. The animated cartoon, however, is not the only form of animated film. There are other kinds which offer to the movie maker opportunities for design and stylized motion and which are less tedious for the amateur to construct. With each the basic principle is the same, that one frame be exposed, the object moved a little, another frame exposed, the object moved, etc. While amateur equipment, generally, is not designed for frame by frame use, by very gently pressing and releasing the button, passable results may be obtained with some cameras.

But, before entering into animated films of arranged surfaces and solids, one may consider the work of the first "absolute" film makers, the Scandinavian, Viking Eggeling, who in 1918 filmed a moving point, and his successors, Hans Richter and Walter Ruttman, who filmed moving lines. This may be done in two ways, by photographing successive positions of points and lines or — an increasingly important procedure — working directly upon the negative itself, just as an etcher works directly upon his plate.

The Japanese have made films of rice paper cut-outs in which both background and performer are cut of the rice paper. The artist works for a pattern of contrasted and harmonized paper designs which are very pleasurable to the eye. The motion is based on the broad movements of the Japanese dance and sword drama. It is not necessary to be a skilled artist with a singular ability to make exact drawings in order to do a cut-out film. The Japanese are deliberately undetailed and broad in their pictures and the effect is all the more suitable because the primitive touch is the right one in a cut-out film. The usual thing is to cut out each position of the performer, though this is not necessary. One might join the parts of the body with paper fasteners that allow free movements and changing positions. Different designs of wallpaper pasted on cardboard can also be used.

In Germany, Mrs. Lotte Reiniger, assisted by Alex Strasser, has made silhouette cut-out films which are another form of animated pictures. I mention this rather as a source for study than as an end to achieve. It took Mrs. Reiniger four years to complete *The Adventures of Prince Achmed.* The problems of such a film are very serious. There is the problem of tones. In *Prince Achmed* the black of the figures contrasted too sharply with the white background and, after a time, the eyes of the spectator were troubled. I prefer her *Dr. Doolittle* and Toni Raboldt's *Cinderella* because the figures in these are less detailed and there is not as much lacework cutting. In this form of cut-out, as in the others, it is not necessary to cut a new figure with each change of position. One may cut a new arm, leg, etc., and paste it upon the figure, or merely use pivots at the joints. Moreover, it is not necessary — in fact, it is even erroneous — to attempt exact variations in positions. The less detailed, the larger the movements, the less frequent the changes, the better the film.

In fact, why does one need human or animal figures at all in the animated film? I think of the "photo designs" — still photographs — made by Francis Bruguière, the American photographer now resident in London. These photographs were meant to illustrate a book. When Bruguière first showed them to me, I experienced the sensations of "flight," "panic," etc. This indicates that the pictures, though stationary, suggested kinetic qualities, qualities of the movie. Bruguière cut paper into a design, then threw light upon it to organize the cut-out into a form with ridges, hollows and contrasting tones. Following that method of Bruguière, on the principle of the animated cartoon, one could produce motion pictures of these "photo designs" with abstract ideas such as chaos, creation, the war of the planets, the seven virtues, etc. An artist with a sense of design that suggests ideas could produce a film of philosophic views. But even if this were not wanted or were too difficult, one could still make a film for the pure delight in the changing appearance of the cut-outs, gained by moving the light source or by movement of the papers, or both. In a 16mm. film intended as a commentary on the play, *Six Stokers That Own the Bloomin' Earth,* the director of the Gate Theatre in London, Peter Godfrey, had a scene in which white cut-outs moved up and down resiliently in black space. It was very effective as motion, most simple in design and "got across."

It isn't even necessary to go into designed cut-outs to make a paper film. By photographing moving light over paper of different tones the amateur may get interesting movies. With the use of colored papers, now that color cinematography is available to the amateur, he may get light changes by means of a variety of colored surfaces. If he wishes to change the forms of the surfaces, he may vary angular with circular, oval with circular, vertical oblongs with horizontal, etc. Extending this, he can use pinpack paper designs for surfaces and thereby approach in his own way Bruguière's "photo designs" in motion, by moving lights and by changes in the paper design.

Or the amateur may deal with three-dimensional objects like paper-cups, by moving light in relation to them. Changing the position of the cups and multiplying the number of them, heaped variously, he may get very interesting films. Man Ray in Paris has photographed lead balls of various shapes in a heap, the light contrasting the sizes further. By varying the heap and the angle of light, a film of moving spheres can be effected. Similarly, A. Sandy, a young Frenchman, in his picture, *Lights and Shadows,* filmed cubes, pyramids, spheres, helices, etc., with most unusual and interesting results.

From these animated solids we may pass over to the animated puppet films. The most famous are those of Ladislas Starewitch, working near Paris. Starewitch won the Riesenfeld short-film medal for his film, *The Voice of the Nightingale.* He places his finger-size actors on his desk, films them, sets the next position, films it, and so on. He uses as many as 300 masks to portray the change in the expression of a single doll. But this elaboration is not at all needed. Starewitch is too eager for organic motion, whereas he might more artistically get actual stiff puppet motion and forego the changing physiognomy. The marionette theatre does not vary the visage of the puppet and yet gives the illusion of normal reality. Indeed, that is the very heart of the puppet theatre. Alex Strasser in Berlin made a toy film, *The Picnic,* in which he used ordinary toys with wooden bases. He gave them a relevant movement, stiff, wooden, without change of expression or limbs, the whole wooden toy moving and not the parts. This is, at the same time, simpler and jollier.

The amateur needs nothing more than ten-cent toys for his toy-film. He may film outdoors, getting the effect of forests by using some potted plants. Scale is the important thing to observe. Starewitch filmed a toy boat on an actual little stream running over rocks and gave the impression of a ship caught in a great sea. A toy keg and some small whiskey glasses would suffice for a cabaret. Here again, color may be frequently used most effectively.

Going back a bit to the geometrical solids, a figure can be made of such units. There have been geometric marionettes in Germany and Italy. By moving the positions of these solids, the semblance of motion may be achieved very easily. And, with the help of light, splendid cinematic variations of motion may be accomplished. Make a figure by simply putting together a cylinder, a cube, a pyramid or other shapes. Move the cube, move the cylinder, and the figure, the robot, will seem to be moving. Or use glass objects — beakers, test-tubes. The opportunities are manifold — a challenge!

MOVIE MAKERS,
December, 1929.

NEW BACKGROUNDS

"Necessity is the mother of invention," says the old proverb, but, in so far as creative artists are concerned, movie makers included, it might better be put, "the necessity of economy is the necessity of art." Sets are necessary to the experimental film maker who undertakes the photoplay type of picture. But, to make a good set would cost a lot of money, and therefore most amateurs use the settings and backgrounds that are at hand, tailoring the film treatment to fit the facilities available.

For the most part, this may be well advised, but sometimes it unnecessarily limits creative imagination, for, if the medium is to be an art, the set should be an integral and fluid part of the cinema itself. The cinema experimentalist and *avant garde* producer have known this and have made use of plain backgrounds, symbolism and even shifting planes of light as sets. An amateur can make cut out sets, such as Robert Florey has created, but these, at least to me, are too pretty and too much like a stage to have cinematic quality.

When Francis Bruguière lacked the means for building sets for his unfinished film, *The Way,* he reflected light through cheese cloth in frames in the background. The cheese cloth was framed variously, and the frames were changed and moved during scenes, although, when the characters were expressing intense emotions, the framed light was at rest. Economy produced art, design, rhythm, drama. Again, since his film was conceived totally in multiple images framed against light, the actors themselves were looming, imminent backgrounds to their own drama. This is a use suited to the mystical, psychic, non-narrative film.

In one of his films, Hans Richter, the German experimentalist, has an up and down movement of gray square planes. Modern art, in its various schools, offers suggestions for simple, toned backgrounds in alternation of rest and motion. The Russian Ballet has used a moving background for its dance — the movie can use a moving background for itself. The background in motion is almost a new idea. Moving backgrounds effected by moving cameras are general, but why not have backgrounds mobile in themselves, with the camera at rest?

Why the full set? Suppose you are filming a cabaret scene. Go to Starewitch for a suggestion. In one of his toy size sets, you will find that only a keg and a few small glasses suffice as properties and background. Bruguière showed only a table, a chair and a bottle in a saloon scene.

Representative objects can suggest the full environment. The expressionists used this method symbolically, but it also can be done as realism. In the symbolic set, the bottle might be magnified; in the realistic set, the normal size can be retained. Amateurs tend to like the detail for detail sets that duplicate real conditions, but this is more or less over, even in the realistic theatre. There is no need of perpetuating it in the movies; for example, a carnival scene can be conveyed by balloons. Avoid, however, those arrangements, too suggestive of a musical revue, which one gets in many specially designed sets since *Dr. Caligari.*

But why use a set at all? The first time I suddenly asked myself that question was upon seeing Pabst's *Secrets of the Soul.* The troubled man is asked to tell what he remembers of the night of the murder. He had seen the figure in a group against a background of houses and ambulance, but he recalls the scene without remembering the background, and, therefore, in the scene presented in the screen, as he recalls it, the figures stand, almost in relief, against a bare, black screen. Figures may be set against lustrous backgrounds by the use of velvet hangings, properly lighted. Jean Epstein, in *6½ x 11,* places a woman before long, flowing curtains, giving a sense of her smallness and loneliness and, at the same time, effecting a lovely design.

Carl Dreyer, in *Joan of Arc,* employed revolutionary backgrounds, revolutionary in their stark white and gray and revolutionary in their flatness. In this film, the flat background set, the figures in further relief and the stucco texture helped the severity and structural qualities of the entire film. The experimental movie maker might try flat backgrounds of different tones and textures — textures suggesting sheerness, textures lustrous, textures hard and metallic, textures dull. Try materials gelatinous, materials selected from the world's raw and manufactured wealth, rough metals, galvanized metals, moist clay, terra cotta, crude homespun, silks and satins, cotton wadding, absorbent cotton pulled loose, excelsior, hides and leathers.

Select the material, to serve as a background, for those qualities that suit the unity of structure and the mood of your film. There are materials suggesting solidity and others that suggest the ephemeral – the constant and the inconstant. Is your background to be a participant in the movement of the film, or is it to serve to accentuate the movement of the fore figures? You will ask yourself many questions before you decide upon your *décor*. The background never should be incidental and never pictorial. (This error has been made frequently by the Germans). The pictorial belongs in the magazine, the structural in the film. Yet this does not imply that it is necessary to build sets; it only means that the *décor*, or background, must be considered as a unit in the structure of the film. In fact, the entire *décor* may be constructed of lines drawn upon a neutral gray background – lines based on the entire structure of the film and not simply pictorial reductions of a decorative scheme conceived for its own delight.

In considering the possibilities of the simple, flat background, either stationary or in motion, also think of the opportunities for special backgrounds for experimental color film. As I have suggested planes of tones in motion, so I suggest planes of color in motion. As I have suggested materials of contrasted textures, so I suggest materials of contrasted colors. And, in the mobile background, I place this possible device, the color disc machine used in psychological tests, with its mounting speed and fusion of colors, its slowing speed and separation of colors. Here is something to play with, both for itself and for what it offers as an idea in color filming and moving backgrounds.

Control of the lighting, diffusion, angles and prisms are all devices affecting or controlling the camera's view – how the acting is seen. But, they help also to create the enactment of a scene. The amateur has at his disposal simple ways and means of "seeing" and "creating" the moving picture. Alberto Cavalcanti films his burlesque ballad picture, *Little Lily*, through gauze to impersonalize the characters. Man Ray takes *Star of the Sea* through mica sheets, liquifying the image and giving it a quality of remoteness. There are numerous "intermediate eyes" through which the camera can see the figures. One may choose isinglass, ground glass, Florentine glass or tissue paper. Frequently, these "before the lens" devices eliminate the need for positive and assertive backgrounds or for any backgrounds.

There is another element of image arrangement which, for convenience, I include in the classification of foreground. That is framing the image. This might be simply the naïve pictorial framing done by cutting a mask to make the image oval, circular or square. But I refer, rather, to the framing done by means of actual elements within the scene itself. Griffith filmed a movement through a window in *Orphans of the Storm.* Action may be taken through an open window or a closed window, through windows with various panes or bars. In *Nevada,* the action is seen within the frame of the cowboys' bunks. Michael Curtiz, in *A Million Bid,* effectively films a man on an operating table, framed by the flanks and arms of the surgeons. This is a construction with interesting opportunities. And opportunities are all that a good movie maker requires.

MOVIE MAKERS,
October, 1937.
(*Published posthumously*).

PLAYING WITH SOUND

My article in the *Musical Quarterly* was published April, 1929, although written in 1927, just when sound first screeched. Between the writing of "Cinema Unity II" and its publication I saw *The Taming of the Shrew*. The "blank verse, recitative film, in which the verbal essence is extracted and refined to meet with the image projected," still awaits its artist. Barrymore is to do *Hamlet*. Will it be as funny as his *Don Juan,* the first synchronized, music only, feature, which I have just seen for the first time. The audience enjoyed its unintentional absurdity. Barrymore should remain Jack, and forego John. [I speak of this more anon]. "Cinema Unity II" (*Close Up,* June, 1930), written as it was more than a year ago, is an early consideration of the non-synchronous sound-sight film, the idea of which has been seized upon at this late day, but only as a statement, by several other writers. The composition of this non-synchronisation has been accurately termed and described by Eisenstein as "disproportion." This includes not only the separation of lip-movements and speech, but utterances — speech-as-utterance — by landscapes. Disproportion as against naturalism.

The Soviet technique of *montage* makes possible this structural unity. Sound will be mounted into the visual-motor composition, compounding it, "on the table." The idea of sound-*montage* has been previously called impracticable by typical studio-practicians. But Alexandrov, Eisenstein's co-director, whom I have just seen off westward, has told me he has mounted sound in his brief experiment. *A Sentimental Romance,* which he made in Paris and sold to Paramount-Publix. He has done in this film a number of things I have thought basic in "playing with sound," such as: running the sound-track backwards, inscribing or designing the sound (sound is after all only inscription). He cut the sound inscription. By such method one may retard or accelerate sound movement. Let us say a note is banged on the piano, impressed on the negative. Immediate cutting — and there are a variety of ways — will change the character of the sound and give it an absoluteness. That is to say, it will not be associated with the instrument from which it will have emanated. One may record a jazz-band and then play around with the sounds as impressed, and get thereby any number of possible arrangements. The same can be achieved with speech: it may be clipped, stretched, broken into stutters, made to lisp, joined with all sorts of sound combinations either in discriminate mélange or in alternating, repeating motifs.

Alexandrov, so he told me, has played with the designs of sound by inscribing it directly on the negative and allowing light to make the final registration. Direct inscription of visual motifs on the negative has been attempted. And direct inscription of sound is more feasible, since in the visual movie human images are wanted, whereas in sound expressive utterances, which can be fabricated, are ultimately desirable. By studying the inscriptions closely one may come to an exact knowledge of these inscriptions and read them as easily as one reads musical notes for sound. The inscription of speech and that of sound differ only in the composition of the intervals and a close student will come to recognise the peculiarities of the different impressions. Actually sound will be created without being uttered!

The problem of fading out sound can be met by cutting. This is anticipated in a visual fade-out used in the Soviet film, *Fragment of an Empire* (*Stump of an Empire*), where, instead of the usual fade-out in a *slope* of deepening density, the fade-out is one of *steps* of successively darker tones. Alexandrov, instead of recording the *slope* up to and down from highest pitch of a siren's whistle, cut the sound into ascending and descending steps, a much more exciting method. Similarly sounds may be made to fade in and fade out.

Cataloguing and indexing of sounds is a step toward conventionalisation. I recall speaking with Charles Lapworth, then production manager for *Sociétè Générale des Films,* on that subject more than a year and a half ago. Lapworth spoke of the simple multiplication of the inscription to get degrees of volume. A sound might be catalogued Mob Scene 1, Index 3. By multiplication one may be able to achieve the volume of a mob of 10 to a mob of 10,000, and with no risk as to outcome.

The companies are cataloguing sounds. First National has such a library of several thousand records and hundreds of reels of sound on film. Col. N. H. Slaughter is in charge of the department. Actually there are very few imitations of real sounds in the films. Natural sounds are fabricated. Companies on location in the mountains have tried to capture thunder but have failed, because it is difficult, impossible indeed, to determine the distance of the thunder-clap, in order to adjust the microphone. Sounds difficult to record, when once ensnared, are made permanent in the library. Bernard Brown finally got the hum of a beehive and it is in the First National collection. But why the effort, when a sneeze in the microphone simulates thunder?

CLOSE UP,
August, 1930.

WHERE IMAGES MUTTER

Muttering images, not as yet uttering. The stutter would be more interesting. The most fascinating experience of audibility I have had in these couple of months since my return after an absence of fifteen good prodigal months was at a hearing of *The Broadway Melody* at a Loew neighbourhood theatre. The mechanism went wrong and suddenly the characters began to hiccough, stutter, blurt, much in the effect I produced in my childhood by shutting my mouth off and on with the palm of my hand while speaking. Receptively, its effect was similar to the effect produced by shutting the ear off and on in an identical manner. That was an accident that occurs frequently, producing an effect which is suggestive of piecemeal utterance of oral, verbal sounds. Analytic sound.

That is exactly the necessity: analytic sound, instead of duplicate. Today the talkie has two divisions: all-talkie and part-talkie. It is apparent to us all, including Gilbert Seldes, that this is a mistake. An all-talkie is not a movie. Silent sequences are determinants. Indeed, even the practitioners recognise this, and ultimately the dialogue-movie is doomed. Or, shall I put it this way: the innovations brought into the present optophonic substitute for the stage-melodrama and revue tend to mobilize the images increasingly, not so much because the producers want it, as because the enterprises attract these devices of movement. Never before has the American film used multiple exposure so much or so well; the revue attracts it as a novelty or "stunt." It is a little cloying because it simpers in the mood of the revue. In *Paris Bound,* the surimpressions had the accumulative effect of a vivacious mosaic. Entirely out of place in this stiff realistic play, but in themselves very successful. Totalities are not thought of in the present "audible film." It is very fragmentary and possesses little structural plausibility.

The present vogue is for the melodramatic play and the revue. (The social drama has its vogue too, but this is out-and-out substitute "electrical" theatre, better, however, than a phonographic substitute for the music-hall). This is not simply for the reasons Seldes assigns: that in the simplicity and broad structures they are easier movie stuff than a more intricate, and sophisticated material, but as the most general of folk affections, they naturally enter as the first materials to choose, particularly since the producer thinks of the talkie as the theater's descendant. He may not be so wrong. It may be that there will be a form of the talkie that will continue the popular theater. (Have not the tendencies in modern theatrical production been toward cinematization? Meyerhold, Piscator, Granowsky, even Reinhardt, and even Gaston Baty. And to offer as a counterbalance to the sonorization of the mute, did not Gordon Craig favor the silencing of the "spoken drama." I am noting an early critic of the talkie. As far back as September, 1913, the dramatic critic, Walter Pritchard Eaton wrote in *Leslie's American*: "A person is a person. A phonograph and a photograph are things. There is a certain fundamental difference which science has not yet succeded in eliminating. Nor does putting two things together make a person. The result is still two things . . . the synchronization of phonograph and film will be less illusive than either film or phonograph by itself. . . ." But then Mr. Eaton was down on the films generally; they had no third dimension — not very prophetic — and without words intellecual appeal was slight, and words did not belong. Sounds a little like 1929–30 among the steadfasts). For myself, I do not object, I do not find the popular talkie — the revue particularly — less attractive than the stage revue. Indeed, the former offers, even in the most banal of structures, a few combinations that the stage cannot achieve, for the stage has not the means for the concentrated bold image which alone permits the following treatment: in *Gold Diggers of Broadway,* while one performer sings, another goes through elastic dance movements, as if limbering up, behind the singer, to the theme of the song. Also, girls move regularly farther in the rear. This presents a three-distanced parallel, with the second image dimmer than the fore-figure and the third dimmer than the middle image. This is a tinted film and, while it adds nothing but slight suspicions to motion picture art, is no worse than the usual spectacle revue. As I have said, I for one prefer it because movements banal in the theatre are frequently rendered attractive by the more perspicacious instrument, the camera, and its associated implements. Other devices becoming general in talkies are off-screen sounds, echoes which have rhythmic possibilities, fades in-and-out of sound, etc. The development of the talkie will be two-wise: as a more thrilling substitute for the quotidienal stage, and as an art in itself.

I do not find in the slickness of *Paris Bound* or the more active, equally competent, *Bulldog Drummond,* anything to get excited over. The reiteration of columned, distributed German studio-lighting I find tedious, despite its competence. (The designer of this lighting is W. Cameron Menzies, who seems to hold first place in Hollywood esteem). Competence! the old sufficiency, the death of art — job-competence in America, aesthetic competence in Europe sometimes, but art the experience?

Paul Fejos' *Broadway* is a director's show-off stunt. It is the instance of a director succumbing to a specious vaunting of instruments, cranes and cameras. I suspected as much when I saw the photos of Fejos on the job with a battery of cameras. The Hollywood L'Herbier. Jean Dreville's *Autour de l'Argent* was an advance give-away of *L'Argent.* Effect-minds both, the director of *L'Argent* and the director of *Broadway.* The effect, in the latter instance, breaks into the impact of a movement built upon short blows. Instead of accepting the relevant structure offered by the play itself, not a singular structure but all it could support, Fejos broke into it with a spectacle, so that it follows in the "tradition" set by *The Broadway Melody,* a spectacle alternating with an intimate drama. The structures differ only in the proportions of the spectacle and drama, the viewpoint is the same, save that *Broadway's* is the more inflated. *Broadway* further indicates the defeat of comedy by speech. Glenn Tryon was most inept. The only comedy that can endure verbal utterance is the animated cartoon, but here the entire structure simply follows the melody of a simple jingle, as in Walt Disney's *Mickey Mouse* cartoons, where the distortions of the linear images are timed elastically in the swing of the synchronized melody and sounds as basic as la-la-la are used, without rhythmic variation.

The revue mind persists even in a film purporting to enfold the life of a people: King Vidor's *Hallelujah!* It is formula, fabricated, unconvincingly illogic and the meritorious effects impress as effects only. It is more facile than other films but its facility does not vindicate its banality and purposelessness. The Negro actors are frequently good and generally photographically interesting. Good things are to be found in the resilient and dramatic use of bold images, which I am sure were not thought of without some recourse to the Russians and Carl Dreyer. Particularly is the tilt of the boy's bold image in a corner of the screen reminiscent of *Joan.* There are occasional good sound combinations but they are rudimentary and irregular, so irregular as to evoke the suspicion that they are chances only, since Mr. Vidor is of the school of spontaneous combustion in direction.

The momentary novelty of a new actor — the Negro — the spiritual, the ritualistic frenzy, the crap-game, all the trappings of the legendary negro, as the white man likes to see him, amidst a set reminiscent of *Roxy's* — in a false reference (how like *The Crowd* in its stretching of a banality to become a significance) serve as a basis for a film which accepts this basis as the determining idea. Don't say this is literary! I am talking about a false conception which becomes the final form and experience. Vidor is always at the determination of the scenario. He does not determine it from the highest and profoundest reference of the potential material and theme, nor does he reconstruct its idealogy that he may realize a superior form and higher level of experience. The film is not even a sound-sight picture. The sound does not appear to be irrevocable in the structure. The film might have been a simple literal (as it satisfies the uncritical mind) trivial but momentarily effective mute movie. Momentarily effective — that characterizes Vidor's work.

The Cockeyed World is not even that. It is uninterrupted lambast and its professed raciness is not even accurately stressed nor is it anything but ulterior. The acting is uncomfortable — if this isn't "overacting," what is? — and the lack of organization in the film crowds the verbal impacts until one can be beaten into deafness by them. How typical of Raoul Walsh, its director. *What Price Glory?* crowded every corner of space with pots, pans and people.

The confession of Mr. Monta Bell (see New York Notes) that he dislikes sound in films may be descriptive of other directorial attitudes. No good can come from submission because of expedience. That is a form of moral compromise which is a detriment to artistic achievement. I have felt such a confused mind in *The Great Gabbo,* directed by James Cruze and starring Erich von Stroheim. The film is listless and diffident in construction, the lighting is bad, and the full use of the ventriloquist-and-dummy opportunity for sound-sight counterpoint is never even suspected. The resultant is a simplism with very little of either intuitive or intelligent sense of the new medium. It is a conglomerate of various sources with no central structurual intention. And after all Cruze is not one of our least. Perhaps Stroheim should have directed. I found his performance, as well as rôle, a bit painful. It made me a little ashamed to watch an adult and not inferior person taking the thing seriously. I remember Cruze as an actor — *The Million Dollar Mystery* — perhaps he should have been Gabbo.

But then with Stroheim directing the result would have been a probable exaggeration of the importance of the material plus some Viennese commentary. So let us spare a bad thing and ask no more!

The best-planned talkie I have yet seen is Hitchcock's *Blackmail.* There was some sense of the necessity of the long silent interval, and of reiteration, even though the plan was elementary, obvious and the reiteration too "psychological." The English are inflating the importance of the film. It has no real meaning and is poor suspense-filming (as poor as *Bulldog Drummond* and *The Man with the Tree-Frog* in this respect). Its competence is only competence after all, for Hitchcock is not a singularly inventive mentality. *Hallelujah!* is, being American, livelier, but the nature of its material makes its achievement more lamentable. The significance of *Blackmail* is its recognition of a first necessity, the plan. The doubling of Anny Ondra just to get her boudoir-eyes is faulty: the entire idea of the double will be dropped as soon as the film-world understands that there is no such thing as a film-voice. Perhaps I am too optimistic: the error of the camera test remains, and *"photogénie"* (historically the term "photogenic" goes back to the first production of a photograph in England, about 1802; a photograph was called a photogenic drawing). has been used to refer to a particular cinematic quality present in every substance. There is nothing intrinsically "photogenic" (or is it photogenetic?"). The cinema and not the substance determines that. (In *The Gramophone,* January, 1929, John Thorne writes on "The Fallacy of the Recording Voice," in which he says no such thing as a "recording voice" exists; all depends on sound vocal technique – and in the talkie, I add, to the directorial employment of the voice).

The necessity of the bold image in the sound film has brought out the Grandeur Movietone, a 72-mm. stock with a proportionate screen. This is not the previous magnification, but a new screen, new negative, new projector. The result, with *Movietone Follies,* is as yet only partially pleasing. For long lines breadthwise on the screen it is splendid because the screen is unproportionately a wide-film and not a high-film. It is good for the movement of masses from left to right and right to left, good for synchronization, good for a figure reclining across the breadth of it, it offers the split screen a "grandeur" opportunity and Mr. Bakshy's frame-within-a-frame. The problem lies in its too panel-like form and in the occupation of the screen when, say, one lone image is upon it vertically. This may bring about more studious image-construction, which in uneducated hands can thwart the cinema, or the final recognition that the screen need not be occupied all of the time. It may also evoke the knowledge that follows this, that the eye may move with the image. We have not done much with a procedure which I shall reduce to a simple movement. A figure enters minutely from the lower left of the screen and grows larger as it moves up the screen, passing and increasing in size rightward. In other words, a use still passive, but receptive, of the screen as a planted base for the movement of *an* image, where the image in a sense will be created on the blank area. I lament, however, that the magnification of the screen promises to desert its first form, offering such rhythmic opportunities, where it expanded and contracted, for a matter-of-fact, immobile enlargement.

CLOSE UP,
January, 1930.

MUSIC AND THE MOVIES

Music has been associated with the movie since the latter's prehistoric days. It was accepted from the very beginning that music was to accompany the film, and the entrance of many film-entrepreneurs was made through the avenue of the accompaniment. Yet the justification and the ideal utilization of the musical accompaniment must be sought solely in inherited "custom." There is no *absolute* justification for the use of music to accompany the film. The fact that in a straw-vote taken of some 300,000 London cinema "fans," thirteen per cent asserted they had been attracted to the movie by the orchestra, is a commentary upon the audience and not upon the legitimacy of music-with-the-film. Russian movie audiences attend a musicless *kino,* because they are not *accustomed* to the musical accompaniment, and trained film-observers, viewing pictures in preview projection-rooms, often find the absence of music enjoyable. But for the western audience, accustomed to the music of the organ or the orchestra, the absence of music would, I am certain, prove ominous and even terrifying. Moreover, profound silence demands too much of the human species, western style. The problem is to discover a beneficent compromise. Since music must be present, let us make the most of silence!

I do not intend to write a panegyric upon silence. I am not one who believes in it as superior to verbal utterance. I leave that exaggeration to my younger colleagues, endeavoring to absolutize the cinema, by making silence the absolute ideal of human achievement. But—silence is the medium of the movie, as it is the medium of the clown. In the movie it is a paramount virtue, and an art can transcend its material lineaments only by the play of its virtues, or better, by virtue of its inherent characteristics. This does not mean that there will not ultimately evolve a legitimate, authentic, and distinctive cinema-form in which sound will be a part. But the present cinema in its exploitable potentialities — despite the contradictory practices of its eminent exploiters — is intrinsically valid through silence. And it is with the present cinema that we are here concerned. Of the sound-film I shall say more at the close of my examination.

Silence, so intrinsically a part of the cinema, was anathematized in the very beginning of the movie by those concerned with the cinema's development. In the first days, Alexander Black, the novelist, accompanied his film showings with lectures. Song-slides — even until today present in the neighborhood houses — alternated with movies in the first *kinos*. I can recall as a small boy being hired by a movie owner to follow the action of a picture behind the screen, not only with my voice, but by pounding the screen, to emphasize physical combat. We have always been afraid to let the movie carry itself by its own intrinsic devices. We are afraid of purity. Mr. Edison, being an inventor, has never been concerned with the æsthetic attributes of his inventions. He never saw any "commercial" value in the silence of the film. In 1912 he presented his premature "talking" picture. Four years previously Gaumont had presented a verbal film. The sound-film is today still premature. But the inventor is abetted by the investor and the impresario. The major share of the responsibility for the inflation of the musical accompaniment rests on the last of these three i's.

Sigmund Lubin, among the first film magnates, sold phonograph records to accompany the films he leased. The synchronized music on disc or film is an extension of this first mechanical music. The experimental Studio 28 in Paris is a direct derivation; its films are accompanied by an arranged selection of music on the mechanical piano. Numerous small houses still retain the Wurlitzer mechanical band unit, and the recently revived Orchestraphone. In all instances the orientation is toward the grand ensemble: the orchestra. Its first realization dates back to Loew's Broadway Theater, 1911, when Ernest Luz arranged the accompaniment and directed the orchestra. Luz gave some good advice in a contemporaneous film journal, reprimanding the random accompaniment. In 1913 there appeared several "musical films." (A recent "musical film" has been projected, which is a visual description of the music. Since this is not an independent film, but a film by analogy, it does not concern us here). One produced in America and another in Germany, to which Luz wrote the accompaniment, pronounced "a score practical for the average pianist." Therein begins the large-scale music. It prepared the birth of the impresario

S. L. Rothapfel (Mr. William Fox's "genius"). In 1913 the Regent Theater in New York was showing the George Kleine production *The Last Days of Pompeii,* one of the earliest feature films. Mr. Rothapfel supplied an orchestra for the film, and at certain intervals an actor recited passages from the novel by Bulwer-Lytton. The author, whom Hawthorne called "the pimple of an age of humbug," would have enjoyed the atmospheric environment given to his tale. Sweet singers appeared from charmed recesses. Soft lights hallowed them. Atmosphere, be it noted, is Roxy's (that is, Mr. Rothapfel's) *sine qua non.* It is expressed in his tall, blond, military, straight-nosed attendants — not to be called ushers! The quality of this atmosphere is suggested in Mr. Roxy's fond term for his employees, "Roxy's Gang." It was the yearning for atmosphere that has made Roxy the premier movie impresario, the archetype of the magnanimous benefactor of mankind. For, if we are to believe the trade journals of both movies and the music, or the critics of amiable disposition, such as Richard Watts, Jr. (for the movie), and Charles Henry Meltzer (for the trade of music), America is a nation experiencing emotional exaltation through the movie "temple." Mr. Watts finds in the combination of music and the movie the greatest *assault* upon the emotions ever known to man. While Mr. Meltzer says: "The movies have accomplished more than a dozen opera houses to help good music. When they have harrowed up our souls with dramas of adventure, or fretted us with futile comedies, they have made amends by interpolating on their bills movements from symphonies, classic and beautiful, or scenes from operas." Mr. Watts is a strange protagonist for the silent art in his assumption that the good movie needs any outside assistance in *assaulting* — as he crudely and inexactly puts it — the audience. Poor audience! are they always to be passive, and never participating? Are they the "friendly enemy"? As for Mr. Meltzer's view, I quote it because it is typical. In fact, he confesses himself true to "type" by his blessing of Roxy, Riesenfeld and Mark Strand, who supplied the theater for the advancement of the educational work. Mr. Meltzer's view is the view that has advanced music in the movie from solo-sandwiches between films to film-sandwiches between solos. The movie has passed into concert, and is progressing backward to the "chaser" in the vaudeville program. Today one finds in the presentation cinema — the "palaces and temples" — the anomaly of a movie house inhospitable to the movie.

Few have stood by the movie. The movie's own have been easily duped by the superior attitude of the so-called music-lover. Dr. Georg Goehler, a German critic, has been emphatic in his attack upon music in the movie. A good picture, he says, needs no assistance from music. And music is altogether too proud to divert our attention from a bad picture to obscure its faults. This is an acceptable criticism, but its tone calls for further criticism. It is the tone of the musician, who is too often the snob. He thinks of music as the first and greatest art; therefore it cannot yield its place anywhere to another, let alone a vulgar medium like the movie. But whatever is the position of the art of music, in its milieu the movie must be permitted its proper place. Music is, in the present cinema, incidental.

In 1915, the *Movie Pictorial* began to crusade through Mabel Bishop Wilson to raise the standards of movie music. By raising the standard has been meant raising the music in eminence. What about the movie? Mr. Carl Van Vechten, in 1917, published an article in *The Seven Arts,* entitled "Music and the Electrical Theater." In that essay he congratulated the cinema impresarios upon their promotion of the musical art, and suggested an extension into Wagner, Beethoven, Debussy, Schoenberg and Loeffler. By 1917 the movie orchestras had rendered Bizet, Gounod and Rimsky-Korsakov. In truth, the "classicism" of the movie musical program had become tedious by 1917 to Mr. Van Vechten, who would have preferred a "let-up" *via* Irving Berlin. The "let-up" has become quite tedious by now, without having created any suggestion towards the ideal movie-music.

Hugo Riesenfeld contributed, in my opinion, notably to the hybridization of the cinema program. He has done much to further the imposition of music, a fact he avoids, it seems, when he complains of this hybridization. However, in the program of the new Colony Theater with which he was associated in its first months, Riesenfeld subdued the glaring insolence of the non-cinema performance by fashioning a music-movie entertainment. When the program first began at the Colony, one was pleased to hear but not see the music. "Ah," one thought, "at last the non-intrusive orchestra! At last a movie spectatorium, in place of a movie auditorium!" But no. It was just a device, a device of the jazz-age. The orchestra rises up from the depths and stands in our visual way. Leopold Stokowski has favored a hidden orchestra at the symphony concert. At the cinema the orchestra before the screen is an anachronism. Riesenfeld freed the program from what has been called, wittily, "Roxy's noisy good taste," and has given us a polite entertainment. However, there is still too much music, despite the fact that Riesenfeld believes in the right of the movie to pre-eminence in the cinema program.

It is this program idea which has worked back upon the making of the film. If the bad film can be strengthened or obscured by music and "acts," why worry about making good films? If we are to see the art of the movie fulfill itself, we must do away with a number of conditions, and one is the elimination of the three i's: investor, inventor and impresario. We must recognize the independence of the movie. Since 1917 Mr. Carl Van Vechten has awakened to the fact that "writing music for the movies is a new art." He has been brought to a recognition of the need for "a new point of view." Others have come to a recognition of the same need. Mr. Van Vechten has based his changed standpoint on the tenet that "a moving picture is not unlike a ballet in that it depends entirely upon action." He had evidently been reading Alexander Bakshy, a prophet among cinema critics. Mr. Van Vechten qualifies this tenet with a statement which is a confession of limited understanding: the movie, he says, "differs from a ballet in that the action is not necessarily rhythmic." A fully realized movie must be rhythmic. The rhythm, however, is not ballet or literary or musical. It is cinematic. It is this inherent rhythm which provides the key to cinema music. We will consider that later.

The supporter of music-with-the-movie may find his authoritative precedent in the first musical accompaniment. He may go back to the antecedent of the movie house, to a time when the movie was a curiosity in the dime museum. This precedent, however, should indicate that it is the small orchestra that historically belongs to the film. The musical progress of the movie accompaniment was, first, an increase in the number of instruments: from piano to drum to percussion accessories to violin to 'cello — inclusive; the thirty-two piece orchestra; the organ, the Hope-Jones unit. Concurrently with this development went that of content: from running accompaniment to scores. At present several forms of musical program exist in the movie. There is still, in very small neighborhood movies — remnants of the old movie alleys and converted stores and stables — the running piano accompaniment, sometimes aided by a fiddle. Then there is the large central house with a full orchestra of very competent musicians. The orchestras in the Philadelphia houses include many of the former members of the Philadelphia Orchestra. A third form exists, which I believe will be the increasingly accepted one, as it is the most relevant one: the small chamber-orchestra. This last and ideal form of orchestral accompaniment has been sponsored by the Little Cinema. The Théâtre du Vieux-Colombier and Studio des Ursulines in Paris, parents of the Little Cinema, have excellent orchestras whose musicians prepare the music for the program. But as yet the Little Cinema has proven itself of little consequence in the exploitation of its enterprise. It is thwarted by a number of things, mainly by the fact that those active in it have as impertinent a conscience as that possessed by the so-called commercial movie-man. I refer particularly to the American Little Cinema: it possesses the general unscrupulousness and sanctimony and incompetence and trusting-to-the-æsthetic-accident of the movie. It has become quite complacent, thus intensifying its sanctimoniousness. The small orchestra is not enough; good taste is certainly not enough; prettiness is not enough. The music, where it has not been interpretative, as in the great part of movie music, has been indolent. The orchestra of the Little Cinema is ideal; it is small, it is intelligent, it need not go out of itself for matter; and, moreover, it is usually hidden from the orchestra audience. It is non-intrusive, an essential element for movie music.

Essentially the music of the movie, whether it has been catch-as-catch-can or prearranged, whether it has been written entirely and only for the particular film or has been an organized *mélange* of musical selections, has not realized itself as other than interpretation. So that in principle all movie music is identical. It may be the score for *The Birth of a Nation,* organized from Hebrew chants, etc., or *The Covered Wagon,* with its old songs, etc., or *The Big Parade,* with its war lilts, etc. (These borrowed antiquities may be considered as documents, and justified as such. The "documentary film" or film-portion is an exception to this general consideration. The Congo music to the dances in *The Black Journey,* is an excellent example of *concurrent* documentary music). It may be music as purposeful as Antheil's "Ballet Mécanique" for the film of that name; or a score such as that arranged by Mendoza and Axt for *The Trail of '98;* or simply the quick response of the agitated pianist in the small slum house — it is music out of place. The movie needs no explanation or interpretation, it must rise or fall of itself. The music must be subservient. Nor does Mr. Meltzer's pronouncement answer the need of the movie-music, that "its purpose should be to study the moods, the minds, if you will, the souls, of audiences and help them sympathize with the dramatist." Does not answer the need, did I say? This is a fantastic bit of impudence. *"Stimmungsmusik,"* indeed! Do the program-annotations at the symphony abet the composer? Mr. Meltzer wishes the music to do what the movie must do, convey the intent and sense and inference to the spectator. He wishes to further reduce the movie's emprise. Certainly, the movie has been innocuous enough!

The ideal cinema will be conceived as a ramified and rhythmic graph, a rhythmic cine-graph. The music accompanying it should be the *mean* of the graph, not the mood of the interplay built upon it. It should attempt no commentary, no interpretation, no augmentation of the film, but simply seek a subdued, non-intrusive, reticent time-concordance with the film. Its highest aspiration should be non-conflict. If you think I have reduced the music of the movie to a humble place, what will you think of the French critic who suggests that the highest purpose film music can fulfill is the drowning of the distracting noises in the audience? Or what will you think of the suggestion of the evangelical Vachel Lindsay, America's first movie critic, to do away with the music because it interferes with the conversation of the spectators?

I have no great hope that my position will be accepted by those influential in the cinema. Nor will it be taken by those who desire to extend, as they believe, the province of the movie. In Germany, Hans Heinz Ewers, the author, and Joseph Weiss, the composer, have joined to create what to me is not an art, but a monster: a *Kino-Oper,* a Movie-Opera! I have not heard that others have followed their example. But to have shadow-forms sing — well, isn't that the contraption of the Vitaphone, the Movietone, etc.? Why not attach a phonograph to Mona Lisa? Then there is the continual urging of certain critics, composers, conductors, etc., for the synchronization of the movie score with the film. George Tootell, an English cinema organist, conductor and composer, has said: ". . . under existing conditions we have arrived at a point from which further progress and improvement is almost impossible, and yet, far from achieving an ideal, we see many features which are undesirable." The music of the movie has passed from the running accompaniment to the suitable setting. Roxy would have music lift the picture from its flat screen to — the gods; every genuine artist knows that if there is to be any transcending of medium it must be done by virtue of the characteristics of the medium itself. No outside help. This holds for the movie as well as for sculpture, painting, and music. The suitable setting has been supplied by adapting music already written to the film. For instance, eight measures of the opening movement of Coleridge-Taylor's "Petite Suite de Concert" were suited to the Jealousy Theme in *The Four Horsemen of the Apocalypse.* This was not a mere casual rearrangement or a more or less trivial alteration, but a precise adaptation with a transference of the melody to the basses and a re-timing of the measure. The musical director who does this well must be credited with considerable ability. Still, this is not creating music for the movies. In some instances — in most instances — such scoring approaches nonsense in its meticulous following of the action, viz:

Cue	
I Hate This	Intermezzo — Whelpley.
Dolores Enters Church	Andante Religioso — Fletcher.
Let Him Go	Dramatic Tension — Borch.

The director times each passage to the film, so many minutes to so many feet. The musical Theme, in this instance Micaela's Aria from "Carmen," is repeated at exact intervals, creating a unity. The caption serves as a cue. This type of scoring is, in its exactness, superior to the chance playing of the movie pianist who was advised, "as the musical interpreter of the emotions depicted on the screen, the player must be *emotional,* and respond to the often quick changes in the situation." The player was told to "size up his audience," as if he were a salesman. In fact, if "not his knowledge of life," he was further cautioned, "his knowledge of the picture must enable him to *anticipate,* so that his music is always slightly ahead of the film, preparing rather than reflecting. Therefore, *the player's eyes should be on the screen as constantly as possible,* and never for too long a stretch on the music or on the keyboard." This is reminiscent of the agitated musician of the movie of the early days. However, the agitation was soon, of necessity, lessened, and stereotype music took its place. Less improvisation and more job music. The pianist was liberated from the hysteria of following and reading facial expressions, moods, scenes, gags, etc. His place has been taken by the manipulator of the effect-organ. The program music that followed on the piano was the forerunner of the present orchestral scoring of big movie orchestras. As the handicraft age still persists in the industrial, so there are still improvising pianists — some of whom play "by ear" — and program pianists in the movie. A repertoire was provided for the program pianist which included the following:

Nature

Grieg .... Morning-Wood
Nevin .... Country Dance
Saint-Saëns .... The Swan
Helm .... Sylvan Sketches
Friml .... Iris
Bohm .... Murmuring Brook

Love Themes

Cadman .... Melody
Elgar .... Salut d'Armour
Liszt .... Love Dreams

Light, Graceful Moods

Chaminade .... Libellules
Delibes .... Pizzicati, "Sylvia"
Moszkowski .... Canzonetta

For "Elegiac Moods" there was music by Debussy, Wagner and Rubinstein, as well as by Bernheimer and Friml; Wagner for "Impressive Moods"; and Enesco, Meyerbeer and Handel; Nevin, Wagner, Meyerbeer, Verdi, Gounod, de Koven, Chopin, Ketterer for "Festive Moods"; composers and compositions for "Exotic Moods," for Comedy, Speed, Neutral Music, Waltzes, Standard Overtures with "brilliant and lively passages which will fit scenes in the Wild West, hurries (speed), chases, fights and mob scenes, etc., many of them also contain slow movements which will prove useful as love themes, etc.," and Special Characters and Situations; Tragedy: a. Impending; b. Aftermath; Death (N.B. – In the presence of actual death, observe silence!). The parentheses and exclamation mark are not mine, but they are appropriate. By "actual death" whose death is meant, the musician's or that of some sensitive soul in the audience? (The answer is obvious. "Actual death" may occur in the filming, by our ever-ready and ever-present camera men, of catastrophies, railroad or aeroplane wrecks, involving the actual loss of lives, such as the newsreel presents almost every week for the entertainment of the morbidly curious. When it is not merely the case of an actor "playing dead," in the featured thriller, but when the lens has caught the picture of life destroyed, silence – even parenthetical silence – would seem more fitting than an indifferent performance of the first sixteen measures of "Ase's Death" or the "Funeral March of a Marionette." – *Ed.*).* Music for Battle Scenes, Storm Scenes, Villainous Characters: Robbers (in Drama), Robbers (in Comedy), Sinister Villain, Roué or Vampire, Revengeful Villain – for Youth and Old Age. There was, in fact, music for every flick, every flicker, every flea. There was music for The Feature Film, the Animated Cartoon, Slap-Stick and High-Hat Comedy, News Reel, Educational and Travel Films. For African movies Coleridge-Taylor's "African Suite." The French Little Cinema has surpassed this. For the splendid *Black Journey* (the Citroën expedition) authentic "Congo Jazz" was played, the one instance of music "suited to subject" which was neither a stretch of logic nor an interference with the picture's rhythm. The same theater, encouraged by the reception of this music-movie combination, presented a North African film with North African music, in which instance the music was an intrusion and a torment. The first venture was successful because the music was modest and kept within its boundaries.

This *résumé* of program piano music for the movie is not a study of a thing of the past. Refer to Erno Rapée's "Encyclopædia for Movie Musicians"; Mr. Rapée is insistent upon suitable settings. A Spanish Overture for a Spanish picture. How Spanish is a Spanish picture filmed at Hollywood? For patriotic tableaux he favors such compositions as Weber's "Jubilee Overture" and Herbert's "American Fantasia." For Scenic Pictures there are the andante movement of Dvořák's "New World Symphony," Goldmark's "Rustic Wedding," and the 5/4 movement of Tschaikovsky's "Sixth." For North American Scenics with their "massive rocks and thundering waterfalls," there is Herbert's "Natoma." Mr. Rapée's sense of the fit is insulted by such an incongruity as playing "Swanee River" to accompany a picture of President Grant, "where a more martial air would be more fitting." In fact, according to Mr. Rapée, there is music suitable to each and every President of the United States of America. The conductor must be quite scientific in his selection of music for the film. In the case of the feature picture he is advised to (1) determine the geographical and national atmosphere of the picture and (2) embody every one of his important characters in a theme. This may seem like a synthesis, but is really a hodgepodge. The musical director is, as a matter of fact, told to hybridize his music to avoid monotony. He has a great list to select from, from A to Z, from Abyssinia to the Zoo. He can have orchestral music for Country Love — a simple and sweet ballad, and he may have music for Society Love — from Victor Herbert or Chaminade, and for comedies he may use old songs as burlesque, preferably in medleys. That is the status of orchestral music. Though Roxy may boast he has presented Strauss's "Ein Heldenleben," any one attentive to the condition in the movies must admit that George Tootell is right when he speaks of an *impasse* in the present cinema music. The boast of Roxy's Music Library is an indication of this massive stoppage. This Library owns 30,000 orchestral numbers, including Victor Herbert's own complete library. There are in this collection 1000 overtures — 600 of which were once owned by Herbert. This permits of a different overture each week for over nineteen years. In addition there are suites, short pieces, marches, waltzes, ancient and modern dances, etc. But this is a collection, not a growth within. Mr. Tootell believes there is only one way out, and that is in the simultaneous preparation of the movie and the music. He has had the experience of preparing the score for a completed picture, an inferior one filmed by Stoll of England, called [*à l'américaine*], *Frailty*. He wrote 2000 bars of music and is convinced of the validity of *original* music for the movie. Only, he asks for synchronization. Allowing that we have intelligent, honest and eagerly progressive producers, interested in the art of the film, we would still need to face a physical limitation in the cutting of the film after the picture is taken. To cut the film would mean to cut the music. Which would be equal to demanding new music for a film already completed.

This would of itself defeat synchronization. Then there is the problem of censorship. The censorship of the picture would leave the music at certain places out of keeping with the film and might produce not harmonies but anti-forms or, at any rate, affect the timing and the sequence. Pathos in the film might be reduced to bathos by an antipathy in the music or *vice versa*. But to me there is in this synchronization a larger evil. It still speaks in too large terms of the music and is still subject to the vicissitudes of "interpretation." I believe the alternative Mr. Tootell suggests to contain the solution.

Mr. Tootell suggests as an effective chamber-quartet the piano, organ, violin and violoncello. Any small orchestra is satisfactory. He believes that the organ of large dimensions could be supplied with works of the modern Russian school, and for the feature film he wants his special, original music. I am against these distinctions. The concept "feature" has alienated the movie from itself; it has loaded the industry with unnecessary expenses and equipments that impede its development æsthetically; it is a false idea. If the word "feature" is to be kept, make every picture a feature picture. *The Last Laugh* was not considered a feature film in America, yet it is one of the few rhythmic, cinematic entities. The organ of the movie is monstrous. I am aware that certain musicians, like Firmin Swinnen, have made excellent transcriptions for organ use, but the movie organ is not one of music, but of effects. It is the confounding that is apparent in a Fairbanks or Lloyd film, of the antic or gag with cinema movement. The legitimate diapason organ can find a place, as George Tootell has indicated, in the small cinema orchestra. We want to get away from the persistent notion that every waver, every close-up, embrace, pie-throw must be interpreted or reproduced in the music. The typical organist follows a plan for describing "specific emotions, moods, and situations" in the register. Love, for instance, has its equivalent in solo flute 4′, Joy is Happiness (Springtime, sunshine) intensified in volume and can be found in the flutes 16′, 8′, 4′, 2′ and strings. Think how simple it is to produce by prescription Hope, Victory, Exaltation, Prayer, Suspicion, Entreaty, Yearning, Anxiety, Temptation, Hatred, Disaster, Defiance, Treachery, Rage, Cruelty, Torture, Grief, Despair, Passion, Renunciation and—Dreaming, to quote a movie caption, *The Gold Wings of Youth*. This all reads like a caricature of the movie actor's profession. He, the actor, is a register that always registers on the same key when a particular emotion is called for. Adoration—his grey eyes bulge in glazed vacuity. This concept of programming the movie situations is a ridiculous statement of the business of the movie musician.

Good incidental music has already been written. Directors here and abroad know of the concise pieces of Maurice Pesse. Firms like Chester in England and Schirmer here have published Swinnen's organ transcriptions of Baron's "Indian Legend," Cesék's "Twilight," Coleridge-Taylor, etc., and the incidental music of Borch, Jungnickel, Bergé and Langey. Certain of the short pieces of Schumann, Sibelius, Buck and others indicate a basis. Stravinsky might be called in. Primitive music is an excellent source. Jazz converters like Copland and Antheil, or John Alden Carpenter, might find a profitable field in the cinema. The hope is in the small orchestra. Symphonic music is too grand to be submissive to the movie.

The notion that every trough and crest in the movie action must be followed or interpreted in the score is juvenile. When a composer writes music to a song, he does not inflate each accent in the written ms. to a musical utterance. One of the weaknesses in Emerson Whithorne's music to Countee Cullen's *Saturday's Child,* is that frequently he "interprets" a word with a musical equivalent producing, not a *relevant,* but an effect that obtrudes out of the total pattern. This is a sentimentality. The purpose of the movie composer should be to get the rhythmic mean, not the bumps and hollows in the action, and construct music in this rhythmic mean. This will avoid conflict between music and movie and will keep the music toned down to its lesser position in the cinema house. The action, that is the incidents, in the picture are only details in the rhythm. The rhythm is the dynamic sequence which includes everything. It is the repetition in variation which produces the visual and dramatic totality. Look at a movie like *Sunrise!* Observe how the players, the settings and the occurrences enter into the unit flow of the film. The Movietone effects are insulting to the purity of this rhythm, just as occasionally the orchestra has deceived us into believing a rhythm occurred before our eyes when it really was apprehened by our ears. The senses are related. Arthur Rimbaud, the French poet, gave colors to the vowels. We speak of "sour music." What is the figure of speech if not a recognition of this relationship? It is because of this close affinity that I would keep music away from the film as much as possible. At least until the cinema realizes its tremendous potentialities. Let us purify the movie and at the same time develop a new field for the composer. This will be a fine beginning for the young musician or the worker in small forms. The movie theaters could afford to employ talented young composers as staff composers. A number of small theaters might combine to employ one composer. This, however, is all incidental.

The movie house will henceforth take two tendencies: one toward the enormous theater, and the other toward the intimate Little Cinema.

There is one danger in the latter. It, too, has been discovered as profitable by the business man. With that has often come the collapse of a promise. Already the Little Cinema has developed its own evil, the importation bug. There is extant in the Little Cinema a bug which bites the owner till he goes *Ufa*-mad and will take anything, good or bad, that the German film company sends. It is the Little Cinema's expression of the American sycophancy. The big producer brings over the German director and actor, the Little Cinema imports the film. However, the Little Cinema indicates one direction away from the non-cinema movie-vaudeville presentation house. I am optimistic enough to believe this direction away will increase and may eventually be the determinant of the æsthetic of the movie architecture and the movie proper—and of the music for the movie. It may work back to a revaluation of the movie and a definition of its form and content. The musician may think himself deprived of a legitimate and profitable sphere of enterprise. But in the small movie forms there may be revealed a very fundamental and pure music which may offer new and fruitful exploitation areas to the composer. This is in keeping with the tendency to purification present in all the arts: in music, painting, sculpture, literature, and cinema. We want to free our categories from confusions. In that way we are freeing life itself from its current confusion, which borders on bewilderment. I believe the composer no longer has a contempt for the movie because it is mechanical. There is no quarrel between the mechanical and the non-mechanical, the quarrel is between the artistic and the non-artistic. The moving picture asks the musician not to impede its progress toward the realization of its inherent qualities. It asks the musician to respect *its* rhythmic content or possibilities. That is a request every artist should respect.

Throughout this essay I have concerned myself with the relation of the movie to the present cinema. I am, however, not one of those dogmatists who cannot see the possibility of a legitimate form in which music and film will be conceived and realized simultaneously and in interrelationship. A form of the cinema may evolve in which the stage and the film may constitute a harmony. A form of the cinema may evolve in which fluid color may be an important constituent. (The color-organ is now being manipulated in several movie-houses). There may be a *Kino-Oper* which will not be monstrous. But such legitimate compound cinemas are distinct, or will be distinct, from the movie as we at present know it. To attempt a compounding with the present cinema is to create a monster out of a man. That is the principal objection to the sound film. These compound cinemas are premature, and what is premature is unlovely.

The indolence and ignorance of the film-practicians (augmenting the irresponsibility of the inventor, the cupidity of the investor and his sanctimoniousness) have betrayed the silent movie. In the silent movie there was never a reason for the lip-mimicry of the spoken word. The sound-film protagonist may well urge the practice of this illegitimate pantomime as justification for going the full way to the spoken word. It is highly ridiculous to conceive of the movie as a screen on which mutes grimace. Ridiculous and even horrible! The practicians who defend the silent movie have made no defense in their utilization of the cinema's silence. They have always showed a nostalgia for the word by mimicking the word. But if the practicians of the "silent drama" have been incompetent in the silent movie, what shall we say of the same people at work upon sound films? It is a small matter to learn the mechanics of the sound film. It is another thing to pattern sound-sight in a distinctive and complete art. Cecil De Mille learned the mechanics of the movie in a moment, but he has never learned anything about the making of a beautiful film. The problem of the sound film is not being met, but the first of the cinematic arts, the silent movie, is being further deflected, confused and thwarted. Music in the sound film is being thought of solely as an experience as yet novel. It is thought of solely as a commercial reduction in costs, as a commercial advantage to the small house, as a commercial attraction to the audience. That explains the intrusiveness of the music. Not simply that the music has been clamorous (as in *Seventh Heaven*), or hodgepodge (as in *Four Sons*). But that the sound is not corporate in a medium conceived in sound-sight. The sound is expedience.

I have stressed non-intrusiveness. This is the emphasis upon silence. To define silence we must avoid confusing, as one writer has done, the present cinema with the cinema of incorporated sound. That writer has said: "In the film-work of the future, music will accompany the picture when its employment materially aids the sensual or emotonal phase of perception." The film which employs music to aid it is not the film of silence. And in the film employing music to aid it — the future film of the writer — the film will as much aid the music as the music the film. In other words, such a film will be a sound-sight compound working in an interrelated sound-sight pattern. The simple film of silent images refuses any aid from another sensory medium. The writer continues to prophesy that the music "will not necessarily be played in a straight, unbroken score." This is a fragment possessing meaning to the present, simple film. The film need not be followed continuously. Silence should be stressed. Not as the quoted writer says, "interrupted or punctuated only by an occasional outburst of symphonic rhapsody to heighten the mood." The movie has its own devices to heighten the mood. It needs no rhapsody or symphony save its own eloquence. The writer plays further into the hands of the conspiracy against the movie with these words: "And frequently, to strengthen the effect, the orchestra will be split, stationed on two sides of the screen and numerically arranged to meet the tonal requirements." An ambitious musical circus, perhaps a future agency in the cinematic arts, but certainly of no value to the movie of plastic fluidity of non-sonal images, of images that may suggest but not express sound. The movie has no concern with "musical agencies," "music plots," with the assistance of any other music than that of its own images. It can very easily convey sound visually. It needs no help for this. And the stress of silence is available for the moments of greatest intensity. It is banal to utilize expressed sound for intense moments, when the movie has its own silent devices. In *Wings* the screen is magnified, and against huge grey clouds two specks — airplanes — combat. The orchestra and all sound should have been hushed. What could have been more terrifyingly breath-taking than silent combat upon the seemingly limitless screen? But no, a specious, infantile realism gave voice to the combat, reducing the emphasis. Recently, in a small house in Paris, I witnessed a revival of Abel Gance's 1918 war film, *J'Accuse!* There is a scene in it where the dead arise from the battlefield and march. The orchestra ceased. The effect was terrific! What vaudeville "fan" does not know the effectiveness of silence during an acrobatic feat? This is the point: since music is inevitable, we can make the best use of silence by selecting the intervals carefully at which the music will be hushed. At all other times the music is to be subdued — I might even say, made bashful. Long periods of silence separated by music will emphasize not the silence but the sound. And only by emphasizing silence can we stress the silent image. Though in the emphasis of silence in sound there is still an emphasis of the sound arrangement. To this I answer: subdue the silence in the sound, use it sparingly. But see that the music neither distracts nor deceives the sight. Hide the orchestra. Perhaps that will satisfy Sir Thomas Beecham, who is so justly enraged against the present orchestral organization of cinema music. The sound-film may drive more spectators into the Little Cinema. That may aid the ideal movie house.

MUSICAL QUARTERLY,
April, 1929.

* [Gen. Ed.]: Page 103 — Note in text is presumably by the editor of *Musical Quarterly*.

REELIFE: WIDE SCREEN PROJECTION

The pun is as old as the movie. M-G-M with Vidor's *Billy the Kid* presents "Realife" wide-screen projection realized after two years of experimentation. The introduction of this new attraction attests to the fact that the talkie, introduced prematurely as fiscal salvation, has reached its saturation point as an audience-bid. The new type of "grandeur" projection has the advantage of the earlier in that standard-size film print is used, not requiring a special battery of projectors to supplement the standard. The latter is used with a special lens that enlarges the image to the size desired. The picture is made on special-size stock and reduced to standard. The image is not blurred, and the grain of the emulsion is eliminated. The grain that is revealed is that of the image, notably in the case of landscape, which benefits most from the new invention, gaining definiteness of edge (a tactile conquest), contour and spatial relations: depth, contrast of hollow and ridge, placement values, etc.

The earlier wide screen was wider but not higher than the standard. "Realife" enlarges the total perimeter. The screen will be adjusted to the particular theatre, and the lens image will be enlarged "much as a commercial artist enlarges a photograph." Flexibility of screen is decidedly a victory! But will literalness not thwart its potentialities? An adjustable screen suggests multiple uses, a screen changing in dimensions, an active screen.

Vidor sees the change in screen as solely a visual change, having nothing to do with the audible. But any visual change in the compound cinema is an audible change. If there is pictorial relief—as the distant approximation of the stereoscopic achieves in "Realife"—there is also, inherently, sound relief; pictorial perspective, sound perspective; pictorial variety (in the intrinsic), sonal variety. Vidor the chronologist has never used sound and speech with the zeal of a discoverer or even a scrupulous student. Literalist he is, but not artist. He sees the new device as doing "away with a good many of the 'cut-backs' and close-ups to which we have become accustomed." The literal mind confesses: the devices of "cut-back" and close-up to him were not rhythmic compositional utilities, but merely expediences! Expediences to satisfy the momentarily effective. *Billy the Kid* possesses a few ingratiating moments and nothing more. "Action on the screen can be told in more direct, flowing style." This means, as illustrated by *Billy the Kid,* nothing other than the rudimentary 1, 2, 3, yarn-spinning structure of the western, initial in Broncho Billy of two decades ago. But to allow Mr. Vidor his own defense, I quote him:

"For example, in one sequence of *Billy the Kid* we have a hold-up scene in the foreground of the picture. By means of the depth illusion . . . a rescue party is seen starting, in the background, several miles away. The oncoming party does not know what is happening in front, but the audience observes every moment of both with more suspense than could be possible by any system of 'cut-backs.'"

The simultaneity achieved does not destroy the function of the "cut back," for the latter is not merely a narrative or suspense expedient, but as the Russians have indicated, a part of a process — psychological, physiological, dramatic, pivotal (as in *Fragment of an Empire*), rhythmic.

The major victories of "Realife" are photographic and the selection of details from a mass. The victories are not so sure with the human players as with the natural setting, and it was therefore wise to begin with *Billy the Kid.* The screen is less apparently framed (perhaps this is because the new screen is a novelty, though its not being square helps too), and it is freer in its receptivity to masses and movements and the participation of background with fore-players — although Vidor has barely hinted at these in his film. Movement backward into the depth is more convincing, not merely because it is more "natural" — as Vidor puts it — but because there is a sense of placement, of changing relationship between the thing or person in motion and environment. In other words, focus is rendered more elastic too. Vidor comments also upon the "sideway" sight of "Realife." The façade and thickness of an erect structure are visible, and distances are more definitely established in ratio. But we are still very, very far away from the stereoscopic film!

And what do all these inventions avail finally, if there is no intelligence to use them, and if, above all, the point of view toward the theme remains as uninformed as ever? *Billy the Kid* is just another western of "the good bad man" who goes good for the girl, a theme and a treatment which date from the first *Broncho Billy*. About a half-dozen years ago *The Covered Wagon* was filmed to ludicrous applause. I don't think many besides James Stevens and myself rejected it or questioned its being a work of importance. It was another — if longer — *Broncho Billy*. Fred Thomson gave us *Jesse James*, one of the few westerns to appear on Broadway before the talkie. This was a mixture of Tom Mix and Doug Fairbanks. Neither the legend nor the historical period found expression in the film. And *Billy the Kid* is another stereotype.

Billy the Kid was an emotional moron who played in the frontier era of economic warfare the rôle of the gun-ready racketeer. Legends never develop around him of the Robin Hood and Jesse James "he did it for the poor" brand. He shot twenty-odd men "not counting Mexicans and Indians," and omitting, I suppose, the ranch foreman who was "only a Jew." Billy the Kid is the high-water mark of the economic desperado unrefined. In the more refined sphere he has numerous counterparts in contemporary society.

The Governor of Billy's state absolves William's misdemeanors as resulting from a "keen sense of justice," and undersigns the Vidor film as authentic despite aesthetically warranted "liberties" with the truth. It is humorous to watch these blunt boys suddenly turn to art for argument. The deliberate degrading of Melville's "Moby Dick" into *The Sea Beast* was defended as artistic expedience. The law and order which came into the wild and woolly west was brought there to paternalize the "organised" rustlers of the new variety, the "land-rustlers." Vidor's film makes the paternalism of the White House a father's wish for peace in the family. And Billy goes off with the girl — reformed. Actually, he was shot dead in his tracks. Might it not have been because he would not give up his "sphere of influence," when the big racketeers came west with the sanction of the government? In *The Spoilers,* the Rex Beach novel recently paramounted with speech (Selig made a silent of it years ago), the identical relationship enters, but is never stressed for what it means: the government backing the big racketeer against the small man. In our land of opportunity, the big racketeer always gets his chance; land-grabs, mine-grabs, Teapot Dome. That's the simply story of *Billy the Kid,* a "saga" that can't be told in the movie. Especially since the west is building a monument to Billy, murderer and emblem, and tourists are wanted.

CLOSE UP,
November, 1930.

3

THE DIRECTOR'S MEDIUM

FIELD GENERALS OF THE FILM

The war of the film faiths begins with the discovery of field generalship. David Wark Griffith appears about 1908; art and the spoils system enter. Before that the movie had no arena because it had no plan of attack; since then the audience has been assaulted plenty. The assault has been aggravated by the critic who, in the need to vindicate the popular taste and identify himself with his environment, has proclaimed this director and that a creator.

There were directors before Griffith. But historically, the first director must be the first important director. Eisenstein has called Griffith "the Grand Old Man of us all," though he is rather the Russian's step-father than father. But D. W. did introduce effective tactics and a major strategy. Tactics and strategy have, lamentably, left flimsy tradition in their land of birth. What "the U. S. A. Cinema" recalls of Griffith are his blue-grass sentimentalisms, his false good taste. This negative tradition has been relayed by Griffith lieutenants like W. Christy Cabanne, rivals like the late Thomas Ince, and by a whole string of directors (film-actors of yore), such as Edwin Carewe. There has been one positive by-product of this false good taste: Mack Sennett's jack-in-the-box humor, the "churlish" slapstick, begun as a tongue-in-the-cheek restatement of Griffith's idyllic refinement. Griffith, himself, has collected all his weaknesses into one film, *The Struggle,* which was withdrawn from public view after a few days.

Good taste works in two directions. If Griffith tripped one way with his false good taste, Cecil de Mille, the goldbraid generalissimo, has lollopped in the other direction with his bad taste. Two influences have primrosed his path of glory: the Bible and the Bathing Beauty. He has borrowed the phalanx from the Gospel and the flank from Mack Sennett. He likes his war meretricious. For lesser comrades-in-arms he has Fred Niblo, Rex Ingram, William Nigh and Allan Dwan; and on the plane below, Alan Crosland, Sidney Franklin and Frank Capra, the gem of Columbia's ocean.

To seek a contemporary extension of De Mille, we must enter the land of cult. In décor, De Mille may differ from Josef von Sternberg, but the latter has become no less a general of Graustark. De Mille believes in Art. Da Vinci influenced his *King of Kings*. And Sternberg, we are reassured, "wears black shirts made by a special black-shirt maker." He is above, so he says, reference to the works of European directors, yet his three productions as impresario of "Legs" Dietrich are full of the "antiquated novelties" of the German studios. In the early days of his career, Sternberg presented, in films of simple climactic progression, the honest American idiom of the open attack. But soon he was cultivated by cult. For a time he appeared out of the reach of the sycophants. To resist cult, however, requires stamina; Sternberg yielded. He traded his open style for fancy play, chiefly upon the legs in silk, and buttocks in lace, of Dietrich, of whom he has made a paramount slut. Sternberg is, by his own tokens, a man of meditation as well as action; but instead of contemplating the navel of Buddha his umbilical perseverance is fixed on the navel of Venus. His diligence was frustrated when he met the innate sobriety of *An American Tragedy*. The result is an aimless, lugubrious mess. As for his direction of melodrama, there is more honest stuff in John S. Robertson's *The Phantom of Paris* than in *Dishonored*—more honest because less egregious. The fireworks may dazzle the schoolboys of criticism, but they will contribute no permanent color to the motion picture. Whether Sternberg is a man of ability or not, I place him on less honest a level than even George Fitzmaurice who made *The Unholy Garden*.

Between the self-consciousness of a Sternberg and that of a Vidor—who is also cult—there is a great difference. Sternberg's has the smoke, but not the flame of battle. Vidor's preoccupations merely bespeak the innocent; King Vidor aspires to an important expression he cannot achieve. He has more zeal than intelligence. *The Big Parade* remains his best film, because it is a chronology, and Vidor is a chronologist. *The Crowd*, which reduced a large, if debatable, theme to an arbitrary pamphlet, was further confused by a mismating between a simple sequence and expressionistic symbolism. Similarly, the conflict between ability and aspiration was present even in the sincere *Street Scene*. This film again reveals Vidor's immaturity. He is obsessed with details remembered from other pictures; they explode as spontaneous combustion — that is his method, which is no method at all. The cult-position Vidor holds distracts him from his logical field of action — matter like *Billy the Kid,* which he directed diffidently. The result is inevitably the setup of the tear-jerker and descent to the level of a Frank Borzage. Only Vidor's innocence and goodwill — and Beery's acting — preserved *The Champ* from the cheapest properties of the subject matter.

Strong statures usually resist cult. No cult has fastened upon Lewis Milestone. He is not obsessed with himself. And yet he has been, in *The Front Page,* the second American director since Griffith to advance a major strategy.

Milestone's contribution in *The Front Page* is the first American contribution to the "philosophy" of the sound-sight cinema. It puts forth the principle of pace set by the verbal element. The film itself is a *tour de force,* a vehicle which by its speed makes a superficial cargo appear profound. That is no small achievement in generalship. Milestone is our only director who treats each film as the solution of a particular problem. He may make only an approximate solution, as in *All Quiet,* but it is a maximum approximation within the barbed wires of Hollywood.

To appreciate Milestone's achievement in his environment, one may refer to W. S. Van Dyke and *White Shadows.* Here is a minimum achievement with potential material. Or, we may refer to Clarence Brown. He has shown himself an apt chameleon. There are three kinds of this creature: the passive, like Herbert Brenon; the apt, like Brown; and the selective, like Jacques Feyder, a foreign importation whom Hollywood has never learned to use despite his responsiveness. Brown in *Flesh and the Devil* showed an aptitude for a maturer idiom, which controlled him rather than submitted to him. In *Emma,* Brown has illustrated that directorial integrity may keep a sentimental idea chaste, when a chaste personality like Marie Dressler is the pivot. In *A Free Soul* he assembled his film as Frankenstein assembled his monster, though, for the Academy of Motion Picture Arts and Sciences, to more self-satisfying consequences. Mention of *Frankenstein* brings up the image of the film made from Mrs. Percy Shelley's novel by James Whale, a man of picayune imagination, who, in three pictures, has revealed his total inadequacy in the cinema and his talent for using the incorrect treatment for the subject matter.

The degradation from director to pasticheur is a continual process in Hollywood. Two studios, Warner and Fox, have especially enjoyed it. The former now delights in the historical curio called George Arliss, for whose formula the sole technique needed is that of the call-boy. There are differences, however, even in the talents of call-boys. These constitute the superiority of John Adolfi to Alfred Green, or vice-versa. Yet we must be grateful for any sign of competence on the job. Therefore two pictures ground in the Warner mill, William Wellman's *Public Enemy* and Mervyn Le Roy's *Five-Star Final,* have a special interest. Mr. Wellman is a man of sporadic ability, however naïvely shocking his great moments may be. Mr. Le Roy is also facile, if overpitched.

The worst sin on the bad record of Fox is its treatment of F. W. Murnau, who completed his great career with *Sunrise.* (I consider *Tabu* an unfortunate throwback). Frank Borzage, among others—John Ford included—extracted from *Sunrise* what was spurious to add to his sentimental attack. Borzage has set the style for Fox, the assault on the helpless civilian. Now Fox has made Henry King into a soldier of ill-fortune, using every malignant attack from tear-gas to dumdum bullets. King has been one of our most talented directors. But for years his direction has been a study in antipathy, between the bold pattern of his work and his indigent subject-matter. Today the discord is no longer a conflict—it is pathetic. Oddly enough, Fox has been the proving ground for the best gangster film of the silent era, Irving Cummings' *Dressed to Kill,* and the best of the garrulous era, Rowland Brown's *Quick Millions,* the first film of a new director. Brown and Rouben Mamoulian are about the only new directors of the last couple of years who may seriously be called promising. The hubbub that greeted the latter's *Applause* confused a bad picture with an ingenious director. In *City Streets* he again separates himself from a trite story to give a sensitive treatment, but one far too heroic for the story. Mamoulian needs to be cautious: his ingenuity threatens to become a routine of excess mobility and other fallacious devices. Rowland Brown's single work is spectacular only in its clean economy. Its performance is subdued, but not emasculated; it does not depend on the trigger-pull for excitement. Therefore it excels the ballyhoo type of picture directed by George Hill or Wesley Ruggles, who made loose-linkage episodes of *Cimarron.* More adroit ballyhoo is the barker-business of Tod Browning.

All causes have their Ichabods. In the movie they are lost souls. A Lubitsch, glib in his chit-chat, keeps remaking the selfsame film. A sensitive artist like Stiller is slain with humiliation. Victor Seastrom, greatest of the directors before the Russians, is another "eucalyptus tree in Siberia." Sometimes a change of camp cleans the cobwebs from the directorial mind. Raoul Walsh made his best picture, *Sadie Thompson,* when he left the stuffy confines of Fox for United Artists. John Ford's *Hangman's House,* made for Fox, was indeterminate; far more resolute is his direction of *Arrowsmith* for Goldwyn. Charles Brabin, after leaving Fox for the Metro stables, reveals nice gifts in *Sporting Blood.* Other directors have been unable to remold themselves in the new talking medium. James Cruze, once the highest paid director, a man of talent for humorous fantasy, plainly shows his dislike for the talkie. Monta Bell admits it in print. William K. Howard, whose reputation was made with *White Gold,* reverts to the earlier era of *Variety* in *Transatlantic* – a refreshing reminiscence. Eric von Stroheim, overrated by cult and abused by the arbitrary ministry of the studio (a man, in spite of many blind spots, of backbone and purpose), is relegated to the has-beens, directors-become-actors. Somewhere in Europe is Maurice Tourneur, one of the best, now a man without a country. And making wretched *Pimpernel* films in England is T. Hayes Hunter, whose dignified *Earthbound* once made Basil King seem genuine. Nor has any studio developed the talent for the macabre shown by James Flood, hardly a novice.

In the meantime, we have a host of drawing-room officers who use the new medium as so many epaulets, so many gold frogs.

VANITY FAIR,
March, 1932.

REMARKS ON D. W. GRIFFITH

David Llewellyn Wark Griffith has been called the first genius of the motion picture. This characterization needs to be qualified. When Griffith entered the movies, in the days of AB (American Biograph), the director was a sort of assistant to the cameraman, who was then George William ("Billy") Bitzer. Griffith came into the AB studio as an actor, and remained to direct. The director of a film was absent one day. Griffith had shown an active curiosity in the new medium, and he was told to take the menial task. He did. With that assumption the director — the artist — of the movie was born.

The development of Griffith is the development of the American film. It has not gone beyond D. W. in idea, composition or human interest. That is to say, it remains quite juvenile. Indeed, there has been no director quite as intuitively gifted as Griffith. Thomas Ince was made of sterner, but at the same time, of weaker, stuff. Griffith it must be allowed, and because of his romanticism, has been more devoted to the motion picture than Ince. If grandiose, as his compositions have been in his large attempts, he has not been flamboyant, like Herbert Brenon or George Loane Tucker or Tod Browning. He has been anxious to present the materials of his own literary conscience.

And that is his first limitation. It is the limitation of a man poorly endowed with content-discrimination. He is an American and Southern gentleman of a desiccate aristocracy. This heritage seeps through all his films. He said not long ago: "The maturer motion picture of today has yet to turn its attention seriously to the kind of themes that we used back in 1908." Mr. Griffith referred to his penchant for "Poesie" and classics, not the purest of tendencies. The Southern gentlemen traditionally go through a training in Xenophon and Ovid, in a classical school remote from the progressive centers and uninformed by the new education, and forever wear this dubious learning as a pathetic blossom in the buttonhole of their intellects. In his penchant for *"poésie"* Griffith is the American Gance — or Gance is the French Griffith. But it is true that within the penchant there was the expression of a need for intensely-felt human episodes. Griffith, as an American, mistook platitudes for criticism, but these platitudes were, if only vague, statements of social impurities. Guided by an intuition fed on unplumbed prejudices, Griffith's social history was articulated in *The Birth of a Nation,* the anticipation of the recrudescence of the Ku Klux Klan! When the Negro, threatened by the bad temper provoked by the film, objected to the picture, Griffith, supported by the liberal and white hypocrisy of "free speech," issued a printed tract and a film-tract on *Intolerance.* A Houston, Texas daily was quoted as saying that the white citizen was not yet prepared to accept orders from the black! Griffith's expansive love of mankind, itself a platitude, did not extend to the Negro. Nor did his *Intolerance* educate him in the skepticism of a true lover of mankind, when America entered the war. He went to England and directed the activities of society dames in support of the war, and produced *Hearts of the World,* a sentimental film urging allied sympathy.

His latest film, *Lincoln,* is another bit of "sweetness and light" in patriotism. After spending months and reading 180 books (he will play at being a scholar), Griffith hired Stephen Vincent Benet, prize-winning author of the unimaginative free verse "John Brown's Body," to write the scenario. A child would have been ashamed of such a presentation of the American legend, Abraham Lincoln. American history and folk-ideology are expressed in the terms of the crudest, most flatulent myths. *Lincoln* is an unintelligent Drinkwater chronicle play on the screen, further reduced to innocuousness by an uncritical director and a bad poet. The fact that it draws tears is rather against it than for it. The pathos of a tremendous social occurrence should not be refined or lachrymose, but revealing. The social occurence seldom gets a chance here. Slogans of spurious manufacture explain the motivations of the Civil War. It would seem that all of America was discovered, developed and directed for the sole purpose of the Lincoln wise-cracks.

The legend of a people may offer as much substance for revelation as the actual unmythical source. But such revelation demands a critical understanding which alone assures a surpassing of the elementary myth. Griffith possesses no critical penetration. The nostalgia of a desiccate aristocracy seeps through this film. In this he is the same old Griffith. His very insistence on Lincoln is a phobia which, as a defense, Southerners, especially one descended from a Confederate Brigadier-General (*sic*), are cultivating. *Lincoln* submits a questionable penitence in the silly pretense, with music, to toleration of the black, a sort of rococo Americanese "Volga Boatman" with Negroes. The Southern gentleman is forever present, as in the tiresome reiterations of the virtues of the protagonists, those of the Confederate leader, Richard E. Lee[?], in particular. The whole film waits like an obsessed schoolboy for the crack of a Lincoln witticism known to the ritualized audience. The Struss-Menzies collaboration in the photography and "art" fulfills all the horrid sentimentalism of the conception and treatment. Abe Lincoln's lip-rouge attests to the dwindling care of Griffith for conviction. The finale of Lincoln's monument is a specious bid for patriotism. Who says the American movie is against propaganda? The innovator of the silent film contributes nothing to the improvement of the garrulous. He has no George William ("Billy") Bitzer to realize his needs, nor has he any needs. His days are over.

Lincoln is the epitome of Griffith's sentimentalism. The portrayal of Ann Rutledge is shamefully simpering. One is happy to have her pass away. The sentimentally idyllic cannot be endured in an "Historic" film. It may be tolerated in a film inherently idyllic, like *The Idol Dancer,* one of Griffith's smaller pictures, or even in an excerpt that might, in better hands, have become an epic, *Scarlet Days,* another of his pictures. But Griffith has never been able to escape the sentimentally idyllic, no more than Gance has, even in his broadest films. *The Birth of a Nation* is soaked with it. However, his compositional sense, of repeated motifs (the "out of the cradle endlessly rocking" of *Intolerance*) has made these films important in cinema history. His invention of the "flash-back" or "cut-back"—a directorial device in montage before the establishment of montage—has been perhaps his greatest contribution to the cinema. The first dramatic use of the "close-up"—in *The Mender of Nets* with Mary Pickford—and of the "long distance shot," the "soft focus" (with the rapid close-up in *Broken Blossoms*), the camera angle and mobile camera (of *Intolerance*), etc., may be attributed to Griffith and his collaborator, Bitzer. But neither Griffith nor his successors in America have developed these uses. They were expediences for Griffith, just as were the insertions of titles into films originally graphic only. Even the critics in the U.S.A., like George Jean Nathan and Gilbert Seldes, have called the "close-up" a banality, unable to recognize it for the structural pivot and pictorial beauty it offers.

It is in the handling of mob scenes that Griffith has accomplished his most original and powerful work. Here again he resembles Gance, the Gance of the resilient march in *Napoleon*. *Lincoln* is pathetic in its scrawny manipulation of the soldiers, who appear every bit like a revue chorus of men of feminine persuasion. In the control of the individual player, Griffith has been undoubtedly zealous and stern, as a director should be. But his code of the gentleman, converted into "refinement," has impoverished his actors and his films as dramatic and human experiences. Samuel Goldwyn says that Mary Pickford ran away from Griffith to rescue her identity. Lillian Gish is a puppet, an inactive puppet, in her mincing portrayals. Only a childish idolater and inane quibbler would insist that Gish is Gish and not the part she plays. The actor is a portion of a conception and must yield to it. If it demands understatement, she must provide understatement; if hyperbole, she must provide hyperbole. Elasticity is an essential of the player, but Griffith stretched that quality in his players beyond the point of elasticity. He established a tradition, by now noxious in the American movie: the tradition of "refinement," a mincing innocence, the pout, the petulance that persists in all the cute players, down to the Farrell-Gaynor combination, and most offensively in Dolores del Rio (griefs of the river!). It will not vindicate Lillian Gish to say: "I have often been called a Griffith product. Well, in a way I am, of course. In a great many ways I am not. Nearly all my early pictures were directed by Tony Sullivan and Christy Cabanne . . ." Lillian Gish was brought up in the Biograph studio, the Griffith tradition in its own four walls, and Cabanne was an assistant to Griffith.

Griffith has undoubtedly been the most important director of the American movie. He was less diverted by careerist ambitions, or by the lure of money than all the others. Indirectly, he was responsible for the beginning of American comedy. Sennett, one of Griffith's players, certainly learned much from Griffith's handling of a comique like Billy Quirk. And Sennett's slapstick parodied the refinements of the Griffith troupe. It is a commentary on both of them, and on the American movie, that they never learned to adequately see the grand talents of Mabel Normand.

Griffith was, in his early days, most impressionable. As he saw the movie progress in its capabilities, and able to handle larger themes running longer, he was the first to seize the opportunity, as in *Man's Genesis* and *Judith of Bethulia*. When the spectacle film came from Europe, in particular Italy, he saw the uses of grandeur and scope (although he rendered these platitudinously) in such films as *The Birth of a Nation* and *Intolerance.* No one in America has gone beyond him in this regard, neither Cruze nor Vidor.

The extensions of Griffith are to be found elsewhere, particularly in the Soviet Union. Pudovkin is a direct extension of Griffith, strengthened by a society of profounder and stronger impetus, and by a cinema of firmer analysis and closer scrutiny — as in the selection of authentic types. In the alternation — amounting to a physiological process — of close view and distant "shot" (as in *Storm Over Asia*) Pudovkin creates a form out of neglected devices. The "flashback" is used in a dramatic and rhythmic process . . . but Pudovkin resembles Griffith in weaknesses of sentimentalism, expressing themselves in poorly chosen similes (the weeping statue in *The End of St. Petersburg*) and in an overstress of the person as against the social occurrence. The latter fault has been increasingly apparent in Pudovkin since *Mother.* In Griffith we see what Pudovkin might have been in America 1910–30, although we must allow a technical-aesthetic understanding in Pudovkin superior to that of Griffith — in 1930. In Pudovkin we see what Griffith might have been in the U.S.S.R., sustained and urged by a challenging criticism and a relentless discipline. Griffith has been, sadly enough, too much his heritage and environment. He has not risen above them. And now he is through!

RÉVUE DU CINÉMA,
February 1, 1931.

MORE REMARKS ON GRIFFITH

Eisenstein has just called Griffith "the Great Old Man of us all." Now, I do not oppose Griffith as the father of the cinema, but for Eisenstein to speak in capitals and so affectionately of a man whose temper makes him his step-father, his kino step-father, is much too generous. Yet it cannot be denied that every singular director takes his hat off to Griffith as an ancestor who was worth something.

At this late date, however, to find commentators writing uncritically of the contribution of D. W. is somewhat exasperating. One may for documentation accredit Griffith with the first dramatic uses of the close-up etc.; but every contribution must be viewed in the total light of the progress of the artist, his success, his failure, his strength, his weakness.

Looking back from *Lincoln,* we have been able to see Griffith as a man of personal integrity, but of that anomalous personal integrity which may tolerate the most vicious social conduct. By a confusion arising perhaps from an ambiguity in manuscript and correspondence, a footnote in the *Révue du Cinéma* corrected, but did not correct, an inexactness in many *"Remarques sur D. W. Griffith."* I intended to call *Lincoln* a proof that Griffith was an unintelligent Drinkwater. That is a redundancy in itself. The lord knows, if Carl Laemmle doesn't, that John Drinkwater is specious enough. The translator has done me a good turn when he says: *"**Lincoln** est la chronique d'un buveur d'eau intelligent."* The pun is accurate in two ways: Abraham Lincoln was a teetotaler, the film has the vivacity of a glass of water at a feast.

Among the directors who owe something to Griffith, I mentioned

Pudovkin. I must clear up the resemblance I have indicated to Griffith. It is twofold: the weak figure of speech, and the tendency to emphasize, in a film of social currents, the individual to the disadvantage of the social emphasis. In a Soviet director this is a more grievous fault, since the character of the Soviet kino is its conveyance of the sense of society; whereas the American movie is habitually forgetting the society to stress the star. But Griffith has been a singular American director in that he has been almost alone in thinking first of the general idea. In the final statement the general idea is lost, but not completely: in *The Birth of a Nation* it persists insidiously.

Closer than Pudovkin is Gance to Griffith. Indeed, one might call Gance the French Griffith. I think that the early Griffith gave us a more compelling and integrated work than Gance, but they both show the sentimentality of the weak simile in their figures of speech: Napoleon and the eagle, Violine and the lily in *Napoleon.* Gance has the affliction which marks the French artist, carried over into the film: the predilection for dissociation. Whereas this is somewhat allowable (though I object to it as immaturity) in a film like *Entr'acte,* where the whole idea is dissociation *per se,* the delight in the irrelevant; in a film moving, at least in intention, to a definite single cohesive idea, the failure to advance the dissociations to associations is certainly not praiseworthy. Gance has done this in *La Roue.* Griffith, perhaps because he is a simpler soul than Gance, follows the path of associations more precisely. Yet the analogies he incorporates are as innocuous *"poésie"* as Gance's. In *Close Up* (July 1929) I said: "The French need to be vigilant against two related faults, sentimentality and refinement. The French sentimentality is not moral sentimentality, as in the case of the English and the American, but aesthetic sentimentality. . . . it is a diffusive, a soft sentimentality in Poirier and Gance. . . . I have said Gance was Hugo without Hugo's vision. That makes him the counterpart in cinema of Eugene Sue." In the personal characterizations — Lillian Gish for instance — the art of Griffith is also very much like that of Sue. Do you recall the girl in *The Wandering Jew* whom the author accepts as the most hypersensitive soul because she loves perfumes? That's Violine and the Lily: that's *Broken Blossoms,* the girl of which Lillian Gish has been in every succeeding film.

Writing on Griffith in *The Miscellany* (New York, March 1931), Mr. Dwight Macdonald would take possible exception to my portrait of a Griffith player. Speaking of *The Birth of a Nation* Macdonald says: "The acting is exaggerated in its expressiveness (as in the playing of the two girls, who flutter about with the greatest vivacity on every possible occasion) but it *is* expressive. And in the movies that is the big thing—the languorous stolidity of a Garbo to the contrary." Now, expressiveness may or may not be the big thing, and Garbo's "languorous stolidity"—when directed sensitively, by a Feyder, a Pabst or a Stiller, rather than meretriciously by a Niblo, or half-heartedly by a Clarence Brown, may be an intensive adjustment to the structure of the film. As a matter of fact, Griffith's honeyed expressiveness is nothing but the traditional sentimentality of the "romantic South" and its suitability is to the "tremendous moral earnestness" of the Griffith film, the earnestness which when finally distilled is a reactionary and malicious platitude and lie.

It is not an accident that Griffith is, as Mr. Macdonald sees him, "a typically American product." Macdonald quite rightly sees that Griffith "never really understood what he had discovered—which accounts for his not developing montage beyond the see-saw stage used in his finales, and for the fact that his latest picture, *Lincoln,* is less interesting technically than *The Birth of a Nation.* . . . During the past ten years Griffith has gone to seed with a thoroughness possible only to the American artist." I am not sure it is "possible only to the American artist"—it is possible to all bourgeois society, centripetal society, at the end of its evolution, in an impasse. It is not true, on the other hand, of a centrifugal society like the U.S.S.R., discharging fresh momentums. However, the seediness of Griffith is important less as an individual case than as an epitome of frustration in the bourgeois cinema. Observe how the American director, including Griffith himself, has relapsed completely into the chronological film, rather than developed the associative, constructed, back-and-forth reference film. The failure of a Vidor in *The Crowd* and *Hallelujah!* is a failure both of conception and—since form is the conception informing the structure—of treatment. *Hallelujah!* is a dwindled *Birth of a Nation* with whatever sense of mass the latter contained altogether lost.

Macdonald, who has done a very good, if brief, bit on Griffith doesn't sight the full story because he doesn't tie up beginning and end from the standpoint of ideology. Therefore there isn't a full picture of Griffith in his account. The details he cites point to an organic disease—very American, very bourgeois. As, for instance, in the "absurd, banal, sentimental, bombastic" subtitles of *The Birth of a Nation*: "The Master Paraded in Chains before his Former Slaves" and "The Black's Mad Proposal of Marriage." Macdonald agrees with me in applying his devastating epithets to "his reflections on human nature, i.e., his treatment of character in action. His people act according to the conventions of the popular novel"—or better according to the conventions of an introverted nostalgia for a lost South — "yet what superb cinema he gets out of their actions. From any point of view *except a cinematic one,* his pictures are earnest absurdities. Even cinematically he is far from impregnable, his fitful talent throwing off the wretchedness as well as the most inspired productions." Macdonald corroborates a statement I have already made on the isolatedness of Griffith who has left no school to follow him. But — he has left traditional fallacies and malpractices: the pseudo-aristocratic "good taste," refined acting, restraint without structural intention, "expressiveness" as against emphatic pronunciation of type and adjustment to the structural scheme, insipid symbols, etc. These have been sustained by a literal movie which has not had its writhing energies released due to the lack of the necessary social impetus. Granting Griffith's intuition for "montage," his sense of economy, his use of the outdoors, his pictorial sense, handling of crowds, we must still inquire what was the quality of these elements. Macdonald has already admitted that the economy in relation to titles condensed the nauseating sentimentality and I add anti-social "moral earnestness" of Griffith. The instance of economic character comment — he conveys the kindliness of his Southern landowner by a close-up of his hand fondling a puppy — is not only sentimentality, very trite and much too simple a statement, it is also hypocrisy, the hypocrisy of an exploiting class. The attitude of Griffith to the Negro (we may find a simile in the landowner's fondling of the dog) is a mixture of patronage and hate with hate preëminent. The *Birth of a Nation* employs no genuine Negro in the rôles — miscegenation will not allow that. In *One Mysterious Night* — Griffith initiated the churlish mystery-comedy — the Negro, thrust forward at every chance for hilarity, is blackface and not real. This is not meant as consideration for the Negro, but as an unwillingness to feature a Negro. It is a double victory: you avoid the Negro and ridicule him with a makeshift. In *Lincoln* the Negroes are in the background, almost in the shadows. The persistence of prejudice is typical of a centripetal society and a small mind.

This lack of productive energy in intelligence accounts for Griffith's speedy decline. Griffith in *Birth of a Nation* and *Intolerance* — even, in a sense, before that, in *Man's Genesis,* and *Judith of Bethulia* — used the extensive theme. Macdonald speaks of the first-mentioned films as "the movies to make use of the *extensive* powers of cinema." Would he dismiss the Italians? Or would he say they were extensive in plan but not in their use of the cinematic powers? They were, at any rate, the overture to Italian Fascism — Antica Roma — as *Birth of a Nation* was to American Fascism — Ku Klux Klan. Macdonald continues on the two American films: "They are the first movies conceived on such extensive scale that the individuals are less important than the vast background . . ." I have already indicated that Griffith's discipline, submission to the inclusive idea, sags frequently. "Griffith treats his epic subjects as Eisenstein does, not as historical narratives running through time but as cinematizations in space of abstract themes." Macdonald is misleading: Eisenstein is at the other pole from Griffith, especially in *Ten Days* which Macdonald compares to *Birth of a Nation*. Good versus bad in *Ten Days* is one thing; in the Griffith film another. *Ten Days* is one of the pivotal films: the objective canvas. *Birth of a Nation* is grandiose melodrama aimed with vengeance rather than with criticism. Again I draw upon Pudovkin as the valid resemblance. One cannot compare Griffith's similes (the simile is always a weaker structural device) with Eisenstein's metaphors. Griffith shapes his themes "primarily to express an idea"; the idea is platitudinous ("war is terrible," "through the ages love and intolerance have been at strife") and its expression is in a very literal and doggerelly symbol – the spider and web, the cradle for "out of the cradle endlessly rocking." Eisenstein is the most efficient instance of a director making use of the reality as symbol. Moreover, in *Old and New* he has built a structure which anticipates this reality as a symbol and provides a rhythmic place for it. Griffith's sense of rhythm has never been that disciplined, that intelligent. As to Griffith and the Russian film, Macdonald says in a footnote: "Griffith's influence on the modern Russian film was probably small compared to that of the Constructivist theatre, Pavlov's theories of reflex action, and, above all, the experiments of Kuleshov in cinematic theory." Still, Kuleshov's cinematic theory found its object lesson and start in Griffith's work, as well as in other Americans, Tod Browning's, for instance; and Pavlov was the scientific authority for the intuitive work of Griffith and further, it went far beyond its naïve origin to a montage which is a physiological process ultimately intellectual. If Pudovkin cites many examples from Griffith films in his book on *Film Technique* and though he says that Griffith's *Intolerance* opened his eyes to the possibilities of the cinema, it is because Griffith is very close to him. I think it is correct to say that Pudovkin's "association with Kuleshov must have been the prime formative influence on his art" only in the sense that Kuleshov was his pedagogic signpost, indicator, the electric button that put the lights on – to grant Kuleshov a more active role. He started the inquiry – served, in a sense, a midwife's function – certainly very important, but less than that of the planter of the seed.

In the same footnote Macdonald says: "Pudovkin's turning from epics like *Storm Over Asia* to the domestic drama of *Life is Good* is curiously parallel to Griffith's progression from the epical *Intolerance* to the intimate human drama of *Broken Blossoms* and *Isn't Life Wonderful?* Let us hope Pudovkin's artistry suffers as little by the change as Griffith's did." The change is more than a change of drama type. Pudovkin is perplexed. He has repudiated his *Film Technique* for a theoretical agreement with Eisenstein. But he has organically repudiated *Film Technique,* has he repudiated his two previous *films?* I omit *Mother* for it stands alone. It is, I think, Pudovkin's best, since most convincing and honest film. Each succeeding film has been poorer, as experience, than the preceding. And this is true despite Pudovkin's increased mastery of the craftsmanship. Here is another affinity with Griffith. They are both expert — or Griffith was — in the alternation of scenes to create a process at work on the audience; the sense of duration of a sequence is especially precise in Pudovkin. They both are highly skillful in the alternation of close and distant scenes: as witness the episode in *Storm Over Asia* when the soldier takes the Mongol to shoot him. And this is another affinity: whereas both lose the thread of the idea, the social mass sense, in the play of the individual in films built on a grander scale of montage; in films where the concentration is on the individual from the very inception the experience is at least unified. Of Griffith's pictures I recall most vividly his *Idol Dancer* and *Scarlet Days;* the latter gave through a ballad idyllism some sense — Griffith sense — of the Indian wars. *Mother* is a highwater mark as a film, and it is a proof that if one starts with and sustains profound individual relationships amid an immanent social mass, he will convey the social meaning. Whereas to break into a mass film with the antic of a player is to injure the cumulative idea, the social motivation. I have said many times before that Pudovkin has had the wrong method for his material; it seems he now admits it. The colleagues who have chided me, more out of perversity than judgment, for my arrogance in anticipating Pudovkin's dilemma, now pompously repudiate Pudovkin's *Film Technique* with him — why? The book is still valuable — although they persist in reasoning and writing fragments of scenarios that are schoolboyish imitations of the suggestions of the Pudovkin book. The truth is that Pudovkin was too near to Griffith; the material and mind of the Soviet society demands another intelligence, even another intuition — profounder, more perspicacious, less sentimental, more precise, more unrelenting. And the technique of this Soviet kino — which is the technique of the world's cinema *en avant* — demands an attention to the intensive within the progressive. Macdonald finds the film an extensive medium, but he is speaking only of the "exterior movement," rather than of the "interior movement" — the movement constructed in the montage.

That Griffith's intensive units are "jerky" at times is due to the failure—success at such an early date was not to be expected—to construct the intensive units within the progression of the film. Pudovkin looked too much upon the intensive unit as the determinant; it is determined by the progression. Concentration on the individual actor is the working equivalent for the theoretical emphasis on the intensive unit—the *cadre*—as the determinant. But—the film is a progressive medium working towards the intensive: that is, its evolution toward intellectuality—it is, however, always a progressive medium . . .

Another point of resemblance between Griffith and Pudovkin is the histrionic art. Griffith derives from it, indeed, as Macdonald said, he has "the lantern jaw, the aquiline nose, the wildly gleaming eye of the old-style Shakespearean actor." Pudovkin has a yearning for acting.

[Ed.]: The manuscript breaks off at this point, obviously incomplete. The missing pages have never been found.

(UNPUBLISHED MANUSCRIPT,
Circa 1931–32).

DREYER, IN THEORY AND PRACTICE

In America *The Passion of Joan of Arc* was received with an enthusiasm hardly surpassed by the reception given to *The Cabinet of Dr. Caligari* or *The Armored Cruiser Potemkin*. Yet strangely no investigation seems to have been made of the artist who created that momentous film. One of his works, *Michael*, a Pommer-Ufa production, had been previously exhibited in America; and a ten-year-old creation, *The Witch Woman,* still esteemed in Europe succeded *Joan* here. But who is Dreyer and what is his creative attitude?

Dreyer is the author of *Joan*. The scenario is accredited to him and Joseph Delteil, the novelist, but its entire conception and construction are his. The realization of the scenario is also his. For Carl Dreyer is that long-sought unique creator of cinema, called director. He is completely the creative disciplinarian. The procedure of the inception and fulfillment of a Dreyer work is epitomized thus: thematic idea, structural idea, establishment of the coincidence of the two ideas in the literary scenario, the definition of the structural plan, the continuity, the performance, the final organization. The thematic idea is the subject and its inferences, the structural idea is the general sense of the theme in the imagery. This articulation is to be found in what has been wrongly called the Dreyer use of "close-up." Close-up is of American connotation and refers to the bland closing in and away of an image for momentary effect. It is this banal literal ulterior use that has led Gilbert Seldes and George Jean Nathan to condemn the close-up without recognizing its relevant potentialities. I call this use "ulterior" because it does not include the execution of the film's rhythmic unit. Dreyer has always thought in terms of the bold image, well connotated by the French term *"gros plan."* He has always thought in terms of structure in relief. *Joan of Arc* is only the culmination of an aesthetic attitude uttered in his very first film.

It is more than a decade now since Carl Dreyer made his first motion picture. Previously he had been a journalist and had entered the cinema as a converter of novels into scenarios, and a film cutter. He was a journalist in the morning and a cinematist in the afternoon. His training as a scenarist has survived in the importance he places in the literary script, which he constructs like an episodic and descriptive novel. His training as cutter is visible in the flexible interrelationship of images and sequences.

From the very first, Dreyer was intolerant of specious themes. He turned from the literary initiation of pictures and their final cinegraphic disposition to produce for the Great Northern of Denmark *Pages From the Book of Satan.* This inaugural film was divided into four parts: Christ, The Inquisition, The French Revolution, the Finnish Revolution of 1918. The Great Northern was then lord of the cinema industry with Vitagraph of America and Pathé of France. Its polar bear vied with the French rooster. The Satan film was followed in Dreyer's chronology with *The Witch Woman* issued by Biograph of Sweden, his native land. This film immediately brought Dreyer into European notice. One might parallel this recognition to that experienced by Eisenstein whom Dreyer esteems above any other director. Eisenstein was eulogized after *Potemkin* which followed his own initial film, *Strike.*

Dreyer was elected to cinematize Hans Christian Andersen, the Danish folk writer, in a film *Once Upon a Time,* privately subsidized. A similar honor was accorded him when Swedish Biograph chose him to direct the Norwegian national film, *Glomdal's Bride.* He followed with the picture which is listed in all of the considerations of notable films, *The Master of the House,* produced by Palladium of Copenhagen. He had made these five and *Michael* when the Société Générale of France gave him the direction of the national French film, the tale of La Pucelle. And it is in keeping with Dreyer that he chose not the heroic Joan the Maid but the lowly, oppressed, doomed, bewildered child. He left to Mario de Gastayne the spectacular armor-clad heroine of Orléans, his was the "passion"—the agony and devotion of the peasant lass of Domrémy, called "Jeanette" at home. How well he fulfilled his austere selection has already been told. But what must be reiterated is that the selection and the fulfillment are not the achievement of a single film, but the expression of a doctrine of cinematic conduct.

Three things are important in the Dreyer methodology: the script, the player and the montage. In the script he places the episodes successively and so worded as to afford a total conception of the film's intention and treatment to the director himself, his co-workers — cameramen, architect, artist, players. It might be said generically — that the film is complete with the scenario. All that remains is to enact it. However, Dreyer leaves room for inspiration, for the "idea born on the lot." To assure this flexibility he does not prepare the continuity, the immediate working-paper or blueprint until the night before the filming. Then he will know the exact placement of the decor and where each player will participate. And not until he gets "on the lot" does he determine the physical relationships of the materials, inanimate and human. The scenario has determined the total graphic and cinegraphic structure. He and his co-workers have understood the scheme of construction, they have decided upon and effected the decor and the lighting system and make-up and costume that will unitedly carry out this scheme. No trial and error once the work has begun, no accident. But inspiration is different, it is the moment's seizure of the defined whole, and it never diverts from this unit scheme. That is why there is no virtuosity in a Dreyer angle, it is a detail of the entirety justifying and justified by all that precedes and follows. Similarly Dreyer is drastic in his omission of images that are handsome in themselves. Like Poe he asks will this detail be necessary to the singular structure? His construction of the image is rhythmic, cinematically rhythmic, and not pictorial, although the pictorial is a constituent. He has even regretted not varying the bold image in *Joan* in a rhythmic plan of three scales: head, head and torso, full body. He believes he might even have varied the bold relief with the distant, non-relief image, although he admits that the persistent bold image is stronger. However, it is penetration and not impact that Dreyer seeks. Nowhere can that be better seen than in the use of the "backfiring" camera — the camera moving forward and quickly back — in the exposive mob scene at the end of *Joan*. In the Russian film the intention is "impact," in the Dreyer film it is more poignant in its resilience. Dreyer's montage attains to the heights of elasticity, and in it we find a suggestion of the "reflective processes" which Eisenstein calls the next Russian development in the kino. Dreyer is the indicator to the future intensive, philosophic inferential motion picture, and his entire career is a progress toward that film. And yet he has done nothing more than to reestablish the film at its source.

Indeed, this pronunciation of a principle by studying the source of cinema is an important tenet in the credo of Dreyer. He is a staunch advocate of the study not only of the film's source in itself but in the other graphic and plastic experiences of mankind. His movie is not "painting in motion," that anomaly first uttered by the evangelist of poesie and movie, Vachel Lindsay. Painting and sculpture suggest textural treatment and may even indicate stylistic values. French miniatures of the middle ages, Flemish genre art and Brueghel paintings of fairs and crowds are rich with textural and motive suggestions.

Mankind's experiences are sources for the cinema as they are sources for every other art. Experience as a source in art, and experience as the ultimate end. Dreyer builds the rhythmic, dramatic, psychologic to this end. Therefore, the human material, the player, will be for him the most important of his instruments. It is an instrument that is more than an instrument; it is the experience of the film to be conveyed to those viewing it. He demands not passivity from his players nor will he allow them — as does Cecil de Mille his actors — their own ways; he asks for intelligent receptivity, a great deal to ask of actors.

Dreyer does not think that it is always necessary to look for the intelligently receptive player in the professional actor. His next film he hopes to make a social comedy without professionals. The Russians seek generally their "types" for less subtle purposes than the sophisticated satirical; Dreyer would select the intelligent layman for his human material. It is the human material he wants, and it is the human identity he sought in the so-called historical film, in which he telescopes the years, discards the ephemeral marks of costumes, the gratuitous checks of ritualistic practice and makes one thing the decision: the film — the aesthetic, dramatic, human experience.

Dreyer's method, as he and commentators have observed, leads inevitably to sound. The bold image offers a basis for intensive, stylized verbal-visual imagery. This piecemeal incorporation of the caption in the visual motor rhythm, the intervaling of the images in time, his sensibility of time less autocratic and more refined than the metronome — all indicate that he is right in favor — the new compound cinema as his milieu. He would like to do a social satire of New York. "And if," he once said to me, "your American friends reject my wish because I am not American, tell them I am not French, and yet no one has said my Jean is not French." Two of the great directors of Sweden's golden age of cinema have come to America, Stiller to die, Seastrom to perish aesthetically, will the third great Swede, Carl Dreyer, come to America to be destroyed? I think not, for he is a man of forty who has made his films as every artist creates, each film in itself as the expression of a philosophy. He is seeking no Hollywood career, but wishes only to make another film, an American study. In anticipation of this possibility, he is studying available sources in American letters. He is disciplining himself for the creative work. He wants no fantastic America. Always he has sought not realism, but the reality in experience that his film might be an experience of a human and aesthetic reality. He believes that the worker must be the slave of his work, not in the American sense of being obliterated by it, but in the more transcendent sense that one must dream of his task for love of it. This is in keeping with his unvacillating values – non-Hollywood, non-Ufa, non-Bohemian, non-juvenile. He is circumscribed by these values, his own structure, but they create his films and keep him from diverting his aesthetic energies to what is experimentation for other directors but would thwart his fulfillments. The sole experimentation he must allow himself is the study of speech in the visual-motor structure.

BOSTON TRANSCRIPT,
March 29, 1930.

JEAN PAINLEVÉ'S MOVIES

Some time ago the French press stated that the only son of the Minister of War, Paul Painlevé, had gone into the movies. Jean Painlevé, whose father is a member of the Institute and a former President of the Council, had previously shown an inclination for but one of his father's vocations: science. And it was in behalf of science that he entered the cinema.

Jean Painlevé had just discovered at the laboratories of the Sorbonne the matter to color the cells of the human body, to enable the photographing of the cells in the fight against cancer. The laboratories were in need of money, and Jean, skilled in the use of the camera, accepted an invitation to make a romanticized documentary that would yield revenue. The film was to have been *The Unknown of the Six-Day Race,* celebrating the famous bicycle competition. It was never realized, but the film company saw to it that the laboratories were not the losers.

Young M. Painlevé was a gainer, too. He had had the opportunity of seeing and studying studio operations, and had conceived the idea of turning his knowledge of science to the art of the motion picture. The first thing he did was to adjust the focus of a magnifying glass that enlarged the image ten-thousandfold. Then he invented a periscopic objective that permitted submarine filming. With his operator, Raymond, he left for Port-Blanc, in Brittany, and there installed a laboratory with the little money he had. An expert on submarine fauna, he became the artist of undersea life.

The results of his patient and sensitive work appeared in Paris. His study of the respiration and expiration of an octopus was shown at the

Studio Diamant. It was more exciting than the Brigitte Helm feature to which it was a filler. The intentive little film now bears the title of *Passion and Death of the Octopus,* as it appears for the first time in the United States at the Eighth Street Playhouse this week.

Painlevé has, himself, expressed the principle, born of necessity, which presented the concentration of the life of the octopus, rather than fragments of its activities.

After the success of *Passion and Death of the Octopus,* Painlevé, faithful scientist and sensitive artist, turned to *The Daphnia,* a study in transparency revealed by microcinematography. His films were projected at the programs of Pathé in Paris. The last moment of the octopus, the loves of the daphnia, the romance of *The Hermit Crab,* told not with embellishments but suggestively, through sensitive directness, have won for Jean Painlevé first rank among the film artists of France. He continues and extends the tradition of the French nature-film, since *The Germination of Plants,* a tradition of artistic delicacy in the service of science. Scientific institutes throughout the world have invited him to present his microcinematographic studies in person. Painlevé, however, thinks of his works as motion pictures that, though based upon scientific researches and knowledge, are dramas of the screen, human films. He has become one of the young French independent film-producers whose work is awaited with eagerness among the film-minded.

[Ed.]: Published without a by-line. Found among the critic's printed articles and unpublished manuscripts given the editor by the author's widow, Mrs. Elizabeth Goldman, and purported to have been written by Potamkin.

THE NEW YORK TIMES,
June ?, 1929.

THE WOMAN AS FILM DIRECTOR

I have been asked a number of times, "Can a woman become a film director?" My answer takes two forms. First, I make the obvious retort that women are in demand as players, as scenario writers, and as film editors. Then I go on to say how few women have ever created films. There was Lois Weber. She was one of the earliest directors and one of the few to act in films and direct them at the same time. She and her actor-director husband, Phillips Smalley, appeared in and produced the first talking pictures back in 1908 for Gaumont. Olga Tschechowa, Russo-German player, had a company built for her in Germany, and did some brief direction. The talkie seems to have forestalled her aspiration. Now we wait to see what Jacqueline Logan, formerly starred in American films, will do as player-director in England.

The unique American is Dorothy Arzner who developed from a film-cutter to a competent director of light comedy. Russia has Esther Shub who builds factual historical chronologies out of fragments of diverse pictures, and Olga Preobajenskaia, the estwhile ballet-mistress who directed *The Village of Sin*. We may expect to see many more women directors issue from Soviet Russia. There is a State School of Cinema which accepts women in its courses. The young daughter of the astute Chinese general and statesman, Eugene Chen, is now studying camerawork there, and will then go into the course for directors. In France, a young movie journalist, Mlle. Lucie Derain, has made her own documentary film of the streets, rivers and incidents, the *Harmonies of Paris*. Mme. J. Bruno-Ruby, novelist, journalist, former golf champion of France, has directed films too. But the outstanding example and highwater mark among women movie-makers is Germaine A. Dulac.

Mme. Dulac last year was elected a Chevalier of the Legion of Honor in recognition of her staunchness for the film as a distinctive art. Her career in the cinema goes back to 1915, after a successful one as journalist. The press and the pen have been the way to the cinema for many noted directors, such as Carl Dreyer, the great creator of *The Passion of Joan of Arc* and René Clair of *Under the Roofs of Paris*. Mme. Dulac has by no means let go of the pen since she took hold of the camera. She has been a persistent literary crusader in defence of the intrinsic motion picture. Press and platform have encountered Mme. Dulac's attack on producer and exhibitor who assume that a film, the work of an artist, is anybody's merchandise, to be mutilated as anyone pleases. She has also insisted upon what she accepts as the axiom of cinema, that the motion picture is inherently "visual" and when it wanders away from that it isn't a motion picture. Moreover, she has been active in presenting new young artists, like Joris Ivens of Holland.

Her first picture was *The Enemy Sisters*. Following this she made *Geo the Mysterious* and *Venus Victrix*. The war invaded the peace of the cinema. One worked desultorily. Mme. Dulac filmed *Souls of Madmen* in 1917. After the war, in 1919, there came *The Cigarette, The Spanish Fête,* upon a scenario by the late Louis Delluc, pioneer of the art-film as director and critic, and *Mischance*. "At this period," says Mme. Dulac, "the French film began to reassert itself, and the possibilities of a cinema aesthetic were apprehended." In 1920, there appeared under Dulac's direction *La Belle Dame sans Merci* and *The Death of the Sun*. In 1922, Obey's scenario, *The Smiling Mme. Beudet,* was produced. She then pivoted to the ubiquitous serial, endeavoring to create in *Gossette* a sustained style to renew the declining idiom of the film-by-installments. From the serial she turned to a scenario by Bouquet and realized the fantastic *The Devil in the City,* in which she showed her sensible and sensitive understanding and use of virtuosities. Then, in *The Artist's Soul,* she introduced some absolute manipulations of pure film processes. In 1925, came a "visual poem," based on a narrative by the Russian writer, Gorki, called *The Folly of the Valiants*. *Antoinette Sabreur,* a classic of the French stage, was next, "mutilated," she maintains "by the producer." Her latest works include the ingenious *The Seashell and the Clergyman, Invitation to the Voyage, Oblivion,* from a novel by the Rider Haggard of France, Pierre Benoît, and an *Arabesque*.

Of her own films, Mme. Dulac prefers, among those "which have permitted me to work toward the evolution of the cinematographic art," *The Spanish Fête, The Smiling Mme. Beudet, The Devil in the City, The Folly of the Valiants, The Seashell and the Clergyman* and *Arabesque;* among those strictly commercial, *The Cigarette, Gossette, The Artist's Soul.* Her attitude towards the film is concentrated in these words:

"To my mind, in the present state of the cinema, films have only two values: market and research . . . The director must seek, forever seek. The cinema has not yet arrived at the zenith which permits creation in repose. Yesterday prepares today, today prepares tomorrow."

A viewpoint such as this is fitting to the Gallic mind which creates a film as the problem of an individual artist at work in his own *atelier,* studio. Indeed, Mme. Dulac, like other French film directors of merit, has been most interesting when the work she has done has been a personal adventure. She has failed, as most French directors have, in the long, commercial, popular, shopmade film. That is why it is so pitiful to find these directors forfeiting their independent graces to make foreign versions of American talkies. Mme. Dulac has not, I think, made that sacrifice yet. Pictures by her for competitive exhibition, for the box office, have been bad, straining to make poetry out of the banalities. The result is usually *"poésie,"* paste jewelry, a sentimentalism of imagery and figure of speech frequently found in the work of our own important director, D. W. Griffith.

But whenever Germaine Dulac makes a film that is her own intention, there will be something worth one's interest. She herself has said to me, in one of our many conversations in her home encased in old maps and studded with antique curios: "Unless the French director prepares everything in the film himself from the script to the cutting, his film will not be fully realized. We are not a people as yet for collective filming." A change in the social makeup may effect a change in this mentality, but tentatively we may say that Mme. Dulac is right. That is why, as I told her, it seemed so strange to me to hear the Frenchman insisting upon a quota to protect the French film from foreign competition, mainly American. Mme. Dulac, however, favored it, not to keep American films out, the intention of the French producer and politician, but rather to urge French fans to watch the film work of their compatriots.

French pictures, when they are well done, are films calling attention to a method or a viewpoint or a quality necessary to enrich the evolving motion picture. They have special, élite merit, and are not the rudimentary pleasantry enjoyed as a popular art. But the French being folk, and being distracted by the carefree exoticism, the pretenses of the land *outre-mer,* do not seem to be yielding their preference for American movies. The creation of popular entertainment, especially in this world of corporative economy and the industrialization of art, is not the Frenchman's forte. The French director, if he could preserve his own identity, would be the cinema's aesthetic stress, rather than the popular victualer. Germaine A. Dulac surely has her emphasis to lend.

She is, like many French directors, very clear and articulate in her conception of the motion picture. This critical comprehension is to her, at the present point in film history, more important than the films themselves. The critiques, the studies, the polemics, she asserts, cast "a luminous ray into the obscure future and, with altruism, guide the cinema toward a precise destiny, revealing the cinema in its ideal strength, its perfect image." It will be seen that Mme. Dulac is eloquent in her love for the tenth Muse. As to herself, she belongs, she says, "ideally, if not in effect" to the school of pure movement, the *extra-visual,* as opposed to the "anecdotic school." Her aspiration is "the union of the two by means of their common factors: sincerity and the knowledge of the visual." The lack of artistic sincerity, which means to her finally the absence of devotion to the nature of the art, is the real cause of the failure of the anecdotic film to realize "the spectacle of a *work*." The only liberty the commercial producer allows the director is the freedom of choice of theme, a freedom which is no freedom, because the choice is among a limited number of specific scenarios or plays or novels. The success of the Russian film, Mme. Dulac finds, is its devotion to the image. The best of the films of all nations are, she maintains, devoted to the expression of national experiences through significant images. The Russian, for instance, subscribed to the Stalinist formula of an art "proletarian in content and national in form."

"The great fault of the cinema," says Mme. Dulac, "an art uniquely visual, is its failure to seek its emotion in the pure optic sense. Visually, by the movement of rhythms, the cinema composes its complex life. The cinema certainly can tell a story, but it must not forget that the story is nothing, a surface only."

I cannot say that I totally agree with Mme. Dulac. Let us not speak of a story but of an experience, a human experience. Its force, the social persuasion of the Russians, for instance, is the impetus of the film. Having been motivated, the film then seeks to convert this initial experience into the final aesthetic experience of the picture. It does so by the means Mme. Dulac urges. But since the cinema has a "complex life," too broad a characterization of it can be misleading.

Of such means Mme. Dulac is a delicious master. Take her best film: *The Seashell and the Clergyman.* There is not in it a definitely apprehended story, but one does follow it as the succession of the image-experiences of an inhibited mind. They are most convincing as a mental state and very lovely as a rhythm. The ingenuity of the effects of imagery achieved is startling; though, as with all ingenuity, the method by which these effects are achieved is very simple. For instance, in one place, a body divides into two. It was effected so: the player must stand at severe rest. His head is propped by a brace to prevent the least movement. A thread is drawn midwise down the face. The camera is moved left-right with the thread as the limit of the scope of the lens. One half of the negative has now recorded a movement while the other half has been masked to prevent any imprint. The movement is reversed to capture the second half of the figure upon the second half of the negative. The result on the screen is of a body moving away from its center in the opposite direction, a body splitting, although actually the body has never moved.

Germaine Dulac was one of the first of the artists to experiment with prisms, for distorted or multiple effects. She was one of the first to look for the kinetic effects of moving things.

American Cinematographer,
January, 1932.

FIRST FILMS

There is perhaps no greater indictment of studio practice than the frequent superiority of a director's first job to his later work. How many young men have begun with "promise" only to submit apologies. For that reason the critic, cautious because of past lessons, restrains his enthusiasm on encountering a promising debut. Still, such a debut must be recorded, if for no other purpose than to point the finger of scorn at the "art-industry" which lacks the momentum to sustain and encourage the good talent.

A good talent has appeared in Rowland Brown, who works, of all places, in the Fox den. That lair has yielded about the worst of American pictures, on par with the Warner product. The Fox film I recall most vividly out of the silent era is *Dressed To Kill,* a much more variegated racketeering film than *Underworld.* And to date the most interesting of the Fox films in the compound era is Rowland Brown's *Quick Millions.* That the gangster picture should be the most vivacious today is neither surprising nor flattering. Its bravado contains indictment that attains to no more than a rough sort of cynicism, but that is much more than the sweet junket of fillum. This fact is hardly a compliment to our society or our cinema.

The virtue of the Brown film is its clean cool economy. It is as unsentimental and as objective and aloof a treatment of a melodramatic subject as one can expect. The performance is subdued but not emasculated, the groups composed so that the very contours are sharp, and not one margin has a loose fringe. Indeed, this is one picture in which there are no loose ends, such as one finds in the chronologies of *The Secret Six* and *Cimarron.*

Unlike most racketeer pictures, *Quick Millions* does not depend upon the trigger of a gun for its excitement; that is contained within the structure itself, it is a directorial excitement. The machine-gun has served the movie as a sort of *deus ex machina* to get the plodding picture out of the slough of despond. *Quick Millions* is too level headed for that, it is a self-assured film. And yet the East Coast critics — to halo the reviewers — passed it by, preferring to dwell upon the hokish *Public Enemy*. And Brown, I am told, for some overt act of disrespect has been penalized by being sent back to the scenario department. His term of sentence is over. What will follow *Quick Millions?* Only a valuable theme can urge on development. *Quick Millions* was an exercise well done. Brown should be given an important idea to realize — but he probably won't. He is going over to Universal.

Another gangster picture serves to reintroduce a director of insight. When Reuben Mamoulian appeared in *Applause,* there was a hubbub which confused a bad picture with an ingenious director. Mamoulian, wise enough to see the futility of tolerating the story he was given, decided upon playing above the level of the tale. *His* performance was good, the film's — well, nothing could have been done for it, anyhow. On the screen two things were visible — a bad picture, and a new inventive director. In his second film, *City Streets,* Mamoulian again separates himself from the trite story. He gives it a bold *Joan of Arc* treatment — *gros plan,* facade at an incline, flower and flight of bird — a treatment far too heroic for the picture, but *per se* sensitive. Of course, it was impossible to sustain such treatment and the film sags. But even when it does, Mamoulian vindicates himself by doing a thriller which is as breathtaking as the railroad serial, *The Girl and the Game.* The one constant relation between the director and the picture is through the heroine, Sylvia Sidney, who, one must sadly admit, seems too good for the movies — too authentic, and hardly the staple article as to looks.

Mamoulian is scheduled to compound *Jekyll and Hyde.* In the mute period, John Robertson made a film of the Stevenson story, and, in spite of the praise it was given, the picture was meretricious, of the age before cold cream. It is a pity a man like Mamoulian who evidently can handle experience, should be awarded what is by now a literary curio. But what with *Dracula,* filmed as a drawing-room affair, and *Frankenstein,* reality has no column in the double-entry books of cinema. The one satisfaction in this appointment of Mamoulian is that it will allow for the play of inventiveness, if the supervisor will allow it, without separating the treatment from the narrative.

First films — last sincerities? This business of looking for the sport of treatment and to hell with the scenario — the intellectual idea becomes very soon a pessimism or cynicism which says: "What's the use?" There is a director like Henry King. He was one of our best. The critics were "enthused" with his *Stella Dallas,* never recognizing that this was a case of antipathy, between the bold pattern of the direction and the indigent subject matter. The antipathy has apparently become a constant, and King gives us either a matter-of-fact *Lightnin'* — as much as that pleasant insipidity can endure — or a *Hell Harbor* — overlooked by reviewer and critic — which posits a rarity in American films, grand canvases of open space, distance, clouds . . . in another of the decrepit quasi-Conrad South Sea malices. The discard is no longer a conflict — it is pathetic.

It is in keeping with the low energy of the movie at this moment. Will another mechanical element enter to stay collapse? Even vivacity, the literal gaiety, seems to be in a condition of apathy, and, when it is agitated into something resembling motion, it looks like locomotor ataxia. That there are potential artists among the directors of Hollywood cannot be doubted. But the impetus, the nutrition is not there, and Hollywood is not a magnet to character.

(UNPUBLISHED MANUSCRIPT,
Circa 1931–32).

"The hope for the film and for the society which includes them, is in a thorough inquiry into society. Dissociated aesthetics must today be re-associated with its source. The attempts at synthesis through literary materials must fail for lack of a precise and constant measure or instrument. Only a social ideology can supply the efficacious instrument."

HARRY ALAN POTAMKIN

PART TWO: FILM AND SOCIETY (1930-1933)

4

SOCIOLOGICAL CONSIDERATIONS

THE MIND OF THE MOVIE

The film reflects the social mind that has created it. It expresses with a grandiose expansiveness the economy and the politics of a land. The British cinema was a scrawny thing before 1926, when English finance became concerned with the building of a cinematographic industry to support a threatened imperialism. Thereupon the British intellectual, a puppet in the Empire, became interested in the lowly art. His superciliousness toward what is hardly a gentleman's interest is expressed in the flippant tones of his critiques. But to talk cinema has become a gentleman's sport, and the sons of the élite, from Margot Asquith's to Lord Swaythling's, have entered the practice of the film. Before that, the motion picture was left to the care of the adventurer, as the business of horse racing is left to the tout. The pleasure, and a good deal of the profit, of horse racing, is the gentleman's. The motion picture, however, is a more stupendous sport. It can reinforce the Empire or speed its disintegration. Hence English quota films to combat the American movie; hence the encouragement of Indian films made by the favored classes of Indians and remote from the facts of Indian life; hence film making in South Africa, Australia and Canada. The content will express, in a general and often particular way, this aspiration to beat the U. S. A. and to render the Empire profitable to the mother country.

Or consider the Italian cinema. Fascism was anticipated in the films of 1913–1914, such as *Quo Vadis, Antony and Cleopatra, Spartacus* and preëminently *Cabiria,* D'Annunzio's moving picture. *Antica Roma* was erected in its pasteboard glory in anticipation of the pomp of the march on

Rome. Today Italian imperialism, looking toward North Africa, is sentimentalized in the film which tells of the love of an Italian soldier for an African girl, a film like *Kif Tebbi.* Here the national chauvinism is personalized, and the native of the land awaiting prey is symbolized as willing in the reciprocal love of the girl for the boy. Numerous pictures of this kind have been produced in Italy.

Another instance. The battle between the "old-drama" film and the "new-drama" film in Japan is a battle between the old and the new, between the declining aristocratic society and the dominant bourgeois. The confusion in which the Japanese cinema finds itself is the confusion of the class rôle, the aristocrat enacting the middleman. The threat of a third class will probably make itself felt in the film, negatively as a protective weapon of the threatened class. It has already expressed itself in literature, as this quotation from a conservative periodical, the *Japan Magazine,* indicates:

> It appears that the greatest demand for the year was for proletarian literature, due perhaps to the excitement over the arrest of so many youths and maidens for being guilty of dangerous thought. The result is that henceforth there will be a more clearly marked distinction between the writers of this school, and authors in general.

The film will be the last instrument the workers will capture to use effectively, but in some lands beginnings have already been made. Several workers' films have been produced in Germany. This, omitting any question of the films' merits, indicates the strength of the workers in that land. Workers' film societies have been started in several lands, but production as yet is very negligible. However, any beginning is significant.

The relation of the worker to the film, and the film to the worker, provides a major entrance into the study of the mind of the American movie and of American society. Writing in the *Harvard Monthly* of 1910, Horace M. Kallen expressed the attitude of bourgeois society toward the entertainment of the masses. He said that the movie might "reestablish on its pristine eminence, the discarded and abased melodrama," which was, he thought, excellent, because melodrama was to be preferred to "the intellectual drama," since it "keeps the mass from thinking." Mr. Kallen had observed that the spectators of the new art, "the rival of the musical comedy," were "self-respecting petty bourgeois and workers." These were to be kept from thinking.

As American society has become less and less diffuse, and more and more concentrated, with a corresponding concentration of the economy of the land in fewer and fewer hands, the motion picture has become less and less expressive of "independent" manipulators and more and more the merchandise and instrument of consolidated enterprises, until at the present there can hardly be said to exist any "independence." The movie industry was a frontier enterprise with its murderous Billy the Kids and gang-warfare until the leaders consolidated. Warfare of a more refined order continued with the trust threatened and even riddled by the offensive of a strong independent. But the days of the strong independent are over in the films as in commerce and industry generally, as in the whole of American society. The threat can come from only one other trust: labor. The movie is concentrated in the hands of the financial powers along with the various other media of rapid intelligence — radio and television, and, as of old, the press. There is the alignment. It expresses itself in the total impasse of American society.

During the more-or-less free-for-all days it was still possible to get a film made of Upton Sinclair's "The Jungle." It was still possible to have Essanay produce a picture condemning the exploitation of the poor house-owner and farmer by the sellers of marshlands. Today the worker is either a clown, or a populist swashbuckler who gets the girl. The America that boasted of its creed of labor has the young toiler reveal himself as the son of the millionaire. The building worker, together with the thug, can shout his manhood, but evades the implications of his "career." It is a part of bourgeois populism to inflate the worker by making him a hero along with the "good bad man" of Wild West mythology and the Prohibition racketeer. But to create a drama of actual relations, as did "The Jungle" and that early Essanay film, is possibly too engrossing a problem.

The problem that may be faced is that of the "restless rich." The movie here accepts the problem which other more élite forms of amusement, like the novel and the theater, have drawn from their environment. The problem concerns itself generally with the love-irritations of those who were born to the purple. Forty-seven Workshop motion pictures, fabrications according to a formula of wit and anguish, dealing not with profound realities but with literary possibilities. Conversations upon conversations — speech has helped these to become glibber and more fictitious. The audience accepts these films as experiences of polished folk, actually distant from their own yet so near to them, in imagination. There comes the thrill of escape in the sense that one is attending the polite ritual of sophisticated people, so lucky to have such tremulous heartaches and such easy access to liquor. The ambient degradation is, of course, distilled; one senses but the remnant perfume. Nostalgia in evening dress. A people who have been taught to respond only to appearances cannot be expected to recognize how callow and callous this evidence of our society is. It exposes the mind of that society, but, lacking social stimulus, it does not expose it critically to the light. Social criticism has dwindled in the American film. All that remains is a gaiety uninformed by sincerity or intelligence, a literal gaiety, which is even now festering, since it has no outlet, no further process.

II

We have had pretenses to social themes. A great rhapsody greeted King Vidor's *The Crowd*. The film, however, is a poor literary perpetration of "touches," pre-established irony, not the irony that is organic criticism.

I have chosen Vidor as a special instance, because a cult of Vidor has been created among the intelligentsia, including Gilbert Seldes and the whole of Paris. His *Hallelujah!* was hailed as a masterpiece in revelation. It was a revue-film purporting to be a picture of humble life. Its attitude was that of the white American toward a disparaged people. The momentary novelty of a new actor — the Negro; the spiritual, the ritualistic frenzy, the crap-game, all the trappings of the legendary Negro, as white men like to see him, amid a setting reminiscent of Roxy's, in a false reference, serve as a basis for a film which accepts the basis as the determining idea. The false conception becomes the final form and experience. Vidor is always at the determination of the literary scenario, though his direction seems more spontaneous combustion than penetration of the material. He does not determine the scenario from the highest and profoundest reference of the potential material and theme, nor does he reconstruct its ideology that he may realize a superior form and higher level of experience. Momentarily effective — that characterizes Vidor's work and the American movie at its best.

Momentary effectiveness may suffice for a "churlish comedy" or a revue film, but as the achievement of a picture of human existence it can mean but one thing: the impotence of the society producing it or the suppression of that society's creative energy. As an achievement in a rendition of Negro life it reflects, it is a product of the white man's society. The Negro is not new to the American film. The late Bert Williams appeared in a film before the war. This got very little attention due to white antagonism in the South. The picture of the Jeffries-Johnson fight shoved the Negro entirely out of the picture, save in certain farcical instances. Before the war Sigmund Lubin had produced all-Negro comedies in Philadelphia. White impersonations of Negroes have been frequent, either in slapstick or in the perennial *Uncle Tom's Cabin.* Negro children have in the last years been appearing in such slapstick films as Hal Roach perpetrates with his tedious and unconvincing "Gang." The treatment of little black Farina is typical of the theatrical (variety and film) acceptation of the Negro as clown, clodhopper or scarecrow, an acceptation which is also social. No objections have been raised by the Solid South to Farina's maltreatment by the white children – an adult falsification and unpardonable treachery of the director.

The plight of the Negro is amusement. The evasion of the toiling Negro in the film is only a duplication of that same evasion of the Negro-at-work in literature and of the worker altogether. America, the laboring nation, avoids the contemplation of the fundamental fact of labor. The middleman's mind.

The Negro has been fantastically presented. The Jew is another far-fetched clown, churlish or à la Pagliacci. In 1912 the American Solax Company, in advertising their film, *A Man's Man,* said:

> Up to very recently the stage Jew was the only type which furnished amusement. Long whiskers, derby hat down to the ears and hands moving like the fins of a fish. His manhood, his sentiments and his convictions are not burlesqued [that is, not in this film, *A Man's Man*] but are idealized.

Laborer, Negro, Jew, foreigner generally, become butts or objects of a quasi-pathos. The terminal of "the final kiss," the happy ending, or even its arbitrary reversal in the unhappy ending, is evasion of experience. The level of experience, as the American movie understands that term, is Hall Caine. When Victor Seastrom was brought from Sweden, he was given as the American equivalent for a Selma Lagerlöf portrayal of localized, bourgeois society, a Hall Caine novel, with its semblance of tragic episodes, but none of the cumulative *exposé* of tragedy, as contained in Lagerlöf. Hall Caine and Herman Sudermann – the difference is but one of finesse – have supplied the social theme to numerous American movies. Sudermann, the German borrowing, has the pretenses of a social attitude, but not the convictions. Andreieff becomes an idyll in the American movie, and Tolstoy a posture.

Epics out of the history of America – *The Covered Wagon, The Trail of '98* – are reduced to trivial narratives of personal enmity. Prison-breaks become the responsibilities of pathetic individuals, rather than of society. Evasion. The social criticisms in these films, as in the war films, are merely remarks, they do not inform the progression of the film. An incisive, informative point of view is lacking; and lacking this point of view, the film lacks the impetus to impel the structure beyond its literal and rudimentary level. D. W. Griffith said not long ago: "The maturer motion picture of today has yet to turn its attention seriously to the kind of themes that we used back in 1908." Mr. Griffith referred to his penchant for *"poésie"* and classics, not the purest of tendencies. But it is true that within this penchant there was the expression of a need for intensely-felt human episodes. Griffith, as an American, mistook platitudes for criticism, but these platitudes were, if only vague, statements of social impurities. Guided by an intuition fed on unplumbed prejudices, Griffith's social history was articulated in *The Birth of a Nation*, the anticipation of the recrudescence of the Ku-Klux-Klan! His expansive love of mankind, itself a platitude, did not extend to the Negro. It produced a composition more grandiose than grand, one that has not been improved upon as such.

The movie comedy has alone extended beyond its rudiments. Not very far beyond; it is constantly threatened with relapse. Indeed, at the present moment, there seems to be no material and no director capable of sustaining this position of the comedy, as it is held by a performer like Harry Langdon. The slapstick or "churlish" comedy of Mack Sennett was the expression of a frontier contempt for authority—the Keystone Kops. This contempt was tolerated because it was not serious, and the threat did not come from a challenging group. There have been some half-dozen American films, lively with their inheritance of "churlishness," and more specific subject-matter, which punctured the sobriety of such myths as fraternity and heroism, and the High Hat of gentlemanly vulgarity. But instead of a furthering of these quixotic valiants, the comedy has followed the influence of such spurious "satires" as Chaplin's *A Woman of Paris* and those of Ernst Lubitsch, with their trite axioms of love, sex, greed, etc. Instead of sharpening the specific attack, and enlarging upon the rhetorical foundations of the comedy, the mind of the movie, the mind of a vicarious society, has bestowed upon the High Hat the order of the élite, rather than the value of an anachronism. Chaplin brought in a subtlety embodied in himself, an expression of the London music hall, influenced by the Frenchman, Max Linder, and the American, Mack Sennett. It cannot be called American in its quality. Nor can it be said that Chaplin's comedy has come very close to its promise of social exposure. He too has been frustrated, in part by himself, in part by the cultist stress placed upon his achievement, but mainly by the environment in which he is active. The hope of American comedy remains a hope. The "churlishness" remains, and it becomes, to the passive mentality, a vindication of America. The French aesthete finds in it a stimulant for his saturated senses. The American producer serves his country by lending the brazen muscular impact of "churlishness" to the various legends: "join the Navy and see the world!" (*A Girl in Every Port* and *The Cock-Eyed World*); "the valiant little tailor" or "the meek shall inherit the earth" motif (Harold Lloyd, Jack Oakie, etc.) . . . Again, the movie expresses the low ebb of creative vitality here . . . its cynicism, its delusions.

NEW FREEMAN,
August 20, 1930.

THE FILM EVANGEL

The movie is the contemporary American folk ritual. And Will H. Hays of Sullivan, Indiana, is its evangel. The foe of Mr. Hays who makes the issue personal or private and calls Will a "flop" is deceiving himself. It is Mr. Hays's duty to serve the movie not as a business man but as a politician — strategist, press agent, soft-soaper, decoy — in sum, evangel.

Mr. Hays, church deacon (of the older theological Christian church), is definite enough in his comprehension of his work. He is an arch-religionist. Speaking before a convention of Rotary (which makes the world go 'round) in 1925, *Anno Domini,* St. Will said:

> . . . religion is the one essential industry in the world, make no mistake about that. To do right for the sake of right — that is the highest phase which animates our being.

If you have seen the Hidalgo wax figure of this holy man, you will know from that ikon what spark it is that animates the supernatural body of the former chairman of the Republican National Committee.

Contemporary religion, St. Will asserts, is articulated in the ritual of the movie, which

> . . . is, indeed, almost a living breathing thing which has the greatest influence upon the ideas and ideals, the customs and costumes, and hopes and ambitions of countless millions of men, women and children.

Will H. Hays knows the permanence of the cumulative effect of the movies on the mind of the masses. That is why the evangel has carried his message of international good will to Europe — A.D. 1930 — urging the German producers not to perpetrate any films containing social, political or economic ideas. What other ideas are there? Oh, the esoterically moral, of course. The evangelical innuendo is directed against the films of Soviet Russia — the only land whose social, political and economic ideas might influence the "millions of men, women and children" and thereby offend the holy arbiter. This political whisper does not prevent Will from dividing — in loud tones — the world's talkie-apparatus market with Germany, keeping the Soviet Union for himself.

The language of an advance agent is always euphemistic. Evangelism is clerical advance-agenting. When the Motion Picture Producers and Distributors Association was established in 1924, with Mr. Hays as "czar," the agreement among the parties was named "The Formula." Hays appropriated the slogan of the National Board of Review, "Selection not Censorship," in the delightful "Supervision from Within." As the true evangel he began at once to steal the thunder of other groups. His thunder-stealing act is genuinely clerical. How many times has the church appropriated a folk-ritual which it could not demolish! But, of course, the church does not take altogether kindly to Mr. Hays's usurpations of moralingering, expressed in the two "Codes," the first for the mute film, the second for the garrulous. Mr. Hays knows his obligations. He became immediately the seismograph to groups of self-interest sufficiently powerful and unified to be coercive. His seismograph reactions become forms of action in the interests of the powers he is serving. He has said as much:

> One of our first steps was to give the organized public an opportunity to express its opinion for the betterment of pictures . . . If the subject involves a Protestant church, advice may be sought of the Federal Council of Churches of Christ in America . . . In the event the Catholic church or faith is involved, we are authorized, as a final arbiter on any matter pertaining strictly to religion, to approach a distinguished prelate appointed by those in authority with the view to making suggestions either for changes before the picture is started or after it is completed but before it is released.

It has not been observed that the American movie has produced a single "sacred" film comparable to *The Passion of Joan of Arc,* made in France. *The King of Kings* is a product of this sycophancy — it is the pimple of sanctimony. The respect for the "organized" public is further expressed in a delicacy toward group sensibilities. "No film or episode may throw ridicule on any religious faith," but a reformer may be scoffed at, as in the metamorphosis of the inhibited clergyman in "Rain," called "Sadie Thompson" in the movie. Religions may not be offended, but a Swede, in *The Big House,* may be pictured as devouring and enjoying the prison-swill against which even the American moron (I.Q.) revolts. Yet "the history, institutions, prominent people and citizenry of other nations shall be represented fairly." The emphasis is on "prominent people." The newsreels of democratic, republican America are replete with kings and queens, lords and ladies, and Mussolini staging a Roman holiday for us latter-day Greeks.

Among the organized groups, Mr. Will Hays includes Rotary, the Boy Scouts, Women's Club, the D. A. R., and the United States military. His addresses for adult Rotary and adolescent Boy Scouts are almost identical, with a change of paragraph sequence, down to the moralizing doggerel. Carbon-copy morality typifies the evangel from St. Paul to Aimee McPherson. In his recognition of the rising womanhood, Will Hays again performed his thunder-stealing act at the expense of the National Board of Review. I quote from his report:

> Only this past year, a national conference of representatives of public groups was held in New York. At that time a suggestion was made by Mrs. John F. Sippel, President of the General Federation of Women's Clubs, that a woman be stationed in Hollywood . . . to interpret to the studios the viewpoint of the organized women of the country. I asked the women at the meeting to nominate a woman for the position and they suggested the name of Mrs. Thomas G. Winter, past president of the General Federation of Women's Clubs . . . Mrs. Winter is in Hollywood . . .

The democratic mechanism is at work. For the M. P. P. D. A. is nothing if not democratic. Again the evangel speaks:

> In the pattern of its structure the association is not unlike that of the Federal government of the United States itself. Independent organizations have solemnly and voluntarily joined together to do certain things in the interest of all, just as the colonists joined together in defense of their liberties and in the defense of self-government.

The simile is not altogether ill chosen. The typical democratic jargon is employed.

> There is no attempt to say 'You can do this' or 'You can't do that.' There are, however, many carefully considered suggestions which may be made to the studio officials, growing out of the years of consideration of

enlightened public taste and a continued effort to interpret it as well as remembering the industry's duty.

Altruism, flattery, litotes -- more poetry than truth — capitalist buncombe. The same authority dictates to Mr. Hays, "Dictator," as to Mr. Hoover, President. Will is the voice of the inevitable concentration of the movies in the hands of high finance.

Knowing that the newspaper is the Bible in another *format,* the evangel immediately gave the glad hand to his fellow-clerics. He sent out "feelers" to the daily reviewers asking them "what's wrong with the movies?" The most assertive replies issued from the erstwhile Confederate States, D. W. Griffith's homeland, and referred to a peculiar bias towards the Negro. The suggestions have not gone unheeded.

The democratic blarney of international good feeling is recurrent in the Hays Code.

For instance, if the story affects a foreign government, the association asks the ambassador from that government — or the official of the government who has been designated for such contact by the ambassador or minister — and obtains from him suggestions as to the proper treatment.

Did the Chinese minister write the scenario for the insidious *Dr. Fu Manchu* and *The Return of Fu Manchu,* as well as for Harold Lloyd's *Welcome, Danger!*?

. . . careful attention is given to every film which has a foreign background or which in any way affects the nationals of any country in the desire to remove any cause for agitation against our films.

"The foreign problem," Mr. Hays admits, "is chiefly an economic one." Where is the altruism? The American cinema offended France in the portrayal of a ratty Frenchman in *Beau Geste.* In *Beau Sabreur* the rat was not only a Frenchman but a rebel. "No political ideas," Mr. Hays? In *Forgotten Faces,* to get the film through the French corridors, "Froggie" becomes "Broggie," but to any American he is still Johnny Crapaud.

The Last Command, in its sentimental glorification of a Russian Grand Duke, and the balancing portrayal of the revolutionists, does not, in its sympathies, exactly recall the pre-War movies that attacked Czarist persecutions. Mr. Hays might answer as a statesman that we have no diplomatic relations with Russia. That does not prevent him from hinting against Soviet films and exploiting the Soviet market.

When we come to the moral "ideas and ideals," aphroditic and bacchic, of the Hays Code, we find the most titillating wit. Wherever more than one dominant group is concerned, Prohibitionist and bootleg, the rule is as equivocal as a Republican strategist can make it.

> The use of liquor shall be restricted to the actual requirements of characterization and plot.

Whenever liquor is consumed in a film distilled in America, it is always in keeping with the characterization or plot. Who's going to quibble?

> Law, natural or human, shall not be ridiculed. Sympathy shall not be created for the violation of the law. Crime against law shall never be presented in such a way as to create sympathy with the crime as against law and justice.

Perhaps Mr. Hays means to differentiate between sympathy for the crime and sympathy for the criminal. He is such a sophist! Certainly the deluge of racketeer films, in which the Arnold Rothsteins take the place of the "good bad man" of the Western, do not induce a respect for the law.

"Revenge in modern times shall not be justified as a motive," yet in *The Big House* the entire romance between the girl and the escaped convict is brought about by the latter's plan to revenge himself on the girl's brother for framing him. If this is not explicit vindication of revenge, it certainly is implicit. If Mr. Hays had meant the barring of explicit vindication, there was nothing to keep him from saying so — nothing save expedience. He has ordered that

> Adultery shall not be explicitly treated or justified; scenes of passion shall not be introduced when not essential to the plot.

He is absolute about two subject matters: "sex perversion" and "white slavery." No powerful "organized" group has urged the advertising of these special traffics. Profanity, on the other hand, is a commerce of fundamental and universal affection. Therefore Will Hays forbids only "pointed profanity," thus satisfying the moralists and saving the art of the motion picture for *double entendre*.

The Code is decoy. Mr. Hays is foremost the political agent of the film business. Where severe political challengers seem to assert themselves, there is no equivocation. Despite the fact that Mr. Hays is out to forestall national censorship, the legal authorities and he coincide where certain "social, political or economic ideas" are expressed or implied in films. The Hays organization called for the burning of the Sacco-Vanzetti demonstration newsreels, and it kept off the market the films exposing the police brutalities of March 6 and the procession of May 1. On March 6 the Cameo, a house of the R. K. O. (circuit), a member of the Hays organization, was requested — request complied with — to remove the Sovkino film, *China Express*. Several months later the picture was reexhibited. No protest has been heard against the showing of the Bombay rioters. The Indian revolt is not altogether unpleasant to the particular interests behind Mr. Hays.

Will H. Hays knows a good — and true — idea when he sees one. He reiterates the fact that religion is an industry, and that the movie is "capable of wielding a subtle and powerful influence upon ideas." The film is said to give the public what it wants, yet, says Mr. Hays, "No one knows whether a motion picture is going to please the public until it has been produced and exhibited." Then what determines the choice of a film for production and exhibition? "The timeliness of the subject matter is a factor." By timeliness, critical veracity is not meant.

Many apparently unrelated things enter into the situation and influence the picture's exhibition.

All the way from buying the story to showing the picture in a theater there are complex problems to be solved . . .

Beyond all considerations of the practical business developments of the industry, there is consideration of the motion picture's influence on ideas, customs, tastes and habits.

Politicians reason in a circle because the circle is a loophole.

As a barrage and a decoy, the evangel serves his interests well. Will Hays is serving the business of film imperialism adequately. He knows that: "More and more is the motion picture being recognized as a stimulant to trade. It is advertising America to itself," and the world. The recrudescence of the defunct British film industry and impelled by the American film-imperialism. "England is being suffocated by American films!" was the cry. Quotas and contingents have not thwarted the American movie's march, led by Will H. Hays, a major-domo with a warrant.

New Freeman,
November 26, 1930.

THE DEATH OF THE BOURGEOIS FILM

Should you be teased by the superficial vivacity, the literal gaiety, of the American movie, and deduce that all is well with the film of bourgeois society, darken your assurance with these reminders:

The Swedish cinema, the highest peak, as human experience, hence as art, reached by the film of the bourgeoisie, is dead!

The German kino of its golden age is dead!

Dead also is all hope of the realization of a strong French cinema from the effete *atelier*-efforts of the adventurers in "purism"!

Fascism has struck the Italian cinema dead!

The motion picture of the buffer-states exists to enjoy the flattery and cajolery of Europe's marplot, France.

England had hoped the opportunity of speech would permit her to seize the film-imperialism from the U.S.A. – England is still hoping.

And the American movie – is in an impasse, before a blind wall.

The Svenska film, subsidized by the powerful omnivorous Swedish Match Trust, started, after the War, the moment of retrospective agony and prospective frustration. It began on an eminence. It ended at exactly that height. Selma Lagerlöf was the constant source of the Svenska film of that day. The Swedish motion picture, in other words, was born on the high level of Swedish literature – the level of the Swedish society. A society provincial, intensive, self-centered, self-tortured, a masochistic society. It was self-critical of its vices, but not of the motivating vice: the bourgeois society itself, whose positive centrifugal energies were spent. Inebriacy, homicide, religious hysteria, the tortuous sex intrigues, greed –

were dealt with, not flippantly, callowly, in the puerile callousness of an American film — but with emotional profundity, fathoms deep — ending in the sea of futility, despite apparent redress. The Swedish film, like the Swedish society, fed on its own heart. It was unsustained by new life, borne upward from the rudimentary and impelled by basic energies. Nor could the outer world, the emotionally decrepit, cynical, evasive world that admired the "art" of the Svenska film, sustain the passionate introversion of its content. This film was the flower of the cinema until then, a flower without local roots.

The flower was recognized for its gardeners, by the American trust. "Trust" is an ironical label. America bribed the talents of the Swedish directors, and of a few of its actors. Seastrom (Sjöstrom) went to the U.S.A. — to become an echo of himself, a shadow. They "wanted" to give him human experience — his experience — and they handed him Hall Caine! Stiller was flattened into a silhouette, a Peter Schlemihl without a shadow. He was placed under the supervision of a talented German studio-showman, Pommer, who had built U.F.A. in Germany, but who was a steam roller over the exquisite talent of Stiller. The latter died — in his art — and in his life. Dreyer moved to Germany, to Norway, to France. Brunius . . . Molander (the last of them, after the heart had congealed) . . .

And today Sweden, thinking of the film as competitive melee, is making imitations of American flapper films — of "the cat who dared to look at a queen."

The bourgeois film died, with the first Svenska, at its peak.

The War and the Inflation had made the German petty bourgeoisie self-conscious and self-pitying. Films came forth pitying the plight of the old doorman who has lost his job (*The Last Laugh*); the cabby destroyed by taxi competition (*The Last Fiacre of Berlin*); the son-and-husband persecuted into suicide by wife-and-mother feud (*New Year's Eve*). There were simplistic fantasies of escape, dated films now: *The Cabinet of Dr. Caligari* and *Torgus the Coffin-maker*.

The Germans thought if a character was anonymous, he was universal. They started from that premise, and while near the premise (the beginning of the film), there was a type-universality about the character. The film ended by being ridiculous: the extreme instance is not the convincing instance. To make an instance convincing it must carry the environment, integrate with it, be normal in it, however concentrated by the film's portrayal of the instance. The Germans were not scrupulously devoted, however, to the conviction of experience. They were concerned with virtuosity, platitudes on human nature (the defense of an evasive society), with pathos in its most sentimental form. The aspirations of pathos to become tragedy, social indictment, were not heeded. Only so far and no farther dared the German petty-bourgeoisie and bourgeoisie estimate the plight of their society. To evaluate it as more might mean to condemn utterly the source of that plight. So they put the pathetic individual in a mist to obscure the environment. They turned to the spurious literary simulation of tragedy — Sudermann. The fate: the vamp from the city (*Sunrise*). To the effete glossings of surface, feigning "super-consciousness" (Pabst). The desolation of a social stratum they could never sustain, and ran away from it into the rancid butterfat of German melodrama (*Joyless Street*).

When you run away from society, you hide in the four walls of the individual — irony-and-pity etc. You run, if you are a movie man with a knowledge of your tools, into the cloistered walls of the studio. The Germans ran so completely into the studio that they sought to drag all art, all life, the outdoors and all emotion into the studio. What they dragged in was a molehill, and they called it a mountain — *Homecoming*. Artisanship satisfied every craving: art — human experience — was prattled. The result, most often, *kitsch* (*Metropolis*).

Today the German cinema — in the hands of the Fascist Hugenberg — is devoted to "national honor" — an equivalent for the American successes of the L.C.D. — "least common denominator" — not of aesthetic appreciation, but content-discrimination. The bourgeois cinemas everywhere are devoted to the gratification of the "minimum" — the maximum of illusions to guarantee a minimum of dissent. They are all, in brief, *negative*.

The French have been pictorial *cinéastes,* who made, of occasion, films of merit as personal lyrics. One of them has shown that he is perhaps the sole *director* of satire extant. René Clair can create his commentary directorially, with the actors as service. Yet he has not *said* very much in satire (social humor) as yet. And he yearns back to the dissociations of *dada.* To *Entr'acte* — where there are ideas (formal) but no Idea. Automatism, the dwindling of will, the depletion of social, creative impetus. *La belle France, l'avarice,* is a static economic nation and a static social nation. The weight of a goldhoard burdens the energies of a land. It is not felt altogether as a displeasure, for only when one moves is a weight exceedingly oppressive. However, some of the young men want to be on the go, and . . . — they are wasting their energies in inconsequences, in apathy, defeatism, — the boomerang of missionary zeal for the film-as-art, or in the making of foreign versions for American talkies.

The grandiose Italian film (*Cabiria, Quo Vadis, Theodora,* etc.) influenced all other "national" cinemas, including the U.S.A. It anticipated the "march on Rome," the Fascist film-show. And now there is an Italian cinema writhing and steaming (in manifestos) like the burnt out crater of Solfatara at Pozzuli near Naples. There are films which sentimentalize Italian imperialistic aspirations: the last utterance of capitalist hope. There is Mussolini: there is bombast. There is the Pope: special interest in the interest of capital. And there is a cinema which may be written Nil.

Fascism, a dictatorship for the past, cannot create the energies (essential) to a vital motion picture. Spain is a similar case.

And Poland . . .

Poland makes many crude braggart films that are distributed, financed, and praised, bourse-high in France. Poland, the stool pigeon, sits in the Corridor pivoting its fowl-neck from the U.S.S.R. to the Republic of France. Cf. similarly Roumania and Czechoslovakia.

England snubbed the film, but since 1902—at least—she has been worried about "the Americanization of the World"—principally, of course, her colonies. She tried to edge in and edge America out, and hoped the moment of opportunity would be the pause when silence went into vocability. She was conceited enough to believe she spoke a superior therefore more attractive mother tongue, and after the pause would dominate the kinema. (Note: Confuse not the instrument—opportunism—with the end—imperialism).

But—it's more than a hope or wish that makes a film. One cannot condescend to the movie and win it over. Nor can one offer another's "inspiration" simply by trade-marking it "British" and expect it to be recognized as singular. England rejects her own nativity and yet wants to be accepted as a man with a country. I deliberately mix the sexes. Read intermediate as indeterminate. England must still worry about her ineffectiveness against American "exoticism" in the British Empire.

I bring Japan in as an instance of an indeterminateness of another color. Japan is an instance where the past is struggling with itself in the cinema. The day-before-yesterday with yesterday, so to speak. It is the confusion of the aristocracy enacting the middle class. The results are: the sword-and-cloak drama of antiquity; and the German, American influences in the middle class—intrigue, the nemesis of the brothel, etc.

In the meantime, a militant proletariat asserts itself. The confusion present in the Japan cinema is part of the quantitative change in the Japanese society. The assertive class, the laboring, will be the qualitative instrument effecting the synthesis—a great and positive cinema will be born!

The Death of the Bourgeois Film—the Rise of the Proletarian. Two films from revolutionary sources have been presented by Germany. In one case, we have just another German futilitarian pathos film of *Die Strasse* — the nemesis of the brothel — the prostitute from whose hands "the pearls of happiness" are snatched. In the second, the cartoons of Heinrich Zille are filmed with human players. The result is a lugubrious episodic film which has its moments of intimacy in *Rote Wedding,* but still another film of pathos, uninformed by a dialectic point-of-view. The tag of a May Day demonstration is only a confession of failure in the systemic film. The spirit of the May Day demonstration should have informed this film for proletarian makers. A much more relevant film was made in Germany of fragments of newsreels. The document pointed with propaganda is the veritable first proletarian film.

Just as the politico-economic experience of the workers of the Soviet Union is the educative example for the workers *"za rybezhom"* — "beyond the borders," so the kino of the U.S.S.R. is the educative example for the workers' film *"za rybezhom"* and *outre-mer.* With Marxist objectivity, the Soviet cinema has taken what could serve it from the bourgeois cinema — especially the U.S.A. — and has urged the motion picture toward its inherent fulfillment. As Léon Moussinac has said, speaking of *Potemkin* and *Mother,* "these films entered into the history of the cinematograph *because* they have entered at the same time into revolutionary history" — that is the Soviet film, "proletarian in content, national in form" (the Stalinist formula). But a national form serving an international medium and an international experience.

The Soviet Proletkino is many categories beyond the bourgeois, the high level of today (U.S.A.) and the higher level of yesterday (Svenska). The bourgeois movie, U.S.A., still treats as rudiments, statements, experiments, — occasional devices — those intrinsic utilities of the film which in the U.S.S.R. are structural pivots and essential composition. The difference is discoverable "at the source" — in the aim, the social mind, the subject-matter.

L.C.D. — the merchandising principle for cheap wares. Film-as-merchandise is also film-as-vicarious-experience, to be worn but not analyzed: the maximum of illusions to guarantee a minimum of dissent. "There is no truth in the superstition that it is good for the public to think" (Horace Kallen) was pronounced in 1910 in reference to the movie, the "laboring-man's university" (D. W. Griffith). This negation, by being rubbed, becomes the unctuous bribe, "Give the public what it wants."

What the public wants is what the producer — his backer, his class — wants, as his "philosophy of life" and as the illusions with which he wants to amuse and deflect the lowly. The film is at once *response* of the mind which the dominant class has *effected*; and the *agent* of the dominant class to *affect* the response. The resultant of response and agent is a complex of falsehoods: the agonies of the social register — the Blue Book Blues — the sorrows of the Almanach de Gotha; churlish comedy — slapstick insouciance; "the good bad man," the boulevardier of romance; approximate rape — its thrill and compensation; "the prince and the serving-maid — she got her man"; distance as enchantment — A DANCE IN A CUL-DE-SAC! What perfection is here is all in the surface — you may legitimately suspect the wood.

FRONT,
(The Hague, Netherlands)
April, 1931.

ANTI-SOVIET CINEMA

The destruction of the Russian monarchy in 1917 was seized upon by American statesmen and film producers as vindication of the slogan: "Make the world safe for democracy!" But at the same time Russia's defection was threatening. Herbert Brenon, the chameleon who had directed the pre-war pacifist *War Brides* and was to make the postwar pacifist *Sergeant Grischa,* issued *The Fall of the Romanoffs,* in which Rasputin is the villain, the Tzar a duped innocent, and the pogrom-maker Iliodor, "the mad monk" of Tzaritzin, now Stalingrad, "the saviour of Russia." Iliodor was advertised as appearing "himself" in the picture. The film was urged as an argument against "the Kaiser, the Rasputin of Europe," and, by suggestion, against the Revolution. *Anton the Terrible,* a Lasky film, admitted the guilt of the czarist officer, who apologizes for his cruelty, and condemned the revolutionary.

To follow the trail of Mr. Jesse Lasky is to pursue the progress of the reactionary American movie. Under his aegis had been made *The Only Son* which, in 1914, glorified the strikebreaker and told the whole story of unionism as the worker's betrayal by a leader. The first full-fledged wing-beating against Soviet Russia came from Paramount-Lasky when Josef von Sternberg directed *The Last Command.* Since then Mr. Sternberg has romanticized the imperialism of the Foreign Legion in *Morocco,* just as Mr. Brenon did it in *Beau Geste,* and has initiated the underhanded attack on the Chinese Soviets in *Shanghai Express. The Last Command* sentimentalized a Grand Duke, and insulted the revolutionary leader, forcing, finally, from the latter a tribute to the former, though hardly vice-versa. I shall not go so far as my younger colleagues in asserting that the collapse of the bridge and the wreck of the train carrying the revolutionists as the symbolic prophecy of the collapse of the U.S.S.R.; for the only symbol Mr. Sternberg seems to understand is the sexual, and that must be very vociferous. However, certainly the intended mood of the film is anti-Soviet and pro-tzarist Russia; dishonest and tawdry, quite indicative of the later development of a director who wears "black shirts made by a special black-shirt maker." In Hollywood *Il Duces* are running wild; perhaps capitalism will find its salvager there?

As long as Soviet Russia was considered more ludicrous than threatening by the general (and financial) mind; as long as she was a "beggar" at "civilization's" table; as long as the potentates were not afraid of her challenge and her impress on the popular mind, it was not urgent to propagandize against her very strongly. There were numerous films like *The Volga Boatman* which (stressed) pre-revolution sentimentalisms about gypsies, and more suspect films (from the viewpoint of liberalism) like *The Red Dancer of Moscow* that tended to encourage an inimical prejudice against the new society. But in 1930 the same corporation that produced the latter film yielded from its studio *The Spy,* a direct and vicious attack on the U.S.S.R. By 1930 the Five-Year Plan had raised Soviet Russia from beneath the contempt of capitalism to a position where capitalism had to raise its eyes and stand on a raised platform to see her. The Five-Year Plan was, by the very nature of its growing achievement, influencing the fancy and the logic of great numbers. Communism was becoming a repeated word in popular speech. Something had to be done!

The Spy was directed by Berthold Viertel, imported from Austria. I am told that when Boris Pilnyak, the Russian writer, was in Hollywood preparatory to writing a scenario for M-G-M, Viertel advised him against submitting it, since it would be perverted into a falsehood. Since then Pilnyak's scenario has been laid aside, and Isaac Don Levine, slanderer of the Soviets, has been called in. Viertel should know whereof he speaks, because, as I am advised, *The Spy* was changed into an attack under his very nose. Well, he is partly responsible, as this creed of his will indicates: not until great social themes are handled, Mr. Viertel has said, will there be great pictures; but since that is not permitted us, he continues, let us concentrate on our technique. In other words, instead of resisting the false themes, let us shoulder them and play around with the "art" — to such consequences as betrayal, virtuosity and trumpery.

The story of *The Spy* is this: it relates of the emigrés in Paris and the Tcheka in Moscow. Tcheka spies listen in. The Grand Duke — never once visible to the audience — becomes the more awesome by revealing his presence only with arm and hand. This apotheosis — "Christ" in *Ben Hur* — is a theatrical trick toward emotional enhancement. The picture intends more than "passing amusement." Someone must go to Moscow to assassinate Citizen X, the leader of the Tcheka who, we are told, will not allow the emigré families to leave the U.S.S.R., just out of sheer meanness. The sympathy is all with the emigrés, who, for no fault of theirs, are being persecuted. The noble young Captain risks his life for the deed, which ain't, according to Fox, so dirty. He goes because he has left behind him in Moscow a wife and son.

Nobility just oozes from the pores of this movie. The preternatural nobility of the invisible Grand Duke, the more mundane but still idyllic nobility of the Captain, the wife, the son, the waifs. On the other side there is only ignobility or the coldness of steel. Of course, to make the lie more tolerable, a last leniency is accredited Citizen X; he merely exiles the Captain to Siberia. But this gesture is really allowed in order that the wife may further show her devotion by going with the husband. This, of course, is a borrowing from the films of earlier days when the revolutionary was the hero, when such devotion was typical. Anyone who has witnessed, as I have, counterrevolutionaries on trial knows that, because their class or foundations have collapsed, so do their vertebrae. There may be vindictive tenacity remaining when one's class utility is vitiated, but rarely is there the larger courage which accords with magnanimity: that belongs to the class with the historic future.

The contrasts of nobility and ignobility are accentuated in a number of ways: Tcheka uses a "renegade" nobleman, in love with the Captain's wife, to betray the Captain; the wife is imprisoned on a pretext, her child goes astray, joins the *bez prizorni* or "wild boys," is found by the mother singing on a street corner, she enters a state gambling house as hostess because the revenue succors the homeless waifs, who are now her best friends – they kill the "renegade" nobleman when he intends assault on their benefactor; the Soviet "police" pursue the waifs; several fall to death from the housetops – anything to increase the horror of the Soviet "regime." When the disguised Captain enters Soviet Russia, he is trailed by a Tcheka agent who recognizes or suspects him as a counterrevolutionary. The Captain dispatches him in a dark corner – and this is, I take it, a victory for honor. The film by its very use of the term "Tcheka" should necessarily have its concoction refer to some years back, but it is actually presented as to have the audience believe the lies not only true but of this moment. The waifs are dragged in to make use of the vilest of bourgeois sentimentalism, childhood, hardly cared-for in our United States. For eight years I worked among our own *"bez prizorni."* The method of *The Spy* is the method of treachery. No suggestion is made of the victorious solution of this homeless child problem in the Soviet Union – a problem we do not, in our own national instance, care even to face. Soviet Russia has never hallelujah-ed her successes. In her films she has included the travails. We have had "Lenin's Address" (*Children of the New Day*) which indicated the depredations of the wild kids, and recently the excellent *Road to Life*. Incidentally, this latter film, circuited generally, because of its commercial as well as human attractiveness, by R.K.O., has influenced our movie moguls. *Hell's House,* an independent (that is, non-Hays) production was booked for Broadway showing, despite its technical weakness, because it could be offered as "the American *Road to Life*." It adds, by comparison, to the stature of the Soviet film. And once more have homeless waifs entered into an anti-Soviet film, *Forgotten Commandments*. Having seen male urchins treated, R.K.O. has invented *Mistress of Moscow,* with an imported *mittel-europa* actress, to tell the story, as R.K.O. cares to tell it, of the female urchins, the prostitute.

Having been forerunner, Paramount, not to be outdone, has produced two anti-Soviet pictures in two months, with more to come. The first is *The World and the Flesh,* starring George Bancroft of the explosive guffaw and Miriam Hopkins, a comedienne constantly miscast. Bancroft is one Kurlenko, leader of the Petrograd sailors. (Is the name taken from Krylenko, notable in the Soviet military and court-of-law?). On the Black Sea are some white guardists, among them the dancer who has risen from the slums. Kurlenko captures them, he is captured, they are recaptured — within which time love has enflamed his manly heart. The dancer goes to him, to keep him in his cabin, while the helmsman steers the boat back to white guard territory. But the moujik posted to watch reads the stars, though he cannot read the compass, which is being guided in reverse by the trickery of a magnet; and the dancer, who fearing now for Kurlenko whom she has learned to love, confesses her treachery, begs him to escape, only to learn they are entering among the Reds and not the Whites. The dancer is sentenced to death, but Kurlenko, because of pledge and passion, exploits the illiteracy of the turnkey and liberates the dancer. The Soviet of that station condemns Kurlenko — who speaks of himself in the third person as the Carlylean hero responsible for the Revolution — unless the dancer is returned. (Compare this to *Cities and Years,* the Soviet picture of a betrayal). She reappears, and both are condemned — aren't Soviets masters of duplicity? But just then enter the Petrograd sailors, Kurlenko lifts his dame in his arms, the sailors cheer, and out walks Kurlenko with an explosive guffaw. Is this the Hollywood picture of a Trotskyist dream? The germs of this Oliver H(orse) P(ower) Garrett scenario appear to be (in addition to the old seed that produced *Dishonored* too) the Kronstadt counterrevolution and the exiling of Trotsky. What a pity Emma Goldman and Max Eastman could not have assisted on the scenario. The Soviet that condemns the hero is composed of men in Windsor ties, and thick spectacles, intellectual-looking dames and people very Semitic in physiognomy. The suggestion that Kurlenko, the he-man, was to be betrayed (not ultimately by love, for isn't sexual love above revolutionary devotion?) but by malicious parlor-Bolsheviks and Jews is not accidental.

Paramount may have been worried that perhaps this film might have left an iota of sympathy for the revolutionary. *Forgotten Commandments* was produced, incorporating the migration-from-Egypt section of De Mille's *Ten Commandments*. This insert is a parable against the Soviet Union, the Satanic contrast. The story deals with a young couple come to Moscow to study. They are placed into a barracks-like makeshift residence, a stall per individual or couple (this is made to seem typical of conditions and a deliberate regimentation). The husband becomes assistant to a great scientist who is at the same time an ardent Communist, speaking always as never a Communist would that "the state is god," "the party is the family," etc. The scientist influences the young man away from his wife, they are divorced. The divorce scene, without referring to the sensible philosophy informing marriage and divorce in the Soviet Union, for the children, for the general well-being of man and woman, is rendered as a sort of Ford rationalization device to the laughter of the audience. And this comes from Hollywood where marriage and divorce are frivolous, tantamount frequently to promiscuity; comes from the land of divorce mills, Reno, for instance; from the land of the greatest number of divorces, of which there would be more could people risk the scandal or the money involved. Again, to prove sexual love above revolutionary devotion, and egoism greater than socialism, Paramount has the scientist, who loves his feminine assistant, kills her and wounds the divorced young husband when he finds them together. And again, to enhance the condemnation of the Soviet social idea, which it never dares to present in its truth, the scientist saves the boy by operating on him and then confesses to the crime. Departing he says, "the finger of fate." And this from a Communist! The young wife comments: "the hand of god!"

God has entered some time before. Into an appropriated church, "desecrated" by being turned into a home for the wild boys — and made to look like a stable — enters the old soft-voiced priest, who stops the lads from destroying, in their benightedness, a Bible. He tells them the story of Moses. A reversal of analogy is suggested: not the tzar and the church are Pharoah, but the Soviet government; and the children of Israel the "abused" people of Russia. When the scientist interposes, priest and young innocent peasant-wife (of the blond boy-to-be-demoralized) object that "he has done no harm" save, of course, to incite the boys against the socialist society. The priest applies the commandment "Thou shalt not steal" against the Soviets, saying they have encouraged thievery among these children — a heinous libel upon a people who fought so heroically and successfully to reclaim these young boys; the commandment "Thou shalt not kill" is referred again to these children "born of blood and revolution," and not of imperialist war, of clerical hatred, capitalist intervention, leading to famine. The prize commandment is voiced by the scientist who says "Thou shalt covet thy neighbor's wife," before the wild boys. "Nationalization of woman" is inferred by this, as it is also contained in the words of Kurlenko in *The World and the Flesh,* when he says: "Every man for himself" — communism is anarchy, you see — and "every woman for any man who can take her."

The lascivious films are only beginnings. R.K.O. had planned a picture starring Constance Bennett, gowns and all, to be directed by the regisseur of the drawing-room, E. H. Griffith, and written by the author of the books on American espionage, "The American Black Chamber," Major Yardley. This has been laid aside, and *Mistress of Moscow* is announced. Lily Damita is promised in *The Red Temptation.* Even the lowly serial is to go anti-Soviet.

This campaign can not be left unchallenged. Malice and prejudice inform these films; there is no possibility of objectivity — "we'll treat communism as a religion" — and no wish for sympathetic treatment among producers controlled by Wall Street. Cecil de Mille returned from the U.S.S.R. saying only the Russians could make films, and stating he was returning to make a film there. He was dropped from the Motion Picture Producers' and Distributors' Association by Will Hays, charged with "inactivity." Rowland Brown, who gave so much promise in his first picture *Quick Millions,* has resisted the attempt to have him direct a Hollywood-chosen film about Soviet Russia; let us hope he is victorious — since he seems to be a person of social conscience. But a more concerted opposition is needed which will amount to a boycott of theatres showing such unscrupulous, such reactionary films. There are enough Soviet sympathizers, enough individuals of liberal and radical tendencies, organizations like the Workers' Film and Photo League, the John Reed Clubs, etc. to make the producers, whose keenest sense is the fiscal, hesitate.

(Unpublished Manuscript,
Circa 1931–32).

POPULISM AND DIALECTICS

The major problem confronting the film maker of the U.S.S.R. is the thorough treatment of the social theme. By thorough treatment is meant non-sentimental or critical treatment. It is the *social idea* as against populism. The latter is the concern with the popular expression as a fact in itself, uncritically. We have known it in politics here; we have known it in the "highbrow" inflation of the popular idiom: "jazz," "slang," "movie," etc. In Russia it evinces itself in professional peasant-poetry exaggerating the peasant as an ideal, an inimical propounding in the proletarian dictatorship. The critical expression of society in the U.S.S.R. is articulated in the Marxian dialectics, and its conversion into the form of the cinema is a structural problem. The solution of this problem determines the degree of achievement in the single instance of a film, as well as in the entire Soviet kino.

Dialectics as drama is conflict – and that is its structure in the film. There is the THESIS – the status quo. The ANTITHESIS asserts itself – the proletariat (combatant, antagonist-protagonist) or the new force. The result is the SYNTHESIS – the new order. The idea-dynamics of the Soviet film is dialectics.

One may divide the history of the Soviet kino to date into three periods: the first is the pre-dialectic period, so to speak, and while it has vestiges even in the present, it is not over-important in the present consideration. The dialectic-film divides itself into that typified by Pudovkin and that being typified by Eisenstein. Pudovkin typifies the usual, and what seems to be the more popular brand. In this film the individual represents, as accumulant, the social movement: first (Thesis) as the apathetic of the order, second (Antithesis) as the collection of the antagonism, third (Synthesis) as the positive explosion of the new. Examples are: the peasant migrant in *The End of St. Petersburg,* the Mongol youth in *Storm over Asia,* the amnesia victim in *Fragment of an Empire,* the peasant brother in *The China Express.* Of these the amnesia victim is more deliberately a dialectic-symbol than the others. He is, in fact, about ready to pass into the objective milieu of Eisenstein.

The dialectics of Pudovkin is more symptomatic than purposeful; it is an expression of the social occurrence which is being presented. In Eisenstein the dialectics is the intent and not the incident. It is expressed completely as structure and conveyed as idea. In Pudovkin it is more literary. *The End of St. Petersburg* is the dialectics of the individual expressing the mass. *Ten Days* is the dialectics of mass. Even in his latest film, *The Old and the New (The General Line)*, Eisenstein does not divert from pure mass dialectics, although he has in Martha the individual representing the new collective aspiration. Martha is not an accumulant, since she is convinced and collective minded before the moment of climactic change, the qualitative moment. The mass, peasantry, is itself Thesis, Antithesis, Synthesis, a very much more absolute realization than the individual-accumulant. The stress of the dialectics in *The Old and the New* is the machine — the milk-separator, thresher, tractor — which is present at the moments of crises to concentrate the mass-processes into assertions.

The Old and the New is the first statement of dialectics in unfolding. Dialectics is the theme. It comes as an advance and simple statement of the official Dialectic Film, the film whose theme will be Marx's *Capital.* The casual examiner may find in *The Old and the New* traces of populism. The narrative is in its bare fable the Broncho Billy ranch-film of the battle between two economic kinds (in the old western cattlemen versus sheepmen); just as *The China Express* in its fable-skeleton is the American railroad serial, and *Storm Over Asia* the western-Fairbanks combination — Fred Thomson. But — the difference in the stresses, in the mass-emphasis, the proportioning of caress to indictment puts *The Old and the New* far away from the populistic.

Populistic impurities are more apprehensible in the romantic Pudovkin, who begins with the individual combatant rather than with socio-structural motive. To the extent that populism diverts the Soviet film from the dialectic motive, that film is unsatisfactory. *Motele Spinder, The Simple Tailor,* directed by V. V. Wilner, is a flagrant instance of a film which divides itself into an overplay of the individuals (though they are supposedly social indicators) and a mass-experience, a people's plight. Here the individual-symbolic does not move within the mass, accumulating the force, as in a film by Pudovkin or as in the case of the peasant-soldier in *The New Babylon.* First there is the individual or individuals within a narrative, then there is the mass. There is no complete, nor even, a considerable degree, of synthesis. The fact that the film deals with pre-revolutionary days, in which the Synthesis, the new order, was not yet achieved does not modify the criticism of its unsynthesized structure. The dialectic-idea can inform *any* subject-matter that is social. The glory of the Soviet kino is that it possesses just that sort of unvacillating motivating idea. *The New Babylon* deals with the Paris Commune, which achieved no Synthesis. Yet the dialectic-idea was contained within the peasant soldier who expressed the mass verging on the Synthesis.

The problem becomes a simple statement of choice: shall it be sympathy with the individual or sympathy with the social idea? The former tends to be retrogressive in its answer, as witness the recent film by Petrov-Bytov, made of Gorki's "Cain and Artem," which belongs actually to the Polikushka (Germany-style) period, before the Soviet cinematists had, under the tutelage of Kuleshov, built a kino by studying the cinema at its source in the American folk film. Petrov-Bytov makes folk an end, POPULISM; the film of sympathy with the social idea makes folk a source and the social experience an end. The latter category is the category that moves forward with the evolving cinema, which intensifies its speculations, extends its human preoccupations and compounds its utilities. It is in this category, the insistent Soviet film, that the U.S.S.R. serves the cinema of the world and becomes its mentor.

EXPERIMENTAL CINEMA,
June, 1930.

THE AFRAMERICAN CINEMA

The Negro is not new to the American film. The late Bert Williams appeared in a film before the war. But this did not get very considerable circulation due to southern antagonism. It was the first of the Johnson-Jeffries fight that thrust the Negro out of films and created the interstate commerce edict against fight films. Sigmund Lubin produced all-Negro comedies in Philadelphia before the war. The Negroes themselves have been producing pictures on the New Jersey lots, deserted by the white firms that migrated to California. These companies have starred actors like Paul Robeson and Charles Gilpin in white melodramas like *Ten Nights in a Barroom*. White impersonations of Negroes have been frequent, either in farces or in the perennial *Uncle Tom's Cabin*. Negro children have in the last years been appearing in such slapstick films as Hal Roach perpetrates with his tedious and unconvincing Gang. The treatment of Farina is typical of the theatrical (variety and film) acceptation of the Negro as clown, clodhopper, or scarecrow, an acceptation which is also social. No objections have been raised by the solid South to Farina's mistreatment by the white children (to me a constantly offensive falsehood and unpardonable treachery of the director) nor to Tom Wilson's nigger-clowning.

The present vogue for Negro films was inevitable. The film trails behind literature and stage for subject matter. There has been a Negro vogue since the spirituals were given their just place in popular attention. Many Negro mediocrities have ridden to glory on this fad. Many white dabblers have attained fame by its exploitation. The new Negro was suddenly born with it. Cullen and Hughes were crowned poets, but Jean

Toomer, a great artist among the Negroes, has not yet been publicly acclaimed. He first appeared before the hullabaloo was begun. The theater took the Negro up. First Gilpin, and eventually came *Porgy*. Now the film. Sound has made the Negro the "big thing" of the film movement.

Of course, the first Negro film in the revival had to be *Uncle Tom's Cabin*. I praise in it the gaiety of the first part and the friendly, unsupercilious treatment of the Negro and the general goodwill of the actors. I condemn in it the perpetuation of the claptrap sentimentality. This is not the day to take Harriet Beecher Stowe too seriously. *Uncle Tom's Cabin* should have been produced as folk composition, or better not at all. It is not important as matter or film. Sound is bringing the Negro in with a sort of Eastman Johnson–Stephen Foster–Kentucky Jubilee genre, or with the Octavus Roy Cohen–Hugh Wiley crowd satisfiers, where the Negro is still the nigger-clown, shrew sometimes and butt always. And Vidor's *Hallelujah*! with a good-looking yaller girl. As for me, I shall be assured of the white man's sincerity when he gives me a blue nigger. I want one as rich as the Negroes in Poirier's documents of Africa. I am not interested primarily in verbal humor, in clowning or in sociology. I want cinema, and I want cinema at its source. To be at its source, cinema must get at the source of of its content. The Negro is plastically interesting when he is most negroid. In the films he will be plastically interesting only when the makers of the films know thoroughly the treatment of the Negro structure in the African plastic, when they know of the treatment of his movements in the ritual dances, like the dance of the circumcision, the Ganza. In Ingram's *The Garden of Allah* the only good movement was the facial dance of the Negro performer.

The cinema, through its workers, has been content to remain ignorant. It might have saved itself a great deal of trouble and many failures and much time had [they] studied the experience of the other arts. Well, what can the Negro cinema learn from the White Man's Negro and the Black Man's Negro in art, in literature, in theater?

Graphic art: The Greek and Roman sculptors of black boys were defeated because they did not study the structure of the faces. In modern art, there is Georg Kolbe's fine *Kneeling Negro*. There are Annette Rosenshine's heads of Robeson and Florence Mills—elastic, lusty miniatures. And there is the vapid, external, gilded Negro by Jesper in the Musée du Congo, Tervueren, Belgium. Compare. If you want to see how a principle can be transferred and reconverted, see what the late Raymond Duchamp-Villon learned from African sculpture. Relaxation among angles. Study Modigliani for transference to another medium. In painting examine Jules

Pascin's painting of a mulatto girl and Pierre Bonnard's more stolid Negro. But always the source: the sculpture of the Congo, the Ivory Coast, the Gold Coast, the bronzes of Benin, the friezes of Dahomey. Observe their relation to the actual African body, coiffure, etc., to the dance. What do you deduce?

Literature: In America I know of but one white man's novel that has recognized the Negro as a human-esthetic problem — which he must be to the artist — and not either a bald bit of sociology or something to display. I refer to Waldo Frank's *Holiday*. This eloquent though monotoned book is not a bare or ornamental statement of the interrace. Its concern is not with the culmination of the tragedy in the lynching, but with the relationships involved. The horror and the sacrifice of the lynching are certainly unavoidable, but greater and above these are the relationships, and the denial of the beauty of these relationships by the final mob act. This is the one book I know of that has recognized the entirety as ultimately human relationship, which determines the aesthetic unity. There is not in this book the ethnographical-archeological-sociological preoccupation that obscures the major motif in the other books. This is a novel, it is art, it is distillation, condensation, purity. Shands, Stribling, Peterkin, Van Vechten all strive to reveal their intimacy with the details of life and vocabulary of the strange folk they present. Shands' *Black and White* and Stribling's *Birthright* do free the central motif from a number of these interferences, leaving a clearer path to the culmination. But the motif should determine the book, which it does not in either case. Peterkin wishes to be genuine (but to be genuine is not to be unselective) and sympathetic and impartial. This makes her work a less questionable enterprise than Van Vechten's *Nigger Heaven,* the conscience of which must be severely doubted. *Black April* is better than *Green Thursday*. The former obscures the relevant data with data on folk idiosyncracies. It is the artist's business to evaluate the relevant data that he may be better able to know its potentialities, and not to record every detail contributing to the formation of that material. *Green Thursday* indicated no sense of the potential materials, their convertibility and relevant form. They were dark waters poured into Hamlin Garland jugs or Mary Wilkins-Freeman ewers, taking the form and conveyance of the receptacles.

Theater: The film may find instructive analogies and sources in three plays: *Earth* by Em Jo Basshe, *Porgy* by the Heywards, and *The Emperor Jones* by Eugene O'Neill. *Earth* is an instance of a play with a concept in its theme, but no recognition of that concept perceptible in the language or human-arrangement of the play. The theme was meant to articulate the struggle with the Negro between paganism and Christianity. Instead it is a struggle of personalities we witness. The theme indicates what the Negro film promises in the way of experience, when the philosophic cinematist will be present. *Porgy* is more immediate indication. It lacks all concept. It lacks significant intention. It lacks valuable narrative. Its tale is that of Culbertson's *Goat Alley* and the old white melodrama – the wicked man, the lured girl, happy dust, the cripple, sacrifice, vengeance. But its virtue is folk, always a good source. It has caught the folk in its rhythm, and whatever idea the play possesses is in its rhythm. This "rhythm as idea" makes of it a better play than Torrence's *Granny Maumee,* in spite of the latter's effort to convince us of folk authenticity. The tragedy of *Porgy* is no more important than the tragedy of *Goat Alley.* It is rendered more poignant simply because it has taken place in a folk structure to whose rhythm the individual participants contribute. That is why the character of the crab-vendor, suggested by one of the actors and inserted into the completed play, does not obtrude. It is of the total folk structure and easily finds its place in it. In the Theatre Guild production the play failed as a rhythmic unit, leaving us to enjoy, not the entity, but the details. This may be due somewhat to breaks in the authors' construction. The authors and the director failed to sustain the rhythmic counterplay between Crown's sacrilege and the Negroes' religion in the hurricane scene. This was a play meant to be produced not mimetically but choreographically, and moreover – as folk – to be stylized. It laid too much stress on a bad story, the songs were not intervalled with precision, and – most serious of faults – the diction was stereotype. This last, of course, has nothing to do with the production, it is the authors' weaknesses: The authors confess they did not take advantage of the original Gullah dialect because it would be incomprehensible to an audience not familiar with it. Should Synge have avoided the Gaelic on the same score? Synge exploited, and converted the difficult speech, suiting it to the language of his audience, which was his language medium, and attained thereby a tremendous eloquence. Any author, intuitively gifted and philologically and rhythmically aware, could go to the documents and records of a Gonzales, a Bennett, or a Reed Smith and recreate a diction at once original, relevant, convincing – and comprehensible. Yet Peterkin and the Heywards, operating in the very environment of the dialect, could do nothing with it but run away from it. These immediately foregoing words are full of meaning to the Negro film with speech.

Coming to the Negro talkie, we can find no more complete entrance than by way of *The Emperor Jones.* In itself *The Emperor Jones* is not particularly Negro. One may question the thesis of atavism which runs through it, as one may easily deny the too patent psychology. But it is excellent theater, a theater of concurrent and joining devices. It is, in fact, better cinema than theater, for its movement is uninterrupted. The uninterrupted movement can be borne only by the film and screen, for the necessity of changing sets obliges an interruption in the theater. There is a central motive of the escaping Jones. The theater has not the capabilities to reveal the textural effects necessary to the drama, such as the increasing sheen of sweat on the bare body. Here is your "photogenic" opportunity! The theater can never equal the cinema in the effect of the gradual oncoming dark, also a dramatic progression in the play. The ominous and frightful shadows, the specters of the boy shot at craps, the phantom gallery—the cinema has long been well-prepared for these. And now the sounds. The play is dependant on the concurrences and reinforcements of sounds. The sounds are part of the drama. The drumbeats, the bullet-shots, the clatter of the dice, the moan of the slaves, and the recurring voice of Jones, his prayer—what a composition these offer for a sound-sight-speech film! This is the ideal scenario for the film of sound and speech. Here silence enters as a part of the speech-sound pattern, and becomes more important than it ever was in the silent film! Here one can construct counterpoint and coincidence, for there is here paralleling of sound and sight and their alternation. There is intervalling, a most important detail in the synchronized structure. But all this does not end *The Emperor Jones*. It must be Negro! How? We can switch back to my earlier words: "The Negro is plastically interesting when he is most negroid. . . ." The Negroes must be selected for their plastic, negroid structures. Jones should not be mulatto or Napoleonic, however psychologic requirements demand it. He should be black so that the sweat may glisten the more and the skin be apprehended more keenly. He should be woolly, tall, broad-nosed, and deep-voiced. The moaning should be drawn from a source in the vocal experience of the Negro, the medicine doctor's dance from a source in choreographic experience. But beware! We do not want ethnography, this is no document. I am not asking for the insertions of *Storm Over Asia:* I am asking for a tightly interwoven pattern. The sources are only sources. Folk, race are not complete in themselves. Dialect is not an aesthetic end. I am not asking for the duplications such as Langston Hughes writes. We shall have enough of these, and they will be nothing but records, and records lacking even intelligent selection and commentary. What I have said in my remarks upon the Negro in art and literature will indicate what the ideal Negro film must not be and must be. The documentary film is ethnographic. The documentary film is a source, but even in a document one cannot place everything and there must be concessions to the form. In the constructed film of the Negro, the art film let us say, the problem will always be, not the Negro in society, but the Negro in the film. The problem will not be that of Edward Sheldon's *The Nigger,* filmed years ago with William Farnum (Fox Film, *The Governor*). That sort of play in reality omits the Negro, just as *A Doll's House* actually gave us no woman but a thesis. We are, I hope, far away now from films about "the black peril" — although *The Birth of a Nation* is still with us and "the yellow peril" is a constant offering. The problem of intermarriage and interrace is not likely to be honestly dealt with on the American screen for a long time, but I do not complain of that — the problem play has generally been dull drama, it would be even duller cinema. When the cinematists have shown that they have intelligently examined the Negro as subject matter, that they know a great deal about him and his experiences, then the problem film of the Negro can be attempted, for the problem will be comprised then, and only then, in a complete experience of a people. It is indeed reassuring that literature in dealing with the Negro has become more sympathetic. The sympathy, however, has not extended as yet to the formal material, the convertible raw stuff — it is humanitarian, and that is good. But in the humanitarian sentiment one still detects considerable patronage, indulgence, condescension, and an attitude hardly judicious, that of the examiner of an oddity. In the documentary films of Burbridge and the Cobham journey, the captions are frequently supercilious, and in a document of a polar trip, a bit of nondocumentation is perpetrated for humor: a Negro hand runs off scared upon seeing a polar bear, safely bound, hauled upon the deck. These Caucasian evidences will persist a long time, and wherever they will persist there will be no proper attitude toward the Negro as subject matter.

Then is the hope in Negro films turned by Negroes? That would be a hope, if the American Negro had given evidence of caring for and understanding his own experience sufficiently to create works of art in the other mediums. But the American Negro as graphic artist has shown very little awareness of this experience; as writer he is imitative, respectable, blunt, ulterior, and when he pretends to follow Negro materials, he does little more than duplicate them. Of course there are exceptions. The exceptions, I believe, will eventually create the rule. But that rule will be created only by artists who are strong enough to resist the vogue which would inflate them. We are now entering into a vogue of the Negro film. Perhaps when that is over, the true, profound, realized Negro film will be produced, and perhaps Negroes will produce them.

It will have been observed that my preoccupation has been constantly with relationships. I have been preoccupied with relationships only because they are constantly present. The relationship between the African dances and the sophisticated Charleston and the Black Bottom is unavoidable, the relationship between native Negro song and jazz is evident. We are always what we were: that is perhaps a platitude, but it is also an important truth for the Negro film. It suggests a synthetic film, a composite film, in which the audience's experience of a girl by [?] Tanganyika becomes the audience's experience of an idolized Josephine Baker. Folk, race dominates the world. There is a theme. And the movie with its devices for simultaneous and composite filming offers the opportunity. Someone might similarly make an incisive film deriving the hooded Ku Klux Klan from the leopard-skin-hooded vendetta of the black Aniotas of Africa. In that way lies penitence for *The Clansman* which became *The Birth of a Nation.*

CLOSE UP,
August, 1929.

NOVEL INTO FILM: A CASE STUDY OF CURRENT PRACTICE

A platitude persists that the movie, being a distinct medium, has its own way of telling a story, and therefore should be permitted the freedom to use it. No one will dispute this too simple and broad defense. But when it is used ambiguously as the countenancing of *Moby Dick's* conversion into *The Sea Beast,* one may charge the defense with bad faith and betrayal of trust. The platitude becomes a demagogic sophistry.

The question involved in the conversion of a social novel into film is one of the treatment of an experience in which "society has an equity." (Dreiser has, in conversation with me, granted that "equity" to a novel as exotic as *Thaïs;* but I choose to confine it strictly to our common right in any re-incorporation of what the social entity, or any living part of it, has apprehended *texturally*). The fight for the integrity of this experience is not a personal one, nor even for the rights of authorship. It is a struggle against the debasing of the intellectual and social level of an experience.

In 1926 Paramount purchased the film rights to Dreiser's *An American Tragedy*. Will Hays, acting as the junction between one self-protective agency—the church, and another—the movie, achieved the temporary shelving of the novel. In the half-decade Paramount has had over 1,800 days to consider the nature of its problem. But Paramount, being a medium of middle-class society to affect the social attitude, resolves the problem of film-making into that of dispensing the cultural minimum—a maximum of illusions or evasions to assure a minimum of dissent.

The technique of minimisation is most drastic where a critical idea is concerned. In 1922, James Oliver Curwood sued the Affiliated Distributors for infidelity to his story, *The Poetic Justice of Uko San,* appearing on the screen as *I Am the Law*. The Court decided:

"I take it that, while scenery, action and characters may be added to an original story, and even supplant subordinate portions thereof, there is an obligation upon the elaborator to retain and give appropriate expression to the theme, thought, and main action of that which was originally written."

Frank Packard sued Fox on the film version of *The Iron Rider,* and the Court sustained him, saying:

"No person has the right to hold out another as the author of literary matter which he never wrote."

In these instances there was no question of the lowering of a social idea. Both Curwood and Packard were purveyors of the cultural minimum. The question involved was purely a monopolistic one, of property rights. But when Upton Sinclair sold his friend, Ben Hampton, the film rights to *The Moneychangers,* in which Morgan is accredited with the panic of 1907, and the film appeared as a Chinatown dope traffic tale, the monopolistic question was answered to Sinclair's disadvantage. Sinclair was not in accord with the cultural minimum and its dispensers.

The case of *An American Tragedy* is subtler, more acute and therefore more insidious. The defense insinuated immediately extraneous biases to prejudice the Court against the plaintiff: his high regard for the Soviet Union, the "Bolshevist affiliations" of S. M. Eisenstein, whose original scenario Mr. Dreiser favoured. The New York Supreme Court has decided to the disadvantage of the socially critical idea. It has, in other words, decided negatively, for the cultural minimum.

A film, like any other work of art, is initiated in experience, converted through performance and conveyed as experience. The initial experience of *An American Tragedy* – the theme – is contained in Mr. Dreiser's "ideographic plan" of his novel:

"It was to be a novel which was to set forth in three distinct social, as well as economic phases, the career of a very sensitive yet not too highly mentally equipped boy, who finds his life in the opening phase painfully hampered by poverty and a low social state, and from which, because of his various inherent and motivating desires, he seeks to extricate himself. In his case, love and material comfort, as well as a foolish dream of social superiority, are his motivating forces.

"Part One of my book was purposely and particularly devoted to setting forth such social miseries as might naturally depress, inhibit and frustrate, and therefore exaggerate, the emotions and desires of a very sensitive and almost sensually exotic boy most poorly equipped for the great life struggle which confronts all youth.

"Part Two particularly was planned to show how such a temperament might fortuitously be brought face to face with a much more fortunate world which would intensify all his deepest desires for luxury and love, and to show how, in the usual unequal contest between poverty and ignorance and desire and the world's great toys, he might readily and really through no real willing of his own, find himself defeated and even charged with murder . . .

"Part Three of the book was definitely and carefully planned to show how an inhibited, weak temperament, once in the hands of his dreams, and later the law, might be readily faced by an ignorant, conventional and revengeful background of rural souls who would, in their turn, by reason of their lacks and social and religious inhibitions and beliefs, be the last to understand and comprehend the palliatives that might have, but did not, attend the life of such a boy, and therefore judge him far more harshly than would individuals of deeper insight and better mental fortune."

The first and second yellow and white scripts, prepared for Paramount by Samuel Hoffenstein and von Sternberg omitted entirely the first part of this design and the end. When produced and presented, the film has a beginning and end, makeshift "equivalents" for the processes of *An American Tragedy*. The picture is, as Ralph Fabri has said, "no 'American Tragedy,' not even a local one, not even a small personal tragedy." Seldom is the thematic conception of *An American Tragedy* even palely present in the film. When it does show itself even faintly we are led to suspect its right in a film that has no constantly informing theme, no intellectual social idea up to that level. Every repeated social incident – a murder or a marriage – contains an inference, a principle, a theme. It is the operation of a social process. Therefore, in the presentation of such an incident in some expressive medium – novel or film – the theme may be detectable. Whether it shall be there intrusive in a banal plot or structural in a thorough realisation of the thematic conception depends on the artist. The occasions when it is given faint recognition in the Sternberg work may be due to the grudging concessions made to Theodore Dreiser. Paramount altered isolated scenes to agree with Mr. Dreiser's viewpoint, thereby unwaringly [a] confession to the existence of a theme. But Mr. Dreiser, upon seeing the whole job, recognised the subterfuge. Though these isolated scenes were dimly theme-informed, the unit-structure lacked thematic motivation.

The lack of good will on Paramount's part goes back to the treatment accorded Eisenstein, first assigned to the conversion of the novel into film. Paramount has said Eisenstein's scenario was too long and that the U.S. authorities didn't want the Soviet director to remain. In answer to the second alibi, we may note, first, that the associated directors of Hollywood didn't want Eisenstein around, perhaps because he was too great a pace-setter. But, we are told, the Eisenstein scenario was too long. We may reply that the objection to a long scenario or a long film is itself arbitrary, and that, the Eisenstein scenario is flexible enough to be modified to incorporate the *theme* in the normal-length feature-film. But Paramount did not want to exploit the *theme*. Sternberg has admitted that Dreiser did not ask for a mere fidelity to the incidents of the novel. And ironically enough, what Sternberg has given us is the bare legend, the fable. He has given us the newspaper account of the case of People *v.* Gillette, Dreiser's initial material. (The attorney for the defence, Judge Lynch – *quel nom!* – has maligned the novel as a bad transliteration of the recorded case. Strange then, commented the plaintiff's attorney, that Paramount should have paid $138,000 for the rights to data available to any newspaper reader. Lynch's insolence has a tangent in the argument of disparagers of Dreiser who assert that the author, to prove the integrity of his opposition, should have returned the $138,000. This would not have helped matters, and moreover our interest is not in the mere personal ethics involved, which are not absolute but variable). Eisenstein, the sequence of whose scenario parallels that of the novel, transcends the mere recital of the narrative and achieves *An American Tragedy* within the compound of sound and sight that is the motion picture today. His structure is constantly informed by the conception, *An American Tragedy*. In Sternberg's work we do not experience the milieu of the boy and his evangelical family. We are not allowed to know the process that evolved him and the girl Roberta. We see Sondra solely as another movie doll playing the usual rôle of an upper class favourite. But what is the social-psychological operation within Sondra that fastens her to Clyde? These people are only digits in the Sternberg chronology, digits never vitalised. After the rejection of the Eisenstein scenario, Dreiser and H. S. Kraft had made suggestions that sought to inject more of the motility of the theme into the film. The claim of the defense that it has "equivalents" for the necessary moments of relationship does not hold on inspection. So literal, so naïve, so unimaginative are our movie-makers, they cannot see, lack all docility to learn, that a statement is not a proof, it is not a process. Nor can they claim that a 6 or 8 or 10 reel film cannot re-render the process of 700,000 words. The film is a progressive medium aspiring to intensiveness. It is an evolving medium, developing from the simple metric structure to the overtonal. Eisenstein has written upon the nature of this evolution and the consequent cinematic categories. The overtone is no mystery. It is achieved within the structure of the film, through the intensive within the progressive.

The picture has been called "lively." We do not ask that a monument bounce like a rubber-ball. But the film is lacking in all resilience. It is not leavened by an idea, it is dismal, tedious, aimless. How completely Sternberg has missed the import of the theme is evinced by the introduction of the picture. Before the story opens, there are repeated shots of water disturbed by a thrown object. And throughout the picture the captions are composed upon a background of rippling water. Sternberg saw the major idea of the matter in the drowning. How lamentable! The drowning is the physical climax of the process; it is not the informing idea. And the film, lacking a process, lacks a climax. The drowning is the sum total. I need not urge how banal and antiquated a tedium is this self-conscious device of anticipating the act even before the film opens.

The district attorney, played by Irving Pichel, is as relevant as the falsifying script and direction will permit. A glance at Eisenstein's scenario suggests what Pichel's rôle might have revealed. That scenario unfalteringly insists upon the political nature of the controversy between the defense attorney and prosecutor, ulterior to the immediate case against Clyde. The entire trial is conveyed in the film, not for what, in its own instance, it reveals of the theme, *An American Tragedy,* but as blatant showmanship of the self-conscious order.

Whereas, in the original Paramount scripts the boy's history begins with his work as foreman in his uncle's collar factory, and the presented film goes back to Clyde as bellboy, Eisenstein's scenario sets the lad as a child in the drab mendicant sanctimony of street evangelism. Paramount asserts it has an equivalent for this in the film, when the boy, running away, goes through the mission – a glimpse never related to the boy. The integrated organism of the boy in the mission, and the mission in the boy, we do not perceive, therefore the process is really never begun. We do not feel the attempt, the dream, of the boy to rend this integration. Eisenstein, however, sets the process off atmospherically, suggestively, emotionally:

Darkness.

The low inspired voice of a woman is heard rising and falling in the sing-song of a chanted sermon. Gradually there mingles with the voice the sounds of the city and the noises of the stret. The siren of an ambulance – the anxious ringing of a street-car. The characteristic cries of news-

boys. The tooting of automobiles. Gruff music through radio horns. With the ever-increasing sound of the various noises, views of the city flash upon the screen. Views that express a well-defined contrast. The infinite contrast between the chant of the sermon and the life of the city.

And the woman's voice continues, exalted, speaking of the harm of drink, of the horror of sin and the love of Jesus Christ. A small thin chorus follows the voice of the woman as she starts singing the 27th hymn:

"How sweet is the love of Jesus."

As yet we see neither the woman whose voice is heard nor those who sing with her.

Of the many indifferent passers-by, there are one or two who listen to the sound of the song — persons slow their walk and look in the direction of the hymn.

A group of curiosity-seekers at the corner of a narrow street, they are busy watching.

The crowd watches, pitying. Various of its members speak of them in varying ways. Some mock them: "You'd think they'd find a better racket than this." Others pity them. Yet others patronize them —

Finally — the street missionaries. An old man with thick grey hair; a woman, large, heavily built; and their children, two little girls and a boy of about seven — CLYDE GRIFFITHS. It is they who were singing the Psalms.

One woman wishes to know why they drag their children along with them. And a second woman clinches the comment by adding: "Better for them to be sent to school." The children, uninterested, listless, devoid of enthusiasm, their eyes astray, sing their hymns of praise while their parents try to gather alms from the little group of curiosity seekers. No alms is given.

The bystanders disperse, and the missionaries, folding up their music, pick up their small organ and move into the cavernous darkness of the towering narrow streets.

Seven-year-old Clyde, sensitive and ashamed of his surroundings, looks no one directly in the eyes.

The family of missionaries move slowly down the street. "I think they were kinder to-day," says the mother.

They approach a dingy, low-built old-fashioned building, over the door of which hangs a sign, "Bethel Independent Mission." The rest of the family disappears within the small doors of this building and only Clyde remains on the threshold. He hangs back because the street urchins are making fun of him and his family — because he irks to answer them and pay them out for their mockery. But no words come to him, and with a typical movement he shrinks into himself.

We find the character of the child described in relation to other children; his sister Esta (entirely omitted in the Paramount version) is also portrayed:

> . . . she peers through a stone gap between the houses onto the street, alive, bathed in light. Clyde sits down beside her as though hypnotized, as though enchanted; the children stare at this tiny piece of life, listen rapt to the sound of an old waltz, the strains of which float up from an unseen restaurant. They look, listen and dream.

They are placed within the mission, its melancholy almost morose oppressiveness, in which the only glow is the mother's exaltation, a glow, however, that obscures her children's plight. The discord is enhanced—symbolised—by the conflict between the restaurant music and that of the mission. In the film the father is mentioned, but only verbally and vaguely; in the scenario he is present to establish further the setting for the child's life. The film omits the elopement of the sister; the scenario includes it—it is important. There we have Clyde Griffiths.

In the film Clyde gets a big tip as bellboy. He utters an appreciation. But the tip is momentous to Clyde. Eisenstein builds the proportions of the incident within the formative experience of the boy by a technique we may call *disproportion*. The literal folk of Hollywood follow what's in the patent narrative. Eisenstein has other resources. It is a rhythmic procedure he introduces. The stature of the incident, its content, determines the particular proportion he will allow. He does not build his film in a simple arithmetic or geometric progression, chronologically. He breaks up the rudimentary ratio and introduces a voice from without that will effect instrumentally the *sense* of the boy's exultation.

> The man . . . takes a 50 cent piece out of his vest pocket and gives it to Clyde. Clyde cannot believe it. He is numb with astonishment. To look at the garters the man turns on the light, and with the click of the switch the room suffuses with brilliance, as the glow of happiness suffuses Cylde's face.
>
> "Fifty cents."
>
> An unknown voice is heard screaming it, and a smile almost of exaltation brightens the whole face of Clyde.
>
> "Fifty cents."
>
> . . . still louder screams the strange voice, and together with the cry

the orchestra is heard playing a wild, happy march. As though at High Mass, the music peals forth, and the hotel resembles a mighty cathedral. Like an organ swells for the huge proud volume of music and a tremendous chorus of human voices rends the air asunder behind the whole small being of the youthful Clyde clasping in his fists his 50 cent piece.

And as the screen fades and grows darker, so the mighty notes of the music grow fainter and their sound slowly fades —

And there rises the images of the poor mission hall and the sound of its congregation singing psalms.

Clyde runs through the mission hall into his room, closing the door behind him.

This is disproportion — a non-literal process. In the relevant symbol of the cathedral-anthem is the disproportion, the extramural introduction, which interprets the proportion of the tip to the humble delights of Clyde. In the succession of the threadbare mission is the colliding image which binds the organism that is Clyde to its source.

Later we meet a similar construction. In the scenario, as in the film, the immediate inspiration for the plan to drown Roberta comes from a newspaper account. But — the Sternberg version seeks to impress this inspiration by the newsboy's *ad tedium* repetition of the headline. Actually this attacks the audience without exposing the process within Clyde. Nor is the image of an overturned boat and a straw hat more than an excerpt. Eisenstein exposes the process by constructing it:

ACCIDENTAL DOUBLE TRAGEDY AT LAKE PASS
UPTURNED CANOE AND FLOATING HATS REVEAL
PROBABLE LOSS OF TWO LIVES

He reads it at first mechanically, without comprehending it.

"The girl's body has been found, but remains unidentified. As to the man, he has not yet been found. Fifteen years ago in this spot a similar accident occurred, and the body was not recovered."

Clyde finishes reading the article, throws the paper off the table, turns out the lamp, and sits wearily down on the couch. And suddenly he hears a whisper:

"And what if Roberta and you ——"

And in the dark corner, he imagines he sees an overset boat. Jumping up Clyde turns on the light.

He sits down on the couch again, nervous and shivering, he picks up the paper he has thrown away, and rereads the article. And while he is reading it with wide-open eyes, the whisper from afar gradually creeps up until it forms the word "KILL."

In a strange, gradual way, the phrase spoken by the whisper forms and forms until at last it pronounces the whole word: "KILL! KILL!"

And from this moment the action begins to work along the line of thoughts of a distracted man, leaping from one fact to another, suddenly stopping—departing from sane logic, distorting the real union between things and sounds—all on the background of the insistent and infinite repetition of scraps of the description in the newspaper.

In this scene, in which the idea of murder is born to Clyde, he acts separately from the background, which keeps changing after him, either dashing in a mad tempo when the background is slow, then falling when there is no reason to fall, then unsteady on a rock, then transformed into stone-like motionlessness in the midst of a busy street.

With the aid of the technical use of transparencies, this effect of the inharmonious actions of Clyde to his surroundings can be attained. Around him is first his room, then a street in busy movement, or the lake, or the mean dwelling of Roberta, or the summer residence of Sondra at Twelfth Lake, or the machines in the factory, or running trains, or the stormy sea, in each setting of which he moves, his movements being discordant with the scene.

And the same with the sounds. These are likewise distorted. And a whisper becomes the whistle of a storm, and the storm cries out "Kill!" or the whistle of the storm becomes the movement of the street, the wheels of a street car, the cries of a crowd, the horns of motor-cars, and all beat out the word "Kill! Kill!" And the street noises become the roar of the factory machines, and the machines also roar out "Kill! Kill!"

Or the roar of the machines descends to a low whisper and it whispers again: "Kill! Kill!" And at this moment a pleasant, unemotional voice slowly reads the newspaper article: "A similar accident occurred fifteen years ago, but the body of the man was never found."

And at the climax of this symphony of madness, Clyde jumps out of this nightmare hell, perspiring, disheveled, excited. He runs to the telephone and calls up Roberta. Through the phone he speaks to her in a hoarse voice.

"This is Clyde."

Not every single element in this process is of itself novel. But novelty—*nouveauté*—is what a Sternberg seeks, and it comes forth antiquated enough. Eisenstein has constructed a relevant process that accumulates into "This is Clyde," a poignant clause.

He tries to put tenderness into his voice, but in his effort there is too much affection. His voice, through the phone, sounds loving and soft; it seems unbelievable that a man in his state of frenzy could be so kind.

The expressionistic disproportions — dissociated images re-associated within Clyde — co-ordinate the event with the state of mind, and — this is the important thing — collecting as a process, they participate in the total structure of the film, which is present in the very last passage quoted. The construction recurs, it is rhythmic and dramatic, when Roberta and Clyde are together. In variation, it is in the court scene. Filming this scene, Sternberg, intent upon violences, stages the rowboat of the tragedy in the courtroom. Eisenstein, realising where to stress, avoids what would sensationalise the pitch without exposing the tactic. Sternberg makes a hullabaloo of the incident where a spectator yells "Hang him!" It appears as horseplay rather than as an exhibition of the hostile rural temper. The film hasn't prepared this temper. Having no process wherein to function, it's violence without elucidation. Eisenstein brings the boy's environment into the case, and stresses the minds at work — the rural antipathy, the political play of the prosecutor. The character of Roberta's parents, fanatics, is in the scenario but not in the film.

The original Hoffenstein script terminated with the mother's faith in the boy's innocence. The film terminates with the boy confessing his guilt — he might have saved Roberta. Eisenstein brings the boy to his death — *that* is his terminal. And swings back to the beginning, the mission. Cause and effect tie up the process, which will be repeated again in other lives.

Blackness and quiet.

A sharp crackle and the sharp light of an electric contact — and again quiet — again blackness.

Grey smoke rises against the dull sky and loses itself in the quiet air.

A tall chimney, a roof; the camera descends past the windows and balconies of the mean building, and the lower descends the camera, the stronger sound the voices of a little choir singing psalms.

In a dirty lane by a mission, surrounded by a crowd of curiosity-seekers, to the sound of a harmonium, some street preachers are singing, as at the beginning of the picture. There they stand, but now the hair of the mother is white as snow, the father is old and ailing, and Esta is grown to a sickly woman, and, instead of Clyde, is her little seven-year-old son.

"How long since you wrote to Mother?"

. . . says a notice by the entrance to the Mission.

"Everybody's happy"

. . . sings the white-haired, broken mother. Pitifully wheezes the harmonium and the strains of "Everybody's happy" fade distantly as the scene Fades Out.

Reading this end as it stands here alone, one might find it sentimental, but since it refers back to an early scene, since it insists upon the outcome and continuousness of the tragedy, its social nature, in the film rendition it would have concluded the inevitable process. (This conclusion is different from the cliché [prolog-epilog tag] of *Street Scene* where the children resume their play after the murder – "life must go on" or some such platitude. It is organic and "emotional rather than merely sentimental").

Superior as this scenario is to the Paramount film, there are still within it indications of concession to the reigning mood, concessions, to be sure, kept at a distance from too ready hands. The scenario, I take it, is a vivid suggestion of the completer thing Eisenstein would have made of *An American Tragedy* had he filmed it – and under more self-respecting control than that of Hollywood.

For Paramount never intended to respect the integrity of the idea it bought. The Justice trying this case has put the legal stamp on the subterfuge of the movie. He has given high judicial authority to the Hays Code and the cultural minimum. Is this precedent? Although the defense argued that the Sternberg film was the equivalent in its medium to the Dreiser novel, the Court supplemented with a blessing that contradicts the defense, which the Court has upheld:

In the preparation of the picture the producer must give consideration to the fact that the great majority of people composing the audience before which the picture will be presented will be more interested that justice prevail over wrongdoing than that the inevitability of Clyde's end clearly appear.

The Judge has corroborated the charge of the plaintiff that instead of an indictment of society, the picture is a justification of society and an indictment of Clyde.

In strict orthodoxy the Court places the responsibility on the "public," and so evades responsibility. This lofty dictum ties up with the dedication that introduces the film: to the men and women who have done so much for youth. Probably by giving birth to them.

CLOSE UP,
December, 1931.

DOG DAYS IN THE MOVIE

The Rin Tin Tinnabulation of the melancholy bells: "Hollywood's canine prince" is dead at the age of 14, after 13 good-luck years of mute but glistening heroism before the camera. "Rin Tin Tin," an obituary reads, "was essentially a gentleman. That is why audiences were so fond of him." He earned $300,000 for his owners and kept Warner Brothers from going to the dogs. His name must be joined with that of another gentleman and hero, the cowboy Tom Mix, who for many years kept the Fox corporation in the saddle. Like the puncher, the hound was to have made a comeback in the era when the bark must be as good as the bite — inevitably to as little success. They never come back! or if they do, it is not to glamour as of old. For in this cynical period even the dog stars are suspected. And though statesmen and men of perched brow may assert their devotion to "the art of the western" or "the art of Rin Tin Tin," and thereby vindicate Hollywood and Hays, as well as the aestheticians of the primitive, there is no vindication of Tom Mix or Rin Tin Tin — they need no vindication. In these elementary cinemas of literal and undisturbed action — and audience reaction — with their unvarying formula of suspense and climax and relief, there is no criterion but this formula. The audience delighting in the simplicities of this melodrama does not debate photography, direction or even performance, and recognizes little or no difference between a Tom Mix and a Buck Jones or even a Buddy Roosevelt, between a Rin Tin Tin, Sr., and Rin Tin Tin, Jr., or a Ranger, between a Mickey Mouse and an Oswald the Rabbit. Once there was Strongheart the dog, and he became one with Rin Tin Tin — distinctions are affectations in this category, dog is not plural. The applause of the audience is not for the singular entree but for the staple condiment, and any brand will do — the average housewife can not distinguish between different brands of salt. Claims of superiority are made by the populist and it is he who betrays the primitive, the elementary, the staple by branding it "art."

Rin Tin Tin is dead and therefore, being a dog, he must be happy. It is invidious to enshrine him as artist or even as gentleman, though we may permit the latter as a conceit. Yet can I not hear the enterprising critic, in an effort to make his snobbery popular and profitable, submit the marketable but questionable suggestion: "What the movie needs is another good dog." Marketable because it is cute and for the moment inveigles the simple audience into worthless self-esteem. Yesterday such elegances were reserved for effete magazines like *The Soil, Broom, The Dial.* Today they are doled out with blessings like on slapstick and "autographed bathtubs" to the vast millions, so easily tantalized and betrayed.

No longer will staples sustain. The need is for diets. The movie "art-industry," as Jesse Lasky called it, is in a hell of a fix. It is between the devil (Hays the evangel) and the deep dead sea (Holy Hollywood), and what lies between is morass. My metaphors are mixed, but then so is the movie, despite the more direct control of that spasmodic jack-in-the-box by the mechanism called Wall Street. The mechanism itself is askew. Rin Tin Tin evolved during the ascent of cinema and at his peak, after having borne Warners through difficulties, he could support them no more. It was then garrulity succeeded the mute hero. He was still vital but Hollywood was not, and so he was discarded by Warners who needed more than the b.o. appeal of Rin Tin Tin to safeguard their stock-juggling. The noble beast typified the contradiction of the movie: it, intrinsically, was still vital but Hollywood was not. Not that the talkie was not inevitable, but only that it was unanticipated in the understanding of the practicians, therefore premature. Even today there are few who can comprehend the talkie as a sound-sight compound. And today the talkie cannot salvage the movie, and no other technical development can salvage it, for sound-and-talk brought a new sense into play and with that set the limits of compounding, wide as they are. All other innovations are heightenings within these limits.

The trouble with the movie is a chronic one. Had its own body been more properly kept it might have resisted the epidemic crisis better. The cure, that is the improvement of the body politic of the movie, is simpler than supposed, perfectly obvious, therefore avoided by all those who sell slogans about the art of the horse-opera or the recrudescence of the serial or the unimpeachable Walt Disney — with all due respect. The answer is "subject-matter." Subject-matter, the content of daily life. I shall not gainsay "fantasy" altogether, for in this imperfect age the vicarious is insistent. Audiences have long been conditioned by the ideals of *nouveau-riche* producers who "give the public what it wants," more easily when what the public wants coincides with what they want the public to want. But in a time such as this, when uncertainty and dread are each man's portion, an audience will respond to more than Rin Tin Tin, will desire an explanation of its own state. Films like *Bad Girl, Seed, Emma, Young America, Bad Sister, Are These Our Children?* containing approximately normal types, indicate, incipiently and despite their fraudulences, the tendency essential to the movie. But does the producer recognise the tendency as one toward drastic reality? A Hollywood director wished to make a picture of a typical American family caught in the "depression," but the young producer said: "We'll give the public horror instead." Now, it is true, in a period of economic anguish, there are two mental, social tendencies: toward realism, toward the fantastic. Germany's cinematic "golden age," coming upon the War and the Inflation, was a duality: the German middleman looking upon his plight pathetically, the German simplistic mind indulging in abberations. The control, however, insisted on the second tendency and the German *kino* disintegrated into innocuous *lichtspiel*. Had the control favoured the tendency toward reality, the German film would have remained integrated much longer. The unreal cannot sustain over long periods.

But our producers are thinking of expediences only; long periods, despite all this talk of "plans," does not adhere, it seems, to capitalist production any more. Get what you can while you can get it, even though you enhance the evil in so doing. Universal produces *Dracula* and *Frankenstein*—"scarers" that forsake the very core of their horrors, the plague-analogy of the vampire theme, man's creation turning on man. The movie of *delirium tremens*—on near beer! First novelty and then publicity build-up pack in the crowds, who have been led to expect horror and therefore find horror—up to a point. An "independent" produces *White Zombie* at perhaps a tenth or a twentieth the cost of *Frankenstein* and it is just as good, even better. United Artists takes it up, builds it up, the crowd is inveigled, but do I not hear as much laughter as cries of horror? Is there really a fool born every minute, and how long can the movie wait till he grows up, or shall it get him while he is still wrong? The big companies are choking to death. They are afraid. Five-star *Grand Hotels* are not heroisms but steam-whistling in the dark. The so-called independents, "indies," working on little, not obsessed with stars and salaries (actors can be got cheap) have the opportunity to make good films and market them. And what do they do? The same old stuff; they take none of the risks of independence. Every one is scared!

At last the movie, being a topical medium too, must recognise the "depression" as subject-matter. The audience is lured to see a film pretending to tell the truth and they are shown another picture on the glib studio formula, *American Madness*. With a grand flourish this film opened at the Mayfair. There were spotlights on the theatre but not a flashlight on the truth. Bank runs are caused by a $50,000 robbery augmented, in public rumours, to 50 times the amount. Loans to banks and factors—they will dissipate the crisis; is this film the work of the Reconstruction Finance Corporation? Faith in character, and the love of woman—these would have saved the Bank in the United States, if only people wouldn't gossip. The theme song of this film of redemption, cancellation of evils, might be the popular "You call it madness, but I call it love." The movie has the coupon mind. It is shivering on a perforated fringe! Total collapse will be stayed with these runs of deluding films, and then the downward pace will be intensified. The graph may fluctuate upward now and then but the path is generally downward—until there is the courage of facing reality and elucidating it in the movies. But can that be expected from the Hollywood camp as it is constituted today?

CLOSE UP,
December, 1932.

THE YEAR OF THE ECLIPSE

I shall use quotations from my correspondence to *Close Up*'s last number for 1932 as keys to my first correspondence to 1933, since what I have to say grows from "Dog Days in the Movie." "The movie of *delirium tremens* – on near beer!" . . . The outlook for 3.2 per cent brew is good. The difference between the promised and the present "near beer" brand is the quantity of hope in American breasts, deceived into that hope by the promise of a prosperity that will follow upon the liquidation of prohibition. Hoax upon hoax – the vision of the desperate! And the movie is its immediate image. It reads *concoction* as *experience,* the momentarily effective as the memorable, or neglects the quality of the memory altogether. I asked: "Is there really a fool born every minute, and how long can the movie wait till he grows up, or shall it get him while he is still young?" (The printer put down "young" as "wrong" – not an inaccurate error). The fool today is not constantly foolish, his reaction cannot be counted upon as certainly as in earlier days. 1932 was the year of the eclipse, astronomically and in the cinema. Not even the attractiveness of Marlene Dietrich sustained *Blonde Venus*; it was removed from the Paramount Theatre before its engagement was really over. The crowd was as wise as the critic. The critic should have been wiser: he should have seen *Blonde Venus* in *The Blue Angel* and foretold the inevitable. Sternberg may succeed Pommer at U.F.A. That is ironical, because what is creditable in today's Sternberg is really Pommer.

The most painful partial eclipse was that of Lewis Milestone. Although Tom Buckingham was the accredited director of *Cock o' the Air* and Nate Watts the accredited supervisor, Mr. Milestone had a great deal to do with it. Its wretchedness was partly due to the delicate interference of the Hays troupe. But I am puzzled by the puerility of a field general like Milestone, who uses his prestige and authority, his talent, to toss off rowdyisms stodgy and unprovocative. The fault seems to be the desire to repeat a previous success, *Two Arabian Knights,* just as in *Rain,* Milestone seems to have wanted another *tour de force* like *The Front Page,* a film of major importance in the history of the compound cinema. Others have observed two of Mr. Milestone's limitations: his belief that speech should be uninterrupted, his inability to direct women. The first limitation deserves study. In *The Front Page* Milestone correctly gauged the *quantity* of speech and its velocity (the relation of speech to visual-motor *density*) and thereby, for the first time, presented the principle that though the *plane of correlation* in the cinema is visual-motor, the vocal element in the compound may, if the subject-matter requires, set the pace for the unit. In this particular film (Milestone's milestone) the vehicle gave the cargo an appearance of substance. Indeed, I half suspect that the director recognized that the play had more appearance than substance: it was a typical Ben Hecht imposture, garbling half-truths and circumstantial data into the semblance of an indictment. The glamour of the vehicle rendered the cargo glamorous until the end, when the vehicle could shatter itself and leave no memory, save that of a principle of construction — valuable to the practician but not to the audience. In *Rain* such treatment would find the resistance of a more sullen material, pseudo-psychology, picturesqueness, mood. The interferences crisscrossed to make a picture that seemed to fall apart with every scene, and yet — it was not quite so condemnatory of Milestone as some would have us believe. Elements of sternness were present and, if the *régisseur*'s inability to direct women was apparent, it served to show up Joan Crawford. Without her accustomed M.G.M. directors and flattering cameramen, she became, as someone said, "a female impersonator." The chief fault in the case of Milestone is one of conscience: he is not sufficiently insistent upon the important subjects he can command and direct.

* * *

There were other temporary eclipses. The entire industry has been operating in the dark. Joseph I. Breen of the Hayes office enumerates the besetting evils thus: The industrial depression; Too many theaters; Competition by other forms of entertainment such as radio and dog racing; Destruction of the illusion surrounding screen personalities by too intimate revelation in the fan magazines; A lack of big personalities on the screen. . . . Not a word about the films themselves! However, those in the industry itself recognize that something is wrong with the product. They do not read the difficulty as harshly as I have read it: ". . . the courage of facing reality and elucidating it in the movies." They call it "topical films." It is interesting to see how the different studios interpret the topical. Columbia, the latest recruit to the Hays organization, issues completely dishonest pictures like *American Madness* and *Washington Merry-Go-Round*. The latter boasts of a "courage" that insults the unemployed veterans, who have no representative in either Washington or Hollywood. Less sycophantic films are those produced by Warner Brothers, a previously dull studio that has awakened with some vigor to the current scene. Jack Warner, production chief, announces that: "Newspapers will be watched this year as they were last for ideas and plots."

* * *

We may divide these topical films into two categories: social segment films, personality films. Unfortunately, the individualistic, star-systematized cinema makes no strenuous effort to make one of the two, which is the Soviet intention. Of the Warner pictures the two that come nearest to this unification are: *The Cabin In the Cotton* and *I Am a Fugitive.* This approximation is made possible by two facts : these are not stories about "prodigious" personalities (as in the case of *The Match King* and *Silver Dollar*) where the social happening is popularly obscured by the quasi-legendary figure; they are stories having widespread reference quickly discernible in the current scene. Because they have widespread reference, it is worth our while to see how this reference is handled in the film. *The Cabin In the Cotton* is not an exceptionally arresting film in its direction, its central person is earnestly but not vibrantly enacted by Richard Barthelmess, remnant of the Griffith camp, but its subject-matter is the most important the American film has risked in years. It is the *class struggle.* Does this mean, however, that the movie has yielded its restriction on films of the struggle between capital and labor? Not at all. The newsreels still keep out clips that might refer to that warfare, the steel trust has time and time again stipulated that it will not permit the use of its premises to enact that struggle. A film like *Taxi* was not borne along its logical motif of the struggle between the taxi trust and the privately-owned taxi. I understand Cagney wanted such a story, but it was rejected as being "labor v. capital!" I know a young man in the publicity department of one of the largest companies who wrote a scenario situated in Pittsburgh. His scenario won him a job in the editorial department, but the scenario itself was rejected as being too much on the labor theme, although the author was very careful to keep any semblance of that theme remotely in the background, where everything important is usually kept (in the capitalistic cinema). And then there was the controversy over the Boulder (Hoover) Dam scenario, when the delegated scenarists found "forced labor" in the American enterprise. The net result of the controversy was two scenarists "canned" and a strengthening of the dictum against "capital-labour films."

* * *

The class struggle as expressed in *The Cabin In the Cotton* is agrarian. The action is set in a locale not the most remunerative to the film, not the most influential in effecting opinion and not on the most intimate terms with industrial and finance capital. Observe that no tie-up is made between the agrarian and the industrial South, a tie-up very real today in our economic Society. Our world is an industrial one basically, and it is in the basic segment that no study is even remotely attempted. Therefore, while the movie will dare an *I Am a Fugitive,* it renders prison life in the industrial North as truly reformative (idealistic penology) in *20,000 Years In Sing Sing,* a preposterous title for another story of a self-sacrificing racketeer. Further separation occurs in *The Cabin In the Cotton,* the Negro sharecropper and tenant farmer from the white. The only presence of a Negro is in the blind singer who chants as he passes the jazz-festive home of the planter. Yet the outstanding phenomena of the agrarian South today are the revolutionary self-assertion of the Negro peon, the class-amity between erstwhile foes, black and white dispossessed. Amity is urged in this film, not intra-classamity (as in *Kameradschaft*) but inter-class-amity (as in Phyllis Bentley's novel, *Inheritance*). And who is to effect this impossible conciliation? The hyphenate, whose father has been cheated and sent to an early death by the planter who is now the son's benefactor because he recognizes in the boy profitable material. In politics the hyphenate is easily characterized, in an ostensibly non-political novel or film he is not so readily stamped— he becomes first pitiable then heroic —when he shows up the greed of the one "bad" planter in order to have him shake hands with the tenants. A proper conclusion would have been the boy's assumption of tenant-leadership against the planter. Two falsehoods are presented to strengthen the drama of conciliation; the tenants steal the planters' cotton and seek to set up their own broker in Memphis (how long could a tenant conceal the bales before he were apprehended?), the collaborator of the hyphenate in making the peace is the district attorney — an agent of the planters who is presented as a friend of the tenants! There are other details equally suspect. Yet, it would be sectarian and dishonest not to say that this film, in its argument and mood, balances the sympathy to the credit of the tenants. That is assuredly a victory! a concession to a rising temper. Then tenants are facially well chosen, not non-professional players but professionals chosen and controlled upon the documentary principle — director Curtiz has evidently learned something from the Russians. For the first time, in my immediate recollection, the movie has dared to approach lynching as a contemporary American custom. Here the victim is a white peasant who has been sorely driven to the murder of a planter. More should have been made of the scene since it submits the climax to the hyphenate's evolving attitude. We must recognize also that this is not a typical instance. The typical instance is lynching not on a "real" but a framed charge; the most frequent instances are the organized mob murders of Negroes, but that is an indisputable fact to which our conscience is too sensitive — we can argue the lynching in *The Cabin In the Cotton* as rare and therefore chance. Still, the incomplete presentation of the pursuit and lynching of a white man by wealthy men of his own race is an incipient suggestion of the fact that lynchings are economic. Therefore, for all its distortion of the social theme it particularizes, *The Cabin In the Cotton* is an advance in the movie's content. A more truthful production would have sought its material in works like *Georgia Nigger, To Make My Bread, Call Home the Heart, Strike!* or *Gathering Storm.*

* * *

As a work of cinema, *I Am a Fugitive From a (Georgia) Chain Gang,* is superior to *The Cabin In the Cotton.* Its young director, Mervyn Le Roy, is as yet an eclectic of the second or third order. He has made as bad a film as *Numbered Men,* films as inflated for their tiny intelligence as *Big City Blues* and *Three On a Match,* and pictures as reputable as *Little Cæsar, Five-Star Final* and *I Am a Fugitive.* His career is an argument for the importance of content: the better the story, the better has been his direction! Le Roy is gifted in the American open-play tradition that has been deserted by von Sternberg, but which Milestone enlivened in *The Front Page.* His last films show Le Roy's indebtedness to Milestone, but he has not the older man's proficiency in timing. If the talkie has damaged anything in the American idiom, it is its metric. I do not lament this disturbance for it serves to break up the confounding of time with speed-uninterrupted action. In *I Am a Fugitive* Le Roy shows skill in the alternations of speech and silence, but he fails to convey lapse of time, despite his use of the archaic calendar-leaves (an archaism improved somewhat by the coincidence of hammer beat) and distance (which must be conveyed conjointly by space of time) by means of an inanimate, inexpressive map. Le Roy exhibits the Milestone weakness in his direction of women; he was successful with Aline MacMahon in *Five-Star Final* because she is a superior player with a masculine emphasis (her roles are "hard"). The young director was more successful in the sensational or spectacular scenes (although the second escape was, in its scenario, quite routine), and less successful in the scenes away from prison — as in the period of the fugitive's rise to success. This attests to the immaturity not alone of Le Roy, but also of the American movie mind. Le Roy's faults are as much environmental as personal. They arise from the American aspiration to be momentarily effective, which coincides with the unwillingness to be thorough in the treatment of social material. *Five-Star Final* overpitched its tragedy — stretched it beyond the point of elasticity — neutralized the indictment with humour and terminated the drama with a cute remark. Of competence there was much, a competence of verve and of a quality superior to the blue-print workmanship of a Frank Capra, for instance. *I Am a Fugitive* is too spectacular at times, the chain gang is clustered in two sequences of the film to serve as a lavish background for the innocent prisoner played honorably by Paul Muni. By the end of the picture we are thinking not at all of the chain gang but of the fugitive, and mainly because he has been made a man of the hour whose hour is destroyed by the vindictiveness of a state, which breaks the promise exacted by the insistence of the popular voice. It is in its characterization of the state (through governor et al) that the picture achieves its main importance. Were it not for the inspired conclusion, when the fugitive's agonized face disappears in the mist, I doubt that the antecedent action would be recalled. Not often does a last image work retroactively *in favor of* the narrative. The "shocker" at the end of *Public Enemy* is memorable solely for its own violence . . . The reason for the existence of a medievalism like the chain gang is not indicated in *I Am a Fugitive,* as it was in *Hell's Highway*. If these two films could have been mixed for their better elements the complete chain gang picture might have been realized. The latter film was begun by Rowland Brown and, by its first part, reassured us that we were not wrong in admiring that director's initial picture, *Quick Millions*. He seems to have the surest, cleanest directorial hand of any newcomer in the last several years, and is as resistant to curleycues as he has been to the film hierarchy. The original scenario of *Hell's Highway* had in authors Samuel Ornitz and Brown, two socially-conscious individuals, and that possibly accounts for the fact that the film has a base to start from: the chain gang exists for the private contractor that he may have cheap labor for his competitive bid. It is this fact that *I Am a Fugitive* needs. However, *Hell's Highway* absolves the state from connivance in the sweat box; *I Am a Fugitive* provides the state as nemesis. In the latter also, a cause, unemployment, leads to a result, the chain gang, in the instance of the central person; in the former there is no such relationship, and the central person is a cliché. Neither film avoids the picturesque, particularly in the Negro singing—operatic in the Le Roy film, vaudevillian in the Brown. Unless the singing can be related with penetration to the setting, it is dangerous diversion and is better omitted. Similarly, the scene in the hangout in the Le Roy film between the runaway and the sympathetic girl is better omitted than presented hurriedly and lacking in the essential qualities of tenderness and poignancy, for which the film has not prepared the way and from which there is no development. In its literalness, the American movie includes every episode and renders too kaleidoscopic a film demanding scrutiny. But, for all its insufficiencies, *I Am a Fugitive* is an advance in American film content and to that extent its form is shaped. Will it be a jumping-off place for more progressive films or an end-stop? Indications point to renewed concessions by the social segment film to the aggrandisement of the personage who should be the character-convergent for the happenings. Though *The Match King* does contain some probable Krueger data very glibly set into motion in the effrontery of Kroll ("Kr" from Krueger "oll" from Toll) it is a delectable cad we get and not a peak-phenomenon of egregious economy in collapse. Any suggestion of a possible deduction of general pertinence is subdued, although in the bribery of the Polish minister something did slip through. *Silver Dollar* is the tale of an all-too-human superman and not the striking instance of the battle of the financiers. The defeat of silver is treated almost as a hastily improvised snubbing of Yates Martin (H. A. A. Tabor in reality), whose vulgarity, we are somehow left to feel, brought on the defeat.

Close Up,
March, 1933.

THE CINEMATIZED CHILD

Educators and critics alike have, in their considerations of the child, too often obscured the fact itself, the child. Today we are indulging in a "cult of the child" which, however amusing it may be to the zealot, is baneful to the child. We have had numerous volumes of verse and prose by individual children and as many anthologies of such work, whose enthusiasts have presented such work as "art." Such work, however, has but one importance: as the expression of childhood. No matter how clairvoyant, how precocious a child may be, his apprehension is limited to his childhood's awareness. The child cannot anticipate his experience. He meets it as he becomes aware of it.

The resistance of the child to advance contacts is his protection. But it is not completely a resistance. The child resists the *experience* of which he is not aware, but he cannot resist the influence. Between resistance and influence there is the distance between the systemic and the external. To be controlled by experience is to be controlled by oneself. To be controlled by influence is to be controlled by a motivation which is an imposition, and therefore false and insidious. And here we must pause, lest the purist embrace this distinction to make it serve his fallacies. Experience — control by oneself — implies an environment wherein the vicarious is minimized, where one is called upon to realize oneself in complete, or approximately complete, coincidence with society. I think it fair to say that now there is but one environment of that discipline, the Soviet Union. The discipline of our other societies is either a shiftless one or incisive maladjustment. The environment of accord between personal and social morality is one wherein influence is a part of experience. Such an environment proves that the awareness of a child can be materially extended, therefore eliminating the danger of unappreciated influence.

It is a curious condition of a disproportionate society that while we are willing to believe the child an "artist," we are unwilling to admit he can understand himself as a part of the socio-economic world. As a matter of fact, he is intrinsically more prepared for comprehension of what makes the world go round than for what might render it exquisite. But, even in the belief in the child as an "artist" we find aberrations, due to an ignorance of the components of "art." For instance, we will talk to the child about drawing, take him to the museums, etcetera, but never about the forms of expression most intimate to him – in America, the comic strip cartoon – throughout the world, the motion picture. We do not talk to him from *his* experience – consider it, in fact, anti-pedagogic and even insolent.

Experience. . . . When the child becomes aware of sex, the contacts he makes which stress sex are his experience, and as such can be condemned only when they are not proportioned to the child's understanding. But then one's contacts are always ahead of one's understanding of them – especially in a disproportionate society. To assure rational growth to the child, comprehension must be urged to the control of the contact. That is, criticism must be developed in the child. To continue with sex: the cinema is another experience of sex to the child who is aware of sex, but the dictionary is also an experience of sex at that time. The first awareness is always through symbols – that is to say, the first registered awareness operating for self-delight. Experience is symbolic first and physical later. No, I am not Platonic when I say this, and I agree that the terms "symbolic" and "physical" are somewhat arbitrary for the sake of economy. But its implication is that mental self-delight precedes genital. But since the first enters into the individual's apprehension toward the synthesis of his outlook, it is experience. The cinema is a *detail* in it.

I have chosen the experience of sex because in this disproportionate society which is ours it is a major insistence, and because it is the instance worrying the moral-minded and the moralistic-minded. There is some basis for that worry. But it is to be found as well in other instances than sex. The danger, however, is not that the cinema will hypersexualize the child, that it will disintegrate him, but simply that it will hurry his experience and thereby condense his childhood to defeat the very essence of development, gradualness in growth. This is the imposition of influence. It gives the child an attitude which contradicts childhood. This attitude is all the more baneful because it is alien to childhood. It is, however, as prominent in the so-called moral instances as in the immoral. The attitude is present in the very manner of presentation, as much in the spurious gentlemanliness of Adolphe Menjou, his suavity and the elegances of social attainment built around it, as in the forcible rape of the young innocent; as much in the social sentimentalism of a supposed picture of childhood like *Skippy,* as in an out-and-out crook film. Indeed, it is not the violences of the latter film that render it dangerous, but the suggestions of wit and redemption. The dangers are present in the hilarious social values of American films — and that means of European films, since they accept the level of the American — in the conceptions of love, splendor, achievement, patriotism, etcetera. But — the cinema is not the initiator of these values, it is the reflector of them — response and agent of the society expressing these values. The child is environed by these values and must imbibe them from many sources. What the cinema does is to concretize these values and make them permanent through inevasive images. The mind of the child is as wax to receive these images and as marble to retain them. The film defines and gives the "working image." It pictorializes for the child the language of his text, his story-book, his periodical, his parents, his friends; pictorializes and animates, so that words, even when they are true and accurate, may borrow and become the fraudulent animated image of the screen. This image is repeated *ad infinitum*; it is the formula of the moving picture.

In regard to this phenomenon, Dr. Bruno Lasker has interesting things to say in the exemplary investigation, "Race Attitudes in Children." (*Race Attitudes In Children,* by Bruno Lasker, The Inquiry. New York: Henry Holt & Co., 1929; pp. 197–203). The objectivity of this research is not injured, but assisted, by the critical comments of the editor. The few pages allotted to the influence of the film in the formation of race attitudes are explicit. Lasker's words introducing this section deserve quotation and are included here because they reënforce my statements: "Looking back, we are apt to exaggerate the influence upon us of specific things seen and heard; their weight in most cases was that of the proverbial last straw, that of a particularly vivid impression on top of many others in the same direction." The film is the cumulative visual-motor emphasis of an experience. Lasker quotes a report from a teacher who overheard two of her high-school pupils discuss the merits of Joseph Hergesheimer's novel, *Java Head:* "One of the girls had read the book, the other had seen the film based on the story. The first referred to the Manchu woman as having given her new light in her conception of the Chinese. 'But,' said her friend, 'you should have seen her in the movies! She was just like all the rest of them. It's all right to read about them; but I don't like to see them.'" If the book-informed girl had seen the film, the likelihood is that the visual-motor image — unless she were not eye-minded — would have dominated the verbal. And now with oral speech added, the "reality" is further affirmed.

Before we can decide what to do about it, we must admit that the full correction lies not with the film but with the society — it must find the cure in itself. In anticipation of that drastic change, we may still find ways of meeting the influence of the film. First, we must consider the preferences of the child, the fact of our concern, although the end is society. We must try to distinguish between inherent preferences and conditioned. The University of Chicago Press has issued the results of the Wieboldt Foundation for an investigation of "Children and Movies." The results appear in a volume by that name, prepared by Alice Miller Mitchell. (*Children and Movies,* by Alice Miller Mitchell. Chicago: University of Chicago Press, 1929). "The material for the present research was furnished by 10,052 Chicago children representing three groups: average public-school children, juvenile delinquents, and a specific group of children who have a certain degree of organized leadership in their lives as the Boy Scouts and the Girl Scouts." Written quizzes furnished the greater part of the working material. "Of the 10,052 children studied there were only 168 or 1.7% of them who reported that they did not go to the movies at all . . . the majority of the 168 . . . gave religious restrictions as the reason . . . two children . . . said that they did not attend the movies because they did not like them . . . 90.6% attend the movies at regular intervals . . . from once a month to seven times a week. Isolated cases, especially among the delinquent group, reported as many as eight or nine movies a week, explaining that they went twice on Saturdays and Sundays. Several delinquent boys said that before they were committed to institutions they would spend an entire day going from one show to another. . . .

"If frequency of attendance can be taken as an indication, it appears that boys care more for movies than do girls . . . early adolescents seek movies more frequently than do the later adolescents. In the case of the delinquent group, however, the opposite is true. The older the delinquent child, the more frequent a movie-goer he appears to be. This does not necessarily mean the older in chronological years. It applies more specifically to those who are older in delinquency experience. . . . The most outstanding factor which apparently influences the frequency of juvenile attendance at the movies is the degree to which some organized recreational interest enters into the life of the child."

What does this research tell us of our fact, the child? First, children like the movies. Second, delinquents like it more than do Boy Scouts. But are these categories polar absolutes? What are in reality the offenses that constitute delinquency and are they absolute and apart? Are the characteristics of competitive sports always more able than those of film participation? Does the child participate more critically in sports than in cinema? We must remember that both scouting and movie-going are rituals. The nature of a ritual is to render the participant uncritical. The movie is enveloped in trapping of publicity, plush chairs, organ music, etcetera; scouting has its uniform, its platitudes, its prizes, etcetera. Both excite imaginations inherently active—to what ends? Less serious a danger is the impulsion into "offenses" than into sentimentalism. Less serious is "delinquency"—save that this disproportionate society makes of it something inimical—than the sentiments provoked, of chauvinism, racial antipathy, and the like. Scouting is national sectarianism in many cases, the movie is that in as many. A presumably wholesome (since farcical) film like Harold Lloyd's *Welcome Danger!* is a thousand times more vicious in its picturing the fiendish Chinaman and Negro than the vilest sex film. The pitch of race dislike is reached, because of earlier suggestions, sooner than the pitch of sex interest, which is biological, therefore innate, awaiting fulfillment. The first is *all* influence. Sport antagonisms, separation of racial groups, uniformity of ideology (verbal usually, hence hypocritic), which typify our favored group organizations for children, are sometimes more socially delinquent than larceny or arson. Of social attitudes this research says nothing beyond recording the film preferences of "delinquents" for killings, robberies, evasions of police. But the attendance of adults at movie theaters, where these films are in abundance, attests that this is no particular enthusiasm reserved to "delinquents." Incidentally, it is interesting in this report—if one does not already know it—that children do not generally list war films first in their preferences. But that is proof of nothing. Western films are war films in a more romantic *milieu* and usually contain an even more intensified hatred of a foreign people: Mexican, Indian, Chinese (if not burlesqued). Again it is a mistake made in this research not to recognize identities of kinds of films and identities of preference. Is the preference of the delinquent for films showing the victories of criminals any different from the general adult affection for comedies where police are fooled or beaten? In the history of disproportionate societies, this is not the worst of preferences, although it is nothing but a vicarious satisfaction in the victory of the weaker depending on his nerve and wits—the more romantic—or simply sympathy for the protagonist.

Miss Mitchell quotes some delinquents on the way in which the film was a provocation to "sin" or offend. The tales really indicate that the urge was there before the film, rather than arising after it. The movie was probably a climactic influence. The research is incomplete in that it does not attempt to seek into the preferences of children encouraged toward criticism: children in the progressive schools, in radical environments, etcetera.

That the film submits its problem is undoubted. But until we can reorganize the social conscience that includes the film, we must accept the existence of just the film we have. And how to meet that film is the problem. Certainly the child is ultimately susceptible to the niceties of art, but we cannot speak to him in view of the ultimate, nor babble to him of abstractions. We must first be sure he is responsive to the experience of art, or of the particular work. The child is assimilative, or more correctly, adaptive to the extent of dissemblance. He may even reveal what is apparently a critical sense, critical of methods. But the appreciation of art is, in its infancy, visceral. To attempt to divert it to esthetics is to give it a premature effeteness. The period of childhood is the period of the visceral cliché. The child enjoys mischief, but he prefers it broad and violent, as in the antics of Fairbanks and Lloyd. He enjoys pathos too, but it must have the impact of physical emphasis, as in the Jannings performance in *The Way of All Flesh*. He enjoys battle when he can be a partisan — as he always is, in the movie. He enjoys the discomfiture of others. He enjoys the sagacity of those he favors. This is the essence of the comic film, in which the weakling conquers, the imbecile is victorious. It is most enjoyed when it is exploited in the violence of the gag: the popularity of Harold Lloyd. As yet there is not instance here of the awareness of either the implication of the subject-matter or the aesthetic organization. For this two things are needed: comprehensive experience and training, granting the possession of a good visual-motor sense.

Too often the consideration of the cinema-for-the-child becomes a matter of what the child *ought* to like. He ought to like Chaplin, but he prefers Lloyd. By every apparent reason he should have enjoyed *Chang*. But what were his reasons for not greatly liking it? I refer to the preferences of the American children whom I have met in my work, American children and children of European parents. They varied enough in intelligence, experience, age and nativity to lend my observations authenticity. *Chang* was objected to because there was no plot, there were animals in it, there was no star. There was a plot in *Chang*, but to the child conditioned by studio films it was not discernible. The child likes animal pictures, when the animal is a person of the drama, like Rin-Tin-Tin. Children want a star, that is, a personality who is to them intimate and constant. This, of course, is due partly to the bad training of the previous and present movie.

The answer is generally — reeducation in cinema. How?

Through special performances? These may do a little good, but only a little, quite negligible. The American child goes many times during the week to the movie. He enjoys going to the theaters which his elders visit and seeing the films they see. He wants to see advertised films and actors.

Bar the questionable film to the child? What is the questionable film? The harm is present in the social attitude and in the social value extolled or exploited. Censors represent that attitude, have the prejudices of that attitude, and at best accept the common logic as to what *ought* to harm the susceptible, and this may be the least baneful. Moreover, who will guarantee the non-admittance of the child? The proprietor? He will use the prohibition as a bait — this is an old American custom. The parent? He or she is usually too weary, too indifferent, or must yield to expedience. And how many times a week can one say No? The child will go anyway, borrow, beg, steal or sneak in. The prohibition only whets.

There is the institution, such as school or settlement. They provide a medium. A movie in the school has the value of instruction, and also a relief from tedium. What a child will enjoy in the schoolroom, he may not enjoy in the theater. In the theater he looks for the absolute enjoyment, in the school he accepts the relative. The settlement or neighborhood house can offer selected films but the theater is *the* locale of entertainment.

But the school can perform a more direct task. Hughes Mearns has suggested education in film art. Inferring from his work in verse instruction, I take it he is concerned with what he thinks are art values. If he has taught his students to avoid the cliché of words, he has led them into a cliché of attitude, much more injurious. The trouble is that Mr. Mearns has wanted his students to be art lovers, rather than to be lovers of sounds first. Mr. Mearns thinks of education in cinema as a way to develop the child's dramatic judgment. But I see it as two things: training in a major contemporary device, and as development in social (not "moral") judgment. I advocate the actual taking of films, beginning with the filming of stationary objects, advancing to the filming of moving objects, proceeding to the filming of moving compositions of objects, and on to the filming of animate things — directing the interest to the task rather than to the sentiment, a mechanical arts, shop course, graded from the visceral to aesthetic discernment, at about the time the child has advanced to that appreciation. The concentration upon the mechanism would lead the child to look for the mechanical base in the films he sees at the theater, thereby diluting the effect of the inimical content. But this is an indirect result of the instruction. The content of the film should be officially recognized in courses dealing with the film as a current topic with free opportunity for the expression of opinion, reserving to the teacher the tool of Socratic stimulus — to be used in calling to the surface the ritualistic suggestions of press, fan magazines, ads, films, rumors. The relating of fact to fancy *within the experience of the child* would stimulate the critical judgment of the child to a reappraisal of the misleading illusion. It would not need to be violent. The influence would arise from the simple relationships within the experience. The child would be encouraged to make his own deductions. We are attacking the evil influence and not the child. What is meritorious within the film would gain special force through propulsion within the relating of fact to fancy.

FILMS,
November, 1939
(*Published Posthumously*).

THE RITUAL OF THE MOVIES

I would like to describe the motion picture as the major contemporary ritual, and I do that not to be high sounding, but to define the characteristics of the movie as we know it.

Professor Morris Cohen, of City College, New York City, once said that baseball is our religion today. I take exception to that, because though the baseball spectator has long been called the fan, he is, in a sense, a critic of sport. There is almost no baseball fan so-called who does not know the game, and when he goes to the baseball game, though he may be an enthusiast and may lose his head, nevertheless he knows a good play when he sees it and he knows a good play on the enemy's side as well as on the side he is cheering, and that is a characteristic which the movie fan does not possess. The movie fan is strictly a fan, the word fan being an abbreviation of fanatic. So that we have at the bottom of the hierarchy, the laity, the fan.

The moving picture industry has done everything possible to intensify the ritual itself but not the work of art. In the building of these large temples and cathedrals—and I say they are rightly called temples and cathedrals—everything has been done to merchandise the show. The money changers are in the temple. What have they done in the last few years? Have they improved the pictures? They have done things to the stage show which is part of the ritual. They have done things to the basement: into the women's room there may have been introduced a Helena Rubinstein demonstration of preparations, cosmetics; in the men's room there may have been set up billiard tables and demonstrations of golfing;

and there may have been needle swallowers and a gentleman playing the piano. In the upper regions there may have been quartettes and quintettes making chamber music. And always, of course, there are the ushers in their armor. Everything has been done to inveigle the audience, and it is my contention that not until the audience ceases being a part of the ritual does it become an audience. In a ritual there is no audience because the fan is part of the ritual. The observer has no objective attitude towards the thing that is going on. That is what has happened in the movie, and not only in the larger theaters, but also in the smaller ones, where premiums are handed out. The ten cent movie house on Third Avenue hands out dinnerware premiums. As attractions these are means of bolstering the boxoffice; as influences they inveigle the audience. The film on the screen has remained much the same.

The movie is at present constructed to be momentarily effective, and even when major ideas are carried the result is usually a momentary result. But take a film like *I Am a Fugitive From a Chain Gang,* probably the best film in a long time from Hollywood, were it not for the last moment the film would not be memorable. That saved the film in the memory of the audience and made everything that went before it remembered. This very seldom happens in motion pictures, that an incident can be retroactive. Try to think back to pictures that had important subject matter, and see if they are memorable in your mind. You will find it very difficult to remember motion pictures for their point, for their idea, because they are so built as to simply assure a response from the audience at the moment, and that is, by the way, to my way of thinking one of the reasons audiences are not coming back to the movie theatres. We are all, in our way, philosophers — I will put in quotation marks — "quasi-philosophers, pseudo-philosophers" — but the very fact that we have proverbs existing proves we like to make deductions, and when individuals go to a movie they like those movies, which seem to give them what they call an idea, philosophy, a thought.

For instance, I do not object to the horror film because it is horrible. As a matter of fact, most of the time it is not horrible; it is funny, because when you give to vague notions concrete forms you make them ridiculous. My objection to the horror film is that it does not stress the possible, even psuedo-idea in it. I remember going to see *Dr. Jekyll and Mr. Hyde,* one of the best as far as construction is concerned. I sat next to a young man who all through the antics of Mr. Hyde kept on saying, "Hully gee, gee!" He could not grasp it. He knew there was something meant, but the exaggeration so overrode the idea of dual personality that finally he went out. I walked out with him, watching him. He was sorely perplexed, but he could not associate in his mind the antics with any notion that he was after. And that is why after a time horror films do not attract audiences or a film like *The Island of Lost Souls* does not have much of a response from the audience.

In the whole aspect of the ritual, as I have said, you really eliminate the audience, and that is one of the things that the movie wants to do, it wants to eliminate the audience, wants to make he audience uncritical. But what has happened in the last years?

Conditions being what they are, people have become a little more skeptical, they do not fall for certain things, and even the industry itself has realized that it has no longer a uniform audience. It can not say that even a Tom Mix picture will have a uniform audience as it has had in the past. It has a split audience reaction and it is afraid of it. At first it was very much afraid of it, indeed, so much afraid of anything resembling disagreements of the audience that one company sent out a dictum to its house managers to eliminate from newsreels any clips that might remotely resemble Bolshevik propaganda, and they meant by that the elimination of any scene of a bread line, because they were afraid of audience reactions. The reaction occurred once during the showing of a clip on prohibition and one of Mussolini, where the audience reacted the opposite way.

Where you have a ritual you will eventually have cults, and the cults may arise from two sources. They may arise from dissent with the ritual or they may arise from the exaggeration of certain points in the ritual. One of the first cult tendencies came from France. After the War the young men of France, some of them who went in for film production, some critics, some writers, began to view the movie again, and they were displeased with what they called the shop-made film and they began the Film Club. Among the individuals was one who went under the name of Canudo who is now dead. I have called him the missionary of the film-as-art. He was enthusiastic, he loved the movie. There was another man, Poirier, one of the finest of the French directors; another the late Louis Delluc, really the pioneer in the new French forms, and another was Moussinac, a critic. They formed the first Film Club. From the first Film Club many have derived. In France itself in 1929, when I was there, there were probably a dozen by various names, some of them fantastic affairs to which people came simply to have fights, where they would debate the merits of the particular film shown. There the young Frenchmen, who always like to squabble, could get up and call the others names. I remember one incident where one man got up and said not only was the picture rotten but the piano player was just as bad. Actually what evolved was either this kind of vandalism or the tendency to create the cult.

We have had cults in America, the cult of *Caligari,* for instance. I agree with Moussinac that this film is a date and not a milestone. There have been other cults. The French began the Charlie Chaplin cult. They went into the special cult, which may amuse Americans, of the art of the American film. The favorite picture in France today, the favorite artistic film, is generally an American one, and what we consider here trash, aesthetically or ethically reprehensible, will be exhibited in Paris as art. There was a picture *A Girl in Every Port,* a Victor McLagen picture. There were some young and lovely women in the film and the picture was clever and well timed, so it became an art film, and in one of the leading highbrow periodicals in Paris there was a review in which Victor McLaglen was called *"un grand artiste."* Anyone who knows him knows he is only and always Victor McLaglen. This sort of exoticism is in the French Film Club, and we have the same attitude here in America toward the foreign product.

The film club came to America not as the film club. It was carried over in its diluted form, the little cinema.

What happened in those places in America "dedicated" to the little cinema? We had one cult, the Ufa cult. All the films from the studio of Ufa – which in early days produced films like *The Last Laugh,* still one of the greatest pictures ever made – were called art in America. Finally even the critics got wise to it, so that they began to pan the little cinemas. Today we can hardly speak of them as little cinemas; they are houses showing foreign products, sometimes good pictures. Nevertheless, we can accredit the little cinemas for introducing to American audiences some of the leading films that have been made which otherwise would never have entered America.

I may say also for the film club that a great director, perhaps not great, but certainly important, René Clair, the young Frenchman, is decidedly a product of the film club movement.

The film club has come into America and that is what concerns us. The film club has come into America as a growth of the original film club idea – for instance, the Film Forum and the Film Society, and as a member of both I consider them from the same standpoint, not by what they are doing so early in their careers, but what they must do if they are to observe the organic principle of the film club, and that is, that the film club has its ultimate justification only when its recognizes itself as an educational forum. That is why I am justified in bringing the film club into this discussion. I want to oppose in this discussion the cult idea of the film club, where gentlemen and ladies in high hats and evening gowns are shown Mickey Mouse to satisfy their sense of the exquisite. I oppose also the Messianic film cult which thinks that the movie is a thing absolute and apart, that has no relation to other arts or has no relation to life. We have had much writing in which the whole tendency is to say that the movie is pure when it has no relation to anything else. We have to fight both the populist cult and the Messianic cult. The movie is not going to save the world and we are not going to save the movie, but we have certain functions to perform, and through the film club we may realize the conception of the movie, whether entertainment or instructional or educational, because it is a medium of propaganda and influence.

I would say, then, that the film club is to the audience generally what the critic is to the spectator; that is, the film club provides the critical audience. But I do not want it to end there.

I have no feeling for, no faith in the film club, in the esoteric film club, which wants to remain apart from the general problem of the motion picture. That is why I rather dislike the idea of such high rates being asked for membership in these organizations, but the situation at present makes it necessary in order to pay the expenses.

In London there is the largest of all film clubs, the London Film Society, and the London Film Society has been influential because its audiences number some two thousand, which is already a mass audience, so to speak, and that was possible in London because of the absence of Sunday afternoon showings so that people could come to showings of the Film Society. The influence was through the large membership, and eventually theaters began to take the films recommended by the Film Society. Also, the Film Society through its efforts weakened the political censorship, so that certain important Russian films like *Potemkin* and *Mother* were able to be shown to general audiences.

The film club has to correlate its programs in two directions, the aesthetic and the social. In the aesthetic direction it has to take part in the history and evolution of the motion picture. That is why sometimes it is important to show pictures which may not be today so entertaining, but which are important in what they have contributed to the history of the film.

Then, in the social direction, it must correlate the movie with the manifestations of society. Therefore, in the end it must show those pictures which are important to what is occurring in society, and I, for one, though I am supposed to be a critic of art, maintain that purpose is the more important, the social purpose. I say otherwise the film club is nothing but a high-hat affair and no art can be furthered by being isolated in exclusive circles. That is why I am interested in what has been begun in the way of these Motion Picture Study Clubs, in the Better Films Councils, because the tie-up with the community is present.

NATIONAL BOARD OF REVIEW
MAGAZINE,
May, 1933.

THE CHILD AS PART OF THE CINEMA AUDIENCE

Since the film club, as a force in audience building, is in principle educational, it is related to the problem of the child and the cinema. But this problem of the child and the cinema is not a problem in itself; it is only one of the problems of the child in relation to society.

We cannot hope to solve the problem of the child and the movie until we solve the problem of the child and society, until there are fundamental changes in society in relation to the child, and, of course, the major change we have to make is to break down the wall of ambiguity and hypocrisy that exists between society and the child. We do not want children to see certain things in the movies, but what are we doing about those things in society? The movie is nothing but a reflection of society.

For five years I was director of a children's play village in Philadelphia, a very interesting experiment. It was in the very worst section of Philadelphia, the worst slums, the red light district, the center of the dope industry of America, in the hooch neighborhood, where I have seen many a man go blind in the early days of prohibition. These children were (and still are, I assume) very sophisticated in their knowledge of vice. That does not mean, however, they were not still children, because a child does not anticipate his experience. The child only knows what he experiences, and while he may be abnormal or adult in certain things, he is still a child in other ways.

Into this work I took my own principle, which is that everything in education begins with the child. You do not begin with *Ivanhoe*; you begin with the child and you bring *Ivanhoe* in in relation to the child.

And one of the experiences of the child, the most intimate one perhaps of all his experiences, is the motion picture. I used to start with the motion picture and the comic supplement of the Sunday paper. And I did not care how bad they were. There were some objections, but I said, "This is the beginning. We are not going to start by asking the child to make wedges for rattling windows, about which he doesn't care in the least. We are going to start with the thing the child cares most about." We began and I learned many things about the child and the movie. For instance, I learned that what we think a child ought to like is not what the child likes. That is very obvious, nevertheless it had to be learned.

Chang, for instance, was a very fine picture. Ordinarily we would say children would like it. The children I have met with were rather representative, they came from various nationalities, various age groups, from different levels of life — that is, they came from the pauperized class, from the unskilled laboring, the skilled laboring, or from families of storekeepers in the neighborhood — and I found the children did not like *Chang.* I wanted to know why.

Well, first, "It is just an animal picture." That is funny, they did not like an animal picture. Maybe it was because they lived in close areas and animals became something they had to kick around. There are multitudes of such children in this country and they are increased as conditions get worse.

They did not like *Chang* because there was no central hero that they could recognize; they did not recognize their stars. That is an influence of the ritual. It is not something intrinsic in child psychology, but the influence of having seen certain actors in single type roles all the time. And there were other incidental reasons.

When I spoke about Chaplin I said, "I like him." They said, "You are silly. He is so silly, so foolish." They became my superiors, my grownups. I said, "Whom do you like?" Harold Lloyd was the child's comedian. Film after film we discussed, and they liked those films which we consider films not for children.

The point I want to make is that we have got to study the child and not the motion picture first if we are going to know the relation of the film to the child, and I do not think we can do it by surveys only, because something happens to the child when he answers questions on paper. When there is no intimate responsible relationship between him and the questioner he often becomes a liar. Even though it may not be in the schoolroom, he rather likes to answer as he would like to think you would want him to answer. There is something the matter with an educational system that makes children that way, but it is so. You get such answers—I know, I have gone to school; I know I have answered in college papers according to the professor because it means a good mark. English was always my good subject and I always got a very high mark. My only low mark, a mark that was below what I expected in English, that I ever received was from a professor who took off a number of points because I did not put in everything he had said in his lectures on that particular subject. I had my doubts about them so I left them out. He did not like that, so he marked me down. That happens with the younger child even more so; he is less assertive.

The only thing I can say is that only through the most intimate relationships with the child, where the child feels a real faithful relationship—that he will not be betrayed by the questioner, that he does not have to hide something—is it possible to get the child, and it was possible in this play village institution where I taught because the child did not have to come to it. He came after school hours as a relief from school; in fact, he was wilder than ever because he came from school where he had been held in check. We would get not only honest objections, but sardonic and cynical, his angriest reactions even at times; and there I came to these conclusions:

I said you cannot solve the problem of the child in relation to the film unless you solve his problem in relation to society. We are not going to solve that problem very soon. There are fundamental changes necessary before that problem is solved. The only way I can see it is again through certain educational means.

It is pretty well agreed that the motion picture is a pedagogical instrument. I do not have to discuss the merely mechanical aid that the movie can supply to the instructions of the teacher. I am thinking now of the movie *per se* as a subject, and for some five years now I have been urging that the motion picture be incorporated as a subject in schools—that is, in two ways: first, as a manual art, where a child can understand how a motion picture is made, and even make films; and secondly, as a course in current topics, whatever title is given to such subjects in schools.

I do not stress as yet the aesthetic because children do not begin by being aesthetic in their reactions. For instance, in relation to verse, they begin by reacting to sounds. They take my first name and they say, "Harry ka-Parry." I have objected, for instance, to Hughes Mearns' work with children, where Hughes Mearns wants to destroy the verbal cliché. I say let the child have his clichés of language. The child *should* say "white as snow." What do you want him to say? Why shouldn't he use clichés when he is 10 or 12? Is it better that he should have clichés of attitudes and language affectations than those elementary clichés? When a young child says, "The moon was a battered dishpan" it may sound very unusual, but to me it is very definitely a cliché of attitude; it is a borrowing from certain types of modernistic verse which no more belongs to the child than other experiences that are remote from him. Let him like these stereotype things, but let him understand gradually. Teach him what is the mechanism of his reaction, and that can be done, I think, in two ways in a movie. Let him study; let him be taught how to make movies. Why should he be taught how to hammer horse shoes when we do not have horses any more and not taught the movies which are so much a part of his life?

In my own work with children I did this: they were going to see a film, *Camille,* with Norma Talmadge. I did not say to them, "Don't go to see that picture," because I knew they would go anyhow, even if they had to sneak in. So in advance of the film I said, "Look in the picture. You will see two things are going to be done." For instance, there was one scene where Fred Niblo used stationary photographs for his effect. I said, "Look for that. Then you will see in the picture also, instead of having a man go through all the details of taking off his clothes and putting on his clothes, they simply have him go this far with his jacket and then go on," which was one of the first attempts at eliminating the unnecessary transitions.

They went to see *Camille* and I asked them how they liked it. Many of them had not seen the picture because they were looking for effects, but in looking for these technical things their pleasure was enhanced through their particular experience at the motion picture theatre that day, without accentuating the sexual suggestion.

In the social treatment the method to pursue is to have the child relate, with assistance from the teacher, the fancies of a film to the facts of his own experience. What does he see in the picture? Can he extract from the film the truth or the falsehood? I think that can be taught.

We know that children have grown up with the films. In growing up with films there has been developed the individual who is movie conscious. That is to say, there are many, many young people who want to make films, and I am not thinking of the children who want to be Greta Garbos or Clark Gables, I am thinking of those children who really want to make pictures, want to direct, want to act, want to write scenarios. There is no provision made in our society to instruct these young people. Well, they are going to take care of themselves until such a thing takes place; they are going to form amateur groups, which at present are a bad imitation of

Hollywood. Or there is an organization which perhaps has a firmer base, the Workers' Film and Photo League where young men and women go out and make records of labor events. They are not remarkable works of art, but I think they are important as beginnings.

What are we going to do for these movie-minded young people? We must establish out of this whole educational pattern from the early days, a program by which they are taught movies in the manual arts and movies in the social subjects. Gradually they will take the movie up in its refinements of art and then they will be taught direction. There must be established universities of the cinema. The only ones of the kind that I know of today are in the Soviet. There they found it necessary to make the movie organic with their life, and to stimulate a sure, steady flow of new talents into the production.

Today the young man who wants to make films, or young woman – young women especially, there is only one female director in Hollywood, Dorothy Arzner – cannot reach Hollywood. Some of them are too sensitive to pull the necessary strings; some of them do not have family connections, and they are having a drive to get in. Hollywood is so far away. But shall they be kept down? There must be a way provided. Several months ago I drew up a tentative plan for such a possible system where degrees will be given so that the parents may be satisfied that the children who go to the school of cinema may get an A.B. degree; may even get a Ph.D. The school will teach not only the motion picture, it will teach also the necessary subjects of history, history of the motion picture, the fine arts, aesthetics, sociology, languages.

I will give you an instance of the University of Cinema in Moscow. There they teach cameramen chemistry, physics, and they teach German as the language; to the directorial students they teach English as the language because they believe that American direction has offered more in the way of direction than foreign. They teach English, the history of art, economics, sociology and scenario writing.

Now, with the establishment of such courses we may have a career for those who have grown up from audience relationships to critical and creative relationships – I give this as a sort of beginning and end for a body that may prove the vanguard for the movie audience.

National Board of Review
Magazine,
June, 1933.

FILM CULTS

The mass movie-fanatic is a part of a grand ritual. He does not specialize in the adulation of the rudimentary. That is left to the élite, the effete, the intelligentsia of cinema. As far back as 1910 a lone American crusader for movie as against theater based his defense of the former on its ability in melodrama, that agent of moral absolutes. Today, after a multitude of cults of single films, single personalities, products of certain studies, we find the aesthete raising movie melodrama to the summit of the movie's province. Actually the graph of enthusiasm has long ago reached its climax and now is about where it was at its point of origin. Film cultism had its inception in France. There it began, however, with more earnest zeal as dissent from the popular ritual. It might have materialized into actual guidance had it not deteriorated through propinquity to Dadaism, the cult of dissociations. The super-refined lads of the salons found their paradise in William S. Hart and Pearl White's smile, "that almost ferocious smile announcing the upheaval of the new world." Chaplin was the key cult, and although the brightness of his talent has dimmed, and he has never given us the quixotic film towards which his early pictures points, the cult still persists with a vengeance in Europe, and its echoes are dull but present in America.

About 1917 the echoes began to shout loud in America. We were propelled into cults of the slapstick or "churlish" comedy, especially of Mack Sennett, whose cult is still alive in France and in Gilbert Seldes. France had no experience of the American movie prior to 1917; she discovered it in that year (the year of America's entrance into the war) and

Bill Hart, Pearl White, Charlie Chaplin became the tin gods of the aesthetes. The resonances motivated the American boys of delight. They began to write with seriousness, if not with critical insight, upon the rudimentary film, such as the serial *The Girl and the Game,* a railroad thriller, *The Exploits of Elaine,* with Pearl White. The most namby-pamby love-films were considered as exalted art. The boys were trying strenuously to reconcile the hostile environment with their sensibilities, and, in doing that, they became disproportionate populists. That was the era of machine-worship, to be followed by its equally hyperbolic reaction, machine-rancor. The aesthetes were thinking archaeologically, in terms of the major tool, and not, as contemplation of a social phenomenon demands, sociologically. Otherwise they might have seen the true nature of their object of worship. Or, had they been less academic, and looked into the film as a form of evolution, they might have been less content to idolize it at its primitive source.

And along came Charlie. "Charlie Chaplin has freed the moving pictures from the morons. This was easy for him because he is a poet. Poetry is a more violent acid than any other known acid. Its presence ruins the richest, the most powerful combinations, demands totally new beginnings." Chaplin did give a push to the comic film, but for the American comedy the push was a little off the right path, and Chaplin himself has trailed too far away from his original relevant mood. It is difficult to know today the point of his later works, with their overdose of maudlin pathos. He has developed much in aimlessness and directorial looseness. The enthusiasts have failed to see that in their eulogy of Chaplin the personality, the *raconteur,* they are actually offering a negative. A film is a whole, and the whole is greater than any of its parts, including Chaplin. Chaplin the personality has been up until lately generally successful, but the film of Chaplin has not always been realized. Eisenstein has said he likes most that Chaplin film where Charlie is everywhere yet nowhere, namely *A Woman of Paris,* one of the few American films expressive of a new principle of direction. In his last picture, *City Lights,* the first few moments are the peak. The remainder is an unleavened procession, now and then enlivened with a brief episode, a gag of quality. The film does not seem to proceed by its own motility. Its major motif, the relation between the millionaire and "the classic hobo," becomes subsidiary to the minor motif of the blind girl and Chaplin. The author-director-producer-star has weakened. He has fallen very far beneath the indications of *The Kid,* its social satire, its insistence on the major relationship, as against the formula romantic relationship. Reinhardt will continue to insist that

Chaplin is the beginning and end of the cinema. What a "fixation!" The quasi-philosopher will find Chaplin the epitome of "the American Mind." Commentators will re-hash Chaplin's data. Popular writers will stress over and over again the nature of Chaplin as a man of moods. The muckraking columnist and pseudo-critic will take the opportunity to rush in a few doubts, mostly slander. But honest fundamental criticism of Chaplin as a digit of the motion picture, placing the motion picture above Chaplin, and society above the motion picture, will be disregarded.

In France, among the young *cinéastes,* looking for new fields to furrow, there has been an agitation to dethrone Chaplin. In order to do this a new tin god was to have been erected. Harry Langdon was to have been that fetish. But the American movie being less than its most gifted comedian, Langdon has found no film and no director to sustain him. No film-person has recognized in Harry's talkie-technique the only personal contribution to speech-as-sound made by an actor. Yet Langdon did, in his few shorts, introduce a verbal pattern paralleling his pantomime, a contribution which Chaplin has avoided. The French *cinéastes* have deserted Langdon for the four Marx Brothers, of whom only Groucho has a personal inventiveness. The *cinémas* of Paris specializing in American compounds are the new base for the Parisian cultism that looks to America for its fetishes.

That was in the days of the "little cinema," which began as an idealistic boycott of the shop-film. The cult *par excellence* of the little cinema was *The Cabinet of Dr. Caligari,* which still persists in the dreams of *arts-decoratifs*-minded "cinema-goers." Especially is this true in America, and even more especially in England, where the young men of Grub Street have only in the last few years discovered the cinema. They have followed the Old Lady of Threadneedle Street in her devotion to the lowly democratic art. Only gigolos follow old ladies. In 1927 the English critic was uncovering the western "horse opera" as "art," just ten years too late. And *Caligari,* long ago rightly called a date by the more conscientious French critics, is still pinnacle. *Caligari* may have hinted at a principle of integration, but it was certainly not an example to be followed. And it was not, save by the poseur reveling in banal fantasy.

The influence of a cult does not end with the cult itself. A residue may deposit itself in the recesses of an *atelier* to mingle with the dust and agitate less vivid senses to recreate the object of the cult. Years after France has given us the best of machine films, *Ballet Mécanique, Of What Are the Young Films Dreaming,* etc., and has shown us the best films where water is the subject-matter; after Soviet Russia has proven the validity of these instructions by incorporating them into human dramatic films (thereby invalidating them as forms in themselves) along come the American faddists presenting a program of machine and water films. And moreover, when the day of the separable musical accompaniment, the chamber concert, has passed; when even the little cinemas of Paris, that once encouraged the small unit orchestra playing to the film, have installed the mechanical medium, the faddists, too late, taking such a music-movie association unto themselves, applaud what they see and what they hear as achievement. And the films, mark you, have just been made here in the United States and stamped as "original." Fortunately, this inept stuffed-shirt affair can never be more than a family gathering, where the proud relatives inflate the precocious scion.

The main film cult, however, seeks identity (thereby comfort) with popular taste, and not with the recalcitrant or rebellious element in that taste beginning to make itself felt. Hence it builds melodrama to an ultimate category, and says that is what belongs most to the movie, that is what the movie does best. For "best" read "easiest." This melodramatic cult concentrates itself in some personality, a film or individual. It defends its position on the ground that in a movie it is the treatment and not the material that counts. This attitude must be fought as a form of intellectual selling-out. The movie is more than a "passing amusement." And deceptive platitudes limiting it to the snobbery or laziness of the cultists must be exploded. To explode it, the non-populist, non-cultist intellectual must join with the rebellious section of the popular audience in demanding a respect for a more substantial point of view.

The cultist mind abhors all discussion of theme, yet will categorize certain material as not movie stuff, and other as pre-eminently movie stuff. Anything in life is stuff to the film, given the mind that can handle it. And that includes literature. The Swedes made honorable pictures of Selma Lagerlöf's novels: that as expressing their life at its highest consciousness.

The most powerful of cults at the moment is the *Mickey Mouse.* I do not wish to be ungrateful: Mr. Disney has contributed a pleasurable bit to the screen, particularly at a time when the short film is moribund. But to exaggerate the repetitions and duplications of the Disney idiom as colossal or pace-setting is to thwart the progress of a form, the animated cartoon, which is still lisping. Indeed, it is this conception of the animated film as a "cartoon" in motion which refuses to see that Disney both in *Mickey Mouse* and *Silly Symphony* has only reiterated first statements. A comparison with the more varied Soviet animation or "multiplication" film will indicate the first statements as: a graphic that is not much more than a scrawl, line-contours with an occasional dull wash for setting, a lycanthropy with a bit of puerile sophistication, an absence of a pointed, developing narrative-idea, an unoriginal turkey-in-the-straw musical motif, "perpetual motion." On those rare occasions when the Disney cartoon emits a fresh yipe, we may get an inkling of the further possibilities of this medium. There is too much gag in the Disney film and not enough idea. Not to indicate this, but to say instead, as Diego Rivera has preposterously asserted, that Mickey Mouse will be the American personality of our generation to carry himself into our future national consciousness, is to be a foe to the very thing being eulogized.

This cartoon cult is not new. Seldes has continued his precious kowtowing before the newspaper strip. And several years ago, the British poet-novelist, Robert Nichols, advanced with great temerity — so he thought — the notion "that the theoretically ideal cinema-picture is of the type of the motion picture cartoons" (such as *Felix, the Cat*). This is a kind of cult of the child. The critic, knowing little or nothing of previous writings on the film, its cult-history, avoiding the contemplation of the intrinsic film, its future, retreating from any examinations of the basic evils frustrating the advance of the movie, and perishing to be at one with the easy-going movie fan, persists in the adoration of the infant cartoons. Cults are never self-critical. And being never self-critical, they are never objective. So that when they do turn on the idol of their creation, it is not a progressive act but an act of treachery.

MODERN THINKER AND
AUTHOR'S REVIEW,
November, 1932.

HOLY HOLLYWOOD

"In the valley of the Cahuengas" lies the Holy City, "God's Country, land of sun flowers," where it was "easy to close one's eyes and dream—dream of a past which is a fuel to flitting shadows and fancies as the day with its ever-changing lights, as the songs of the birds with those endlessly varying notes and trills." 1905 dreams thus of 1769—in 1931 this is still part of the "poésie" of Hollywood, though by now somewhat rancid. Like all Holy Cities, Hollywood is also a Mythical City. The myth is sung in cinema, and the picture of the city in the visions of the world is not single but various: the Sodom of America or the Paris of America. Paris, in our nostalgic chauvinism, is modern capital of exquisite corruption. And Hollywood is "the capital of cinema," "the Mecca," the Rome. It is the city of the modern pilgrimage, the goal of the new Luther. The mixed picture of the mythical city agrees with the multiple image of contrasts that is America in the eyes of the world—and her own.

A flamboyant tract, "Hollywood's Alibi," an extract from "The Ripening Harvest," amid amazing descriptions of art and the artist, makes a statement of whose full critical truth its authors are hardly aware. "Hollywood," they say, "is symptomatic of a general condition. Hollywood's alibi is America's alibi." The alibi is undersigned and okehed by the appraisers of sin. "It is no shame to America that she is a nation of neurasthenics! Those blots on her reputation are in reality the scars of conquest . . . her overstrain, her perfervid exertion. . . ." This aphorism adorns the tract: "Out of putrid matter the fairest flower may bloom." The cinema is cleared of sin by these optimists, and given an absolute status in the annals of art, "because, for the first time in History, Art has attained the status and dignity of an Industry." Jesse Lasky calls the movie an art-industry. The hyphen purifies art. The pamphleteers conclude emphatically: "And Hollywood is synonymous with America."

Hollywood is the pimple of the American process, just as America is the pimple of the capitalist process. The process in either case is at the blind wall of an impasse. America is vested interest: Hollywood is vested interest. America is ultimate concentration: Hollywood is ultimate concentration. America is frustration: Hollywood is frustration. Hollywood is epitomé.

America is boom: Hollywood is boom. The boom of self-conceit, called prosperity, has drowned the threats of collapse. The boom of publicity resounds to obscure the cries of help, as theaters close, employees — artistes as well as bureaucrats and white-collar slaves — are discharged or have their salaries cut. Hollywood has identified herself with the illusions of perpetuity, however ephemeral her indiscretions called movies. The initial reason for her existence no longer abides. Sven Gade, a Danish director who has left Hollywood behind, has said that the movie no longer needs the sun of the heavens but that of a diversified community.

In aboriginal Hollywood reigned Chief Cahuenga. About 1770, a half dozen years before England lost its American colony, the Spanish padre Junipero Serra came along and preserved "the valley of the Cahuengas," today the name of the main thoroughfare that intersects the Hollywood Boulevard and the Pass that leads into San Fernando Valley. An historian (publicity writer for a bank) smirks upon the "comic opera" Spaniards that overran Hollywood before the Great Migration of "stars." Evidently it was small beer compared to the super-comic-opera Hollywood of today. And what has given him the figure of speech if not the movie itself? The Spaniards ousted the Indians, the Yankees ousted the Mexicans, and the motion picture ousted them all. Why doesn't Hollywood make a movie about its history — there's "Greek" George who was brought in from Smyrna with his camels to serve as transportation through the southwest deserts. There's Tiburcio Vasquez, the bandit who robbed Yankees to avenge his Mexican honor. It is said that the American he robbed visited him on his deathbed. But come to think of it, hasn't that romantic buncombe been treated a million times in the film — "the good bad man" of vicarious fiction. And so has the fable of the Senora who horsewhipped an American land-grabber, only — the land-grabber isn't called by his true name, and he wins the dame. Always the molasses to sweeten the lie. The popular commentators like Herb Howe call it "romance." Everything is halcyon in Hollywood — according to the rumors of press agents.

The development of Hollywood from the Indian playground to the Mexican "land of cactus" to $1.25 an acre government ground is interesting enough but typical in a virgin land. The cynical Herb Howe edges the "romance" a bit by adding to his tale of how Hollywood got its name the remark "Hollywood started faking as an infant." And here's how: "In 1883 Mr. and Mrs. H. H. Wilcox arrived in Los Angeles from Topeka, Kansas, with their Arab horses, Duke and Royal, and their Negro coachman, Sam. Mr. Wilcox, a cripple, enjoyed taking long drives through Cahuenga valley. He was attracted particularly to the ranch of apricots and figs located on the land which John Bower had sacrificed for $1.25. He moved a farmhouse onto the land and took up his residence there. Mrs. Wilcox perfected a process for drying the figs that made them famous.

"On a trip East, Mrs. Wilcox met a woman on the train who spoke glowingly of her English estate, Hollywood. Mrs. Wilcox liked the name and, when she returned to her ranch, she posted it over her gate. Mr. Wilcox, feeling a bit sheepish no doubt, imported two English holly trees to justify the name. He planted them by the gate, but they perversely died." There is something prophetically symbolic in this. What happened to other imported trees: Stiller, Leni, Murnau . . . Seastrom? And this reminds me of an exchange of wit between an American young woman and Eisenstein. "Everything," said the American, "that you find in Hollywood is imported—even the trees." "Yes," said Eisenstein, "and even the directors."

Exotic Hollywood of the cinema was anticipated in the Hollywood of pre-cinema. The pre-movie was florescent in Paul de Longpré. M. de Longpré, probably to help his easel-paintings of flowers, built himself a Moorish home with flower gardens. Today Mary Pickford owns a de Longpré. Boon and Boom are one. The Hollywood of 1930 is only a more rococo Hollywood of 1905—in its tone. But a quarter-century of American economy has reflected itself in the mentality of Hollywood. Its legend does not belie its mentality.

In 1904 a camera had shot a picture of an airship in old Chutes Park. In Los Angeles Colonel Selig had a studio in 1908. There he made the first complete West Coast picture, *In the Sultan's Power*. Quite in keeping with Moorish architecture. In 1910 D. W. Griffith came with a Biograph troupe including Mary Pickford, the first Mr. Pickford, Owen Moore, Mack Sennett, Arthur Johnson, since died, Florence Lawrence, Marjorie Favor and Lee Dougherty. Other troupes came during 1909 and 1910 from the east. But these came to Los Angeles. A year later Nestor established the first permanent producing company in Hollywood. More romance, as told in the writing of old Nestor himself, David Horsley:

"The hieroglyphicked monuments of Egypt have, until recently, been accepted as the longest-lived story-telling media known to man, but tablets found among the fossil remains in the Le Brea deposits near Hollywood have been deciphered and they take us further back into history than Cleopatra's Needle.

"The question who discovered Hollywood was being discussed with much heat in 250,000 B.C. A wordy war was being waged between rival claimants for the honor. Each claimant had his own staff of tablet carvers (press agents). These tablets were the motion pictures of that time. The tablets found in Le Brea pits have been deciphered, but the translations cannot be given here as unprintable epithets occur frequently.

"The translations reveal that the noisiest claimant was a young tablet carver who had left the employ of the pioneer to announce to the world that he was the discoverer. The real pioneer finally got sore and told the truth.

"Passing lightly over the intervening years we find a similar situation. . . .

"I came direct to Hollywood and arrived on October 25, 1911. A badly abandoned roadhouse — the old Blondeau tavern — at Sunset Boulevard and Gower Street was the only immediately available site for a studio. I leased the property on October 26 and it became the birthplace of motion pictures as an industry in Hollywood."

The sense of *blague* in this recital must not be considered sport, no more than was the boast of an early American settler sent back to Europe, that "we have the longest rivers and our waterfalls make the loudest noise." The sense of "the world belongs to me" has contributed to the spirit of carefree, if vapid, exoticism that has made the American movie the world's fad and fancy, even today — when that exoticism is festering with the germs of decay. But Horsley's recital, for all its swagger, its feeling that "I have been prophesied through the ages," is the preposterous attitude of self-conceit which has befuddled the American movie time and time again — right now — and America herself. National vanity, national inanity.

The first picture filmed in Hollywood was *The Law of the Range,* directed by Milton Fahrney. Dorothy Davenport, later Mrs. Wallace Reid, appeared in another of that ilk, *My Indian Hero.* Her husband was an extra then. He was destined to be one of the scapegoats of the Hollywood ritual.

By 1912 the Hollywood boom was on, and 1914 may be said to be the real beginning of Hollywood as a capital of the film, and the land of world legend. 1914 saw America's definite ascent to the financial mastery of the world, and the entrance of Jesse Lasky, cornetist and show promoter, with Cecil de Mille into the movie. The film was *The Squaw Man,* which has recently been made as a talkie. Dustin Farnum was the star. The picture was made in a barn. As Herb Howe says: "Cecil de Mille in a barn is a picture incredible. Perhaps it was rebellion against this stable environment that led him to glorify the bathtub and attendant luxuries." From barn to brothel. The showman's road to glory.

I have called Hollywood the new Rome, others have called it Mecca, a third the American Paris, and a fourth: "Hollywood has within it probably the greatest number of highly cultured, world-famous people any city of similar size has claimed since the Periclean age of Athens." The catch is "any city of similar size." Waldo Frank, among other good-hearted men of letters, has said Hollywood is just another normal American city. It is, as we shall see, but not as the apologists suppose.

Ramon Gomez de la Serna has seen Hollywood from the distance of a continent and an ocean, and he has visualized the mythical city so:

"From the distance Movieland looks like a Constantinople combined with a little Tokyo, a touch of Florence and a hint of New York. Not that all of these are jumbled together here, but that each of its districts represents one of them.

"It is like a Noah's ark of architecture. A Florentine palace, seized with the salaciousness which exotic buildings produce, looks longingly at a Grand Pagoda.

"All this is in the heart of the city, in its nucleus of tall buildings. All around it the city spreads out into a thousand little square white houses, like filing cabinets with clear visages. It is a glittering city of seashore bungalows, without a shore.

"Strange panorama, looking like nothing so much as an immense Luna Park!"

Perhaps the delineations of the city are not exact, but it is difficult to find contours in a myth. Yet the fantasy of Ramon is not amiss in so far as the pervasiveness of its aroma is the breath of Hollywood. Atmosphere! The rarefied air of the movie. The delusive odors. We shall have the "smellie" soon. The rustic becomes citizen and builds a swimming pool for a bathtub. He has learned that from the film, and in turn he will carry on the circle. Little boys die and go to heaven. Once dead souls were falling stars. Today they are stars in the firmament of a city of rococo mirage, which dominates the fancies of the world. This is the world-religion. America controls the coffers and Hollywood the mind's eye. Shopgirls wear lace dresses and marry princes. Pedestrian souls, by sycophancy, nepotism and pederasty — paternal virtues — establish the national idea of manhood and womanhood. They buy motorcars to run from the studio to the tennis courts, and tell the directors, the pathetic "creators" of cinema, where to get off. "You can't 'shoot' my back, I get paid for my face," said N. T. to L. M., and the face won. Artists come to this place pretending to hope for the salvation of Hollywood or their own — the latter is recorded in \$. The more poignant and sensitive, not able to extricate themselves from the morass, drool dog-stars or cry destruction. The by-product is paranoia. The fortunate, indifferent to the attractions of activity, report daily to the shop and go out to the links. "In its cafés the most popular movie stars come together, all the great men of that Cinema City whose plebiscites pertain only to the things of the movies."

Before one comes to Hollywood, one is assured of every courtesy. One is "yessed to death," and when that low, one yields to the suasion of the counting-room. Plausible excuses are given. "The technical staff says it can't be done. And, of course, you know, we can't buck the Union." In a popular soap ad. B.O. is "body odor"; in parlance cinematic it is Box Office. The odor from the body politic of cinema, Box Office, is the most emphatic of the incenses of the Holy City. It is not, however, a direct odor. By a subtle mechanism it issues from the protective glands of the dominant class.

The gala sun won for California over Florida. The sun and other bribes. Hollywood was accumulated out of the numerous film localities: New York and the metropolitan area, Chicago, Philadelphia, Nevada, Arizona, Jacksonville, etc. The concentration coincided with the concentration of the small companies into the larger corporations, and the beginning of Wall Street domination. Once started, the centralization went on unimpeded. The too simple-minded opponent was dealt with racketeer-fashion: a mode not limited to the movie, always enjoyed by the movie. Hollywood, zoroastrian paradise, collected the energies of America, of the movie originated in the east. It has not improved upon the movie in its intelligence. Though sun is no longer essential to an art whose instruments are now hypersensitive, the creative center persists thousands of miles away from the critical center of America. Such a separation is in itself disastrous. The separation persists because of two reasons: vested interest in Hollywood, and the lack of an impetus to provoke migrations or new centers. In the Soviet there are many centers throughout the Union. An autonomy of inspiration allowed the various republics assures a diversity of schools of cinema. In America concentration means identity, sterility. The importation of talents is no aid to the liberation of suppressed energies nor to an extension of the art of the movie beyond its rudiments, its folk-rudiments which, not allowed to grow beyond this stage, finding themselves frustrated, threaten to collapse through lack of assertion. The American movie has been in that predicament many times, and has been saved temporarily by a new invention, legitimate if premature, and by artificial stimulation.

Were the movie less ritualistic, less the operations of a vested hierarchy, it might be de-localized. But this would mean that the performer is to live his life of a human being outside of the immediate studio-frame, wherever his extramural contacts are concerned; and the independent artist would be encouraged, in so far as valid ideas are concerned. This is impossible in an economy which resolves its "individualism" into corporate control, where the performing artist — in baseball or film — is private property, where the prestige of this artist is in the hands of his proprietor who may create him as a popular myth or degrade him as a villain. The "star" system is vested interest. Hollywood is the composite city of "stars," the trademarked city of lure, which it pays the producer to maintain for the symbolic value — in money.

Hollywood is maintained, as any Holy City is maintained, as obfuscation. From it the icons issue ordered by the controlling interests. There in the city of the temples are pampered the gay courtesans who bespeak the glory of the faith and the profits of religion. There in the lush live the Harlows of adoration, platinum halos. Evil things occur there — rape, seduction, suicide, murder — as much a product of the age as of the city, though the latter may more virulently, by its exaggerations, incite these. To hush the cry of wrath, from zealots and the envious, a scapegoat is sacrificed, and the evangel purchases the authority of great minds. Fifteen years ago Professor Hugo Münsterberg, under the behest and the subsidy of the film industry, absolved the film as an art. Today Will H. Hays, film evangel, gathers the "organized" bodies of America into a protective screen. The cry of the film as a moral agent is advanced. "The cinema is the enema of sin! The enema of the people! Sin is not the synonym of cinema. The film is Virtue!" I ply here, descriptively, the preposterous trade of the Hollywood wisecracker, "the wizard of wit." Rape shall be committed only by double-entendre. For the preservation of virginity. Murder shall be effected by inference, and liquor drunk through a straw. "Religion is the world's greatest industry," and the movie is the new religion. To the faithful simony is allowed. And to the priest his courtesan. The movie is defended by its simonized disciples as a catharsis: a ritualistic purgative. What it leaves in the body systemic is more vicious than what it sets free. Its function is to free from all the pores the currents of criticism that might ultimately assail consent. They go off as steam. Its function is to obscure all the major issues by calling them profane or by stressing the trivial. Hollywood, created by a sanctuary of the myth, must stress and re-stress the trivial. And Hollywood believes the trivial, however she blow this up to enormity. Hollywood, no matter what the critics within it may say, will not perfect herself through herself. For Hollywood is vested interest. What remains within it too long loses its combativeness, and rationalizes its submission, or shriek rancor ineffectually. Hollywood is normal indeed. Holy Hollywood is Holy America, is the Holy Alliance and Entente of capitalist society. It is the aspiration and criterion of that society. The distance of her Hollywood from her sphere of influence lends her an added authority, just as the distance of America from Europe lends America an added glamor. Things near being what they are in an oppressive society, distance is always enchantment. The Pope is in the Holy See!

in BEHOLD AMERICA,
by Samuel D. Schmalhausen.
(New York: Farrar & Rinehart, 1931).

EUCALYPTUS TREES IN SIBERIA

Boris Pilnyak went to Hollywood and returned perturbed by the "eucalyptus trees in Siberia." More serious matters than horticultural anomalies face us the coming months. Hollywood has become interested in Soviet Russia as subject-matter. Not that revolutionary Russia has not been treated before in the movie with all the impartiality for which Holy Hollywood is famous. Lasky, always in the vanguard of reaction, pulled off *The Last Command* some years ago. And the Fox den has been very engrossed in the affairs of the white guards, as *The Spy* attests. But these were only guerilla attacks, sporadic and with no follow-up. Now we have the war in earnest, according to reports from the general staff of the various studios. To build up just the right tremulous state in the audience, the advance rumors are being circulated that "the cycle of Soviet stories in the offing for studios is bumping into its first snag in the fear of certain writers and executives to become involved with the radical mob." Now, it may be that there are a few scribes on the coast with comparative consciences and relative pro-social instincts. They might have more sensitive nostrils and can smell a rat in a sewer. But the trade's explanation of the disinclination to join in the anti-Soviet racket is that the literary gangsters are suddenly motivated by the "fear that they might displease radical groups and run into trouble." The trouble that they might run into, one executive at a major studio went so far as to say, "this nitroglycerine thrown by this communistic crowd." Yet, in typical Hollywood courage, "several studios are going ahead with plans for Soviet pictures to cash in on the present interest in Russia." Well, they can have the help, I am sure, of such amenable cashers-in as Mother Eve Grady, Karl Kitchen, the gourmet of slop, and Ding Darling.

I don't need to tell you that American film studios are, like the *Literary Digest,* impartial. So, naturally, they "will stick to a middle course, laying off either praise or blame of the Soviet system." But if you've got to compromise, you've got to compromise in favor of some proposition. And Metro, "first to try the Soviet thing, plans to treat communism in its story as a religion," thus being impartial to both the Pope of Rome and the Archbishop of the Greek Catholic Church. One of the potential non-committal advisers is a Russian *émigré* not long over from Paris.

Metro's example has been followed by that eminent follower-up, Laemmle. Universal has bought a story called "Ural," by one "Nevin Brooke," "unofficially reported a fictitious name, the author said to be a woman, not wanting her connection with the story known." "Why not? if the story takes the 'middle course.'" And now Columbia seeks a Soviet writer, probably one like George Agabekoff who has been impartially telling preposterous stories about the G. P. U. for the readers of the most ardent anti-Soviet sheet, *Le Matin,* which wrote its Russian policy a moment after the Bolshevik coup in 1917 in this laconic headline: "The coupons will be paid!" They weren't. . . .

Paramount and Radio are thinking also of filming "modern Russia stories." And "other studios are reported working on such stories privately, the film companies not wanting their plans to get out until the picture is actually in the making to forestall any opposition." The mystery thickens! Nor must we think there is no sentiment of love in this passion for Soviet Russia. It is a nostalgic sentiment, for "Russia has always been a favorite locale for film dramas." The Grand Duke and the Comsomolska marry and one-sixth of the world goes back to the Bank of France. Real hot stuff! "Studios now feel that Russia is still an excellent spot in which to brew heavy plots" — strong tea and moonshine vodka. I submit gratis this nucleus for a picture:

It will tell of a certain relief administrator who halted the shipment of quinine to an epidemic-ridden country, because he was afraid the Reds might overrun America. For a happy ending the studio might invite Gene Tunney to write a denouement of Catholic conversion. The relief administrator falls in love with the daughter of the Czar, they find a miraculous ikon which holds back the revolutionary hordes while thousands of infants are slain by the *"cordon sanitaire."* And then enters Father Edmund Walsh who, in the name of Pope Pius, takes over the property of the Greek Catholic Church, the United Synagogues, the Doukhobortsy, the Skoptsy and the Khlysty. "Chief difficulty to date has been to find writers who can *concoct* the Soviet yarns." The italics are of course, mine. It shouldn't be difficult to find people to "concoct" their white lies — in the interest, you know, of better understanding, between General Denikin and Andrew Mellon. There's Princess Kropotkin, who can advise also on proper manners; Count Ilya Tolstoi, who isn't at all interested in a culture which has paid more fruitful homage to the art of his father than the one from which he and his father sprang; and Rachmaninoff, who might write the prelude to the film intervention.

We have been told that timid writers fear Communist bombs. Well, let us hope that these films will be greeted by demonstrations of workers contradicting the hypocrisies of Hollywood. Here's something for the Workers' Film and Photo League to prepare for! Just as these studios are working on their new field of malice, news also arrives that the steel trust will allow Universal to go on location in a foundry, if the film contains no reference to the labor-capital hyphen. Also, that John D. Sr. has undersigned the scenario of the film on his life, to be called by his Christian name. This is cinemapotheosis indeed! about the first film purporting, without change of identity, to be the life of a living man. There was, of course, a Pancho Villa movie years ago, but it made no pretense of being anything but makeshift. Mr. George Arliss, who looks as cadaverous as old John D., will play the role. Nothing, you don't need to be told, will be said about Ludlow.

NEW MASSES,
November, 1931.

THE EYES OF THE MOVIE

This material was published as a pamphlet one year following Potamkin's death. Put together by Irving Lerner from lectures, scattered notes, excerpts from reviews and articles, it is perhaps the most doctrinaire of the writings attributed to Potamkin. Sponsored by the Film and Photo League, as a memorial, it was published by International Pamphlets in their series of propaganda publications. — Ed.

The movie was born in the laboratory and reared in the counting-house. It is a benevolent monster of four I's: Inventor, Investor, Impresario, Imperialist. The second and fourth eyes are the guiding ones. They pilot the course of the motion picture. The course is so piloted that it is favorable to the equilibrium of the ruling class, and unfavorable to the working class. This is truer in the realm of the film than in the other arts, for the film more than the other arts is the art of the people.

As far back as 1910 a commentator recognized the movie as the entertainment of "the self-respecting petty-bourgeoisie and the working class." In 1916, D. W. Griffith, pioneer director of the film, called the movie "the laboring-man's university." In 1925, a well-known American writer called it "the laborer's art." The commentator of 1910, a Harvard philosopher, asked for a motion picture that would solve all problems for the audience in melodramas of right victorious over wrong — in short, hokum — because "there is no truth in the superstition that it is good for the public to think." He wanted "social stability." And that is what the makers of the movie want today, even though "social stability" means social stagnation.

The owners of this "art-industry" insist that "their" merchandise is merely entertainment, "passing amusement." They point the finger of reproach to the Soviet film, which is straightforward "propaganda," the urging of a positive and persuasive idea. Now, the movie is for the great majority of people the art to which they most impressionably respond. That has been admitted, as quoted in the first paragraph, and by the evidence of the movie's popularity. Most people are eye-minded. The things their eyes see become the things that affect them. The suggestion of the movie, because they are given in active dramatic images that seem real, with recognizable persons in recognizable settings, and because they are repeated in film after film, become the beliefs of the impressionable audience, whose mind receives the suggestions like wax and retains them like marble. The movie is the modern ritual, and though its invitation — its benevolence — is "entertainment," its influence is "propaganda."

The owners of the movie industry know that the movie is "entertainment as propaganda" — in behalf of their class. Statesmen, churchmen and others serving capitalism have been aware of the effectiveness of the movie for reactionary propaganda ever since that art was invented. As far back as 1902, when the movie was just creeping out of the penny arcade peep-show stage, England was already talking about the "Americanization of the world," in which process the movie was assigned an important part. Mention was made of how alert the missionaries were to the possibility of the "kinematograph" as propaganda for Christianity. By 1911, the very élite London journal, *Country Life,* in an editorial wrote that the cinematograph in England "soon became utilised for propagandist work. Missionary meeings were enlivened by moving pictures of the heathen in their blindness bowing down to wood and stone." We see, however, how this same journal in the same editorial gets excited against the film-propaganda of another country, that of the United States.

The movie is the climax to the impressions of other forms of propaganda — school, church, press — and since these are controlled by the same class controlling the movie, the spectator is influenced by one driving class — propaganda implanted in his mind by the decisive impression made by the film. Direct tie-ins of magazines with motion pictures go back to 1912, when the Edison serial film, *What Happened to Mary?* ran in the McClure magazine, *The Ladies' World.* Since then the newspaper, the magazine and the published book have worked hand in hand with the film. We find a capitalist like Hearst powerful in press, film, (His outlets being Hearst Metrotone News, produced by Fox Film Corp. and distributed by Metro-Goldwyn-Mayer and Cosmopolitan Productions, released and distributed by M-G-M. Hearst specializes in making films for Marion Davies and in the so-called political films: the notorious *Gabriel Over the White House* which was serialized in the Hearst press simultaneously with its public release, and *Washington Masquerade* for instance), and radio. The printed word helps to create the atmosphere of romance around the personalities of the players the movie-goer sees on the screen. A glamorous priesthood lures the laity and tells them "all about life." And since the other great industrialized art — the radio — is joined with the movie, the impression is made even stronger. The sound film has made the movie seem more "real." And television, because it will pretend to come direct and untouched from the source, will add to the effectiveness of the propaganda.

To indicate the relative strength of the movie, I quote "from a teacher who overheard two of her high-school pupils discuss the merits of Joseph Hergesheimer's novel, *Java Head*." "One of the girls had read the book, the other had seen the film based on the story. The first referred to the Manchu woman as having given her new light in her conception of the Chinese. But, said her friend, you should have seen her in the movies! She was just like all the rest of them. It's all right to read about them; but I don't like to see them."*

This is the medium that is in the hands of high finance. The independent producer hasn't a chance, except to stick close to the average merchandise. The independent distributor is being pushed out speedily, he is now negligible; and the independent producer is not independent in conscience or courage. He makes "horse operas" — cowboy pictures — fake Africans, cheap sex rot, to edge into a controlled market. By 1917, the popular serial actor and director, J. P. MacGowan, writing in a little-read highbrow magazine, could say: ". . . the day is passed when small capital, coupled with boundless presumption is capable of creating a millionaire overnight. Daily it is becoming more substantially commercialized, which is but another way of saying the conservative element is coming into the ascendant." It would seem that today, with the movie industry at low ebb, an independent might risk a film of more honest subject matter, but the producer, the so-called independent, as well as the movie trust, is part of "the conservative element" — the middle class that is becoming more and more self-protective. Only one independent can offer the necessary challenge: militant labor.

A glance at the composition of this "conservative element" is enlightening. First, there is the producer, who is also, dominantly, the distributor

* [Ed.]: This quote originally appeared in *"The Cinematized Child."*

and the exhibitor. The three-in-one producer is a former small merchant, a manufacturer, a gambler or the like, under financial hegemony. Then there is the director and those pertaining to him, the scenarist, the cameraman, etc. The director, *et al.*, are seldom near to the social experience, the economic life, of the audience who is to be reached and touched. The actor is usually a conceited, glorified upstart without experience, or an actor whose experience in life is framed rigidly by the proscenium arch or the perimeter of the silver screen. Together they express the *nouveau riche* and gross aspirations of "the conservative element." And it is the actor who especially colors the film, since he is the golden trademark of the movie-merchandise. All together they are concentrated in Hollywood, a circle of vested interests whose circumference does not go beyond the perimeter of the screen for a knowledge of life.

In 1914 an independent producer might possibly risk a film sympathizing with the plight of labor. In that year Upton Sinclair's novel, *The Jungle,* was made into a movie. The company that produced it was permitted to go bankrupt. We must not forget also that *The Jungle* has been persistently read down by the middle-class as a tract for pure food, and the middle class has an interest in that. In the very same year, Jesse Lasky, always a leader in the reactionary film, produced *The Only Son,* a film vindicating the strikebreaker and condemning the labor agitator.

Upton Sinclair sold two other stories to the movies. One was an unpublished play, afterwards the plot-within-a-plot of *The Potboilers.* This was turned into a story of a lost will, having nothing to do with the original. Sinclair's novel, *The Moneychangers,* which describes J. P. Morgan as causing the panic of 1907, was sold to a personal friend, Ben Hampton, who bought it with the promise of respecting both letter and spirit. It appeared as a melodrama of Chinatown dope traffic. Sinclair sought to prevent the use of his name, but Pathé had the contracts, and ideas and names are merchandise in the courts of law, if the idea is *The Moneychangers* and the name is Upton Sinclair. (Ben Hampton doesn't mention this incident in his *History of the Movies,* 1931). In 1933, Upton Sinclair steps into Ben Hampton's shoes and refuses to eliminate Eisenstein's name from the distorted version of *Que Viva Mexico,* made by Upton Sinclair and Sol Lesser. See *New Masses,* September, 1933, for elaboration on this point. We have another instance in the case of *An American Tragedy.* Every year Sinclair gets an offer to picturize one of his stories, if he'll "leave out the Socialism." And "socialism" implies, to the American producer, anything that might remotely favor the viewpoint of labor.

In *The Little Church Around the Corner,* the movie definitely asks labor to *believe* in the boss through the church. The scene is set in a mining town. An orphan lad, whose father has been killed in the mine, has an itch for holiness; but he is derided by the villainous boy because he can't effect a miracle on a mute girl. The operator, persuaded by his young daughter, takes the young and frustrated saint under his wing. The boy becomes a clergyman. A delegation of miners calls on the operator demanding safer working conditions. The hard-hearted boss refuses to listen. Since it is only a question of the heart, a way must be found to soften that organ. The clergyman goes back to his people. A cave-in takes place. The clergyman digs in and rescues the entombed men. The church, you see, is the saviour of labor. But the workers want revenge on the boss. "What," cries the young minister, "would you use violence?" Now really. . . . The mute girl, grown older and dumber, stands near him. He prays, she prays. The lips move. My God, she speaks. A miracle! The mute girl speaks and the boss sees the light. The men too. They are convinced. The boss's hard heart is as soft as a woman's now. All is honky-tonky (or is it honky-dory) and hotsy-totsy. Capital and labor embrace. To strengthen the religious appeal, the doughnut-damsels of the S. A. (Salvation Army) stand by to help. The war isn't over yet. . . .

But today the theme of capital-and-labor is carefully avoided. The laborer is either a clown or a romantic swashbuckler who gets the girl — "Should a riveter fall in love with an heiress?" — another gay racketeer hero. In this way labor is cajoled and flattered and diverted from the fact at hand, the fact of struggle. In the farcical comedy it is usually one of the lower classes who is the buffoon. He is a goof, "a classic hobo," "a Christian innocent," who, however, most often, like the "valiant little tailor," wins by the accident of wit at the lucky moment. Of course, the successful class cannot admit its success is entirely luck. It is wit turning accidents into account. So that in effect luck isn't luck at all. Dominance is due entirely to the "divine right" of quick thinking, inspired by the devotion of a pure maiden.

The Negro gets special Jim Crow treatment. He is not new to the American film. Long ago Bert Williams appeared in the movies. Before the war Sigmund Lubin produced all-Negro farces in Philadelphia. They portrayed the Negroes as indolent idiots. It was the film of the Jeffries-Johnson fight, in which the Negro pugilist won, that thrust the Negro out of the movie. The battle took place on July 4, 1910, and was the climax to the bitter racial sentiment that followed upon the panic of 1907.

The southern bosses had seized the opportunity and intensified the breach in the working-class as a way of deflecting the class-attack: a typical strategy. There was the Atlanta railwaymen's race war. In the popular theater, announcement had to be made, on the showing of *Uncle Tom's Cabin,* that "a completely white cast" was playing the Negro rôles. It is only very recently that this perennial has been filmed with Negroes, and then in a genial manner, hardly indicting the white masters of today.

The Negro

There have been films with so-called Negro themes. Years ago there was Edward Sheldon's play, *The Nigger,* filmed as *The Governor.* Pretending to charitable sentiments toward the Negro, it was actually an attack on miscegenation, intermarriage. America's greatest director, David Wark Griffith, son of a Confederate officer, gave us *The Birth of a Nation,* from the Reverend Thomas Dixon's *The Clansman,* which has served, in book and film, as the bible of the Ku Klux Klan! The rise of the twentieth century Klan was inspired by the revival of the picture. And today, when race feeling is so acute in the South, the film is again revived to circulate in provincial towns, as well as cities.

When objection was raised by Negroes and whites to this film, Griffith, behind the barrage of "free speech," issued a pamphlet and a film upon *Intolerance.* He quoted from the press North and South in defense of "tolerance." The Houston (Texas) *Chronicle* said:

"The time has not come when the people of Houston are to have their standards of thought or taste set or fixed or regulated by the Negro citizenship. . . ."

The Negro is treated in the film as an amusement: a clown who sings all the time, dances, shoots crap and men, is dissolute, wields a razor, etc. He is the butt. Even films with children, like the Hal Roach Our Gang comedies, make the Negro child, "Farina," the receiver of the blows. This has a double insidiousness: it abuses the Negro, and it falsifies childhood relationships. If white children accept a Negro child in their play — as Our Gang accepts "Farina" — then the Negro is accepted on equal terms or not at all. Children are not naturally race bigoted. Such sentiment is instilled by adults who are themselves within the influence of a class society.

The southern upper class doesn't want even that much mingling. When the "czar" of the movies, Will Hays, sent out "feelers" to the press, L. F. Hart, reviewer for the Fort Worth (Texas) *Star,* wrote that he "would protest promiscuous mingling of races in such pictures as Hal Roach comedies as Texas has Jim Crow statutes, and intermarriage of whites and blacks is punishable as miscegenation."

Griffith introduced another racial film. His *One Exciting Night,* the parent of mystery farces, has a Negro as the "scary William" of the haunted house. But, since a part is a featured one, Griffith's southern tolerance cannot accept an authentic Negro; he blackfaces Tom Wilson, a white man, for the rôle, adding insult to injury. In his recent film, *Lincoln,* our director employs Negroes in a Roxy setting, but keeps them remotely in the background.

Hallelujah! pretended to be a sincere picture of the agricultural Negro, but it was another revue-film, with all the trappings of the legendary Negro, as white men like to see him. He is held to blame for his own sorrows. He is his own nemesis — with the devil in him. The white exploiter is completely absolved. When this film was shown in New York, the Negro audience was segregated in a Harlem theater — to "keep them in their place."

The whites saw the film on Broadway, the Great White Way. The southern upper crust objected to *Hallelujah!* They did not like this relation of the Negro as "star," and themselves as "customers." The Negro was not ridiculous enough (no "Amos 'n Andy"), a little too romantic for the southern boss, worried by signs of working-class solidarity. It must be noticed that the film took care to avoid Negroes too emphatically black; they had to serve "yaller" Negroes to the sexual pander of the white audience and to the "dignity" of the Negro upper class. No objection was raised by the Negro upper class to *Hallelujah!* as was raised to *The Birth of a Nation.* The former did not offend the class dignity of the Negro élite — it was "so elemental," you know — although it falsified the Negro tenant farmer.

To make the Negro ridiculous, he is put into all sorts of situations that are out of keeping with the particular film. A documentation of a polar voyage intrudes a Negro to be frightened by a bear tightly bound. The animated cartoon contains "black" animals personified invidiously. The news reels have shown Negro boys in battle royals and grease-pole fights, degrading sports, for the amusement of the guffawing Tammany clown, Al Smith. They have relished the demonstrations of frenzied baptisms, which are as common, certainly, among the southern whites as among the blacks. But white baptisms are not shown on the screen.

Negroes have produced films with Negroes as actors. These duplicate white productions. They avoid the real life of the Negro. They do not dare to criticize the society that produces racial antagonism, because that would mean issuing films on the life of the Negro worker as a worker.

The Jew

The Jew has had special treatment, too. He too has been a clown or a sentimentalized scarecrow. In 1912, the American Solax Company, in advertising their film, *A Man's Man,* said: "Up to very recently the stage Jew was the only type which furnished universal amusement. Long whiskers, derby hat down to the ears and hands moving like the fins of a fish. His manhood, his sentiments and his convictions are not burlesqued (that is, not in this film, *A Man's Man*) but are idealized." The Reliance Company produced *Solomon's Son,* so their notice read, "with dignity, minus the burlesque atmosphere usually attending the Gentile's version of a Jewish story." So that between the comic Jews and the idealized Jew there are no gradations. To find the real Jew we must turn to the Soviet film. (The Jew and the Jewish problem has been dealt with in such Soviet films as *Cain and Artem, A Jew At War, Horizon,* and *The Return of Nathan Becker*— the first Soviet sound film in the Yiddish language). We hear no objection to this distortion of the Jew, but when the shoddy film *King of Kings* appears, Jewish upper-class dignity is offended by the portrayal of historic (biblical) characters, and what a lamentation is heard! To these silk-hat Jews Cecil De Mille, the director replies, beating his breast, "Would I insult the Jews? I'm half-Jew myself." And so we get the Negro on the half-shell, the Jew on the half-shell, the worker on the half-shell, as an appetizer for middle-class attitudes.

In the meantime, the film evangel, political decoy, of the Americanned art, Will Hays, in his ambiguous code of the Motion Picture Producers and Distributors of America, Inc., says that "The history, institutions, prominent people and citizenry of other nations shall be represented fairly." Not the foreigner or foreign-born worker in America, God and Wall Street forfend! but only the "prominent people" are to be treated with courtesy, people like an ex-Grand Duke, still called by his title, a Siamese king, a prince of Japan, the Prince of Wales—anyone high-hat enough. The news reel and dramatic picture present him as superfine merchandise. The Swede prisoner in *The Big House* devours all the prison swill that even the moral moron, the American machine-gun murderer Butch, revolts against.

"Give the Public What It Wants"

You see, we need the swell folk. The movie business believes in "Give the Public what it wants!" Which means: "Give the public what we want the public to want!" By "we" in this reference, I mean the dominant class. That oppressive stratum wants the public to react away from certain "prejudices" — they have been dealt with in this pamphlet up to now — and it wants the public to act toward certain illusions, vicarious experiences, distractions, glamorous falsehoods.

The "problem" that may be faced is that of the "restless rich," the love-irritations of those who are born to the purple. The audience is served these films on polished platters as experiences of witty folk, so lucky to have such tremulous heartaches and such easy access to liquor. The agonies of the social register. The Blue Book Blues. The audience feels the thrill of escape from the major problem of reality into a life of fancy which appears real. Repeated succession of such films makes the audience, "the self-respecting petty bourgeoisie and the working class," forgetful of their plight — that at least is the hope of the class serving this dish. As more and more doubt creeps into the audience through the pressure of circumstance and positive radical education, the illusions served will be augmented to overwhelm dissent.

"The Nouveau Riche"

The ideas of the *nouveau riche* are constantly fed the lower class audience. Distance in time, place and experience is offered as enchantment. There is the thriller, the carelessness of the slapstick, the boulevardier comedy of an Adolphe Menjou, the comedy of the glistening high hat. There is approximate rape — the thrill of it, and the compensation — rape with virginity preserved. There is the final kiss, the happy ending; and even the unhappy ending has its compensation, arbitrary redemption, the acquittal of social institutions or the tears of solace. There is the princess and the serving-man, the prince and the serving-maid motif — a cat may look at a queen; "she got her man." There is a good bad man — rural in the wild west film — cosmopolitan in the racketeer picture. The bluffs at exposing racketeering merely hide its basis in our competitive society. There is the picture glorifying the magnate as human: George Arliss in *The Millionaire* — "there's no lace on his underwear." The one picture on the life of a living American is prepared on John D. Rockefeller, Sr. It is to be called by the name of the paragon himself, and he has ok'd the scenario. It is announced on the occasion of the capitalist's 92nd birthday anniversary, when the country's press spends its talents in eulogy, and John D., Jr., writes to one newspaper saying how gratifying it is to know that though "Two or three decades ago he (John D., Sr.) was being bitterly assailed for the alleged predatory tactics of the great oil company with which he was identified; since that time sentiment toward him appears to have undergone a radical change." A reactionary change. The process of bourgeois society is one of vindication, and how well the movie serves it. While the press and the pictures pretend to go thumbs down on racketeering, urging *The Secret Six,* the "vigilantes," to get after the gangster (Pathé has even its news reels serve in this racket), the racketeer *par excellence* is deified.

A number of these self-defense films pretend to be social criticism. We get epic subjects like *The Trail of '98, The Covered Wagon* and *Cimarron* reduced into films that are narratives of attempted rape and the "eternal triangle," personal enmity and personal vanity. We get prison films like *The Big House* that shift the social guilt from society to the individual and from the individual to nowhere. We get *An American Tragedy* that debases a criticism of society to a justification of its vicious process by having justice redeemed—a tragic social document becomes a duplicate murder story and the Court says: "That's fine! The people want to see justice prevail rather than the inevitability of a social process."

War Films

And we have the war films.

The film has served the war from its infancy. The American movie had its start in the Spanish American War. Rumania used pictures of her troops in the Balkan war to stir enthusiasm for the World War. And Japan did the same with pictures of the Russo-Japanese War. In 1915, when we were ostensibly neutral, films like *The Treason of Anatole* were produced, sympathizing with French and German soldiery, but making of a war a wistful attraction. That year England perpetrated films with a dual purpose: to stimulate enlistment and to encourage Anglophile sentiment in America. An English producer said to an American journalist at that time:

"Our days—and nights too—are spent in glorifying the British and showing the Germans up in an unfavorable light. . . . American exhibitors have no desire to violate Uncle Sam's admirable desire to be neutral."

The tone, as well as sequence, is ironical. *Fooling the Fatherland* became, for American consumption, *A Foreign Power Outwitted.* "The explanatory matter of the play is to be so altered that it mentions either a nameless or fictitious power at war with Britain." But — "for all our scheming we fail to cover up the fact that the enemy wear German uniforms, and a 'doctored' photoplay may always be detected by others."

In September, 1915, Hudson Maxim's preparedness tract *Defenseless*

Peace, was filmed as *The Battle Cry of Peace.* Ford attacked the picture in full-page newspaper ads. "He pointed out that Maxim munitions corporation stock was on the market." Thomas Ince served the quasi-pacifist dish *Civilization,* which strengthened Wilson's campaign on the "Kept us out of the war" ticket. The dubious pacifism of America produced *War Brides,* provoked by the acuteness of feminism at that moment. It told "how a woman, driven to desperation by the loss of loved ones, defied an empire." Its romantic futility satisfied the uncritical pacifism that subscribed to, and was betrayed by, the Woodrovian slogans "too proud to fight," "watchful waiting," "he kept us out of the war." How simple it was to convert these into one glamorous "Make the world safe for democracy"! *War Brides* was suppressed. The suppression was justified thus: ". . . the philosophy of this picture is so easily misunderstood by unthinking people that it has been found necessary to withdraw it from circulation for the duration of the war."

Hearst, more interested in Mexico and Japan than in Europe, took the serial *The Last of the Cannings* [*sic*],* glorifying the Dupont family and American womanhood, and converted it into *Patria,* an attack on Hearst's phobias. We were not yet at war with Germany but close to it, and Japan was an ally of Britain, an enemy of Germany. Woodrow Wilson asked that the anti-Japanese touches be removed. The Japanese flag was lifted out, and, by contiguity, the Mexican too. Preparations for the war-objector were part of the preparedness propaganda. In the last months of 1916, *The Slacker* told of the conversion of a society butterfly into a flag-sycophant. It should be indicated also that the soldiers in *War Brides,* against whom Alla Nazimova rose, were out-and-out German.

Films appeared romanticizing British history and espionage; *The Victoria Cross,* the English in India; *Shell 34,* the heroism of a spy; *An Enemy of the King,* the days of Henry of Navarre. In 1914 the outdoor war-news film-showings of the New York *Herald* brought counter-applause from Allied and Entente sympathizers. "We were neutral with a vengeance in those days." Germany tried to edge in for sympathy with *Behind the German Lines.* But the interests were concentrating popular interest upon the Allies, and pro-British, pro-French films appeared. Geraldine Farrar played in *Joan the Woman,* a Lasky picture. Pictures of our troops in Mexico, and the war abroad, had served to create an ennui for battle. The yearning was there, at first weak and confused, but steadily strengthened into violence by suggestion and direct hypodermic. The rape of Belgium was perpetrated in the studio of America, abetted by our Allies. An uninterrupted propaganda turned America about face, seemingly overnight.

Actually, this propaganda had been increasingly at work, ascending toward a climax, and America had turned quarter-'bout, half-about, until full about, facing the Entente "squarely." The need was to create and sustain a war-temper, to eliminate all doubts, and to extract devotion, moral and material.

The impressionable directors set to. The Ince producers of *Civilization* emitted *Vive la France.* Slogan films were plentiful:. *Over There, To Hell with the Kaiser, For France, Lest We Forget.* Love for our brothers-in-arms was instilled by films domestic and imported, such as: *The Belgian, Daughter of France,* Sarah Bernhardt in *Mothers of France, Somewhere in France, Hearts of the World,* D. W. Griffith's contribution to the barrage. The strifes of France were presented to America: *Birth of Democracy* (French Revolution), and *The Bugler of Algiers* (1870). The vestiges of admiration for Germany were eliminated by films like *The Kaiser, Beast of Berlin, The Prussian Cur, The Hun Within.* German-American support was bid for in Mary Pickford's *The Little American,* a tragicomedy describing "the German Cavalry of bestiality," "the hell-hounds" and "the repentant Kaiserman." Chaplin ridiculed the Kaiser in *Shoulder Arms.* The fair sex was intrigued by films like *Joan of Plattsburg.* As far back as 1916, "when everybody but the public knew we were going into the big fight overseas," a glittering Joan on a white horse, contributed by the movie people, had paraded in the suffrage march on Fifth Avenue. The movie stars—like Mary Pickford and Dorothy Dalton—became the symbolic Joans of American divisions in the war. A miniature Joan, Baby Peggy, joined the abominable harangue that children spat on fathers of families: "Don't be a slacker!" An insidious propaganda among children was instituted and developed. The "non-military" Boy Scouts had films made especially for them: *Pershing's Crusaders, The Star Spangled Banner, The War Waif, Your Flag and My Flag,* serials like *The English Boy Scouts to the Rescue,* and *Ten Adventures of a Boy Scout.* The objector was shamed by "don't bite the hand that's feeding you" movies: *My Own United States, A Call to Arms (The Son of Democracy), The Man Without a Country, Draft 258, The Unbeliever, The Great Love, One More American, The Man Who Was Afraid.* German atrocities were insisted upon: *The Woman the Germans Shot.* All branches of the service were gilded: *The Hero of Submarine D2.*

Governmental organization found incentive in conjunction with England, citizen bodies and the film corporations. An American Cinema Commission went abroad. England had organized one with eminent individuals like Conan Doyle. D. W. Griffith not only was at work in England on *Hearts of the World,* but he also coöperated with high society in recruiting British sentiment. The National Association of the Motion Picture Industry, William A. Brady, president, was organized but never functioned, although it served as a stimulant to the movie companies' enthusiasm. The Red Cross had begun to use films, but not satisfactorily enough. With Creel's Committee on Public Information, the Red Cross set up the Division of Pictures, which released four films to one-third of the movie houses, "about the same number of audiences as Chaplin audiences." In New York there was the Mayor's Committee of National Defense, Jesse L. Lasky, motion picture chairman. The movie companies organized a War Coöperative Council. In 1918 the films were said to have put about $100,000,000 into the war chest. Movie stars spoke and carried on for the Red Cross, the Liberty Loan and enlistment. A propaganda slide in the cinemas read: "If you are an American, you should be proud to say so." The sale of Liberty Loan bonds was helped by 70,000 slides. Douglas Fairbanks jumped from a roof for $100 for the Red Cross, and Chaplin sold autographed halves of his hat. The movie actors joined the California Coast Artillery, others organized the Lasky Home Guards. Lasky received a title for his work in many divisions. His coöperation with the government was balanced after the war by the government's willingness to help in the aviation film, *Wings*. The popular star, Robert Warwick, now a Captain, was quoted in the fan-press upon war's ennobling qualities.

The period since the war resembles in a general way the period before and during the war. There are films like *The Big Parade* and even *All Quiet on the Western Front* which explicitly condemn war, but implicitly, by their nostalgic tone, their uncritical non-incisive pacifism, their placing of the blame on the lesser individual and the stay-at-home, their sympathy with the protagonist, their excitement, their comic interludes, make war interesting. Their little condemnations are lost, amid the overwhelming pile of films in which war is a farcical holiday, or a swashbuckler's adventure. The momentary pointing of guilt is made so naïve, so passing that it never gets across to the audience—*The Case of Sergeant Grischa* and *Hell's Angels.* It simply serves as a betrayal supporting the bluff of disarmament conferences.

Carl Laemmle was suggested for the Nobel Peace Prize for *All Quiet.* During the war he made *The Kaiser, Beast of Berlin,* after the war he wept upon the plight of his *Vaterland* in his advertising column in the *Saturday Evening Post,* and after *All Quiet* he issues a series of sergeant-private-girl farces in which one of the agonized Germans of *All Quiet* is starred. Well, he still qualifies for the prize; he is no less noble than Wilson or Grey.

We have also governmental coöperation. The Navy, however, has declined to coöperate in films kidding officers. It's all right to make fools of gobs, but it's bad business to invite gobs to laugh at the officers. The class distinction is important in the capitalist army, more and more important today. Further coöperation between producers and military is found in the Warner Brothers' instruction in sound to officers. The battleships are being sound-equipped. How easily the movie can be put on a war basis! And, of course, we still have the films glorifying individual branches of the service, from diving to aviation. Film producers and impresarios carry honorary military titles.

Let us not be led astray by objections to pacifist films like *All Quiet* and *Hell's Angels*. The neurosis of "national honor" is today so active in capitalist countries that the slightest abrasion sets it off. The Fascist Germans find in these films insults to German officers. The Fascist French accept them for the same reason. In the meantime, Germany issues a film like *The German Mother-Heart,* in which a mother who has lost six sons is made to feel how exceptional was her opportunity. In America a similar theme is handled in *Four Sons*. And with it all we have "educational" films flaunting patriotism; R.K.O. has a Patriotic Week that is praised by Vice-President Curtis . . . the total is rather threatening. Only the workers' movement is a potent factor against imperialist war.

Imperialist war is completely indicted in the films of the U.S.S.R. alone. The Soviet kino selects images at once real and symbolic that concentrate the horror of war and relate war to its source. Andreas Latzko, in his book *Men in War,* created a picture of war whose images are at once real, symbolic and relentless. No film producer has proven his sincere condemnation of war by filming this book. Capitalism wants its pacifism delectable. The Soviet kino goes beyond Latzko. It sets war directly within the society producing it. A film developed entirely to war can do nothing else but make of war an ominous, therefore compelling, universe. The Soviet film makes war a portion of the film, the hideous peak of a competitive society. (The best example is Boris Barnet's *The Patriots* — released in America by Amkino in 1933. See also, note by Irving Lerner in *New Masses,* August, 1933, p. 27).

The movie is valuable as a merchandise in itself, to sell other merchandise, as a vehicle for the "national idea," and as an instrument of imperialist control. In an editorial — quoted at the beginning of this pamphlet — in the November fourth issue of the London *Country Life,* 1911, we are told:

"Some recent events in Canada have caused many of us to consider more seriously than heretofore the purposes to which the cinematograph can be used. The business in moving pictures was practically monopolised by two American firms, and they, moved no doubt, only by pecuniary motives, followed the practice which has long been that of our cousins of twisting the lion's tail. The particular twisting which appeared to find favour in the United States consisted in showing an American soldier in the performance of deeds of unheard-of gallantry, and a British soldier in an attitude correspondingly contemptible. This might very well pass as an amusement in some of the more remote and less enlightened towns of the United States. It does not concern us much here, because there has always been a considerable amount of raillery passed between John Bull and Uncle Sam. . . .

"But a very different situation arose when those exhibitions were carried into one of the most important Overseas Dominions of the King."

England doesn't care what America thinks of her, but she's worried about what her colonies may think. However, in dealing with another power, diplomatic care must be taken. Therefore the Overseas Club handled the matter without, of course, criticizing "the taste of the American manufacturer in pandering to the anti-British element in the United States." The Ottawa branch met and protested strongly against the exhibition of too many motion pictures — does this imply that a limited number were acceptable? — "showing deeds of valour performed by the Americans to the detriment of views exhibiting the glory of the British people." British war pictures were substituted in Canada. The New York press called the Canadian sentiment anti-American. Today, 20 years later, when the nationalist temper is hot and bothered, oh, what a lot of rancor in Ottawa! Some fifteen years after this pre-war strife, the same sentiment was expressed, with scurrility, by the British press, which saw before it the enormity of the American movie. A Fascist journal, *The Patriot,* wrote on "American Film Propaganda":

"We hope, but do not expect, that the agitation over British films will arouse English people to the danger in their midst of American propaganda through the agency of American films. England is being suffocated by American films; they lead in East and West. . . . The historical films have for their motive the belittling of the Monarchy as an institution." Come now!

J. W. Drawbell, editor of the *London Sunday Chronicle,* said: "We are suffering from too much America!" But, he added, "We are fools if we delude ourselves that we have nothing to learn from these same people at whom we rather look down our noses." The Prince of Wales was called upon to urge an empire movie for England. The imperialistic motivation is easily read between the lines of Premier Macdonald to the House of Commons in 1927:

"There is one serious reason why everyone of us is interested in British films being shown abroad, and that is that British films should uphold to foreign nations a better conception of the moral conduct and social habits of people who profess to belong to the leading nations of the world than, unfortunately, is the case with so many films that are being exported, for instance, to China . . . these people, who, a few years ago, regarded us as being a dominant and ruling people."

The Labor Party premier is worried about British financial prestige in the Far East. Two years previously, the Tory Baldwin had showed himself in accord with the premier to follow when he said to Parliament:

"I think the time has come when the position of the film industry in this country should be examined to see if it is not possible, as it is desirable on national grounds, having regard to the enormous power which the film has developed for propaganda purposes, and the danger to which we in this country and our empire subject ourselves, if we allow that method of propaganda to be in the hands of foreign countries."

Mr. Baldwin is less ambiguous than his successor. England is most disturbed about the influence of the film in South Africa, where white hegemony is threatened by the increasing cohesion between black and white workers. Therefore the censorship is very severe in regard to the possible effect of films on the natives. Anathema are "all subjects which are calculated to wound the susceptibilities of foreign people, and especially of our subjects of the British Empire." These are "political" anathema: political hypocrisy. Among the "social" are "stories" showing any "antagonistic or strained relations between white men and the colored population of the British Empire, especially with regard to the question of sexual intercourse, moral or immoral, between individuals of different races." The divisions of the censors' code dovetail. Under "military" we discover that the movie may not show "officers in British uniform in a disgraceful light," "conflicts between the armed forces of a State and the populace," "reflections on (the) wife of (a) responsible British official in the East." These are quoted from specific restrictions. In 1928 films were censored on "political" ground of "references to H.R.H. the Prince of Wales," "libellous reflections on Royal Dynasties," "British Possessions represented as lawless sinks of iniquity," "white men in state of degradation amidst Far Eastern and Native surroundings" and — always this reiteration — "equivocal situations between white girls and men of other races." How about white men and girls of other races? Was not a scene deleted from *Piccadilly* where the

British star, Jameson Thomas, kisses the Chinese-American actress, Anna May Wong? Under "administration of justice," we find that "no film coming into Britain or born in Britain may show police firing on defenseless populace." That, of course, has never happened in the magnanimous British Empire.

Lately the British press has been feverish in the demand for even closer censorship of films for South Africa. It protests the "deplorable impression of the morality of the white man, and, worse still, of the white woman," which American films convey. "The establishment of a Board in London . . . to censor all films for exhibition in tropical Africa . . . will readily commend itself to all those who have the best interests of the native races . . . at heart, as well as the prestige of the Europeans." ". . . the silly tosh . . . on American films does materially help to lower the prestige of the white man in the eyes of the unsophisticated native." "The increase in crime out here is in many instances due to the film, and anything that in any way decreases the prestige of white women in a black country is an abomination which should be firmly put down."

Yet the British film sees nothing deplorable in picturing an Arab resistance to British invasion as the act of a "dirty dog," in *The Lost Patrol.* England may reply that it is competing with the American movie, which purchased a British novel, *Beau Geste,* and put it under the direction of an Englishman Herbert Brenon, to be made into a movie glorifying three Britishers in the Foreign Legion against the Arabs. Incidentally, a Frenchman is portrayed in the film as a "rat." France protests and prohibits the film. U. S. A. produces a sequel, *Beau Sabreur,* in which the "rat" is not only a Frenchman but a rebel, too. To assuage France, Hollywood then issues *Forgotten Faces,* wherein the Americanism for Frenchman, "Froggie," becomes, for French circulation, "Broggie,'" but the type, a crook, is a French steretoype of American idiom. What does Will Hays say about respect for the citizens of other countries?

England applauds film-making in India, as long as the makers are upper caste Indians, waiting on British approval and the films obsolete and meaningless legends around Indian princes. Under various other guises imperialism is supported, defended, vindicated, honored. England films Sir Alan Cobham's aeroplane tour of Africa. The White Man's Burden becomes lighter in the air, especially when the "burden" itself is kidded. France films the automobile expedition of the Henry Ford of France, André Citroën. The trek is recorded through the "black heart" in dances by the natives, but never are we permitted an insight into the imperialistic nature of this expedition and its meaning to these black dancers.

America issues boastful "hunt" films in which the Negro is a coward and a lazy wretch. These films have become such a formula that they are patched up in studios from fragments and "shots" taken in zoological gardens. In such a film *Africa Speaks,* the perpetrators dare to stage the slaughter of a Negro boy by a lion, and to mourn the death hypocritically. It is obviously a fake, but that a Negro and not a white man is chosen as the victim is itself significant. The two false "explorers" are most offensive in their enacted authority toward the Negroes, whom they would never dare to treat so in the open veldt. Their conduct is a commentary on the "white man's negro." Lions roar and the white men boldly face the beasts with their cameras. The Negroes dive into a cave and hide. The goateed white man remarks upon a Negro: "He is tired. L-a-z-y, tired." Will Hays threatened to expose the bogusness of this film. The Columbia company, its distributors, joined the Hays organization. The film is still circulating. . . . If it isn't contempt the chauvinistic film heaps upon the Negro, then it is patronage, the faithful slave, as in *Trader Horn.*

The evasion of the human subject-matter in the films of colonial and semi-colonial peoples typifies most American pictures of that kind. We have a film around monkeys, *Rango*; or a film in which the native is an isolated unit, *Chang*; or a film in which the natives are "forgotten people," *Grass;* or a film of a remote and unimportant legend in which the imperialistic suggestion is safe in the background, *Tabu;* or lyrical studies of a ceremony like *Moana.* In *White Shadows In the South Seas,* the struggle is platitudinously, abstractly, stated as between "civilization" and "romance," and concretely as between a gang of thugs and a derelict doctor romantically inclined. Never is this struggle depicted as the advance of imperialism, and never is the conclusion more than a wistful shrug of the shoulders: "It's very, very sad, but nothing can be done about it."

In reference to the Indian, since the tale is retrospective, we may see the film lamenting the "vanished Indian." This is the gallantry that slays and then forgives. Or it may idealize the "lost paradise" as in *The Silent Enemy,* or vindicate the white man by having the hero or the hero's son marrying the chief's daughter—never, of course, the lowly Indian girl. This occurs in *Cimarron,* where the hero murmurs distantly about the $1.40 paid the Indian for his land, and the wife talks about the "dirty Indians," and the son marries the Indian hired-girl, who, I'll have you know, is no humble menial, but an Osage chief's daughter. By 1930, the marriage becomes respectable, even élite. And there are the innumerable films in which the Red Man is a vicious murderer, or a sneak. If he is a half-breed, well, of course, he's got to be a sneak. *Cimarron* has such a character. From the heights of his superiority the white exploiter may condescend to see the Red Man as a loyal person—loyal, that is, to the white Gentile, happy to be the "White Man's Burden," along with the Negro and Jew. It is interesting that in this one film, *Cimarron,* the devoted Osage, the loyal Negro, who dies in his loyalty, the soulful Jew (whose soul grows from a peddler's wagon into a department-store) are assembled for the entertainment and education of the audience. In this way the imperialist, the oppressor, is complimented and his imperialism is redeemed and glorified. Other tactics are used to aid the machinery of whitewashing and covering up the deeds of the imperialists.

In the last few years the screen has abounded with films glorifying American aggression. *Old Ironsides* dealt with the War with Tripoli. *The Rough Riders* makes an idyll of the Spanish American War and *Flight* says sweet things about our Nicaraguan occupation.

Nationalistic self-glory, to the disadvantage of the oppressed, fills the screens of the capitalist world. Italy anticipated the Fascist "march on Rome" with pictures glorifying the Roman past: *Cabiria, Quo Vadis, Theodora,* etc. Since the Fascist coup, Italy has been producing films sentimentalizing her imperialist aspiration in the love of an Arab for an Italian, and of an Italian for an Arab. (One has only to follow the news of the German film industry since Hitler came into power for further confirmation of this fact. For some time before Hitler's regime, the government turned out pro-Fascist and imperialist films. Two of them were distributed here: *The Rebel,* and *Morgenrot,* the former a fake historical film preaching Nazi-nationalism with the help of Christianity against France. Universal Pictures Corp., Jewish-owned and Jewish-managed by father and son, Laemmle, the distributors, and they are now making a film in America for the Nazis. *Morgenrot* was distributed by an independent firm).

Only one society dares to issue films exposing imperialism. That society is the land of the Soviets. *A Shanghai Document, China Express, Storm Over Asia, Love In the Caucasus, Salt of Swanetia,* and other films, depict the suppression of autonomy, the aggression in the Orient, the contrasts in life between colonial or semi-colonial and the imperialist, between poor colonial and rich. Similarly the Soviet films are the only ones which expose the imperialistic motive of war.*

The land of this cinema is the present target of the imperialists.

* [Gen. Ed.]: Most of this paragraph originally appeared in *Anti-Soviet Cinema.*

When the Russian monarchy was destroyed, the event was seized upon by demagogues as a proof of the slogan that the war was being fought to "make the world safe for democracy." But at the same time Russia's defection was threatening. Brenon, who made the feminist-pacifist *War Brides* before the war, and was to make the pacifist *The Case of Sergeant Grischa* after the war, directed *The Last of the Romanoffs,* where Rasputin is the villain, the Tsar a duped innocent, and the *pogromschik* of Tsaritzen, now Stalingrad— the "mad monk," Iliodor, "in person"—is the hero, the saviour of Russia. The film was directed against the Kaiser, "the Rasputin of Europe," and the Bolsheviks. It was meant as a discouragement of the Revolution. *Anton the Terrible,* a Lasky crime, admitted the guilt of the Tsarist officer, who apologizes for his cruelty, and it condemned the revolutionary. In the years before the war, America had issued films sympathizing with the revolutionary, usually a Jew. The films were made by Jews not as yet in established social positions and therefore not too suspicious as yet of the revolutionary suggestions of such films as *Nihilist Vengeance, The Heart of a Jewess, The Terrors of Russia, The Black Hundred,* etc. Moreover, in many of these films an effort was made to reconcile the persecuted with the persecutor in morganatic marriages or in the sudden "ennoblement" of the tyrant. The solution of the discord was carried very emphatically into the film that echoed to the February revolution and the threat of October. With this propaganda at work, America, through an official Bureau, let it be known that

". . . the American economic mission in Russia will use the motion pictures for the advance work of enlightening the uninformed people of the most remote parts, as well as Russians in general who have been entirely misled by German propaganda.

"Because of existing conditions in Russia, and in effect of German propaganda, no amount of printed matter could possibly accomplish so much as the widespread showing of motion pictures. Films will open the way for effective later use of printed matter.

"For the Great Russian film campaign the motion picture companies have been called upon for *forty miles of film,* providing not only the directly educational and news films which show America's war activities, troops in France and the German devastation of Belgium, but also a certain proportion of typical American screen dramas.

"If Ivan laughs at Charlie Chaplin, and falls in love with Mary Pickford, he comes appreciably nearer to reaching a receptive state of mind for the subsequent work of the American mission."

Since the war,* suggestive films have been issued in which the attempt is made to influence the mind of the audience against Soviet Russia by idealizing and romanticizing Tsarist days — the court, the love of an aristocrat for a girl of the people, etc. Other films, like *The Last Command,* glorify a nobleman, the Grand Duke, and by direct contrast, degrade the revolutionary. In *The Last Command,* a train carrying the revolutionists collapses through a bridge. I shall not go as far as to say that this is intended as a symbolic prophecy of the collapse of the Soviet Union, but it certainly excites an emotion prejudicial to it. Every land has been guilty of heinous film-propaganda against Soviet Russia. The Fox company of America, which has recently gone thumbs down on all newsreel "clips" showing unemployment lines and all that might even remotely be construed as "bolshevist propaganda," has recently issued a film called *The Spy* which hallows the Grand Duke and invites the assassination of the Soviet official. This film has had diligent circulation to family audiences. It relates of the *émigrés* in Paris. "Cheka" spies listen in. The Grand Duke — never once visible to the audience — becomes more awesome by speaking and revealing his physical presence only with his arm and hand. This is a theatrical trick that was used in *Ben Hur* to deify Christ. Someone must go to Moscow to assassinate "Citizen X," the leader of the "Cheka," who, we are told, won't let the *émigrés'* families leave the U.S.S.R. The sympathy is all with the *émigrés* who, for no fault of their own, are being persecuted. The noble young Captain, whose wife and child are in Russia, risks his life to do the deed, which ain't, according to Fox, so dirty. A "Cheka" spy trails him; he beats the spy off.

Nobility just oozes out of the pores of this movie. The nobility of the invisible Grand Duke, the Captain, the wife, the son, the *bezprizorni.* These last, the homeless waifs, are presented so as to suggest they are still rampant in Russia, when, as a matter of fact, the Soviets have heroically solved their problem. In the film, the Soviet "police" pursue the waifs. Several fall to death from the housetops. Anything to increase the horror of the Soviet "régime." So noble, in contrast, is aristocracy that the Captain's wife willingly becomes the hostess in a state gambling-house because the money from the den goes to succor the waifs, with whom her child lived while she was purposely falsely imprisoned. You see, one of the aristocrats is now a "traitor" to his class. The "Cheka" uses him to

* [Gen. Ed.]: Much of the following two paragraphs repeats material in *Hollywood Looks at War.*

trap the Captain because they know he loves the Captain's wife. And when he wants to do her further dirt, the waifs kill him — they love aristocrats so. How noble are the enemies of the Soviet Union; how ignoble are the friends! The film was made about the time Soviet Russia nipped the intervention plot of the Industrial Party, about the time Denikin's "history" appeared in English, wherein the interventionist of 1920 avows the *émigrés* have not yielded their "ideals."

The immediate motivation behind the picture is explained by the identities of the members of the Fox directorial board. They include: the president of the Utilities, Power & Light Corp.; chairman of the governing committee of the Chase National Bank; the son-in-law of Andy Mellon who is, at the same time, a director of the U. P. Railroad; Corny Vanderbilt; the prexy of the Central Trust Co. of Illinois; other bankers, industrialists, etcetera. The interlocking of control means a unity of purpose, and the imminent purpose is war — against the Soviet Union.

Every reactionary agency and institution in our society has its hand or wants its hand in the movie. The Daughters of the American Revolution has a Committee for Better Films. The National Chairman, in her annual report (1928) said: "I am sure that every one present will agree with me that the motion picture today holds what is probably the greatest power for good or evil in the world; and I am sure that you agree also that it is up to you and to me, and to our prototypes among the 116,000,000 citizens, which influence shall predominate." Under the hypocritical guise of "Better Films," the influence that shall predominate is apparent enough. The influence is to be borne by patriotic films of state and national history, with the emphasis on a "George Washington" picture. The D. A. R. coöperates with the Hays organization in the interests of this "patriotic service" to glorify the incidents and personages of American history, from the Battle of Saratoga to the imperialistic flights of Colonel Lindbergh. Among the ten films favored by the Chairman of the Committee are four pictures sentimentalizing military training, mother sacrifice in war, jingoism generally; two are of a religious nature; one romanticizes the subjugation of the American Indian; and one is anti-Soviet. The D. A. R. advertises itself in "patriotic trailers" taking "3 minutes for showing." The first of these reveals "our flag waving in the breeze, with a boy and a girl, either scouts or members of the Children of the American Revolution, properly saluting the flag and pledging allegiance to it, using the uniform flag salute adopted by the D. A. R. and 67 other patriotic organizations." We find the D. A. R. poking into other civilian bodies like the National Board of Review and the Amateur Cinema League, whose executive director sports the title of "Colonel." The various state chapters boast of having shown patriotic films on such occasions as George Washington's birthday anniversary — waving the flag ostentatiously. In the chairman's report care is taken to refer to the help the motion picture industry has given to the Red Cross, and to mention the Church and Drama Association, recently deceased, and the Religious Motion Picture Foundation. The former organization had the chairman at one of its luncheons as "a guest of honor."

The church has been thirsty and hungry for the movie. It has found the film edging in on its province as distraction and ritual and has brought pressure on the industry and government in an attempt to control the "art of the lowly." Finding that it could not dispose of so powerful a folk-pleasure by calling it a "menace," and very early discovering how this medium could serve clerical propaganda, it went into the arena in two ways. First, it has sought to produce films — not too successfully. We have read above of the early missionary films. One of the first pictures made was of the Passion. This was "duped" and repeated over and over again. One may find ads today for such pictures in trade journals like *The Billboard*. In 1925 the Religious Motion Picture Foundation was organized under the auspices of the Harmon Foundation. Its offices are appropriately in the financial district of New York, Nassau Street. As to the productions of this Foundation, we read "All controversial or debatable grounds have been avoided and the subject-matter of all pictures has been confined to simple and well recognized interpretations that have governed Christianity through the centuries." The Foundation wants the church "to compete" effectively "with the drawing power of golf course, beach and motor," not only to lure "the young people of today, and many of the older ones" away from the movies and dance halls — of course, "if you are able to draw large crowds away you are to be congratulated," but to give them at the same time "a living and inspiring religion." The church was losing its grip over young people.

On March 20, 1914, Canon Chase appeared before the Committee on Education of the House of Representatives and opposed the unofficial National Board of Censors, now National Board of Review. Chase has been very zealous for a national censorship that would make it simpler for the church — his church — to control the film. For some time he issued in the joint name of the New York Civic League and the Lord's Day Alliance, his Catechism on *Motion Pictures in Interstate Commerce*. Today he is general secretary of the Federal Motion Picture Council which wants a government commission to control the movie. Similarly the Women's Christian Temperance Union endorses the Hudson bill which amid the usual decoys of moral supervision places the *real* aim of capitalist control: the suppression of films that "ridicule or deprecate public officials, or other governmental authority, or which tend to weaken the authority of the law, which offend the religious belief of any person or ridicule recognized leaders or symbols of any religious sect; which 'unduly emphasize bloodshed and violence.'" This is obviously class legislation and really nationalizes the Hays code. The question is solely as to which reactionary agency shall directly benefit from the profits of control. Our fight against national censorship must be solely one to prevent further suppression of films made by the possible courageous independent, by labor, or the Soviet studios. We know that the censors of Pennsylvania suppressed *The Armored Cruiser Potemkin,* and that *Seeds of Freedom* was emasculated beyond any possible showing. Since the latter film revealed the synagogue's betrayal of young Jews in the 1905 revolution, Jews of Philadelphia "society" refused to "pull strings" for its freedom from gross destruction. We know that while Hays wants to keep national censorship off, and control in his own hand, he was not averse to—in fact, induced—the suppression of the Sacco-Vanzetti newsreels and those of the March 6, 1930, unemployment demonstration in New York. We know that on that day, the police commissioner "requested" the Cameo, a house belonging to R. K. O. of the Hays organization, to remove the Soviet film *China Express,* which had another week to run. The Cameo complied immediately with this "request."

We know, also, that various excuses are used in the suppression of a film of challenge. The British Board of Censors prohibited *Potemkin* because "it deals with recent controversial matters." Local bodies like the London County Council and the Middlesex County Council refused to pass it. When the agent tries to put it through other local councils, "he suddenly receives a visit, the first of several, from officers of the special department of Scotland Yard." The agent "wants no quarrels" with Government inspectors. He makes no further effort to show the film, and is even scared to let a Parliament committee look at it. The Pudovkin picture, *Mother,* was not allowed "on the ground that its scene was Russia, that its action concerned a strike, and that forces of order were depicted firing on a mob. Reply by the agent that many films of American and other origin dealing with the Russian Revolution, or the events preceding it, often in a manner unsympathetic to authority . . . had been approved. . . . *The Red Dancer of Moscow* and *The Volga Boatman* as well as other films like *Intolerance* and *The Three Passions* showing the shooting of a mob. The exception taken was then altered and explained to cover rather the tenor of depiction of scene and action than the scene and action themselves. . . ." We need not go on with this argument. This was a Soviet film — that was enough. Always does capitalism object, so it says, to the "controversial." That's what Fox said when it ordered unemployment and "Bolshevism" out of its newsreels. (But it could launch a malicious attack on Communism and Communists in a Fox film, called *Shanghai Madness*). It said that a mixed reception to Mussolini provoked the thumbs down on "controversial" matter. But right after the order, Benito was on the Fox screen, and Fox was exploiting *The Spy*.

France, most fearful of the nations when Soviet Russia is mentioned, has suppressed the Spartacus Film League which exhibited Soviet pictures, and prohibited the best of these films, mutilating others and permitting those most negligible in persuasiveness or political theme. The English soldiers in *Storm Over Asia* were vaguely called "whites." In the meantime, French capital is invested in the movies of the bluffer buffer-states of Poland, Roumania and Czechoslovakia and these pictures — jingoistic and most often wretched — are shown in Paris to exaggerate praise of the press. The stool pigeon must be petted. It serves in the anti-Soviet attack. The poor exhibitor, having a bad Polish film forced on him, is frequently obliged to lure his patrons by calling it a Russian film. At the same time, the Fascist youth of Les Camelots du Roi attack *The Golden Age,* the film of a young Spanish aesthete. The reasons assemble so: Buñuel, the director, is one of the super-realists, a friend of artists who have become Communists; his picture, hardly direct, seems to make fun of the clergy; and — there's a small man with a tall wife — he is mocking the king of Italy! That's how acute "national honor" is. In Nüremberg the beautiful picture, *The Beggar's Opera,* a film far from drastic in its satire, is suppressed because it broadly kids the clergy and the police.

The clergy are very sensitive, you know. Hays had to say: don't laugh at a minister in the films. He even called in the sects to act in coalition with him. He has been especially close to the Catholics, even though he himself is a Presbyterian elder. The Catholics are internationally unified. They have their movie congress and they can use the sacred weapon of excommunication. In 1916 they placed a ban on *Power of the Cross.* A. M. Kennedy, its author and producer, was threatened with excommunication if he showed the picture. Today Hays has on his Committee on Public Relations the National Catholic Welfare Conference and the International Federation of Catholic Alumnae, as well as the D. A. R., the Boy Scouts, the General Federation of Women's Clubs, the Russell Sage Foundation, the National Congress of Parents and Teachers, the

National Education Association, the American Library Association, the Young Men's Christian Association, and the National Recreation Association — schools, church, playground, club, etc. "Less actively associated were representatives of various religious organizations, including the Federal Council of Churches," which recently had a skirmish with Hays, it wants to be heard more, "labor organizations, patriotic societies, and health, civic and welfare bodies." When the coalition was started, labor was "represented" by the A. F. of L. demagogue, Hugh Frayne, lately included by Matthew Woll in his 100 citizens to combat Communism. But the A. F. of L. is perfectly content to let Hays do the job of making the worker a "100% American." It subscribes to Hays' address to German movie-men in Berlin in the summer of 1930, to veto all films containing "social political or economic ideas." This was a suggested attack on Soviet films, the only ones whose "social, political or economic ideas" might consistently offend Hays or Hugenberg, the Fascist owner of the German U.F.A., with whom Hays was so convivial. The attack is also directed against any "ideas" critical of the *status quo* that might even moderately be present in a film made outside of the Soviet Union. Hays has admitted that the movie is "capable of wielding a subtle and powerful influence upon ideas."

So do the proponents of national censorship. These include the Federal Motion Picture Council, launched in 1925. "Its first president was the . . . general director of the Department of Moral Welfare of the Presbyterian Church in the U. S. A." In this Council we find the "national motion picture chairman of the W.C.T.U., previously . . . in the Department of Moral Welfare" of the Presbyterian Church, and another member, "general secretary of the Women's Coöperative Alliance of Minneapolis," as well as church rectors. Other bodies favoring national censorship are: the Disciples of Christ, the Woman's Foreign Missionary Society of the Methodist Episcopal Church, the Woman's Missionary Council of the M. E. Church South, the North American Home Missions Congress, the Northern Baptist Convention, and the notorious National Grange.

All these are thundering on the right. We on the left must build both defense and offense to their reaction.

The answer lies with the audience of the movie, which D. W. Griffith called "the laboring man's university." The movie magnates are looking for a new audience. They cannot see that the new audience is the old audience with a new mind, a mind in advance of the reviewers and the producers. This audience can be directed to see the fraudulence of reactionary films. Showings of Soviet pictures and other revolutionary films are themselves initial arguments against the shallowness of the American film, which has only prejudice as its basis. The Film and Photo Leagues, the John Reed Clubs, and other workers' cultural organizations through revolutionary film criticism and through their own revolutionary films must instruct this film audience in the detection of treacherous reaction of the bourgeois film.

We must build – On the Left – the Movie!

—International Pamphlets
(sponsored by The Film and Photo League),
Number 38, 1934.
(Published Posthumously).

* [Gen. Ed.]: Page 253 – ". . . the Cannings" – reference is to *The Last of the Fighting Channings,* by Louis Joseph Vance.

5

NATIONAL TRAITS

THE PLIGHT OF THE EUROPEAN MOVIE

Europe has America on the brain. America is either the last bulwark, proof, or justification of European civilization, or America is degraded and degrading—hope or despair. This interest in America is filled with a distrust because of America's enormous financial and economic power. The result is a resentment against America intensified by the intrusion of Americans into the industrial life of every other country. And in no enterprise has the presence of America been so treacherously felt as in the movie—of England, Sweden, Germany, France, Italy and even Russia.

There is no English cinema to mention. A few pictures have been filmed by Stoll, who owns the best kinema theaters, patterned upon the popular successes from America, and starring an idol like Ivor Novello, or a darling like Lili Damita. Some war films relating the activities of British troops in the War have been successfully produced. But English films are few and far between and the crowd would rather see Tom Mix or Gloria Swanson. In England, as elsewhere in Europe, Chaplin, Lloyd and particularly Valentino, since his death, are great legendary figures. English film entrepreneurs are desperate. It has been proposed to build a film industry in some colony, preferably Australia, whose youth and climate correspond with those of California. The press, already fiercely resentful of America, is frequently protesting against this American popularity. The people have no theories, they like what they like. To them *The Big Parade* is a big movie, to the newspapers it is bad diplomacy. But then, American movie directors have not been trained in schools of diplomatics as have English statesmen. The results of diplomacy, moreover, are not always most favorable to the nation or the art. Objections are made to details. But still the people crowd to see the tremendous war film from America, even though G. B. Shaw defends it as excellent pacifism.

Movie critics with a few honorable exceptions, like that of Miss Iris Barry, seize every opportunity to attack the American movie, even going so far as to praise a bad German film when such praise gives an opportunity to assail American pictures. The English, one critic writes, may feel that a particular German film is too long, but that is due only to the fact that "we are too much accustomed to the rapid tempo of the American picture." A pathetic little journal, *The Patriot,* trembling at every imaginary thrust at an even hypothetical king, writes thus on "American Film Propaganda":

"We hope, but do not expect, that the agitating over British films will arouse English people to the danger in their midst of American propaganda through the agency of American films. England is being suffocated by American films; they lead in East and West, and, thanks to our apathy, a promising British industry is being strangled before our eyes. The war, of course, was America's chance, and, with her genius for money making quickened by the jealousy of English commercial supremacy, she grabbed it. England was fighting on every front throughout the world; she had subordinated everything to the task in hand; her civil industrial life was in abeyance for nearly five years. America had a clear field. We are concerned now with only one branch of America's bid for world supremacy in trade, but there is no more progressive industry than the American film business. Money has been lavished upon its establishment, improvement and advertisement. The film magnates take their business seriously, and they plan ahead. No sooner does one film company produce a masterpiece (treating of American affairs one instinctively reaches out for superlatives) than every other company immediately strains every muscle to achieve a super-masterpiece. In detail and in representation the American films have been brought to a high pitch of perfection. We do not grudge this tribute to America's sole art." The slur must be there with the praise, the movie is America's *sole* art. But what is particularly England's art today?

Various objections have been raised to the American film, but the above-quoted writer extends his objection, a most unique and ridiculous one. "The historical films have for their motive the belittling of the Monarchy as an institution." The American movie has the object of destroying the English throne! To see the American film as "red" in its purpose is a remarkable instance of hysterical color-blindness, which is a result of the insidious American phobia distempering England. Heavy tariffs are being

Lloyd Bacon's *Moby Dick* (1930)

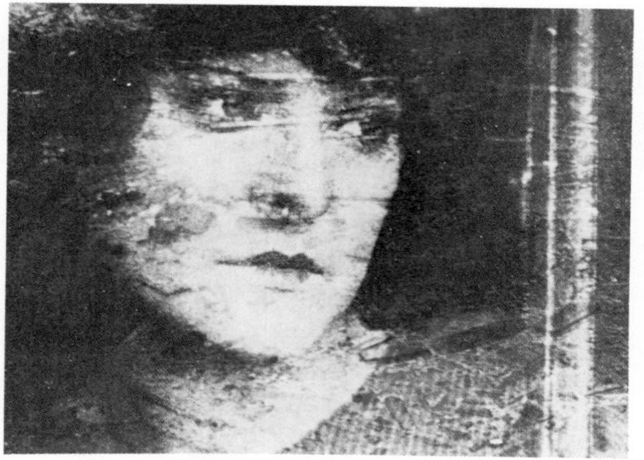

above: Jean Epstein's *Coeur Fidèle* (1923)

below: Cecil B. DeMille's *Male and Female* (1919)

right: A. Capellani's *Theodora* (1913)

facing page, bottom: Ernst Lubitsch's *The Wild Cat* (1921)

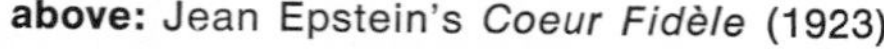

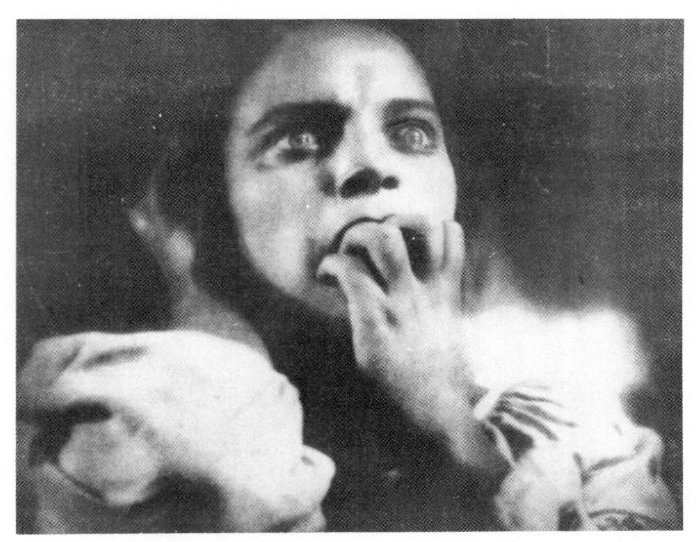

facing page, top: A. Dovzhenko's *Earth* (1930)
left: Carl Dreyer's *The Passion of Joan of Arc* (1927)
above: G. W. Pabst's *Westfront 1918* (1930)

left: Sergei Eisenstein's *Ten Days that Shook the World (October)* (1927)

facing page, bottom: René Clair's *The Italian Straw Hat* (1927)

above: F. W. Murnau's *Sunrise* (1927)

below: Fritz Lang's and Karl Freund's *Metropolis* (1927)

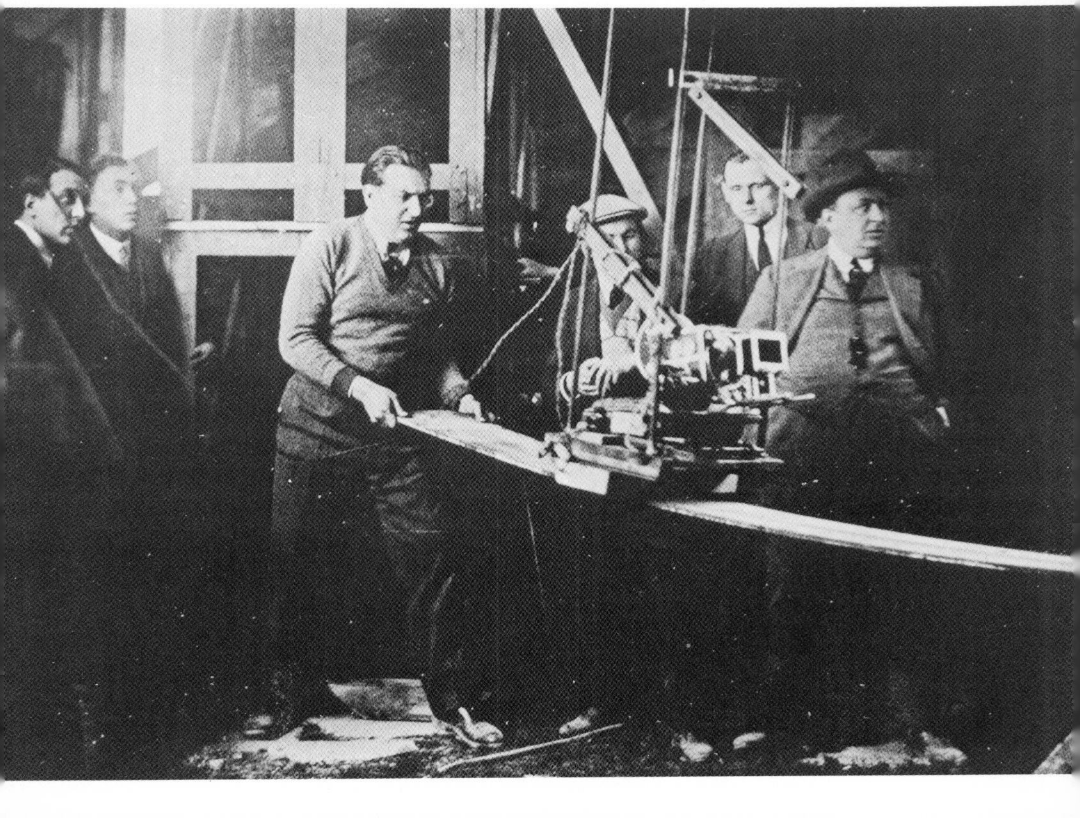

HOTEL DE LA

facing page, top: Mikhail Kalatozov's *Salt of Swanetia* (1930)
far left: G. W. Pabst's *Loves of Jeanne Ney* (1927)
left: Chaplin directing A. Menjou in *A Woman of Paris* (1923)
above: S. M. Eisenstein's *Potemkin* (1923)

facing page: D. W. Griffith's *The Birth of a Nation* (1915)

above: Josef von Sternberg's *The Case of Lena Smith* (1928)

ieft: D. W. Griffith's *The Love Flower* (1920)

left below: *Frank Capra's American Madness* (1932)

left: D. W. Griffith's *Abraham Lincoln* (1930)

above: Edward L. Cahn's *Laughter in Hell* (1932)

facing page: Howard Hawks' *Scarface* (1932)

facing page, top: Michael Curtiz's *Cabin in the Cotton* (1932)

facing page, bottom: Cecil B. DeMille's *This Day and Age* (1933)

above: James Cruze's *Washington Merry-Go-Round* (1932)

below: Rowland Brown's *Blood Money* (1933)

above: William Wellman's *Wild Boys of the Road* (1933)
below: Cecil B. DeMille's *This Day and Age* (1933)

asked to keep American films out. England has no film industry, the colonies have none. One lone amateur film, *The Light of Asia,* oozing with soft sentiment, soft acting and deliberate ignorance of the craft, has come from India. It is a bad business, and one to be regretted by Americans too. For if the movie is to be something more than a money game, each nation must develop its own, as it has developed its other arts, major and popular. But fright, resentment or vindictiveness will not help the British cinema. This popular favor for American films may be just the thing to keep the English film free of the thing threatening the development of the cinema art here; it can for the time, until the moving picture is sturdy enough, divert the attention from the immediate satisfaction of spectators to the furtherance of the convention and art of the film. As it is, the English compensate themselves with the dubious brag that the best American stars and directors are English: Fairbanks, Pickford, the Gishes, Griffith and Chaplin, though the last was born in Paris.*

An interesting development in the British industry is the formation of the British Incorporated Pictures, Limited. This corporation has "already secured guarantees of success" — among them a five-year option on film stories by fourteen of the best known British authors. The authors, artists and actors associated with this corporation include Galsworthy, Caine, Bennett, Sabatini, Phillpotts, Doyle, among the writers, Gordon Craig, Dulac and Brangwyn, among the artists, while among the actors are Mme. Karsavina, Sybil Thorndike, and du Maurier. Affiliated companies are to produce in Canada and Australia, South Africa and India. The enrollment of these artists is no guaranty of success. This procedure has in the past greatly handicapped the American cinema artistically, in thwarting the development of original screen talents, and has not proved the best thing financially. The most popular American movie actors — and the best — are not those taken over from the stage, at least not the well-known stage stars. Moreover, a survey of the tastes of London "fans," based on 300,000 questionnaires, indicates that Londoners are attracted by a particular picture rather than by a particular movie star. England has begun on the star system with a vengeance, enlisting Talullah Bankhead at a large salary. This at a time when American film producers have decided upon cutting the salaries of stars whom they alone have created. J. W. Drawbell, editor of *The London Sunday Chronicle,* says "We are suffering from too much America! We hate Yankee bluff and bluster, but we stand for hours in queues to see American films that distort our own war efforts,"

* [Ed.]: Chaplin was born in London, 16 April 1889.

and he says "We are fools if we delude ourselves that we have nothing to learn from these same people at whom we rather look down our noses. We have too little of American enthusiasm and freshness; the dogged determined will to work; the tireless driving energy and the daring virile ideas that lie behind the success of her vast campaign."

No other nation has done so much in the kino as Germany, in the utilization of cinema story and cinema craft. It anticipated French abstract experiments; its exploitation of light has realized the finest color values, thus rendering useless the technicolor film. The principle of movement has in general been more respected by Germans than by any other producers. The German cinema actors understand better than any other, except the American comics, the nuances of cinema pantomime. The German public knows this. Actors like Jannings, Krauss and Veidt have not the attractiveness of the Valentino school to offset bad playing. The German actresses have not the obvious sexual charm of the little American coquettes. It is the knowledge of their art that puts them across. But America has made its presence felt here also. Fox has established a German branch to film in Germany. Ufa (the Universum-Film-Aktiengesellschaft) owns the finest motion picture theaters in Germany; the Ufa Palast-am-Zoo in Berlin is perhaps the most appropriate theater for movie presentations in the world, unadorned but beautiful. Ufa controls the German film world, which means really all of central Europe. But what has happened? Ufa has entered into a combine with Paramount. Ufa's stars, Negri, Jannings, Veidt, Krauss, da Putti, Dagover, are brought to America and submerged.

Lubitsch, a very intelligent director, is trapped into innocuous or unimportant films. Why has Ufa done this? A gentleman of my acquaintance in Berlin who has been associated with the industry for some years explains it so: bad management, the duplication of office jobs, heavy office salaries, and poor business acumen; and, the superfilm. Germany has fallen for America's game. Even though *The Last Laugh,* her best film, was perhaps her least expensive. Example: the new film *Metropolis* cost $4,000,000. All that can be realized from it in Europe are $2,000,000. The consequence is evident.

Sweden has filmed splendid pictures. But no sooner does America learn of a performance in playing or directing than she shows her golden bags. The two leading Swedish directors, Seastrom and Stiller, have been purchased by America. The two most talented actors, Greta Garbo and Lars Hanson, have been imported by America to their own esthetic damage and the injury not alone of Sweden but all Europe. For European actors interchange without loss to their well being. Krauss in the French film

Nana, Greta Garbo in the German production *The Street Without Joy,* Veidt in the French picture *Comte Kostia,* the German Henny Porten in the excellent Viennese presentation *Baruch,* etc. The lone vitality in the Italian motion picture is supplied by these foreign players. And the actors grow with this, for they are given the chance for growth. Krauss gave his best performance in *Nana.* There was something to do, worth doing. But what has happened to Pola Negri in America? She has grown old, and—where is her *Passion* of yesterday? Stiller in Sweden directed *The Atonement of Gösta Berling* with Greta Garbo and Lars Hanson, a picture of vigilant rigor, as native to Sweden as the Selma Lagerlöf novel from which it was taken. His first American picture, *Hotel Imperial,* opened with a fine instance of European movement and photography, but quickly flattened down to a most banal sample of American literalness. Seastrom in America produced *The Scarlet Letter* with Lars Hansen. The Hawthorne novel is also rigorous, but the film failed to convey the eloquent sternness of the book. And Lars Hansen's native ability, so well-suited to the demands of the novel, was mashed into softness by the scenarist, the director and the actress opposite him, Lillian Gish; in short, by the American cinema practice. The migrations from Sweden are not looked upon altogether with fear by Swedish writers. One, Folke Holmberg, says: "The Swedish cinema is not yet singing its swan song." He hopes the emigrants will yet return to their native land; it will be too difficult for a director like Seastrom, he believes, to so transform his whole cinema-psychology, which is purely Scandinavian, to the satisfaction of the American mentality. But even should they not return, Mr. Holmberg says, there will still be a Swedish cinema. Although the films have been few, they have nevertheless been and are meritorious. It is to be hoped the Swedish motion picture prospers, because it has a distinctive character and an "impeccable photography."

Italy produced the first grand film *Cabiria.* But it now seems to have been an accident of birth. There is less of an Italian industry than there is of an English. The theaters show almost invariably American films, some German films, now and then a French film. The American films are the most patronized. The fight for dictatorship of Italy will some day be between Mussolini and Tom Mix. Arbuckle is still active on the Italian screen, and Charlie Chaplin's Odyssey is attracting more enthusiasts than ever Homer's did. The Italian film photography is really the photography of the old magic lantern. Scenic films are always a succession of post cards without motion or flow one into the other.

Douglas Fairbanks has called the Russian cinema the greatest in the world, the only one fully understanding and creating a "drama of motion." Russian films are in America, and it has been rumored that the young director of *Potemkin* is to become an American director.

One country has met the onslaught of America, and met it with grace and self-preservation. France, which recognized the merit of the American film long before America did, promises, despite little progress, to develop a distinguished film art. This would be quite in keeping with its reputation and tradition. Although most French films are bad imitations of bad American films, and French audiences are Wild West mad, there are independent producers who, if faulty, have integrity; and there is an intelligent critical interest in the movie. The first movie criticism appeared in France in 1913 and there has developed a body of critics, as authentic and authoritative as the critics of the other arts. Among the critics, in fact the best of them, are men and at least one woman who are among the leading producers of films in France. This, too, is in keeping with the French tradition. Whatever there is of a cinema criticism in America stems from France. There are fewer praiseworthy pictures in France than in America, but the commercialism of the American motion picture industry has not yet found a counterpart in France. The hope lies there.

That's Europe's motive [?] story told briefly. Europe's plight will serve neither the cinema nor America. Certainly, let us exchange films, thereby exchanging ideas and experiences. But let each develop its own idiom.

NATIONAL BOARD OF REVIEW
MAGAZINE,
December, 1927.

CINÉA-CINÉ

The cinema in France has influenced French letters before it has influenced itself. Cendrars, Romains, Clair, Montaud and Dermée have written novels and poems drawing form or plot from the cinema. Joseph Delteil avows openly, "the cinema is my father, I owe my life to it and love it. The cinema is the pink pill of literature; it gives it blood and color." The *Nouvelle Revue Française* publishes *cinarios* [*sic*] by René Bizet and others in the endeavor to establish a new and relevant literary art for the cinema. In the work of Louis Delluc and Jean Epstein, France has the nucleus of a new criticism. It is interesting that the most important ciné-critics in France are leading experimentalists in the craft of the cinema itself. This provides for the sensitive interrelationship between the two which exists in France. There is a notable absence of such interrelationship in our cinema world.

Architecture, music, painting, have, if we are to believe their prominent practitioners, drawn from the cinema. "Modern architecture is essentially photogenic . . ." (Robert Mallet-Stevens). If the influence on music is not always actual, it is certainly, according to Paul Ramain, potential. In painting the evidences of cinematic influences are discernible in futurism — the succession of positions of an object in motion — and in surrealism — the *shunting* of varied separate patterns into one pattern.

But the cinema in its intrusions does not find immunity from counter-influences that are unsalutary. Literature demands payment with a plot intrusion that thwarts the inherent tendency of the film. It furthers also the malignant parasite on the action, the caption. "The error of the cinema is the scenario," says Léger, the director of the *Ballet Mécanique,* although the *Nouvelle Revue Française cinarios* do contain the idea of a movie-plot, based on qualities of cinema technique. But nevertheless the French motion picture has gone farther and farther away from its inherent character. In the early *avant la guerre* films there was the bare cinema story untroubled by too many details or captions. Of course these films were ridiculously crude, as their republication in 1926 shows, but they were not overloaded with a luggage not theirs. The first film was screened in Paris more than 30 years ago, and since that time there have been very few moving pictures manufactured in France that were not burdened with short stories, novels, plays (in themselves bad theatre), or even narrative poems. Today Pierre Benoît's novels are utilized for stupefying movie-dramas "shot" at a stupendous cost; Lamartine's already sentimental *Graziella* is further sentimentalized as a picture, redeemed only by the first "serious" (though pale) use of slow motion as a vehicle; and the cleverest large-scale directors, Baroncelli and Pruniéres, perhaps present another atrocity made out of Napoleon. This tendency, alien to the natural tendency of the film, has been accentuated by the very worst aspects of the American and German movie, the super and costume cine-monsters. The newspaper serial for the movie, written to advertise public favorites and for a specific star, has been borrowed also from America. Only in several isolated instances have the literary origins of a film not obliterated it. There was the recent *Nana* from Zola, directed by the son of Renoir. In places there was vivacity of movement, as in the play of Nana's capricious plump legs effectively carrying her emotional temper, or in the restatement of a Degas ballet and a Renoir garden group, but more particularly in the establishment of definite, mask-like ratios between the players, who were unbelievably (as compared with American stars) intelligent and aware of these ratios. But cinema it was not, it did not sustain its movement. It was apparently not conceived as cinema, but rather as the graphic interplay of character units.

Another film was the equally recent *Poil de Carotte*. Its visual honesty of domestic detail and its sympathetic apprehension of the tragedy involved made of it an emotional experience far more powerful, probably, than the original novel. To an American it was simultaneously the experience of a human tragedy and the experience of an intense and rancorous humiliation. For it was another evidence of a superiority of French values to ours. What domestic detail would be the turning point in an American tragedy of mother hatred? Of course no such tragedy could ever occur in an American movie. But the detail, if given the movie? The son brings home his first play and things are sweet thereafter, or . . . The French movie, however, is relentless: the mother hides the pot, and the boy befouls the fireplace. That is the determining detail and nothing of it is spared the spectator, who, being French, enjoys it without comment or protest. The young protagonist, André Heuze, does not need to turn his rattling freckles into obvious, sentimental farce or barefoot-boy pathos; his freckles are his tragic destiny. However, *Poil de Carotte* did not serve the needs or the demands of the cinema. That has been served by only one French film whose origin as story was outside itself: *Vanina,* produced in 1920. The first and only completely plastic film France has created, a fluid *contrast aux formes.* The first and the last.

Vanina bore no issue. Nothing followed; nothing was learned from it. Not because it had nothing to teach. For its re-presentation in 1926 at the Studio des Ursulines proved it to be still the finest thing France has done. But because there was no one who was receptive to its teaching. The French film has improved upon the lighting of *Vanina,* Man Ray has done much better ciné-portraiture, the experimentalists Chomette, Cavalcanti, Clair, Epstein, L'Herbier, have extended the possibilities of ciné-virtuosity by the isolation of certain plastic details, but *Vanina* as a complete motion-picture stands alone. It is in fact better than anything done in America and Germany, from the standpoint of flow. *The Last Laugh,* Carl Grune's *The Street, The Beautiful Blue Danube,* are German pictures that have exploited the motive drama contained in an incident far more completely than has *Vanina,* and of course speed is an American monopoly, but plastic motion has been nowhere else so sustained and continuous as in *Vanina.* In this respect it is superior to *Potemkin.* The exploitation of movement in the latter was patent, it was a movement of surface masses sufficient to carry the drama which had in itself tremendous motive power. Whereas in *Vanina* the movement is integral and attenuated, showing a thorough and intensive understanding and manipulation of both subject and medium. The plot fuses into the movement, so that the relationship between the movie story and the Stendhal novel from which it was extracted and rendered casual. Here is a total conversion of potential movement into plastic movement. In America no such conversion has been attempted: *The Big Parade* moves as the story moves, it is chronological and matter-of-fact, its effective progress an accident of the story. *Vanina* begins immediately and proceeds in accumulative flow toward the critical pauses where the flow is precipitated in a dramatic burst, thence to proceed further. Captions are reduced to minimum, and no descriptive captions are used—the action explains itself. This frees the flow to an intensification of the motive drama.

Vanina was not succeeded by other pictures which continued the development. The *films abstraits* cannot be said to be extensions of that lone product, nor to have been created in its light. No more than they have been aware of the German kino-dramas which have anticipated them in the use of the virtuoso technique for purposes of vehicle. The abstract film, in fact, has been born not of cinema at all, it is illegitimate. Abstract painting derives eventually from Cezanne, it is the ultimate isolation of one easily grasped aspect of the manifold in Cezanne's graphic. It is legitimate as painting. But as cinema it is not acceptable. The French artist and those others who think in terms of graphic cannot perform the metamorphosis necessary for thinking in cinegraphic terms. The French cinema is in need of "the compleat ciné artist," as intelligent about cinema plastic and cinema presentation as the painter and sculptor are about their plastics. Picabia's surrealism, haphazard, unaware, directionless, is not meant for a new art, it is the ultimate language of an art which has been vigilant a long time. The cinema cries for organization, alertness, definiteness. It cannot flourish on distortions which do not re-establish relationships, on isolations remaining isolations, on violence without vitamine. The cinema has not yet learned self-consciousness. Its convention has not yet been established. It has no traditions, no schools, and is not yet ready for an *avant-garde*. The laboratory films of Chomette, Picabia or Cavalcanti have revealed nothing to further the detection and comprehension of a convention, which will be found, I believe, not in linear plastic nor in prismatic distortion, but in the key to *Vanina*: plastic fluidity.

In Jean Tedesco's journal, *Cinéa-Ciné,* Mm. Henri Fescourt and Jean-Louis Bouquet ask very decidedly, if delicately, shall it be *"Sensations ou Sentiments?"* Shall the *Images-Idées* be accepted "solely to charm the eye" or shall they be a means "to give birth, through the play of sentiments, to the divine Emotion?" The ancient debate has been carried over to this infant. If a cargo without a vehicle is so much dead storage, what is a vehicle without a cargo? The answer to the riddle is not direct; it is, however, conclusive. What the cinema needs is not to borrow but to establish out of itself. The late Louis Delluc wrote: "The Cinema is painting in motion." Jean Tedesco replies: "The screen cannot be compared to a painting." Pierre Porte defends Chomette, the *metteur en scène* of the Beaumont film, by an analogy with music. Fescourt and Bouquet reply. "Why cling so tenaciously to the word *music* when you can say cinema?" The controversialists are alert: therein lies the hope of the French film. If they can be on guard diligently to keep the cinema endogamous and uncrossed until it has borne of its own by its own, it will then be ready to borrow from other plastics.

NATIONAL BOARD OF REVIEW
MAGAZINE,
October, 1927.

THE FRENCH CINEMA

Jean Lenauer, writing in the May *Close Up,* has said some true things which, because they are not qualified, are dangerous. To say, for instance, that to him the French have no sense of the cinema is no light charge, and, one may counter with one of two remarks: this is a prejudice and not a critical judgment, or the question, a sense of what cinema? For M. Lenauer, like his young French colleagues, is all for the American cinema. It is true that he charges the French directors with aping the American successes, but from every indication his cinema mind has been formed by the U.S.A. movie. He is in this a European and particularly a Frenchman, although his nativity is Viennese. Like the young Frenchmen, he claims the movie as his and only his, and to have been born before the film or with it — as in my own case — is to be put beyond the pale. The young Frenchman delights in saying the French are without a cinema-sense. Lenauer has in the May *Close Up* only repeated M. Auriol in *transition* No. 15, M. Charensol in *La Revue Fédéraliste* of November, 1927, and the first utterer of this condemnation, the late Louis Delluc. There are a host of others. In truth, the young Frenchman is developing a defeatist mind, and Lenauer is throwing on his little pressure.

One of the slogans of the French counter-French critic is the denial of youth in the French cinema world. Everyone I have met has complained of this, and Cavalcanti was glad to have even an inane actress in *Captain Fracasse* because she was young. Youth! Youth! it is a perennial cry. And what does it here signify? What does Youth claim in this instance? That the cinema belongs to it. And how does it substantiate its claim? By repeating the attitudes of the Frenchmen who first began to swear fidelity to the film. Auriol utters Soupault's adorations of the American action-film. And everyone of them echoes Canudo. Except that, typical of youth of all ages, these youngest Frenchmen are rebelling against the old cinema — of France. The Revolt of Youth? Nonsense. The Rebellion of Youth! Impatience and arrogance mostly. There is little development here in France of that salutary skepticism among intelligent young men which includes in its scrutinies Youth. For Youth is not a fact, it is a symbol, and that symbol has no reference to the date of one's birth. It is true that art and youth are related, but it is not the youth of which Lenauer talks, but youth which means fervor. Will Lenauer say that the older Frenchmen whom he condemns are all without fervor? And am I, are we, to deny sincerity and depth of devotion to the film to all those who do not love the film in the way Lenauer says he loves it? And just how does he love it? Is it a sign of love to condemn all who challenge the beloved? That is chivalry in the wrong category. And just when did Lenauer begin to love the film? Of course these questions are not for M. Lenauer himself. (I am not, it is self-evident, directing my words against M. Lenauer. I am thinking of all the lovers of the cinema who cry their love aloud. I know too many parallel instances in America to be convinced too readily by the declaration: "I love the cinema." The American enthusiasts of 1923 — and now — were superior to the film only a few years before their discovery of it as "art." Their interest came only as a consequence of popular enthusiasm, and an urge to be of the time. But no critical affection is worth anything unless it has grown from the visceral pleasure of childhood. Are the young Frenchmen, and young Europeans, experiencing a belated childhood? [I dwell upon the American phenomenon in an article, "French Opinion and the American Movie," appearing in *Du Cinéma*]). Nor do I ask for an answer. These questions contain certain implications:

I. The cinema was not born with the motion picture. It has its origins in the first experiences of mankind, and its sources are all the manifestations of life.

II. To care for the film only may be a good way to a career but it is certainly no assurance that the film will be enriched. Creation in one art, or activity in one profession, does not, even in this age of specialization, bar one from another art or another profession.

The cult of youth has produced some interesting conditions in the French cinema. There is no differentiation here between the amateur and the professional. And this is bad for the amateur, the beginner. The group of young men which includes Auriol and Lenauer will agree that what I say about the inflation of the amateur is true, but they will not agree that they are contributing to the very condition they mock. If there is snobbism in France, and there is, they are strengthening it by their attitude, and one of them is youth. Any number of youngsters (some of older age) put out a film deriving rudimentary from *Rien que les Heures* (without full awareness of the principle) or *Berlin* and enter the ranks of the *metteurs en scène,* with the footnote: forgive the transgressions, they are young and they had no money. To produce a film without money always excites the professional (or better commercial) world, but it should mean nothing to the beginner—that's just how he should begin, and moreover, why should his first work be made public? In America we distinguish between the amateur and the professional, and that is the amateur's salvation. It is a part of the discipline of any artist to "be rejected" or to be ignored—that he may learn how really insignificant his infant labors are. If youth is not favoured in the large French companies, its favor in the specialized halls is certainly less creditable.

If the young Frenchman really cares about the French film, he will not heed the cry of defeat (which is really a self-inflation) but will examine the French film to learn the French idiom, which must be his. That the American film, by its very remoteness from his own physical experience, enchants him is not enough reason for him to mistake that enchantment for the complete and sole experience of cinema. If he really loves the film, he will not show it by talk upon the influence of the movie on customs, such as gum chewing, to which he is an addict, or physical gestures after James Murray or George Bancroft. Nor will he show it by damning the French girl for Joan Crawford or Louise Brooks. Nor by an ignorance of the past of the American film, which he so much idolizes. Nor by limiting motion to antic, action, speed. Nor by finding Victor MacLaglen a great artist, whereas that lucky Irishman has a constant (hence non-artistic) personality no matter what the film. Nor by denying the meritorious Catherine Hessling because she casually recalls Mae Murray. He will stop chattering and go to work. He will discipline himself and question his enthusiasms, or at least examine them to know where to put them. AND HE WILL STUDY THE FRENCH INTELLIGENCE IN ITS EXPRESSION IN THE FRENCH FILM, whether he likes its makers or not. His head is now stuffed with American idioms, but he will need to be re-born an American before he will make an integral film of them. The Frenchman remains a provincial all his life.

To remain a provincial is no limitation to an artist. The Frenchman's Frenchness has been one of the chief reasons for his cultural and aesthetic survival amid influences that should have long destroyed or reduced him. He creates within his own boundaries. Nowhere is this condition more apprehendable [*sic*] than in the cinema. The French mind shows itself constantly in the success and the failure.

The French mind is, first, a pictorial mind. The French cinematist is pictorial minded. He is not in the least, as is the American, action minded. This is as noticeable in the old serial thrillers, whose idiom is action, as in the absolute films of the *avant-garde*. Nor is the pictorial mind counter-cinema. Nothing is counter-cinema. *And no people are incapable of making films.* The task is to use the mind where it can legitimately function. It cannot function in police films: do not attempt police films. It functions in documentaries, films of restricted areas, films psychological and metaphysical, etc.: set it to work in these milieus. The pictorial mind can be set to work badly or well. It is daily perceived in the "grand" French films where it is resultant in a tedious, over-adorned spectacle like *Koenigsmark*. The pictorial mind does not lend itself very easily to "big" films. Action alone makes these supportable. That is one reason why the French cannot compete commercially with America. But the cinema is not justified by commerce, no more than Balzac's right to exist is determined by the public taste for Dekobra.

The pictorial mind succeeds best when it functions independently within limited areas. Germaine Dulac does a fascinating film in *The Seashell and the Clergyman* and a charming film in *Mme. Beudet,* but when she turns to do a "large-scale" film she puts out the sentimental *"poésie"* of *The Folly of the Valiant. "Poésie"* is the pictorial mind forced to extend itself out of its non-literary milieu. Gance is full of *"poésie."* He belongs to the France of Rodin, and with Poirier, to the France of Lamartine and Hugo without their vision. The best instance of the pictorial mind rightly applied is Jean Epstein. He insists upon the image, lingers over it, penetrates it. What does it matter that *Finis Terrae* is slow? What does it mean that it does not satisfy those who wanted the subject treated *physically* instead of *psychically?* Epstein has shown how the physical material may be rendered psychical by persisting in the examination of the physical image. The pictorial mind here transcends itself.

It is in keeping with the pictorial mind that the French have made so much of the term "photogenic," that Germaine Dulac indefatigably urges the *film visuel* as against the *film anti-visuel*. It is right that Man Ray should have found his center in Paris, and that the best short, nonnarrative films should come from France: *The Octopus* of Jean Painlevé as well as that early nature study, *The Germination of Plants, The Zone* of Georges Lacombe, *The Petite Lily* of Cavalcanti . . .

This leads to a second deduction, the source of the French film is in the traditional *atelier* of French art. It is true, in the main, that the film dependent upon collective labors has a hard row in France (but, from another point of view, does it have such a good time in America?). (The collective difficulty in France is mainly the natural indifference of the French working man, and the financial closeness of the producer. As for the major collectivity, between the artists, I think, on the whole, a better *esprit* exists in France than in America. And as for the intrusion of the mercantilists into the enterprise of the author, what grosser instance than that of Hollywood?) This is not irremediable. My deduction is not, however, made from negative conditions but conditions which are organic and positive. All that I have said before leads to the deduction, and the most interesting films are those made from the *atelier,* single-artist viewpoint. This does not infer that the French film must rest in the *atelier,* as the pictorial mind does not infer that the French film must remain in the framed set. Not in the least. The instances of *Finis Terrae, En Rade, Two Timid Souls* are sufficient to gainsay such inferences. Yet these films are film with their sources in the *atelier*-mind and the pictorial-mind. With Epstein the *atelier* becomes the study, for speculation and metaphysics. *En Rade* is the pictorial mind providing an enveloping environment. *Two Timid Souls* is evidence of the pictorial mind creating comic rhetoric of the picture. Comedy in America is action. The gag in *Two Timid Souls* is a pictorial gag, in Harold Lloyd it is the antic gag. Chaplin makes very little of the picture.

The *atelier*-source does not (the word "source" is the explanation) limit the French film to the laboratory where Jean Lenauer confines it, although the experimental film will always be a French contribution. Nor does it restrict the film to its absolute forms. It means simply that the film companies must recognize the *mind* of the French artist and work according to it. The Société Générale des Films promised to be just that sort of corporation, allowing the director, and not the fiscal policy, to set the pace. At present the Société Générale seems to be biding its time amid the confusion caused by the talking picture. But its single-film policy is the accurate one for the French cinema. For that cinema, because of the characteristics detectable in it (which I have considered above) will not be a world's popular cinema, and no *contingement* [*sic*] make it that. In fact, the French have not, in their entertainment, the gift of the popular, whether in the revue, the vaudeville show or the motion picture.

The French need to be vigilant against two related faults: sentimentality and refinement. The French sentimentality is not moral sentimentality, as in the case of the English and the American, but aesthetic sentimentality. (A signal instance of refinement applied wrongly is Renoir's *The Little Match-Girl,* where the operetta-Russian Ballet's [which is really French in its mincingness] decorative sense was exercised upon a Danish folk-theme. Decorative refinement is one of the main obstacles to the creation of a French cinema comedy). It is present in almost every French film, but where it is held within the boundaries of each instance it aids rather than oppresses the film. It is sensivity in *The Seashell and the Clergyman* of Germaine Dulac, and in her *Cinegraphic Study Upon an Arabesque;* it is sensitivity bordering on collapse in *En Rade;* it is sensitivity avoiding collapse by larger references in Epstein; it is a diffusive and soft sentimentality in Poirier and Gance. Leon Poirier has made beautiful documents in *The Black Journey* and the second part of *Exotic Loves* where the image is the end, but in *Verdun* and *Jocelyn,* where the image refers to its sources in national and literary experience, he offends with his superfluous stresses of sentiment, and that is sentimentality, or one form of it. Gance continually associates his image with some "poetic" phrase: Violin and the lily, Napoleon and the eagle (in *Napoleon*), "the rose of the rail" (in *The Wheel*). And both enjoy the surimpressed [*sic*] symbol: The Spirit of France. I have said Gance was Hugo without Hugo's vision. That makes him the counterpart in cinema to Eugene Sue. The French "big" film is eighteenth-century romanticism. In that it is very much the France of today. Eighteenth- and nineteenth-century romanticism.

Of this ilk is the recently sponsored humanitarianism of the French film. Another sentimentalism. For an inclusive humanitarianism is not in keeping with the French temperament of non-projection and dispassion. Therefore it is frequently false, particularly when uttered by those who find in the slogan profit. M. Tedesco hails the "new humanitarianism" of the American film, finding that sympathy in films like *The Crowd, Lonesome, Underworld, A Girl in Every Port,* etc. I shall not here go into any examination of the American films. But to discover one's human experience at this level of cinema content, indicates that the discovery is hardly profound. This acceptance of American "human interest" films as human experience accords with the frequent French declaration that the movie is not an art. This is the Frenchman's justification of his affections. The whole matter of art is resolved in the levels of experience. The level at which the matter of life is experienced, determines the category of art or non-art.

The dispassion of the French keeps them, on the whole, more rational towards the love-life than other peoples. Therefore the Frenchman who declared against the need for Freud was not so much in error as Lenauer implies. But this dispassion does make it difficult for the French to project themselves into the lives of a less indifferent, more passionate people. But to say that they never project themselves into such lives is to forget that the French have been the most persistent admirers of the Swedish film, the only fully realized passionate pictures. Here I think French critical rationality recognizes the level of tragic experience at which the Swedes have conceived their films. I do not like the way in which *Sunrise* was received by the French multitudes, but I must admit that the level at which it was conceived, sustained though it was throughout the enfoldment of the narrative, was a level at which it might just as easily have been rejected. For the material may have attained to the tragic, in the German conception it reached only pathos, and pathos is not far from sentimentality, emotional sentimentality. (I say all this despite my admiration of the film and its director). The French reject emotional sentimentality, but they accept decorative sentimentality.

There have been a few French instances of *approximative* tragedy in the cinema, and these few instances indicate a milieu which the French have not nearly begun to exploit. I refer at this moment to the domestic tragedy, which provides immediate activity for all the French qualities of provincialism, limited locale, pictorial mind. The film that first comes to my mind is *Poil de Carotte* of Julien Duvivier (with continuity, I am advised by Jacques Feyder). The film was poignant and convincing and in every particular French. *Thérèse Raquin* belongs to the French acceptation, despite the pronounced German qualities of the exterior lighting and the acting of the two male players. (Feyder, a Belgian, is assimilative). The French, if they but knew, would do the domestic film. Dulac gave us *Mme. Beudet,* sensitive in its irony carried pictorially. Nine years ago Albert Dieudonné made *Une Vie sans Joie* (called *Backbiters* in England) and had he ceased where the tale demanded, he would have presented to a sympathetic audience a tragic idyll. Instead he continued the film into the episode of the runaway tramway, where it looked very much like a take-off of an old French tinted film of a locomotive's dash. Jean Benoît-Lévy and Marie Epstein have recently produced *Peau de Pêche.* It is a mélange of many themes expressed in the images and the captions. But amid this mélange one detects certain promises: in the images of both the city and the country, in the characterization of the chum of Peach-Skin, and in one episode which should have been the film. The little stream which is the sustenance of the neighbourhood runs dry. The peasants have assembled to hear the radio of one of their neighbors. While they listen a cry comes from one of the lads: "The river is back!" An old man says: "Of what importance is the world to us now? We have a river back." A monumental theme expressed in the area of a small village in the provinces. A theme that obscures the entire film. A theme that indicates a possible point toward which the French film can strive. It is a theme for Jean Epstein.

Jean Epstein is an artist the rest of the French directors might study with profit. He is, although, I believe, a Jew, born in Poland, French in his virtues and his faults. His faults are almost always rendered virtuous by an all-inclusive mind which is not far removed from French sentimentalism, but which, by nobler intention and speculation, becomes mysticism. Epstein deals with inferences, the inferences of the penetrated image. His film *Finis Terrae* is, I think, of highest significance to France. I can indicate some errors, like the shifting of the point of view from the boys and their mothers to the doctor, but they do not contradict the contribution. The film is entirely pictorial-minded. It takes the natives as it finds them and builds the image of their stolid movements. I detect in this, not the snobbery Lenauer finds, but relevant intelligence. However, I do not intend speaking upon Epstein here. I reserve that for a paper wholly upon him. I wish only to indicate that here is one source for the French cinema.

And what will the French film take from *Joan of Arc?* It's perfection does not mean that it does not contain the germ of propagation. It too is built of the image. True, it was done by a Scandinavian. But it was done with French material and it's method offers an opportunity for the French intelligence. Another source — and this is one out of the boundaries of France — is the Swedish film of the days of Seastrom and Stiller. The American film, whose "technique" so infatuates the French mind, is not a source for that mind.

Sources: that is the first investigation every artist should make. I have dwelt upon the systemic sources for the French cinema. But, since the cinema, no more than any other art, is isolated, it will find its sources, not only in itself, nor in the mind immediately referring to it, but also in the other aesthetic articulations. Dreyer went to the medieval French miniature for a source to embolden the imagery, and hence the drama, of *Joan*. The French theater is full of sources of identical mind with the French cinema mind: take Gaston Baty's production of Molière's *The Imaginary Invalid*. The pictorial mind dominates. The French *cinéastè* must cease his absolutes of non-accord between the theater and the cinema. He must look into all his experience and expressions to discover himself. He must believe he can create cinema, if he is faithful to his own intelligence, intuition and experience.

CLOSE UP,
July, 1929.

THE FRENCH FILM

The French cinema was, in the first days of the new art, the most important of all. As far back as 1895 the French magician, Georges Méliès, had begun to use the new medium at the Théâtre Robert Houdin for the purpose of furthering the illusion, which is the secret of magic. In 1896 he constructed the first studio for making films. He began to manufacture pictures that even today are amazing for their knowledge of the fantastic possibilities of the movie. He was the scenarist, the designer, the director and the star of his pictures. The company was Star Film. Méliès is responsible for the entire practice of film cutting, which today, under the name of *montage,* is the philosophy of the Russian film. Méliès used cutting for tricks, like sudden transformations. The animated cartoon finds its ancestry in the pictures of Méliès, where heads of humans are notes in a bar of music. Chairs and tables move unaided. America had a replica of Méliès in Sigmund Lubin, who cut his films to make autos jump from peak to peak. The name of Méliès was important in the commercial history of the film, too, along with the names of Pathé and Gaumont. Those were the days when the creators still owned the films, the days of the movie's infancy in the laboratory.

As late as the war the French film was dominant in the movie world. The rooster of Pathé vied with the polar bear of the Danish Great Northern and the V of the American Vitagraph. Max Linder was, until Charlie Chaplin appeared, the one screen comedian known to the world by name. Indeed, Chaplin is not entirely without somewhat of an obligation to Linder as a forerunner.

The war came and the European Cinema well-nigh collapsed. The American movie became dominant, although two nations, when the war ended, contributed more than America to the actual advancement of motion pictures: Sweden and Germany. But when the Frenchmen saw their first American film, *The Cheat,* with the venerable Fanny Ward and the Japanese Sessue Hayakawa, they were captivated. They saw too, Pearl White in *The Exploits of Elaine* and William S. Hart the Westerner, and J. P. MacGowan the best known of the serialists. Of this discovery of America in the film, a noted French writer, Philippe Soupault, wrote: "One day we saw great long bill-posters stretched along the signboards like serpents. At each corner of the street a man, his face covered with a red handkerchief, threatened the peaceful passers-by with a revolver. We heard galloping horses, chugging motors, screams and death-rattles. We dashed into the movie house and realized that all was changed. The smile of Pearl White appeared on the screen, that almost ferocious smile announcing the upheaval of the new world."

That was the pitch of the French enthusiasm. It let down for a time. But it was again restored with the coming of films like *Underworld, Dressed to Kill, The Crowd, Lonesome, A Girl in Every Port, The Cat and the Canary, The Last Warning.* These films are shown not only in the neighborhood houses, but in those élite places that specialize in art. Art, evidently, is the enchantment of distance. France it was that discovered first that Charlie Chaplin was an artist.

That is a picture of the French attitude towards our movie. I personally think the French enthusiast exaggerates the virtues of the American film. But whether that is so or not, he certainly diverts the French director from the thing he can do best to a confused imitation of the American product or to a pessimistic assertion: "The French are not a movie-making people!"

The confusion goes back to another source too. The motion picture was getting on to a differentiation between the stage play and the photoplay when the classical theater of France, La Comédie Française, began to turn its traditional dramas into pompous movies. Sarah Bernhardt entered the films. The Bernhardt movie, *Queen Elizabeth,* was imported into America, and from this was born the "famous players in famous plays" idea of Adolph Zukor, which has not been the best thing for the movie. Therefore, when, amid spectacle plays, the lively American film – the rudimentary movie – appeared, the French felt, as Soupault said, that "everything was revivified with a single stroke."

After the war, writers and painters turned to the film. Louis Delluc, novelist and critic, began to turn out pictures. These were the beginners of the "new French cinema," although Delluc asserted that the French have no mind for making films. This has been repeated frequently, but I do not accept it. With Delluc at the time appeared the writer, Canudo, who, with his declaration that the movies were the seventh art, began the "highbrow" interest in the motion picture. Delluc sent the new film makers searching into the film itself to find just what it was: its quality and its possibilities. From him stem the experimenting and adventurous film-makers, still active: Mme. Germaine Dulac, Jean Epstein, the Brazilian Albert Cavalcanti, René Clair, and numerous others. There are these others who have been important in the development of the French film, but whom I feel to be quite finished: Abel Gance—the French D. W. Griffith, Marcel L'Herbier, Leon Poirier.

Canudo is responsible for the origin of the film club, the "little art cinema," and for the film criticism. He was criticizing pictures as far back as 1911. His judgments and anticipations are important even today. He founded the French Film Club, and today there are almost a dozen of these organizations.

There are about a half-dozen successful movie houses specializing in selected films. By putting the movie into the Autumn Salon of Art, and into the great International Art Exposition of 1925, Canudo gave the motion picture film a definite place of honor among the arts.

Now both Delluc and Canudo are dead. Their work is still evident: the positive work of both and the negative statement of Delluc. This latter might be put to study by the French. Perhaps Delluc implied what I believe: the French have not the mind for a certain kind of movies. They cannot do the action film, that is an American product because the American mind is an action mind. A French serial of the old days was never active, possessed little suspense and was more posed than played. The French spectacle film is unwieldy in its overcostumed and overpicturesque way, just as the German spectacle film is clumsy in its stolid movement. But there are films the French can do and do well.

The French are a nation with eyes for the pictorial. Go to a French vaudeville theatre. You will see an endless succession of acrobatic acts that would bore most Americans. But the French see the form as well as the feat. Their sense of the design is more refined than ours. Jean Epstein, using a slow-motion camera, captures the texture of sea spray or a floating veil as no one else has ever done.

Moreover, the French are people who work alone. So Madame Dulac, who has been named a Chevalier of the Legion of Honor, has told me.

"We," quoth Mme. Dulac, "are most successful when we have made the film alone from beginning to end." You will find the French are therefore best when they make films that are short and lyrical instead of long and continuously active, like a Fairbanks film. Indeed, let a director in France make a film needing Fairbanks' agility, and the bet is, the film will be stiff and lacking in sprightliness. Cavalcanti, a Brazilian but French in his mentality, made such a picture of the novel by Gautier, *Captain Fracasse.* It lacked the poignant or mischievous quality, the dance quality, of a short Cavalcanti picture like *La P'tite Lilie.*

The French can do the domestic tragedy. The best of such films is *Thérèse Raquin,* called here *Shadows of Fear,* directed by Jacques Feyder, who has done his first American film, *The Kiss,* starring Greta Garbo. The French can also make good films of a pathetic nature or tragic nature about a child. American films of a child or children are usually false, making the kid or kids too adult or smart or cute. The Germans make good films about children – groups of children. In France the individual child is the subject and frequently the case is very exceptional. Good instances of child films made in France are: *Faces of Children* and *Gribiche,* directed by Feyder, and *Carrot-head,* directed by Julien Duvivier, with the continuity by Feyder.

"Feyder," the young French director, René Clair, once said to me, "is our greatest director." I don't accept this, for I consider Clair no small beer himself. Clair is the only important French director of comedy. He is for me, about the only real director of comedy in western Europe, and there is no one quite his equal in America as a director of subtle movie fun. In America the comedy director depends on his actors, they are usually greater than he. There isn't any director up to Harry Langdon or Raymond Griffith. Clair lacks, contrariwise, the comic actor worthy of his talents. It is interesting that his star in *The Horse Ate the Hat,* Albert Préjean, resembles Ray Griffith. But he isn't a Griffith – Clair needs such a genius for comic performance to help him make his greatest comedy. But there is this about Clair: he is a director and he makes everything serve him. Not only does he work the actor, he uses the screen, the film stock and the camera to produce laughter. Clair has a memory and he employs it. In *The Horse Ate the Hat* he recalls the table-and-chair film of Méliès. The serving-man has whispered to the groom, being married by the mayor, that the irate soldier waiting for his return has threatened to destroy all the furniture. The groom visions the furniture issuing from his home in accelerated motion. In the film, *Two Timid Souls,* the novice-attorney describes the idyllic bliss of the marital life of his client, the defendant.

The latter enters in slow motion. The young lawyer forgets what he wanted to say. The defendant is seen moving back in slow motion. This describes the state of mind of the lawyer, who has gone back to the beginning again. Suddenly the movement stops with the husband and wife in a stationary position. Then the lawyer's mind goes blank and the domestic scene explodes from the screen leaving it blank. All this is told, not only by acting, but by the movement of the camera and the film. Clair splits the screen into two parallel panels picturing the young lawyer and his rival showing what they'll do, one to the other. The film ends with the screen divided into three pictures, the rival on the left, the father on the right, the young newlyweds in the center — all in bed. First the left goes dark, then the right, and lastly the center, and with it the picture.

I have dwelt on Clair because real directors of comedy, even more than real comedians, are as rare as Kohinoor diamonds; and also because Clair remains the single director of comedy in France. Though why, it is difficult to say: France has comedy and satire, writers of such, actors in such, and the early French movie made much of the comic like Rigadin and Max Linder.

There are hopeful indications in France in the film of the Breton seaweed fishers, *Land's End* made by Jean Epstein, who has made also the best film of soul-torment in a long time, from Poe's *The Fall of the House of Usher*. The former film is made without professional actors. The Breton natives themselves perform in this simple but poignant film. Another good sign is a film made by Clair's young assistant, Georges Lacombe, which tells in simple, straightforward fashion the life of the rag pickers who live in The Zone and sell their wares in the Flea Market. It was this market by the way, that served as the locale for Maurice Chevalier's first American film, *The Innocents of Paris*. Young amateurs are constantly making films in Paris and having them presented in art cinemas. This hospitality is both good and bad: good in that it gives the newcomer a chance, and bad in that it inflates the young amateur.

Paris is the convergence-point for all artists. And to Paris come also the individual and independent makers of films from the world over; Cavalcanti from Brazil, Buñuel from Spain, Deslav from the Ukraine, Man Ray from America, and Carl Dreyer from Denmark. The last directed the great picture — to me the greatest picture — *The Passion of Joan of Arc*. To show the cosmopolitan character of the French film world, let us see who made this film. The company is made up of Russians, the director was born in Sweden but has lived in Denmark, the star is Italian in origin although long a French stage actress, the cameraman Polish. In Cavalcanti's company making *Captain Fracasse* there were a Brazilian director, a Danish operator and a Dutch heroine. But then take Hollywood, the greatest directors are not American. But somehow America does not preserve the greatness of her foreign directors, a genius like Seastrom for instance. On the continent interchange is constant and no one is the worse for it. Some day this fact will produce very, very great pictures in France. Even today, singly, the films of France are important for one thing or another. As a commercial competitor, however, France is small potatoes, and the sooner she knows this the better for her directors and her films. France has been a great influence and is still, and can be so for years to come. We have learned much from her as to the art of the film. Her artists are experimenters, ours are job holders who do good jobs. We need to be constantly taught, and France can teach.

When the world gets to a point where it no longer expects to be hit into excitement or tickled into guffaws by every film, when speed isn't the test of a film – and that time isn't so far distant – the French film will come into its own in the world's eyes and the eyes of France. For the present, the individual film maker works at his camera and there is much talk and writing about films. This is a sign, a good sign – the air will be cleared. As it is, the most sincere and ambitious World War film has come from France, *Verdun,* by Leon Poirier; the best domestic tragedy; the best tragedy of the single child; the best film of mystical torment; the best technical comedies; the best ballad-films; one of the best documentary romances of native life; some of the best films of machine movements and the like; the best psychoanalytical film; the best Napoleonic film; and so on. This record isn't bad. France might respect it a little more than she does.

The French waited long until they began to make the talkie. And now the good news comes that the first real talkie will star Yvette Guilbert, directed by René Clair's brother-in-law, Henri Chomette. Why is this good news? Simply because Yvette Guilbert, at least to me and thousands of others, is the greatest personality of the French – and perhaps modern – theater. This great chanter of medieval songs with a voice of abundant tones, and a pantomimic sense not equalled by anyone else, with a poise beautiful and colorful, I have been urging as the beginning for the French audible film. France has failed to build a theater with Mme. Guilbert as a foundation – perhaps France will build a new cinema with her at its beginning.

CINEMA,
February, 1930.

THE GERMAN FILM: KINO AND LICHTSPIEL

There is a similarity between the German film and the French. It is the similarity of the studio and the atelier. But the similarity ceases very soon, for the French cinematist takes his atelier outdoors; the German cinematist puts his outdoors into the studio. The German film has never left the studio. That is one of the gravest limitations in the German kino. It thwarted a film like *Homecoming,* made the entire rendering of *Asphalt* false. Certainly the studio structure is essential to some films: it was the success of *The Last Laugh*. But if the Germans insist upon their studio filming, they must be willing to omit certain themes and contents from their consideration.

The problem, however, is larger than this. The German mind, as revealed in the film, is the mind for the principle. The Germans have given the cinema some of its major principles, but have seldom been the ones to realize these principles. To the world's cinema the German film has been most important. But to itself it has contributed only formulas in theme and construction. Therefore the German is the artisan-mind that prevails, not the artist-mind. The principle-mind, not the creation-mind.

The principles the Germans have given to the cinema are:

(1) The integration of light, decor, performer . . .
(2) The thematic narrative . . .
(3) The cinema pre-plan . . .
(4) The effective submission of the actor . . .
(5) The camera as a major instrument . . .
(6) In sum, control and discipline . . .

As details or stresses of these principles one may include: the maturity of the actor, the constructed, in place of recorded cinema, the film as uninterrupted visual imagery, and so forth. It is apparent that the German contribution is most tremendous. But how far have the Germans gone in the realization of these principles? Take certain examples: *The Cabinet of Doctor Caligari, Torgus* or *The Coffin-Maker, The Last Laugh, The Last Fiacre of Berlin, The Wax-Figure Cabinet,* The Street* . . . Take the work of Ernest Lubitsch, Paul Leni, Lupu Pick, Arthur Robison, Ludwig Berger, Fritz Lang, Georg Pabst . . . *The Cabinet of Doctor Caligari.*

It will seem sacrilegious on my part, to many enthusiasts, were I to say that this is not a great film. Indeed I shall say with Leon Moussinac that it is not a work of art, but a film date. You will find that the enthusiasts are usually painters or people who think and remember graphically, never cinegraphically. Gilbert Seldes, the American journalist, writing in the new volumes of *The Encyclopædia Britannica,* speaks of the film thus:

"Without immediate effect on public or producers, this film is memorable because of its effects on the critics; it may be said that *Caligari* created motion picture criticism in England and America. (This is not altogether true, and I shall have something to say of this in a later paper. What Mr. Seldes may mean is that it made movie criticism for Mr. Seldes). French critics hold it in low esteem because of its elaborate scenario; yet even they allow its chief virtues: that it worked chiefly through the camera (although the subtitles in the American presentation were lengthy and frequent) and broke entirely with realism on the screen . . . *Caligari* means that the motion picture must be created not photographed . . . ."

Mr. Seldes has said nothing in his commentary to indicate the merit of the film itself as realization. He has indicated the principle or principles which it exemplified. Nor is he correct in asserting that the objection of the French critics was to the elaborateness of the scenario. The objection of the *absolutists* — Léger for instance — was, at that time, to any scenario at all, any narrative scenario that is. *Caligari* was, if anything, naïvely simple in its content. Indeed, one of my objections is the general objection I have to the simplism of Germany fantasy, of which I shall speak later. But the major objection to *Caligari* was and still is that, while it intended integration of light, decor, performer and mood of narrative upon a defined sequence, its structure, its quasi cubist-expressionist structure, was that of the stage-illustration. That, in fact, with its infantile nonrealism, was its appeal. Of *Torgus* I have spoken in an earlier article. *The Last Laugh*:

Seldes says of this film:

"Films without subtitles had appeared before; the distinction of this one was that everything the picture had to say, and it said some subtle things, was said by the means of the camera. What is more, the correlation of scenes was perfect, the separate sequences held together, and needed no connection or explanation." This is rather elementary discovery. The importance of *The Last Laugh* is multiple and more transcendant than Mr. Seldes indicates. It set down the first form of the cinema: the simple universal theme without complexity of narrative details. *And* it realized, as well as articulated in intention, the principle of constructed, unvacillating environment converging upon the character in relief. It is, to my mind, the only German film I have ever seen that, working upon an inclusive principle and a definite preconception, has realized *itself*. That is why F. W. Murnau remains for me the most effective of German directors, although for philosophic sincerity I look elsewhere: perhaps to Paul Czinner.

An exception. I think here of *Vanina,* made by von Gerlach, who died prematurely. I leave this film out of the consideration of German films. It is *the* film of films which indicated the path of *plastic fluidity* the cinema should have taken but never took. Its rhythmic structure is not German, nor has it been apprehended as a pivotal source by the land where it has been most appreciated, France. Perhaps there have been attempts to follow *Vanina,* but those films which may have been such ventures (as I detect the likely ones) seem to be following its faults rather than its rhythmic precept. Indeed most directors of Paul Wegener [?] seem to remember *Vanina* for Paul Wegener rather than von Gerlach.

Karl Grune made *The Street.* (The failure of both *Vanina* and *The Street* before the tribunal of American movie critics indicates the absence of any instinct for first laws in that high body). It too was admirable in its reduced statement of the pathetic adventure of the man. It too emphasized the organisation of the light in the mood. But it did not maintain its mood nor its temper of pathos. I think this is due to two traits exhibited by most German directors: the infidelity of their emotional concern, and their unawareness of the difference between the structure of melodrama and that of tragedy. I should go on to say that these two traits are the same and they are closely related to the artisan-outlook of the German director and his affection for the studio.

I have never seen a German film that attained beyond tragi-pathos. What is a most frequent literary source for the German film? The writings of Sudermann. Certainly Sudermann was not a writer of the tragedy of man. He was a fabricator. He has the episodes of Lagerlöf, of Hardy, of Ibsen, but not their cumulative exposal. Or similarly Frank Wedekind.

He compiled social dramas. His works were fabrications too. Therefore Pabst's *Lulu* is a fabrication. The film (I am speaking generally), like water, never rises above its source. That is a first law of art. The entire German cinema, with several notable exceptions, turns toward the fabricated. That is the artisan-mind, the studio-mind, the mind that delights in virtuosities, in camera sketchings, in fringe-filmings rather than penetrations. This mind is as apparent in Pabst as in Leni. This is the mind that is not concerned with the material at all, but only with the instruments. Pabst works over the surfaces of his films, along the edges. Never does he look *into* an object, as does a Jean Epstein. It is significant that the word, *photogenic,* is French in origin and not German. When Jean Epstein sketches and moves up and down a line or an object, I recognise the intention as speculative, even though the result is sometimes only tentative. That is the philosophically experimental. When Pabst uses his camera non-assertively, I see no such relevant intention, it is something apart — and what is apart in a film purporting to reveal a human adventure, is unscrupulous. That is the artisan's experiment.

This same unscrupulousness is present in Ernst Lubitsch, in Paul Leni, in Fritz Lang. Lubitsch with his "pictorial repartee" (high-school sophomore brand) and his "touches" (see also von Stroheim "the master" and Charlie Chaplin of *A Woman of Paris*), (I am not now referring to the important contribution of the Chaplin film, but to its gratuitous intelligence). Leni with his decorator's camera-play and smart-boy comics, Lang with his big-scale insipid architecture: the same concern with trivia. The wastes of able craftsmanship in Berger's *The Burning Heart,* in Kurt Bernhardt's *Die Frau nach der man sich sehnt*: what is the cumulative intention here?

The German film *pretends* to tragedy and that accentuates the falsity. Instances are Dupont's *Variety,* and the numerous moral films of Germany, such as *The Woman's Crusade* (*Must She Go On?*). The German penchant for the moral further burdens the pretension. The effect is generally ludicrous, as in the Ucicky film dealing with sterilization, the many "flaming youth" pictures . . . The law of art has not here been understood or even, I fear, suspected: the conversion of the material, which includes the moral idea. Never is the moral intention as offensive as it is in the French film, of a L'Herbier or a Benoît-Lévy, for in the German film we sense the honesty of that intention, whereas it is only an *etiquette* of decorative sentimentality in the French film. But the Germans have never learned to embody the moral idea in the unfolding motion picture, as have the Swedes of the great Swedish film period.

Yet in this affection for the moral I find a hope for the German film, once it learns to wed the moral intention with its first victory, the simple theme of general reference (*The Last Laugh, The Street,* etc.). The success is just beginning to expose itself in the stories of children and young folk. The films of children are as yet superior to those dealing with young folk, simply because the problem of the latter is more ponderous. But the fact that the Germans, of all people, care for their children *en masse* promises genuine films of the lives of the children. Max Mack's *Der Kampf der Tertia* is an excellent indication, and the sensitivity of Hans Behrendt's *The Robber Band* is another indicator of hope. The American films of children are most wretched, from *Our Gang* to *The Innocents of Paris.* Childhood is made egregious in them. The French film of children is usually the film of a child and the reference is seldom far-extending (*Poil de Carotte, Gribiche*). Moreover, the French have little sense of the child as child. The Germans, I think, have shown they are best fit to deal with childhood. The group-mind of the German comprehends the child as group-individual and this is fortunate for both the verity of the performance and its cinematic effectiveness, as well as for the child participating (but this is a matter beyond this essay).

There have been accumulating in the German kino for years local, domestic films of Berlin low-life (Liedtke in *Wochenendezauber* and Kampers in *Lemkes sel. Witwe*) which should long ago have provided the folk-basis for a great German film comedy. But only recently have we been favoured with the first instance of this awaited comedy, in the film rendering by Hans Behrendt of Carl Sternheim's *Die Hose,* with its blend of grand burlesque and satire, its infusion of the extraordinary — in the person of the court poet — into the ordinary — gloriously done by Werner Krauss. The film made from Hauptmann's *The Beaver Coat* might have been another transcendent comedy, had its director understood the law of the conversion of material, with its two divisions: the retention of the essential narrative and the creation of cinematic correlatives in the performance. Hans Behrendt has understood these two demands adequately.

Two promises remain with the German film. First, the rise of new directors, with the hope that the studio-mind will be modified or new uses will be found for it. Second, the maturity of the German actor. The latter has been constant amid the fluctuations, even non-development, of the German kino. Werner Krauss, Fritz Kortner, Heinrich George, Hans Schlettow, Bernard Goetzke, Wolfgang Zilzer — Asta Nielsen, Grete Mosheim, Henny Porten, numerous others whose names escape me for the moment, performers who fuse with the cinema. The performance of a Grete Mosheim as a *backfisch* reveals what intelligence and talent might do for Clara Bow. These German actors have kept the German film from perishing in the hands of the artisan. If there has been any fault to find with these artists it is that they have been *too* submissive to the director, although frequently I have felt Werner Krauss setting the pace for his *regisseur*. It is very likely that the German actor will elucidate for the director his legitimate art, by clarifying for him the nature of cinema performance. The German director has been, like the German schoolmaster of the past, the sort of disciplinarian who believes in getting the most out of his pupil. He demanded *Mehr, mehr!* So that very often the actor became apoplectic. Jannings and Veidt are typical instances. Fortunately, in *The Last Laugh* the co-ordination and convergence of the environment upon Jannings served as a rein and Jannings was brought back into the film and a powerful unity was preserved.

In this consideration, I mentioned at several points the bluntness of German presentations as revealed in their moralizations, in their fantasies, etc. I assume these evidences of bluntness under the general head of simplism. It is a term I have used many times in these pages, and which, I believe, my readers will understand by connotation. If we take the fantasy of *Caligari* and compare it with that of *Die Hose* we will note the difference in the categories. *Caligari*'s narration contains no intricacy, no larger reference . . . it is *Peer Gynt* without the philosophy and the poetry of the Ibsen drama. Am I stretching my comparison? Certainly, deliberately, I wish to indicate where the Germans have gone for their experience of the fantastic. To *Torgus*. These fantastic narratives—these fantastic films, ended with themselves. Epstein's *The Fall of the House of Usher* rises to a sense of universe-torment. Stiller's *The Treasure of Arne* was the poignancy of the primitive. Yet *The Treasure of Arne* was a very simple film, its intricacies were in its transcendental references, in its experience. (Further studies in simplism German-style are: *The Three Wax-Figures, Warning Shadows, Secrets of a Soul,* and *The Man with the Tree-Frog*). I especially include the other as an evidence of German bluntness. Here is a mystery-play where the mystery is not introduced until the film is well-nigh ended, and immediately solved. In other words, here is a mystery-play without a mystery. Which is mystery enough, I suppose. Murnau's *Tartuffe* is an instance of a great idea gone stodgy because of simplism.

In *Die Hose* we find a very simple narrative, but the references save the film from the simplism which is the tale only and nothing more. The secret lies in the unconcern of the German directors for the experience of the unit, the theme and its references. Again we may compare with *The*

Treasure of Arne a German film, made from Sudermann's *The Cat's Bridge*. All the appearances of tragedy but no tragedy in this latter film. Or the film made from another Sudermann, *Dame Care*. What is the meaning of these films? What do they intend? That they intend no peculiar experience is evident in their impurity. The film is constantly blemished by parts of the narrative that have no place in it. If the film cannot rise above its source, it certainly can fall below it. An instance of this decline is the Zelnik cinematization of Hauptmann's *The Weavers*. Captions alone cannot make a film universal. What did Zelnik intend here? What was his social apprehension of the theme, and what form should this apprehension take in the film? There is no evidence that he asked himself these questions. This was another film-job.

CLOSE UP,
November, 1929.

* [Gen. Ed.]: Page 298 — The film was released in the United States as *The Three Wax Figures*.

THE RISE AND FALL OF THE GERMAN FILM

No sooner was the War over than the German film began to re-create itself and rise to eminence; when the complete history of the cinema is written, no land will tell a more important tale than this rise of the German film. Germany gave the motion picture many of its most valuable principles and a number of its devices, and in Germany the cinema's first form was realized, the film of simple reduced human narrative about a single personage: *The Last Laugh*. The pre-eminence of the German film was not held for long. Save in the instance of this one kind of film, the Germans have given the principles but not effected them. Therein lies the fall from pre-eminence. But that is a story with many details, and what follows is the account of these details in the rise and the fall of the German film.

In German a photograph is *lichtbild* (light-picture) and a movie is *lichtspiel* (light-play). This light-play is accepted to the full by the German film maker. To him the entire creation of the film is light. It is because of this emphasis upon light that the German film has made its major contribution to the cinema; and because it has made light of the film, it has declined. Moholy-Nagy, a Hungarian photographer at work in Berlin, expresses the German viewpoint completely in these words: "The film is the motion-relation of light-projections."

The Germans are a people of scientific mind, interested in principles and mechanisms. Light became a principle and the all-in-all of the technical method. Light was distributed in columns and diffused in umbra and penumbra, luminosity and shadow. Light was organized into a harmony with the setting and the actors and the scenario. A design was planned and carried out in the performance. This principle and method produced films known to American audiences. On the fantastic side there was *The Cabinet of Dr. Caligari* and on the realistic side there was *The Last Laugh*.

The Germans decided that a camera was an instrument by which you looked at the things to be recorded: from above, or from a corner, or from beneath, or from whatever point of view was demanded. Thus was created the *camera angle,* presented in America in the film *Variety,* which burnt its way through these United States and came near demoralizing the matter-of-fact technique of Hollywood.

Originally the movies were without captions or subtitles. But the economical director, like David Wark Griffith, inserted words to save time and negative. The Germans saw the ideal of a picture that told its tale without the help of words, and they produced films like *Warning Shadows,* which was directed by an American who had become a German director, and is now working in England: Arthur Robison.

The importance of the scenario as containing the complete film was first comprehended in Germany. The greatest scenario writer is a German, Carl Mayer. It was he who prepared the manuscript for Murnau's American production, *Sunrise.* But his most singular contribution in scenario-writing is his literary plan for *The Last Laugh.* It is written almost like a free-verse poem, and, without directions, gives the movement, the tempo, the camera position (in a general way), the mood and the character's expression. The scenario brings together the director, the actor and the cameraman in a common understanding of the film. When it does this scenario writing becomes creative and not mere adaptation.

The Germans sought to give the film flow, fluidity, and to relate the actors together in the flow. The difficulty arose from the fact that this attempt was made by men more intimate with the framed stage than the screen, so that the performance seemed, or seems from the distance of years, somewhat ridiculous. Nevertheless the idea was there, and it was given the form of motion picture by von Gerlach, who died prematurely. He did this in the film, *Vanina,* which, when first shown in America years after it was made, was dumped by critic and exhibitor. However, in Europe it is still esteemed as an artistic film. In it starred Asta Nielsen, to my mind the greatest of film actresses.

Speaking of the theater coming to the movie reminds me that many of the leading directors and actors of the German film received their training in the theaters of Max Reinhardt. Reinhardt is a good trainer, an expert impresario, even though he is not so great an artist as is usually proclaimed. The good training of the German actor accounts for much that is excellent in the German cinema.

The Germans stressed the mature actor as against the milk-and-water, baby-face, brainless type who had no understanding of form or of the intelligence of the motion picture. America has imported an outstanding example of the mature German player, Emil Jannings, but the greatest of them all are still in *Deutschland.* The German actor has a genuine consciousness of movement and structure; he understands too that he is a part of a film and not *the* film. If at times he jumps out of the picture, it is because the director is not up to him. But it must be admitted that Jannings, despite his tendency to burst out of the screen, was held in rein in Germany and not in America. The failure, like the success, belongs to the director.

In Germany was developed, quite logically, the cameraman who is a creator, the film-engineer, so to speak. Chief among these is Karl Freund, who has just come to America to further color cinematography. Freund is responsible for the *camera angles* of *Variety,* the first use of the perambulating camera, the camera following the player, in *The Last Laugh,* the miniatures that loomed like giant edifices in *Metropolis* and a number of minor devices to modify the vision of the camera: prisms, haze-glasses, etc. Freund also first made use of the automatic camera.

Now with all these virtues and contributions, why, it will be asked, has the German cinema declined? Where is the German film of its golden age of the '20s?

When an art declines there are two reasons, exterior and interior. In the case of the German film, the exterior reason is the importation by America and England of leading directors, Murnau, Lubitsch, Leni, Berger, Dupont, etc., and other important film people. But this is a lesser cause, for after all, there are other directors in Germany, and Leni was not so much a director as a designer—and the man probably in a great measure responsible for the work of many German directors, namely Erich Pommer, has been away from Germany only for a time. The real cause of the decline is an interior one. The cause subdivides itself into several. First, there is the fact that German film has never left the studio. That is like rearing a child in a closet. The rudimentary health of the American film is attributable in part to its early outdoor life, and the Swedish film moved in the open, as has the Russian since its post-revolutionary birth. The French film, I once said, brought the studio to the outdoors, which is good;

the German has tried to create the outdoors within the studio, which is vicious.

The result can be seen in the film, *Homecoming,* where the Siberian landscape, with flowing waters, is built in the studio, quite noticeably. Freund filmed most of *Berlin: a Symphony of a Great City* outdoors; there is one sequence in a studio, the effect of which is an intrusion. This film, taken without actors, a composite newsreel, should have started something in Germany. It was scientific, and therefore in keeping with the German mind, and it was documentary, a wholesome basis for the new cinema. But it has not been Germany that has developed this genre of film; France and particularly Russia, in the work of Dziga Vertov, have gone on with it. The Germans have kept on with studio reproductions, as in the film *Asphalt.* It must be said that the studio lighting of Germany has remained much the same through the years, and its formula is recognizable in the work of certain American companies, Metro-Goldwyn-Mayer particularly. The Russians, an infant film-land, have gone way ahead in tonal quality of light, in *The New Babylon.*

A second reason for the decline of the German film is the over-simple, or *simplistic,* narrative it delights in, particularly the infantile fantasy it indulges.

A third reason is the German's penchant for the spectacle film and the film that contains more architecture than cinema, the unwieldy film, like *Siegfried, Metropolis* and *Spies.*

A fourth reason is the German director's disregard of the subject-matter in films involving human experience, or for their complete disdain of content. He is in reality not an artist but an artisan who is interested only in the workmanship and not at all in the fabric.

A fifth reason is the failure to develop the type of film Germany can do well. One is the film of children. The German is interested in children, not in a child. The latter interest is French. The German attitude of the child in the group is the correct one for the cinema. Nothing is so bad for the movie or for the child as the *starring* or individualizing of the latter. There are two German films I think of at the moment, in which the mass-child is the theme: *The Battle in the Third Class,* relating of the crusade of a class in one of the new progressive school-communities to save the cats of the village, and *The Robber Band,* dealing with the play-life of a boys' gang.

A second type of film the Germans have not developed is the small-town or local comedy. There are numerous local comedies and farces that remain local, but I know of only two films which have attempted either in form or content to make the local comedy more extensive. They are: *A Royal Scandal* and *The Beaver Coat.* The former has been exhibited in America.

A sixth limitation of the German motion picture is the Teutonic penchant for social moralizing. If this moralizing were not far-fetched and were completely converted into a film, no one could object. But the instances selected in the urging of a social action are so extreme as to make the argument ridiculous. I think of a film that deals with the abortion law, *Unwelcome Children* (called in Germany *The Woman's Crusade*), and of another that dealt with the sterilization of hereditary criminals, *Inherited Instincts.*

Even in scientific films, of which the best are German, there is sometimes a moral viewpoint which has no place in an objective film. I recall an astronomical film which ended with the destruction of the world for its impurity, a theme conveyed in other terms by *Metropolis,* which certainly was childish in its over-simplification.

The best animated cartoons are American, but Germany, in keeping with its technical, studio mind, has produced animated cut-out silhouette films, like those of Lotte Reiniger and Toni Raboldt, and animated toy films, like the charming *Picnic* by Alex Strasser. The Germans are noted also for films dealing with absolute contents, like moving lines and planes, such as the films of Hans Richter and Walter Ruttman.

And that is just where we leave the German cinema. I believe it needs to re-educate itself. I do not think the union with the Russians will effect this re-education. It must be *interior,* come from Germany herself. Directors there are a-plenty, but they may be too much of the old school to learn a new viewpoint. Yet if they can be re-educated, they have ability. I include among these such directors as Kurt Bernhardt, Hans Behrens, Max Mack, Gustave Ucicky, G. W. Pabst, Martin Berger, who made a splendid film on Rasputin (this is not to be confused with the film by that name circulating in the U. S. A.), and others. The players are many: Jannings, Werner Krauss, Fritz Kortner, Bernard Goetzke, Henny Porten, Greta Mosheim (the best interpreter of the 16-year-old girl I have ever seen), Mady Christians, etc.

In the process of re-education the Germans will need to look for new sources for their material. They will need to stop making films from a would-be tragic writer, Herman Sudermann (a practice carried over to America in *Sunrise, Flesh and the Devil,* etc.) and turn to the truly great writers: Gerhardt Hauptmann, Thomas Mann, etc. The Germans, it is

The Russian social idea is composed of the following: the social-revolution, the criticism of the bourgeoisie, the dictatorship of the proletariat, the ultimate of collectivism, the re-education of the mass and the individual in the mass, the conquest of the egocentric mind. Each of these is identified with the other. The Russian film, confronting these social intentions, must solve its problems, its construction, with these as insistences and total experience or final "message." That the Soviet kino has been preoccupied with the integral national idea of collectivism is more than evident. The preoccupation has been called too facilely "propaganda," with its negative connotation of counter-art. But propaganda, when profoundly conceived and realized structurally in the form, is art. The Russian cinema, and the Swedish before it, have alone approximated form.

That the approximations have not as yet been extended into a completed structure is due to a number of disturbances, vacillations in the inclusive idea, which induce vacillations in structure. These vacillations are: the concern with the egocentric and the deflection from the relevant method. The latter refers to the failure to discover the correct conversion of a profound and inferential social material into a motographic treatment. Or to put it more simply: the Russians persist, generally, in a method ill-suited to their material. The method is the American muscular movie, which served as initial instruction to the Soviet Cinema and which has persisted, in the work of Pudovkin especially, as the Russian medium, perfected beyond naïve American uses. However, the Russians have recognized that this technique can go no further and, as Eisenstein has said, cannot satisfy the *reflective* processes. We begin to see the new and intrinsically Russian film in Dovzhenko's *Arsenal*. In this film the early Russian juxtaposition of the individual and his analogy (the simile) become, at least in intention, a structure of integrated symbolism with a new non-verbal continuity or logic. The symbol *in* the realistic structure—a simplism intended ultimately as a kino language—is substituted correctly by a structure incorporating the symbolic conversion *of* the realistic detail, such as the human personality. So is one problem of the Soviet cinema being met.

A vexing problem is that of the individual in the film, to what extent shall he be *expressed*? Russia is troubled by this matter, as the criticism dealt Protazanov's *The Man From the Restaurant* testifies. Eisenstein, interviewed in France, has remarked with severity upon what he terms the retrogression in the Russian film, the backstep to the single personage. He adds, however, that this is only a momentary withdrawal for an accumulation of strength toward a further advance. To Eisenstein, the constructor of mass-film edifices, the intellectualist and classicist of the Russian film, complete objectivity is possible. He does not penetrate the individual and there is a question in my mind whether he has penetrated the social inference contained in the mass-expression. But to the other film makers of Russia, the individual is an experience. The problem becomes more simplified when we ask: how can the individual as an experience become the social idea as an experience? The answer is contained in a number of films: from Pudovkin to Dovzhenko. In these the treatment is not concerned with the narrative of the individual caught *pathetically* in the social morass, or fate — the German and American evasion of the social criticism contained in the plight of the individual (see *The Last Laugh* and *The Crowd*). The individual in *The End of St. Petersburg* and *Arsenal,* in *Storm over Asia* and *In Old Siberia,* is the concentration of the social force. For a moment one expected such concentration in *The Man From the Restaurant,* when the walk-out occurs, but the film disintegrates into a palpably American story of the rich villain and the young hero and pure heroine.

A third problem arises from the educational purpose of cinema production in Russia. How can this purpose be rendered cinematically? Eisenstein approaches this problem from the objectivity of the newsreel. A very delicate operation is involved, to subtitle the didactic. Nothing is impossible in the film, everything is its material. The problem is an intellectual one. That is where intellectuality enters the cinema.

A lesser problem, but an important one, is the criticism of the bourgeoisie. Up to the present that criticism has been mostly a too Dickensian caricature of certain gross types, not a revelation of basic errors which are expressed in vicious tendencies. In other words, types have been ridiculed, but the bourgeois ideology has not yet been criticised. An attempt at organizing a critique condemnation is the sequence of two conducts such as, men dying in battle, the exploiter indulging his appetite. That is, of course, elementary, but it is necessarily so. The first criticism had to be visceral. The criticism of the fundamentals is a development.

EXPERIMENTAL CINEMA,
February, 1930

LIGHT AND SHADE IN THE SOVIET CINEMA

The Moscow School of the Cinema is an institution unlike any other in the world. To this college of film making young men and women (increasingly sons of workers and peasants) come from all parts of the Soviet Union, from remote Tartary and Siberia, as well as from Leningrad and Moscow and Kharkov, to be trained and educated in a profession which is not only an art but also, in the missionary atmosphere of contemporary Russia, almost a sacrament. Lenin had said: "Of all the arts, the most important for Russia, in my opinion, is the cinematographic art." And so, to Communist Russia, it is. Here in the Moscow Cinema School such artists teach as Eisenstein, Pudovkin, and Nikitin, who played the part of the shell-shocked soldier of *Fragment of an Empire*. It is a university devoted to the making of artistically literate and socially intelligent film creators. The fruit feeds the root — that the root may feed the new fruit.

The entire attitude of the Russian toward the motion picture is so different from ours as to be incomprehensible to the intellectual who wrote me: "You take the movie too seriously, it is after all only a passing entertainment." For the Russian writer the film is a dignified medium. Victor Shklovski, most astute and scholarly of critics of Tolstoy and Dostoievsky, writes scenarios as he writes his treatises, not with condescension but with respect. Kavaleridze, the Georgian sculptor, comes to the film because it is an art of greater power. To him was entrusted the Ukrainian epic-film commemorating the tenth anniversary of the expulsion of the Denikin counter-revolutionary armies. Kalatozov turns from economics to the art which can best serve human economy. Men debate their ideas as film material.

Actually, we have but an inkling of the magnitude and the variety of the Soviet film. We have seen its most singular products, but a cinema as fluid as the Soviet, constantly feeding from the roots up, cannot be judged by its high trees alone. We must understand its social stimulus, and its organization.

Before the Revolution, Russia was making some two dozen films a year. Meyerhold directed the effete *Picture of Dorian Gray* of Oscar Wilde. It expressed the exquisite sadism of a courtly society. After the victory of the workers and peasants in November of 1917, Russia turned to the film as the most direct and persuasive of mediums. The first films made in revolutionary Russia were derived from literature, like Tolstoy's *Polikushka,* or dealt with historical personality, like *Czar Ivan the Terrible.* The former showed the influence of the German motion picture of the golden age (*The Last Laugh* period) in its concentrated pathos, but was enhanced by a sincerity and a poignancy that brought the Soviet film immediately to the high attainment of the short-lived Swedish movie, the highest reach of the bourgeois cinema. *Ivan* was also related to the German picture of the extreme historical personality, but was improved by a better sense of historic setting. In this it transcended considerably the expatriate Buchowetzki's *Peter the Great,* made in Germany.

Since then the class struggle has been the consistent theme of the Soviet cinema. But a theme may have many facets, many versions, and many periods. The first of the class sruggle or dialectic films (dialectic is synonymous with class struggle in revolutionary terminology) was concerned with the pre-Revolutionary insurrections. *Potemkin* by Eisenstein dealt with the Black Sea mutiny of 1905; *Mother* by Pudovkin, with the 1905 period in St. Petersburg. *Mother,* to my mind Pudovkin's most convincing film, has never been shown in the United States. From the pre-November film the next step was the re-living of the November Revolution. Eisenstein made his *Ten Days That Shook the World* and Pudovkin his *End of St. Petersburg.* The Paris Commune has been filmed in *The New Babylon.* From the retrospective film the Soviet cinema has turned to the prospective: to the anticipation of revolt of the oppressed in the Orient, as in *Storm Over Asia* and *China Express;* to the construction of the economy and morality of its own land, as in *Turksib, Old and New,* and *Soil.*

In the reconstruction of morality the film serves as immediate propaganda to make personal morality coincident with social. Sex among the comosomols (young communists) was treated in Ermler's *The Paris Shoemaker,* bureaucracy in *Three Comrades and One Invention,* drunkenness in *Life in Full Swing.* All of these are comedies. Alexander Room, a director unknown to America, remade the "eternal triangle" into a film dealing with the sexual consequences of limited lodgings. *Bed and Sofa* was a social satire in which Russia laughed sympathetically at its new morality. Ermler in *Fragment of an Empire* ended on a note which struck us as petty and irrelevant, an anti-climax. To the Russian however the old marital relationship of harangue and despotism is not merely a private matter but a disturbance to social well-being. As the problems disappear the films dealing with them vanish. Such is the case with *The Paris Shoemaker.* It is a bit of history now, a coin out of currency. The shopping line — which is being dissipated as the Five-Year Plan makes scarce articles plentiful — has induced a witty film which tells of an individual who, contemplating suicide, pauses to contemplate. Immediately a line forms behind him.

Frequently a film will not placard the screen with one poster but with several. *Life In Full Swing* in a normal sequential narrative, with good folk humor, advertises the evils of drunkenness, the rights of the woman to her own life, the values of the nursery, the advantages of the new architecture with its centralized cooking, and community pride. It does it in a simple yarn in which these points are not obtrusions but incorporated details. The audience has enjoyed a film and carried away a few suggestions socially valuable. Sometimes, as in *The Paris Shoemaker* and *Fragment of an Empire,* the different ideas are stressed with equal virulence and crowd the progression too densely. The lustiness in these films, however, is able to support this density. The lustiness arises from the complete devotion of the director, Ermler. Ermler comes from the Soviet province of White Russia. He suffered branding by the counter-revolutionary terrorist troops. Today he is a member of the Communist Party, a discipline granted only to the most stalwart and responsible. Many ask but few are chosen.

The major current material of the Soviet film is the land's economy. Nothing could be more fallacious than to characterize these films on industrialization and collectivization as "machine-worship" pictures. These films are urging machinery as a means toward a social ideal. They are not the so called abstract or absolute films glorifying a piston for its own self, and aestheticism that arises from the sad disparity between the aesthetic sense and the social conscience. They are preeminently human films, in which the piston is an instrument to serve the common welfare. Of course, the conversion of the idea into a persuasive form requires a treatment of the piston that will be structurally convincing. So that just there the purist and utilitarian meet. But only there and no farther.

The Soviet film aims not to please but to persuade. To persuade one must convince. The basis therefore of the Soviet film is in the document —

the newsreel and the travel film. Esther Shub has made films without the use of a camera. She has mounted in sequence fragments of films made in the past. Czarist society is historically presented in that way in her orderly compilation, *The Last of the Romanoff Dynasty*. Dziga Vertov uses his camera documentarily and places the findings of its eye in a juxtaposition that is intended to convey a unified sense of an environment of limited or extensive area. *His Man With a Movie Camera* is known here. He has made also *The Eleventh Year, One Sixth of the World,* and lately, with sound, *The Symphony of the Don* (coal) *Basin*. Blok's *Shanghai Document* uses the documentary in simple sharp contrasts: rich and poor, oppressor and oppressed, invaded and native. It is a fundamental film which should instruct the conscientious amateur and independent in other lands.

A document that is paramount in the Soviet cinema is the ethnographic film. From the scientific expedition film in *Pamir,* the Soviet movie makers are passing, have passed, to the film of the backward people. Not solely informative will such a film be; it will also urge an interest in these people. Perhaps these people suffer from trachoma; the film will stress their need of medical help. Perhaps they are suffering from an economy depleted by superstition. *Gateways of the Caucasus* describes the pagan-Christian festival wherein the cattle are exterminated and the grain gozzled (*sic*) leaving the natives to starve the remainder of the year. The films will contrast the drudgery and oppression and ignorance of the life of the peoples before and their enlightenment now, to stimulate the same contrast in the communities not yet reached.

The summit of the ethnographic film I saw in Moscow last year. It was made by a young Georgian, Mikhail Kalatozov. Kalatozov was formerly an economist and later a cameraman. This was his first film as director. *Salt of Swanetia* relates of Swanetia, the saltless land, where "birth is a sorrow and death a holiday." This is a grand dire film, built on peaks of pathos. The figures are large, as in *Joan of Arc,* but they are dark and liquid. From the opening, with the tall snow-clad mountains, to the explosion of the women demanding release from their bondage to the infamous ritual, the picture is unrelenting and its indictment of a life wherein malaria and blood-hemorrhages are the daily increment. "Salt!" Salt!" Beast and man seek it. The widow drips her milk into the open grave of her husband. "Salt and roads! And no more nutriment to the grave!" one is ready to cry. The picture cries this in its epilogue. Strictly it does not need this conclusion, for the entire film evokes into hope—road-building has commenced! We must extend the road. . . . Here is an ethnographic film incorporating the major facts of the Swanetian life in a drama that calls forth high emotional response and commands immediate action.

The granting of social and cultural autonomy to the minority nationalities of Russia has enriched the Soviet Union culturally, as well as politically and economically. These ethnographic films are a direct result of the establishment of these nationalities on par. Ethnographic film units are placed in numerous locales throughout the Soviet Union. This multiplication of production centers is permanent in the dramatic cinema also. Instead of a single Hollywood (with its offspring Astoria), the Soviet cinema has film studios in Leningrad, Moscow, Minsk, Kiev, Odessa, Tiflis (the Georgian Republic), the Armenian Republic; and corporate units who devote their attention to specific areas — the Vostok or Oriental-Kino (makers of *Turksib*). No studio has monopolistic control; there is no Hollywood of vested interest.

The censorship in Russia is no negative thing. It is intelligent and positive. It asks: "Does the film fulfill the idea?" The censors answered the doubts of sympathetic critics of *Salt of Swanetia,* who said that the film was not informative enough and was over-pathetic. They gave, quite correctly, a first class endorsement to the film. The censors thought that *Soil* was not persuasive enough. That was not only a political criticism; it exactly characterizes the film esthetically.

No category of the motion picture is left unexploited. While we are gurgling over *Mickey Mouse,* the Soviet animated cartoon is busy with the transmitting of ideas. The Soviet film has been making animated political cartoons for years. But if it is the whimsy you still want, the synchronized whimsy, the Russian movie can offer you the very best animated cartoon. It is superior to the animations in rice-paper that come from Japan. *Post* is now a children's storybook in animated figures, the central structure of which is the profile poster-drawing. The pattern of *Post* is, however, multiple. It is a film manifold, not a patterned repetition of figures dancing, set to barnyard or other familiar music; it is synchronized in a sound-sight harmony, wherein the music, incorporating verbal utterance, is an original modernist composition that might well be rendered as an autonomous symphony. The graphic artist is Sehenovsky, student of the eminent poster-artist, Lebedev; the composer is Dershenov. *Post* corroborates the suspicion that *Mickey Mouse,* with all its merits, is still immature and coddled beyond all good sense.

And what I have said but hints at the abundance and variety of films in Russia.

THEATRE GUILD MAGAZINE,
July, 1930.

THE CINEMA IN GREAT BRITAIN

Britain has played a rôle of considerable eminence in the creation and advancement of the cinematograph. In June 1802 the first photograph, called a "photogenic drawing," was made in England by Thomas Wedgwood, son of the famous potter. In 1839 William Henry Fox-Talbot of Wiltshire put photography on a commercial basis.

In the meantime there had been steps toward the camera of moving images. Before the Royal Society in 1824, Dr. Peter Mark Roget had read a paper on the principle of the "persistence of vision," which is the basis of the cinema, and a year later came the Thaumatrope of Herschel, a machine born of Roget's "explanation." Faraday, the scientist, developed upon Roget's theory, and in 1834 Horner of Bristol followed Herschel's Thaumatrope with his Daedaleum. Thirty years later Rudge invented his *Life in the Lantern* and followed it with the Biophantascope equipped with a rotating handle. Beale, Linetti [*sic*]* and Ross introduced their machines.

The English contribution, however, was exaggerated by Talbot, who first wrote on the cinema's history. Talbot was English. Ramsaye, the American, has authenticated or invalidated the various claims of nations and individuals, so that the efforts of certain Englishmen, like William Friese-Greene, become matters of curiosity (complicated, non-working machines or belated practices) rather than historical contributions.

However, in a history of the cinema, two English names enter, and these two English names are the beginning of the commercial film in England. These names are R. W. Paul and Cecil Hepworth. Paul invented the Theatograph upon Edison's Kinetograph, improving the latter in compactness, portability, economy, etc. He made the first English films, shown in "peep shows," and called *Bootblack At Work in a London Street* and *A Rough Sea At Dover.* Ramsaye, in *A Million and One Nights,* tells of an interesting, surprising collaboration in a patent anticipating the present motion picture art between Paul and H. G. Wells the novelist. This was in 1895!

Herein came the Theatograph projecting films to a screen. Armat in America, Lumière in France, Paul in England, brought the film into the theater out of the penny arcade. Cecil Hepworth comes in now. A young mechanic-inventor, he sells an arc lamp to Paul. Later he evolves a machine for developing films for the Warwick Trading Company. This Company was really Charles Urban, who, urged on by the British demand for British films, produced microphotographic films, ancestors of our present "nature and science" pictures, and who ultimately turned to color films with Kinemacolor. This is another English contribution. Hepworth turned to story-filming, with pictures like *Rescued By Rover,* and became a dominant figure in British cinema until the present era.

In pre-war days England was a film competitor. Firms like the Hepworth, British and Colonial, Cricks and Martin and London Film were very successful. The war broke in. America became dominant. Still, England cannot excuse itself simply by crying "the war!" for failing to make good films after the war. Sweden produced great pictures. And if England says: "Well, Sweden fought no war and the richest trust in the world, the Swedish Match Trust, backed the Swedish Biograph," one can still answer: "Germany, certainly a war-sufferer, produced great films after the war, greater indeed than America's."

The English somehow have trailed the other nations in the cinema, as they have trailed them in other arts. Companies were making films right after the war, not many indeed; they could not hope for world circulation, they might at least (or at most) have made good films. Stoll had movie theatres and made an occasional film for them and neighborhood houses.

But England, dwelling upon trade dominance, determined to create a strong cinema with world ambitions. In 1923 the Prince of Wales said: "It is well worth the British nation's while to take the film industry seriously and to develop it to its utmost as a national industry . . . It is up to us to see that the British film-pictures take their places in the theaters of the world, and particularly on British screens."

At one period in 1926 not a single studio was working. I was in London then. Diatribes against the American film were being issued but at the same time America was being urged as an example to Britain in the cinema. The British parliament had paid very little, almost no attention to the motion picture in its first days.

The English did not foresee the movie's commercial and imperial importance, and moreover, English snobbery looked down, and still does, upon this commoner's art. I recall a story told me by Leslie Ogilvie, formerly manager of the Shaftesbury Pavilion, the art cinema off Piccadilly. In 1914 or thereabouts, before the war, Ogilvie was running The New Gallery on Regent Street, an art gallery converted into a movie house. The youngest art ousting an ancient one! An English beau was about to enter when the changed aspect of the place stopped him.

"What's this?" he asked.

"A kinema," Ogilvie replied.

"And what's that?"

"Go in and see."

"But what does a gentleman do?"

"He buys the best seat."

"But a gentleman can't be sitting next to a — a —"

Curiosity however got the best of him. After the show, he came out murmuring, "Not so bad." Most "gentlemen," however did not go in. The artists — well, even today the American poet, John Gould Fletcher, has to reprimand his London colleagues — Fletcher lives in London — upon their neglect of the movie.

The City, however, high finance, saw in 1926 the need for backing the English film. In October of that year the Imperial Conference met in London and appointed a committee on Empire films. After a stubborn fight the Cinematograph Films Bill was passed in the last days of 1927 and became an Act on the statute-book. Films had to be registered, and classified as foreign or domestic. A British film is one made by a British subject or a British company in a British studio after a scenario by a British writer. Seventy-five per cent of the labor costs must have been paid to domiciled Britishers. Then the quota determines a percentage of British films that must be exhibited.

Theaters followed upon this bill, studios sprang up, existing studios brightened. I was in England just last year. About two dozen companies were actively making films. A couple of foreign companies were making quota-films in England. Half of the British firms had been born with the Act. In 1928 British International, the largest of the producers, had made twenty-two films. This company owns numerous theaters and is going after more.

Foreign directors were imported, some Englishmen who had worked in America, several Germans, Americans, etc. Foreign cameramen like Mary Pickford's cinematographer, Charles Rosher, who filmed also *Sunrise,* was brought over to work for the great German director, Dupont. Actors came from everywhere, defunct Anglo-Americans like Percy Marmont, Wyndham Standing, Carlyle Blackwell (some Englishmen went to America) and English performers who had done work on the Continent. "Stars" were being trumped up, and a struggle was being made to put "it" into what May Edginton, English authoress, called the "it-less English girl."

English authors who had made film stories before, like Caine, Phillpotts, Wallace, Deeping, etc., were drafted again, and others were called upon. Studio cities sprang up around London. A weekly fan journal appeared. Fans began to shout "Up with the British films!" but the non-jingo fan still prefers American livestock. And there's the rub!

The British, to beat America, tried to do American films. All over the Continent we find the same effort. But an English film is attractive both to Englanders and Americans wherever it is English in theme, characterization, setting—which means eventually wherever it is rural. England, from all indications, has recognized that, so that we get such pictures as:

The Farmer's Wife, directed by the best of the English directors, Alfred Hitchcock, who also made the first English talkie, and a well-organized one, *Blackmail*;

Widdecombe Fair, directed by Norman Walker;

Under the Greenwood Tree, from the novel by Thomas Hardy, directed by the American, Harry Lachman;

A Cottage On Dartmoor, directed by the Hon. Anthony Asquith for British Instructional in conjunction with Swedish Biograph;

The Loves of Shakespeare; etc.

The English have gone to other parts of the Empire to make films: to India for *Shiraz* and *Emerald of the East*; to Ireland (in subject-matter at least) for *Juno and the Paycock*—the actors too are Irish—and (in authorship) *The Informer,* starring Lars Hanson and Lya de Putti; to Scotland for Harry Lauder films, etc. At this point we may consider the Empire in relation to the mother country and as to its own film production. Before the revival of the British cinema, Australia first saw British films from two to five years after their British release. American films reach Australia four months after American release. Sentiment is cinematically rather pro-American, due as much, perhaps, to better advertising than to better films. In New Zealand in 1914 half the films were British, but the war crippled English film trade there. New Zealand has attempted film production, like that of the native Maori film, *The Romance of Hine-Moa.*

South Africa constitutes a film monopoly in the person of I. W. Schlesinger, "The Uncrowned King of South Africa," who has control of theaters, cinemas, radios, cabarets in the Union. This monopoly is taking up British films, and under the name of African Film Productions has produced at its studio near Johannesburg such films as *The Blue Lagoon, King Solomon's Mines* and *Die Voortrekkers.*

As to Canada, England is just beginning to drive a wedge or trying to, into American domination there. In India anti-British sentiment does not promise well for England. An English report says: ". . . the great majority of Indian audiences prefer home productions and therefore in cinemas which provide for purely Indian audiences, an Indian film is ordinarily more profitable to the exhibitor than a Western picture." But the report goes on: ". . . the large number of cinemas which depend mainly on European audiences have a natural preference for British pictures."

There is one more phase of the English cinema that awaits our attention, the progressive, artistic phase. One begins naturally with the Film Society of London. This society was founded in 1926 for the exhibition of selected films. It meets monthly in the New Gallery and presents choice films, such as Pudovkin's *Mother,* which it showed intact, following the film club principle laid down in the conduct of the Parisian film clubs. Recently the Film Society showed the first feature-length British film to appear on its program: *The Lost Patrol,* directed by Walter Summers, the best maker of war films in England. The Society had shown various English short-subjects like the scientific *Secrets of Nature,* but Summers' film was the first full-length film to receive the signal honor.

Active in the Film Society have been Iris Barry, novelist and film critic, author of *Let's Go to the Movies,* Edmund Dulac, the painter, Frank Dobson, the sculptor, E. A. McKnight Kauffer, the American painter working in London, and the Hon. Ivor Montagu, a new film-director, who has made a film on *Table Tennis* (ping-pong) and directed three so-called "inventions" by H. G. Wells. He is a partner of another young director, Adrian Brunel. The Film Society may be said to gather together those London intellectuals who do not quite disdain the cinema. A typical program would be as follows:

2:30 *A Glass of Water,* 1928 (British).
2:43 *The Girl and the Englishman,* 1911 (American).
2:57 *Vormittagsspuk,* 1928 (German).
3:04 *Jorinde and Joringel,* 1922.
3:15 Interval of five minutes.
3:20 *Nosferatu* (Dracula) 1922.

The last two films are German too. This is a "balanced" program: a scientific film, a pre-war Griffith with Mary Pickford, an experimental absolute film from Germany (no story, no subject-matter, combinations of devices only), a silhouette cutout picture, and a full-length horror film. The printed program contains descriptive and historical annotations.

Sometimes a speaker is presented. Pudovkin, the great Russian director of *Mother, The End of St. Petersburg,* and *Storm Over Asia,* spoke once upon the principles of film making which are contained in his important book, *Film Direction,* translated into English by Ivor Montagu of the Film Society.

There is a great deal of amateur film production on standard and substandard stock throughout England. Some of the clubs have elaborate studios and have made numerous films, most of them very crude imitations of commercial junk. The more important societies include the Manchester Film Society and the Film Guild of London. There are a number of good independent amateurs in the universities. I saw a meritorious motion picture made on 16mm stock by a Cambridge undergraduate, Basil Wright. In Cambridge there is quite a deal of interest and talk concerning films. Too much of it is effect and faddist, but a great part of it indicates the realization of a new art in the awareness of young Englishmen. Many will turn to the films as a vocation, now that the cinema has been made respectable by vote of Parliament, and the presence of aristocratic scions.

It is interesting that the first international periodical for the film-as-art should be an English project. The editors, Kenneth Macpherson and Bryher, live in Switzerland, but the magazine, *Close Up,* is issued from London. There are correspondents in all the main film centers: Robert Herring in London, Jean Lenauer in France, Kraszna-Krausz in Berlin, Chevalley in Geneva, Attasheva in Moscow, Howard in Hollywood and myself in New York. *Close Up* is continually stern with England; the one consistently critical voice. It is helping, with other agencies,. to build up an active English critical body. A number of the English critics have turned out films: Herring, *Between the Lines;* Blakeston, *I Do Love to Be Beside the Seaside*; Macpherson, *Monkey's Moon*; Grierson, *Drifters.*

This also must be said for England: the publishers are always readier to take a chance on a book dealing with cinema than the American publishers. The latter say there is no public for such literature. The future will undoubtedly show a great improvement in English film criticism, much of what is belated and inexact, and a great increase in works on the film, translations and originals.

Two other film societies have recently been organized in England:

the Masses Film and Stage Guild, by the Independent Labor Party, and the Workers' Film Society. The societies aim to enroll the working population in the interest of exceptional films. Fenner Brockway, Member of Parliament, is chairman of the Masses Film and Stage Guild, whose fee is a shilling. In the Workers' Film Society a number of important names are present: Hon. Ivor Montagu, who has resigned from the board of directors of the London Film Society, John Grierson, critic and director, Oswel Blakeston, critic and experimentalist, and Kenneth Macpherson, editor of *Close Up*. These societies are meeting with official opposition, which is prohibiting private film showings. They will most likely open regular movie theaters.

Among independent films in England is *Light Rhythms,* the joint work of Francis Bruguière, a Californian living in London, and Oswell Bruguière. Bruguière is still a photographer who has made "photo designs" of cut-out paper organized by light. This film is an animation of "photo designs." Bruguière made an unfinished film, *The Way,* in America, in which his wife, the actress, Rosalind Fuller, and the dancer, Sebastian Droste, played the symbolic story of man's life from birth. *Light Rhythms* is a first venture in the "pure light film," of which I have written in various journals here and abroad.

CINEMA,
May, 1930.

* [Gen. Ed.]: Page 318 — "Linetti" [sic] — references to Linnett's Kineograph books?

THE ENGLISH CINEMA

England sits atop her globe looking down upon her dominions.

England hoped to sit as neatly upon her quota and look down upon far-flung film dominions. But the eye of England is on the U.S.A. cinema, the cinema of the presumptuous American offspring. There is little talk of cinema in England, but a great deal of talk of movie. That is, the questions of film conduct refer almost entirely to: how can we duplicate and beat the American success? And, of course, the answers amount to: by playing the American game. Look through the pages of the film journals and you will see from editor to fan that the same concern is uppermost: America.

I was in England in 1926 when the quota was hot on its birth. A typically English sentiment was expressed by a paper, *The Patriot,* in the following words: "We hope, but do not expect, that the agitation over British films will arouse English people to the danger in their midst of American propaganda through the agency of American films. England is being suffocated by American films; they lead in East and West and, thanks to our apathy, a promising English industry is being strangled before our eyes. The war, of course, was America's chance, and, with her genius for money making quickened by the jealousy of English commercial supremacy, she grabbed it. England was fighting on every front throughout the world; she had subordinated everything to the task; her civil industrial life was in abeyance for nearly five years. America had a clear field. We are concerned not only with one branch of America's bid for world supremacy in trade, but there is no more progressive industry than the American film business. Money has been lavished upon its establishment, improvement and advertisement. The film magnates take their business seriously, and they plan ahead. No sooner does one film company produce a masterpiece (treating of American affairs one instinctively reaches out for superlatives) than every other company immediately strains every muscle to achieve a super-masterpiece. In detail and in representation the American films have been brought to a high pitch of perfection. We do not grudge this tribute to America's sole art." The slur must be there with the praise (the crude, aristocratic gallantry of the Englishman): the movie is America's *sole* art. But what is particularly England's art today?

Various objections were raised at that time to the American film, but the fore-quoted writer advances his hilarious one. "The historical films have for their motive the belittling of the Monarchy as an institution." Dear Patriot, to so libel my America, my Monarchy-idolizing America. The American movie to be accused of aiming to destroy the English throne! Perhaps the accusation is symbolic. Since the throne depends upon the commerce of the Empire, and the American movie threatens that commerce in numerous ways, the throne is threatened. But I attribute the accusation to petulance, the same petulance with which America has been charged. Indeed, the U.S.A. is in many ways, in many of her most unlovely ways, still the child of her mother.

Petulance, however, builds nothing so positive as either an industry or an art. And England in the cinema is following not the art or the industry of the movie, but all its commercial processes, with their involvements of nepotism, braggart expenditures, favoritism, exploitation of personalities (the star system), duplication of successes, etc. Well, Napoleon called England a shopkeeping nation. Indeed, the aristocracy has surprising shopkeepers' traits — those traits usually attributed to shopkeepers. A little while ago no gentleman (as gentleman is understood in England only) would go to the movie, it was vulgar. Today he finances the vulgarities of the films, and goes to see them. And he laments the fact that the English film cannot be as briskly vulgar as the American, which calls in the pence. We shall touch upon the "vulgus" later.

Writing in The London *Sunday Chronicle,* 1926, its editor, Mr. J. W. Drawbell, epitomized the English attitude of mind which still prevails: "We are suffering from too much America! We hate Yankee bluff and bluster, but we stand for hours in queues to see American films that distort our own war efforts . . . We are fools if we delude ourselves that we have nothing to learn from these same people, at whom we rather look down our noses. We have too little of American enthusiasm and freshness; the dogged, determined will to work; the tireless driving energy and the daring, virile ideas that lie behind the success of her vast campaign." And does England think that mere wishing will give her these qualities? And does she think that by duplicating the evidences or results, the shadows of these results, of these qualities, she will do what America has done? The mistake is in her thinking at all about America. She must probe herself. If she fails to create the greatest cinema, and here I am shifting to my interest of the cinema that is art, she must find that failure in herself, in the Englishman, and she must be satisfied with what lesser thing she can offer.

Art is experience. I do not mean the workaday experience that is easily acquired, but the experience which is the systemic being. The Russian movie began at once with experience, for the Russian is the most experiencing of men, and therefore you have a Russian film of such grand proportions. The American movie has been one of gay, muscular adventure, superficial if pleasant; today it is making weary, ineffective attempts to attain to experience, as in *The Crowd* and *Lonesome*. Experience can be attained to only if experience has been the source. The Americans are not notably an experiencing people; in this they are kin to the English.

The Englishman is afraid of experience. He is suspicious of emotion. I am not now referring to the English "vulgus," but to the more knowing, the literati. The uniform reaction to Dreyer's *Jeanne* was almost funny in its commentary upon the English fear of tears, the pseudo-Nietzschean disparagement of pity. (The analogy to Nietzsche was suggested to me by an Englishman. There are still Nietzscheans among the English, I am told. Well, the English are a warrior nation). Dostoievsky, the most cosmic of writers, embraced pity as the completest of human contacts: thereby is man-in-the-universe discovered. There is a direct relation between Dostoievsky and the Russian cinema.

There have been expressions in *The Film Weekly,* of London, of the English need for Russian films, and the need for English directors to learn from the Russians. There has been talk by a number of more open-minded Britons of the urgent necessity of importing talents to fashion films in England. If one is interested in a competent and competing cinema perhaps importation is acceptable, though its value is questionable, when one looks at the outcome of Stiller, of America, of the effect of Lubitsch's "touches" on the American film (a false charm). And as to learning from the Russians or from any one, what is one to learn? A camera angle, such as America learned from *Variety,* and, in its utilization, confused further an already confused milieu? Here is a lesson to learn from America, since England wants to learn from America: if you are going to use an approach of another people, be sure you have the receptivity to incorporate that approach into your established attitude. The lesson to learn from the Russian film is: find your source.

Mr. Anthony Asquith determined to do a film of the lowly. Good. The Germans had established such themes as their particular contribution to cinema subject-matter. Mr. Asquith opened up with underground train lights, very reminiscent, perhaps learned from the Germans or the French absolutists. Mr. Asquith may deny this, he has even expressed himself rather condescendingly, if kindly, upon German and Russian films. But what was the experience of an unprejudiced mature spectator to *Underground*? A hybrid film produced by a coincidence of absence of a precise cinema viewpoint and a remoteness from the lives of the protagonists of the narrative. Mr. Asquith is a case in point: he is young and, let us assume, he is willing to learn. He is given at once, in the American fashion, a "big" film to do, instead of being put on a small, personal "errand." If it is London he wishes to film, why not grant him some corner, Petticoat Lane, or Trafalgar Square? Let him sketch with his camera the Regent Quadrant. The film document is the legitimate exercise: it is a test and an education. Could Mr. Asquith do as capable, if unpretentious, a film as M. Georges Lacombe's *La Zone?* This training is vital in two ways: in its demands upon the understanding of life and its requisitions upon a cinema viewpoint. Instead of such training, Mr. Adrien Brunel's does hobbadahoy parodies of the newsreel, without revealing any cinema instinct or sense of pertinent commentary. One conceit alone remains with me: the use of musical notes to represent insects in flight. I am aware when I suggest the documentary film as apprenticeship that London authorities are still hostile to having their city exposed. Yet the Honorable Anthony Asquith filmed the underground. Moreover, one may construct a document about the contents of a room, although this may call for a penetration denied most people. The end to be willed is the attainment of a viewpoint. Of course, the documentary film transfixed by a genius like Flaherty can become something beyond a document. In this instance, however, I am not thinking of a completely converted material but of a training. I am thinking not of the work, although the work may prove most meritorious, but of the one to be educated. Is England serious enough in its cinema intentions to educate its worthy young men? Or does she think that the building of studio cities is more necessary?

In this matter of studios England is again aping America, without realizing that Hollywood is one of the chief obstacles hindering the advance of the American film. The day of the studios is over. Mr. Charles Lapworth, an Englishman who is production manager for the Société Générale des Films, producers of *Jeanne d'Arc*, urged his company against the studio. The European cinema has all Europe and northern Africa for its studio, and England has the globe. If the studio is needed, it can, as in the fashion of France, be rented for the time desired. To maintain studios is to have the pace set by the overhead expenses, and not by the director, as is the policy of the Société Générale.

Joining the idea of document and the idea of the circulating "studio," I approach the suggestion which seems to me to offer a way to English cinema. I would certainly centre the film industry in London, to keep it near the active critical opinion yet to be fully articulated. (The English artist, literary and graphic, is, in typical English fashion, still indifferent to the movies — although from the start of the motion picture, the French artist was curious, even enthusiastic. It is true, Mrs. Virginia Woolf and Mr. Aldous Huxley have expressed themselves upon the need of the films, but their very general and repetitious judgments were evidence of a non-participation). But the English countryside offers the documentary zone for the apprentice, the natural setting for film placement, and the peculiar English contribution to the cinema theme. This was hinted in Mr. Alfred Hitchcock's cinematization of Phillpotts' *The Farmer's Wife.* Perhaps after a long experience of this material and environment there will be developed from the source an experience which will be able to convert such a novel as Hardy's *The Mayor of Casterbridge* into a film. But in going to the source the English director must first understand that pictorialization is not conversion. In the film, *Widdecombe Fair,* a typical American narrative as major plot was threaded by a dull literal pictorialization of the old ballad, after which the film was named. This sort of illustration-song parallel belongs to the magic lantern era, which, in many ways, the film has not yet left behind. But to have taken the sense, the native sense, of the ballad and by re-rendering that sense in a structure suggested by the ballad-structure, to have attained what may be called a ballad-film, would have been an achievement and the establishment of an English idiom. I do not mean parody, such as Cavalcanti so pleasantly attained in *La P'tite Lilie.* I am again stressing conversion.

The English ballads and the English dances offer a source. There are more suggestions for filming at the Children's Theatre, near Shaftesbury Avenue, than on the stage where Tallulah Bankhead rants. The English music hall is another tremendous opportunity. How early the English cinema could have learned this, if it had listened to Mr. Alexander Bakshy, who anticipated what I am saying many a year ago? Why did the English cinema let this prophet of the motion picture escape to America? Bakshy might have given English films their first-needed impetus. But the English cinema may still benefit by what Mr. Bakshy said long ago: that cinema performance "is the most abstract form of pantomime," and should be left "to the dancers, clowns and acrobats who do know something about the laws of movement." This is a recognition almost oracular in view of what has transpired: the success of the dancer, the clown and the acrobat. Englishmen are always indicating the English origin of Chaplin, and Lane, and others, are always hinting that America benefited by the war in taking these artists into the films. But what is England doing in regard to other good and qualified artists, Beatrice Lillie, for instance? Instead of going to the musical hall to discover both performers and forms, the English film-producer puffs a Mr. Alexander d'Arcy as "the new Valentino" or expends tons of publicity on a Mr. Carl Brisson. Playing the American game, and getting where? The source of all art is in the "vulgus." Shakespeare is to be found in *The Shepherd's Play* and *Gammer Gurton's Needle* and *Ralph Royster-Doyster*. By the way, these are splendid film subject-matter. The area of the film is to be found in the distortions of the excellent English music hall, or in the genre themes of the countryside and London, or in the old ballads and dances — these are the sources. Comparing English stars to American will only further obscure the logical players in the variety houses of England. Talking, like Mr. Asquith, that treatment and not plot counts will only, in its demi-truth, obscure the essential convertible and suggestive content which lies at the fingers of the English cinema. It is not plot, Mr. Asquith, it is content, subject-matter, the human theme, that must be talked of, and the treatment (or, as I prefer to call it, the cinematic viewpoint) in relation to this content is Conception. English films lack Conception. Your indifference, Mr. Asquith, to the plot, as you term it, allowed *Underground* to begin as a light superficial comedy (which, I think, you should have kept it), pass into the idyllic, the quasi-pathetic, the arrantly melodramatic, so that it was nothing as an experience and unreal as a revelation of the people it purported to represent. There was no indication of the insinuation of their Underground existence in their lives. Just to have had certain adventures occur in the Underground does not allow you to offer your film as a document of the lives of the Underground people. You did not experience these people, your experience of these people would have been the "plot" which you scorn. You are very old-fashioned in your progressiveness, Mr. Asquith.

I am sure that by now we do not need to be warned against the novelist or the novel in the films. We know that the unselective borrowing of novels for film narratives has been baneful, and was brought in as a practice by the film commercialist. But we know also that, given the mind for it, anything is convertible into film. However, the selection must be based, among other things, in the case of England, on the English experience. What I have said before will explain my present point. If there is no one (and it seems there is no one) in the English cinema able to create a subject-matter of this experience, there are subject-matters waiting in many novels: those of Thomas Hardy, for instance. And will not someone go to Scotland and do *The House with the Green Shutters?* Or to Ireland and do *The Playboy of the Western World?* Or to the English mines and do *Sons and Lovers?* Or to Australia and do the novels of E. Grant Watson? The Russians have never bickered about original plots, but at once seized upon existent "experiences" published in novels: *Polikuschka* and *Mother*. I am afraid no one in England's cinema is up to the dimensions of even the least of the books I have mentioned. Perhaps it is wiser to depend upon the novels or plays of an Eden Phillpotts, until the conviction of sufficient power impels the director to attempt grander themes. But the English must not expect the rest of the world to wax violently enthusiastic over her first films-at-source. The world will find them pleasing, because they will be peculiar to the folk enacting them. But I am not interested in their appeal or selling power, I am interested in placing the stress at the right place, away from a nostalgia for American success. What is the good of taking a director like T. Hayes Hunter, who in America was responsible for a film as worthy as *Earthbound,* if in England he is accredited with two banal films like *The Triumph of the Scarlet Pimpernel* and *One of the Best?* Or an actor like Monty Banks, hardly the brightest of the comedians, and permitting him to film such wretched stuff as *Gin and It?* Or a Mr. Harry Lachman and having him do *Week-End Wives,* which has all the details of American high (hat) comedy and none of the gaiety? Or worrying about the "it-less" English girl? What is the value of the numerous amateur cinematographic societies — working with normal and 16mm stock — if immediately they are concerned with camera tests, scenarios, thrillers, etc., and evidently are playing for the attention of the large producer? I believe I have indicated possible procedures for the serious English cinema. Certainly, even as far as monetary success is concerned, what I have suggested could hardly be less profitable than most English films produced under the suasion of the present state of mind.

CLOSE UP,
March, 1929.

FILM BEGINNINGS IN BELGIUM AND HOLLAND

The small lands of the Flemings, Walloon and Dutch cannot be said to have a full-fledged cinema as yet. But there is much activity in Belgium and Netherlands, especially in the latter. Belgium has produced a number of very bad commercial films, like the one which depicted the heroine of Tournai, the *Belgian* Edith Cavell, in which an actress from the theater, Renée Liëgeoise, grimaced after the fashion of films of the first vintage. The Belgians have inscribed their martyrdom and heroism on their minds and consequently the resultant film is both crude and offensive in sentiment. A number of other war films have been produced in Antwerp where there is the Flemish Cinema. On one Sunday morning I attended a showing of its first production called *Leentje van Celee* [?] (Peggy of the Sea) a most hilarious film atrocity. The story dealt with the recovery of a castaway infant and her rearing to radiant maidenhood, her love for a wastrel suitor, the devoted crippled idiot (never was there such an idiot or such a cripple), etc., etc. Postcards were sold of the stars in true Woolworth fashion. In the middle of the film, the screen was emptied and its contents, the players, in sober Sunday garb, dumped before the doting adherents: "Our Mary Pickford, Douglas Fairbanks—and Lon Chaney!"

But this is not the real story of the film in Belgium. In Brussels, the capital and cultural centre of Belgium, where it contacts with Paris, there is more earnest and progressive and intelligent endeavor. The Cinema Club of Brussels, founded in 1927 upon the example of the Paris film-clubs, has developed to the position of owning a permanent theater, established in the vast Palais des Beaux Arts in 1929. The programs are changed weekly and the theatre is open each week end. The first efforts toward a Cinema Club were made in 1926 by Albert Valentin, a very able young writer and editor of the monthly review, *Variétés.* Valentin led the Club in its first season and was followed by Carl Vincent, film critic of *L'Indépendance Belge,* a daily. It is Vincent who has said: "It seems a little strange that Belgium should not by this time have developed a local industry and her own school of cinematography on a considerable scale. All the necessary elements are to hand: method and the capacity for teamwork so essential to cinematographic enterprise, intrepidity in business undertakings and, what is even more important, those particular characteristics, to be observed in the work of Feyder of Brussels, which give her artists a peculiar sensibility to rhythm and to the plastic in people and things. But historic circumstances we need not here specify in detail have decided against her, and Belgium, where the film industry is conspicuously prosperous, is still dependent upon the outside world for the filling of her screens."

Still, although Belgium possesses no well-fitted studios, no actual film players and no organized film production, there are films being made there which participate in the art movement of the cinema. First, there is a young Fleming of about twenty-five, Charles de Keukeleire. With a musical background, this young man has turned to film making. In 1927 he made *Boxing Match,* "a series of rhythmical impressions, alternately objective and subjective." There are two themes in this film-study: first, the fight itself, and incidentally, the crowd. De Keukeleire's work has been shown about Belgium, in Germany – at the Film and Foto Exposition in Stuttgart, last summer – and in France.

In Brussels there is, or was, an advance-guard stage group, the *Vlamen Volk Toonel* (Flemish Folk Theatre), and with this group de Keukeleire planned to film an old Flemish legend, *The Infant Jesus in Flanders.* The project fell through, and the young creator went ahead on his own, producing *Impatience.* It is called "a cinegraphic poem," showing the increasing frenzy of a woman in a motorcar, interrelated with the landscape, the player and geometric forms.

Another young adventurer is Monsieur Gussy Lauwson, who has produced *Reflections* upon the theme of "life is an illusion." Carlo Queeckers has made *Flemish Kermesse* and *The Emigrant,* a study of the interesting Antwerp docks, to which and from which the world's vessels sail.

These are mild beginnings, but they are basic. It must be remembered that the entire cinema has its origins in the documentary film. Documentation is an instructive start for the young film man. These young people show perception. A Belgian critic (the union of the critic and creator in Belgium is a good promise) has said of de Keukeleire: "He imposes the sensation of speed solely by the trepidation of cylinders or of the indicator. His end is attained with force and precision." De Keukeleire has been called "the seeker."

The young men of Belgium, Brussels before Antwerp, will build a Belgian cinema which will ultimately record the life of the industrial areas, like Charleroi, the coastal fishing districts, the ports, instead of war sentimentalisms. The Cinema Club of Brussels, now in a permanent theater, and its extension in Ostend, the cosmopolitan bathing resort, provide a base for consolidated production. The reader will be interested to know what American films are considered "notable" and included in the programs of the Cinema Club. Since these programs are typical of the film-club programs throughout Europe I will name those American films which are considered pivotal and historically important in the art of the motion picture. These include:

The early comedies of Chaplin.

A Woman of Paris (called abroad *Public Opinion*) by Charles Chaplin.

Grass by Schoedsack and Cooper.

Way Down East by D. W. Griffith.

Nanook of the North and *Moana of the South Seas* by Robert J. Flaherty.

The Marriage Circle by Ernst Lubitsch.

The Cat and the Canary by Paul Leni.

Greed by Erich von Stroheim.

The Mark of Zorro with Fairbanks.

Beggar On Horseback by James Cruze.

White Gold by W. K. Howard.

A more consolidated and extensive body is the Filmliga of Holland. In Amsterdam, the central and inaugural unit, the Liga has recently erected its own theater, de Uitkyk. Originally an organization in Amsterdam for the exhibition of important films, the Liga extended itself throughout Holland: The Hague, Eindhoven, Haarlem, etc. It went into production through the sponsoring of individuals. Now it plans a collective production, *The Flying Dutchman,* with sound. The Flying Dutchman is the recurrent storm, and the Filmliga intends sending its players and director and cameramen out into a genuine storm with Dutch fishers of the Zuyder Zee and the Ocean.

Among the individuals associated with the Filmliga is young Joris Ivens, a trained phototechnician who has turned to the motion picture.

Ivens' first film was *The Rotterdam Steel Bridge.* This documentary film has been widely recognized for its very sincere and sturdy qualities, the angles, the sense of steel and concrete, of volume and mobile weight, the slow but sure movement, the balanced rhythm, the accumulation of movements about the bridge. A very sober film. Sobriety is the nature of the Dutch and it is the heart of the Filmliga. It is, as I shall indicate, also its danger.

Joris Ivens' vocation of phototechnician is especially revealed in his film *Rain,* a product of angles and filters. Ivens, despairing because of the continual oily autumnal rains — those thick, sober, well-fed rains of Holland — came to Paris and complained to his friend, a Dutchman, too, M. H. K. Franken, of nature's perversity and his own dire condition. "Well," said Franken, "why don't you film the rain?"

Ivens went back to Amsterdam, took his portable Eyemo and his Japanese assistant and into the rain went he, not crying any more: "Rain, rain, go away!" but diving under legs, horses, wagons, trams to get angles on the deluge. What do you look for in the rain and how many ways can you look at a rain? There are such things as texture of the drops, speed of the fall, angle of pour. There are glistening streets, glistening oilskins, overshoes, horses' hooves, splashing feet, umbrellas. An umbrella opens and shuts forward to the spectator. A leg moves, hose moist, water-sogged or lustrous, according to the texture. Ivens showed me this film in its uncut state in his projection room of the Capi photographic establishment on Amsterdam's main business street, the Kalverstraat. Although it was not in its final form, I could proclaim it a little gem of persistent sombreness, conveying its mood without literary aid. How superior to *Autumn Mists* by the Russian working in Paris, Dmitri Kirsanoff, who intrudes his wife, talented Nadia Sibirskaia, weeping over a letter which she burns, to force the mood of the dismal upon the spectator. There is purity in Joris Ivens' film, sentimentality in Dmitri Kirsanoff's.

Ivens made a film of a pile-driver in action and has taken it to Moscow with him. He is staying at the home of Serge Eisenstein, the director of *Potemkin* and *Ten Days.* Ivens is thought highly of by Eisenstein, and I too add my modest voice to accredit Joris as a cinematographer. As yet he has proven himself the man who can make an objective film — that is quite an attainment. The film *The Breakers,* for which he was cameraman under the direction of his good friend Franken, does not show off his camera work as well as his more objective film, *The Bridge. The Breakers,* based on a scenario by Franken from an idea by Jef Last, who acted as the main character, told a simple love story of an unemployed fisherman.

I had suggested to them to see *Land's End* by Jean Epstein, the French director as a good example to study, but they objected, saying Epstein lacked sobriety, meaning in reality that he was delicate and interested more in the psychical than in the physical. Pumpernickel does not always build structures. Sobriety must be analyzed, bluntness is not alone enough, or sincerity or pompousness.

Another of Ivens' products is a film of *Skating*. The last film Joris Ivens made before going to Russia was *Dredging the Zuyder Zee.* He has taken his films with him and the *Luxemburg* film by Franken and Ankersmit. *The City* by Bon and *Crystallisations,* by Mol. He has been invited to lecture in Moscow, Leningrad and Kiev. His first Moscow lecture was introduced by the great Russian director, Pudovkin. So many people were refused admittance on account of limited space, Ivens had to repeat the lecture a few days later.

Other Filmliga members who have made good films are J. C. Mol, director of the Multifilm factory in Haarlem, and the late C. Aafjes, operator for Polygoon, makers of industrial films. Mol has made a fine scientific film, a work of art, *Crystallizations,* of a crystal of salt in water. When this was originally shown in Paris, a triple screen spread the crystallisations over a vast area, a startling composition of dazzling dancing minutiae. Aafjes made a notable advertising film celebrating the anniversary of the newspaper *Handelsblad*. This *Handelsbladfilm,* made in collaboration with B. Ochse, shows that as immediate a thing as an advertisement can be unusual and artistic. Instead of the typical matter-of-fact blurb, this film is a continuous movement of back-and-forth resilience with a composite exposure — one impression on the other — of machinery, titles, workers. It is one of the few films of continuous motion and continuous multiple exposure. In this intensive way, uninterrupted by remarks, the maker could tell much in a small space and within a very brief time. It is a film which can stand as exemplary.

Aafjes made a film in collaboration with J. Meza, *The Life of the Bees,* for Polygoon, his company, and left about a dozen meters of another film, *Hollandish Circus*. He died prematurely.

A new film is *When the Ears of Corn Bend Over . . .* , the joint work of a young Dutchman, J. van Canstein, and a young Frenchman, Jean Dreville. It is a film of the farm, without staging or professional acting.

William Bon, a young Dutch student, has made a short film called *The City,* for which he received considerable technical advice from the master, Joris Ivens. It is this coördination of the more experienced with the inexperienced that promises so much for the future Dutch cinema. The Filmliga has recognized the need for clarification and in its periodical, one of the best in the world, the members and others discuss a variety of subjects in Dutch, German, French and sometimes English. The Dutch, speaking a provincial language, are linguists. To the Filmliga are brought also the leading directors: Walter Ruttman from Germany, Mme. Germaine Dulac and René Clair from France and Pudovkin from Russia. The last is, as the Liga has itself said, tied up with the development of the Filmliga, its past and future. Fortunately, the Russian film is a very great force in the lives of these beginning artists of Holland.

The Filmliga unites with the independent and progressive activities throughout Europe. It has representatives in Europe, Franken and Ankersmit in Paris and an affiliated exhibiting group in Copenhagen. Franken and Ankersmit have made a small film together of the *Luxemburg Gardens* in Paris. The Filmliga has staged an international film exposition, and the films of its young men have been exhibited regularly in Paris. The Studio 28 there makes it a part of its program to exhibit Filmliga productions like those of Ivens and Mol. Ninety per cent of the films shown in Holland are American; whatever commercial film production there is is mainly newsreel and publicity films. Sometimes the latter are works of art. But the outside world gets to know of the increasing activity in film making there, and directors like Pudovkin, Eisenstein and Dulac praise the makers. If the Liga keeps its sobriety from being inflated to conceit, it will do very, very much.

Such organizations as these in Holland and Belgium, together with the ones existent in England, France, Spain, Germany, Czechoslovakia, Alsace, Russia, Switzerland, North Africa and South America, can do much to advance and safeguard the art of the film. We need such an organization in America, where films of the past, of the world abroad, of independents and of the future can be shown. An international organization was begun in Switzerland last September to consolidate the work of these clubs, and the Filmliga of Holland is represented on the international council, as it should be, being the one producing club which is the source of a national motion picture.

Belgium will no longer need to content itself with the vicarious self-praise that the noted director, Jacques Feyder, who has made fine films in Germany and France and directed Greta Garbo in *The Kiss,* is a Belgian. Nor will Holland need to point out that two Dutch beauties are known to Europe's fans as stars: Lil Dagover, who was the woman in *The Cabinet of Dr. Caligari,* and Lien Deyers, the young stool-pigeon in the German mystery film, *Spies,* and heroine of the French film, *Captain Fracasse.* Nor will Holland need to depend for its film releases, its shows, solely on the Tuschinski chain of theatres, now that the Filmliga is centralized in a house of its own.

It is of greatest importance to the morale and culture of Belgium that the land should be diverted from its introverted self-regard, from the continual brag of how staunch Burgomaster Max of Brussels was when the Germans invaded the land, and how brave every woman – symbolized by the heroine of Tournai – was. I dropped in one night to see a play in Flemish at the Royal Flemish Theater. Again a terrible hamfat production of the heroism of the Flemings. The young film makers, turned to art by the example of their Parisian confreres, can save the land from dwelling upon its heroism, an incident of war's monstrosities. These young people are turning to the permanent things, the land and the folk: festivals, men departing for new hopes – and, it is true, platitudes about life. They had better first concern themselves with the physical realities constantly recurring and from these to extract finally truth. Indications point to such preoccupation, and it is all for the good.

Belgian experimenters in the art of the cinema are helped toward their ends by the Belgian law which requires that certain films shall not be shown to children under 16. This takes the place of absolute censorship – that arbitrary and unfair external supervision – and allows ultimately films to be produced on serious themes which will not be impaired by the fear that kids will see them. The law is respected: notices are put in front of the theaters announcing the non-admittance or admittance of sub-sixteeners. Such a law would hardly succeed here: it would probably be used continually to entice youngsters by pretending to forbid them but overlooking their entrance. This trick has been played here. But in Europe the people are better disciplined socially.

CINEMA,
June, 1930.

THE GOLDEN AGE OF THE SCANDINAVIAN FILM

In the first days of the world's cinema the polar bear of the Great Northern or Nordisk of Denmark vied with the rooster of the French Pathé and the wings of the American Vitagraph for preëminence. It was the Danish company that gave the impetus to the topical picture or newsreel when, in 1909, it showed the arrival in Copenhagen of the pseudo-discoverer of the North Pole, Dr. Cook, as he was received by the King and Crown Prince of Denmark. About 1907 the Nordisk staged a "lion hunt" – one of those early "travel" pictures – under the direction of Ole Olsen on one of the Danish islands, tiny Sprogoe. It contributed to the methods of "duping" and staging, developed highly by Sigmund Lubin in Philadelphia. The climax of the Nordisk was reached in the war period. The Scandinavian nations did not fight but they felt the war positively and negatively. In 1916 the Great Northern produced *Money,* the novel by the French writer Emile Zola – recently again filmed in France under the direction of Marcel L'Herbier. The film was produced by Dr. Karl Mantzius, now dead, who also played the main role. Other actors included Augusta Blad and Robert Schylberg. All three were from the Royal Theater of Copenhagen. The trend was then the "Famous players in famous plays" idea, an idea that may have been remunerative, but not altogether to the good of the film. However, this first version of *Money* was more sincere and convincing in its time – than the second version. Sincerity has always been a portion of the Scandinavian film when it has been Scandinavian and not, as in later years, Hollywood duplicates.

The first player to become known nationally was Psilander. He became a post card favorite and haberdashers began to sell Psilander shirts, Psilander cravats, Psilander etceteras. He committed suicide, a frequent end to a satiated favorite. But from Denmark came too the first actress to evolve a film form of playing, Asta Nielsen, who remains the most accomplished of artistes. She has been in Germany, on the stage and in the film, for a long time now.

It was at the Nordisk studios that Carl Dreyer, the great director of *The Passion of Joan of Arc,* began. Dreyer was born in Sweden but has lived in Copenhagen. He was a journalist. About fifteen years ago he entered the Nordisk—devoting half his day to journalism still—as cutter and scenarist, continuing in those capacities for some years. In 1918 he made his first pictures, *Pages from the Book of Satan,* divided into four parts: "Christ," "The Inquisition," "The French Revolution," "The Finnish Revolution of 1918." After his first film he went to Sweden, his native land, to make for the Swedish Biograph *The Fourth Alliance of Dame Marguerite,* called here *The Witch Woman.* He then succeeded with a film drawn from motifs by Hans Christian Andersen, the Danish folk-writer, called *Once Upon a Time.* This was privately subsidized. Swedish Biograph asked him to make the Norwegian national film, *Glomdal's Bride.* Back then to Copenhagen, this time to work for Palladium, for whom he made *The Master of the House.* This film and *The Fourth Alliance of Dame Marguerite* gave Dreyer a great repute, and no book on the art of film which has appeared in Europe has failed to include his work. He was unknown in America until *Joan of Arc,* save for a German UFA film he made, *Michael,* which starred his compatriot, Benjamin Christiansen, who made a film in Scandinavia, *The Witch,* and is now directing in Hollywood.

Dreyer was at work in Sweden in the golden age of the Swedish cinema, the most beautiful cinema in the world before the appearance of the Russian. If I seem to be over-enthusiastic, let me quote the best and most judicious of French critics, Leon Moussinac. "The Swedes," says he, "have transposed upon the screen their character . . . transfiguring a tale or a Scandinavian legend by the contact of their very souls . . . tragic calm, noble serenity, puissance." Yes, as Moussinac goes on to say, these Swedish pictures unite lyricism, hallucinating and poignant lyricism, with passionate zeal, and tenderness, the soft familiar intimacy, nuances of sentiment, in a gesture or a glance. Says a sober English writer, L'Estrange Fawcett: ". . . I believe the finest examples of screen art so far have been Swedish."

The greatest of the Swedish directors were Victor Sjöstrom, now a Metro-Goldwyn-Mayer director known as Seastrom, and Mauritz Stiller, who came to America to make films and died. Actors include Greta Garbo and Lars Hanson, well known as players in American films, and Gösta Ekman, a noted stage-actor and film-player, who was *Faust* in the German film of that name. Conrad Veidt and other German actors played in Swedish films. There is an easy exchange of players in Europe without harm to their art. It is different with directors.

The Swedes did not idle about for subject-matter. They found it at hand in their literature, which was so close to their life. The novels of Dr. Selma Lagerlöf have served for most of the Swedish films: for *The Driver,* or as it is known here, *The Stroke of Midnight* (in England: *Thy Soul Shall Bear Witness*; in France: *The Phantom Chariot*); for *The Treasure of Arne*; for *The Accursed,* etc. *The Driver* was enacted and directed by Seastrom. This is built on a Swedish legend which tells of the last man to be slain on the stroke of the parting year being sentenced to drive the chariot of the dead until the next year. A drunkard and wife-deserter is beaten in a brawl in a cemetery, and visions himself pleading for release from his soul's debt on earth with the salvationist who has sought to rescue him and has fallen ill unto death because of his recalcitrance. The vision clarifies his heart, he returns to his wife and family. A typical Swedish tale of soul's salvation: a persistent motif in Lagerlöf's works — sentimental in its mere fable but intense, piercing, cathartic in its Seastrom direction, with the most exquisite sustained use of transparent movement — double exposure of the driver — upon the substantial structure of the world of reality. There has been no film quite like it. It is continually revived in the art cinemas of Europe, in whose programs Seastrom holds an eminent place. So eminent is his position that the Free Tribune of the Cinema in Paris revived his epic film, *The Proscribed,* and presented it in its integral and intact original state for the true student of the film to see.

Stiller directed *The Atonement of Gösta Berling,* starring Greta Garbo and Lars Hanson, a terrific dramatic narrative of a triangular relation, illicit love and penance. Sin and salvation are the evangelical motives of these Swedish pictures, growing from the intense moral conscience of the Swedish people. In *The Treasure of Arne,* directed by Stiller and starring Mary Johnson, a medieval tale of a murder of a feudal family, theft, conscience-pangs, love, betrayal, sacrifice of the loved who betrays, penance — a procession of the women of the village across the ice to the murderers — becomes a film of tormenting poignancy, with strange black undercurrents of the soul's intermittences, those moments when deeds are committed which are diabolic but logical. What moved these men to murder? And was the murder of the sweetheart justified because her love was not greater than her debt to her father whom her lover had slain? Nature acts in the Swedish film, it is not simply a passive setting as in an American western: it plays, it propels the women across the ice with their slain. The women are Earth crying condemnation. The wolves in *Gösta Berling* are the threat of Nature; the wife's return to her mother to grind the grain is the compensation of the soil. In *The Accursed*—based on Lagerlöf's *Jerusalem,* the narrative of the mystical excitation among the peasants of Dalecarlia which made them migrate to the Holy Land—the mother would drown her child because her husband had followed another woman upon the pilgrimage. Nature here is passionate and embattled, the soul as well as the blood are in turbulence. While this film seems more the formula than the art of the Swedish cinema, it is still, being very near to its nativity, a better film than those copied after the Swedish. The director, Gustaf Molander, has never, in all the films he made in Germany, quite approached *The Accursed.*

Even Hollywood has tried to copy the Swedish film. I can name a number which are echoes, but how distant, of these great pictures. There is *Captain Salvation* with Lars Hanson: you have the evangelist, salvation, and some scenes like those in *Gösta Berling,* e.g., the harangue of the populace. This however, is like the mockery of a dirge. It is not heroic, as are the Swedish films, but mock-heroic. It is a fabrication, not an experience.

Flesh and the Devil is related to the Swedish film. It has two Swedish actors, Garbo and Hanson. Its plot was based on Sudermann and Sudermann is an echo of the Scandinavian. He perpetrates tales, but does not create experiences: he has all the tragic episodes but no tragedy. Incidentally, Germany has shown that its cinema has no real love of the tragic by making Sudermann a sort of national film-source: in *The Cat's Bridge* (a *Treasure of Arne* without conviction), *Dame Care,* and the German-American film, *Sunrise. Flesh and the Devil* is German in set, a studio attempt to produce a natural setting that will *act,* as does the Swedish of yesterday.

Seastrom's American films are, of course, reminiscent of the films he made in Sweden, but only reminiscent. His first picture here was *Name the Man!* based on Hall Caine, who is a dismal tawdry reduction of Lagerlöf. That was America's idea of starkness, and what was the result? Imitation, trumpery—not art. Seastrom did as well as he could and the only one who helped him was Mae Busch. Conrad Nagel, sourfaced and unimaginative, was no Lars Hanson. When Seastrom was given *The Scarlet Letter* of Hawthorne to do, here was something very close to the rigorous

Scandinavian. He had Lars Hanson; but alas! he had an actress not trained in the stark, severe school of the tragic, but in the cute, mincing, waxen school of pathos of D. W. Griffith. Lillian Gish softened the drama and the film and quite killed its possibilities. Frankly, I saw years ago a version of this novel done by Fox Pictures — when they were making the worst stuff in the U. S. A. — which was superior to this more recent production. Stuart Holmes was the minister. America even went so far as to give Seastrom a Lagerlöf novel to film, *The Emperor of Portugallia,* which became *The Tower of Lies,* with Norma Shearer, Lon Chaney and Ian Keith. Not a bad picture, but not a Seastrom of the golden age. *The Wind* echoed the Swedish act of nature. I should say it vociferated nature, rather than, as in the Swedish film, entwined it with the conduct of the people. It blurted the oppressiveness of nature very much like the old melodrama's "and the villain still pursued her." It was insistent but not stark, and entirely missed a final experience. After a Swedish film you felt something complete and definite.

Stiller came to America, worked on *Hotel Imperial,* with a great German supervisor, Erich Pommer, trained in an entirely different school, above him, and all about him American shop methods and formulas. A vacuous James Hall, with the glazed eyes of a drowned cat, stalked through the film, which collapsed completely after the first fifteen minutes into an ordinary picture. Stiller died, and *Confession* was put out as his. Stiller may have had a hand in this dreadful picture, but I refuse to accept it as even the shadow of his ghost.

Folke Holmberg, who represents the Scandinavian cinema in Paris, said, when Seastrom and Stiller left for America, that he did not believe they could survive as artists away from their native lands, because no people are quite so consolidated, so localized, so folkish as the Swedes. He appears to have prophesied well; now let us hope for the fulfillment of his prophesy that other artists will appear equally good. Films are still being made in Sweden, but they are attempts to retrieve the motion picture commercially by doing American comedies. The backers of the Swedish Biograph are the powerful and wealthy Swedish Match Trust. They gave their money to the films — that is, a very small fraction of it — and in a few years the best, sincerest, most beautiful and moving films came out of Sweden. Why the Match Trust needs to make money on films is beyond me; why there are not other artists to continue the work I cannot see; and what is there to prevent a balance of these tragic films with gayer films? Dreyer, who made the heroic *Joan,* is preparing a light comedy now, but not in Sweden. There must be Dreyers, Stillers, Seastroms, Bruniuses (Brunius made a film upon the life of *Charles XII* of Sweden) in Scandinavia. Swedish Biograph and Nordisk combine with British companies, to what avail? Palladium of Copenhagen does Cervantes' *Don Quixote* with the slapstick comedians, Pat and Patachon, and makes of that great satirical novel a series of quotations illustrated by slapstick poses. The work is L. Lauritzen's, but he should not boast of it. A. M. Sandberg directs films made of Dickens' novels, such as *Great Expectations* and *David Copperfield,* and an imitation of a French commercial product, *The Golden Clown,* starring Gösta Ekman. Ekman turns to film making and directs a trite antiquated picture which gives him the opportunity of acting a double rôle, of a fop and a peasant. Dreyer moves about Europe making films, Christiansen, Seastrom, Stiller, Sven Gade leave for America (Gade is now back in Germany) – and we who have seen the golden Swedish film and who recall the preëminence of the early Nordisk ask whither have these gone?

I am not alone in suspecting the Swedish film to have gone to Russia. Sweden and Russia have been closely united culturally. The literatures of the two lands bear close resemblance one to the other: undercurrents, deeds of anguish, introspection, self-debasement, penitence, salvation are ingredients of the novels of both lands. The first films of Soviet Russia, like *Polikushka,* were drawn from extant literary works. *Polikushka* reminded me, when I saw it in Paris, of *The Treasure of Arne,* in its poignancy, the impotence against fate; the immaculate last moment of the funeral in *Polikushka,* the spirit of the slain girl pursuing her slayer in *The Treasure of Arne.* The revolution in Russia, however, releasing, as it did, the energies of a land, soon released the creative forces, and the film went beyond concentrated tragedies of individuals to vast social canvases, in which the individual was a symbol of the collected social forces. With this there was also a development of the film-technology up to the subject-matter. It must be said the Swedish cinema never reached full technical development, therefore never attained to its artistic summits, however great the height it reached. I do not think the subjects which formerly went into Swedish films will make up the Scandinavian film of the future. Nor will Knut Hamsun's novels be made into movies, as was *Growth of the Soil – and how amateurishly!* I believe the new Swedish and Danish and Norwegian cinema will deal with social movements, perhaps like the pilgrimage motif in *The Accursed.* But such movements must be treated *en masse* and not for the individual cases. As yet Scandinavia is not prepared for this, as can be discovered in the film directed by Schnedler Soerensen, *The Enslaved,* dealing with the fight of Schleswig-Holstein to liberate itself from Germany in 1914. The film was sincere but its viewpoint was too naïve and the direction was concerned more with individual heroes and villains than with historical and social forces.

We must look for hope in other corners. In Copenhagen there is an experimental theater, Forsogscenen, which includes a division dedicated to the showing of films, films which have little chance for runs of any length in the commercial houses, films too special as yet for general showing, censored films which are worth showing, etc. This group is connected with the strong Filmliga of Holland, already producing. Ultimately perhaps this Danish group will also produce films. Copenhagen has available studios. Norway, I believe, has but one minute studio at Oslo, but it has several men trained somewhat in direction, like Breistein, Sinding and Ivarson. It has actors and actresses, like Lillebel Ibsen, the granddaughter of the great dramatist, Henrik Ibsen. She is a lesser, but good, Beatrice Lillie. Ibsen's *Peer Gynt* would make a marvelous talkie and I know that Carl Dreyer would not be averse to doing it.

Sweden has a list of available directors: Brunius, Gustaf and Olaf Molander, Edgren, Wallen, Hasselstrom, etc.; actors: Ekman, Mona Martenson, etc.; a tradition; a highly cultured audience, social-minded; what will follow?

CINEMA,
September, 1930.

CINEMA ITALIA

In 1913, Italy sent the Cines six-reeler of Sienkiewicz's novel, *Quo Vadis?,* to America, where it was presented in regular legitimate theatres at one dollar admission. This was the beginning of the sumptuous historical spectacle film. It was brought to America by George Kleine, who also released here at about the same time as the Palermi-Genina production, *The Last Days of Pompeii.* This film began the career as impresario of "Roxy." He presented it at the Regent Theater in New York with a full orchestral accompaniment and the recitation (at intervals) by an actor of passages from Bulwer-Lytton's novel.

Quo Vadis? started something. Zukor had already brought over the French film, *Queen Elizabeth,* with Sarah Bernhardt, and three and four-reelers such as *The Fall of Troy* and *The Odyssey* had been exhibited. *Quo Vadis?* brought the historical spectacle to a head and rushed producers into the conversion of famous plays and novels into films. Griffith went into antiquity to make his last Biograph picture, *Judith of Bethulia,* with Blanche Sweet. In 1914 another Cines film of the spectacular sort came from Italy, *Antony and Cleopatra,* followed by *Spartacus.* The climax was reached in the production of *Cabiria,* written and realized by the poet, D'Annunzio. The probable stimulus for Griffith's Babylonian scenes in *Intolerance* was *Cabiria. Ben Hur* is a descendant of this pre-war stuff.

Antony and Cleopatra is the glorification of Rome. "It is equivalent to waving the Italian over the Egyptian flag, quite slowly for two hours." The words are those of one of America's first movie critics, the poet Vachel Lindsay. "From the stage standpoint, the magnificence is thoroughgoing.

Viewed as a circus, the acting is elephantine in its grandeur. All that is needed is pink lemonade sold in the audience."

"The famous *Cabiria,*" we are still listening to Lindsay, "a tale of war between Rome and Carthage, by D'Annunzio, is a prime example of a success, where *Antony and Cleopatra* and many European films founded upon the classics have been failures. With obvious defects as a producer, D'Annunzio appreciates spectacular symbolism. He has an instinct for the strange and the beautifully infernal, as they are related to decorative design. Therefore he is able to show us Carthage indeed. He has an Italian patriotism that amounts to frenzy. So Rome emerges body and soul from the past, in this spectacle. He gives us the cruelty of Baal, the intrepidity of the Roman legions. Everything Punic or Italian in the middle distance or massed background speaks of the very genius of the people concerned and actively generates their kind of lightning.

"The principals do not carry out the momentum of this immense resource. The half a score of leading characers, with the costumes, gestures, and aspects of gods are, after all, works of the taxidermist. They are stuffed gods. They conduct a silly nickelodeon romance while Carthage rolls on toward her doom. They are like sparrows fighting for grain on the edge of the battle.

"The doings of his principals are sufficiently evident to be grasped with a word or two of printed insert on the films. But he sentimentalizes about them. He adds side-elaborations of the plot that would require much time to make clear, and a hard working novelist to make interesting. We are sentenced to stop and gaze long upon its array of printing in the darkness, just at the moment the tenth wave of glory seems ready to sweep in. But one hundred words cannot be a photoplay climax. The climax must be in a tableau that is to the eye as the rising sun itself, that follows the thousand flags of the dawn.

"In the New York performance, and presumably in other large cities, there was also an orchestra. Behold them, one layer of great photoplay, one layer of bad melodrama, one layer of explanation, and a final cement of music. It is as though in an art museum there should be a man at the door selling would-be masterly short stories about the paintings and a man with a violin playing the catalogue. . . . But the mistakes of *Cabiria* are those of the pioneer work of genius. It has in it twenty great productions. It abounds in suggestions. . . . As it is, the background and mass-movements must stand as monumental achievements in vital patriotic splendor.

"D'Annunzio is Griffith's most inspired rival in these things. He lacks Griffith's knowledge of what is a photoplay and what is not. He lacks

Griffith's simplicity of hurdle-race plot. He lacks his avalanche-like action. The Italian needs the American's health and clean winds. He needs his foregrounds, leading actors, and types of plot. But the American has never gone as deep as the Italian into landscapes that are their own tragedians, and into Satanic and celestial ceremonials."

Cabiria has left its history in many ways. There are Cabiria-vestiges everywhere. The studio has a term "Cabiria" for a usage of film technique. Rex Ingram is a director of the Cabiria school. Maciste, the giant of that film, still displays his Italian muscles in his Maciste strong-man series in the side streets of Paris, Berlin, New York and elsewhere. An entire cult of the spectacular historical film was built up in Italy with films like *Itara, Inferno, Christus* and *St. Francis of Assisi*—these last two directed by Antomaro; *Cavalleria Rusticana, The Carnival of Venice* and *The Patrician of Venice*—these Venetian spectacles the work of Almirante; *Messalina,* realized by Z. Gazzonni [*sic*]*; and *Theodora* by Carbucci. There was another D'Annunzio film, *The Ship,* "a hymn in frescoes," with the noted actress and danseuse, Ida Rubinstein, in the stellar role.

These films have an importance beside their merit. They are, in their glorification of the Italian past, the stimulants of Italian "futurism" and ultimately of Italian "Fascism." Just as there is a direct relationship between the recrudescence of the Ku Klux Klan and Griffith's film, *The Birth of a Nation,* so a film like *Cabiria* is the song before the occurrence. Italy is said to be a land that introduces its social changes with songs. Just now there are being whispered songs counter-Fascist. *Cabiria* was the cinematic hymn that evoked, in its measure, the inflated nostalgia for *Roma Antica.* Today there is exhibited in Italian film production, depleted as it is, the imperialistic sentimentality of the Adriatic land of the boot. Films like *Kif Tebbi, Sun,* and *Miriam,* among many others, deal with the love of a native for an Italian hero. The Italian director, Enrico Guazzoni, has made several such films, from novels of popular native authors like Guido Milanesi. A whole horde of Italian actors and actresses participate in these pictures: Donatella Neri, Marcello Spado, Piero Carnabuci, Ugo Gracci, Dria Paola, Lia Bosco, Isa Pola and Carlo Gualandri (to name a handful only). The last two were the Miriam (Arab) and Mario (Italian), respectively, of *Miriam,* directed by Guazzoni. The preceding were in the cast of *Sun,* directed by Alessandro Blasetti, from a scenario by Aldo Vergano.

The decline of the Italian film, so dominant a decade and a half ago, began about 1916. The historic film deteriorated, by its very nature, into "pasteboard" structures. This characterization has been given to the film, *Theodora,* by the pioneer French film critic, the late Canudo. And it has occurred recently in a summary by the most conscientious of French writers on the film, Leon Moussinac. Moussinac finds that the "pasteboard" splendor of the film has now been replaced by its equivalent in politics, "the march on Rome" theme of Fascism. He says that despite all the urgings of an Italian motion picture, there is no rebirth. And he is right.

There was an attempt at one time among young Italian enthusiasts to create a "latin" cinema. There was a picture called *At the Frontier of Death,* directed by Toddi, called "one of the best masters of the modern film," and presenting Mme. Vera d'Angara, "so aristocratically beautiful and sensitive." The desire was for a folk film, an ethnic film, rather than a political film, but the promise was never fulfilled. Instead there have been Maciste muscle-films, Luciano Albertini (*The Invincible Spaventa*) daredevil pictures, pictures like *The Supreme Beauty* and *The Gaze That Dies* with Mme. Yanova, an importation from the Czarist cinema, a social comedy with Pina Menichelli or Francesca Bertini, or an occasional cinematization of a novel by Manzoni, with a noted chanteuse as star, Emilia Vidali. In 1929 only ten films were produced. The institution of a film "dictator" could not stir production. The Pittaluga monopoly did not make a single film. That may be excused by the preparations for sound-film production, which began with a rendition of *Ave Maria,* and has gone into the production of the novel, *Mercy,* by Grazia Deledda, Nobel prize-winner. For this film there were recalled from France two Italians who have played in Continental films, Carmen Boni and Augusto Bandini. The scenario is by an Italian, Michetti Guastalla, the direction by so Italian a name as Macini, and the artistic supervision by another native of the boot-shaped peninsula, Aldo de Benedetti. In Palermo, Sicily, there has been founded the Imperia Company, which has on its schedule the film *Porto.* As yet, however, there is nothing resembling an efflorescence of cinema in the Kingdom of Italy of the Dictatorship of Benito Mussolini.

The whole situation in Italy has something of the futility of a man trying to rise by his bootstraps. Italy is trying to rise by the straps of the Boot. Or to put it in another figure of speech of the Italian physical scene: it resembles the energy of the burnt-down volcano, Solfatara, at Pozzuli near Naples, the lava swinging ferociously in the crater, but getting nowhere. Film dictators, new companies, etc., do not supply productive energies. The Fascist propaganda film institute, Luce, will not convert propaganda into art as the Soviet studios have, and while the International Film Institute of the League of Nations, located at the Villa Falconieri in Rome, may be meritorious as an agency for the educative film, it will not have any relation to the popular, dramatic, artistic Italian film waiting to see the light. The Rome Institute is a sort of sop, it seems to me, to the intellectual world, to show Fascist Italy's concern for world enlightenment. This is not taking away from the merit of the work itself.

Nationalism can be national distemper as well as national glory. The Italian politicians endeavor to *save,* meaning actually to give birth to, a national cinema by laws, combinations with foreign countries against the domination of Hollywood, quotas, etc., and give expression to their rancor in words typical of wits' ends: "The Italian public has been excessively saturated with projections in which the effort of the allied armies during the great war is exalted. This constitutes indirectly a depreciation of the glorious efforts of the Italian armies under the sun of the Fatherland and upon the battlefields of other fronts. Among other things, in these films, there are often scenes truly macabre which impress the public inimically and depress the whole-hearted spirit, especially among the women and the young men who represent the security of the nation, just as in other war-films ridiculous or humorous scenes are introduced contrary to military discipline." The verbosity of this official manifesto cannot be fully conveyed in a translation which has omitted a number of epithets, but the jingoist sentiment is there. And a silly jingoism which fails to see that any film of the war exciting partisanship or making warring a lark actually excites pro-military sentiment everywhere. But Italy wants "pasteboard" awe. And of actual creation there is less manifestation than manifesto, more explosion than power.

The orally expressed aspiration to bring into Italy the glory of *Roma Antica* explains, in a great measure, the sterility of all Italian art, including the film. We may contrast two lands of dictatorship: Russia and Italy. The former, a dictatorship for the future, releases the creative energies of a suppressed land and produces the finest films in the world. The latter, a dictatorship for the past, increases the oppression upon the energies of the land and produces almost no cinema. The expression of this political negation of progressive forces is petulant and childish, as witness the suppression of the American film, *The Street Angel,* because "the girl of joy" strolls the streets of Naples! The fact that the lass is treated sympathetically doesn't count, and that she is vindicated is overlooked — Naples is pure, "See Naples and Die"! In Shanghai this film was burned by patriotic Italian sailors. A "patriotism that amounts to frenzy."

Italian artists like Italian politicians are continuously writing manifestoes. The Italian futurists preluded the Fascist *coup* with fourteen explosive points. But explosion is not power! The noise of Marinetti, Prampolini, Bragaglia and others are not creative of enthusiasms, basic and thorough, or of momentous energies. Italy's painters, the two greatest among them, Amedeo Modigliani and Giorgio di Chirico, went to France to live and work, even though Modigliani is related, in his work, to the Italian primitive, Cimabue, and Chirico was a futurist, and has Italian art-ancestry in Pannini. Similarly the leading Italian directors, Augusto Genina (who is director of *The Beauty Prize* starring Louise Brooks in her French film), Carmine Gallone and Gennaro Righelli, are at work in Germany and France; and the favored stars, such as Carmen Boni, Maria Jacobini, Marcella Albani and Francesca Bertini are also, for the most part, French or German players.

The stagnation is apparent in the very movie houses themselves. I once said that the Italians would elect Tom Mix to succeed Mussolini as dictator. That's about the taste for Italian pictures in Italy. Tom Mix—Roscoe Arbuckle—Charlie Chaplin. Going to a movie in Italy is a desperate affair. When the nozzle of the King's horse or Il Duce's horse is detected just crossing the frame of the screen, an anthem (there are millions of them!) is played and everyone rises to block the vision. This happened numerous times in a house in Venice. Everything is classical in Italy. There was announced at one movie *The Odyssey of Charlie Chaplin.* It turned out to be the original Mack Sennett production of *Tillie's Punctured Romance.* In Florence there was a showing of the German film, *Othello,* with Jannings in the title rôle. The picture was shown at the Royal Opera; about six spectators appeared. I sat in the royal box.

There are about 3000 film theaters in Italy, of which about two-thirds show films exclusively, and of these a few hundred show films only several days a week. There are about 600 that may be said to take films seriously. I recall some of these, remnants of the days when the motion picture was an "electrical theater." Double-decker houses like some in Paris: one auditorium in the basement, another on the ground floor, charging separate admissions to separate programs. In Naples there's a basement movie which is divided in half, as an architectural necessity, by pillars. To utilize all the space for patrons, two screens are placed on either side of the poles, and the film projected to the two.

An Italian explained the condition of the cinema in Italy by saying, "the Italian soul is too artistic for the movie, it prefers the traditional opera." If so, too bad!

CINEMA,
October, 1930.

* [Gen. Ed.]: Page 348—"Z. Gazzonni" [*sic*]—the director of *Messalina* was Enrico Guazzoni.

CINEMA IBERIA

The Spanish film world is dominated by Hollywood. A Madrid house advertising its season's program lists sixteen American films, three French, three German, one Scandinavian, and one Spanish. Spain is very eager to create a domestic cinema. I know that Carl Dreyer, who made the great film, *The Passion of Joan of Arc,* was asked to come to Spain to supervise production. Production has been switched from Barcelona to Madrid, with the former remaining as the distribution center for foreign films. From Barcelona the distribution radiates into the Peninsula: Catalonia and Aragon, Valencia and the East Coast, Northern Spain, Castile (inclusive of Madrid), Andalusia (with Spanish Morocco) and Portugal. Films made at Barcelona before the shift included *Barcelona and its Mysteries* and *The Daughter of the Fisherman,* starring Lorenzo de Omo.

Production in Spain dates from 1923. One of the earlier Spanish films was *The White Gypsy* with the famous chanteuse, Raquel Meller. It was received everywhere as mediocre in conception and in execution, lacking unity of development, rhythm, and all persuasiveness of action. Raquel Meller, however, was found alert and vibrant, intense, fine and pensive. I condense here the criticism of the French writer, Canudo; it is an epitome of the general reaction to the film. This is the story of *The White Gypsy*: A Spanish husband and father believing himself betrayed by his wife, deserts her leaving their two children to a band of gypsies. The children grow up, the boy into a bullfighter, the girl into a danseuse. They meet and fall in love. But learn they are brother and sister. The father finds them and finds also his wife, innocent and dead. They return the body to the shattered hearth. Canudo's condemnation of this film was undersigned by the eminent writer, Enrique Gomez Carrillo. The best "Spanish" film I know of is the French version of *Carmen,* with Raquel Meller, directed by the Belgian now in America, Jacques Feyder. This version is based, not like the Geraldine Farrar or Theda Bara edition on the Bizet opera, but on the original Merimée story.

About twenty films are produced in Spain annually. The most successful are those which convert popular novels and plays, like *The House of Troy* and *The Way of the Cross.* The public has liked romanticized or semi-historic films. This has encouraged the producers toward more ambitious ventures. In the period of the great painter and caricaturist, de Goya, is placed *Pepeillo,* which relates the life of the popular folk-hero, the bullfighter of that name. This, self-evidently, was well-liked. It is one of the Madrid productions. Another is *Long Live Madrid, My Native Town!* In this a well known toreador and one of the prettiest actresses of the capital played the leads. The Spanish producers believe that, despite difficulties, the Spanish cinema is destined to prosper, especially in the markets of Latin America.

A young Spaniard, Luis Buñuel, who followed the Latin trek to Paris, has showed ingenuity in a sadistic film, *Un Chien Andalou.* One would hope that Señor Buñuel might be allowed to turn his gifts to more ambitious, less treacherous, introverted ventures, in his own land. He remains in Paris to do a second film of similar, reprehensible tendencies—of cruelty, over-refined—called *L'Age d'or.* His first picture, with two talented young players, Pierre Batcheff and Simone Mareuil, dealt with a sexually inhibited mind. It contained such fantasies as a razor cutting the pupil of the girl, ants eating the palm of a hand, a hand lying in the street, the putrefied head of a calf flung over a piano, hands caressing a nude torso, two priests being pulled up a floor while attached to a piano, etc. The razor-cutting sequence was ingenious. The razor is near the girl's eye. A cow's eye is cut, giving the sensation of the girl's eye being severed. Ingenious, but rather shiverful. Pity it is that Spain cannot find a real, wholesome environment for Buñuel's talents. But the Latin lands do not seem hospitable to their most sensitive artists. From Italy migrate the best painters, Modigliani and Chirico, and from Spain geniuses like Picasso and Juan Gris. Buñuel does a clever film that has no survival-value.

The Spanish cinema is seeking to realize itself from within, not from the exertion of the government. This may account for what little vitality there is in it. The paternal attitude of Fascist Italy toward the Italian cinema has produced nothing but more repression. The Spanish cinema is more self-assertive. Even during the dictatorships of Primo de Rivera, a Spanish writer, in *The Literary Gazette* of Madrid, questioned the revolutionary, health-giving character of Fascism. It was political only, he said, not social, moral or aesthetic, and therefore, the implication is, Fascism cannot produce a robust national expression in the arts, of which the cinema is the most primitive. In this same journal considerable space is devoted to the Cineclub's activities. Of all the film clubs in Europe, there is perhaps none so lively as the Madrid organization. Buñuel is, in a sense, a product of this cinema group. One hopes it will pass eventually from the adulation of Buster Keaton to an examination of the possibilities of a Spanish cinema, guarding it from the too special super-refined influence of the French private art studios, and from the too-nationalistic film of pompous jingoism.

Like most other lands, Spain at first refused to accept the inevitable sound film, *cine sonoro,* for a variety of reasons: the popular enthusiasm for American films, which they thought would be destroyed by alien speech; the beginnings in the mute cinema already made in Spain; the wish to compete internationally, which would be thwarted by the Spanish tongue. There were lesser reasons like: increase in ticket prices; less frequent change of program. And "custom." But the inevitable is inevitable, and Ibañez's *The Vintage* has been made into a talkie, directed by the leading director Benito Perojo. Playing in this film are Conchita Piquer, José Mora and Maria Luz Callejo. The verdict is another success! Another film, *The Songs of Songs* is being synchronized in England.

A movement has been begun in Spain to establish an Hispano-American Film Congress. This movement intends to establish cinema centers in Madrid, Havana, Mexico City and Buenos Aires, whose first work will be propaganda films, films, that is, to "sell" the Hispanic lands to tourists and to the good will of the world — films of persuasive documentation.

There is an interesting personality "not on the screen" of Spain, but who bears some relation to the motion picture. That individual is Ramon Gomez de la Serna, known by his first name of Ramon. He is 38 years old and the author of some 80 books, among which is *Movieland,* his first to be translated into English. "Ramon," his translator says, "has never been in Hollywood. Not even in the U. S. A." and yet he presents a composite Hollywood based on the evidences of the screen and his own fantasies. His picture is of a "super-real" fantastic community. (Ramon has also written a number of scenarios for films which have not yet been made). Here is his description of "Movieland, The Grand Burg":

"From the distance Movieland looks like Constantinople combined with a little Tokyo, a touch of Florence and a hint of New York. Not that all these cities are jumbled together there, but that each of its districts represents one of them.

"It is like a Noah's ark of architecture. A Florentine palace, seized with that salaciousness which exotic buildings produce, looks longingly at a Grand Pagoda.

"Strange panorama, looking like nothing so much as an immense Luna Park!

"One of the best paid people in all Movieland is a good drunkard.

"A good moving picture drunkard is a very difficult thing to find. He is not a drunkard who reels and staggers about. No. He is a drunkard who is in full command of himself, a presidential drunkard, capable of presiding over a world congress of drunkards."

Ramon here represents that ultra-sophisticated, yet naïve, school of France — once called "dadaists," now "super-realists" — who have tried to make an aesthetic out of the unrelated but have merely produced a cult of the nonsensical. His book expresses a little of the Spanish film's rococo bombast and adulation of Hollywood.

The impulse for self-determination in the motion picture extends to Spain's neighbor in the Iberian peninsula. On May 6, 1927, the government of Portugal decreed that: "In all moving picture exhibitions in Portugal one film of Portuguese production must be shown, of a minimum of one hundred meters. This film must be changed every week and must be, if at all possible, alternatively of nature and Portuguese drama." Since then an attempt has been made to manufacture films as well as laws. An historical film, *José do Telhado,* with Aida Lupo as principal, is one of the first Portuguese movie dramas. A film has been made documenting the life of the Portuguese fishers. It is called *Nazaré.* At Lisbon there has been produced *A Castela das Berlengas.* Porto Film Ltd., just founded at Oporto, has begun on a series of purely national movies, based upon the most important pages in the history of Portugal. The first two pictures are *Rainha Santa Izabel* and *Ignez de Castro.* Carlos Moreira is technical director of this company and Maria-Emilia Castelo Branco artistic director.

At Lisbon there has been made a film on the capital, an anecdotic film chronicle in ten parts dealing with Lisbon life. It is called *Lisboa,* the Portuguese name for the city. This film, directed by Leitao de Barros, has been enthusiastically received by the Portuguese critics. The interpreters have been assembled from the native theater and include José Alves da Cunha, Erico Braga, Aura Abranches, Palmira Bastos, Ester Leao, Chaby

Pinheiro, Adelina Fernandes, and others. Another Portuguese film is *Maria do Mar,* directed by Leitao de Barros.

José do Telhado is based on the novel by Eduardo de Nohonha and is the filmwork of Director Rino Lupo. José is a figure in Portuguese legend. He is the Jesse James, the Dick Turpin, the Robert Macaire of Portugal. His activities, which terrified the north of Portugal, took place between 1835 and 1862. The romantic character was given him by the popular mind, who called him a "good bad man," a brand which romanticized the outlaw, however vicious he may have been in life. We have given such a romantic quality even to the unemotional cold-blooded murderer, Billy the Kid, and today the most anti-social bandit, the racketeer, is romanticized in our films like *Underworld, Street of Chance,* etc. José is pictured as a devoted husband and fond father, and what a lover! A friend to the poor and the oppressed. A victim of fate who paid for his crimes on the African coast. Intrigue, love adventures—a very sympathetic personality for the Italian director, Lupo. The outdoor scenes are set in the locale of José's manoeuvres, and the camera work is the Frenchman's, Maurice Laumann, who has worked in Portugal many years. Among the supporting players in the film are the leading Portuguese actors: Julieta Palmeira, Maria Emilia C. Branco, Zita d'Oliveira, Luiz Magalhaes, Carlos Azedo and Rafael Alves.

From the Latin Peninsulas of Europe to the Latins of the Americas is a logical journey. Production of films is almost nil in South America, nothing at all in Mexico and Central America. That erstwhile Spanish possession, the Philippines, has one company making three or four pictures yearly. Peru makes a couple annually. Ecuador some, Brazil a bit. A young Brazilian, Alberto Cavalcanti, is one of the best-known of independent directors in France. Argentina, the wealthiest of the lands of South America, has a film production of four or so a year. Mario Parpagnoli, an Italian actor now in France played in one of these, *The Knight of the Canyon,* produced by the Sociedad General Cinematografea, and directed as well as played in some others including *Galleguita.* It is natural that Argentina, land of the *gaucho,* should follow the American western.

The Argentine is one of the largest consumers of films in the world, although it is still one of the smallest producers. At present Soviet film—*Potemkin, Ten Days, Krassin, The Yellow Pass, Storm Over Asia*—are in the vogue. German films like *Variety* were successful, but *Metropolis* and *Spies* did not altogether appeal to the Latin temperament. The French film, *Money,* appealed because, like France, Argentina is a moneyland, a land of investments and speculations. The French satire, *The New Gentle-*

man, did not click. American films in favor have been *The Broadway Melody, The Iron Mask, Docks of New York, Four Devils* and *The Wedding March.* H. P. Tew, writing on the Argentine in *Close Up* for February, 1930, has said: "Buenos Aires is the perfect cinema cosmopolitan town. In the grand assimilation of the films of all countries it is a successful melting pot. And the purely artistic, the purely political, the purely propaganda, the purely cultural: all these ideas are sifted and taken. And no one minds what tendency as long as there is good cinema." What will the victory of American imperialism mean?

Now Cuba is going to make Spanish audibles. The Barrio Picture Production of Habana has made a single silent film, *La Virgen de la Caridad,* and is now intending to manufacture garrulous films for 108,000,000 Spanish-listening people outside of Cuba. Raymond Peon is director, and the stars include the Roy d'Arcy of Cuba, Guillermo de la Torre.

CINEMA,
December, 1930.

NEW YORK NOTES: I

I shall not speak of Hollywood in these notes, except as it refers to my province, New York. I believe it is time the movie found other locales. Perhaps the talkie will help that. Paramount has a studio at Astoria on Long Island, within greater New York, and Mr. Monta Bell, who was educated with Charlie Chaplin, is director. That is still Hollywood in derivation, but Mr. Rouben Mamoulian, who directed *Porgy* for the Theater Guild, has made a film at Astoria, *Applause,* and Mr. Mamoulian may be included in our New York school.

Not only I have felt the need for another school than Hollywood. Sven Gade, returning to Europe from the western Paradise, declares: "That just as it was inevitable that the movie should have sought the sun of California, it is now essential that it return to the east. It is now too far from the cultural, critical center of American life." You may read the full story in *Der Querschnitt,* January 1929.

I have not yet seen *Applause,* but in subsequent Notes I shall tell you what I think of it. In the meantime I am quoting from the words of Mr. Monta Bell, the supervising director of the studios, and from those of Mr. Rouben Mamoulian, director of the film itself. The comments of the two men are very interesting and very enlightening, if not entirely novel to the readers of *Close Up,* who have not just begun to hear about the contrapuntal organization of sound and sight in the "audible film," as our New York reviewers now call the talkies. But these observations coming from America may promise something. Therefore, I take the trouble and liberty of quoting them.

Monta Bell writes in the Motion Picture (September) number of the *Theater Arts Monthly* on "The Director," in relation to the new compound cinema. He says: "I feel like an amateur in my own business. . . . I believe that the director of silent pictures is far in advance of his brother director of stage productions, as we both approach his new medium. . . . At the time I came East I did not like talking pictures. I do not like them today. . . . If some one company had the courage — perhaps it would have taken a very rash courage — to hold aloof from the hysteria that brought these things about so rapidly — to produce only silent pictures during the year, I am not sure but that they might have found a considerable market for these same silent pictures. However, that is past. Talking pictures are here and here to stay." Mr. Bell came East though he disliked sound — not a happy confession, but most talkies seem to have been made by people who disliked them — and Mr. Bell had several theories: that a talkie was still a movie, that sound and speed used to enhance the movie was the right way for the talkie. He quotes from an article written a year previously for *The North American Review,* which he is all the more convinced is accurate. In that article he said: ". . . that which the eye sees is the chief attraction of the screen." An image held too long for the sake of sound is tedious; the screen should be made "continuously interesting." Directors are recognizing this. Bell suggested a year ago a number of devices now being used whose intention is not the synchronization of the sound with the issuer of the sound, but of sound from one source with an image not issuing the sound: in other words, non-coincidence of sound and image. He points out in his current article that directors now know it isn't the thing to have too much speech. He points to *Applause* as an instance of the correct compound: no unnecessary speech, dialogue and sound effects for the movement of the film. Bell sees the director as a writer, making his own transcription; and the writer who can manage people, he recognizes as a potential director.

Rouben Mamoulian has this to say about his film *Applause,* "The picture that you will see is an example of the perambulating camera along with the ordinary use of the microphone, an instrument that is not as yet a selective earpiece. . . . I lifted the sound-proofed camera off its feet and set it in motion on pneumatic tires. Scenes moved out of one room and into others without halt. I tried to introduce what I call counterpoint of action and dialogue." (This idea will not be new to readers of *Close Up,* however, novel it may seem to readers of *The New York Times*). "The camera flew, jerked, floated and rolled, discarding its stubborn tripod legs for a set of wired wheels that raced over the studio floors.

"The camera here becomes descriptive in a new sort of way. Where a break in the ordinary film to allow for a close-up has been the *modus operandi,* I now guide my lens along a straight and continuous line, without breaks in continuity, without needless explanatory speeches and also sans the printed subtitle.

"As in music, I have tried to attain counterpoint in the film. Not alone in the action on the screen, but in sound. For example, when the mother bends over the child singing it to sleep . . . the camera leaves her for a moment and goes to the head of the child, who . . . whispers her prayer. . . . Two unconnected sounds heard at the same time, that form a melodious whole.

"I have also tried to keep design in mind. There is always one force in motion played against another, and the camera rises and falls to catch the decorative element whether still or in motion.

"The camera then becomes an invisible spectator.

"By carefully timing the sequences and exercising stopwatch precision in rehearsing the cast, I believe I have a completed film that needs but a minimum of cutting."

Gilbert Seldes, our critic emeritus of the movie-as-art, writes in *Harper's* for September on "Talkies Progress":

"Not one of the talkies shown by midsummer, 1929, is worth a minute of any intelligent person's time. In themselves, that is. A number of them are good enough entertainment because they are transpositions to the screen of good stage melodrama or of good musical shows; some are good entertainment in the accidental moments when they remain movies. But as a self-contained, self-sufficient form they are wholly negligible and are worth consideration only because they are beginning to show signs of knowing what direction they want to take. Up to the present they have lived on borrowed material; and the trouble with living on the energies or emotions of others is that one doesn't live." The general sense of Mr. Seldes' epitome is accurate even if the analogy in the last sentence is amiss. If the sound film finds something that can be borrowed and incorporated that is its prerogative. Mr. Seldes objects to the early practice of focusing the camera on the throat or gullet of the speaker; he objects to it as unpleasant — why so finicky? — and because it doesn't permit us to see the voice's effect on the other characters. He says that now directors know they do not need to locate the voice by isolating the speaker. Seldes, like the logician that he is, says that in the nature of the instruments lay the answer to the problem — the stability of the microphone, the activity of the camera. But the microphone need not be immobile. The points upon the talkie which Mr. Seldes makes I have previously considered and presented in these pages. These points refer to the apparent non-synchronization, surmountable (though the writer does not say so) by the very camera-concentration to which he objects. As to the aesthetic necessities that "the art of cutting the new films has yet to be developed," and "a convention of speech must be effected." I must say that Mr. Seldes sounds like a weathercock. I have myself in *Close Up,* not merely expressed the needs for these instruments of the compound film, but have recorded tentative methods for the realization of the needs. And more await publication in these pages. It is true, Mr. Seldes says some theorists have expressed possible methods, but his summary is at this date a little behind times.

Simultaneous with this article of Mr. Seldes appears his book on *The Movie and the Talkies.** It is of necessity a brief book, and one must acknowledge that the author has done a good job. Indeed, I know of no one else who could remember to say as much as he has contained in the volume. (This little book is crowded with the various phases of the motion picture. At times Mr. Seldes is eloquent in his condensations, viz.: ". . . the movies can annihilate space and show the aggressors, the victims and the rescuers; it can subdivide time and multiply suspense; it can give the maximum of threat and of fear and hold them to the last fraction of intensity before it gives the maximum of joy." This arises out of a reference to an early Griffith film). It is a pocket critical history of the American film, despite tangential references to films elsewhere. Mr. Seldes might have carried out the work even more effectively had he placed stresses (in the sense of length of passages) more judiciously. He begins: "The moving picture is an illusion. It is also an industry." He spends a number of pages on the evidences of the illusion, implying that the illusory nature of the cinema differentiates it basically from the other arts. But—is not painting an illusion? Is not literature an illusion? Is paint any more a reality than the static image? Is a picture formed of paint any more a reality than a motion made of static images? But beyond this is another question: the illusion that becomes the reality of art (the reality of imparted experience) is not the illusory physical basis of the medium, but the organization which we call performance. (The confusion here is of the illusion of the origins with the illusion of the expression. The latter, while it relates to the former, is in a category, not isolated, but singular. That is, it does not depend solely nor—after being created—much upon its origins, it has its

* [Ed.]: Gilbert Seldes, *One Hour With the Movies and the Talkies.* (Philadelphia: J. B. Lippincott Co., 1929).

own peculiar experience to impart. Mr. Seldes, by his reasoning from the illusory basis of the cinema, concludes that the chief error has been the "over-emphasis of the actual side," that the cinema's "essential quality has been put aside in favor of an incidental." Still, the "actual" — the incidental, the factual — has been a source for the development of the essential: the newsreel and the romantic documentary, for instance; the newsreel and the Russian montage-film; the newsreel and *Potemkin*. The essential quality of any art subsists and survives against odds. These odds are the materials — obstacles if you will — to be mastered and converted. All art is victory and every artist, despite his beliefs, must be an optimist in so far as his art is concerned). Mr. Seldes has tried to concentrate into his slim volume the movie's technical foundations, its commercial history (which he might have packed into a couple of lines — "It was born in the laboratory and reared into the counting-house"), and the aesthetic development and principles. There are films made strictly upon the physical basis of the film: the animated cartoon, etc., but these are not the most important of the cinematic forms. Montage is, in a rudimentary sense, this physical basis of the film. But to build up a syllogism leading to a law of cinematic aim upon the premise of the film's illusory nature is to make the mere material rudiments the complete aesthetic experience. This has been an American error among the aesthetes of the cinema. Mr. Seldes does not make, however, the full mistake of being literal as was Mr. Matthew Josephson. He recognizes the American blunder that saw action as motion. I have put it before in these words: Cinema movement is not simple recorded motion, it is organized motion (rhythm). Seldes is wise enough to observe that the American folk film is rudimentary but not realized, and the reason for this is not the crass and stupid commercialism — which Seldes rightly indicates has proven its ignorance before the tribunal of actual developments, which has vindicated the aesthetician — but the congenial rudimentary and literal-mindedness of the American cinema, too expressive of the American non-creative mentality. It is because of this bred-in-the-bone-and-blood limitation that I urge a New York cinema. The Hollywood film colony is a vested interest community of phlegmatic imaginations and a circle of imitations. When I think of the reader of Mr. Seldes' book, I accept Mr. Seldes' reiterations of erstwhile axioms which by now are platitudes. No one in America — or very few — read serious critiques of the cinema. People have had to be told that the movie is not a hybrid, despite reference to other arts. Still, Mr. Seldes might have stressed certain qualifications such as: while the movie is not a mobilized sculpture or painting, and while it was a confusion that considered the movie an "electrical theatre," the unawareness of other mediums is no guarantee of a unique motion picture art. This qualification should further stress that no longer do we need to think of a particular theme as cinematic or not, if there is the artist who can convert it into cinema. The entire experience of mankind belongs to the film as it belongs to every other art, and mankind's graphic experience (painting and sculpture) can inform the structure of the motion picture. I repeat myself to the readers of *Close Up,* because this statement of "sources" is most important in a land whose cinema is literal and matter-of-fact.

It is this literal mind which explains the fact that Mr. Seldes correctly states: there has been no development beyond Griffith in composition. Only the American comedy has got to any distance beyond rudiments. It is not Chaplin alone who extended the rudiments. Indeed, it can barely be said that Chaplin is the extension of the American movie. Though he derives somewhat from Mack Sennett and – Seldes forgets – Max Linder, he is more validly the extension of the English music hall and, to an even greater extent, the development of himself. Much nearer to America in structure and temper are films like: *Hands Up!* with Raymond Griffith, and *A Commercial Yankee in King Arthur's Court* [*sic*] from the Mark Twain novel. Chaplin the personality is perfection, but he is not the sole realization of performance in the cinema. For the actor is not the achievement of the film – Mr. Seldes will agree to that, I know. If in America the film has not been fully realized it is only because the director has been unable to realize it, and this goes as much for Chaplin as director of his own comedies (yes, and of *A Woman of Paris,* too) as for Griffith and Sennett and the lesser men, including Mr. Seldes' favourite King Vidor. (Mr. Seldes wishes his text to culminate in two queries, the first of which is: Why has no figure comparable to Chaplin in slapstick comedy appeared in any of the other types of the movie? I have answered this query in my own way above but I wish to add, that if Mr. Seldes means: figures comparable in their *understanding* of the nature of film performance [and that should be the question, not degree of excellence]. I offer Werner Krauss, Asta Nielsen and the maligned Catherine Hessling. If he means directionally, I submit the Victor Seastrom of Swedish Biograph, Eisenstein, Dreyer. Frankly the "cult of Charlie Chaplin" needs some investigation. As for Mr. Seldes' enthusiasm for Vidor, it is not so exacting as his judgment usually requires).

Seldes very soberly and with some courage meets the Russian film and is not rhapsodic over it. But he fails to name its cardinal fault: it is a perfection and elaboration of the American physical method, a thousand times superior to the latter, but unsuited to a material more inferential, more social-minded, more profound than the usual American content. With all his urge to transcend the literal, Griffith was also held back by the experience of the American impact-film and as ultimate experience his films never attained to more than sententiousness and a *"poésie"* which was reflected in the false and tedious restraint of a Lillian Gish or a Mae Marsh, whom Mr. Seldes sentimentally remembers.

Mr. Seldes does not venture into a discussion of categories of the film which might lead him to consider forms out of the immediate range of the American experience. He does not treat at all of the future film, the psychically intensive, whose first and probably archetypical utterance is Dreyer's *Jeanne d'Arc*. He repeats the objection he has contributed to the *Encyclopædia Britannica* to the close-up, confusing its banal and sentimental effect-use in the American film with its intrinsic offering as a rhythmic employment or bold imagery for intensiveness (where it ceases being a close-up). He will not talk of the stereoscopic film — because he has not seen one — save to condemn it as false realism. Of course, it need not be that any more than sound is only extraneous duplication, simply because the practicians have no minds beyond the literal. (He blunders somewhat rankly in referring to rhetorical uses of instruments as "tricks." And a correction: *Entr-acte* is usually accredited to René Clair and not to Man Ray, as Seldes assigns it; and the film of Chomette's was sponsored, not made by de Beaumont. A last tribute: *Close Up* is referred to twice in the little book [which by the way costs $1.00], once as "fascinating." Dorothy M. Richardson is quoted).

The New York movie has individual articulation in the work of a few independent artists. The first of these whose films I have seen are Watson and Webber. They have made a short cinematization of Poe's *The Fall of the House of Usher*. It is done under the impetus of the French school of the multiple image, with prismatic multiplication of an image, gelatinous construction, limpid movements, sustained fluid rhythms. The technique of it is quite professional, but the effect is broken by two intrusions: first the amateurishness of the players (fantastic stylization is the severest test of the player) and the presence of solid forms in a contained structure of gelatinous, obscure, impersonalized, sheer, non-solid forms. Solidity defeats the mood and the visual apprehension of the digits in the film's collective symbolism. This is a film too brief and too intense to permit of a dual structure. The characters should never appear as human entities in a world of solid affairs, such as food. There is no quotidienal (*sic*) reality in the transparency of this Usher-world as Watson and

Webber establish it and the establishment of such a non-human world denies (particularly since the unit is so brief) anything beyond it that can be seen with morning-eyes through no intermediate eye of gelatine and collapse.

The film is creditable, but we must not exaggerate its achievement. It is important as a capable independent effort, and as an indication of an interest in the non-literal in America. But how important will such enterprise be to the realization of a new American movie? To me the new cinema will build with the healthy rudiments of the film we have so far effected. We have our mythology, our legend, our lore, our folk-film. That is our *source*.

I suppose the question will be asked: how does this film compare with Epstein's Usher-film? I say first: there is no similarity. Then I say: Epstein's is more profound, it achieved a complete and precise sense of universe-torment. The American film remains with me as an excellent achievement in physical materials. It does not impress as a psychical experience. I feel no transcendence in the use of the physical materials. The enthusiasm for it – and it deserves disinterested praise – is due to the weariness among appreciative sensibilities of the world of the American film which will not venture in the sheer nor in the more delicate utilization of the film's instruments.

One critic has preferred the American Usher-film to the French and has dismissed the latter as using age-old (as age goes in cinema history) devices like rising mists. And why not, pray? Devices like words are determined by their affiliations in a definite unity. The mists are integral in the Epstein film and they allow his penetrating camera the scrutiny his film demands. A new device does not make a new film; an old device does not make a film out-of-date or trite.

* * *

The readers of *Close Up* will recall my words on the olfactory cinema. I discover in the September 3rd, 1917 *Artcraft Advance*, issued by the Artcraft Pictures, a division of the Paramount [*sic*] at that time, these words by Douglas Fairbanks: "There is now on foot a scheme to suggest sentiment or emotions by odours and perfumes. There is an odour for every emotion if it can only be discovered. A certain Italian is now working on a symphony of odours. You know how you associate an odour with some place. Heliotrope for instance has a wonderful effect on me. Should a symphony of odours be scientifically developed we may get as much from it as from sight. They will be able, in conjunction with what you see on the screen, to shoot out an odour into the auditorium which will produce the same effect as sad music such as Beethoven used to play. Belasco tried it when he used incense in the *Darling of the Gods*."

* * *

Mr. Ralph Steiner is a New York artist of photography. He has made a film, *H20,* which has won the *Photoplay* amateur prize. I have not yet seen the film but I hasten to record this victory which may be significant of further independent films. Or may not. Still, that an American may be willing to film such an untypical (from our fans' standpoint) subject, one so pictorial, as water, is no small evidence of a new attitude. Or is it an old attitude? Is this the influence of Paris upon a mind essentially graphic in its interest? Therefore, the Paris influence — traditional in American, and the world's graphic art. But, you say and I agree, hadn't I better wait until I see the film? I assure you, my friends, I bear it no prejudice. Only — I am remembering Philippe Soupault's good advice of some six years ago, that the American film must not go aground [?] the "antiquated novelties." It has its own character to consummate.

CLOSE UP,
December, 1929.

NEW YORK NOTES: II

I have just come from a trip to the Bronx whither I went to see and hear a Yiddish talkie called *Ad Musae* (The Eternal Prayer). It is about the worst film ever made, indicating absolutely no knowledge of the cinema, even the most elementary, on the part of the makers. It is a succession of "acts" with groups keening or singing Hebrew ritual songs, *Kaddish* and others. The "acts" are actually separated by blank intervals. Yet this film, bad as it is, is of singular importance to any genuinely perspicacious student of the cinema. It signifies the importance of the Jewish physiognomy, like the Negro, an unexploited cinema plastic material, the singularity of the intensive Jewish gestures, and most outstanding, the Yiddish and Hebrew utterances as the material of the sonal film. *Ad Musae* lures me into a survey of the Jew as Movie Subject.

* * *

Very early in the history of the motion picture, Manager Mark Dintenfass commissioned Irene Wallace, a Scotch-Irishwoman, to prepare for the Universal Company a scenario relating the grant of freedom to the Jews of Poland by the good King Kasimir. This might have indicated to alert entrepreneurs a rich field of subject-matter of historic and folk content. At that time occurred the infamous Mendel Beiliss case, with its cruelly absurd blood-accusation against the Jews. Films issued upon this theme and upon the general theme of persecutions in Russia: *Nihilist Vengeance, The Heart of a Jewess, The Terrors of Russia, The Black Hundred,* etc.

In 1912 the American Solax Company, in advertising their film,

A Man's Man, said, "Up to very recently the stage Jew was the only type which furnished universal amusement. Long whiskers, derby hat down to the ears and hands moving like the fins of a fish. His manhood, his sentiments and his convictions are not burlesqued (that is, not in this film, *A Man's Man*) but are idealized. The Reliance Company produced *Solomon's Son,* so their notice read, "with dignity, minus the burlesque atmosphere usually attending the Gentile's version of a Jewish story." The burlesque Jew enters the films very early from vaudeville and the burlesque theater. It is this Jew, John Howard Lawson, the American playwright, put into *Processional* as the American acceptation of the Jew, a caricature of the immigrant's appearance and gestures. If the movie or theatre wanted a valid comic or gesturing Jew there was a stage Jew at hand who was valid, the stereotype Jew of the Yiddish theater, a vivid character amid the shoddiness of that outlandish theater, a character with his own striking idiom waiting for a Gogol to exploit it. Alexis Granowsky drew from this inartistic theatre the stylizations for his marvellous dynamic, ballet-principled productions. The method of the Granowsky theater is highly suited to the film of folk fantasy.

The comic Jew of the films has been a grotesque hybrid caricature of Polish immigrant Jew and German, the German comic typified by the Ford Sterling of pre-Chaplin days. There was such a comedian in Max Asher, who has been continued, a little more Semitized, in Max Davidson. Chaplin himself, of whom more brilliant wit might be expected, has used the burlesque hand-rubbing Jew as pawnbroker. A hand-rub may be insolent or it may, if derived from the hand-rub of the ecstatic Chassid or Jew lamenting, be a movement of great beauty; of joy or despair. Very closely related to these early comic Jews is the Jew who has been urged upon the films by the success of *Abie's Irish Rose.* This play, and its ensuing movies, has two antecedents: the Irish-Yiddish joke, now a further "incongruous juxtaposition" with sentimental optimism, and a film like *Humoresque.* Despite its pretence to sobriety, this film was the forerunner to the grimly funny lot born of *Abie's Irish Rose,* those fearful narrations of Irish-Jewish amities and enmities. *Humoresque* was an impertinent fable written by a sentimental woman, Fannie Hurst, further sentimentalized by the director, Frank Borzage, and almost obscenely sentimentalized in the performance of Vera Gordon, a product of the super-sentimental American Yiddish theater. There was no critical appreciation of the Jewish content, ceremony, domesticity and ambition. It was a highly extravagant and incorrect study of Jewish society. Yet its tear-provocations won it the medal for the best film of the year. Other films which belong to this fictitious group are *His People,* where so fine a player as Rudolph Schildkraut was used so ignobly. *The Jazz Singer* is another "cheap" and spurious Jewish film.

More diligent attempts to do a substantial Jewish film in the American cinema were the ventures with Zangwill's Ghetto tales and an early Vitagraph picture, *The Golden Land.* The latter was a chronicle of an immigrant's progress in America and his desertion of his family in Russia. The sentiment was free of mockery and insolence, and patronage, an attitude which obscures the profound experience of the folk, but the film did not possess a thorough intimate understanding of the people portrayed.

Attempts have been made (to satisfy the Yiddish spectators) to employ traditional Jewish plays, like those of Jacob Gordin, with famous Jewish actors, Jacob and Sarah Adler, Bertha Kalich, Malvine Lobel. Films of complete Jewish casts with Yiddish captions, directed by Jews, usually untrained in the cinema, have been produced. These are about as bad as the Negro films made by Negro companies, because there is not sufficient training or cinematic insight for them. Having Jewish actors is not the sole answer to the problem of the Jewish films. Nor are Jewish directors needed for the Jewish film. The Hebrew Habima was directed by a non-Jew, Vakhtangov. It is even possible a non-Jew may have sufficient aesthetic detachment to use the genuine material most cinematically for full plastic virtue and intensity of the relevant movement. What I have so far summarized may seem to the pseudo-purist literary, but it is actually a statement of the working material. A study of this material implies a study of its cinematic conversion, beginning and end, experience into experience.

The American film being, as I have often said, literal, has never thought of the Jewish material of folk roots and philosophic reference: Ansky's *The Dybbuk,* Sackler's *The Tsaddik's Journey.* Did it want realistic material? There was Levick's *Rags,* far from a great play, but certainly profounder and even more effective than the material of *His People.* Germany with its intuition lusting for fantasy produced *The Golem,* and for dramatic material did not disdain to offer the *spielfilm, Nathan the Wise,* or *Tolerance.*

A film nearer to the American movie selectivity is Dupont's first picture, *Baruch,* called in London and New York *The Ancient Law.* This is not tremendous stuff, but it is far above *The Jazz Singer,* of which it is the continental counterpart. There is more scrutiny of the data of folk and the intensity of the village Jews, passionate of temperament, is rendered. Its reference is not extended beyond its tale and performance, and one can ask here for an expressionism of setting (though it was acceptable being modest) that found its basis rather in Chagall than some German studio-artist. Miss Iris Barry in *Let's Go To the Movies* has justly praised the poignant sensitivity of the performance of Ernst Deutsch, but the most important characterization was that of the rabbi, his father, by Abraham Morewich of the Vilna Players. This was not slobbering, though it conveyed the emotionalism in the rigid orthodoxy, the rigid impassioned orthodoxy, of the parent. *Baruch* is not beyond the American interest. If the American director will look into it, he will find a commentary upon his crude use, whether in comedy or "serious" film, of the Jew. I have said its reference is not extended beyond its tale and performance. It is true that the film unfolds the metamorphosis of the young Talmudic Jew into a man-of-the-world, who has cut his sidelocks and the tie that binds him to his home. It tells of the "blood being stronger than water." It tells of the battle between two worlds: the testament and the drama. But while it tells of these major knowledges of man born of race and parent, the tale does not remain as inference. It remains, however, as a lyric, and that can never be said of the American film treating of the Jew. Sincerity of attitude, directness of presentation — the intrusion of no extraneous sentiment — observation of type, care for revealing details . . . these created *Baruch,* and they are all within the ken of literalness, if it be faithful.

The talkie lends the Jew an added glamour as film subject. I have referred to Granowsky's use of typical Yiddish sounds in the vocal rhythm, co-ordinated with bodily motion. *Ad Musae* indicates the opportunity for rhythm, stylized utterance, tragic utterance in the Jewish chant upon one sound Oi — thought of usually as comic. The shrill voice — North African in its source — the reiterated motif at one pitch — inextricably joined with concentrated angular movements of finger, hand, body — or with the meaningful rock of the Jew — these wait for the thorough student and artist to reanimate the new medium.

* * *

The new medium will serve and be served by philology. Undoubtedly someone will use its opportunity to record dialects comparatively. In the comparisons lies a vital clue to standardized speech sounds and rhythmic variations. Take the dialect of the American Negro for an instance. The Heywards shied away from it when they made *Porgy,* but it is luscious with grand verbal play, which will be comprehendible by suggestion — intonation and reference. Verbal meanings are conveyed by non-verbal sounds. The garrulous saxophone is a handy example. "Babe" Cox in the current Negro revue, *Hot Chocolate,* suggests all sorts of love-nuances, frustrations and hopes and poutings, by sounds sung to a vocal mood. Do you recall the two clowns, The Love-Birds, who carried on an amorous converse by whistles only? These are very, very elementary hints toward my far-reaching "philologic" film. I append two Gullah variations: "W'en oona duh de-day, de-dee' duh no de-day; w'en oona yent dey, de dee' duh de-day." (When one is there, the deer is not there; when one is not there, the deer is there).

"Me yerre um; no shum; too long buffo' me shum, me yerre um." (I heard him; I didn't see him; too long before I saw him, I heard him).

This so-called "phonetic decay" is a direct suggestion of reduced speech, which with monotone, non-inflection, sustained pitch, reduced or modified inflection, metronomic variations, etc., will lay the basis for the conventionalization of speech in the talkie. (And what of the lessons of Esperanto?) Does this sound too effete for the new medium? There is no reason why that medium must blunder in the erroneous path of duplication. Aesthetic organization is the very secret of health for any expression of man called entertainment or art. It is not nearly so arbitrary a method as unexamined dialogue. The talkie is neither all-talkie nor part-talkie, it is a singular compound. . . . (A very interesting suggestion toward this conventionalized speech can be found in *The Mask,* January, 1924. It is made by "The Author of *Films.*" He calls his suggestion, which he offers as an "experiment for a new kind of speech" for the stage, "Acca," the Italian equivalent for H. H is excluded from his speech "because it has got itself entangled with the T's and the W's and other letters, and too many windy words are the result." There is practically no H in Italian. "The absence of the H," says the Editor of *The Mask,* "is one of the best reasons for Opera being sung to Italian words." Upon the basis of the elimination of H the author of "Acca" has, he says, been able to compile a vocabulary sufficient for the improvisation of a small comedy. He is after an actor's language, with speech as sound working with gesture. That is for the stage. The article is followed by three editorial reflections from Landor, Goethe and *The Mask* itself, all praising mime-ized loquacity and silence: says Goethe, "I for my part should be glad to . . . speak like creative nature only in pictures." Here's cannon-fodder for the silentists. Said *The Mask* in 1908, ". . . in silence we will reveal the Movement of Things . . . this is the nature of our Art." But not of *our* Art. An extract from a letter of London may be offered to both sides, silentists and sonorists: "England discovering Stanislavsky promises to be a joke. Are they not funny when these foreigners show them . . . words don't matter, the gestures are so eloquent!" Which argues against realistic or duplicate speech in favour of sonal speech, which is the argument in "Acca".)

Applause for Mr. Mamoulian, though the Paramount ads attribute that film to the actress and the author of the story. Gilbert Seldes finds in *Applause* a gratifying moment to digress upon the mobile camera. Says he in *The New Republic,* October 30th, 1929:

> "The essential problem of the talkie is to find the proper relation between the camera and the microphone . . . a satisfactory relationship can be maintained and that will be found when the nature of the mechanics of each has been understood. . . . The camera is a recording instrument, but the record it makes is an illusion; the microphone is a recording instrument and the record it makes is a duplication (within quite narrow limits) of the actual. . . . Thus, at the beginning we have the juxtaposition of two instruments with different and frequently incompatible capacities. The next point about the two is that the camera is, in practice, mobile almost without limitation . . . whereas the microphone is practically stationary. . . . The problem of reconciling these two instruments is complicated by a non-technical and non-aesthetic fact: the moving picture has accustomed us to quick movement and the microphone, attached to the movie, is an interesting novelty; so that either habit or curiosity must be given first gratification until a compromise is effected."

Let us consider Mr. Seldes' observations up to this point. He is still a fundamentalist, or so he thinks, when he separates the sight from the speech in the film, one as an illusion the other as a fact. An illusory basis does not alone determine an illusion. As I have said previously, the illusion is the organization of the "facts" — images or sounds — as much as in the mechanism. Moreover, is Mr. Seldes unaware of the *fact* that many of the sounds we hear in the sound film are not the actual sounds recorded? It is all in the conveyance, the instrument converts the sound by its very limitations — from this will standardized sound ensue. When Mr. Seldes thinks he hears a dry paper being crushed — so the visual image or his "illusion" informs him — in reality a wet paper is being crushed, lest the dry paper record like the collapse of a ton of coal. When he thinks he hears thunder, he is really hearing the noise made by rolling small sized rocks down a slight incline of less than four feet. If he believes he hears the noise of riveting, it is because a low-powered bell-buzzer taps on steel. Rain on the roof is shelled corn running through sieves. And the wild screeching of night birds is a razor blade scratching on glass. Back-stage is back-screen.

As to the mobile camera and the immobile microphone, we might comment antithetically so: the camera need not be mobile (that is only a *kind* of camera use) and the microphone can be mobilized. As we learn more and more about the nature of speech in the talkie, we will find the microphone can be freed. And also the invention which permits sound recording apart from sight recording (Mr. Seldes will not like this latter) will permit mobility *or its results*. To get synchronization it is not necessary to record both sound and image simultaneously. This physical freedom will do much toward helping the formalizing of speech, such as my suggestions above work toward.

The non-technical and non-aesthetic fact to which Mr. Seldes refers may have something to do with the compromise to satisfy Mr. Seldes' penchant for speed. But that penchant is a habit and an ailment, and if it is, as Mr. Seldes agrees it is, a non-aesthetic fact, not demanded by the public (the usually accredited criterion) looking at and hearing sound films, then Mr. Seldes ought to have accepted this slowing-up as a release from the tyranny of speed. So long as speed is accepted as a universal quality of the film, we will not attain to that ultimate film of "reflective processes." Neither habit nor curiosity need to be gratified by the true artist of the film. He must work toward the fulfillment of the intrinsic, and he will have his audiences for that. There is a difference between fluidity and mobility. Fluidity may be achieved with the stationary camera — in the montage.

* * *

Mr. Seldes continues by commenting on the films of Vidor (*Hallelujah!*) and Mamoulian: "Both of these directors have been happy when they used music and both seem to have struggled vainly when dialogue was imposed upon them." The secret is in the word *imposed*. ". . . good directors are avoiding speech and using sound as much as possible." They aren't so good and they aren't so free. "The solution is in the creation of artificial form. . . ." I refer Mr. Seldes and the directors to the pages of *Close Up* and these notes. Mr. Seldes is "intrigued" by Mr. Watts of the *New York Herald Tribune* who has "caught a hint of such speech in (of all things) a British picture, *Blackmail* (which Mr. Seldes has not yet seen) which brings the speed of the talkie to the pace of the movie." Is this a test of the talkie's success? Mr. Seldes finds the Vidor film "a good movie in which the camera has held the first place." Yes, but it should not hold last place, nor *first* place in the conception. I can assure Mr. Seldes that it would not have been good silent or talking. The singing sequences gave a halo to the entire film, a false halo. The "most effective portion" — which Mr. Seldes finds the pursuit in the swamp — "is virtually a silent picture," but were the little sound of breathing removed then, perhaps,

Mr. Seldes could see the claptrap triteness of it as drama or cinema. Yes, *Hallelujah!* is a silent film that betrays the audience into approval by the *imposition* — intended as betrayal — of sound. And that is exactly what the talkie must watch against, this use of the audible as a "trick" to hide a bad silent film. The movie was frequently made appealing by the insinuations of music. Mr. Seldes himself has been unable to penetrate the non-integral sonority of the Vidor film to see the actual spuriousness of the visual structure and the thematic false rendering in the narration. What is this uncritical approval of a director who continues the worst in the Griffith tradition, the pettiness, the sentimentalism . . .?

* * *

Now at last to *Applause*. First, since I have gone this far in my reading of the observations of Mr. Seldes, let me summarize his criticism of the film. The actress and tale are of little or no concern: it is the direction that counts. The faults are: the director's inability to render duration (why does Seldes want duration, doesn't he ask for speed?); the use of Russo-German camera angles to break up monotony — "but there is no excuse for monotony, in the first place" (that's why Mamoulian wanted to break it up); the overdoing of the mobile camera, "just as the Russians have overdone their trick (sic!) of cutting into brief flashes." "But the principle (of the mobile camera) is sound." And "Mr. Mamoulian has made all his comments cinematically."

Now I can compare my scrutinies with those of Mr. Seldes. In this way the readers of *Close Up* may get a more or less full sense of the film.

* * *

The two major faults of Mamoulian's film are: there is no sustained rhythmic structure, and there is no sense of speech as abstracted sound. The relation of camera to microphone is not the initial, inclusive and ultimate law Seldes would make it, simply because neither camera nor microphone is the sole instrument of visual film or social film. The one positive significance of *Applause* is a vindication of my declaration that an *outré* Hollywood mind will extend the American film. Mamoulian excels Hollywood in its own virtue of competence and even elevates the competence at times by his caress of the angles and movements of figures — as when the chorus women move about the newborn and her mother. It is evident that Mamoulian is more than a job-man, but no matter what sympathetic use of instruments he might evince, the fact that he has not thought of or realized the film in a sustained structure of visual and oral image would have destroyed whatever validity there was in his craftsmanship.

Whether it is the director's fault or not, the voice of the heroine is abominably maudlin. Speech is still realistic. Reality is achieved solely by analysis. And speech demands analysis (conventionalization) as much as non-verbal sound.

The story is no more trash than others. It is another version of *Stella Dallas* and as human revelation it is on no lower level than *Hallelujah!*-or, when it is finally analyzed and estimated as to how much of the theme it finally conveys, even *The Crowd.* These are all fabrications rather than conclusive experiences.

Seldes unwittingly exposes the real fault of the Mamoulian treatment, which just about steps over the boundary out of virtuosity: "Mr. Mamoulian has made all his comments cinematically." The key is in the word *comments.* There are *comments* here with no major structure to be commented upon.

The most important film I have seen since my return — the most important American film that is — has been laughed at, sneered at, reviled by spectators, either ignored or utterly condemned by critics (critics indeed!). It is a "filler" on the programme with *The Last Performance,* Universal hokum by Fejos, with Veidt modifying his usual facial rant. The film is by two amateurs, Jo Gercon and Louis Hirshman, and is called *The Story of a Nobody.* It tells a story by means of objects only, a story of two human beings, a boy and girl, and is the first American attempt at a completely objectivized film. It is perhaps naïve, and too frequently there is a change in the distance between the seen objects and the unseen people, so that at one time the objectivity is about to collapse from proximity to the human personalities. But I do not want to consider details here: I wish to emphasize the principle of objectivity and a realization of it which is entirely in keeping with the American literal mind: there is nothing nebulous here as in the Watson-Webber *Usher* film. I wish also to indicate the first American film (if we except Bruguière's unfinished fragment) to attempt intensiveness as against progression. There is a very good use of intensiveness through multiple exposure. A telephone is stationary center, on either side counter images alternate. This is motion *within* the screen, of the screen. The film is called a symphony and is divided into three movements captioned in analogy to music. I do not favour this method as more than tentative to call to the spectator's attention mutations of tempo in the rhythmic movement, which is also borne by repetition of images, single or grouped variously. I compliment Mr. Alfred B. Kuttner for accepting and exhibiting this film against the counsels of commercial expedience and uncritical disparagement by the layman and those who call themselves critics. His programme note is good if a bit grandiloquent (but then, do I not sound so here too?); by such means the little cinema serves its original educational purpose.

A Hearst Metrotone and Fox Movietone Newsreel Theater now occupies the Embassy where *Hallelujah!* was last shown. An hour's programme of sound newsreels for 25 cents (a shilling), and the house is always full. Theaters will be opened in other cities. In 1908 Pathé opened a newsreel theater in the grand boulevard in Paris, and it is still going. When I went to the Broadway Newsreel Theater I was annoyed by the hypocrisy of the re-elected mayor, of the industrial-captain Schwab, of the Martin Johnsons who made that spurious film, *Simba*. The interesting portions were those that were not ephemeral, such as wine making in France, etc., and a murderer confessing. This latter was poignant and condemned the purposeful gentleness of the interrogator, the ghoulishness of producer and audience exploiting the poor frightened man, the "science" of criminology enjoying its new toy, the circumstances that made a harmless individual a murderer, the tabloid scandal tone of the theater's announcement of the film – and created a pity, where pity could be created, for the man who said "youse" and could not remember what led to the firing. It was an exposé of humanity that was more concerned with the capture of the "criminal" who did not want to escape save by suicide, than with saving the wounded girl. A very dramatic film that should free the actor, but a film which should not be repeated or broadcast.

CLOSE UP,
February, 1930.

NEW YORK NOTES: III

I never read mystery stories, except those which are arabesques like the tales of Poe. The sole mystery for me is the person who writes these stories. Therefore, there could be no more mysterious individual to me than Mr. Edgar Wallace of Albion, who, according to himself, has written "one or two" popular mystery novels. It was accordingly, no small excitement that preceded my meeting with this prolific gentleman at the luncheon of the Associated Motion Picture Advertisers. I shall not comment on Mr. Wallace's Tammany appearance nor on the delight he finds in his own playing at modesty. I shall limit myself, as movie correspondent, to his observations *re* cinema.

"My claim to distinction," said he, "is, I'm the first author to come to the United States with no intention of going to Hollywood. I won't go to Hollywood until the producers charter the Berengaria for me and give me a million dollars in advance. I know well enough that Hollywood doesn't think anything of anybody unless he's hard to get and has cost them a pile of money." I submit this as valuable criticism of the commercial cinema, and I am not facetious.

"I have another claim to distinction," continued the man of mysteries. "I am the president of a film company that hasn't earned a penny yet. We were just about ready to produce when the talkie came along. Well, we're in for the talkies now. I was told it would cost me $100,000 each for the making of four films, $100,000 a film! I turned one out for $15,000. And do you know why? I was on the job all the time. No graft. Every penny spent went into the film." Another valuable, if not original, criticism.

Third criticism: "They made a film called *The Terror* in Hollywood. I wrote a story by that name once. Well, the characters in the film and the characters in the novel had the same names, but I'm not sure the story of mine they bought was the one that came back with the laundry. I'm not one of those writers who objects to a change in his tale, but—."

The "but" recalls the introduction to the "movie" edition, published by Grosset and Dunlap, of Melville's *Moby Dick*. The writer, S. R. Buchman, argues too aptly:

> "In story, the screen version of *Moby Dick* exceeds the book. The discrepancy between the two must not be considered as a profanely wanton alteration. The episode of the book has not been misused; it has been enlarged and clarified. This approach of the producers was dictated not by any aimless unprincipled desire for melodramatic heightening, but by the bald limitation of the cinema. . . . To some minds, any departure from the original in the picturization or dramatization of the classic is censorable. *The Sea Beast* is a clear reflection of the spirit originally infused into the work by Melville."

Here we have a dishonest application of a correct principle of conversion. Omit the "nots" from where they are placed and put them before the affirmative statements and you have the justification for the remarks of Louis Moussinac upon the rankness of *The Sea Beast,* for which that intelligent critic was indicted. The last line of Buchman is a lie or it indicates the shallowness of the man. The test of conversion is: Has the theme been re-rendered? are its inferences included? have the changes aided or thwarted the scope of the original material? is there an equality in the final experiences of book and film?

Yes, I confess, Mr. Wallace has served me as an expedient for this tirade.

He will serve me again:

"Will the talkie kill the stage? Killing the stage is an old, old scare. I ought to know something about the theater, I've got a few plays in the provinces—6 or 7 or 8, I dunno—so take this tip from me: the theater's going to stay, and the talkie's going to help it and it's going to help the talkie. The sound film will be a recruiting ground for the new theater audience, and the theater will be the recruiting ground for the talkie's actors. Why, Henry Irving used to say the theater's dying because people would rather ride on bicycles."

Arthur Hopkins, the theatrical producer, has just said the theater began to decline with the motor car. The truth seems to me to be rather that these popular amusements came opportune with the decline of the *popular* theater. Entertainment is a whole, and what one part loses, another wins. The film and radio have become the popular entertainment. If we list the popular forms that have died or are dying we will find a numerous lot, in America at least: the minstrel troupe (the most defined of all in organization), vaudeville (a city like Philadelphia has lost its one major house), burlesque, the circus (in America the large companies have consolidated), the comic quartette, the ventriloquist, etc. Indeed, the talkie has come in to sing the swan song of the black-face minstrel, the ventriloquist (*The Great Gabbo*), the burlesque (*The Dance of Life, Applause*). . . . These swan songs, like the movie as a whole, have not passed beyond O. Henry fabrication as yet. I have faith, the American film will be more than *feuilleton* stuff some day.

* * *

Mention of *Applause* reminds me I met Rouben Mamoulian, its director, the other day. Mr. Mamoulian does not think his film great, because, as we agreed, a banal subject-matter cannot yield a transcendent film. But he thinks of his work as something of a conquest. His contract allowed him freedom to choose his scenario. This was resolved actually into a choice of the least bad among three. Mamoulian thinks the lack of good scenarii (*sic*) a basic problem. He was given time to study the mechanisms of the studio and then decided, since he was obligated to produce a film, to plunge in. The plunge was taken with astuteness and determination. He let it be felt he had a point of view for which he would fight. Studio practices were disturbed and the disturbances have since become the practice. For instance, Mamoulian used two sound units working simultaneously to get sound receding — sound in distance, mobile sound, so to speak. This was unheard-of: the practice was to get first the sound on one spot and then on the other. Two sound units working on one sequence together was too expensive an operation. But it proved a cost of economy. It has been supposed by some observers that Mamoulian used a crane for mobile camera. He moved about in a bulky cage. "It was," he said, "like playing polo on elephants." I have already commented on the paralleling of two sounds in *Applause,* a banal result so I felt and still do. Mamoulian points out, however, the victory of the talkie in simultaneity of sound. "The theater," he said, "could never accomplish this simultaneous yet separate structure." The film's intensiveness permits such phenomenon in sound as in visual image.

Mamoulian has signed no contract for another film, although Paramount desires him to do another picture. He is waiting until the spring and until he finds a suitable scenario. To find in America a director who thinks, like any other true artist, of one work at a time, rather than of five-year contracts, is itself a discovery of importance. Mamoulian made another comment, a familiar one, on the intensiveness of the film: "Five minutes is an age on the screen." This should have guided him *against* durations of song. But then the movie has a new business: to sell theme-songs. That is another hindrance to the true sound-sight film. But perhaps this will dwindle with the lessening of the domination of the revue film. How far this musical business can go to contradict cinema is apparent in Sydney B. Franklin's production of *Devil May Care,* where the film is divided into acts by means of fade-outs, and the only sensation of legitimate sound is the thud of hooves. Intensification of gesture, physiognomy and voice (even though the principle is not respected in the least) makes what is endurable in the musical play within the proscenium frame, most embarrassing to the spectator of the film.

A third personage, and cinematically the most important of the three is the German visitor, Karl Freund, who has come to America in the interests of the Keller-Dorian color process. Freund digressed upon the making of *Berlin,* attributing the inspiration for the "newsreel composite"—as I describe it — to Cavalcanti's *Rien que les heures* and Karl Mayer (to the latter the idea of a Berlin film). He described the difficulty of deciding upon a scenario, how a story was urged upon him — the experiences of a visitor from heaven being one of Freund's idyllic pretexts — and how finally he decided on the "clean" job. To Freund the film ideal is the newsreel, as basis. He has the usual German penchant for the "little irony," for "great happenings from wee causes," e.g.: a dog crosses Broadway, a motor car crashes, a train stops . . . "for the want of a nail the horse was lost; for the want of a horse the ride was lost, etc." German simplism. *Berlin* was one year in the making. Instead of the ordinary scenario a system of index-cards was used — notes — the cards shifted in order as the film evolved its rhythm and design. Freund would like to do a film of one corner of New York — Times Square, perhaps — 24 hours; or a Central Park bench; or an American composite. I have in the pages of *Movie Makers* suggested such montage-filming as amateur enterprises. "I would," said Freund, "begin my film with *'Ich berichte'*: like a chronicler." The Anglo-American poet, John Gould Fletcher, has published in the University of Washington's Chapbooks an essay on *The Crisis In the Film.** Mr. Fletcher is the poet

* [Ed.]: Seattle: University of Washington Book Store, 1929. Reprinted in the volume, *Screen Monographs II,* in the series, *The Literature of Cinema,* New York: Arno Press and The New York Times, 1970.

appreciating the film. Although mingling in a milieu that disdains the "lively" art, he is able to evaluate it for himself and enjoy it. He condemns "the attitude of that small minority of intellectuals (more common in Europe than in America) who simply despise the film. . . ." Historically, Mr. Fletcher finds, the film is a by-product of naturalism. He declares the movie camera to be:

"Even more unselective than the ordinary camera. . . . In order to produce a series of instantaneous pictures which, by being rolled off one after the other, render the effect of continuous movement, it is not primarily necessary that there should be any study of composition, any graduation of light and shade, any definite control of material. Indeed, all these things merely complicate the film problem. The most commonplace news-roll (*sic*) is, as far as film recording goes, as valuable as *The Nibelungen* or *Caligari*. What makes the difference is the quality of mind at work in the latter, which is unapparent in the former. It is a quality of selection, of unity of purpose, of interplay of episode, of pictorial composition and dramatic climax: a quality, in short, of art."

As a record, Mr. Fletcher is saying, the thing need be nothing more than a statement of thing recorded; as art, it demands organization.

"The film, therefore, in so far as material goes, is rooted in actuality. What gives it artistic possibility is that it can combine actuality of scene and of event to a far higher degree than is possible on the stage. It can relate each episode of a long story to its appropriate background."

This constant inter-reference is one of the cardinal virtues of Dreyer's *Joan,* which alone separates it from any resemblance to the Comédie Française or the Theatre Guild. Of insistent inter-reference I have spoken continually in *Close Up.* It is the means to philosophy and *inference* in the cinema. "Thus the film solves the problem which agitated Ibsen and most of the great dramatists of the later nineteenth century: how to combine naturalistic fact with symbolic significance." This is one of the film problems of Soviet Russia, a problem which overlooks two things: the difference between the symbol and symbolism, the representational detail and the structure; and the error of separating the figure of speech from the content of the film. I refer especially to the iron horse symbol in *The End of St. Petersburg* and the gargoyle analogy in *The New Babylon.* Pudovkin even went as far as giving the horse tears! *Joan* conveys the gargoyle in the Bishop not by analogy but by the structure of the Bishop himself, as his face freezes into immobility. Self-continence is a more disciplined, more integrated, purer structure than the simile, a borrowing from the *language* of the poem or novel. Even in the novel the metaphor is preferable.

Fletcher believes "the most impressive films are those in which reality and fantasy are in some way interwoven in the very stuff of the story," but his examples do not prove the case: *"The Nibelungen, Faust, Caligari, Warning Shadows, The Gold Rush, The Kid, Metropolis."* The fantasy in these films are the weakness of the films, or where the fantasy is amusing it is not important, as in *Warning Shadows.* In this film, a fantasy film, the fantasy is not strong enough to offset the reality. The truth is, simplistic fantasy, whether a part or all of a film, rejects eminence, and it is not interweaving of reality or fantasy that makes the great film, but the fantasy in the reality. Let me put it this way: fantasy is the conversion of the ordinary into the extraordinary — that is Dostoievsky's definition. The satisfying fantasy of Chaplin is not the fantasy-in-itself of the chicken episode in *The Gold Rush* or the heaven scene in *The Kid,* it is the suggestion, the reference, the inference of the personality of Charlie the man of the street, it is the fantasy within the real. The principle is identical with that mentioned above regarding symbolism. As to the symbolic structure, utilizing the human being, the Ukrainian film, *Arsenal,* points to this realization.

Mr. Fletcher finds the major virtue of the German cinema to be its daring. This is an incidental virtue; I have spoken of the chief contribution of the German film (November *Close Up*)*: it has articulated major principles of the motion picture. The chapbook sums up a number of considerations, which have been treated in more detail in many earlier treatises: the questionable necessity of the musical accompaniment, the scarcity of great films, the incompetence of the practitioners, the conflict between the film-as-art and the film-as-industry. The poet does not accept the whimsical compromise of Jesse Lasky, namely, the film-as-art-industry. The former characterizes the American movie as showmanship, which for him is a barrier to the advancement of the cinematic art. Mr. Fletcher fails to see the deeper-rooted limitation of the American film (refer to my Notes in December *Close Up*).** He believes the didactic intention of the Russian film is another barrier. But if the didactic intention is converted into a cinematic structure? If the didactic intention, propaganda, is actually social experience? The Russian film is giving its own adequate answer, or, at least promises to, in a multitude of idioms. Fletcher errs in coupling the Swedish film with the German. The latter has never gone beyond the experience of pathos. The Swedish film transcended pathos. The author repeats the purist declaration that the movie is pictorial and not narrative — it is both

* [Ed.]: See herein, "The German Film: *Kino* and *Lichtspiel.*"
** [Ed.]: See "New York Notes I" above.

and more. The failure of the film as narrative has frequently been its failure as art: the failure to convert the material into the form. Fletcher abhors the talkie as non-cinema. I hope he has changed his mind since this outburst: the speech film may need the poet soon.

Close Up,
March, 1930.

NEW YORK NOTES: IV

Paramount financed the Byrd exploration into the South Polar region, and sent along two "ace cameramen," van der Veer and Rucker. The picture has just been released. *With Byrd at the South Pole* shows alert camerawork of two good artisans, not extremely brilliant. The cameramen were evidently directors too, for much of the documentation seems enacted, rather than recorded. The men of the party played—there had to be "humorous touches" so the young lady reviewers of the daily press (how they multiply!) could applaud. Close-ups of seals are interesting, and the bobbing up and down of the whales is exciting—more so than the trip to the Pole, but, despite the obvious improvement in the mechanisms of cinema which enabled better pictures, the animal records are not better than those made by Ponting on the ill-fated Scott expedition more than two decades previously. Ponting had the disadvantages of his period, including the stolidity of "stills"; and the relative security of the two trips was certainly to the advantage of the Byrd expedition. Somehow the picture of the Scott expedition, which I have seen simultaneous with that of the Byrd, was more ominous, perhaps for apperceptive reasons: the knowledge of the outcome of the one and the other. But there is something in the Byrd picture that belies heroism, risk—a part of the exploration—and that something is composed of faults typical of the American attitude: the forcing of the heroism; the horseplay; the lack of sobriety in the captions; the smug camerawork—alert in the usual way and artisan-like though it was; the smartaleck vocal commentary at the latter part of the film by the "lightning announcer" of the radio, Floyd Gibbons. Gibbons weighted the excitement of the flight over the base of the earth with his hackneyed and ill-tutored exclamations, his rasping voice and his weakness for threadbare similes. The editing by Emmanuel Cohen, trained in the uninspired tradition of newsreel editing, showed neither grace in the titling nor a feeling for composition in the mounting. I do not see why (apart from publicity scoop reasons) Paramount had to go to the Pole to make this film. A much better Polar film, based on the facts of Polar discovery, could have been made in Canada or Alaska; though, of course, here again, the chance of an epic, when one recalls other American "epics" — *The Covered Wagon* and *The Trail of '98* — must be discounted.

It seems ingratuitous to say, after my tirade, that *With Byrd at the South Pole* is not without interest, and merit, but an interest not special — from the viewpoint of execution — and a merit academic.

Another "epic," made independently by Burden-Chanler, directed by Carver, assisted by several others, including an "animal authority," has been a hit at the Criterion on Broadway, where Paramount has put it before the eyes of a gullible public. It attests, however, to the appeal of the silent picture and the weak-kneed primitive. Even the critics found it meritorious. *The Silent Enemy* was praised by the astute Alexander Bakshy of *The Nation* (New York), and Mr. Bruce Bliven, who, possessing the qualifications of sentimentality, nostalgia for lost paradise and a naïve hate for machines — which is enough reason for him to disparage the Soviet films — and a total ignorance of the medium of the cinema, has become film critic for *The New Republic*.

Actually, *The Silent Enemy* is a complete failure. Epic is epic treatment. The stuff of the Red Man fighting hunger and the elements is not novel. Treatment, organisation, pictorial tones for moods, these determine the novelty, the connotation, of the film. There is not the least indication of "montage-feeling" here. The advertised caribou, much applauded by the expectant but prim audience, is dull enough to have been "shot" in the safe corral of a stockyard. Formula scenes are there. I could have foretold the trek at long distance of the sleds and marchers — just as an identical "shot" appeared in the Byrd film. And I could have foretold the applause in the two instances — applause from habit and reminiscence.

The release of satiation, after the victorious caribou hunt (how little of the zeal of victory is in this hunt!), not being properly anticipated by a rightly stressed and pictorially-toned agony of starvation, is a weak and trite "discharge." The fight between the mountain lion and the bear contains only the minimum of fascination present in the fact itself. The camera did nothing, the feeling for montage being nil. The performance of the natives was literal — since the director possessed no instinct for "overtone." The folded arm self-sacrifice may be a fact, but a fact, presented in the fashion of the 1914 "injun" film, is less than a fact, it becomes a lie. The vocal introduction of the chief — banal and sycophantic — anticipated this unleavened structure, and the reduction of a tale of primitive struggles, man v. nature, to a pernicious white man's bourgeois acceptation, the trivia of personal enmity and "the eternal triangle." It is just the sort of film to be expected of the oppressed man's "patrons." Perspicacious sympathy was not in their philosophy, and in technology they were novices with talent. The art of the cinema is technology informed by philosophy, hence. . . . Here an epic to be enacted that was not!

I had just published an essay on "Motion Picture Comedy" in *The New World Monthly* (New York) in which I referred to a delectable memory of John Barrymore in *The Man From Mexico,* made about 15 years ago. Almost simultaneous with the appearance of my essay came the announcement that Warner Brothers had produced F. Anstey's *The Man from Blankley's.* The film is far from my anticipations. Anstey's drolleries are there in the lines, but the film is inactive, and the High (Hat) Comedy depends on the activity of comedy, less boisterous than that of "churlish comedy." Al Green's direction is flat, unvivacious: the photography as bad as the lowest of the usual Warner Brothers' work; the microphone badly adjusted to the voices; the child's acting so much sawdust stuffing. Barrymore frequently recalls his earlier days, but the insistence upon the Barrymore profile, the Barrymore family eyebrow lifting, and the years of depression of beaus and dons and beasts, have left their mark in the dulling of a genuine comedian. No High (Hat) comedian remains. Griffith, the brilliant Raymond, who, in appearance and grace and whimsicality, continued the tradition introduced into the movie by "Jack" Barrymore, has aged — and Barrymore too — lost his svelte lines, and, with the talkies, not found his place, because of a voice almost mute. It was sad to see him in a brief comedy, *The Sleeping Porch,* constructed to the expedience of his low voice by making of him a man suffering with a cold. A real sense of the logic of monotone and non-inflection in the talkie would recover to Griffith his place in the film sun. His low voice is a soft misty hoarseness that can be exploited in the formula of speech-as-utterance. As it is, he appears for a moment as the Frenchman, Duval, slain in the shell hole by Paul, the young German. The performance is mute but intense, it lends some character to a scene awkward, obvious and prolonged. And what will Griffith do now?

CLOSE UP,
August, 1930.

NEW YORK NOTES: V

I have had a season of American film-seeing-hearing and I can say that the U.S.A. cinema remains where it was. The revue film came in and has gone out. It used some stunts brought in by a lesser foreigner, Marcel Silver, among others, and they have remained and died as stunts, never once entering into the mind of the movie, as that mind expresses itself in its structural interests. Dance combinations showed virtuoso skill, especially those organized by David Bennett.

The good-bad-man of the underworld has been having his vocal period in films awkward and an occasionally smooth one, *Street of Chance*. The Lingle murder in Chicago is anticipated in *Roadhouse Nights,* not a bad job, but a little haphazard. Excellent organization of scenes is evinced by director Henry King in *Hell Harbor* for a pesudo-Conrad picture on the "dangerous paradise" motive – we've had a run of that too.

War films: *The Case of Sergeant Grischa, Journey's End, All Quiet on the Western Front*. I've spoken about these in the *New Masses* for June.

Prison films, reflecting the times childishly, now are coming forth. I have seen two: *Shadow of the Law* and *Numbered Men*. The former has the usual Paramount competence at the beginning, but fades out before half-way. The latter is wretched in the typical Warner Brothers' (First National) indifference toward dramatic values, characterization, fluency, the elementary job qualities.

The only American films that are generally sufferable are the light-hearted comedies without high pitch of drama, and never seeking more than the idyllic. *Young Man From Manhattan* becomes, despite an original germ of "human interest," another one of these passing favourites, and I am thankful to Monta Bell; he kept the picture at its level of youthfulness, and did not attempt to make it a "picture of American life," which King Vidor might have tried to do with it. Paramount can get as far as a good job with "passing frivolities," and that is more than can be said for most of the other companies. In the revue-operetta class, Paramount certainly excels. Metro has been, on the whole, very weak in this type of production. I prefer the light tonal quality of a Paramount film to that of, let us say, a Metro, with its penchant for European blacks. Paramount's grays have the matter-of-fact cleanliness suitable to the American film. Sometimes we find a let-down here too. *The Big Pond* was tonally impure, as was also *Innocents of Paris.* They reflect the entire failure of the Chevalier films, a dependence upon a personality that is pleasant, energetic, but not incisive. Chevalier was capable in *The Big Pond,* but the film was kept simperingly gay instead of allowed to become satirical (if not trenchantly so), as the content implied. *The Innocents of Paris* is one of the worst films on record, with its crowded scenes and speech, unbalanced, oversentimentalized, the usual offensive child portrayal of the American film. I am not surprised to find that its director, Richard Wallace, is responsible for *Seven Days' Leave.* I suppose the name of Wallace won him the direction of the Barrie story. How any grown person can write such a fable, and how any grown person can enjoy it, would be a mystery if one did not know the horrible sentimentalism that inhabits mature bodies.

* * *

Why was *Seven Days' Leave* praised? It was such a sweet story. Imagine the stomach that can endure sweet stories that sympathize with an idiotic old lady (a scrub woman, of course — chivalrous kingdom of gentlemen!) who would have a lad killed for her own pride. The fact that there was no girl-and-boy romance, that old ladies made up the story, affected the critical faculties of the commentators to panegyric. Horrible cute old Beryl Mercer! She was just as simperingly Scotch (if her portrayal is not only Scotch out of Barrie and Hollywood) in *All Quiet.* A static film with as little mobility as *Journey's End,* to which it is not unrelated in its Britisher's attitude toward the "lower classes."

How can anyone believe in the sentiments of those who accept the pacifism of the war films mentioned and the romanticism of *Seven Days' Leave?* The answer is plain: pacifism is itself uncritical romanticism, sentimentalism, and it has nothing to do with the actual condemnation of war for its real character. This would imply a criticism, even a negation, of present economic society, and the romanticists would not yield to that.

And Welford Beaton recommends Carl Laemmle for the Nobel Peace Prize on the strength of *All Quiet?* Why not? Was it not bestowed upon Theodore Roosevelt, the biggest peace-bluff of all? It doesn't contradict the spirit of peace prizes that Laemmle is president of the company that made some years ago a film called *The Kaiser, the Beast of Berlin.* And that jingoist fragments are conspicuous in Universal newsreels as in all other "actualities."

* * *

The most interesting of American films that I have seen of late is an industrial, publicity picture, *Business In Great Waters,* of the laying of the Western Electric high-speed cable between Newfoundland and the Azores. The director, Charles Darrell, and photographer, Walter Pritchard, executed no ultra-brilliant conversion of an engrossing, if didactic, narrative—but held to a diligent straightforward record of the enterprise. A very good workman directed, and a photographer who could "shoot" the thing before him, above him and beneath him, sustained an exciting picture in the sequence and light-tonality. Animated drawings added to the tension and interest of the picture, as did the map in *Turksib.* The synchronization disturbed the film. The vocal description of the work maintained an even, moderately inflected tone, but the language and verbal "stretching" rose above the temper of the visual movie, which told the tale unaided. The major offense of the synchronization was the insertion of sea-chanteys into a straightforward, unfabricated account.

* * *

Where is the amateur film during these accumulations? The amateur in America, like the amateur in England, has generally an exaggerated interest in the film. By exaggerated I mean that he thinks of his relation to the movie as something which passes beyond the limits of amateurism. He has his eye on the large-scale film. He mimics it, is nostalgic for it, and organizes his groups pompously for the exploitation of his personality and personalities like his. Therefore his films are egregiously histrionic. I recall during my visit to England being made aware of groups with studio-divisions and sub-divisions. I recall a number of terrifying imitations of Sennett and Fritz Lang. In America Eastman Kodak has circulated a "model" film, *Fly Low Jack and Play the Game,* in which the hero runs through a series of sports in William Haines fashion. For these amateurs Marion Norris Gleason has written a book, *Scenario Writing and Producing for the Amateur,* with an introduction by C. E. Kenneth Mees, D.Sc.,

Hon. F.R.P.S. (Boston: American Photographic Publishing Co.). As Dr. Mees says: "The book has been written to provide a simple and clear account of the construction of a motion picture as a drama. It should be both interesting and valuable to the rapidly increasing army of cinematographers." It is not a bad book of its kind, but it serves the egregious histrionic movie-amateur, and as such it is entirely too esoteric for me, who thinks of amateurism as an interest in the intrinsic film and film as social document. The author has some good instincts, visible in this quotation: "As to the limitations of amateur productions, don't worry about them unless they are obvious. Limitations often turn out to be creative stimulants; witness the two-by-four stage of the Provincetown Players and their significant contributions to our national theater. And in the realm of the motion picture amateur, one of the best contributions yet made to the art of cinematography in this country, Dr. Watson's *Fall of the House of Usher* was produced in a stable fitted with homemade sets and contraptions." There is some good elementary advice, but the chapter headings will indicate that the author is concerned more with the expression of individuals acting than in the discovery of authentic material, the development of correct attitudes toward social subject-matter, and the cultivation of the aesthetic sincerities: 1. Dramatic Construction of a Scenario. 2. Writing the Scenario Continuity with examples of tedious film narratives. 3. The Home Movie with similar examples. 4. Children's Scenarios, as original as Rip Van Winkle (never asking just what is legitimate child-in-film stuff). 5. Holiday Scenarios (isn't this social settlement stuff?). 6. Scenarios for Organized Groups. 7. The Experimental Field. 8. Directing Amateur Motion Picture Production. Chapter 7 on The Experimental Field begins: "It is far outside my province to suggest how the experimenters are to experiment or what the pioneers are to discover." Which aren't the same thing: experiment and discovery. "The whole interest of an experiment lies in the fact that the result is uncertain; the whole adventure of exploring is just that one doesn't know what lies ahead." The trouble here is the author made the typical error of talking about experiment, when she would have done better to talk about principles and variety of cinema kinds. As a matter of fact, she begins to have an inkling of the correct sobriety when she writes: "It is he (the amateur), and not the professional, who is going to put the scenario into its right place—the foremost place that it must have in any great art, or an any real art. After all, it is Shakespeare, not Richard Mansfield. . . ." "Scenario-conception" the author says she means, meaning "the message," "the gist," "the idea," not "story-scenario" merely. One would not have known that by her scenario examples. There are scenarios for a talkie and a color film, again not statements of principles to be enacted, but stories to be acted. Not a word or suggestion of the method of cinema unity called "montage." If the author had really thought through what is meant by "scenario-conception" she would have realized that the amateurs to whom her book would go and appeal could not make use of a "conception," for that demands a point of view. The amateur with "conception" will appear among the social-minded, not among the country-club-minded, tea-party amateur of the Gleason society.

* * *

In the June 1930 *Close Up* — in an article written a year previously — I suggested that "the cinema is not so remote from the theater as dogmatists insist. The cinema has a source in the theater, the theater has a source in the cinema." Eisenstein called the motion picture a stage in the development of the theater. He did not mean that the movie had no character of its own. It is, he believes — as I do with him — a part of the historical continuity of the "show" — the popular amusement. The movie did not defeat the theater. The latter, as a popular form, is now at its minimum; the movie, as a popular form, is at its maximum. But a form must pass from the rudimentary to the realised, from the popular to the elite, from the ritual to the art. The movie, in its international evolution as cinema, has passed out of the rudimenary. In America it is held at the rudimentary because of the repression of the vital energies that will propel it.

* * *

The first American writers upon the film wrote against it, just as the first writers of the sound film wrote against it as an interloper. In either case the opposition was prompted by a defense of a seemingly threatened art. Walter Pritchard Eaton in 1909 called the movie "canned drama." Other descriptions were: "moving-pictures ad nauseam" (1908); "nickel madness" (1907); "startling development of the bi-dimensional theatre" (1909); "silent stage" (1909). Carl Van Vechten characterized it as "the electrical theatre." The commentators could not see beyond the film's character as a "nickelodeon" (1908) or a "nickel theatre" (1911). The chief preoccupation was a moral one: how would the child be affected? Or a protective one: the "theatre's new rival" (1909). In 1910 Horace M. Kallen wrote the first piece of real film criticism. It appeared in the *Harvard Monthly,* and strange to say a good deal of our movie commentary has since issued from the academic precincts of Harvard University. Professor Hugo Münsterberg wrote his book, *The Photoplay* (1916). *The*

New Republic, as early as 1915, published an article by Harold Stearns on the films. Kenneth MacGowan was called, in 1917, "the first film critic in America" – he wrote for the *Seven Arts Magazine.* Alfred Kuttner, the only one of these writers to retain an active interest in the cinema, wrote also for *The New Republic,* as did also Gilbert Seldes, another Harvard johnny.

Kallen wrote of the film as a part of the historic continuity of the popular theatre, but was at the same time able to extract the distinct qualities of the new form, namely, "concentration and expressiveness." (Kallen saw as another distinct characteristic of the movie "rapidity of movement." By this he evidently meant "speed." Critics have insisted upon "speed" as an essential of the film – it is a quality of the "primitive phenomenon." Another characteristic he designated was the "dominant æsthetic paradox," the customary in unaccustomed media. This may be looked upon in two ways: through the eyes of 1910, as seeing the new art treating of the materials of the old and, by this juxtaposition creating an "æsthetic surprise"; or, through the constant eyes of art, as seeing in the film a means of disturbing desiccate logic, in the sense that Eisenstein speaks of the "pathetic treatment of non-pathetic material." So that Kallen has listed three categories of principles: the law of art, the law of the cinema, the law of the film's first form). He, however, inherited the academic limitation of seeing processes as terminated things at the moment of inspection, rather than as forms in evolution. The movie has had few critics who have seen it as a form in evolution. Of all who have written in English, Alexander Bakshy alone has been perspicacious. Kallen could not see the film beyond its rudiments in the melodrama and "churlish comedy." (The 1910 attitude toward comedy in the cinema is shared by the German, Professor Konrad Lange, who said in an address [1912] before the Dürer Bund in Tübingen that the comic or grotesque film depended entirely upon eccentricity. It could not be compared, he said, to the art of the circus clown, for the latter spoke once in a while and uttered witty remarks. [It is then the circus clown is least the artist]. Chaplin had not yet appeared by 1912 to disprove the charge that the film could not carry wit. Both Kallen and Lange saw speechlessness as an obstacle to anything but churlishness in the comic film. To Lange the comic film was a *"Schundfilm"* – rubbish-film; its humor *"Hampelmannhumor,"* jumping-jack humor. He must have had in mind Mack Sennett's Keystone Kops and Ford Sterling. They were basic, folk jesters). His attitude was snobbish, patrician, but not inaccurate for the time. The "primitive phenomenon" of the film was as Kallen saw it. He said: "The rival of the musical comedy has appeared and with it a totally new and unexpected force in the theater, a force that may have enormous power for dramatic good and evil, a force that will moderate and perhaps re-establish on its pristine eminence, the discarded and abased melodrama." Kallen's preoccupation with the pristine was not altogether altruistic—æsthetic that is to say; it was aristocratic, defensive. He wanted the mass to be kept from speculation, for if it were not, something might ensue, something dreadful, like a revolution. This may have been but the aloof air of a young man, but it has served as a principle in the film industry. The movie has been a fairy tale and has had its existence as a compensatory mythology. Only a new social mind can stir it to actuality and positive experience.

* * *

The mythological nature of the American movie becomes hideous in the instance when social turbulences are the subject-content. M-G-M has just issued *The Big House,* "inspired" by the recent prison riots. Since this is the best of the films that followed these explosions it offers the most advantageous of opportunities. Here is certainly a social material. What does it reveal?

The film begins within the prison, begins, that is to say, with a promise of *intensiveness.* But to sustain the intensive there is required a disciplined and rigorous mind, which is not the mind of the American movie. The intensiveness is one of theme and structure. To assure such sustained intensiveness only one thing could suffice: conception. A conception of the theme is lacking. The intensiveness of locale is not maintained. The thief, Morgan, escapes from the infirmary. The story follows him into the city, the bookshop of the heroine, the heroine's home. The intensiveness is *relieved. Relief* is a constant in the American formula. Not the relief which enhances the tragedy, or the criticism, but which neutralizes it. There is further relief in the whimsicality of the machine-gun murderer, Butch, who commits an offense, only to say "I was only kiddin'." With these words he dies after he has attempted to kill his pal, Morgan, whom he has wrongly suspected of squealing. The winsome pathos of hard men. There is much winsomely pathetic relief in Butch's pretending reading of a letter—which he says came from a girl crazy over him—but which Morgan deciphers for the illiterate gangster as the announcement of his mother's death. Sob-hokum according to formula. And the film offers no relief from that.

The burden of the guilt is shifted. The warden forebodingly complains of overcrowding. The film does not convey the sense of that. The film directors hope to have the dialogue carry the charge, but only the unit film is vehicle. (The same failure characterized *All Quiet*). The warden speaks of 3,000 idle men, brooding. They seemed to be having a charming time of it, even though the jailers were tough. They had a cockroach race (see *Journey's End*) which ended in a fight between Butch and Morgan: but that's the holiday spirit, heroics. The genial guard (there must be one such) warns against putting the boy — in for ten years because of running down a man while drunk — with the hardened Butch and Morgan. These are only verbal statements. They do not create, as they should, the basis for the informing *temper*. When Butch, revolted by the food, explodes, provoking the outburst of 3,000 men and his own solitary confinement, the literalness of the director is apparent. We should be convinced, not by Butch's explosion (which is simply a crude statement, coming from one we should hardly expect to rebel at bad food), but by the food itself; just as the maggotty meat in *Potemkin* was the explanation and argument of the revolt. (To show the international content of American dungeons, *The Big House* includes all the nationalities. These are present in ridicule, the short, baldheaded Jew in spectacles grimacing and twisting his jargon to amuse the customers. This is churlishness in the wrong place. The Swede, portrayed as a stupid loose-jawed glutton by Karl Dane, swills himself on the food which the fastidious Butch discredits. Butch evidently is more refined than his patent idiocy allows. Really, this is much too complicated for simple minds).

These are the accusations. But the burden of the guilt is shifted from the prison to the individual, the boy who frames Morgan. Factually, the prison seems to have provided the boy with the instigation to stool-pigeonry. Factually, I say, for though the warden deplores such method, the film does not convey the sense of the social guilt involved in such provocation. The boy is the guilty one. And he is redeemed twice: by his own death in the riot caused by his revealing of the plan to escape and by the stupendous consequences of his framing of Morgan. If he hadn't framed Morgan, Morgan would not have been put into the dungeon, from which he was released feigning illness, to escape from the infirmary. Morgan would not then have called on the boy's sister to wreak vengeance, the two would not have fallen in love, Morgan would not have returned to the prison determined to go straight, would not have saved the prison guards from massacre, and been pardoned into his sweetheart's arms, which await him outside the gate before a hedge of flowers and a sedan. The guilt, whose burden has been shifted from society, vanishes completely.

* * *

Those who believe the true æsthetic attitude is to separate the form from the content will not like my treatment. But the content provides the form by *informing* the structure. An heroic form cannot be constructed of a frivolous content. *The Big House* is shop-competence which, not urged toward scrutiny, does not attempt the instrumental uses which only scrutiny provokes. The intensiveness is not sustained because there was not the mind to sustain it. The approach was frivolous, facetious . . . and the result is not even physically exciting. The mess-room explosion and the riot are too recognizably the elementary formula to excite a reaction or tension. It is all too plausible. Scenes that should be poignant, like the boy's entrance into the supply department for his prison garb, provoke snickers. Guffaws are very generous in the audience. The mind of the film and the mind of the audience coincide, it is the mind of that section of America which created the film.

* * *

There is another type of film which is now in vogue. The film of the "restless rich," provided by the popular play and novel. The latest of these is *Holiday,* and since it has most efficiently, all the qualities typical of this sort of film, it is worth looking at. *Holiday* is from the play by Philip Barry, a Harvard 47 Workshop product. It treats of the ineffably rich, about which movie audiences read a lot, but who are no more than invidious creatures of mythology. America's experience of them is a vicarious experience.

Edward H. Griffith is the director of the picture. His *Paris Bound* was another such. Mr. Griffith possesses style. That is an aristocratic virtue, but not a profound one. It is suited to this kind of film, the kind that supposes the narrative of the entanglements of the oppressed rich is a social problem — *the* problem of art. Of course, such a narrative, penetrated to the social core and referred to the complete motivating process of structure, might become a revelation of society. Henry James approached that, Edith Wharton was less close to it — usually the product of the environment of which the narrative deals has not felt any process organically enough to do more than narrate the story of some individuals within a certain area. The effect is generally of a fabrication, and that is the effect of *Holiday* — veneered, suave, civilized — as that word is used by the people blessed with remoteness and unconcern. The film remains a literary story, a parlor play — it depends wholly upon the actors — and these must not go out of the drawing room. Smart lines must follow upon each other . . . the gaiety, is it? of the nations, their aristocracy, of course. I can see the wife of the shopkeeper, the twenty-year man-of-the-world (though born of the people), and even the mill-dolly revelling in this whiff from a romantic world. They whiffed it in *The Laughing Lady,* in *Paris Bound,* in *This Thing Called Love* . . . less crude than Clara Bow in *Love Among the Millionaires* . . . and therefore all the more to 'ware of.

I have spoken of processes. Montage is a process. Films like *Turksib* and *Joan of Arc* are processes. The process of the film is, in its evolution toward realization, in the opposite direction from the theatre's development. The theater is an intensive medium aspiring to progressiveness. *The cinema is a progressive medium aspiring to intensiveness.* The film in its progress toward progressiveness — the latter sought to further *cinematize* itself. At this point the two came closest together.

* * *

The failure to recognise the method of montage as an integral process is the explanation of the sad attempts to sovietize films outside of the U.S.S.R. I have had the opportunity of seeing Grierson's *Drifters* at last; and it is the immediate provocation for my statement.

The zeal of the British, and Mr. Grierson himself, has been unfair to *Drifters.* The film does not deserve the anticipation the English comments have caused. As a first job of a young man, it is commendable. As an attempt of cinematic art, it is far from meritorious. Grierson has said he derived the *energies* of his film from the U.S.A. cinema, the *intimacies* from that of the U.S.S.R. If these could be joined together, the result would be hybrid. Why did Mr. Grierson not seek his energies also in the Soviet kino? Montage is an expression of the energies as well as of the intimacies. That is to say montage is the progression and the intensive unit. Moreover, I suspect that Grierson has defined energies as muscular impact. The American film is a film of muscular impact. It cannot be said to contain anything so plural as energies, for the energies — the creative expressive energies — of the U.S.A. are suppressed. The energies of a film are the energies of a land.

Grierson, it must be said to his credit, sought to re-vitalize the documentation with a structural intention. Yet he did not bring to his desire for intimacies the scrutiny — the *over-tonal interplay* — which such a revitalisation demands. Where are the people in his film? He is more engrossed with the *independent graces* of fish in the water — well-done details in themselves, but no part of the human process which the film was to be. The picture therefore is indeterminate: it is not the straight document such as *Business In Great Waters,* which satisfies its own demands; it is no re-vitalized revelation of human activity.

Nor does the film achieve the simplest of processes: that of accumulative muscular impact. It does not compel response to the fishers, to the sea. The filming of the nets as they are thrown overboard is good—catching them "on the go," but this too remains an independent grace because it is not integrated in an ascending structure. This was a film intended to show labor. If Mr. Grierson thought to extend it to inferences beyond the facts of toil, to the total economy of exploitation, his attempts at inter-reference between sea and market, fisher and broker, were certainly too inadequate. The intention of labor is not fulfilled.

* * *

I dwell at length upon *Drifters* because of its meaning to America. I have long urged the film makers to begin with the simple documentary. Instead of seizing a Paul Fejos and putting him on *Lonesome* or *Broadway,* such a young man should be presented with an exercise in documentation. The document is a basis, and the document transfigured is the ultimate work of art in the cinema.

The fishing trade is of especial interest to me. I have planned a film of the fish docks, the "live car" bringing in the live fish from the ponds and streams of midwest and far-west U.S.A. I have followed the fish since swaddling days.

* * *

What do our enthusiastic young men do? H. W. has made a film called *A City Symphony*—an ambitious and reminiscent title. It is a montage-film—if montage means, as it does not, the pell-mell piling of fragments. Herman knew of the use of the negative as positive; so he loaded his film with that utility. Any device has its specific values. Haphazard and dense application of it is disastrous. H. W. should have asked: "What is the pattern and tonal value of this bit of negative in the order of my film?" He employs the negative in instances where its value is lost. For instance, when the locomotive comes in in negative it is nothing but a frozen block. If H. had intended a frozen locomotive, O.K., that would have been ingenuity, but he was after a mobile something—and this was not it. The entire film is unorganized, no pattern, rhythm, formal intention, is apprehended. And as for the photographic work: it is a beginner's. I think of the Lods-Kauffman film, *Aujourd'hui*: it sought parallels of movement, but destroyed the organization of the film by putting too much into it. Not knowing where to end the picture, they terminated it with an *Etc.* And that's how I feel about *A City Symphony,* it's all et cetera. First films like first poems should be writ and discarded: unless the light of inspiration is vivid in them. Paris has spoiled enough novices by professionalizing them. It is the prerogative of the swaddler to swaddle in this basin or that trundle. H. W. could first play in an "excentric" milieu making "stylized" films. Stylization here means lining one's face with smears and moving like a scarecrow: a mixture of Robert Florey and *Beggar on Horseback.* It is not what it should be: the intensification of a structure, the fantasy of the ordinary-into-the-extraordinary of the Japanese, Nielsen, Hessling, Krauss – the capture of the mean and the construction upon it. Not possessing a complete understanding of the choreographic nature of stylization, the "excentrics" ("excentric" is their spelling and the word itself exposes the spuriousness of the venture) did not take care that every detail should be "stylized." A number of the persons of the drama were not altered a whit from their native pedestrian selves. The film has not been released. I present it as another instance of "love among the independents."

CLOSE UP,
October, 1930.

6

THE POLITICS OF FILM ART

RENÉ CLAIR AND FILM HUMOR

René Clair is the likeliest directorial playboy of the western world . . . in the present ebb of film sportiveness. In his very first film, *Paris Qui Dort,* 1922, his talents for the rhetoric of humor, schematized humor, were apparent. In *Entr'acte,* film of dissociations born of the aristo-idiosyncratic dada, he presented a holiday of high hats of Luna(cy) Park. This picture has been the film of passion for the exquisites who have pronounced dada the word of wisdom and surreality the surpassing experience. It was Francis Picabia's idea, the idea of that Picabia who is, according to M. Ezra Pound, the arch-cogitator of modern life. The enthusiasts' attempts to make of it a satiric film fail, for satire must be edged with precision, and its aim must never be ambiguous. In this film the specific object of the thrust is indiscernible, because there is no objective; the picture is an oneiric procession of inconsequences, where unity is destroyed and never re-established. The main value of the film is its instructions to René Clair and as an index to the understanding of René Clair; it is the film of his complete self-indulgence toward which he constantly yearns. It is, for all its sophistication, a "primitive film," based, like fairy tale and animated cartoon, on the phenomenon of metamorphosis.

Entr'acte is present in all of Clair's succeeding films. Since Jean Renoir, the son of the painter, produced the dream episode in *La Fille de l'Eau,* the vision of slumber and somnambulism has played a perennial rôle in French film fantasy. *Le Voyage Imaginaire* collected its wits in the autosuggestion of the bank-clerk. *Un Chapeau de Paille d'Italie* (called here *The Horse Ate the Hat*) has the recurrent image of the play within the disturbed fancy. *Les Deux Timides* bases its rhetoric on the parallelings of mental attitudes expressed physically. Clair's least successful film, his non-comic *La Proie du Vent,* is based upon mental aberration. *Le Million* is a "fantastic comedy" whose construction is as artificial as a dream; *A Nous La Liberté* is a diffused fantasy à la horseplay, though it wants so much to be satire. As for *Sous les Toits de Paris,* that is Clair's occasional complete romantic submission, a slumming tour in the idiom of a street-song, itself make believe. This dream-*tendency* is symptomatic of French bourgeois aesthetic: Bergson says "Comic absurdity is of the same nature as that of dreams."

But whereas the other French directors indulge in fantasy by submitting to its control — the results being too often lugubrious — M. Clair manipulates the fantasy with tongue in cheek and fingers crossed. His fantasy in a sense mocks fantasy, as the *leitmotiv* is one of genial contempt for a social foible. The humor of a comic film is, in proportion to its completeness, threefold: farce, the humor of situation; comedy, the humor of character; satire, the humor of society. Clair's comic films include the three, but in his talking pictures he has declined in the third humor. His milieu, the French cinema, does not supply the impetus, and he himself is too self-indulgent to accept the discipline required by this third humor. Nor has the American movie provided the impetus for such humor in the work of the comedian — European in origin — who promised to bring this third humor in cohesion with the first: namely, Charlie Chaplin. Chaplin has never given us the socially quixotic film toward which his fun-play pointed. The introduction of Chaplin into this essay is not amiss, for Clair has frequently been compared to Chaplin. When he completed his *Les Deux Timides,* he found it quite correct to accept the suggestion of Miss Edna Purviance, Chaplin's most steadfast leading lady, that Charlot receive a print of the film. The relation of Chaplin to Clair has been more casual than causal: the resemblance is generally due to the fact that both are active in the field of humor and go to first statements for their enterprises. Similarly the resemblance to *Mickey Mouse* which has lately been discovered in Clair is due to the fact that this animated cartoon is itself not epochal but a development of a first statement.. It is true, however, that in Clair's latest film the parallels to Disney and Chaplin are more apparent; indeed the diffusiveness and evanescence of the Clair film, which I like to translate as *And Freedom for All!,* seem to remember *City Lights*: this I read as the augmentation of a fatal tendency in Clair, rather than as a beneficial influence through Chaplin. Both Clair and Chaplin, it may be added, have heretofore depended not at all on the caption or isolated gag for laughter; their last films are inferior in this regard.

These two men must be compared, if at all, only as directors. They are poles apart. A Chaplin film is the film of a *raconteur* who enacts a personal legend: it says "I." The humor of incident and the humor of society blend in this personality, the humor of character. A Chaplin film is as good as this personality, this eccentric, this "classic hobo," and as bad as the domination of this personality to the disadvantage of the integration. It is as good as *The Kid* and as bad as *The Circus*. Eisenstein once said he liked that Chaplin film wherein Chaplin was everywhere and yet nowhere, the film in which he does not appear but which he directs, *A Woman of Paris*. In Clair's films, Clair is everywhere and nowhere: his films say "They." But — the tendency to self-indulgence sometimes oppresses the "nowhere," or objectivity, with "everywhere," or subjectivity.

René Clair's films are not, being directorial comedies, dependent upon the tug of the individual *comique*. In America we recall our comedies by the comedians, and American film comedy has deteriorated because there are no directors and no stories up to the talents of comedians like Raymond Griffith, Harry Langdon and Edward Everett Horton. The original dramatic source of a Clair film may be Labiche or Berr-Guillemaud; the scenario conception is Clair's own. His experience as novelist (author of *Adams*), journalist and critic aids rather than hinders the play of the literary idea awaiting conversion. The younger Frenchmen who yesterday spoke of the "intellectual" quality of Clair's work, are today complaining of that quality, and proscribing Clair with the vocationless substantive "An Intellectual," that dread term of isolation, social quarantine, which identifies the proscribed with introspective Hamlets and aspic Cleopatras. The complaint is twofold: the human performance is not warm enough; the pattern is too schematic.

These supposed faults are, within the category permitted by the subject-matter of Clair's films, virtues really. The films achieve humor by directorial composition, and the actors are part of this arrangement. In the performance of the humorous film, rhetoric is paramount. Slapstick is rhetoric, the churlish rhetoric of the animate instrument, the actor. Clair, a good student, possesses the sense of tradition, along with the perspicacity for its manipulation. He develops first statements into principles, composition or rhythmic structure. In *Le Million* this edifice is slight though merry. Slapstick abounds in Clair's work, sometimes penetrated for its essential design and manipulated for its most effective arabesque. *Le Million* is the original chase re-devised, not literally but rhetorically. Clair has developed from automatism to principle. In his latest film, however, Clair's self-indulgence is too "exuberant" — too *Entr'acte* — and the burden of chase and kick in the pants weighs down an already confused and diffuse attack on — ? Heretofore the chief shortcoming in the Clair idiom was in its very virtue: its rhetoric was somewhat blunted by unrhetoric players, whimsical enough and agile, even acute and appealing in a Mona Lisa blandness, but unrhetoric. Ideally this idiom demands a player with the sense of under- and overstatement dovetailing, that balance of litotes and hyperbole which informs the work of Clair at its best. Such a player was Raymond Griffith.

I recall a conversation with Jean-George Auriol, the young editor of *La Révue du Cinéma*. "Clair," I said, "needs an actor like Ray Griffith." "That's interesting," said Auriol, "Clair has tried to secure Griffith for his films. So has Henri Chomette." (Chomette is Clair's brother-in-law, known here for his direction of the de Beaumont "absolute" film, *Of What Are the Young Films Dreaming?* He has also directed after the Clair idiom). The lack of a Griffith is, however, not an overwhelming loss, since the pattern of a Clair film carries the objects within it, characters included. Before "montage" was emphasized by the Soviet directors, it was a term in French ciné-currency. Clair wrote an excellent essay on "Rhythm," in which he characterized movement as dual: "exterior" and "interior." Exterior (external) movement is the movement of the performing objects. Interior movement is the movement of the film, the integration. He has placed his stress on this movement, the composed progression; it has been his determinant, in theory, and in practice — often but not always.

Therein lie his rhetoric of the instrument and his rhetoric of composition. They tie up with his sense of tradition. He re-discovers the film at its source, goes back to the early devices of his countryman, Georges Méliès. In *Un Chapeau de Paille d'Italie* the groom awaiting marriage has been told by his butler that the soldier who awaits his return with the lady's hat has threatened to break everything in the apartment. A vision of furniture running out on all fours through the portals plays upon the screen. It is a reminiscence of the early days when Méliès, *le père du cinéma* or perhaps *le grandpère,* was making films around stories of ambulant kitchen furniture. This reminiscence coincides with the period sense instilled in the film, the lighting, the actions, the byplays, and the fantasy of a pasteboard horse in a garden of paper cut-outs. In another director, a Renoir or Cavalcanti, this last would have obtruded as a sentimentalism; in Clair it comments upon sentimentalism.

In *Les Deux Timides* Clair makes use of slow motion, reverse motion and stop motion in one sequence. The young lawyer describes the blissful home life of his client sued for divorce. The screen is large with a close-up of the face of the attorney pleading his first case. The idyllic picture he draws enters as an image superimposed across his forehead. His face vanishes, and the idyll carries on. Again the tongue-in-the-cheek sentimentalism — in setting, garb and performance. The husband enters in slow motion, with a bouquet. The young lawyer forgets his lines. The husband is reversed in slow motion. The young lawyer repeats his lines. The image repeats the movement. Suddenly the image stands still, and then — it breaks, explodes off the screen, leaving the screen blank. The entire speech of the lawyer, and his stagefright, are told without the presence of the lawyer on the screen. Instead of the literalness of the American movie, the instruments of the cinema are used rhetorically.

Later in the picture the rivals are pantomiming what they will do when either meets the other. The screen is split in half with the movements counterpoised and concurrent, but with each performer oblivious of the other. An old forgotten custom. The picture ends with a triptych, three panels. On the left the defeated suitor in bed, on the right the elder "timide" in bed, in the center the newlyweds in bed. The left goes dark, the right goes dark. The film is a narrow central panel collecting all eyes mischievously upon the couple in bed. The groom presses the button, the panel goes dark, and with it the film. This is one of the few instances of a film ending with the end, with itself.

Sous les Toits de Paris, Clair's first audible film, was less schematic than his silent ones. America received it as the first picture of a European "genius," but America had had, not long before, the opportunity — if limited — of seeing a Clair film, his testimonial, *La Tour,* to Eiffel. Here again his use of a simple device for structural effect is at work. He succeeds still photos of the Tower in process of being built — at higher and higher levels — so accurately timed as to impart a sense of actual growth. And by precise angles, he conveys height, weight, and solidity. It is a brief, sensible acknowledgment. The scheme of *Sous les Toits,* I see it, is one less of achievement than compromise. I was with Clair when he was filming *Les Deux Timides.* Next door Jacques Feyder, now with Metro, was completing a picture. "Our best director my friend Feyder," said Clair. I did not agree; the Belgian Feyder, who has made the best film of domestic tragedy *Thérèse Raquin,* is too much the chameleon. And moreover his comedy, *Les Nouveaux Messieurs,* is not without Clair's influence. Feyder was then leaving for America. Clair was hostile to the idea, because he was at the moment hostile to sound in the film: "It is the death of the film." I could not agree. I told him the Brazilian at work in France, Alberto Cavalcanti, awaited sound effects eagerly, although he was not prepared to accept speech. Clair was wholly ill-disposed toward any interruption in the *film muet.* As time went on, he must have recognized that the inevitable is ultimately correct, and compromised by working out a modest compound in which sound is used in an elementary way as parallel and synchrony. Clair by his compromise has effected a simple arrangement, wherein silence is an integer.

In his second talkie, *Le Million,* Clair moved back to his more personal idiom. Rhetoric enters the compound. He has found this rhetoric in the occasional lapses of the sound mechanism. For instance, in the burlesque of the opera, the singers reach a high note. No sound issues . . . after the caesura, a screech. Hollywood conventions from the musical film supply another bit of rhetoric repeated in different measures: the march of the creditors to Michel's room. The song, for all its improbability, becomes a plausible incident because a plausible structure, sustained from beginning to end, has been prepared to incorporate it. From slapstick and terror-film has been borrowed the collapse of the chandelier when the tenor reaches the top note to prove his identity. These are churlish and quotidianal enough movie-isms but they become aloof and winking-elegant in the Clair arabesque.

Le Million was sustained and fully realized; however, so slight an idea built entirely on a beginning-to-end chase could be sustained without hardship. In the *Liberté* film Clair, probably appreciating with others the need for a maturer thought, does not control the thought, first, because he has not clearly "divined" it, and second, because of self-indulgence in antics. The confused "divination" results from an epidemic condition in the French, and the world's, muddle class, and from Clair's own chronic deficiency: he is, regretfully, not "intellectual" enough. He is betrayed by his self-indulgence. A friend of mine has said that Clair is too much the amateur, and that is true. While his amateurism endows his film with a personal affection, it also makes it sprawl impulsively: chase and tomfoolery are not meted out according to the structure's needs but according to impulse.

In his two best silent films, the straw hat and timid soul features, the environment was specific, provincial (even though possibly Parisian) France, the people detailed explicitly, the rhetoric operative in behalf of the idea. That preciseness should have been developed to an improvement of Clair's third humor, the humor of society; such improvement would have enriched his first and second humors. Clair, in his latest film, sought this improvement in satire, but the only clear attack is upon his *Entr'acte* windmills, the high hats of the bourgeoisie, so that again the emphasis seems rather on foibles than on fundaments. For the first time he almost deteriorates into moralizing, though he'd have his film answer the "moralists," and to rescue himself from it he seems to be kidding his own heart's delight—the abstraction and platitude "liberty"—with an extravagant idyllism at the termination of the film. Clair is quoted as having said in London that the film had not turned out as he had expected. Seeking a responsible idea he produces an irresponsible manoeuvre. In a cablegram to his American distributors he states his intention, and its components criss-cross each other just as in the film:

"*A Nous La Liberté* is not a film for the serious folk. If you believe that work is the only important thing in life do not go to see *A Nous La Liberté* but send your children to see it. There would have been fewer unemployed today if the moralists had not created the religion of work yesterday. We ought to work to live but it is stupid to live merely to work. If work were well organized, if the machines were at the service of man this film would have no sense. . . ." The French word is "*sens*," direction; alas! for all of M. Clair's directorial skill, the film is as directionless as the thoughts in the cablegram, vagueness and vagary, naïve platitude. It sounds, more plaintive, though, like the pompous John Cowper Powys saying laziness will dispel the depression; and goes back to the papa of dada, Tristan Tzara, who hated America because America extolled work. As an analysis of the crisis it might be an extravaganza on Stuart Chase, or in fact a strict visual-motor rendition of Mr. Chase's samurai-mexico counterbalance. Coming from a Frenchman it is an abstraction purely, a Gallicism: the French are farthest from adventurism of all folk; and this "run-away-from-work" theme, detected in two recent films, *Cain* and the Clair opus, mean something falling apart in the social fiber of France. The thoughts expressed become more decorative than conclusive. Clair kids rationalization, and in this does he mean to kid Capitalism or Communism or both? (the film has foolishly been called Communistic; it lacks any such positive conviction); the factory is handed to the workers—is he joshing social-democratic fancy, the boss, the worker, the factory?; rationalization now frees the worker to go fishing—is he riding rationalization, the notion that the machine will ultimately "liberate" man, work or liberty?; the rich auto kids the libertarians on the road, who is kidded?; the last kick in the pants, the exaggerated idyllism—is this poking fun at liberty or the notion that work is all? And all the incidental fooling—uncle-and-niece; prison efficiency (how easy it is to run away from jail); how easy it is to upset the belt (is this a thrust at Ford or possibly a suggestion of sabotage?); Clair kids the new factory but uses it effetely in his decoration (the atelier-instinct of the French artist); kids love, bureaucracy, flunkeyism, and offers the solution of wanderlust (provided it's summer of course) and then—

yes indeed M. Clair is "exuberant," irresponsible. His self-indulgence upsets his apple-cart and the apples run in all directions; can't he handle ideas after all? Unfortunately the present French society, just emerging from a deceptive self-complacence, cannot offer Clair the necessary discipline, unless Clair is willing to identify himself with that portion of the society which can give him the instruments of criticism instead of platitudes. Clair probably was finally provoked into making this last film by Pabst's *Die Dreigroschenoper*, but he did not learn enough from the German picture: its purposefulness, its conclusive central motif, the minor elements contained in the major development, an exact downright idea and lyrics of content, no overaesthetic delight in the "primitive." Pabst experienced the idea with comparative thoroughness in relation to a social environment; Clair dealt with abstract notions apart from a concrete social reference. One accepted the discipline of the idea to be converted into the form; the other put the cart before the horse, and let the form separate itself and send the idea into detours. One exemplifies a positive direction in art and society; the other a negative. And this is regrettable. Clair is gifted and able; he needs the guidance, not of cult, but of sincerity.

A sincere appraisal of Clair might have indicated to him his own tendencies and at what point he would need to combat the social hindrances to his tendencies. That Clair should have drawn upon Labiche is nothing fortuitous. As Filon says, Labiche has "raised the French farce almost to the level of the comedy of character and manners." That "almost" is significant: Bergson, whose favorite example of *Laughter* is Labiche, omits him from the consideration of "The Comic in Character." Clair is the Labiche of the cinema. He has rendered Labiche's *bourgeois,* "essentially mediocre in his vices and in his virtues," standing "half-way between the hero and the scoundrel, between the saint and the profligate," in terms of his medium — gesture and cross-reference and horseplay — of cinema. It was a mistake to exaggerate Clair's achievement in the film of the leghorn bonnet. He comprehended the principle of "circle of discovery" inherent in the farce-comedy, the constancy of relation between a character and some physical property, he knew where to go for his mechanism, but the film was not an achievement calling for superlatives. Rather there should have been indicated that, although he was, like Labiche, "something better than a public *amuseur,*" it was folly to place him, as yet, "on a level with Molière." From Labiche Clair should have turned to do, not necessarily Molière, but a Molière. Perhaps the coming of sound has disturbed that progress, and now in the *Liberty* film he expresses a wish to go beyond foibles of man and woman as foil to generic ideas. Clair has been quoted several times as disliking Soviet pictures: they are for him ulterior, *trop d'idée*. But the pressure of ambient doubt must have forced him into idea. This idea he did not assimilate; even within his platitudinous cablegram there is an alternative of thesis that might have tied up his thoughts: "if the machines were at the service of man. . . ." But for Clair to have appreciated this clause as more than an abstract or linguistic hypothesis would first have required that Clair yield his bourgeois affiliations. There is a difference between petulance (fault-finding) and satire (criticism), between naming a few characteristics — effects — and attacking causes — structures. Clair needs a re-education, not primarily in technique, but in subject matter. He has, on the whole, been faithful, often militantly so, to art as against commerce. Within this fidelity he should develop a clearer and even livelier understanding of the art of social humor — satire. This is important not only for himself but for his pivotal position as a source for other directors in Europe and America. Clair must advance beyond the *imbroglio*, nor will the substitution of "liberty" for a straw hat or a lottery ticket suffice. Nor is it enough at this difficult moment to think of the *bourgeois* — the middle citizen — as one who will earn the contempt, not of future society, but of past. It was really from that point of view that Labiche, for all his vaudevillism, disdained (not very thoroughly, to be sure) his own class. Marcel Proust's Swann, when angered at Verdurins, could think of nothing more devastating than: "Upon my word, these people are sublime in their smugness; they can't really exist; they must all have come out of Labiche's plays!" For Clair, too, these people "can't really exist" — that is a view from the past — but Clair is not Proust and therefore his acceptations are not so defined. In that he is, in this bewildering period, the middle citizen *soi-même*; when he can look upon that middle citizen through other spectacles than the haze of "leisure" — which he reads infantilely as hoboing — there will be less "exuberance" and more zest, less impertinence and more wit. What is required of Clair is volition rather than a spontaneity which is inimical to schematized humor, especially as it rises to the third category. A volition, clarified of prejudice and unprobed provocation, will not only direct the shafts but time them too; in other words, Clair, by improving his social criteria (since he is fundamentally a humane person), will improve his technique, already keen. Then, perhaps, he will see more than high hats worn by upstarts, and treasury notes floating in the wind — he will see more than extravaganza where satire is wanted.

HOUND AND HORN,
October, 1932.

PABST AND THE SOCIAL FILM

The war was over, defeat its German portion; the inflation was still within the raw feel of the *Kleinbürger*. That class looked upon itself pathetically; its cinema plainted (*sic*) self-pity in films like *The Last Laugh, New Year's Eve* and *The Street*. "Die Strasse" of brothels has been a favored milieu for German pseudo-tragedy, and among its outstanding photodramas is *Die freudlose Gasse* (*Joyless Street*), Georg Wilhelm Pabst's first film.

Joyless Street (or *Streets of Sorrow*) is a picture of the famine-ridden Viennese clerk class, *die Angestellten,* that fringes on the proletariat, dovetails with it, and ultimately is part of it. Abject in its position, this functionary and small-merchant class could be understood in the terms of Pabst, a middle-class Jew from a middle-class city, Vienna, the head to a nation that has no torso. Pabst set a mood of hopelessness, the descending and enveloping oppression of hunger, of pittance and dread. He was as yet the humanitarian, and not the "psychologist," in the *"freudlose Gasse"* (the street without Freud). His sensitiveness placed this picture of the stricken above each other such recital by the more typical German directors: he was not moralistic. His Viennese origin substituted delicacy for *delikatessen;* he did not compound the pathos on the recipe of *"mehr! mehr!"* This same delicacy, finesse, becomes, we shall see, a distraction later.

The German artists of this "golden age" made their characters anonymous in the hope they would be universal. The characters eventuated frequently into caricatures, the converse of Peter Schlemihl—they were shadows without reference. For at least half of his initial film, Pabst preserved the characters from this deterioration, and maintained a mood of relevance and sympathy. However, he was not working in the isolation of his own attitude, nor was his own attitude resolute and apart. The picture did not support itself on this level all the way, though it held up longer than Grüne's *The Street.* It collapsed into the rampant absolutes of melodrama. The German petty-bourgeois class was contemplating itself pathetically, hardly with stern realism. The stratum above it was holding it away from critical inspection, because that superior stratum needed a buffer between itself and the lower seam. It was a simplistic pathos the artists distilled from the war and the inflation: therefore anonymity, therefore the concoction instead of the experience, therefore the failure to sustain the sorrow and the event of which it was the mood, therefore the romancing among scarecrows with perpetrations of "fate." Merchant, flunkey and *knecht* of the abacus did not dare to be drastic. Despite Germany's awful experience, its films were more fretful than tragic.

Through this period Pabst was gaining his cinema knowledge. He worked within the double-tendency of the German *lichtspiel* toward the real, away from the real. He was around when, through the insistence of the dominant control and the straitjacketed studio-mind, the energies of this sturdy film subsided into "ingratiating virtuosities," billows and columns of light, engineering pomposities, architectural shells, remarkable but vain. Pabst brought into the German stolidity something of the volatility of Vienna. He let his characters unfold their plight without the inquisitional rack. As compensation, he found in the intensity of German performance, though often it leaped from the frame, a discipline that enforced his finesse, reined it, made him keep his eyes open. The German film was all pillars, Pabst was mainly nuances. There was a blending of the two in the first part of his first film; the latter part was neither pillar nor nuance, the structure had collapsed under the preposterous relations, the routine of the literary closet, a mockery of the tenants in the *Joyless Street.* The director had not been perspicacious or wilful enough to extract and reorganize from this confusion the probable data that might have continued the social drama. He was himself caught in this confusion, an acceptation not limited to Germany nor to the period of *Die freudlose Gasse.* Periods of great stress incite the self-protective will to deceive and be deceived, and melodrama — its absolutes — is servant of this will.

Pabst moved farther into intensive drama. In *Secrets of a Soul,* the story of a knife-phobia "complex," he relates the case, rather than renders the *mind* of the case. He is still true to the German pillars, does not convert the case into the flux of images of an *atelier* easel-film like Germaine Dulac's *"extra-visuel" La Coquille et le Clergyman,* or Luis Buñuel's *"sur-*

realiste" Un Chien Andalou, films lightly, naïvely subjective. True, our director did include neurotic fantasies in the stolid case study—under the guidance of Drs. Abraham and Sachs—but even these were hardly "pure flow." Pabst had no time for tidbits of self-expression, for pictorial *implicit* films; and fortunately he did not yield to the symbol *ad absurdum* of expressionism, he was too substantial for that. But he could not escape, given the fee-simple case of an obsession, a blunt pedantry in recounting the thesis of the knife and the "soul." If the narrative was warmed to more than a formulation that was because of the zealous acting of Werner Krauss. Because Pabst himself was not, evidently, a Freudian fanatic, the film has no self-excitement; it is orderly, clean and without affectation. The public mind was whirlpooling in the individualized neuroses that flattered and satisfied the middle class: it was having a great, if aimless, time! Pabst had been ricocheted into this vortex, though his own "suppressed desire" was more social than Freudian. *Psychologism* became his preoccupation. In the film *Abwege (Bypaths)*, Pabst's best artisan-job of the silent days, the finesse of this quasi-psychology gives to a bland and cliché story a suavity and clear-edged composition that for the moment inveigles one into accepting the particular theorem of sexual "crisis" (*Crise* is the apt French name for the film) as true and important. But when one recognizes that the thesis has been organized entirely through short-angles and the convulsions of Brigitte Helm, skilfully manipulated by the director, the whole business is discovered as a setup and, crystallizing a feeling that has been gathering insistence as one has followed the films of Pabst, the observer suspects that gentleman of being unscrupulous, of putting over something exceptionable. In motion pictures like *The Loves of Jeanne Ney,* adapted from Ehrenburg, and *Lulu (Pandora's Box)*, from Wedekind's *Erdgeist* and *Pandora,* the polishing of surfaces, the feints, the detachment, the rarefied atmosphere of the ineffable—all the qualities that have effected (*sic*) the cult of Pabst—are as distracting as Herr Pabst's scrutinies are to the Herr Pabst of his abstruse days. Here one has to ask the import of the jigsaw puzzle before one realizes that Pabst has been playing a game. In the effort to put the puzzle together, the client finds many parts missing. Herr Pabst has not been scrupulous, not careful enough of his own integrity and its obligation to earnest witnesses. And this is not surprising: his very sources, if taken "as is," were not profound relationships but only exhibits, more effete than Pabst's earlier ones and therefore more treacherous: they stop Pabst at the surface of his films, entice him into exploits *chic,* pseudo-intellectual, seeming so subtle yet really saying nothing. There is no impetus for him to lift the lid of *Pandora's*

Box. Here is a man meant for character and all that he is submitting is a manner. His intensive considerations temporize in skin-grafting, though he has been called an "anatomist" — an anatomist of surfaces! To the troubled charge "unscrupulous" came the answer "super-conscious," a cult inflation that corroborates the ineffable, the cryptic — what indeed was our director hiding? Perhaps his own weariness, for certainly dabbling with effigies and charting their manoeuvres must be enervating. Never content in the rôle of an eclectic, Pabst could not manufacture completely clever films. His very distractedness is not without a sense of perturbed conscience: he would like to travel "beyond desire."

The sharpening conflict in Germany, the polarization of the forces, would naturally touch a man like Pabst. It would intensify and direct his social suspicions and tend to dissipate from his concern the shallow complacencies of the ladies and gentlemen of euphemy. At the point two things occurred: Pabst saw Carl Theodor Dreyer's *The Passion and Death of Joan of Arc;* the cinema enlarged its prospects with the advent of sound. To Pabst the Dreyer film was the deepest experience. When the Anglo-American imagist H. D. interviewed him — cult indeed! a cynosure of esoteric eyes looks *up* to a movie director — he would not hear one word against Dreyer's film. A year before, H. D. had compared *Joyless Street* with the work of Kuleshov the Russian and had preferred Pabst because, she said, he "takes the human mind . . . as far as it can go," while "the Russian takes the spirit . . . *further* than it can go." Her objection to *Joan* was similar, but Pabst would not subscribe to her fear of the maximum, though he was her maximum.

In these films of Pabst, he had been turned away more and more from his own maximum. In his first film there was social plight, but he had failed to establish its base. His environment was sorrowing, but it did not understand its terror as the resultant of social causes. There were, in the film, starting points for the dynamic relationship which would have explained the resultant had Pabst extended these points in character and not as the conventions of performance. These conventions became increasingly operative apart from fundamental concrete motivations, until Pabst was sending his camera velvet-like over the scene, veneering the picture, squaring the corners elegantly and rounding circles with grace — being "subtile." In *Joan* he found, if not the historic social base, at least a maximum of intensity of conscience and intensiveness of treatment. He who had dwelt on glossaries encountered an artist devoted to the human text who was not pedantic, nor moralistic. His ethical sense was stirred, and consequently his aesthetic sense was revived from specious daydreams.

The artist of keen nerve ends could no longer yield to his periphery, to topographies that gave neither the lay of the land nor its consistency. He sought and found social material whose complexity the new compound of sound-sight could make articulate. His nuances have become elements of structure; his films are no longer circuitous — he has realized a direct character that transfigures the qualities of charm and grace into the incisive and superb. He no longer dallies with "the woman who has been abundantly charged with sex consciousness"; she is only a figure of speech. *Pandora's Box* is inconclusive not because "one should not make films of literature" — that is a sophistry — nor unsatisfying because Wedekind cannot be cinematized. It is inconclusive and unsatisfying because the literary source is a network of negotiations and not the experience of people; and the film, in consequence, figures of speech stalking as men and women. Kraszna-Krausz has listed the "seven essential scenes" of these "variations on Wedekind" and has described the non-climactic scene-by-scene construction of the picture. Though the "ideographic chart" is interesting, it merely strengthens the criticism that the picture is an abstraction and that Pabst has wasted on it his talents for the intensive. That he does not include "pauses, stops or interruptions," which Kraszna-Krausz calls "artificial breaks or breathing spaces," may be due to the film's not containing anything to pause over. "Concentrated atmosphere" allows reflective examination, but the film is "atmosphere" without content. It is "too diligent, too tasteful, too beautiful" because its diligence, taste and beauty are errant, refer to no concrete tangible edifice. The film and its creatures are lustrous, never luminous. Unwittingly appropriate are the film's alternative endings: the lust-murder of the prostitute Lulu *or* the Salvation Army drum-rally. The latter is truer to the value of the film, though the former is the Q.E.D. of the theorem. The picture is skin drawn over a hollow body, and, though tantalizing contours are etched on the parchment, they are ephemera, illusive momentarily. The cultists beat triumphant tattoos on the drum, they were rallying their own fetichisms.

Pabst broke through this aura. His integrity had been misled, diverted, confused but not undermined. Its positive elements, potentialities, reappeared. They had been visible in his first picture but had been increasingly submerged as his "mastery" had developed. He was more vigilant now, he who had been so close to complete self-betrayal. In *Westfront 1918* (*Comrades of 1918*), he has produced the least showman-like of war-films, a picture intensive in its character-convergence, sharply attenuated in its character-relations, not spreading like valiant steam into an ominous yet compelling universe. True, it is a picture not more than pacifistic, it does not assail or divulge causes, but its pacifism is not flamboyant nor self-delusive, it is on its way to an acute attack upon the war makers. With more politicalization, Pabst might produce the film of war that would state through the agonies of human beings the sources of war within our society and the means of shattering its domains. His intensive treatment, now that he has sound and speech, permits the back-and-forth reference of the climax, war, to its social scene, competitive society, imperialism. There is almost no Soviet film in which war is the whole picture.

Incidental to his new tendency is Pabst's program-picture, a provincial farce, *Skandal um Eva*. Not important in itself, the film indicates again that Pabst has thrown off the ulterior trappings of skill: the film is executed with proper modesty and good-humor, the charm is qualitative and not weighed and measured. Pabst knows where to reserve his calculations, where to respect the mild *esprit*. The film, despite its incidental character, is present in the movie goer's reminiscence; and, as a further instance of its director's self-respect, the absence of any eclectic quality, of any sign of touching up the traits of humor with conceits, is lively proof of maturity.

From the war film to *Die Dreigroschenoper* (the modern reconstruction of *The Beggars' Opera*), thence to *Kameradschaft*, the progress of Pabst's conscience has been notable. One has but to compare Pabst's work in the former film with what a Lubitsch, a Clair or a Mamoulian might have done with an identical material to appreciate this magnificent production in its category of the "musical film." It is a proud work, bold in its vertical structure: the pillars are erect and the nuances firm and structural. There are none of the blandishments of the "musical film," Pabst has not organized the relationships into the insinuations of intrigue, the Lubitsch pattern; nor into the Clair arabesque; nor has he yielded to handsomeness for its own sake to attain a Mamoulian statuesqueness and picturesqueness. He has actually transcended the category of the "musical film"; or better, extended its province.

This victory has been achieved through a diligence that found worthy material. Pabst's directness found a substance for his direction, a substance grand and difficult, but, to the right artist, pliable, conforming. It is quite evident that the operations began at the core of the material and worked outward, for there was a core, the heart that was missing from *Pandora's Box*. Mirthful, sardonic; melancholy, sympathetic — here was wholehearted largesse for a director of great proportions and none less. No conceits, no trailings-off or tangents toothsome but extraneous, not one element of virtuosity — but unified character composed of men and women in various settings, song and episode. The lyrics of Brecht, adult and pungent, are sung, recited and spoken, are molded into the dialogue and the total compound structure. The sound values of consonants and vowels are realized in condensation and enlargement. "So-ho" becomes a grand and succulent piece in the utterance of the baritone pitchman, whose voice sets and sustains the vocal pitch of the film, a pitch borne by the relative non-inflection of the Kurt Weill music. The gray encompassing tone, with its gradations and harmonies, the bold figures, not merely guilt or innocence stuffed with straw, the selection of prototypes down to the casual physiognomy in the crowd about the pitchman — all going back to the stimulus of the Dreyer film — achieve a motion picture that is perfect construction. If within the joy of this perfection a doubt arises, it is because of dangerous suggestions the cynical or sectarian may draw from the events themselves. The characters of the film are *lumpen,* and their chief, Peachem, provokes them, out of personal rancor and revenge, to confront Her Majesty on gala occasion. The demonstrators are ragamuffins and frauds, their demonstration the trick of a mountebank who, on learning he has had no cause for vengeance, calls his army back, but — and here is a redeeming irony! — the beggars become militants, their flood of wrath will not be halted, the leader may shout his compromise, but the rank and file demand succor. This is not a revolutionary assertion, simply because it is not asserted by a revolutionary group and is not spoken in revolutionary terms. Still, in its undertones of vibrant social sympathy, and its overtones sardonic in their satire, the picture transforms the raw material of *melodrama* — in its original sense — into a very stirring approximation of the revolutionary march — an approximation that is not triumphant, as it could not be, but which is warm and in the direction of the element to whom the victory belongs, as the film itself unquestionably leaves one to feel. The victory is Pabst's, and it is a further step in his progress toward social conclusiveness. Never egregious, his daring is, however, pronounced. Like Dreyer he reaffirms the authenticity of the event by eliminating the obsession of period curlycues, historicism for the sake of propriety. He indulges in extra-territoriality: China is and yet is not China; this is and yet is not Gay's London, it is 19th century and contemporary London — Berlin or Paris, or even New York. Nor does this keep the occurrence on nebulous frontiers, afloat in the air; the film imparts a very concrete, tangible, immediate milieu whose temper becomes all the more trenchant for the structural reasonableness of the décor and the costumes. The German studio has become a creator, in this film, not merely of studio-marvels but of a dominion of baroque laughter that is not satisfied with its own fineries but directs these fineries into tart notes on contemporary society, where the racketeer and his police chief unite to run the premier bank on the main thoroughfare. The film is lavish but not prodigal: as in the wedding scene, or in the brothel, Renoir reproduced as a picture postcard, where the words of the song are pre-Raphaelitish with fingers crossed. The film terminates with the wearied beggars, who have sent the demeanor of Queen and police-commissioner into consternation, fading into the shadows where, as the *lied* of the off-screen baritone observes, those in the light will not see them. Is there hopelessness here? No, the tone is too sympathetically bitter to be described as hopeless. And assuredly this is progress in our *Herr Regisseur:* and not one tinge of distraction!

Very logically the next picture by this director should have been one explicitly ethical, unambiguous and direct. In *Comradeship* completeness is not attained, but it is progression. The data is [*sic*] not drawn from a literary clinic nor from a robust *melodrama* — musical play — it is a matter of actual record, a mine catastrophe at Courrières on the Franco-German border a decade before the war. The movie, like every art, is, at its highest point, revelatory. It achieves revelation through record, the core of experience, and restoration. Pabst, on the scenario of Vajda, extends his achievement in *Die Dreigroschenoper* by exploiting the studio to remove the studio (an uncommon thing in Germany) and effects a documentary veracity in setting, demeanor and speech. For this he has had the collaboration of the eminent cameraman, Fritz Arno Wagner, and the expert designer, Erno Metzner, himself a director.

To transcend the record, Pabst, with the initial assistance of the scenarist, delays the event thirteen years, until a year after the armistice. This "telescoping" heightens the social import, makes more poignant the biases of the individuals, gives the film a meaning into the future, gains for the film an acuter conscience. A fire in the French sector entombs the miners. The German miners going offshift give up their free time to risk their lives for the French miners, only yesterday foes. The rescuing party rushes in motor trucks through the frontier — it is fired upon! the frontier guard is dutiful. The German mine superintendent phones the French and receives the gratitude with a "you're welcome!" — the risks of capital! This commentary is rather the reader's than the author's. Three miners on duty in the German mine — the trio had been affronted in a French café the night before — dig their way into the French sector. The leader of the three had, not many months earlier, hollowed the frontier — "goes 800 meters down!" — on a less friendly errand. They are entombed with a boy and his grandfather, who has entered the mine unseen to save the lad. The film is then a record of calamity, vigil and rescue, terminating, when the injured men are freed from the hospital, in a festive departure of the rescuers, where devotions are exchanged in words, French and German, whose spirit if not whose letter is comprehended by German and French: We are workers, with but one enemy, Gas and War!

The film needs a further articulation — what and who is this one enemy whose properties are gas and war? — but that completion could be made only under auspices more drastic. Perhaps Pabst felt this when he said he was through with "ethical films." However, we need not take this statement as final, for recently he said he was glad to make *Don Quixote* in Paris, because there he could be freer to make a social film, perhaps by the simple removal from too intimate surroundings that restrict him. He had been able to produce his tentative maxima because the Nero company was beyond the field of the Nationalist magnetism of Hugenberg's U.F.A. But in a *Kameradschaft* success is proportionate to propaganda. Certain flaws will be suspected but hardly substantiated. The quest of the old man will be called too "sentimental" and too "melodramatic," but only because the judges have in mind spurious attitudes that have maltreated similar episodes. The search in *Kameradschaft* is valid because it is entwined in the development of the film. One of the vigil scenes may seem too deliberately grouped, but its place in the evolving structure is so doom-impending that this very arrangement is at least a possibility. Alexander Granach's acting as the leader of the triumvirate is traced with a stylization not quite documentary, but he is so potent a player that his presence does not contradict authenticity. A quarrel on these points concerns merely the question: is the beauty-spot a blemish? The real problem of the film is deeper.

The picture is accurate, indeed so accurate as to be a puzzle to those who expect the heroic in the treatment of such a theme. Pabst is never oratorical in his portrayal of the human element in the rescue, never colossal in his depiction of the mechanics of the rescue: he is always close to the ethical fiber of the event, and from this steadfastness emanates the artistry — a significant development in Pabst and the German *kino,* sluggish amid jingo lost-glory and *bockbier* films set to goosestep measures and ¾ *takt.* Undoubtedly, Pabst has been stimulated by Soviet pictures; less by those of the "masterful" period of Pudovkin and the "immensities" of Eisenstein than by Pudovkin's first and most convincing dramatic film *Mother.* There is something of the same imminence, the same throbbing and lyrical truthfulness, the same intensity of personnel. The Pabst film is, quite correctly for its purpose, less histrionic; but it is also less victorious in its assertion, and that is where it lacks in memorableness. *It is too empirical!* — does not develop its social tendency.

Sound has allowed Pabst an aid in the double-speech, French and German, very specific values, and a lingering quality — "Georges!" called by the old man — that sensitizes the appeal of pathos. The French girl who has refused a dance to the German the night before beholds the rescuing-party, murmurs: "Les Allemands! C'est pas possible!" Here is a speech within the theme, speech that is correlative to the play of the people at the mine gate. The inflection is contained within a subdued range, allowed to break through at strategic points. Its essence is documentary, its contact revelatory, and along the line of its construction Pabst might have extended his message to its fullness, thereby forestalling the criticism that the film lacks warmth. But for this extension was needed the consummation of Pabst's own ethical tendency. He has, in the film, urged fraternity, intra-class amity: his sympathies are with the operatives. He sees international accord not as some vague "brotherhood of man" — social salvationism — but as proletarian solidarity. However, the proletariat does not achieve such unity in the continence of its own class, it achieves it in *conflict,* not solely with resultant conditions, but primarily with the causes of those conditions. It is, in brief, inter-class enmity that strengthens intra-class amity. The operators in *Kameradschaft* are too casual to the occurrence, not corporate in an event to which they have given rise. Some observers have thought that all Pabst needed to fulfill his idea was another phrase to the concluding declaration. But that is a crude conception of relationship in society and drama. Indeed, not another word need have been added had the relationship been developed throughout the picture: the end might then have been grimly inferential and persuasive through its very truncation, "pulling the punch." As the film stands now, to accept the accord which effected the rescue as permanent in proletarian fraternity would be a delusive irony, especially when we recall that the actual vent at Courrières did not prevent the war of 1914. Pabst wanted this film as an "ethical message," as propaganda — for *future* solidarity. As in his first film, Pabst had possible starting points for the relationship which would have transfigured the record into its effective revelation. The miners initiate the rescue, the operator is only distantly interested — would not the operator, as well as the more recalcitrant workers, have resisted aid, with his machinery, for a competitive property? The 'phone call of acknowledgement would then have been, without debate, the film's rather than the observer's irony. The extension (symbol) of the frontier transgression, above and below, should not have rested too close to the factual; then the episode of the French miner recalling the war enemy would not have appeared an intrusion. The film would have been built up to such a contrast. And within this heightened structure the intimate details of the café and homes might have been dwelt upon and thereby kindled to more than evidences. Again Pabst should have been more wilful, again he should have been less statistical. He faces, in an inconclusive propaganda, the dangers of social platitude, and hyphenation. Still, *Kameradschaft,* because it re-establishes the cinema on the firm ground of the concrete record of an event of mass-reference, and that outside the land of the proletarian rule, is of mighty significance.

But will there be a step taken beyond this maximum? (Italy invited Pabst to direct a picture; he suggested Spartacus as a theme. The suggestion was spurned, though pre-war Italy, dreaming of *"Antica Roma,"* once filmed the gladiator — he's too hot now). Since *Kameradschaft,* Pabst has made a film from Pierre Benoît's *L'Atlantide,* a spectacle cinematized in the mute days of Jacques Feyder. He has directed Chaliapin, George Robey and Sidney Fox — what a combination! — in *Don Quixote,* Cervantes or the opera? And now he is to film Kreuger upon a scenario by Ehrenburg — here is his opportunity for a further advance, if he can subdue the fantasies of the scenarist and resist the competitive suction of American romance, tang and unction, as expressed with flair in *The Match King* of the Warner Brothers. What Pabst does is important beyond the work itself: he holds a preëminent position in Germany, where he has succeeded the late Lupu Pick as president of "Dacho," the federation of German film-workers, and in Europe, where he has been a cult and whose strongest director he is today, if one excepts the Soviet Union. His centrifugal nature, momentums issuing outward rather than energies stultifying through introspection and egotistic devolutions, is essential to an art that has been held back from its own destiny. To find in the bourgeois cinema, within its commercial realm, as socially conscientious an artist as Pabst is indeed a discovery! The poles of the cinema in Germany are epitomized by a Pabst and an Erich Pommer, the great studio-showman who supervised Murnau, Dupont, Lang and others, a man ready to serve any job of whatever *studio* dimensions, but hardly an artist of the conscience of Pabst. Around these magnetic poles will gather the film makers of Germany, the poetasters (the ingenious composers of sophisticated kino-doggerel) about Pommer, the poets about Pabst, if Pabst holds to his position of integrity. Somewhere between these two is a Leontine Sagan (supervised by a Carl Froelich): her *Mädchen in Uniform,* meritorious in its actors' work, is sincere but cautious, does not venture upon its own terrain but preserves a respectable distance from its own social implications and aesthetic form (this has been called "dignity"). And there was much less to dare here than in *Kamerad-*

schaft, for a great section of the German people is no longer hospitable to Prussianism: it is of the past. But Miss Sagan was well behaved, an aristocrat; the film does not fail to leave a sense of faith in the Princess, the benefactress, who, had she but known, would have changed all that oppression of arbitrary discipline — there is still a nostaliga for the nobility. One thinks of what Pabst might have done with the same drama, where he would be exposing retrogression rather than agitating a progressive act.

HOUND AND HORN,
January, 1933.

PUDOVKIN AND THE REVOLUTIONARY FILM

The October Revolution found the Russian film industry in as depleted a state as it found Russian economy and expression in general. The Russian cinema had, before the war, produced about two dozen films a year; production was concentrated in four major companies and in Moscow. It terminated in a fever of reaction but contributed nothing to the evolution of the motion picture. In *The Picture of Dorian Gray* is symptomatized, unwittingly, the demoralization of its own social state; in the *Golden Russia* series it sought to stem the revolutionary will. This sequence, among other feats of patriotism, helped, together with the press, to propagate the myth of "German gold" financing the revolutionaries, the strikers in the Lena goldfields and the Petersburg foundries. It is this war-eve period upon which Pudovkin opens *The End of St. Petersburg.*

The war of 1914 effected the "Skobelev committee" of film propaganda. The Kerensky regime merely altered the "Skobelev committee" into the "Skobelev committee of education." The Bolsheviks disbanded this body, attached a cinema committee to the new ministry of education, and nationalized the cinema. The Kerensky committee had produced two retrospective, vague films; the Bolshevik committee's first production was on a theme immediate and crucial. Based on a scenario by Lunacharsky, the commissar of education, and "realised under technical conditions absolutely deplorable, it . . . transposed quite felicitously the idea of the necessity of the fusion of the proletariat and the intellectual class."

Léon Moussinac, the conscientious French critic, has said that the Soviet film entered the history of the motion picture because it entered the Revolution. At the very moment of the Revolution, the positive value of the cinema was recognized. Emergency conditions delayed its systematization, but there was production and none of it temporizing. The faults of these first films were indeed stupendous, but the pictures were not makeshift. By their seizure of authentic themes in the national experience, they established the Soviet cinema at once within the Revolution. Though there transpired the effronteries that occur when a material has been approached and a manner appropriated before a point of view has been systematically attained, this cinema was assured by a progressive conscience, as alert in art as in politics. It could risk the drastic, oppose itself to the pre-established restraints of studio practice and public taste, since the values predicating these were themselves to be destroyed.

The themes in this preliminary period rejected the literary source. Although opposition to the adapted scenario is a sophistry, the direct transference of the social theme to the scenario attests, in this case, to a commendable desire for reality. The desire itself, however, was overloaded with a self-conscious culturism. Relief from this baggage could be left to the maturing Revolution, when it emerged from the provocations of intervention and famine and could enrich its vigilance. In a few years the kino was industrialized and consolidated. *Polikushka* was the inaugural production. By this time, it was not necessary to be absolute against the literary source. In *Polikushka* there was penetrated class relationship, for its author, Count Tolstoy, had been, as Lenin once said to Gorky, the first to draw a true picture of the *moujik*. A few years later, Gorky's novel, *Mother,* a story of a revolutionary strike of 1905, was cinematized as the first dramatic (film) of Pudovkin.

Vsevolod Ilarionovitch Pudovkin, chemical engineer by profession, came to the film from the level of disdain. He was twenty-seven before he found that the lowly art was not reprehensible. His disdain he attributes to the "rubbishy" films existing up to the time of his conversion – the year of 1920 – but actually his attitude was the common intellectual contempt of one for whom there are only élite arts. It was not until 1926 that the English *haut-* and *demi-monde* discovered the cinema, and then only because it had become the imperial investor's protegé. The Revolution revealed the cinema to Pudovkin as an expression of ardor – response and agent of the progressive conscience. It provided him with great and positive themes, and the energies to realize them. Otherwise he might have collapsed immediately and completely into the social platitudes, the moral maxims and aesthetic sentimentalities of a D. W. Griffith or an Abel Gance, to whom he bears psychological resemblance. But the relation between artist and the Revolution is not a fatalistic one; the Revolution demands the artist assume an active responsibility in the maintenance of the relation. Cleavage occurs in the progress of Pudovkin's career that supports his less diligent devotion and accentuates his propensities to pomp.

There had been established in Moscow a film college. Pudovkin as student had been actor, art director and co-editor. As student and later as practician, he was employed in the Mejrabpom-Russ studio, a center congenial to his temperament. Mejrabpom, the cinema of the Workers' International Relief, combined its revolutionary humanitarianism ("solidarity not charity") with the sentimentalities of the old Russ corporation of the Trofimov interests, and this combination was dominated by the veteran Protazanov, whose talent was still vested in the conventions of the preliminary period: the foreface simulations recalled from the Italian and French films that had influenced the Czarist pictures, the embellishments of the theme and the excess narration, the circumscription by the screen's perimeter, etc. Protazanov, however, had a feeling for folk qualities that, when properly related in the Soviet film, has instilled a sense of locale and personage, but which, through overstress, has betrayed some pictures into populism.

This setting received Pudovkin. After an apprenticeship of six years, in which time he directed *The Mechanics of the Brain,* an elementary lesson in conditioned reflexes, and had experimented in enacting a film from film fragments of Capablanca, *The Chess Player* (*Chess Fever*), he realized *Mother*. This picture placed its director foremost in the Mejrabpom studio, and with Eisenstein the leader of the Soviet kino, and made him a world-figure, although the film has never been exhibited in the United States.

Mother is the bridge-film into the present. Eisenstein, in denying flagrant individualism, has declared the mass as hero and the documentary as authentic. Pudovkin, a man of more humane and less abstract sympathies, saw the type (not yet the character), and the mass accumulative and representative in him. In *Mother* there is fusion; the film remains the archetype for the picture of revolutionary *development,* as contrasted to the film of revolutionary *climax,* the Eisenstein contribution. In the figure of *Mother,* Pudovkin concentrates the mass accumulation from denial to assertion. In his following films a similar development transpires: the peasant youth in *The End of St. Petersburg,* the Mongol in *Storm Over Asia.* Where the mass in the narration is close to the figure, the development is controlled so that its general historical meaning is conveyed; where the mass in the narration is at a distance from the figure, the historical meaning is less assured and a partially populist type is presented; in *Storm*

Over Asia what is intended as a condemnation of imperialism becomes an antic show. The mass accumulation in the Mongol is not organic but declarative on the part of the director. He has preserved the formula of sequence, but not converted it in the relationships of the film. Pudovkin improved the conception of the individual in the revolutionary film when he superseded the pantomimist with the type, and at the same time prevented the film's being monopolized by the mass-documentary legalism of Eisenstein. The type — the figure — is emphatically pronounced in *Mother,* because it is pivotal and the relationship between it and the mass is sustained dialectically. That is to say, as the mass advances into a revolutionary body, the figure is experiencing the transformation which is the historical evolution of the mass. Thesis — the apathy of the old order — is negated by the antithesis — the awakened consciousness — to the synthesis in the assertion of the new. In *The End of St. Petersburg,* Pudovkin covered a larger canvas, and there are great lapses wherein the figure loses its pivotal rôle because the mass has become rather an arena than a concurrence which flows into the figure. The first part of the film, the thesis portion, is the best, because here the director had but to set the figure and not to set it in motion. By origin Pudovkin is a provincial from Pensa, the district in which *The End of St. Petersburg* begins and from which the dialectic figure derives. In *Storm Over Asia* the figure is set rather in a showman's field than on the field of battle. It is a remarkable program picture, exciting but not revealing. The figure has become an effigy.

In the preparation of the scenarios of *Mother* and *St. Petersburg* Pudovkin had the same scenarist, Nathan Zarchi. The opening of the latter film is struck in the same mood as the former. Between the former and latter film, *montage* had been exaggerated from an emphasis into a determinant; from *St. Petersburg* to *Storm Over Asia* it was inflated into an entirety. The exaggeration was forced by a number of conditions: the glamorous position held by the Soviet cinema beyond its own borders, the domination of the Soviet kino by intellectuals and art-centered persons, the impetus of a new art encouraged by a new society. When Ivan Anisimov condemns Eisenstein's predilection for the immense, he fails to indicate that this is one individual's articulation of a general attitude. This attitude is not solely fetichist, the idolatry of physical dimensions, it is also a result of the vanguard rôle of the Soviet cinema in the cinema *per se.* The error is one of ill-balance. The correction of the ill-balance is only just now taking place. The self-conscious attitude of the film makers had to be transferred to a consciousness of the social material, and directors had to be provided from within the new organism.

In Zarchi, Pudovkin had a scenarist much closer to the core of the social material than Brik, his scenarist in *Storm Over Asia.* The inspiration for this film is the primitive, populist American western, an inspiration whetted by the "Doug" Fairbanks of his early elastic period. It does not base its stature on experience but on concoction (which places it in the American umbra) and is lavish but not exact in its specifications. Pudovkin undoubtedly enjoyed the indulgences allowed him by O. Brik, Mayakovsky's critical guide; the film does bask in a bland sun. Because of this largesse, Pudovkin tends along the path of least resistance: the path of antic histrionism, of propagandistic reduction, of the extramural figure of speech, of mastery — not of the sense but of the sound, the smoke but not the flame of battle. Certainly no more remarkable onslaught has been achieved than that which concludes *Storm Over Asia.* Always peerless in his command of scene duration and alternation (long distance with closeup, etc.), he produces sequences that are emotionally disturbing, as in the episode where the soldier takes the Mongol to shoot him. But these are not entity.

Storm Over Asia is the natural evolution of the preoccupation with performance. Pudovkin, the sentimental intellectual who came to the motion picture from the level of disdain, made films because he "liked" to make pictures, as a colleague of his once said. His attachment to the human figure invests his first two dramatic films with mood. The revolutionary artist has a threefold aim: to expose, to impel and to sustain. Pudovkin has revealed himself as an artist who can sustain the fervor he impels. *The End of St. Petersburg,* for all its lapses of grandeur, departs from the screen but not from the experience of the beholder. There it remains an intimate promise. More so is this true of *Mother,* whose rhetoric is self-contained and full-bodied. Commentators have been fond of quoting Moussinac to the effect that Pudovkin's films resemble a song and Eisenstein's a cry. This comparison and contrast is an epigrammatic convenience that will not bear analysis. The singer of the Soviet film is Alexander Dovzhenko. Yet *Mother* has the resonance and compactness of song. The Dutch critic Hoyer calls it a hymn (and *Potemkin* a march song). *Storm Over Asia* would therefore be "The Song of the Dawn," externally heroic, internally only a typical yarn. It is the enlargement of a gesture. In its enlargement there is, of course, handsomeness, especially of setting, there are verve and melodramatic ominousness. Occasionally there are scenes of intimacy, such as the episode of the partisan commander's wife. But having accepted a political reality in terms of an hypothesis, an acceptance encouraged by the preoccupation with performance (*montage* or antic histrionism), Pudovkin was beguiled into the demonstration of externals. He may have wished to drive in the knowledge of the manoeuvres of imperialism; what he conveyed was only a series of pictures of manoeuvres, which in their turn were driven out by the impact of the melodrama and antic play. The few instances of poignant exposure, such as the reluctance of the soldier commanded to shoot the Mongol, and of sardonic commentary, the bandaged "Heir to Jenghiz Khan" in full dress and the regalia of the imperialist governor simulating the man (a reminiscence from a similacrum-photo of Chaplin and the ministerial table in *Ten Days*), are not sufficiently resistant to overcome the impact. The hypothetical narrative leads to a grossness in the representation of the hierarchy as a slobbering infant. The Soviet film has established at least one rule of selection, that the most convincing and not irreducible instance shall prevail. That is an objective rather than sentimental approach. Not always has this rule been observed, especially in the selection of enemy types. But the Dickensian caricature is a thing of the past, now that the proletarian-minded artist has entered the cinema, and the Soviet society has matured. Pudovkin's attachment to the human scene has been his personal substitute for objectivity; even in the portrait of the industrialist Lebedev in *The End of St. Petersburg,* he presents, if not the person in full, at least the type in its basic social motivation. But in *Storm Over Asia,* the human materials are distant from him, and he correlates them in formula. The rôle of the clergy is exhibited as a crudity, when the priest-healer tries to seize the silver fox from the young hunter. (This scene and others are not without the influence of Eisenstein, who is partially responsible also for Pudovkin's performance preoccupations). Subterfuge and inveiglement are only once indicated and then in terms of palpable pretense, at a moment of crisis: the governor's dissemblance in the temple when he is informed of the disturbance. In brief, Pudovkin has reduced the process to the machinations of the show. In his two earlier films, the dialectic figure is nourished by a totality in which he is an element; in *Storm Over Asia* the dialectic figure is isolated until the moment his process is completed, which renders him abstract, an actor. Hoyer finds the influence of Freud, whom Pudovkin has studied, in the transmutation of the Mongol, but this change is only a more vivacious re-enactment of the apprehension of villainy conventional in the folk-film.

In *Mother* and *St. Petersburg,* Pudovkin was still being supplied with social, human data from his own memory, a memory as close to the current society as the events of the films themselves. He was within the experience of his material, and though he did not view this experience objectively (he is, as Hoyer says, "no ideologue"), he was safeguarded by the thoroughness of that experience. That is why he set the example for the mass-individual in the Soviet film. But when he came to *Storm Over Asia,* a material distant in its evidences, he gave over a large portion of the film to an ethnographic record of a ritual not built into the dramatic film, because this ritual was one thing tangible in the material. The film is constructed by an impresario. The impresario approach has beginnings before *Storm Over Asia.*

Kuleshov, with whom Pudovkin was associated in his first enterprises, has been his teacher with the pointer. But the lesson on the blackboard had been inscribed by David Wark Griffith, in *Intolerance* particularly. *Intolerance* had first appeared serially in Russia in 1918. Griffith possessed a fine quantitative sense, and, in addition, the feeling for the qualitative overtone that issues from the quantitative build-up. He could anticipate the quality in the progression of the imprinted film. This quality, of course, expressed Griffith's values, his sentimentalisms. Pudovkin, because of a psychological resemblance to Griffith, as well as because of influences from Kuleshov and earlier Soviet directors (and under the tantalizing pressure of the quizzical and authoritative Eisenstein) was encouraged in his deficiencies: the figure of speech that departs from the boundaries of the particular film (a conceit), the oversimplification of performance (mincing in Griffith, antic sobriety in Pudovkin), and the relaxation of the social theme. However, it is not necessary to maintain the Griffith-Pudovkin analogy too closely or too long. One might make a more important identification of Abel Gance the Frenchman with Griffith the American and prove it is not primarily America but the bourgeoisie that has produced Griffith. The positive influence of Griffith on Pudovkin is that of example in kind. Kuleshov is the finger on the electric button, but the electric system is the Soviet society. There is also the influence of Pavlov.

Kuleshov called attention to a self-evident fact, known in practice but not in principle: that the film is a progression composed of intensive units. The progressive composition is *edited* into existence. The French used a theatrical rather than publicistic term, *montage,* which was rendered international by the Russians. To explain, as Montagu quotes Pudovkin, "the fertility of Russian cinematographic theory by the fact that in early years after the revolution there was a shortage of raw film" is to be naïvely deterministic. The shortage of raw film provided an opportunity for research, but the society provoked it. Pavlov provided an authority in science for an approach to the audience. *Montage* and reflexology encouraged experimentation that was not haphazard, an experimentation that had a point to start from and an end to reach. But it was the social need that commanded this experimentation. *Montage* would not have been developed were there not a profound idea and its tangible expressions to enact. *Montage* therefore became a special kind of editing ("constructive editing," it has been called) and no longer was it editing in general. However, because of the concentration on method, a confounding occurred, of *montage* with cinema. This was so much the case that Eisenstein, in speaking of the forms of cinema, talks of "the four categories of *montage*." One recalls William Carlos Williams' dictum: "Rhythm is the poem." Pudovkin, in the introduction to the German edition of his manual on *Film Technique,* declares peremptorily: "The foundation of film art is *editing*." But—the film-progression is by no means the entire film. Eisenstein is aware of this, and in his categories of *montage* includes as the penultimate the *tonal*—light, etc. Pudovkin, it will be observed, does not say, ". . . film art is editing," but that its "foundation . . . is editing." However, in the overstress of his work he has contributed to the confusion, and has himself been victimized. At the present time, when the great need in Soviet Russia is the penetration of the new social values as expressed in the new social conduct, he is busy with "new *montage* experiments."

No more valuable "book of practice" has been prepared for the novice in cinema than Pudovkin's manual on *Film Technique*. It must be accepted, however, not as a work containing the laws of cinema, but as a volume of elementary discipline in the art. It should not, on the other hand, be grouped with the numerous books on "how to make movies." The manual was originally one of a series of handbooks published by the Russian film publishing house. Pudovkin has not yet produced *The End of St. Petersburg,* and the work is at the acute point of contact with Griffith, Kuleshov, and Pavlov. It is bound to the associative practice set by Kuleshov and ennobled by Pudovkin in *Mother,* and whatever faults this practice may possess, it is well that a manual should base itself upon it, rather than upon the speculations of Eisenstein. Unfortunately, when the book reached the shores of Albion it was transfigured into gospel, although the translator did preface it with the remark that "Pudovkin is no Aristotle." This, sadly enough, was not read as a warning.

There are, in the book, frequent instances of Pudovkin's determinism. Since, however, these instances relate generally to matters of immediate practice, rather than to a conclusive point of view, they may be taken as rules of discipline. For instance, the statement that "a film more than seven thousand feet long already creates an unnecessary exhaustion" should be refuted if one looked upon it as categorical. In the sentence preceding the one quoted Pudovkin invites such refutation: "Cinematography is, before anything else, limited by the definite length of a film." But we can overlook the remark and simply take what follows as a guide but not a restriction. Farther in the volume, he says: "The film spectator has no time to savor words." A very terse stipulation well put, explained further by Pudovkin's observation that the title must reach the spectator "in the course of the process of being read." Yet savoring a title is not obviated temporally; savor is also a question of the quality of title. In *The End of St. Petersburg,* Pudovkin repeats certain titles, place names, for instance, in conjunction with words that present changes in the status of people, from "native" to "worker." The very repetition, a temporal device in part, is a savory. The titles in *Potemkin* are even literary, their suggestions color the visual image. However, the advice, as put by Pudovkin, is an essential guide, as indeed is the "ideal" of a captionless film. But the movie is in its evolutionary nature a compound medium in which the *literary* legend plays a part. What should Pudovkin say to the savoring of the spoken word? And to the savoring of the superimposed translation of the spoken word? In 1929 he was bespeaking the attitude of a group of Russian directors who anticipated the sound film in a contrapuntal envisualization. Thus, they argued, the film would remain international. But for the revolutionary artist the internationalism of an art should reside not in its form but in its content. Stalin's principle of an art "proletarian in content, national in form" is an international principle. Certainly, contrapuntal sound-sight composition would enrich the cinema (indeed it has already enriched it), but the Russian group derived counterpoint from an emergency situation (again the narrow deterministic viewpoint), the apparent separation of lip-movement from oral utterance. Soon after, the identification of the two became secure. Such compounding may be a first junction, yet it is legitimate and permanent in the cinema, as much so as the close-up, and can be exploited structurally. Fortunately, the Russian sound film did not wait until these authorities became active, although their absolutism may have thwarted a direct presentation of sound and speech because the masters were expected by the world outside to discover a momentous even absolute collaboration of the two sensory appeals. In the meantime the Soviet sound film has achieved what is not negligible, the relevant orchestral score in the composition of a Dmitri Shostakovitch and the animated films, and speech as profound as their visual image. Dialogue is not alien to the compound cinema. Its use depends on the requirements of the subject-matter, which determine the structure of the entire film. The sound film, including the film of speech, has extended the cinema, in spite of inimical biases and nefarious monopolies, because it has permitted more difficult themes and encouraged production nationally. That this encouragement has not been supported is due to the fact that nationalism, rampant in the bourgeois world today, is the corruption or denial of nationality. But in the U.S.S.R., where autonomous nationality exists, we may expect a diversified expression of the proletarian theme. The universal appeal of medium is a merchandise value; or, an incident of the more naïve compulsive propaganda, a first outcry. The level of political appreciation and cultural satisfaction is much higher today in the Soviet Union (many directors cannot rise to it); the audience has superior critical standards and a facile ritualistic enticement is suspect. The subject-matter is more involved, more delicate, and more individualized, although the themes are recurrent in the social integration.

The seriousness of the problem was recognized in 1929. It was misinterpreted as a problem of method (the challenge of sound augmented the error), whereas method is a secondary concern issuing from the problem of the social theme. The cart was put before the horse. In that year Pudovkin expressed his dissatisfaction with his method, as well he might, after the blatancies of *Storm Over Asia*. A year later he was at work on *Life Is Beautiful!* which was to have been a compound film. Since the manifesto on sound-sight counterpoint, Pudovkin had arrived at a decisive acceptance of the compound film to the extent of drastically separating it from the simple or mute film. It is true that the sound film has been impeded by practicians and theorists still thinking mutely but the sound film is an evolutionary growth from the silent and therefore has instructions to draw from it. The plane of correlation is still visual-motor.

On the flatlands of dilemma, Pudovkin discovered the scenarios of Alexander Rjechevsky. They are, in brief, emotional, suggestive — non-technical, literary scenarios. The overwhelming influence of scenarists upon Pudovkin — Zarchi, Brik, Rjechevsky — is itself a reflection of Pudovkin's instability. His discovery of a scenarist led him to "repudiate" his manual on *Film Technique!* This is an hyperbole in which only a soberly naïve person would have indulged. It is true the book was written in his first directorial flush, but it is an essential guide, "an etymological and syntactic grammar," that is still useful. There was no basic error that had to be invalidated because it threatened the social state — or the art of the cinema. Pudovkin was probably incited into this violence by Eisenstein's taunts at his Kuleshovian associative or linkage-editing, the "brick on brick" method.

What did Pudovkin find in Rjechevsky to spellbind him so? The mere absence from the latter's work of technical directorial directives is not in itself tremendous. What is interesting (and questionable) in Rjechevsky is his literary method, as especially contained in his use of epithets: "At the edge of a naked precipice, under heavy clouds, over endless water — a great river or perhaps blue sea — . . ." Pudovkin thinks "Rjechevsky demands ingenuity"; this assumption is a vagary. In an equivocal phrase like "perhaps blue sea," Pudovkin finds "a precise directive for research and for shooting. . . . A whole *montage*-composition is here given . . . perhaps even the incorporation of other material having no relation to water." The director is evidently enlarging in his mind's eye upon such an associative sequence of unrelated scenes as in *Mother*, (This is a "plastic synthesis" of which Pudovkin has always been proud. "The son sits in prison. Suddenly, passed in to him surreptitiously, he receives a note that the next day he is to be set free. The problem was the expression, filmically, of his joy. The photographing of a face lighting up with joy would have been flat and void of effect. I show, therefore, the nervous play of his hands and a big close-up of the lower half of his face, the corners of the smile. These shots I cut in with other and varied material — shots of a brook, swollen with the rapid flow of spring, of the play of sunlight broken on the water, birds splashing in the village pond, and finally a laughing child.") but actually in the last clause he betokens automatism. This continual major preoccupation with *montage* threatens to cast the artist into dissociations or mere pictorialism. The latter is Pudovkin's yield in *Life Is Beautiful!* a project which started out to reveal the new human being in Soviet Russia. That being, of course, is not discoverable in *montage* but in society. It is not accidental that Pudovkin should have reverted to the period of the civil war to get started in his search; he could not meet the character on the scene. Instead of the certainties of his earlier films we are favored with tentatives, sometimes visually beautiful, particularly where the scene contains no human player. And the human player is an effect and not a being. There is a clue to this further deterioration of the effigy in Pudovkin's remarks upon the scenarist: "Rjechevsky's characters are always composed of *types*. His works are always saturated with the *pathétique*. His heroes do not require any preliminary characterizations, nurtured as they are with the true heroism of our times." This is a lyrical, subjective, indeed passive, self-protective conception which bears no relation to the task of revealing Soviet man and his way of life. *Truth is concrete*: character cannot be created in the abstract. *And Life Is Beautiful!* is an abstraction, a static notion as unrevolutionary as the images of Dovzhenko, from whose moods and frames *Life Is Beautiful!* borrows pensiveness if not mists. Pudovkin was not facing the central problem, though his attachment to the new society is indubitable and not inherently abstract. The problem is a personal one, but not quite so deeply personal as Dovzhenko's, and the likelihood is he will surmount it when he recognizes that *montage* and "slow motion" are really academicisms and not vitalities. It is rather that he has been led astray.

The error is not restricted to Pudovkin. It has been described by a newcomer, Macheret, director of *Men and Jobs*: "The cinema has created a certain conditional language which substituted the demonstration of situations for the analysis of relations — a language which was installing the formal-aesthetic value in place of the social value." The insistence on psycho-physiological manipulation of the audience led ultimately to a situation where the audience was impressed with directorial hypotheses rather than with a social idea that was appraisable. The recovery of the theme, says Macheret, depends upon "making man the core of the work," instead of the commodity, in the cinema the tools of cinema, and the avoidance of "an abstract expression." Macheret is probably referring to influences from Eisenstein, but his characterization refers to Pudovkin as well, although *Mother* leads eventually, despite deflections, to man the core. Macheret concludes that the directors strove "to preserve unbroken the harmony between the subjective qualities and the objective predestination of the type," and overlooked, therefore, the process at work in the re-education of the citizen.

This concrete examination of the social material would necessarily lead to precision of relationship and ripeness of differentiation. "The pseudo-classic type" would be superseded by "the living complex man." It is the substitution of the personification for the person that frequently in as monumental a film as Dovzhenko's *Arsenal* turns the heroic into the mock-heroic. The Soviet film in its staunch directness had achieved the symbol in the reality — this was especially true of Eisenstein. This reality-as-symbol could be enlarged from the single reference to an entire social phenomenon, as, for instance, the whole of *China Express*. The documentary approach has provided a method of authentic selection of type. But when the type is compelled to represent an idea, as in Dovzhenko's *Ivan*, the result becomes picturesque and even elegiac, but hardly representative: it can be sung perhaps but not pursued. And in a society non-ritualistic like the Russian, where everyone may possess and apply the objective measure to an utterance, the disparity between an utterance and its intention becomes a chasm the artist must bridge. That is a brave task, worthy of the artist. Though, in a society where the artist is not burdened with an exceptional and exceptionable position, the audience may be severe in its criticism of the artist's failure, it will preserve him nevertheless, and give him the time and the means to build the bridge. Pudovkin has, for instance, been honored with leadership of the organization of proletarian artists, which is a reflection of popular confidence in an artist who has, for the moment, taken to a byroad. In *Deserter* he may have again re-entered the main highway.

HOUND AND HORN,
April, 1933.

EISENSTEIN AND THE THEORY OF CINEMA

By its inceptual nature, the cinema is a progressive medium, proceeds in time. In its development, it tends increasingly toward intensiveness. The path it follows is opposite to that of the theater, which is an intensive medium tending toward progressiveness. There are points at which they contact, where it would be difficult to distinguish between the cinematic and the theatric. There is, however, a maximum beyond which intensiveness cannot proceed in the cinema, nor progressiveness in the theater. In the cinema, it is the point beyond which the constant of progression is dissipated; in the theater, the point beyond which the constant of intensiveness is shattered. In the mute cinema, *Joan of Arc* is the maximum of intensiveness, and because its intensive nature was respected within the progression, it is cinema, and not, as idle observers have called it, photography. In the theater, Meyerhold's *D.S.E.* exceeds the maximum of progressiveness, departs from the sphere of the theater, but, because it is not realized within the sphere whose constant is progression, arrives at no other art.

Eisenstein's experience in the drama was gained with Meyerhold, the director who has most expansively "cinematized" the theater. It is, therefore, not surprising that the self-assertive younger man should have entered the sphere of the cinema. In crossing this threshold, he believed he was following a "dialectic" of art, one sphere of a planetary system — drama — "negating" the other. Meyerhold chided him for his absolutism, and quite rightly, for the dialectic of art is socially involved, and Eisenstein was omitting the ability of a fresh society to revive an exhausted sphere.

In immediate terms, Eisenstein was forgetting the stimulus of a vivacious audience.

The absolutising of his own actions and reactions constitutes the body of Eisenstein's theoretical writings, "eccentric and fractional." In practice, his alertness and persistence have enabled him to seize the stature of an event and reproduce its configurations suggestively. In extension, this prowess has made it possible for Eisenstein to follow the practice of montage to its extreme. To seize stature and reproduce configurations requires a sharp sense of quantity, and Eienstein, as Anisimov (In his essay on "The Films of Eisenstein," Ivan Anisimov has made a pertinent and consistent study of the relationships within Eisenstein's work. His insistences are often too sectarian, and tend to submerge the director's contributions, in spite of his profession of admiration. Anisimov was a member of the recently dissolved Russian organization of proletarian writers. His essay is an instance of the tendency that finally congealed, to be rendered fluid again by the Soviet society, an organism of fresh momentums. This literary organization did give a judicious tenacity to proletarian expression, but when the judicious became judicial, tenacity became monopoly. In a healthy society, "frozen assets" are readily liquidated.) has indicated, is an artist in the quantitative, which would make him primarily an engineer. That is why Eisenstein is truly the directors' director. He has been pace-setter in the world generally, and very particularly in the Soviet cinema. The battle against the "formal-aesthetic" in the Russian film is largely a battle against the Eisenstein influence. The battle on the challenging side has reached a position where it is necessary to face the danger of of pyrrhic victory. In the zeal to negate the dominance of "externals," the youngest directors are risking the loss of lessons in organization learned from the disciplined though prodigious works of Eisenstein. After all, Eisenstein, in his colossalism and his contours without specifications, was serving the progress of the motion picture in and out of Russia, enlarging its image, enhancing its syntax, dissolving the barriers of literalism. It was in doing these things that he, more than any other individual, turned the cinema again to relationship, the constituency of art.

The relationship of art is vested in the record, the restoration, the revelation, the three r's. Eisenstein's ideal of the cinema has been the synthesis of the documentary, the abstract and the dramatic. Of all his films, *Ten Days (October)* comes nearest to his ideal. To understand, however, the subsequent development of Eisenstein as director and theorist, one must examine his second film, *Potemkin* and Eisenstein's own appraisal of it. *Potemkin* has been called the perfect film, and rightly, with its own category of frontal attack. The film extended this elementary category by disturbing the usual geometric progression with a variation in the metre. This was assured by construction from the viewpoint of the imprinted image itself. Up to that time, the dramatic motion picture had passed through the stages of the camera. There was first the tethered camera, when, so to speak, no directorial point-of-view existed. The actor was a "sedulous ape" and that was the sole consciousness. Later there was invented the ambulant camera. Between the rigid and the completely mobile camera, the panoramic had come into being; the motion picture was an art of its initial instrument. The camera was "the alembic of film intelligence." Of course, during this time continuity was developing too. Continuity may be considered the anticipation of montage. The development of the camera from passivity to activity reached a period when camera was king. Films were conceived "in camera." The domination of an art by its instrument, something that effects but is not contained in the finished work, may become a suppressive burden on the art. The Soviet directors put the camera in its place as an instrument, and themselves began to stress a method.

In the primitive (pre-art) expression the unorganized phenomenon is rampant. The determinant of the primitive film is action, realized in speed and antic. In the intrinsic film the phenomenon is organized as rhythm, realized in tempo and pattern. In the film of frontal attack, heretofore committed to the primitive, Eisenstein constructed rhythm, emphatically borne by the effect-cause-effect construction and concentric intensities of the massacre on the Odessa steps. *Potemkin,* by constructing rather than merely recording the attack, achieved a perfection of powerful surface masses, achieved the perfect "poster," as Eisenstein has himself called it. It remains a film of frontal attack because it was conceived on that level; therefore its perfection, therefore its inadequacy. It is not the historic event but only the single physical episode, the "quick emotional *discharge.*" The designation of his picture as "poster" may have been an afterthought with Eisenstein to disarm criticism of its philosophic shortcomings. The after-the-fact aspect of Eisenstein's speculations and promulgations has been noticed before. His theory is frequently a rationalisation not only of his practice but of his temperament. Absolutes are the usual result.

Himself an intellectual, he proclaimed the mass as hero. He was not alone in this, but the proclamation was personal to him, and of that personality he made a law. To him the professional player was undesirable. Fortunately, what he expressed as a law, others, like Pudovkin, particularized into a principle, the principle of documentary selection, professional or non-professional, the emphatic pronunciation of type. The mass-documentary legalism sharpened the already intensified editing. One extreme concurs with another. If little trust is to be placed in the digit, if he is to be neuter, "it" must be reinforced, activated, by an external will. Moreover, if acting is reprehensible, the player must not be permitted portrayal. He must therefore be limited to a physiognomy or a posture, and these must not exceed their pictorial length: the principle of "laconism." (Victor Turin, director of *Turksib,* a film Eisenstein disparaged as lacking montage, speaks of "associative laconism" [association and brevity]. Eisenstein would probably oppose the junction, and speak, as he has recently, of "extreme laconism," which he finds in the writings of Babel, who, perhaps, has a practical grasp [?] than anyone else of the great secret that ". . . no man can enter into the human heart with such stupefying effect as a full stop opportunely placed"). In this way montage as suggestive inter-reference is further intensified in practice, and in theory becomes "the basic, everlasting, and vital principle." It becomes *tout-cinèma.*

Eisenstein has divided montage, both as a description of the historic sequence of cinema and of the contemporary levels of cinema, into four "methods": metric, rhythmic, tonal, over-tone. The metric film is "the rude force of the motive action," determined solely by the simple arithmetic or geometric progression, effected by the *measurement* of unvarying *time.* It is matter-of-fact, rudimentary impact. Is not therefore the term "metric montage" a contradiction? Rhythmic detail is a breach in the simple progression to stress the content, the *impression,* of a particular component scene. Rhythm is the patterning of rhythmic detail in accord with the distribution of content. Therefore "rhythmic montage" is really a redundancy.

Montage is initiated in the associative process. Hans Richter, German experimentalist, has said: "The conscious formation of associations is one of the most important possibilities of montage. . . . Every kind of combination of successive images evokes peculiar and even powerful reactions. Every combination produces its own effect, and a seemingly slight change in the combination may cause a totally opposite psychological reaction . . . under the head of association one must understand three divisions: formal, rhythmic and content relationships." The severity of the dictum agrees with Eisenstein's "over-tone montage," "the collective calculation of all the appeals of the piece." It is a "synthesis" out of "tonal montage." In the latter order the values are not those of editing but of pervasive qualities—tones of light, graphic composition etc. Is not "tonal montage" therefore a misappropriation, and "over-tone montage" a usurpation? Montage is simply intensive editing, and Eisenstein's conception of it, his conception of a superior montage, is the maximum of intensive editing. Kuleshov, whose associative editing Eisenstein derides, and Pudovkin, whom Eisenstein has confronted with a "conflict-montage" theory, have made contributions to film construction that are not unrelated to Eisenstein's contrast-and-conjunction. Eisenstein would object to the premise of association in Richter's statute. Yet his own work is a development from association, ideally, in speculation, from perception to apperception. His speculations, issued as despotisms, are fascinating explanations of a fact which neither explain the fact, nor provide exact precepts for others to follow. In that sense, "his theoretical reasoning has a negative significance." To build upon practices in *Old and New* a theory of a montage of conflicts, which later finds extensive authority in a truism *Art is always Conflict,* which in its turn finds universal authority in the law of dialectics is a transcendentalism far removed from the concreteness of dialectics. This montage through "collision" and "resolution" Eisenstein calls "the dynamic principle." Anisimov has charged Eisenstein with not thinking dialectically; in the orderly heap of his "Principles of Film Form," Eisenstein has a profusion of quasi-dialectics. Anisimov has called him a mechanical rationalist; Eisenstein writes: "Hypertrophy of the purposive impulse — the principle of rational logic — causes the Art to freeze to a mathematical technicalism." In the same manifesto, Eisenstein describes montage as "the nerve of the Film." Further refinement of this thesis will make montage the neurosis of the film. (The analogies film directors find in music become preponderants in Eisenstein. This is a form of absolutism, which coincides with the concept of a "pure art," an art not verifiable concretely. Undoubtedly, there is a bond between music and movie, as there is between any two arts, but to make the affinity other than mutually reciprocal is to yield to the false concept of "purity." Goethe's declaration, which Eisenstein quotes with reverence, that "Architecture is frozen music," is not a permanent law, but the aesthetic value of a particular period. Terms like "over-tone," "counterpoint" must, in cinema jargon, be only tentative conveniences. Now that sound is organic in, rather than accessory to, the motion picture, it will ask a return of these borrowings, and other explicit designations will be required. In fact, a major enterprise for the critic of cinema is the establishment of a pertinent terminology). "Overtonality" is, in the profoundest sense, not merely "flair, aroma," but what is conveyed to the apperceptions, "the higher nerve-centers," of the observer. It is the memorable residue when the screen is bare. It is the inference." Overtonality" may be achieved *in part* through montage. Eisenstein's films, far away from literal construction, are yet deficient in aftersense, in the qualitative. His montage gives the weight of the physical content, but not the meaning of the social, because the personality of the event is lacking. Yet he is the greatest living master of construction, which, unfortunately, is not enough. Nowhere in his writing does Eisenstein dwell upon the human actor as the material of the experience. There is but negligible reference to the social subject-matter, and then apart from the formalities of practice. Richter also keeps the formal and content relationships apart, parallel but not reciprocal. To Eisenstein dialectics is continent in methodology. Dialectics is, however, at once the subject and its measure, and to eliminate the former is to go abstract, as Eisenstein most often does.

Abstraction and absolutism lead to the exaggeration of indices. Eisenstein is a man of erudition through rabid reading and rapid assimilation. Quite correctly he seeks sources in man's other expressions. The cinema is an art among arts and can be instructed by its colleagues. But a source must not exceed its instructional or corroborative function. Conceiving of ideal montage as a "molecular" process wherein two independent "cells," "placed in juxtaposition, explode to a new concept," Eisenstein recognizes the pictographic language as montage. The use of the term "explode" is significant. "Eye + Water = ('explode to') To Weep." The index is in the separateness of the two images which, juxtaposed, produce a third, a concept. Eisenstein rejects as "vulgar" the "description" of the phenomenon "as a blending," yet is not the first attachment of the ideograms associative, and then propulsive? To enlarge the index into a law of optics, sharing the characteristic of "super-position" with stereoscopy is to make an enormity of a footnote.

The hieroglyphic nature of the Japanese language, its depictiveness, the "ascetic" laconism of Japanese poetry, the separation of the vocal from the mimic in the Japanese theater appeal to Eisenstein as cinema. He would expand them into a system, rather than limit them to indications by asterisk. He concludes that while there is cinematography in every other Japanese expression, there is none in the Japanese cinema. The diagnosis is incorrect, because the wrong instrument of measure is used. The indeterminateness of the Japanese cinema is due to a confusion in the class-rôle. The other expressions were realized in a period of exact class-delineations. The cinema was born and has been reared in a period when the aristocracy is enacting the rôle of the middleman. The conflict between the "old form," based on the traditional theatre, and the "new form," yearning toward America and Germany, has not yet been resolved, and will be resolved only by a revolutionary force. In one branch of the cinema there is no such conflict. The rice-paper animation, being graphic cinema, derives from the traditional.

Eisenstein thinks "explosively," at great velocity and with no "check and double-check." His mental processes are atomic. Yet they are associations. By their intensity his thoughts seem to be in continuous production from the need to qualify the thought previously rendered. This quasi-dialectical succession is not what is meant by "thinking dialectically." Professing to clarify, it isolates the measure from the subject. The procedure is a sort of intellectual quarantine. "Dynamics" is used "in the sense of methodology of form, not of content or action." The result is a great mountain of abstraction, serving mainly the shadow eater. The directors' director becomes the critics' director. The dynamics of the film is not separable into that of method, action and content, save to the anatomist. By anatomy the whole man is not discoverable. If, by Eisenstein's definition, the dynamic is *his* principle, as opposed to Pudovkin's, which he calls "epic," can Lèger's graphic be called dynamic, "linear" dynamic? The dynamic in the cinema is one of several energies of the film, energies not mutually exclusive. It is the resultant of the progressive and the intensive. Pudovkin has described it in these words: "In the method of Griffith are combined the inner dramatic content of the action and a masterly employment of external effect (dynamic tension)." Eisenstein views the resultant as the "effect" of a "collision." That is thinking "physiologically," an intellectualisation of Pavlov's reflexology. The valuable elements of his speculations, however, are many, but seldom enlarged upon. Like his own montage, he conceives in "shocks," in a "linkage" (his characterization of Pudovkin's progression) of "shocks." For instance, his dynamic of directions deserves a close study, as does the entire spatial thesis of cinema. The development of the cinema in intensiveness is largely the exploitation of space. The entire history of man's progress toward cinematography is the effort to record movement (time) in space (graphically). At the other end of the evolution, the screen itself awaits exploitation. Eisenstein has dwelt upon the screen in the cinema, but mainly as to its dimensions—shape and direction—and only incidentally for its variability, "a gigantic new agent of impression as the rhythmic assemblage of varied screen shapes." The screen has entered his considerations in the matter of "Wide Films," but not yet in the organism of the cinema: it can only be inferred in his "conflicts." The Frenchman Claude Autant-Lara has invented a screen-within-a-screen, as yet crude when I saw it in Paris in 1930, within whose normal rectangle the images change their panels—their area and axis—according to the degree of intensity and range of vista of the content.

Commentaries, flashbacks, sub-motifs, visual epithets in and out of different sections to carry on the psychological story. Eisenstein's notes on the screen were impelled by the academicism of Hollywood theoreticians, and one can feel in them a boyish intellectual glee in "putting it over" on the orthodoxy. However, in preparing the notes for publication, away from the hypnosis of his own voice, the author might have rearranged the sequence and allotment to stress the lively use of the screen, the screen's progress from instrument, passive and receptive base, to plastic material. In Eisenstein's remarks on the wide film, one imperative stands out: *"Acoustics help optics!"* At that meeting in Hollywood, he was referring to the "optimum acoustics" of the auditorium, but in the exclamation Eisenstein has concentrated again his concept of a "common denominator" (equivalence) for the sound-sight film. This community is also, according to him, the sum of a conflict – "between Optical and Acoustical impulses." That sum is "counterpoint." With that Eisenstein concludes his chart of the cinema, "the first possibility of devising a *single system of visual dramaturgy* covering all general detail cases of the problem."

He wants a "single system," a monistic mechanism. Both Eisenstein and Pudovkin use the term "motion" very little in their writings. The conception of motion as a "key" is a literalism remaining from the days when films were "motion tableaux," and an open sesame from the ritualistic art-as-magic. But there is a ritualistic attitude also in this voracious "single system." When objectivity becomes empirical, and there is no consistent interrelation of subject and measure, grossnesses occur. What Eisenstein calls linkage-*montage* and the epic principle is association by adhesion; conflict-*montage* and the dynamic principle, association by cohesion. In Pudovkin separate images adhere to a nuclear image; in Eisenstein separate images cohere to render a sum. Emphatic instances are the receipt, in *Mother,* of the letter by the imprisoned son; the rain-ceremony in *Old and New.* Eisenstein once told me that he had re-cut that incident some twenty to twenty-five times for the right overtone, the specific suggestion. Is there then, like Flaubert's one right word, one right series? Richter says there is. But that is too rigid a conception. There are permutations and combinations from which a suitable series is to be selected. The absolute of "one right" is a discipline like the captionless film. Just as in the particularization of a theme into a plot, and in the realization of a plot in a movie, there are many possibilities or alternatives, so within the body of the movie there is more than one way of composing a duration. Unity is essential but not restrictive. Eisenstein could have inter-referred the images (symbols) in other combinations and achieved an equivalent, if not identical, transmission. No difference in quality would have been discerned. As there is a point beyond which impressions are ineffective, so there is a point below which distinctions are evanescent. To insist on exceeding either is to be, respectively, violent or precious. There can, of course, be a wrong selection or series caused by a mis-reading of theme or an incorrect detail of method or a deficiency in temperament. A film may even be perfect in execution and yet, as the realization of a theme, be a wrong film: *New Babylon, Soil, White Shadows.*

To achieve "signification," an art aspires away from the literal. Qualified ratio, or proportion, succeeds literal ratio: that is the development from the metric to the rhythmic. It is proportion (alternation on the basis of content distribution) attained through disproportion. There is disproportion in the expression of the content-values themselves, the ratios of statement. If Eisenstein opposes the narrative-method of Kuleshov (he is wrong in attaching Pudovkin so closely to this method), it is because a statement does not of itself convey a meaning. One must determine the proportion of the idea, and then build for that proportion. Unfortunately, in his practice, Eisenstein sees the physical container for the idea, and the disproportion becomes an heroicism. Not collectivism but certain of its constituent aspects was conveyed by *Old and New.* Of all the principles of constriction, disproportion, because it is the value-relation of measure to subject, is the richest in its dialectic potentiality. Yet this principle Eisenstein has mentioned only casually or by inference.

The most problematic of the disproportion is Eisenstein's "pathetic treatment of non-pathetic material." It is problematic because as it stands it is more a rationalization of the director's sympathy for objects than a completed thesis. What of the pathetic material, the human factor? Is there a converse: the non-pathetic treatment of pathetic material? In Eisenstein's practice there is just that irregularity, due to a temperamental neglect. This converse submits a correct approach to certain human materials: the idyllic, for instance. But until Eisenstein determines the vital proportion in the relation of subject and objective environment, the pathos of the non-pathetic will overwhelm and not elucidate the subject.

From the acceptation of "shot" as "cell" there follows the *intra*-relation of the component picture. Having seen, in practice, that a film cannot be built *in toto* of cohesive particles, but has to be alternate this intensive construction with another intensive construction, the sustained duration, Eisenstein rationalized the need with an "intra-cadre" "conflict." His Mexican film, which I have seen in part in the unfinished state in which he was forced to leave it, shows an increased respect for the intra-relation.

We may expect from its author a new "theory" of cinema based on this increased respect, necessitated in part by the exigencies of production. Eisenstein has discountenanced the antipathy to pictorialism. He is right. So long as the pictorial is not falsely emphasized into the picturesque (the easel-film attitude), but honored as an intensive consideration, it is a value. Eisenstein is an engineer who sees each film as an individual problem to solve. This "objectiveness" explains the absence from his films of the eccentricities, the awkward witticisms and arrogances of his writing. The problem, unfortunately, is seen as a methodological one: objectivity without participation. The new "theory" may either proclaim an elaboration of montage, or, less likely, a departure from montage as an inclusive. Eisenstein did mention that he would have something to say about this "composition of the shot," a phrase that brings him close to Dreyer, whose *Joan of Arc* he found unacceptable.

The emphasis of the component is part of the development towards inference, the "*deep reflective processes*" as distinguished from the visceral attack. The ultimate of "over-tone montage" is, Eisenstein has said, "the intellectual cinema." Anisimov has called the latter a "peculiar defensive device justifying his Eisenstein's limitations." Though there may be a general truth in this characterization, "the intellectual cinema" cannot be treated peremptorily. The mistake of Eisenstein lies in the categorizing of a distinct "intellectual cinema," but an examination of his comments on this cinema reduces the error to merely verbal. If, instead of "intellectual cinema," we say "intellectual appeal," and define "intellectual" as socially inferential, we are arriving at the mature cinema. Eisenstein has indicated that the intellectual appeal is not circuitous, but as direct as the drive of the elemental film. The motion picture must develop, in order not to stagnate, through a serious and profound content, necessitating a treatment permitting scrutiny. The cinema is structurally ready for such content, and when that content is genuinely allowed it, the cinema will realize itself in all its variety.

The literary contributions of Eisenstein since he has returned to his homeland are reassuring. Centering about his work at GIK, the state cinema school, they are a redeclaration of intention. The dialectics of his own experience with the capitalist cinema, commercial Hollywood and the "independent" Maecenas, may have turned him from organization to organism. He quotes Lenin: "Criticism must consist in comparing and contrasting a given fact not with an idea, but with another fact . . ." to corroborate the intention of establishing principles "by critical comparison with the more stadial early forms of spectacle." The fact must be compared and contrasted with another fact in the same sphere: recall Lenin's sundering of Kautsky's eclectic sources. (The terms "stadial" and "spectacle" suggest still the ritualistic bias). But the comparison must be informed by a principle authenticated, not solely in the aesthetic medium, but primarily in the social manifestation. There is a great difference between an elastic and opportunistic judgment. If by "concrete work on individual material," Eisenstein means that he will relinquish, for instance, his "non-coincidence" as the "basis" of the compound cinema, and recognize that while an art aspires away from the literal, it does so as a growth rooted in the literal, he will ascend from the provocative to the preceptorial. He has been and still is a major stimulant.

Hound and Horn,
July, 1933.

"Sartre has said that there can be no great work of literature which does not contribute to the liberation of man and surely this must hold true of film as well . . ."

DAVID CAUTO

PART THREE: MISCELLANY

7

FILM REVIEWS

THE PASSION OF JEANNE D'ARC

We are always waiting in the cinema for the eventual film which will be the vindication of the major cinema devices. We are always waiting for the film down to essentials and yet conveying a profound human experience. For the craft of the movie, like the craft of any other art, is performance — of camera, of film, of player, of screen. (Mr. Alexander Bakshy has stated these four as the different cinema performances or movements, a fundamental statement). But as an art conclusive the cinema must find its source in experience and its final meaning in experience. Where is the motion picture — we are always asking — profound in its exploitation of performance, and profound in its transmission of experience? This query is the key to the importance of plot in the movie, not as detailed or episodic narrative but as subject-matter. The consideration of plot as narrative has been the cause and result of the movie's literalness (particularly in America) and the inability to include in the formation of the moving picture the inferences of the theme, much more important than the narrative. This inability has prevented a film so dramatically effective as Feyder's recent *Thérèse Raquin* (adopted from Zola's novel) from being a film of permanent importance.

In brief, we are always waiting for a film reduced but with passionate human content. The purity of passionate apprehension. A film mindful of the plot as the subject-matter of life. A film using the legitimate emphasis of the camera (or other kino instruments) and realizing an experience of form and content completely fused and fluid. We are always waiting for the expression of a perspicacious knowledge of the medium, and of the matter it is to convert into and by means of itself. The American film has realized in its literalness a pleasant but shallow ease of sequence. The German has stressed, in the main, the device as virtuosity rather than as an incorporate, revealing utility. The Swedish film, like the notable *Atonement of Gösta Berling,* is a rigorous life-exposition, but it has not fully grasped the principle of the conversion of the subject-matter. The French movie on the whole is too banal or too pretty or too frivolous (without being lively) to merit our interest. Yet the film which in this instance satisfies our anticipation is a French film. Its achievement may be explained by the fact that its director is a Dane, Carl Th. Dreyer. The film is *The Passion of Jeanne d'Arc.*

This profound and truly passionate motion picture concerns itself with the last day of Jeanne, the day of excruciating torment. The scenario is the combined work of the director and Joseph Delteil, the dadaist who wrote the prize-winning book on The Maid. It is, I hope, no libel of M. Delteil to suspect that the disciplining will of the director (a prime essential in the cinema industry today) kept the narrative within the strenuous limits of reverence. Reverence is a portion of the intensity of this film, an intensity to which everything submits — the decor by Jean Victor-Hugo, the photography by Maté, with its superb statement of personalities by the skin textures and moles. In total accord with this intense and intensive exploitation of the subject-matter (remember there is really no plot here, only the last moment — the queries, the betrayal, the final conflagration) is the use of the succession of individual cine-photos. These are not close-ups (there is no "closing-up" in the bland movie way), not stills (for the angles and curves are lovely and illuminating), but the bold concentration of individual faces and figures in the active, critical, voracious eye of the camera. This would suggest a static series of pictures, not Mr. Bakshy's "dynamic sequence," rather the mere physical basis of filming than the aesthetic aspiration of the cinema. But it attests to Carl Dreyer's genius that the sequence is eminently fluid, dramatic, rhythmic. The succession has a definite time-order, a definite plastic arrangement in the time-order of exquisite curves (the performers exploited by the camera) and bodily angles, a definite utilization of the screen as the receptive instrument (advocated long ago by Mr. Bakshy, but very seldom realized), and a gradual almost unsuspected rise to the final mob explosion. There are diagonal curves of the moving performers, vertical inclines, a forehead above the lower frame boldly duplicating the moderated masses of the background.

There is no extraneous detail in the film. Not once does a detail fail to directly relate and contribute to the subject-matter. At one point, Jeanne sees the grave digger pull up a skull. Unnecessary? Obvious? There is a swift succession, almost staccato in its brevity, of a field of flowers. The previous detail becomes inevitable, poignant. In fact, the entire film has that virtue, that at any moment the detail on the screen validates what preceded it. This is rhythm, this is art. The beautiful flight of birds, as Jeanne is perishing, the mother suckling her child – the former might be a sentimentalism, the latter a surrealistic simplicism; but by the severe control of the director, they become terrible convictions of the world that would let one who loved free flight perish bound, and one who herself would suckle life burn at the stake. Creation against desolation!

The torment of the young peasant girl, "called Jeannette at home," convinced in her childishness and mysticism of her divine mission, becomes the emotional experience of the spectator. Her fears, persistent under the insistent examination, become heavy with the burden of the torment, become luminous with the momentary glamor and memory stirred by the queries. The heavy tear imparts to the spectator the sense of the days and months of anguish the girl has endured in her steadfastness to her inspiration. The luminous tear elucidates the girl's origins, her free fields, her home, and the momentum of the inspiration that has urged her into this betrayal. The tears of Falconetti, the portrayer of Jeanne, are not the tears of a Clara Bow, insipid, irritating, fraudulent. Her eyes enamored of God borrow no stage-pantomime, but with the grained skin and parched lips, the clipped hair, and chained walk, reveal the entire enterprise of God and land within the girl's body. Falconetti faithfully submits to the intensity of the unit, enters into it, and expresses it while she expresses Jeanne. She is the conception. She is the film. An identical loyalty is manifested by each of the accurately chosen, thoroughly participating cast. No specious prettiness, but hardiness, man in his physical variousness, man in his spiritual diversity serving the same master – Interest. The Interest of State, the Interest of God. Jeanne, serving God, alone of all has served herself, her systemic soul-and-body. She as the servant of herself becomes the everlasting, the others are left to weep upon the torment they have connived. The State alone (Warwick) remains unperturbed, save to halt the conflagration of Jeanne which threatens to burn down the power of England in Rouen. As no prologue was needed, no epilogue is asked for and no commentary from the distance of several centuries. How superior to Shaw's Joan! The inference all embodied in the unit-structure, not tagging along like loose threads, nor stressed like a moral to a fable. One fault alone disturbs the perfection of this grand film, a fault easily elimi-

(continued on p. 640)

"A" IN THE ART OF THE MOVIE AND KINO

Writing in *Monde,* Henri Barbusse's journal, I said: the American movie can be saved by New York. I did not mean to be taken literally. My meaning was: Hollywood redundancies will keep the film rudimentary and lacking in social, philosophic and æsthetic meaning. A new mind is needed to work upon the rudiments and extend them. Hollywood will not supply that new mind. Hollywood is vested interest. Hollywood is uninspired competence — at its best. Hollywood is empty facility. A critical mind is needed. New York is the concentration center of the critical mind. Even in the use of the instruments (putting aside for the moment philosophy), I look to the director who has not imbibed Hollywood.

There's Rouben Mamoulian of the Theatre Guild. He made a first film at the Astoria studios of the Paramount. He put his camera on rubber wheels and glided it to look upon the players from this angle and that. He was given a typical Hollywood story — no more trashy than — the others — and a maudlin heroine, annoyingly reminiscent of Pauline Lord and Gladys Brockwell, and one of those mother-themes (my burlesque good-bad mammy) . . . you know the ingredients — a whore, a pimp, a convent daughter, devoted nuns, a genteel sailor-boy looking for a little wife and a Wisconsin dairy, bichloride of mercury . . . another version of *Stella Dallas*. Given these millstones Mamoulian looked for sympathy to his camera. He proved himself more facile, more competent than Hollywood. But the film *Applause* remains sick stuff. Applause for Mr. Mamoulian must be modified by a censure of him for accepting the theme and the players. A movie, like water, never rises above its source. It can fall below it, but it cannot transcend it. Griffith's *The Birth of a Nation* remains a vindictive platitude, despite its grand composition, because of the thematic, human source in Dixon's *The Clansman.* Vidor could not beat the particularization of the theme of man against the mass in the Johnny Weaver scenario of *The Crowd.* So-called film purists will call my statement literary but I'm too old a hand at movie criticism to be scared by that judgment. What is confusedly termed literary is the substance of the film, its original source, which is converted into the final experience. If the substance is shoddy, specious or spurious, the more dexterous the handling of the instruments, the more remote will be the job from the material. The result is either virtuosity or the inflation of the theme. Mamoulian has proved himself as good a virtuoso as we have in America, but of virtuosity we need no more. We need philosophers who seek great themes told with insight and ultimate import. We need artists who build structures. That Mr. Mamoulian has used his camera as a mobile instrument is O.K. But moving a camera, getting angles, weaving together a couple of different sounds — the mother's chant, the daughter's prayer (what a banal sentimentalism!) — do not build a structure. In the first place the talkie (a misnomer) is a compound film. Its basis is the visual-motor graph (the basis of the simple or mute film). The graph must be constructed with the thought of the placements of sound, simultaneous or progressive placement — in relation to the visual image. There is no such preordained construction in *Applause,* no sustained unified rhythm. Speech is still talkie. Speech should be treated for its abstract qualities as much as sound is. Dialogue is anti-cinema, "speech-as-utterance" is not. I cannot here go into detail with this basic principle; the reader can refer to my contributions to *Close Up* for analyses of my point of view. What I can say here is simply this: Mamoulian has shown himself, in his novitiate, of superior craft-intelligence and daring . . . He brings to the film a proper sophistication in the use of the medium. There is a superb moment where the screen is divided diagonally into two distinct scenes, one of which gradually fills over the second to occupy the full screen. This is an active use of the split screen, surprisingly neglected in America. This alone would indicate what a fresh eye can do for the movie.

Whose fault it is I do not know, but a character of importance in the early part of the film — the comique who is the partner of the burlesque-queen and who woos her — is entirely forgotten. I should like to ask Miss Beth Brown, who wrote the story, what happened to him. He was too devoted to Kitty Darling to disappear. Or was it the fault of the master of the continuity? Well, such little things still happen in Hollywood, and Astoria is just Hollywood's other name. But what happened to the clown? This is the first time I have got excited by a "strange disappearance."

"A" for *Applause* and America. "A" for "*Arsenal*" and Art.

I do not think the Russian kino has as yet found a method that suits its profound material. Once I said: *Potemkin* is a film of powerful surface masses. Eisenstein said shortly after in *The Nation* that it was a poster-film. We agreed, I was vindicated. I said the Russians had better find a new method. Pudovkin said before the Filmliga of Amsterdam he had to find a new technique and Eisenstein in *Close Up* wrote: "Whereas in the first case we are striving for a quick emotional *discharge,* the new cinema must *include deep reflective processes . . .*" (the italics are not mine!). This is exactly my statement. The suggestions for this new cinema are to be found in Dreyer's *The Passion of Joan of Arc* and – in the Ukrainian film, *Arsenal* made by Dovzhenko. Here we have a Russian film that is not didactic but suggestive, that is not a perfection and elaboration of the American film of muscular impact (which is exactly the characterization of the Pudovkin kino), but an intensive, agonized, poignant, introspective film, conceived not as realism punctuated by symbols but as sustained symbolism.

Faults this film has, but that is not to be wondered at. I cannot think of a severer task than creating a structure of symbolism with real solid personalities. But Dovzhenko has succeeded, if not in creating an immaculate symbolic structure, in defining an intention which, by studying the workings of the film, the new Russian director will develop into a form. Russia promises to build a kino where at last thought and poetry and philosophic meaning are active. *Arsenal* renders a film like Vertov's *The Man With the Camera* [*sic*] not obsolete but certainly on a primary lesson for the aspirant.

In *Arsenal* propaganda is freed of its bluntness and becomes a penetrating emotional idea. There is none of the arrogance too often felt in the films of Pudovkin and Vertov. Certainly nothing could be stronger than the ghoulish, garish sights of the entombed soldier and the laughter of the gassed soldier. They are unrelenting as they should be. This is suggestive of the sort of war film F. W. Murnau would make, showing the actual results of the war: cadavers . . . Andreas Latzko's *Men in War*. There can be no pacifistic film which has a central hero, a protagonist – no matter how anti-militaristic its sentiments are. So long as there is participation, as there was in *The Big Parade,* with the soldiers, such a film accentuates military fervor. So long as the ominous rather than the horrible predominates, as in the British film *The Battle of the Colonel and Falkland Islands* [*sic,* see p. 471 *infra*], the military passion is enhanced.

Arsenal is not the greatest of films, but it is one of the most important.

* * *

There is another Russian film which must not be neglected: *In Old Siberia (Katorga)*. It is not the best, but it is one of the most sensitive, and also lacking in arrogance — which is a proof of Russia's adulthood. Another cinematic proof of Russia growing up enough to get a perspective upon itself is Alexander Room's *Bed and Sofa (Three In a Basement)*, not yet shown here. Room's social comedy is Russia laughing at herself, getting a tickle out of her new morality.

Russian films are very often too much caricature and not enough of full human experience. Pudovkin defends this by an analogy with Dickens. Ah! but why not Dostoievsky? Dickens served Dostoievsky — see *The Insulted and the Injured* where even the names and the relationships are paralleled to *The Old Curiosity Shop* — as a "source." Dostoievsky's fantasy was something more than caricature or whimsicality — it was the conversion of the ordinary into the extraordinary. And that is exactly the fantasy — in terms of kino — toward which *Arsenal* tends.

New Masses,
December, 1929.

TWO RUSSIAN FILMS

Conflict in the Caucasus

This film has been simultaneously called here: *Caucasian Love, Love in the Caucasus,* and *Conflict in the Caucasus.* I have chosen the last as most descriptive of the subject-matter. The love motif is incidental. The major and insistent theme is the Cossack usurpation of the homes and lands of the pastoral folk of the Caucasus. Because of the trek, the film has been likened to the American documentary, *Grass.* A more illuminating comparison would be the romanticized films of American mass-migrations, like *The Covered Wagon* and *The Trail of '98.*

This Russian film is assuredly not a great one, but it is a compelling one. It records an actual historical occurrence and relates it through the lives of persons chosen as ethnologically representative. The individual and the document are a unit. In the American documentaries the momentous historical fact is diluted by the insistence upon a trivial narrative of single infinitesimal lives – falsified in the traditions of the movie. No sense of the human, social, economic significance of these immemorial adventures is borne by the American films. The Klondike gold rush is considered less important than a preposterous "western" narrative of a villain bent on rape. Comic relief is intruded to weaken the epic heroism and the larger, more permanent inferences of the trek for gold. The Russian film contains details which ordinarily would be banal. There is the death of the widow, with the ensuing dance, stirred by the courageous patriarch, to thwart the wild grief. This is not a novel device in either theatre or cinema. But it is sustained and justified, even transfigured, by the total intentions of the film, as expressed in the movement and in the theme, and becomes an expression of social optimism. Georgia too has found hope! Significant it is, indeed, that he who provokes the dance against grief is the old patriarch. Youth is not a fact of age, youth — the symbol of courage and hope — is spirit and intelligence. As yet the Russian film has made no fetish of youth, and that is a sign of maturity. Maturity, profundity and the new energies released account for the excellence of the Russian kino. These positive forces will, I am sure, turn back the adulations that tend toward a cult of the Russian film. The Soviet Cinema grows in variety and sensitivity.

The New Babylon

And as the Soviet Cinema grows it comes to new problems and develops new viewpoints. *The New Babylon*, a film upon the Paris Commune, seeks "the temperament of the Paris Commune." I have said "seek" because I find that the particular attitude is too much one of caricature and the treatment too much the sketch to impart the "temperament." The historical statement is over-reduced. The tonal qualities are on the surface. I do not object to the instructions the graphic arts may give the cinema. The motion picture has sources in the entire experience of mankind. But what I desire is that the film, as yet, shall seek profounder instructions than satisfaction with tones.

Yet I cannot withhold my admiration of the consistency of the attitude and the tonal qualities. There is a variety in the attitude and in the pictorial continuity. The latter draws upon different mediums and upon the impressionist painters: Manet, Degas . . . and the arch-sentimentalist Carrière. Indeed, it is amazing how the latter's painting, seen always through a mist, become a portion of the film and lose their sugar-sweetness. No previous film has quite approached *The New Babylon* in the richness of tones, the blackest of blacks, and the arrangements of blacks with grays and whites. I have never seen such filming of black against black! This alone, considered as a new tentative in the Russian kino, illustrates the aesthetic poise that must be evolving in the U.S.S.R. German and American studio lighting become amateurish and drab.

The intention of the film was evidently to satirize the gross superrefinements of the Paris of that era, and incidentally to refer the satire to the same evidence prevailing today. Criticism, with sympathy, is dealt the vacillating artist-leaders of the Commune. There is a logic that cannot be denied here, but its total effect is of an heroic picnic. Sophistication can produce a form of stylized acting, as it has done well here; it may, unexamined by depth, produce an over-simplification which is close to falsehood. Too much is omitted. The picture might have been made after following Jean Renoir's film of Zola's *Nana*. The performance of the soubrette is much like Catherine Hessling as the sexual slut, but I – against all condemnations of the latter – find her performance more structurally firm and intensive. The problems and their tangents provoked by *The New Babylon* could fill a book. That is contribution enough. I urge everyone to examine this detaining film for himself.

NEW MASSES,
January, 1930.

THE OLD AND THE NEW

The third period of the Soviet kino begins! The first period, still persisting in occasional films, is the period of *Polikushka,* the plight of the individual; the second period which will recur in the third, is the period of *Potemkin* to *Storm Over Asia,* the period of the physical and the retrospective. The vigor of this second period endows the film of the third with essential health. Into this sound body, upon its firm strength, is built the new kino of reflection and prospect, education toward the future.

The film which proclaims this new era is *The Old and The New,* (*The General Line*), the General Peasant Policy tract by Eisenstein. Yes, a tract — upon tractors. Eisenstein was confronted with a problem which differed entirely from the compact moment of *Potemkin* or the historical canvas of *Ten Days.* He was to make a piece of social agitation that would stimulate to action and that would be informative of what the new collective peasantry would gain by rejecting individualism.

He was talking to a people of simple and immediate motivations, of not fully criticized suspicions and of certain precise experiences. He was giving them also a moving picture and they, of simple backgrounds, would want a picture that entertained with folk-simple drama. Their logic was a narrative logic, an elementary sequential logic of ideas expressed in a logic of images. Eisenstein's intention was to produce by this expression of ideas in images a logic of dialectics: *The Old and The New*! This film is a first statement of the endeavor to bring the philosophic element into the cinema, an endeavor Eisenstein promises to realize fully in his rendering of Marx's *Capital.*

The problem: an educational end, an agitational conviction, a simple narrative, a folk mood . . . to be made into a film. How was it done?

Thus: the philosophy, or ideological intention, is not kept a thing apart, but converted into the persuasive, folk narrative. Once having recognized and established the problem, the director determined upon a structure. It is the structural soundness and variety of *The Old and The New* that makes it a film superior to *Fragment of an Empire,* which has the elements of the Eisenstein film but lacks its structural rhythmic coordination.

Machinery and the bull-progenitor are the impetus of the film. They are the subject's concentration-points and the film's pivots. How immediately Eisenstein transmits the problems to the peasants! In their terms, in their experience.

The bull is to be wedded to the heifer. This is the splendid ritual of earth. The community garlands the bride and Fomka the groom. The guests wear garlands. And the black kitten, the bridesmaid, wears too a wreath. The marriage is fulfilled. The record on the screen is masterly in camera-alertness and impact-mounting. The gaiety of the preliminaries moves leisurely to a fierce accumulation in the rush of the bull and the cow rearing to receive him.

But the kulak bribes peasant stool-pigeons to poison Fomka. Gloom, despair weigh upon the community. Martha Lapkina, the film's bright-eyed symbol of the collective, falls upon the black earth weeping the death of Fomka. The calf nestles to her: he is hope!

The peasants have just participated in an ignominious religious ritual, from which they have arisen to suspect the priest. From this agitation to the agitation of the agricultural director they go, suspicious of all that distance, heaven or Moscow, sends. Heaven sent a black-frocked priest and a humiliating ritual. Moscow sends a talkative man and — a suspicious milk-separator. The milk-separator invites, however, curiosity as well as suspicion, and when its entrails move, its udders pour — *Abundance!* Martha bathes in the benediction of *Milk.* The clouds burst and pour *Milk!* Eisenstein repeats in the suspensive and glorious movement of the separator's mechanism the success of the Potemkin's getting underway. But here it has more than a moment's meaning: it is the future, the new world.

A tractor is bought. Eisenstein does not spare a third enemy of the people — kulak, priest, bureaucrat — the clerk who holds his soul together with the red-tape. But he gets back as soon as he can to the tractor.

The operator of the tractor has dressed himself in an aviator's helmet, goggles, wind-breakers, celluloid collar and ties askew. But tractors are run otherwise. The peasants, their doubt substantiated, return to the hut and the horse. Martha stands by. The chauffeur removes his coat, his hat, his goggles; he is in shirtsleeves, under the tractor. The trouble is discovered. He needs a cloth. Rip goes Martha's skirt. She submits laughing, masking her eyes for modesty. Virginal Martha, fecund Martha! The tractor moves and Martha rides with the engineer. Hoo-rah! a line of trucks is tied onto the monster. The peasants leap upon their steeds, and the procession winds over the furrows. ALL RUSSIA IS TRACTOR-BLOSSOMING!

The film is a film of wit, folk-humor, shrewdness, optimism, clarity and point, ingenuity, a structurally harmonized duality of viewpoint: of the objective builder and thinker, and of the narrative. It forestalls the objection of two different approaches by its integration of the two toward a single end: COLLECTIVISM! *The Old and The New* is of greatest importance to the future, not only of the Russian film, but of the world's cinema. It proclaims the period of reflection and prospect in the Soviet kino, and enters, as a contributor, the evolving era of the cinema of the world, the cinema of contemplation and inference.

NEW MASSES,
May, 1930.

THE SILENT ENEMY

There are two things interesting about this film: its success with audience and reviewer, and its miserable failure as a motion picture and representation of primitive struggle. Here is a movie being shown on Broadway that isn't a talkie, save for the banal sycophantic foreword by the Chief, and has no familiar stars, and yet it has clicked with picturegoers and commentators. So much for its success. As a film, its failure is complete.

I can think of nothing good to say for this production, unless it be the initiative of the group that made it. The film was made independently by people who had nothing better to do and did that badly. We are told this is true Amerindian stuff. It may be. I have seen this aboriginal injun motif in the aboriginal western movie. Stuff of films is its treatment: its penetration and organization. The attitude of romanticizing the primitive but not presenting the energies of his struggle is typical job-showman's incompetence and ignorance. In this instance the incompetence is accentuated by the pretentiousness of the production.

The film does not show the least understanding of stress or symbol. The stresses of the struggle are placed erringly. There is not the necessary sustained tension of hunger leading up to the satiation after the caribou hunt. Hence the full effect of the satiation is lost. We are told, but not made to experience, the fierceness of the trek and the winter. The movement of a pair of legs with the superimposition of literary legends, subtitles is not stark energy. A thin curve of marchers in the distance — trite image which the prim audience applauds from habit — is not a trek. The symbols are incorrectly chosen, they do not convey the intention — of hunger, terror, doom, recurrent battle for survival. The makers of this film have not the least suspicion of the moods of pictorial tones — the values of gray and white — or of pictorial frames — rectangles and circles. The photography lacks all essential qualities. And even if the documentary material had been successfully converted into the structure of the film, the picture would have been defeated by the reduction of the entire struggle to "the eternal triangle," and personal enmity — concepts of bourgeois society and its "dialectics."

A caribou rush had been advertised. When it appeared the audience sighed "Ah!" and applauded. But this is not the elephant stampede of *Chang*. There is absolutely no camera point of view or composition to effect impact, danger, battle. Blunt literalness only. It might have been shot in the safe corral of a stockyard for all its excitement. The fight between the mountain lion and the bear contains a degree of fascination. This is not in the least due to the perspicacity of the film's makers. Their lack of insight keeps the fascination down to its minimum. Absolutely no feeling for the organization of the images, what the Russians call "montage."

Epic stuff? Yes, even if epic stuff that is by now hackneyed. To make a competent film one needs technology. That much America has achieved. To realize epic material, philosophy — understanding — is needed with the technology. That is still lacking in the American movie, Hollywood-made or Park Avenue-made. *The Silent Enemy* lacks both technology and philosophy.

NEW MASSES,
July, 1930.

TWO PRISON FILMS

The movie is symptomatic of America at its lowest level. It expresses the social mind at that level. The lowest level of the social mind, the least critical level, is the dominant stratum. Dominant as it is, it defends itself by evasions, by the shifting of the burden of guilt. These two films inspired by the social turbulence of prison-breaks are expressions of this shifting of the charge.

We have here two films, the first a product of one of the best American factories, the other of one of the worst: shop-competence, incompetence. But the minds revealed are identical. Both are frivolous even facetious. The burden of the guilt has been shifted by shifting the emphasis of the story. In *The Big House* society is accused by the warden, who points to the overcrowded cells as a foreboding; by the genial guard, who warns against putting the boy, whose crime is running down someone with his auto, with the two hardened criminals, and by the machine-gun murderer, who revolts at the food, provoking the entire convict body into an outburst and himself into solitary confinement. In the first two instances, the charges are only remarks, they do not get into the woof of the film, informing it, giving it meaning. As in *All Quiet,* the director has not sought to make the entire film the vehicle of the attack, but restricted the attack to some verbal statements. Dialogue cannot carry the mood, the film as a whole is the vehicle. The accusations therefore remain incidents — passing and unemphatic. Whatever suggestion of social guilt they contain is dissipated by the events of the story, and their treatment.

We are not made to experience the accusations: the overcrowding, the bad food. The bad food doesn't argue in itself, as did the maggotty meat of *Potemkin*. It does not explain the outburst. The camera does not expose its filth. There was no attempt to construct an unavoidable mood, because there was no wish to construct it, and no ability. The film lacks *temper,* it is another American jest.

The film, concentrating as it does on the major action in the prison, might have been a powerful experience. But the predilection for the comic spirit at once lightens the intensity. The concentration of the theme is severed by moving the action for a period out of the prison into the street, the girl's bookshop and home. The film should have been contained in the close environment of the prison, unrelieved by whimsicality or horseplay or the soft tone of the letter informing the murderer of his mother's death. The film should have been *intensive,* gray, cumulative. Its model might well have been *The Passion of Joan of Arc*. We should have felt the slow process of festering, monotonous, oppressive, bursting in the riot — just as the mob-explosion released the accumulation within the dungeon at Rouen. The film, as an art, is a progressive medium moving toward intensiveness. It is a process, not simply a story. But to create a process in the movie requires awareness of the process of society, and the mind of the movie — the American movie — does not possess awareness.

Numbered Men is an incompetent *Big House*. The idyllic flavor is at once imparted: the farmer's dame who serves the road gang doughnuts, the loyal girl who has taken a job at the farmhouse to be near her lover, wrongly imprisoned. The typical formula is carried out: one of the prisoners is advised his wife is dead — this serves as an impetus to escape (as in *The Big House*); there is a killer here too who boasts, like the murderer in the Metro film, of his prowess (*The Hairy Ape* motif) — the difference is that in the Metro film we are made to like the whimsical brute whereas in the Vitaphone masterpiece he is the nemesis. He is, in fact, the instrument whereby the guilt is shifted from society. Indeed, there is nothing we can hold against society, save the incarceration of the innocent boy. This blemish is eradicated when another prisoner confesses to the crime, sacrificing himself to an extended sentence. So are problems solved. The prison itself is more idyllic than *The Big House*. In the latter the warden complains of 3000 men brooding in idleness, though we never get to feel it. In *Numbered Men* there is a big sunny room where a convict, if he is good, may play the harmonica or read *The American Mercury*. The moment of the riot is brief. It isn't a riot, it's a dash. The prisoners hunt for the runaway to preserve the honor system. Some fifteen years ago Fox produced

The Honor System, a more exciting film on the theme. It was a popular motif in those days. In 1905 Vitagraph manufactured *Escape from Sing-Sing* . . . and a quarter-century later we find the film factories issuing stuff that shows no advance in point of view. The mind of the movie is even more callow now.

Callowness has more than orthographic resemblance to callousness. The society that is callow in its cinema is callous in its attitude toward imprisoned men. The audience that is amused by the spectacle of men being marked and numbered is the society that kills Sacco and Vanzetti, imprisons for life Mooney and Billings, railroads the leaders of the workers in New York, North Carolina, Georgia and California. It is that society which produces *The Big House* and *Numbered Men*; another society produces *In Old Siberia,* that poignant lyrical Soviet film of the plight of the political prisoners in Czarist Russia. As the days go on, the American movie will get farther and father away from the film exposing the social evils. Once it was possible to have *The Jungle* filmed, pictures of Czarist oppressions and anti-Semitism, movies condemning the exploitation of the poor farmer in the everglades of Florida. American society becomes more concentrated, more protective. The movie becomes more concentrated, more symptomatic. A counter-process is at work, the revolutionary threat. This intensifies the instinct for self-preservation in the mind of the dominant class. The movie reveals the intensification. All elements of vital criticism are eliminated, but there is one criticism that is ever-present, the film itself. It is the business of the critic to present in full this evidence of which the movie speaks.

NEW MASSES,
August, 1930.

THE FILM AND THE WAR

My memory of the film of the war goes back to the blithe Wilsonian era of "watchful waiting." The Woodrovian hypocrisy beamed into existence *War Brides,* which was made into a film by Herbert Brenon. The present parleying era finds its movie voice in three films drawn from literary sources. Again Mr. Brenon, in *The Case of Sergeant Grischa,* expresses the pacifist's pity. I do not need to make any comparison between the literary source of the war film and the film itself. However divergent they may be, their pacifist suggestions bespeak in common the incomplete condemnation of war as a social expression. These suggestions play into the social mood that accepts the fraudulences of capitalist conferences on disarmament. *Sergeant Grischa* is presented as a pathetic tale of an individual with reflections of this pathos in the people who encounter him. The director undoubtedly sympathized with the plight of the escaped prisoner, just as many years ago he sympathized with the plight of the war bride. But sympathy with a single plight or individual cases is not sufficient when mass plights, social agonies, human debacles thunder.

Films, like other works of art, convey experiences as well as sensations. The final experience of a film is determined by the *temper* of the presentation. And that is where war films fail. Either in the temper of the particular story of the human relationships involved, or in the temper of the treatment. The failure of *Journey's End* is that of the particular human relationships selected out of the mass and maze of the war. The failure of *All Quiet On the Western Front* is that of the temper of the treatment.

Journey's End treats of the aristocratic milieus of the war, the officers' quarters in the dugout. It is an Englishman's play indeed, a product of a society in which a servant is an idiot and a public-school boy (rich man's son) a gentleman. James Whale, who directed the film, photographed the play with a few insertions of outdoor sports like trench raids, etc. The horrors of war are revealed in the breakdown of three officers, the killing of two and the description of a cockroach race — the whimsical English! No one can call this reproduction of a play a moving picture. There is not even the primary sense of how to film a group and its dialogue to make these exciting, rather than blunt, recording.

All Quiet On the Western Front directed by Lewis Milestone is competent work. There are splendid scenes of the charging soldiers, leaping soldiers, men caught in the barbed wires. There is a good moment of rapid flashes of faces in bold. Unlike the dialogue of *Journey's End,* the speech of *All Quiet* is constructed with some attention to intervals, to time and even emotional quality. But directorial competence is not enough. The temper is lacking.

Lacking the informing temper, the film lacks the structure it demands, the heroic structure. The successions of episodes defeat any possibility of a pervasive experience. A sequence of agony is followed by a sequence of comedy trying to be sardonic — the Maxwell Anderson *What Price Glory?* influence. The agony and the "relief" are discharged with equal force and reach the same pitch, so that the experience is neutralized. The final experience is one of no experience.

What does this mean basically? The absence of a critical mind, the absence of a concern for the inferences of the material. That *Sergeant Grischa* contains a character who says that the one way out is revolution means simply that such a character is in the film. Could not Brenon have extracted, not the language of this character, but the implication of this language, to lend a charge to this film that would have forced it above the level of pathos into something more devastating? My question is deliberately naïve. Brenon is not a sentimentalist expressing a society that criticizes its utterance but not the provocation. The opportunist, president or producer, capitalizes this sentimentality in a parley or a picture. This description is true, not solely of a nation; it describes all of capitalist society.

There is one literary work which, were capitalist society sincere in its pacifism, might be made into a film which would grip the inners of the spectator: Andreas Latzko's *Men in War.* But all war-films are sympathy-films, and become, especially among unsuspecting intelligences, partisan-films. The audience of *All Quiet* accepts the German soldiers as its protagonists. Its heroes are in the war. Amid the ominous, the suspensive, the fascinating! Men are marshalled and mangled and murdered, but the carnage is not offensive, it is attractive, it stirs participation. The drowning sailors in the English chronicle-film, *The Battle of the Falkland Islands* [*sic*]* did not dispell the irresistible ambiance of battle.

I have suggested *Men In War* as a film. The movie is an intensifying medium: it concentrates ecstasy, mystery, horror. War films to date, despite well-meaning sentimentality, have concentrated the fascination of battle. Only the Russian film has concentrated the horror. The concentration has been given social and structural significance by inclusion in a material of which the war is but a part. And these concentrations are unforgettable: *The End of St. Petersburg, Fragment of an Empire, Arsenal.* The French film, *Verdun: Visions of History,* for all its *"poésie,"* achieves import because it has treated the non-military aspects of the war, the shattered meadows, the refugees, and given to the treatment a brooding temper, an ache.

NEW MASSES,
June, 1930.

* [Gen. Ed.]: The film intended here and on page 456 is *The Battles of the Coronel and Falkland Islands.*

TURKSIB

The schedule was 1931, but the Turkestan-Siberian Railroad, under the supervision of our compatriot and comrade, Bill Shatov, was completed in 1930. Turin, a Soviet film director, built an ode of mobile images to Turksib, the regenerator of Asiatic lands. For it was more than a railroad Bill Shatov built. The schedule, a part of the epochal Five-Year Plan, called for a release of productive, meaning social, energies. Turin has composed a cinema ode to this construction and release.

Turksib is a unity of motifs that are repeated in the progressive structure at exactly-timed intervals. Havoc follows lull, storm precedes subsiding: one anticipates or resolves the other in a constancy of rhythm. Flows are paralleled, each lending its quality to the other: water, cotton on the loom, cloth rolling like water, wood on the lathe, smoke, even wooly sheep. Water is the image-symbol of flow and cessation. The film opens in the drought. The land is cracked with aridity. Man and beast watch, brooding, for moisture. The mountain frees the snow. Moisture trickles, ripples, increases in volume and force, a torrent. The land is quenched of thirst. The creviced tongue of the land is healed by water. But not all of the land, and for long. There is not enough water – lull, the cottonfields are athirst. The looms are dry. Men brood, watching for water. All this anticipates the railroad. When the locomotive enters, one feels that all which preceded was the train, so physiological is the process as it culminates in the first locomotive. The sandstorm, terrific and magnificently filmed, is the rush toward the new protagonist, the railroad. Here is a "hero" never obstreperous but always felt. About it life flourishes. "Old and new" meet amicable in the regeneration of the old by the new. Old men study the new images — that liberate them from the thrall of drought, simoom, havoc and lull.

This is a film entirely of structure. It is more absolute than the most absolute of machine-films of a bridge, a press, a turbine. To enjoy it is to enjoy the interplay and repetition of motifs, of constructed harmonies and contrasts. By this construction, the objectivity of the film, inevitable in its documentary material, transcends the mere document. All the documentary materials are assembled to a preconceived end: the release of productive energies, the fusion of the old into the new. The engineers meet the natives and are received by them with bowls of water to quench the thirst. A native child presses the klaxon. The weird utterance of the horn scatters the children. Laughter joins native with engineer, old with new. The children chase after the motorcar. Not perpetrated dramatics but more than mere document.

Rock is unyielding. Mountains must be severed to join Turkestan with Siberia. Rock is to be blasted. Awaiting the explosion all things are lulled. Men, camel, flagpost, flag. Physiologically by this lull we are led in to the explosion: moment of release from lull, moment freeing the road to the rail. Movement ensues. Not melodramatic motion. But graceful bob of camel — into the impact of machines, the sweep of bridges, the U.S.S.R. in construction!

I have called *Turksib* an ode. It is more than an ode. It is more than ode, though it does not become the epic its momentum strives after. This is by no means frustration. An epic tells of a deed that has been accomplished. The road was not yet finished when Turin made his film. But within the ode the urge of the epic suggests the heroic proportions of Turksib, the Five-Year Plan and their significance beyond statistics. The sense of the epic is the *temper* of *Turksib,* product of the Soviet industrial program and Soviet *montage,* the art of the Soviet cinema. Virtuosities of multiple images liquidly fused in the same frame, piston gliding on oil, spinning mechanisms, camera angles, become structural elements and social persuasions.

New Masses,
June, 1930.

STORM OVER ASIA and LINCOLN

In the first chapter of the history of the art of the motion picture, the name of David Wark Griffith will be important. He was the first to suspect the scope of the new medium, and, although the new devices he introduced were conceived by him solely as expedience, they have been utilized by other succeeding directors as experiences. These directors are mainly the Soviet artists. The American movie has not extended in the least the work of Griffith and his early contemporaries. Pudovkin, among the Soviet directors, has developed the early American film to its ultimate. *Storm Over Asia* is the culmination of the romantic technique of the Griffith-Western period. As a culmination or perfection of the primitive film it is a reflection upon the inertia of the American movie. As a perfection of the film of muscular impact, it is still unsuited in method to the profound material of the Soviet kino.

I first saw *Storm Over Asia,* intact, in Amsterdam. I have seen it three times since. My reaction has been always the same. An exciting film, which beats any American audience film. It makes the boasted dramatic technique of America appear a schoolboy's exercise. Griffith's *Lincoln,* in comparison with it, is a mooning idyll. Yet both Pudovkin and Griffith suffer commonly from a sentimentalism which expresses itself in bad "figures of speech" and oversimplification. The theme in Pudovkin's film is tremendous: imperialism. In Griffith's film it is trivial: the Lincoln of the least of the epigrams — a Lincoln that any child beyond the fifth grade in school would disown. Pudovkin, like every Soviet director, had a social theme to convert into a dramatic instance. Griffith had a sentimental figure out of a fairy tale. In the particularization of the theme, the film itself, Pudovkin selected frequent symbols below the level of the theme, and stressed too ardently the personalities and their narrative, so that very often the theme — the implication of the narrative — is not perceivable in the occurrences. That is one reason the film, while possessing strength, physical strength, lacks poignancy, penetration. *China Express,* in contrast, while not grand, remains a more poignant, permanently appealing, film upon imperialism.

In Griffith we see what Pudovkin might have been in America 1910–30. In Pudovkin we see what Griffith might have been in the U.S.S.R. Griffith, possessing social sympathies, expressed these in platitudes on "tolerance" and "free speech," and read his American history in the terms of *The Clansman* (the Ku Klux Klan and the Confederacy, in whose army his father was a General*), and in the terms of the crudest Lincoln myths. His films in the past have been innocuous idylls and grandiose panoramas, allowing his distinction for his instincts of composition. *Lincoln* has everything of the sentimentally idyllic, and nothing of the grandiose. It is an unintelligent Drinkwater chronicle-play on the screen, despite Stephen Vincent Benét's hand in the scenario (why "despite"?). The fact that it draws tears is rather against it than for it. The pathos of a tremendous social occurrence should not be refined or lachrymose, but revealing. The social occurrence seldom gets a chance here. Slogans of spurious manufacture explain the motivations of the Civil War.

The legend of a people may offer as much substance for revelation as the actual unmythical source. But such revelation demands a critical understanding which alone assures a surpassing of the elementary myth. Griffith possesses no critical penetration. The nostalgia of a dessicate aristocracy seeps through the film: in the silly pretense with music to toleration of the black (what an hypocrisy after *The Birth of A Nation*); in the tiresome reiteration of the virtues of the protagonists — Lee especially, etc. Griffith, still bound to the conceptions of refinement and good taste (a tradition set by him by now noxious in the American movie), thwarted a player of more eloquent talents, Walter Huston. And the innovator of the silent film contributes nothing to the improvement of the garrulous. The simple-minded spectator will carry away with him an amiable sentiment toward North and South, emancipation and slavery, and the Union forever! The close, with Lincoln's monument, is a palpable bid for patriotism. Who says the American movie is against propaganda?

* [Ed.]: *Colonel* Jacob Wark Griffith

A last tribute: to Soviet photography in *Storm Over Asia,* as against the sickening "artisticalness" of the Menzies-Struss collaboration in *Lincoln.* To the authentic types (they become prototypes) in *Storm over Asia* as against the dubious histrionics of *Lincoln* (notice Abe Lincoln's lip-rouge). The selection of types among non-professionals has taught the Soviet director to select the authentic even among professionals.

These two films call forth speculations upon the nature of propaganda, which coincides with the nature of art. *Storm Over Asia* asks: "How much immediate impact, how much after-effect? Cannot what drives in too force-fully, just as easily drive out? Is not propaganda the accumulation of what is implied?" *Lincoln* says: "The less critical the propaganda, the less valid art it demands."

NEW MASSES,
October, 1930.

THE RACKETEER PARAMOUNT

The present hero, "good bad man," of the film is not the frontier racketeer of the Wild West. That was a rural contribution to American populism or mythology. This does not mean that the "good bad man" of the past no longer exists in the movie. On the contrary, the advance of the talkie has renewed the stay of that spurious man of courage. He is, to be sure, somewhat more sophisticated, and speech has bestowed on him the semblance of suavity. The city-fication ("civilizing") of America is making a boulevardier of the movie rustler. Even at that, he cannot compare with his 100% city cousin: the hootch-and-vice racketeer. The latter's romantic appeal is much more thoroughgoing. It is one with the emotion of patriotism.

The attraction of the white-hearted western blackguard was "the enchantment of distance" in time and place. The glorification of a moral moron like Billy the Kid, whose "saga" has been immortalized in the movie by King Vidor, is not so simple to condone, since Billy has not been sanctified with a love of the poor as has Jesse James. Are we getting tougher?

The sentimentalizing of a Dion O'Bannion, the florist-bandit of Chicago, and the glorifying of his opponent are a nostalgia towards the present. By reducing the theme of gang strife to a love triangle, the personal romance is heightened. The burden of the social guilt is shifted and dissipated. *Underworld,* Ben Hecht's roseate picture of why gangsters kill, transformed the Dion O'Bannion episode into a vindication of the American scoundrel and a benediction on the society that breeds him. Paramount produced *Underworld.* Fox, nosing for the direction of the business-wind, followed with a more insinuating *Dressed to Kill.* The racket of the racket-film is continuing in the vociferous movie, with Paramount leading in surer, and politer, accents.

Streets of Chance discovered the glib tongue for the racketeer movie. Arnold Rothstein became an altruist sacrificing himself for his brother's soul. A suavest of honorable gamblers — once these were localized on Mississippi boats — was presented in the person of William Powell, elegant and detached. Rothstein was vindicated, and, by inference, the New York police, Grover Whalen, Jimmie Walker, the President of the United States, Wall Street, and competitive society. Paramount was the producer of *Streets of Chance.*

The Lingle murder was anticipated by the Paramount company, through the prophetic Ben Hecht, in *Roadhouse Nights.* Not a word was whispered in it of the reporter's fraternal connections with his murderers. The slain newspaperman died for the glory of the *Chicago Blare,* the Amalgamated Press, and his honor as an immaculate conception — a servant of the people. The second reporter, foredoomed, taps his plight on the telephone — there's a geat deal of tapping in these States. The atmosphere of the liquor war, as pervasively imparted by the newspaperman, is a synthesis of the aroma of Scotch, the fragrance of love, the tang of heroism and danger, and never an ulterior stench.

And now we have reached the heights of the underworld — does one go up or down? — the lawyer. In *For the Defense,* another Paramount picture, William Powell, as smooth and self-contained and relentless as in *Streets of Chance,* portrays, we are advised, an attorney resembling the late W. J. Fallon, criminal lawyer. Mr. Powell is a completely criminal lawyer, though the film ennobles his crime to a sacrifice for a woman, and of the woman for him, and vindicates his support of murderer and thief as a love for the poor. A new Jesse James! The acute observation of fact is evinced in the lovely dame's words: "You know how juries hate a rich man!" It is this hatred of the rich by his peers, as the jury box sees equality, that will be expressed shortly in the election of a poor man out of Wall Street to our democratic presidency.

Underworld, Streets of Chance, Roadhouse Nights, For the Defense, are part of America's celebration of her corruption. They are all Paramount films. This is interesting, not because Paramount alone expresses the movie's portion in the American apology, but because Paramount, the best of the Hollywood shops, anticipates this expression and polishes the lie to a brighter, more insidious, gleam. Therefore Paramount is the best subject for a clinical study of the movie. Paramount gives us the theme-songs for the racketeer: *Underworld* — he did it for the girl! *Streets of Chance* — he did it for his brother's soul! *Roadhouse Nights* — he did it for his paper! *For the Defense* — he did it for the poor!

To this idol we must establish as a positive antithesis the authentic folk heroes of the class struggle. Dialectics against populism. This populism takes many forms: the racketeer paramount, Negro spirituals, the "each blow a caress, each caress a blow" treatment of the worker in the film. Either he is a swashbuckler, flattered by those who commandeer him; or he is a benighted soul being duped into a hatred towards those who love him. This latter attitude is today not so bluntly put; it has been more and more converted into forms of flattery and cajolery. Its history in the film is as old as the popularity of the film. First expressed in delusive aphorisms of loyalty — class-collaboration — by 1914 it was put forth more dramatically thus — I quote from the novelization of the Lasky film, *The Only Son*:

(Schmidt is an agitator)

"He knew Schmidt had been arrested several times in and about New York for attempts to blackmail contractors, and that he was suspected of complicity in a number of dynamiting outrages."

(Lasky was not concerned with exposing "misleaders of labor." This play by Winchell Smith was good movie stuff for Jesse Lasky because, while pretending an attack on a scoundrel, Jesse could disparage the validity of the claims of labor. It was necessary to soft-soap an "organized" group, therefore):

"The Unions were not to blame for Schmidt's power. The man was one who possessed unquestionable ability . . . The men trusted him . . . ."

(An admission):

"Schmidt managed, cleverly enough, to get a show of a reason on his side. He did not arbitrarily call a strike. But he managed to make the men believe that the profits of the plant were much larger than they actually were . . . ."

Should one begin to think that Lasky was truly attacking a labor-racketeer, like John Mitchell or some other eminent, the conclusion of the picture will dissipate that notion. The film terminates with a justification of scabbing, praised by the strikebreaker! In 1930 the labor-racketeer is another "good bad man" awaiting his panegyric in the film: he did it for the worker! There have been pictures recently just skirting the edge of that theme. Lasky's Paramount is again indicator: *Ladies Love Brutes*.

New Masses,
November, 1930.

SOIL

The director of *Arsenal,* that splendid effort toward a symbolic structure and a new logic of the motion picture, enters with *Soil* farther into the intensification of the film as the instrument of an idea. Here is a picture which, as a sustained attitude of a lyrical artist, is singular in its beauty. The sensibility for light-tones and for timing, a sensibility as accurate as a metronome, and an intensity of composition, in which mobile and immobile images collect into a song of death and birth, "old and new," create an experience of poignant plaintiveness. It is, as such, a thing perfect and exquisite.

And that is its failure. It extends the message of collectivism farther into the province of the reflective, whither the film the world over must inherently progress. But in moving to the reflective, it becomes too personal a meditation, it becomes introspective where it should be prospective. There is optimism here, certainly, and there is a statement of inevitable victory of life over death, the new over the old, the future over the past. The development of the process of the Soviet kino presents less Dickensian portraits of the enemies of society, they are more subtilized than those in Eisenstein's last film. But *Soil* has refined the sardonic too much, the irony is delicate and not provocative enough. Indeed, the entire film has a poignancy too plaintive for the intention and sense of its theme. It is not persuasive of man's will. It is a cathartic that purges one of active belief. A sense of "Earth takes – earth gives" remains. Condemnation is balanced by assuage, and the rain on the fruit washes away any residue of assertion. *Soil* is not what it should be, what the material theme demands of the aesthetic treatment, a stimulant to action. It is almost a reduction of a tremendous social material to a personal song, an elegy. It is too elegiac, although it is a surpassingly beautiful elegy.

Soil attests to the diversity of methods that will grow out of the Soviet kino having their roots in one soil: the Union of Socialist Soviet Republics. It attests to the fact of the fecundity of the Soviet film, of its continuous evolution, a process that has developed from an appeal directed at the visceral to an appeal reaching the higher nerve centers. It attests to the fact that "propaganda" in the Soviet film coincides with this climacteric progression, and becomes a more attenuated, more suggestive thing, bringing its message to an apex. Dovzhenko proves that the most physical of activities, a threshing machine in action, may be treated within a film contemplative and lyric, and become a temperament as well as a mechanism. Dovzhenko's failure is the failure of a singer who has chosen the wrong pitch. His success is the control of that pitch. To the art of the cinema, he contributes, as representative of the Soviet film, in the vanguard of the world's motion picture, further instruction in the use of realities as symbols in performance as an element of composition, in textures as emotion, in resonance or suggestion, in the true language of the film. *Soil* is the peak of the mute film, but it may also well serve the valid speech-film as a base. Where the intensification of the silent film concludes, that of the talking film begins.

New Masses,
December, 1930.

COUPONS and PRUNES

Unemployment has entered the movie as a motif! Surreptitiously, of course, through a crack in the back door. And it didn't stay long. In one of Paramount's typical shop-films — trade mark "Nancy Carroll" — the heroine finds her leading man on the street. He's been shot trying to achieve a *Stolen Heaven.* The lad has been a zealous worker, he tells Nancy, at the radio plant across the way, but just the same he was canned. Out of a job, and crazy to go slumming in Palm Beach or Bermuda — millionaire for a day stuff — he solves his unemployment problem by stealing $20,000 from his former boss. Nancy helps him evade the police. Off they go to the land of dreams on their 20,000 bucks, and we never are told they are anything but respectable, true to the Hays code, the evangelical bible of the movie. The code conquers all, the young people give themselves up, we are all redeemed.

Redemption is the keynote of every American film. Bourgeois society is a coupon. *Skippy* (Paramount) puts its bid across through the popularity of young children as players. It bridges class differences: the rich love the poor. The slums are locale for idyllic romance, sweetened with the salt of childish tears. The final romance occurs when Skippy's dad, the self-complacent board of health doctor, brings Sooky, the slum child, a dog to replace the dead Penny, and Skippy brings Sooky another new dog, and doctor dad liberates Shantytown from the dark decree of extermination, and when at last, the cantankerous nemesis, the proletarian dog catcher, is struck down with one blow from the fist of the petty bourgeois doctor, who has removed his eye glasses. The middle class is redeemed, the classes are equal, so equal, in fact, that a doctor is less of a sissy than a dog catcher. And this all takes place in a film dealing principally with pre-adolescents.

The thesis of the leveling and collaboration of the classes is recurrent in the movie. *The Millionaire* (Warner Brothers) presents the fastidious idol, George Arliss, as the golden rule industrialist — Henry Ford mebbe? — whom his workers weep to see going. You can't keep a good man down. The retired manufacturer gets himself a garage and conquers anew — there's no lace on his underwear! That's one leveling. Another takes place before the young partner, who doesn't know his co-garagist's real identity, can marry the millionaire's daughter. The young man asserts he is from a first family; the sale of the garage returns the lad to architecture, as prescribed by his college diploma. The movie is a ritual that purges everything it touches —purges everything of veracity and sense.

Fox film folk have gone thumbs down on all controversial matter. The hireling house managers are commanded to delete from the newsreels all "clips showing breadlines." The coupon-clippers don't mind the breadlines, they do mind the breadline "clips." The managers must delete also anything that might be even remotely construed as bolshevistic propaganda. This from a shop that has been manufacturing the shoddiest anti-Soviet films. It is said the thumbs down was provoked by the split reception to a picture disporting Mussolini. It was O. K. as long as the audience applauded, but when Il Duce was razzed, there was a murmur in the heart of Fox. The movie becomes increasingly self-protective. It is, after all, the response and agent of the class that produces it.

But a dilemma cleaves this class. Its worst enemy is its best friend. It fears the very source of relief for its critical condition. Therefore it boycotts a commodity it needs, wood pulp, from the Soviet Union. Therefore it torments itself with pictures of a monstrosity called the Five-Year Plan, which, at the same time, it tries to laugh down. A publisher recently said to me: "A couple of years ago, you couldn't sell a book on Russia." Now such a book is a best-seller, because American pockets are being agitated by the Five-Year Plan. And Pathé issues a series of newsreels on the Plan with Professor Counts at the microphone. Pathé with extra caution advises the audience the newsreels are impartial, that Pathé has absolutely no axe to grind. Further neutralization of the Soviet item is arranged for in the clip that follows — at one place, the Fish peddles the red herring!

Yet there will be those who insist the movie is no more than a "passing amusement." John P. Miller, officer in charge of a recruiting station in Philly, compliments the Fox film folk on their submarine picture, *Seas*

Beneath. In a letter to the Chief of the Bureau of Navigation, he says: "It is believed that its value as an aid to navy publicity is unquestionable." Enlistments in the U. S. Navy have been "stimulated materially" by the picture. Hasn't Fox any thumbs down on this propaganda? At the same time, Warner Brothers opens its studio to the Army Signal Corps to train officers in making talkies. Later a studio will be opened in the national capital for reserve officers. The film capital is teachers' training school. Vitaphone's chief engineer is a colonel, as well as an executive of the technical bureau of the Academy of Motion Picture Arts and Sciences. He is the professor in the technical phases for the officers' training. Interests — business and governmental — dovetail neatly in the house of Amusement. So neatly do they dovetail that the Coöperative Marketing division of the Department of Agriculture issues a film on the "lowly prune" which shows "the pickers at work, a happy" — oh so happy — "industrious looking group of young people." The government serves the Little Jack Horner who gets the plum and the public gets movies that are full of prunes.

New Masses,
May, 1931.

A SON OF THE LAND

The Soviet film is a process as far from having exhausted its energy as the society itself. In such a process there will exist ambitious and modest expressions, each contributing to the other. The modest expression is the norm.

Among the normal — or, as Tretyakov calls them, the formal — films is Edward Ioganson's *A Son of the Land.* While in the Soviet Union last fall, I saw a film by this director, *Life in Full Swing,* a picture of domestic life. I have spoken of this picture in the *Theatre Guild Magazine* for May. The good humor that we find in *A Son of the Land,* the unobtrusive good humor, was detectable in *Life in Full Swing.* The difference in nature, however, necessitated a different treatment for either film. Ioganson, it is apparent, has understood that — but he has not been as completely successful in his treatment of *A Son of the Land,* a more difficult enterprise. The interesting thing, however, is the evidence of the strong tradition of the Soviet film strengthening the weaknesses of Ioganson's work. Ioganson moves somewhat to picturesqueness — the miscalculated aestheticism of the studio — the Dovzhenko influence — but instead of completely collapsing into picturesqueness, he is rescued by what is by now a law of the Soviet film: authenticity — as expressed in the convincing types, the intensive relations between physiognomies, stern excerpts of landscape, the insistence upon the major experience. These qualities keep the normal film from being simply a routine film, for they require a very devoted study. The norm of the Soviet film is always superior to that of the American — however they may patently resemble each other. The resemblance should not betray us into making false demands on the Soviet film. For instance, it would be easy to say that Ioganson has not prepared his moments of crises adequately for suspense — as when the horses of the *beys* are to trample Aman, the rebellious *dekhan.* But this is not a film built upon the momentary crises of an individual. In its simple, modest way it is the narrative of the rise of a tenant peasantry against the overlord. Less heroic than *The End of St. Petersburg,* it is similar in its tale of the sharecropper Aman who unwittingly betrays his class, and is awakened by his deed to assertion. Less ambitious than *Old and New,* it carries the assertion into a victory over the sabotaging kulak, for the new power — collectivization. Over the dry land the new power flows from the dam built by the poor peasants with the help of the central government. As in *Life in Full Swing,* a sequence of suggestions follows in quiet order — church and kulak, the technical education of the backward people, the coöperation between the Red Army and the rebelling croppers, the vicious tenacity of the defeated class, the victory of folk. The race by Aman when he has released the *bey's* dam to water the lands of the poor peasants — a vibrant view of a laughing face, coats thrown upon the valiant as gifts of gratitude — may well symbolize the return of the rights of folk to the folk. The grant of cultural autonomy denied these native people is as equally a victory of the proletarian revolution as the abolition of the kulak. Ioganson, hardly a craftsman of the magnitude of Pudovkin, has succeeded better in incorporating the festival into the structure and spirit of the film.

The chief significance of *A Son of the Land* is its proof that the process of the Soviet film is a lively one, seldom deteriorating to beneath its norm, but collecting more and more strength — producing numerous new talents — as it moves. I have stated and hinted at several of Ioganson's failings. He needs to improve his sense of timing, sharpen perhaps his emphases, if he is to continue making films more epic than genre, free himself from the instincts of the studio frame. If he did not know this before he started, we may be sure he knows it now — for creation and criticism are in constant touch with one another in Soviet Russia, not solely the specialized criticism of the professional, but also the criticism of the alert worker. This fluidity of relationship is the chief guarantee of the artistic as well as political life of the U.S.S.R.

New Masses,
June, 1931.

LOST PARADISE: TABU

A film that purports to use autochthonous ethnographic materials with native actors must accept the severest of disciplines. The tradition of the American studio is a treacherous one for such films, since it betrays the authenticity by diluting it with sentimentalism — the studio stock in trade. To the extent that the film is distant from the studio it is likely to be successful. Vigilance is doubly necessary because of the literary tradition of nostalgia toward these lost paradises. It is significant that the motion picture has followed the South Sea recipe of the Frederick O'Brien treacle.

The discipline of the valid dramatic ethnographic film consists of a number of selections:

Of performer — the emphatic pronunciation of type;

Of attitude — the control of the idyllic;

Of narrative — the essence of the common experience. *Tabu* fails in each of these three selections. The performer, particularly the heroine, is a concession to the apperception and preference of the western white audience. Far more convincing types, handsome Gauguinesque maidens, appear incidentally in the film. In the selection of type, neither the extreme nor the compromise (the pretty) should be the test. The convincing type is the type structurally pliable and emphatic in its stamp or race or folk or character.

The film is extremely sentimental: it over-idyllizes the idyllic. The causes are several: American studio tradition which is the tradition of the American audience; German studio training which was the tradition of the late F. W. Murnau; the lyrical predilections of R. J. Flaherty. While the camera work, the tonalities, are the outstanding merit of *Tabu,* the quality that marked *Moana,* Flaherty's exquisite film, should not have informed *Tabu. Moana* was a concentration of ceremony within a brief stanza — it was a lyric in conception and treatment, in its very dimensions. But *Tabu* is a dramatic film in the plan of its scenario; planned, not as the tonal statement of a theme, but as the blueprint of a dramatic narrative to be filmed. As such, the idyllic should have been controlled, instead of pronounced and reiterated. At times the graphic compositions are bold and substantial. This is more often true when they are compositions of human beings than of natural setting. Possibly this is due to the German studio bias of Murnau. The Germans have seldom been able to depart from within the four walls and ceilings of the studio. The night scenes in *Tabu* are fearsome chromos with pulsating moons.

The narrative, the initial conception, of *Tabu* is another of those instances of seizure upon the most extreme, the most uncommon, the most exceptional, the most unimportant of native occurrences. Had the approach been through the avenue of experience, rather than of sentimental showmanship, the selection would have been from the quotidianal and most constant of the experiences of the society of the Society Islands, rather than from the trite archives of love forbidden. Murnau and Flaherty should have asked a number of questions to be answered in the film: How do these people live commonly? What are their means of livelihood? What are the social categories among them? What is the nature of their sorrows? How can these be classified for treatment — pathos or tragedy? The first part of the picture, the better part, possesses a physical heartiness, a sportiveness, conveyed in an undulating graph that never pauses. It is an achievement one might have been proud of in an earlier era of the film, although it comes even now as a relief from the tethered movie. The ceremonies flow along within the smooth current of the graph, rather than obtrude in the typical fashion of ethnographic remarks in most films. Had the original conception been profounder, less simplistic, more studious, Murnau-Flaherty might have achieved something more than an O'Brien vulgarization of a Roussellian* lost paradise.

The transition from Part I — Paradise — to Part II — Paradise Lost — is actually a collapse of what is most attractive in the first part. Without having established for Part II more than a formula of the corruption of innocence — the serpent enters the garden — Murnau and Flaherty lose the undulating flow and the fusion of data with narrative. I am not surprised

* [Gen. Ed.]: Rousseauan?

that one critic reacted to the film as bogus. This is not the first time a picture of native life has been ruined by a fabricated literary material. The desire to tell a simple, human, "eternal," universal story has betrayed many an excellent and sincere director who has been misled by the story to a neglect of the tanglible and meaningful experience of the native people. And since form is the conception informing the structure, the perpetration of a flatulent narrative, not relating the poignancies of a people, explains the tedium of the film as it progresses. A pretty girl emerging from tall leaves is much too much Botticelli – it is the tepid romanticism of the pre-Raphaelites.

The wish to emphasize paradise is a typical plaintiveness in the soul of the movie-man. It generally forgets that the paradisiac people have lives that are quite multiple in their simplicity. *Tabu's* failure is the failure of motion picture "art-industry" to respect the experience of a people as something to draw upon seriously for the theme and plot.

As an instruction in what the dramatic ethnographic film can be, when the viewpoint is sober and social rather than that of a romantic job to be put across. I make mention here of a Soviet film which will in time be released in America: *Salt of Swanetia,* the first picture directed by Kalatazov, a young Georgian. This picture, built intensively upon peaks of pathos toward the stature of tragedy, is assertive in its decrial of the enormity that consumes the Swans. Quince-kneed within *Tabu* there are suggestions toward which the entire film should have moved and thereby been enlarged, made heroic, positive, rather than defeatist in its quasi-pathos. Suggestions of revolt against tabus, suggestions of exploitation, of imperialism – *the* universal experience of an oppressed people – loiter weakly and incidentally within the film. These comprise the theme that should have informed *Tabu.*

CREATIVE ART,
June, 1931.

DIE DREIGROSCHENOPER

G. W. Pabst, Viennese at work in Germany, is among the exceptional talents of the European cinema. In the past, I have found these talents, as exercised in pictures purporting to deal with serious experiences, "unscrupulous," delighting in the glossary rather than in the text. The "ingratiating virtuosities" of the German kino are not always tolerable even in the Hollywood-Viennese trivia of Ernst Lubitsch. In Pabst's *Pandora* (after Wedekind) the camera-caress of surfaces, agile enough as *lichtspiel,* was a nonchalance that offended, rather than realized, the theme. I was chastised by the Pabst cultists for not detecting the "unscrupulousness" as "superconsciousness." Read "superconscious" as "distracted." Pabst films have seemed to be built less on thought than on afterthought. All the more reprehensible is this in a man of superior gifts – the most adult among German directors. He need not subscribe to the watch-me-as-I-apply-this-touch of a Lubitsch. Therefore it is with gratification that one discovers the compound cinema – of sound and sight – introducing the legitimate Pabst, the Pabst of integrated films of intelligence and character.

We have seen here three of his audible pictures: *Skandal um Eva, Comrades of 1918,* and *Die Dreigroschenoper.* The first was a small-town bit of mischief, rendered neither below nor above the pitch demanded. The second was a sensitive, poignant lyric of the war within the limits allowed by a society not drastic enough to disclose the war at its source. In *Die Dreigroschen Oper* we find a singular film within its own category, actually transcending the habits of that milieu.

Remotely based in *The Beggar's Opera,* its conception is upon as high a level of honesty and wit. Nominally, it is to be classed among the musical films. Actually, it steps over the boundary of such classification. The musical films cannot be said to have achieved more than the pleasure of a momentary excitation, hardly more than peripheral. Lubitsch's work is tantalizing enough, but Tantalus is no substantial prophet. The Germans have been the most consistently ingenious in their renditions, abetted by the proof that the tradition of the Viennese waltz is less wearying than that of the Broadway melody, however insipid its insinuation may be *per se*. At that one must admit that the one time the American movie diverted from literalness without injury was in the early musicals, such as those made for Fox by a Frenchman, Marcel Silver. But what was their consequence? In the German film *Liebeswalzer,* virtuosity ingratiates itself with dexterous "stunts." I do not like this word and seldom us it, but when the devices play their slickness apart from the suggestion of the food of the film itself, what other terms may be applied? The director himself need not be censured, for a lugubriously trite film has been relieved by the play of the inventions – they are the bid to the spectator and audience. The bid does not imprint itself as an insistence, and is as good as lost. The mind, in this case, is as wax to receive and as wax to retain.

Pabst informs his film with no immature or precious attitude. He employs no schematic rhetoric – the master of which is M. René Clair – but immediately establishes a profound structure which he sustains without a sag. Carrying an unusual narrative, articulated by authoritative players, the director builds a structure large and handsome. None of your stereotype German columns or billows of light – black, white, gray – so enjoyed by von Sternberg – but strong gray tones, without sentimentality. The music of Kurt Weill constructed for sensible – even meaningful – lyrics on stout measures, rounded with German vowels, r's rolled, p's exploded, songs recited, chanted, sung, is inextricable in the sobriety of the pattern, a sobriety that is always vivacious. The undertone of the film is cynicism, the overtone is sympathy – as completely achieved in the optophonic composition as was *Joan of Arc* in its composition of visual-motor images. The mention of the latter is not casual here. The bold intensities of *Die Dreigroschenoper* resemble those of *Joan* in their staunchness, their objectivity, their cleanliness. I am sure the Dreyer film contributed to the Pabst.

The usual curse of the German studio-mind becomes a veritable blessing here. The sense of studio-scope does not burden the film but disciplines, and is disciplined by, the sense of the normal setting, the environment of the persons of this drama. The lesson of *Joan* is grasped, a difficult one to apply, that of temporal extraterritoriality. The setting and costumes are of yesterday, of today — of London, of Berlin. They are proper to contemporaneousness rather than literal to factuality. They are totally in character, because the film has been built to incorporate them — from beginning to end. The care is minute; the bystander who appears for but a brief moment at the beginning is as memorable as the protagonist, Mackie Messer. The humor of the picture is in the structure — no gag leaping above the graph, no bribe of a clever superfluity. The humor is in the conception as realized in the structure — it is the humor of society, satire. The beggar chief sends the beggars against the path of the queen being feted. The suggestion here might have been invidious — revengeful individuals provoke mass rebellion; and the rebels are *lumpen*. But a suggestion is not contained in a single statement; it is imparted by the successive statements and by their interrelationship. The sullenness of the *lumpen* clothes them in the more honest garb of a people in sorrow. The chief cannot return them from the demonstration when he finds he had no basis for vengeance. They plow on stubbornly. The queen and the chief of police, all the festive ones, are scattered in consternation — they reveal their inferiority. The protestants sink into the shadows — so the film ends. In the laughter of Pabst there is bitterness. The beggar chief, racketeer chief, police chief join to direct the City Bank of Piccadilly — the satire is not incorrect, 1931. It is uncensored because it is in a film not apparently "serious." What is deleted for the larger audience is the marriage scene with the frightened clergyman and the climactic scene in the buxom brothel at Tunbridge, where Renoir and the picture postcard join for a hearty play. The self-protective movie will go no farther than a helpless pity. The directors of more vital conscience will need to obscure their indictments in the racketeer melo or *Die Dreigroschenoper*. The Pabst film is peak.

CREATIVE ART,
July, 1931.

HOLLYWOOD LOOKS AT WAR

The Laemmle who professed altruistic heartache in *All Quiet,* followed with a series in which war is a slapstick holiday. This inconsistency is altogether consistent — with the nature of an "art-industry" that is response and agent of the dominant class. The career of Director Herbert Brenon is to the point. He served the feminist-pacifist dish, *War Brides,* before America's entry in the World War. In 1917, when Russia was threatening defection, he perpetrated *The Last of the Romanoffs,* where Rasputin is the villain, the Czar a duped innocent, and the *pogromchik* of Tzaritzin, now Stalingrad — the "mad monk," Lliodor, "in person" — the hero. The film was directed against the Kaiser, "the Rasputin of Europe," and the Bolshevik. In 1930 Brenon turns out *The Case of Sergeant Grischa,* another load of pacifist slop.

The business of "art-industry" carries out the dictates of the central conscience in a patriotic week. No politics in the sinnema, says Will Hays, but RKO celebrates Patriotic Week for the enlightenment of its patrons. Our noble Vice-President, a descendant of an Indian Chief — it's always a Chief — tickles the RKO into making a week out of Independence Day. That means a week of radio, film and vodvil — the concentration is complete, "the mobilization of the entire field of amusements," RKO's public relations bureau ties up the patriotism with State governors, patriotic and civic (virtue) societies, American Legion Posts and outposts. Says V-P Curtis to Pres. Brown of RKO, re last year's enthusiasm: "Your wholehearted acceptance of this suggestion and coöperation in the movement resulted in a tremendous demonstration of an entire week of flag flying . . ." Flag waving.

The Fox company has made a special anti-Soviet drive. Paramount in *The Last Command* — the work of von Sternberg, to whom was assigned *An American Tragedy* in preference to Eisenstein — indirectly attacked the Soviet. But Fox has always been blunter. *The Spy,* circulated diligently to family audiences — it was shown a number of times in and around "Red" 14th Street — is a direct invitation to murder Soviet officials. I am told Fox had a special Russian advisor for this film, a white guard imported from Paris. The sole authenticity in the film is the Red Army uniform.

The film relates of the emigrés in Paris. Tcheka spies listen in. The Grand Duke — never once visible to the audience — becomes the more awesome by revealing his presence only with his arm and hand. This apotheosis is a theatrical trick toward emotional effect. The pictures intends more than "passing amusement." Someone must go to Moscow to assassinate Citizen X, the leader of the Tcheka who, we are told, will not allow the emigrés' families to leave the U.S.S.R. The sympathy is all with the emigrés, who, for no fault of theirs, are being persecuted. The noble young Captain risks his life to do the deed, which ain't, according to Fox, so dirty. He goes because he has left behind him in Moscow a wife and son.

Nobility just oozes out of the pores of this movie. The nobility of the invisible Grand Duke, the Captain, his wife, the son, the waifs. On the other side there is only ignobility or the coldness of steel. The Soviet "police" pursue the waifs. Several fall to death from the housetops. Anything to increase the horror of the Soviet "regime." So noble, in contrast, is aristocracy that the wife willingly becomes the hostess in a state gambling-house because the money goes to succor the homeless waifs. The film is gooey with every vile sentimentalism calculated to influence a simple-minded and uninformed audience.

The motivation behind the picture is explained in the identities of the members of the Fox directorial board. They include: the president of the Utilities Power and Light Corporation; chairman of the governing committee of the Chase National Bank; the son-in-law of Andy Mellon who is, at the same time, a director of the U. P. Railroad; Corny Vanderbilt; the prexy of the Central Trust Company of Illinois; other bankers, industrialists, etcetera. The interlocking of control means a unity of purpose, and the imminent purpose is war — against the Soviet Union.

The existence of a Workers' Film and Photo League and of a Film and Photo Commission of the Workers' Cultural Federation should afford a means of combating the suggestions and invitation of a film like *The Spy.* In the July number of *Worker's Theater,* I have included among the tasks awaiting the League "the use of methods of direct action, boycott, picketing, against the anti-working class, anti-Soviet film." Sooner or later we shall need to become active in our opposition to the monopolized motion picture where it is used invidiously. We ought not delay in circularizing the workers upon movie-manoeuvres of a reactionary nature. We should start in at once upon "the education of the workers and others in the part the movie plays as a weapon of reaction . . . in the U. S. A.; and . . . as an instrument for social purposes – in the U.S.S.R."

NEW MASSES,
August 19, 1931.

MAEDCHEN IN UNIFORM

Among the experiences that entered into the German consciousness after the War and the Inflation was childhood. The new German film, when presenting the child or the young man or woman, has seldom betrayed its material. This love and respect for childhood is a tangible thing for the cinema. It encourages the use of children in mass, and that is always an opportunity for richest expression. Like the Soviet film treatment of the child, the German tends toward the singular through the plural, the individual personality expressive in the mass personality. The French film, like the French adult, is indifferent t. childhood and therefore considers the child either as decorative or as some single instance in an exceptional circumstance. Occasionally, as in *Poil de Carotte,* this has produced a picture of merit. The American movie sees the child as a manipulated spectacle into which a concern for either childhood or the immediate child seldom enters. As for adolescence and youth, we have not yet been favored by Hollywood with an entity that speaks the serious voice of young manhood or young womanhood, although the faintest of whispers is heard in a film like *The Age of Consent.* And whenever one of the elder actors comes down some years in a portrayal (this procedure is less common today than in the Pickford era), it is to offend the image of youth with simpers of cuteness and hoydenish hilarity. There is no one in America comparable to Greta Mosheim in Germany, who, though twice the age of the young women she portrays, never sullies their sorrows nor parodies their joys. It is the Pickford era that has given our present-day young actresses their distasteful coyness, as it is a Greta Mosheim who has set a precept of fidelity for the young women who are their age in German films. This feeling of entity is sensible and sensitive in *Maedchen in Uniform*. It is no Earl Carroll lounge-and-negligée version of life in a seminary, no Hollywood chafing-dish curriculum.

Maedchen in Uniform is a product of the newer film tendency in Germany. Coöperatively produced, it belongs to that sphere of the German *kino* not dominated by the nationalistic *aktiensgesellschaft,* concentrated in Hugenberg's U.F.A., now devoted to *bockbier* and *blutwurst, kostum* and *kaiser*. The important films issuing from Germany are the work of energies not accepting the defenders of the past. *Maedchen in Uniform,* while the mildest of these films, is another proof that only from a progressive declaration can good films come. This should be instructive to Hollywood in its present spasm of a "greater show season."

Girls in Uniform, telling, as it does, of constrictions in a school for daughters of army officers, the love of a girl for one of the teachers, a beautiful woman who defends childhood against the arbitrary discipline of the school, is a film intensive in theme and setting. The sense it imparts is of a single tight event, life in this repressive environment, that does not move on or off the screen but transpires within its rectangular frame. Films are usually expansive, seeming to cross horizontally into and out of the picture. The essence of this German *lichtspiel* is not expansiveness but intensiveness: that is its structural idea. That is the principle the director, Leontine Sagan, and the supervisor, Carl Froelich, have recognized as method and have hesitated to develop.

I say "hesitated" advisedly. The makers of this attractive picture, this modest, almost chaste film, were cognizant of the intensive nature of their material, of an accumulation within a non-expanding area that is to burst finally in the attempt of the girl Manuela to leap to death from the staircase. This is Leontine Sagan's first picture, and she must have found caution in her self-advice and those of a good German studio-director, Carl Froelich. Her work takes no risks and perhaps better so: modesty is preferable to virtuosity. Only a very mature and profound director could have exceeded the picture at its present level and not have fallen into mere ingratiating artifice. German studios have known such spurious achievement often: *kitsch* it is called.

The archetype of intensive cinema is *The Passion and Death of Jeanne d'Arc,* of which the makers of *Maedchen in Uniform,* the latter film indicates, were not unaware. The instructions of *Joan* might have been read more zealously, if not followed to the maximum of that film itself, since *Joan* was an objective tragedy permitting a simultaneous appreciation of its structure and its drama. *Maedchen* is more subjective without being completely so: it asks for a less severe and less persistent divulgence of its plan, and calls for no such stark sense of oppression as *Joan*. Its explosion is not to be historic nor quite so inferential nor so conclusive. The girl is oppressed unto death but does not die; the principal of the school walks away, her shoes creaking as before, under the burden of the tragedy the girls, adoring Manuela, have frustrated. Plaintiveness may enter into *Maedchen* more frequently than in *Joan*: there are differences in pitch, in the limits of severity and poignancy. But, once establishing these differences, the artist finds in the archetype two instructions, two available elements: the relation of physiognomies, the relation of person to object. In its sustained caution, the genuine good taste and respectability that will lead most observers to rate it superlative, *Maedchen in Uniform* does not make enough use of the medium to intensify the relationships, the identities and contrasts among the teachers, among the students, and among teachers and students. The film many times starts to do this, then halts, and entrusts the network to the good sincere playing of sympathetically chosen and endowed players. The direction should have extended this sympathy by the selection possible to the cinema through the emboldened image intensively composed. Texture, light angle, pieces of physiognomy should have been more exploited. Similarly the relation of the persons — the subjective element — to the school's environment, its minutiae — objective element — should have been more explicit and more often present. And, since this is a film compounded of the visual image and speech, more intensive use of utterance should have been made in relation to the dissection of physiognomy, especially to abet the facial accord between the teacher and the girl. One senses in these two physiognomies that there should be a fervid mutual attraction, and this sense should have been analyzed and built upon. Voice tonalities should have been differentiated and bound with the visual pattern and the personalities. Synchrony should have worked in with the details of physiognomy, the disproportion, speech not literally but rhythmically placed, should have enriched the composition for the final experience. To many people the film is meritorious and yet incomplete: the directors did not take full advantage of their prerogatives. Almost every scene within the picture is appealing; almost every scene — the Sunday tedium, the rehearsal, the play, the visit of the Princess, the search for Manuela — falls short of fullness because the entire film is built below its highest possible level. And yet the film is memorable. This is another argument for the primary importance of subject-matter in the cinema and the value of sincerity. In *Maedchen in Uniform* there are no trade-marked actors vaunting their extramural personalities; here is no false spice of greater-show-seasoning, no impresarioship, no pander. The film is therefore more than a moment's excitement, though it is no masterpiece. Moreover, the picture has none of the faults of the serious German film of the "golden age" and after. A film with a social idea and moral preoccupation, it never becomes moralistic nor, like the usual German problem-film, does it hammer the problem until it becomes flat and inactive. It yields to no German film-simplism wherein characters are kept anonymous in the hope they will become universal. The people here are representative, even though they are not always defined.

A film that can compose its experience without recourse to a story of the two sexes (*Maedchen* is all-feminine), without sensationalism where the sensational would be customary treatment, and outside the realm of the monopolistic motion picture, without benefit of the latter's clergy, contributes more than itself to the cinema. The shortcomings of the film are rather to be accepted as lessons for the future than as condemnation of the present picture, especially since the latter's contribution to the cinema is the encouragement of the intrinsic art.

(UNPUBLISHED MANUSCRIPT,
Circa 1931–32).

COMRADES OF 1918

I saw this film in Paris. The post-synchronized French speech coming from German lips was not incongruous. For Pabst has spread the speech like a delicate gloss over the image, and kept the pitch of image and sound subdued to render them the more poignant. The suggestive quality of the film is therefore superior to that of Milestone's *All Quiet,* which was after all, a showman's war. I have previously called Pabst "unscrupulous" in his handling of subject-matter that concerns human experience. I was chided by the Pabst cultists for my inability to appreciate his "superconsciousness." Herr Pabst has not been vindicated in my eyes by that chiding. But his *Comrades of 1918* is more scrupulous, it possesses integrity. The hospital scene is deeper than the pain of young mangled bodies, it suggests the pain of a stricken world. Milestone had a superior opportunity in the episode of the boots of the dead "buddy," but it was not pitched or timed with accuracy. And Pabst, appointed to compensate German production for *All Quiet,* following a narrative very close to the Remarque story, has surpassed Milestone simply because he has forgot to remember Hollywood. Although Milestone gave us the best Hollywood could give us, it was still Hollywood—the Hollywood that overlooks the resonances of treatment.

Yet, I cannot accept *Comrades of 1918* completely. One dare not think of the single war film without thinking of the war film as a whole. What is the indictment of *Comrades of 1918?* A war film cannot be evaluated simply as entertainment or an isolated production; it must be criticized for what it implies and what it omits. The implication of almost all the war films is the attractiveness of war. In *All Quiet* and *Comrades of 1918* the soldier prefers the trenches to the life at home. In these films as in others the basic cause of war is not condemned, the blame finally devolves on the stay-at-home, in *Comrades of 1918* the unfaithful wife. This shifting of emphasis dates from Gance's *J'Accuse*! filmed in 1918. And in almost none of these war films does one ever see the war set in the society that produced it. In the French picture, *Verdun: Visions of History,* despite "poetic" symbols and sentimental characterizations, there was a suggestion, if only an incipient one, of the shattered land, the uprooted lives. But in none of the films of the Continent and America has war been actually and inferentially explicitly and implicitly presented for what it is: the peak of a competitive society. Not to say this leaves pacifism passive, self-betrayed, playing into the very hands that yesterday manipulated the anti-militarism of *War Brides* into the malice of *The Kaiser the Beast of Berlin.*

To make the war the entirety of a film assures an ominous, therefore compelling, universe, however many words of hate of war, explosions against battle, may be uttered. Only the Soviet film has given the war its place as a peak of society, by simply making the war the climax and not all of the film, and by utilizing intensively realities as symbols. It is well to remark that the most drastic of pacifistic books, Latzko's *Men in War,* used realities as symbols in such a way as to render them unforgettable, but no one has dared to film *Men in War,* eminently suited for the cinema.

Moreover, we must consider, in appraising any single war film, what is the strength of this film's attack amid the amibent war sentiment sustained by aviation pictures, war love-romances, and films in which war is a lark, even a slapstick fanfaronade. One must admit that despite its individual directorial merit, *Comrades of 1918,* rather adds a sensitive lyricism to the ambience than helps to dissipate it.

NATIONAL BOARD OF REVIEW
MAGAZINE,
April, 1931.

ROAD TO LIFE

War, intervention and famine deposited on the burdened shoulders of the new Russia thousands of homeless waifs, wild boys. Roving in tatterdemalion bands, they terrified a people striving toward a better commonwealth. Violence upon these unfortunate but harrowing urchins was forbidden. Finally, in 1923, the problem became ferocious in its demand for solution. In consonance with the new conscience, a scheme was impelled to transform the wild boy into the vital citizen. The story of that synthesis is told by the first Soviet talkie, *Road To Life.*

Music . . . voices. Vertically from below, the image of Fomka Zhigan, the Fagin, rises to confront us, with his stiletto marked F.Zh. Not a caricatured offensive Fagin, but an affable chap, insidious in his attraction, facile on the balalaika to which he can sing ditties nostalgic and mischievous; no Dickensian villain but one who accounts for his hold on the vandal children by his sportiveness. Such portrait demands a mature temerity; one slip and the audience may sympathize with the culprit, the marplot. In this instance, the audience apprehends the spell without yielding to it.

From a band of gambling waifs rises the ringleader, the Tatar, "Dandy" Mustapha, played by a boy out of his own experience as a child of the streets. A supreme performance: none of the point-for-point mimicry, the tedious simulation of the sedulous ape of stage and screen; it is composed of surprise and inevitability. We do not know what to expect of Mustapha, his variable and meaningful laugh, his sullenness and delight; he contradicts our expectation from the start, but every contradiction convinces us of the inevitability of the detail – enormous acting, a penetrating reality.

Mustapha plays a three-cornered game whose other vertices are Zhigan and Zhigan's lady-friend; he lifts a fine leather suitcase from a dame just emerged from the terminal.

In a cozy, samovar-appointed chamber dwells Kolka, fifteen that day, with his parents. A congenial home: the mother's long hair graces the picture, her smile embellishes it. The mother goes out. She stops to buy an apple. Across the way, Mustapha, commander, orders "Apple!" One of the boys crosses, appropriates two apples from the vendor's basket; Kolka's mother intercepts him, he trips her, she falls. The cross of the medical aid, perpendiculars bisecting in a white circle, speeds before our eyes. Too late!

Kolka's life is severed. The father takes to drink. He threatens the boy. The boy runs away. He joins with the homeless children . . . In the windy frozen night, social workers and militiamen raid the cellars and dens to round up these boys. The boys fight the raiders, led by a woman. We get a glimpse into the rôle woman has played in the reconstruction of human life in the U.S.S.R. The boys are brought before the commission. Mustapha is brought in. He recognizes his questioners by name; he knows them from previous raids. To each of the queries upon his earlier adventures with this or that Institution, he answers with increasing lustiness that he escaped. When he is threatened genially with more emphatic incarceration his sullenness verges on an explosive counter-threat. The performance is colossal but secure.

The social worker Sergeyev has opposed jail as a place or a method for the wild boys. He undertakes a more voluntary way for the ragamuffins. They take him for a doctor but he surprises them with goodwill. A series of surprises puts them off guard, renders them indecisive. From eight years of experience with boys, five years with American wild boys, I undersign this technique. Whatever the degree of sophistication of a child, there is still some point in his makeup which is still a child's. He is still a child in relation to a new experience: he is wise in relation to what he knows, and innocent wherever the detail is unexpected. When the boys demonstrate against the suggestion of the collective, Sergeyev roars in laughter and draws from his pocket — what? — cigarettes, golden fruit, eager fingers. No counter-attack, no moralizing — humane strategy. The boys consent to go planning to escape en route, but when they find they are not guarded, their decision fades. Mustapha the thief is entrusted with money for food for the journey.

At the collective the cross-engraved doors of a former monastery are the boys' first experience. The surprise is the opening of the doors into a workshop: "The State trusts us!" The surprises become normal in the active life — work, bathing, song. Old habits recur: negatively — the stealing of the spoons, positively — Mustapha's experience as a sneak-thief who cut the rear of a Persian lamb coat from the very back of a woman directs his hand and knife in the cutting of leather.

In the meantime Kolka has become Zhigan's right-hand man. With his boss he perpetrates the theft of a pair of boots, but fails to escape. He is beaten. The attacker is condemned as of the past for beating a child. Kolka runs from the court into the Moscow winter. Bitterly pensive he recalls his home, his present plight. He leads a host of wild boys to the commission to demand that they be taken to the collective.

Spring, thaw, isolation, no raw materials. The boys are nerve-wracked, pugnacious. Sergeyev goes to Moscow. In his absence there is vandalism — gambling, drinking — Lelka kills the community dog, after that a fury of destruction. The more responsible collectivists, led by Mustapha and Kolka, stop the vandals. Sergeyev returns. The boys converge toward him slowly, shame-faced. All he says is: "You had a good time." He unpacks a miniature railroad and locomotive; they will build a real one just like it, Mustapha to be engineer, Kolka conductor, who doesn't care to participate? No reply, Sergeyev smiles. The boys acclaim him by ecstatically tossing him into the air; to which follows-up dirt flying — the railroad is being built to a song of gusto.

Zhigan's gang mourns the loss of its lieutenants. The gang opens a house of pleasure near the collective, to which come first the irresponsible, led by Lelka. The pride of the collective — Mustapha, Kolka and others — follow. They dance, dance, dance wildly then suddenly turn guns upon the Zhigan plotters. Zhigan escapes. The den is emptied.

The railroad is completed. Workers' delegates arrive. Kolka's father comes. Mustapha has gone the night before in a handcar to the starting-point. As he rode he sang a Tatar song . . . and a frog croaked at intervals. Zhigan has been ahead of him and released a rail. The handcar strikes the gap, Mustapha is thrown into the air, he regains his breath — Zhigan is before him. They fight — a groan of pain.

Kolka cannot wait for Mustapha, the time to start is past. The train is off — Hurrahs! — moving at an incline up the screen, until the gap — where Mustapha lies slain. He has his wish the first on the first locomotive, conducted by his pal Kolka. At the terminus the band and the boys polish up. Sergeyev is worried by the delay, but at last — the equipage. The band strikes up the "Internationale," succeeded by the dirge and keen of the siren as Mustapha enters in state.

The mature Soviet mind says: "What we have gained has not been won without travail and profound sacrifice. Let there be no Hallelujahs!" Miss Thirer of the *News,* too busy, I suppose, to see all of this admirable film, terminated it with Zhigan's demise — the American probability.

This film, the first directed by a young man, N. Ekk, is evidence of several conditions in the Soviet film, and in the Soviet society. Having treated the general canvasses of the revolution and the reconstruction, the new study is the detail, the intensive experience, the intimate and humane. Maturity permits the treatment of individuality as the focus of the social composition, individuality but not hero worship. It permits the full story, the losses that add up to victory. In such a picture there will be no oratory, no fetish of the immense or grand technique — that is the first articulation in a new environment, social or cinematic. The instruments will be as one with the idea, the narrative experience. That is what has happened in *Road To Life,* so that the too simple-eyed critics could not see the mastery of the technique, educated, to be sure, by earlier directors like Pudovkin, Eisenstein, Dovzhenko. The camera work is excellent; the photographic defects are due not to the original work, but to the expedience of making prints from a duped negative — and no reviewer knew enough to indicate the fact. The original sound mechanism was imperfect but the film's aesthetic is an harmonious arrangement. This, remember, is the first Soviet talkie; *Potemkin* was not the first Soviet film. And yet *Road To Life* is for the talkie what *Potemkin* was, in part, for the mute film — the fulfillment of a first period. The Soviet film, being the expression of a centrifugal society discharging fresh energies, is the completion of the processes of the cinema frustrated in the centripetal societies. The reviewers seem to have expected a spectacular, browbeating first Soviet talkie. Actually (and I said it more than a year ago) they do not want a Soviet film without the attack which they pretend to dislike, propaganda with a between-the-eyes punch. *Road To Life* realizes purposeful composition — it is the realization that is new — of authentic details: the music of mood and characterization, speaking at times instead of words; speech-as-sound; noise-and-utterance in variation; blank screen and sound; the motif of one instrument taken up by another; or, an opposite motif succeeding — these details are never intrusions because they are within the boundaries of the film.

There are several possible defects in the structure. At times there are too long a stretch of the blank screen — in itself a good device. However, this is not the same as saying that the film is too long: such an objection is due to the arbitrary and bad training of the American movie; speed is no essential of the movie. No film of profound content can move posthaste. Speed is o.k. for an empty vehicle that smashes itself when it comes to its terminus, but films intending an important aftersense belong to another category.

In the Zhigan-den scene the swirl of the images as the pride of the collective dance is a harmless virtuosity that is not wholly an error. It is, rather, the weakest choice from a number of alternatives. Yet just before it there is a triple diagonal image of Mustapha which is appropriate and easy in its participation. Similarly Ekk employs the temporary frozen image (not "still") far more sensitively than it was used by Dovzhenko in *Arsenal,* where, however, a more pronounced use was demanded. A virtuosity alien to the film is the bobbing stuffed doll in the boot-stealing scene.

As to the scenario itself, there are some likely questions. A didactic introduction (by Prof. John Dewey) is no substitute for the dramatic account of the waifs' origin; Kolka's origin, the sole one pictured, is accidental and exceptional, not the mass instance; the death of the mother and the father's consequent conduct smack too much of the temperance tract. Likely answers are: this is not the first nor last film on the wild boys (we have met them before in *Children of the New Day*); out of the vast history of the homeless kids narrative portions were taken to effect a convincing re-enactment; justification for Kolka is found in the fact that he is not an intruded accident but a product of the vandalism of the wild boys, with whom he joins (in itself an irony); further justification is in the visit of the father to the commission to look for Kolka among the rounded-up boys, and in the later scene where he is singled out among the visitors to the railroad's opening; climactic justification for Kolka is found in the moment when his plight meets with his memory to lead him to the collective. And here is where the titling—weakest part of the film—might have helped make more plausible the march of the boys upon the commission. When Kolka sits in intense pain after being beaten on the street, the titles, instead of "Fathers and mothers . . . suppose your innocent young child . . . etc., etc.," might have augmented the accumulation within the boy: his past . . . his present plight . . . the call of the collective . . . Kolka decides! Kolka, tutored, with a background of stability of pride, is the reality-symbol of the social conscience refreshed. As to the degradation of Kolka's father, the mere fact that our *Ten Nights in a Barroom* has made simple recurrences insipid, melodramatic and self-conscious does not, in any way, cancel these recurrences as genuine. Genuineness depends on the fabric in which such a detail is found. And genuine this dramatic document is, surmounting by its total evidence whatever doubts as to details may arise in the beholder. Nor is the total evidence dissipated by too elegiac an expression: there is death but not finality, sorrow but not purgative (as in *Soil*)—the conclusion is an active emotion, reassured by an unobtrusive current of mirth. Optimistic self-critical Russia.

NATIONAL BOARD OF REVIEW
MAGAZINE,
February, 1932.

SHANGHAI EXPRESS

The movie, being a popular art, is also a topical one. But being a popular art, its topic is distorted to the pleasure of its owners. The major topic today is the Sino-Jap war: Thunder on the east has all studios looking for Oriental stories. The motion picture "art-industry" had planned a film of espionage in Manchuria. The narrative was prepared by Major Yardley, author of *The Black Chamber*. International diplomacy shelved the story: Hollywood is neutral. Neutrality means impartiality—to the Chinese nationalist and Japanese imperialist. Neutrality means: find a third party to blame ". . . the villains must be bandits and not identified with any particular country."

When the renegade Chiang-Kai-Shek
Chops ten thousand at the neck
Hardly skittish are the British,
Not a damn gives Uncle Sam,
It seems to please the Japanese.
But when the Chinese Communist
To the peasant gives the land, it
Wins for him the name of "bandit"

Shanghai Express is lead off for this follow-up of slander. Into melodramatic moulds Paramount, through Field General Von Sternberg, has poured virulent counter-revolutionary sentiment. The Chinese revolutionary is an "unprincipled bandit." The "half-breed" commander has a "palace in the woods" to which he would abduct the Nordic harlot,

Shanghai Lily, played by Marlene "Legs" Dietrich. He brands those he doesn't like. His conduct is never motivated by a revolutionary code; he acts upon an egoistic code of revenge.

The neutral and impartial movie reviewer will say that this film is just melodrama "artistically" done. He will not comment upon its base and baseless propaganda, propaganda against the Chinese masses; though he did not expressly relish the propaganda in behalf of the Chinese masses which was so vitally borne by *China Express,* from which Sternberg derived the title and the best technical passages of his film. The "artistry" of the Hollywood claptrap is about as genuine as the Junker name of its director who says he hasn't a thing to learn from Europe, nevertheless swiped the lighting from the German studios, the superficial columns and billow of the *lichtspiel.* Here and there are some glib details generally more picturesque than revealing. Indeed, the entire pictorial quality of the *Shanghai Express* subscribes to the condescending appraisal of an oppressed people as "picturesque." It is supported by the Chinese "philosophy" attributed to the "rebel" or "bandit" chief: "Time and life have no meaning in China." The connotation of "rebel" is negative. It suggests petulance, rancor, unreasonableness and immaturity, never the valor, integrity, staunchness and historic validity of the revolutionary. The term is deliberate, a disparagement of the Chinese Red Army.

The alibi that the film is "just melodrama" is puerile. We assign the category according to the effect, not according to the formula. The effect is plain, and within it Sternberg's intention. Melodrama affords the absolutes of characterization that serve so unscrupulous a director as Sternberg. His actors are in a false equation. The absolutes, from having been served to the audience repeatedly, are now receptive clichés in the mind of the audience. The director does not need to establish the relationship, it is already there. All that he must do is to re-identify the digits and they become at once "authentic" numerals – unprincipled bandit, immaculate whore, etc. The "bandit" is slain by the high-caste Chinese whore – retribution! The Nordic harlot is rescued by the pinch-nosed young English doctor – scientific agent of imperialism – retribution! The strumpet's redemption is set into motion by the sanctimonious missionary – theologic agent of imperialism – retribution! Even the German dope peddler is redeemed by pity. Everyone on the side of reaction is blessed, thrice-blessed – wholesale redemption!

The Paramour Pictures Corporation and its kept man, who "wears black shirts made by a special black-shirt maker," slandered the Russian revolutionary in *The Last Command.* It repeats this proud conduct in

Shanghai Express. And on the tail of this film are to follow other equally "true" and "neutral" statements on the Sino-Jap "imbroglio." RKO is preparing a melodrama to be played against the background of war-torn China. Metro is on the bandwagon whooping it up for this 1932 version of "the yellow peril."

The answer lies with the audience of the movie, which D. W. Griffith called "the workingman's university." The movie tycoons are looking for a new audience. They cannot see that the new audience is the old audience with a new mind, a mind in advance of the reviewers and the producers. This audience can be directed to see the fraudulence of a film like *Shanghai Express.* Showings of films like the Soviet pictures, *A Shanghai Document* and *China Express,* profound and convincing, utilizing no "picturesqueness" and no posed frames, are themselves initial arguments against the shallowness of the American film, which has only a prejudice to inform it. The Workers' Film and Photo League through bulletins on paper and screen must instruct the film audience in the detection of Hollywood treachery.

NEW MASSES,
May, 1932.

MOVIES AND REVOLUTION

Comrades of 1918, a sensitive and intense motion picture of men marshalled, maimed, and murdered in war, never heroic, was G. W. Pabst's entrance into the film of speech and sound. Heretofore he had been a cult of the effete, with peripheral, polished "case studies" in "phobias" and "complexes." This was his Viennese, petty-bourgeois development. The intensifying class struggle, forcing intellectuals of sensitiveness beyond indulgence and "beyond desire," impressed itself into the consciousness of Pabst. He had seen, at that acute moment, Dreyer's *Joan of Arc,* and had defended that profound film against his own cultists' objections. This middle-class fear of maximum, its own maximum, is a phenomenon that exposes the retrogression of that class, vitiated but tenacious. At that moment too came a new sensory element into the cinema and that was encouragement and a fresh opportunity. His conscience stirred, Pabst's talents have realized themselves in a consistent growth from the pacifist war film through the majestic *Die Dreigroschenoper* to *Kameradschaft.*

In 1906 French miners were entombed at Courriéres on the Franco-German border. The Germans came to their rescue. That event of class-solidarity is the core of *Comradeship* (*Kameradschaft*). But with correct insight into the political import of the event, Pabst and his scenarist Vajda project the occurrence into post-war Europe, 1919 . . . A fire has been raging in the French sector of the mine. French Courriéres is encased in the ominousness of that fire . . . Three German miners visit a café in the French town. One of them asks a girl for a dance. She refuses. He says the Germans are as good dancers as the French. Threatening faces collect.

The Germans leave. "Why did you refuse to dance with him?" asks the girl's sweetheart. "I'm tired," she answers . . . Into the French sector the miners go, also the fire fighters. The girl leaves for Paris; she cannot endure the doom immanent village . . . . A grandfather fearfully escorts little Georges to his first descent into the dragon's mouth . . . The mine caves in. The girl leaps from the train at the next village, returns to her home. Her brother and lover are among the fire fighters. The village assails the mine gates.

In the German sector, men are going off shift. A nucleus decides to go to the aid of the French miners. Some of the Germans are hostile to the idea, remembering 1918, thinking of their own families. But the nucleus is magnetic. It asks the management for the rescue equipment. The free hours are given to comradeship.

In motor trucks the rescuers depart. They cannot wait for passports and visas; they cannot stop to explain at the frontiers. They rush through the arbitrary border line; a too-dutiful flunkey shoots. The symbol is real. However, the German management has advised the French of the departure of the rescuers; the frontier guard is told. "Thank you for your kindness," says the French operator. "Not at all," replies the German. The risks of capital . . .

Meanwhile the three German buddies of the escapade in the French café have gone on-shift. Their leading spirit, who recalls that in the war the mine was a road into the French territory, rushes to the mine wall where "the frontier goes 800 meters down." His companions follow him. They hack their way into the French sector. They come upon the grandfather who has found his Georges after an anguished search. The seams have broken. Water floods in. The men hack their way into the engine room and stables. Entombment threatens them there. But they are rescued by a telephone ring . . .

The rescue is done directorially with a fidelity and with a devotion to the human content of the episode and thereby achieves an importance greater than the single incident. Pabst has said this film is "ethical." Its artistry is the complete submission of the technique – camera, set, lighting – and almost complete submission of the acting to this "ethical" intention. No longer is Pabst smooth-finishing surfaces, calling the ambiguous subtle or playing Jack Horner. The denouement of the film, when the Germans have been released from the hospital, is poignant and hopeful. At the frontier the French fire fighter, the girl's brother, says "We workers are one! and our enemies we have in common; Gas and War!" The German who was refused the dance embraces the girl. A German rescuer speaks:

I have not understood the French comrade's words, but their meaning I have felt.

And here we ask for a further declaration. We ask, indeed, that the entire film be pitched to a completer attack, that its explicit condemnation of national barriers, cleavage of working-class unity, and its urging to unity be pointed to a sharp statement as to who is the enemy, who really is this Gas-and-War. Yet we should be naïve or sectarian critics indeed did we not recognize this film as a maximum within the present network of film-control. And what has made this maximum possible? First, the high level of the revolutionary movement in Germany. Second the producing company, Nero, is not within the dominant sphere of action centered in the U.F.A. of Hugenberg, the Nationalist leader. Third, a director of social conscience, responsive, in measure, to the first determinant, was in charge of the operations. It is worth mentioning that his scenarist has been previously accustomed to intrigues like those of Molnar, the Buda pest. Change the determinants and you change the determination. It is also worth considering whether Pabst will hold out or be sustained at the level of *Comradeship*. He has since made *L'Atlantide,* based on the hokum-novel by Pierre Benoît, the French Rider Haggard, and has been recruited to do *Don Quixote* in England. We might anticipate the latter were we not suspicious of Chaliapin as the Spanish windmill-warrior – will we have the grand satire of Cervantes or merely an upholstered opera?

To us here, *Comradeship* places again the question: is it possible to create a proletarian cinema in capitalist America? It is true that of all the media, excepting the radio, the movie is the severest in its resistance. This is due to the nature of the film, the complications involved in making pictures, the expense of making films and the monopoly vested in Hollywood, Hays and Wall Street. Yet, recognizing the severity of the resistance, we know, not solely by an instance like *Comradeship* which is, after all not quite the American case, but by our own evidences mainly, that resistance can be overcome. The Workers' Film and Photo League now extends to several cities; audiences have been established through workers' clubs and mass movie-meetings; the Soviet films have created a critically receptive body of spectators. Slowly but with increasing assurance the movie makers of the Workers' Film and Photo League have been improving the sense of selection and their skill in the documentations they have made. The record by the Los Angeles section of this League, of the "Free Mooney" run across the Olympic stadium is one of the finest of dramatic newsreel-clips I have seen. Such data will never appear in the commercial release.

The sense of selection has still to be educated in the political references of an image and its combination with other images. Certain bad influences or wrong readings from, respectively, the American newsreel or the Soviet kino have to be yielded. And, of course, constant training in technology and its application is essential. Yet, in these first efforts of the Workers' Film and Photo League there is the one potential source for an authentic American cinema. Other groups, amateur or "independent," are frivolous or merely nominal. The League is motivated within the strongest contemporary force, the revolutionary working-class, is self-critical, eager and, as a unit, suspicious of egotisms. The time is perhaps a long way off when it can produce enacted dramatic films. The German proletarian film makers ventured into such enterprises and issued either a duplicate of the simplistic "strasse" film or lugubrious episodic linkages of a period when the German proletariat were more "pathetic" than proud, a period exemplified in the graphic art by Zille. When our comrades of the League are prepared for the dramatic re-enactment, a film like *Kameradschaft* will not be a bad pattern. But even now, in this period of the record, the Pabst film is instructive: it is a record, a restoration that achieves partial revelation.

NEW MASSES,
December, 1932.

GABRIEL OVER ROOSEVELT

The picture *Gabriel Over the White House* was produced by the Hearst wing of Metro-Goldwyn-Mayer and simultaneous with its public exhibition the novel has been serialized in the Hearst press. M-G-M has compiled a newsreel sequence of the life of Franklin Roosevelt. Universal is issuing *The Fighting President*. And the Roosevelt literary opus is shedding its title *Looking Forward* into an M-G-M film originally named *Service*.

Will Hays, juncture between Washington and Hollywood, has always had a tender feelin' for the Metro boys. And Hearst's political essayist, Claude Bowers, himself cordial toward a "benevolent dictator" from his party, is the new Ambassador to Spain. The book *Gabriel* reads much more like a series of political *feuilletons* by Bowers with a Brisbane flavor than a novel. That's why the film is superior; in a movie at least you can *see* the people. The latest Roosevelt-Hearst logroll is the newspaper campaign, endorsed by the Fascist National Economy League and Fannie Hurst, for a Day consecrated to the President. Hearst is competing with the tabloid that floated a swimming pool for the White House denizen.

The Hearst footsteps stalk through the novel in several instances not included in the film. The movie omits the chapter "The War in the East" depicting an American solution to strife between Japan, a Hearst phobia, on one side and Russia and China, "now highly communized," on the other. Hearst's anti-French temper is explicit at one point in the novel. These deletions from the film recall a Hearst picture prior to our entrance into the World War. The picture was anti-Jap, anti-Mexican. But Woodrow Wilson, because we were soon to become Japan's ally, asked the removal of the Nipponese flag, and by contiguity, the Mexican flag was lifted out too. Franklin Roosevelt continues the magnanimous tradition of Woodrow Wilson. The peacemaker role of President Hammond in the book *Gabriel,* identifies F. D. Roosevelt with that other demagogue of the same family (1905) and the Wilson of 1918. Of course, this Oriental war is "merely a fantasy" in a book whose events occur in the future. The film is 1933 – a "prophesy" if not of ten years, then of 6 months. How very prophetic indeed is President Jud Hammond's liquidation of prohibition, and how even more delphic are the labor concentration camps and power projects – cheap labor for the power trust! What we may recognize as a development is the finished fact of the book: wages are pooled and equalized down to the concentration camp scale, out of fairness to all. The pool is administered by workmen – a corruption of the Communists unemployment program. Inflation and remission of the gold standard stressed in the novel, have been a pet theme of Arthur Brisbane back in the less "benevolent" days of Herbert Hoover.

In the novel a peace covenant is signed in London, but in the film the covenant is signed, under duress, in America. Peace is made and the debts are paid. Between the completion of the novel and the completion of the film, Roosevelt decided, with assistance elsewhere, upon the conspiratorial trade conference in Washington. In the London conclave "the Chief Commissar of Russia" is a member of the executive committee; in the American meeting, which is an argument for Roosevelt's aviation program, the Russian is not discernible, no more than he is at the "trade conference." In both cases the moral is "Buy American" in international politics – America "benevolent dictator" of the world!

The film, in several instances, condenses two characters into one. Lindsey, the President's Secretary of Education (Propaganda) and later Secretary of Public Safety, and Beekman, the narrator of the novel and the President's personal male secretary, become Beekman in the film, with the Department of Education omitted. Lindsey is a high-power press agent. (Gilbert Seldes, son of an anarchist and *The Dial's* gift to William Randolph Hearst, has recently urged "a better press" for Roosevelt. Does he want to be F. D.'s George Creel?). Lindsey urges the same, becomes a member of the dictator's cabinet. The Hammond buildup resembles the Roosevelt. Television spreads Jud Hammond into the homes and hearts of America; recall Rosevelt's radio tête-à-tête with the American citizens on the bank holiday. Lindsey, like W. R. Hearst, is a California newspaper publisher and son of a newspaper publisher, and also a film producer. Like Hearst he produces a film in support of the President. The Lindsey picture is to glorify the martyrdom of Bronson, the leader of the unemployed who has been killed by the racketeers. "It was," says the narrator, "a simple matter of arranging for the transfer of cash from the President's private account to Peale . . . ." "The President was secretly to pay for this monstrous ballyhoo out of his own pockets." Beekman, the narrator, is portrayed as one offended by the "bad taste" of the manoeuvre. This, of course, is a device to disarm the critic. The end justifies the means; says Lindsey: "But you don't understand, Beck. Though this is trivial and appears cheap it is a necessary item in a much bigger scheme." In other words, though *Gabriel Over the White House* may be sham, it is for the good of the nation. Beekman found Lindsey's picture "brilliantly done and the acting was above criticism," but I find *Gabriel Over the White House* executed in keeping with its content—in the tradition of Hollywood subterfuge, false-front filming. The film in the book is "A box office success, it did not cost the President a cent." The entire section "Sight and Sound" is the plan for the film *Gabriel,* and is very definite evidence that the perpetrators of it knew too well the fraudulence of their entertainment-as-propaganda. Beekman, sensitive and sympathizing with the public, calls the picture (in scenario) "the most horrible atrocity ever to be inflicted on the patient and docile American cinemagoer." This perfectly characterized the film *Gabriel.* "It appeared to be cheap, tawdry propaganda and absolutely pointless." The picture *Gabriel* is "cheap, tawdry propaganda" but not "pointless." Mr. Lippmann finds it pandering to the public's wish-fulfillment and therefore reprehensible. Is Mr. Lippmann's "learning to deal with reality" genuine or simply a matter of finesse?

Of course the film panders to the public's desire for an expeditious solution of its plight. Hollywood and pander are one. But to what end is the audience's desire manipulated? "Dictatorship, American style." Richard Watts, Lippmann's film-colleague on the *Herald Tribune,* attacks the end, and finds the treacheries of narrative and cinema treatment objectionable. Yet, says Watts in answer to Lippmann's snobbish proscribing of the movie to innocuous themes, the producers are to be commended for venturing into political subject-matter. The producers were *forced* to make this venture: first, to satisfy a changing public taste; second, to primrose the way to dictatorship. In the palmy days, "topical films" were incidental. The racketeer picture was a first cycle of headline themes chiefly because it was cosmopolitan variation of the rural gunplay film. The "depression" was on several years before Hollywood recognized, not the "depression" as such, but certain of its noisiest outcries. Watts has himself indicated, in the instance of the "colyumist"-films, that the movie comes in at the tailend of an outcry against some evil phenomenon to whitewash the culprit. In 1932 bank-runs became subject-matter: *American Madness* is an outstanding instance. Its studio, Columbia, youngest member of the Hays political trust, followed with *Washington Merry-Go-Round,* from which *Gabriel* is a development. Walter Wanger, who produced the two Columbia films, is immediately responsible for the production of *Gabriel.* He took Huston, who was the hero in *American Madness* (and had been *Abraham Lincoln*) and made him Jud Hammond. He took Karen Morley for Pendie Malloy, the President's secretary (in the book she is described as having some Jewish blood, revealed by her "acquisitive nose") because she was the Senator's wife in *Washington Masquerade,* another M-G-M political film.

In *Washington Merry-Go-Round* the unemployed are panhandlers from among whom is distilled a nucleus for a Fascist army, which fights the racketeers. In *Gabriel* also the racketeer is the last enemy of the nation, and a special unit, the Green Jackets, is organized to destroy him. In *Gabriel,* the leader of the unemployed (in the novel it is only a statement, in the film it is a radio hook-up) proclaims his army is free of Reds. Bronson, commander of the unemployed, is shot by the racketeers. While the immediate emotional suggestion is ostensibly the martyrdom of Bronson and the humanitarianism of Hammond, a connection is made between the marchers and the bootleggers.

Jud Hammond, the President, is a party-machine president of the Harding ilk who gets bumped on the head and awakens to an angel voice. Ennobled by heaven, he liberates the American people from Congress (always the butt of comedians and college professors), red tape and hunger. He is a believer in democracy and therefore is not afraid of the "label" of dictator — because the honest people will understand. Sophisticated fans too hopefully believe that the very supernaturalness of the hokum will show itself up; also that the implication that only a crackbrained president can save the country is a joke the people will see. The book has Hammond recover sanity, revert to type, and die before he betrays the people with democracy, bourgeois style. The *deus ex machina* device is an old ritualistic standby. In this instance it sanctifies the dictator, while it provides the loophole of fiction. The American audience, already duped by the glibbest of campaigns, now has an active image of the "benevolent dictator" and "the new deal" (the book calls it "The New Order") which takes on in daily life the physiognomy of F. D. Roosevelt. Meanwhile the movie campaign is enlarged with pictures glorifying Mussolini. At the showing of one of these, the supporting RKO newsreel started with a display of aviation in support of F. D.'s aero program, followed by a Jap nationalist demonstration against the League, concluding with a Hitler parade, approved by the announcer as stemming the "Red Menace." R.K.O. is a component of RCA whose head is Major-General Harbord, America's leading Nazi. In French venal slang "nazi" is syphilis: a correct picture of the virulent stage of capitalism.

NEW MASSES,
May, 1933.

8

BOOK REVIEWS

THE FILM TILL NOW

By Paul Rotha. [New York: Jonathan Cape and Harrison Smith, 1931.]

This book of encyclopedic pretensions is valuable as a compilation descriptive and documentary, despite occasional errors in cognomen. But as a critical history of the motion picture, it lacks a knowledge of the early motion picture—especially American, depends often on hearsay, is full of cultisms and prejudice, and does not observe the *esprit de corps* which should exist among critics as it does among scholars. Rotha, a young Englishman, has accepted, without accrediting, the points of view of other critics, their observations and even their phraseology. His entire treatment of national kinemas as "mindedness" was contributed in a series of articles to *Close Up* by an American cousin. He speaks of the "simplistic studio-mind" of the German kino, the "pictorial-mind" of the French cinema, and the "literal action-mind" of the American movie. This same cousin is indirect source for Rotha's "four movements," originally Alexander Bakshy's. Bakshy has named a fifth and inclusive movement, Rotha does not observe this "movement of the idea." His source hadn't recorded it, but if Rotha understands Eisenstein's "overtonality"—which he footnotes—he should never have failed to remark upon the movement of the idea: suggestion, resonance, flair, ec.

The "mindedness" of a particular kinema is a valid measure, but Rotha has failed to extend his source, as he has failed to name it, to account for the "national mind." For instance, he dwells on landscape in the Swedish film (originally analyzed by a fellow countryman) and fails to dwell on the entire phenomenon of the short-lived Swedish cinema, the peak of the motion picture before the Soviet. Depending for stimulus on a source which is too disciplined for him (he is after all an eclectic with typical aesthete preferences), he gets all mixed up in his instruments of measurement, as witness his consideration of *The Crowd.* His bias is mainly graphic: he cannot see that ultimately the entire matter of "dialogue film" is one of sound density as related to visual-motor density. To be valuable without confusing the reader, the book should be distilled to its documentary base, as a compilation of film descriptions, directors, studios, and the elements of the film-as-art. The comprehensive critical history waits to be written.

CREATIVE ART,
May, 1931.

CELLULOID: THE FILM TODAY

By Paul Rotha. [New York: Longmans, Green & Co., 1931.]

Rotha, introducing this sequel to *The Film Till Now,* complains that some have called him "high-hat." Has he become self-conscious? The high-hat oft shields the low brow. Others, he says, reject him as critic. They are correct. He is a diligent reviewer. And this second book is better than the first because more frequently does he exhibit the virtues of a reviewer who assembles superior commonplaces. Though he takes conventional blows at the Americanned art, he is actually at his best when commenting on the U. S. A. cinema. So long as he does not venture into derivate pastures of social commentary. In his zeal to appropriate the rights to speak on entertainment as propaganda, he reveals only the lack of mental adjustment and the proper instrument of measurement. His essay on Zola is a schoolboy's theme-paper: it is not Zola and cinema. To effect this relation he should have treated the translations into the motion picture of *Money* — done in 1916 in Denmark and a dozen years later by Marcel L'Herbier, *Labor,* Feyder's *Thérèse Raquin,* Jean Renoir's *Nana* which von Sternberg is going to dietrich. The give away of Rotha, that he is only a cultist, a populist, after all, is his overemphasis of Disney's sound cartoons. It is typical of the disproportionate enthusiast to call first statements first principles. The genuine extensions of the animated film, in content, in varied and improved graphic, in montage, in sensory compound, are issuing today from the Soviet Union. Disney's work added sound-parallel with sound-synchrony at intervals to a silent form already built upon an elementary turkey-in-the-straw measure, beyond which Disney has not progressed. The Rotha cultism takes in Chaplin. He finds *City Lights* Chaplin's most "comprehensive" film. Does he mean most diffuse? Satire develops only as it develops in precision, and Chaplin's has been on the decline since *The Kid*. He finds Chaplin's work "untouched." What of the yielding of the drastic in relation to hobo? The blind girl motif is certainly concession. I fear, for all its airs, Chaplin's independence is largely nominal.

Among Rotha's amazing outbursts under the terrific pressure of thinking like a social critic is this: "Nobody will deny that the propaganda of *The Front Page* in all its wildness is nothing more or less than anarchism." Now, I am agreed that Milestone has made a great contribution to the "Philosophy" of the compound film, the first American contribution. But the film's philosophy is nothing more than cynicism. The terrific verbal speed, setting the pace for the entire compound, accomplishes a *tour de force* in that the rapid vehicle makes a superficial cargo seem profound.

Rotha is more comfortable in the realm of technique, and might do very well as a matter-of-fact observer. But he presumes to venture into the problematic and there he has again no instrument and no intellection. Color he objects to, but does not recognize that its failure to date is the absence of color-fluidity and the inability of directors to use color dramatically. Rotha now accepts sound. I can see him suddenly discovering the advantages of color once they are an irrefutable fact. Certainly panchromatic stock has color-values, but there is a vast emotional difference between color-values and colors, between approximation and realization. Rotha remarks upon the Dunning Process: why has he not examined its appropriate uses and the errors of the directorial uses to date? I have seen but one good, rhetorical use of it and that in a terrible picture made by The Masquers. Speaking of "the film of today," in the matter of the variable screen, why is there nothing said of Claude Autant-Lara's important experiment?

CREATIVE ART,
February, 1932.

CINEMATIC DESIGN

By Leonard Hacker. [Boston: American Photographic Publishing Co., 1932.]

There are four grades of integrity in art: artiness, artisticalness, artisanship, artistry. Whether artisticalness is lower or higher than artiness is a debatable matter. I take the epithet "artistical" from a conversation with a Russian-*émigré* official of a now defunct French movie company. That gentleman didn't like American films, they weren't "artistical," like, for instance, Tourjansky's *Michael Strogoff,* a picture that resembled those boudoir receptacles made of convoluted oxidized brass films. The "arty" film has been typified in Paul Fejos's *The Last Moment,* a simplistic platitude on life with a pseudo-aesthetic composition whose chief boast was the absence of captions. This reduction was never more than a first statement, an elementary discipline or expedience. Artisanship is the professional studio's major achievement, below which most films fall. Artistry is the rare attainment, at present seen chiefly in films from Soviet Russia. Sometimes there are combinations, such as "arty artisanship," wherein studio competence is betrayed by spurious virtuosities. The work of von Sternberg is a prime example.

If the book under consideration has any prototype in the "big game," it is von Sternberg. There ought to be a law against such books! Indeed, aesthetic law is thumbs down on this egotistic mishmash of fallacies masquerading as axioms, of platitudes parading as recurrent experiences, valid and basic. There is not, in this book, one true principle or criterion for the amateur. When the author does present a threadbare possibility, "Simplicity will be the keynote of amateur films," his examples contradict the motto. Not content with the severer sequence of direct succession, he fills his scenarios with overlapping dissolves, never organized for the "rhythm" of which he prattles. Close-ups he uses without appraisal, without discrimination as to their structural value in the inclusive unit. Has he not seen or learned anything from Carl Dreyer's *The Passion of Joan of Arc*? Has he not seen or learned anything from Pabst's *The Beggar's Opera,* where the mutation of scenes take place without the tedium of dissolves?

This book can only betray the docile and eager amateur with his "cosmic" talk and its inflation of "relationship" to the "theory of relativity." As there are "vanity" publications in the egocentric field of poetry, so the more objective milieu of cinema criticism becomes a "vanity" boulevard. The designs in black and white, and one in color, by Constance Hacker, are a bit better than the text, though they go well with its artiness. They look like bohemian abuses of the interesting "machine ornaments" of Louis Lozowick.

NEW YORK HERALD TRIBUNE,
July 9, 1932.

THE MAN NOBODY KNOWS

Charlie Chaplin, His Life and Art, by W. Dodgson Bowman. With a foreword by Douglas Fairbanks, Jr. [New York: John Day Co., 1931.]

We have had Chaplinade after Chaplinade — Ivan Goll's bilingual fantasy, poems by Hart Crane and others, drawings by Léger and Cummings and Douglas Fairbanks, Jr., books by Soupault, Poulaille, *et al.* And we have had a few dissenters to the cult: André Suarès, who finds the heart of Charlot "ignoble," and Francis Carco, who recognizes in the comedian only "the false great art." Altogether there have been cult on the one side, muckraking on the other, with very little sincere objective criticism of Chaplin as film maker. One might expect somebody to indicate that the climax of his work was reached in *The Kid,* that *The Circus* was aimless, and that *City Lights* surrendered its main theme of social satire — the relation between the millionaire and the classic hobo — to the minor sentimental motif of the blind girl, a cliché out of Harry Langdon.

The present volume is merely another version of the prayer book of the cult. In the main it is a further simplification of the Pagliacci-with-Napoleonic-dreams, brightened or dulled as you will by a penchant for the rôle of Good Samaritan. Junior Fairbanks, who contributes a foreword, pictures Chaplin as an all-along-the-line antithesis. It is as if the line were drawn down the center of Charlie; to the left is what the world sees; to the right is what Junior detects, the Man Nobody Knows. It is all too consistent, too literary, too Hollywood-all-over. The best thing in the book is an anecdote:

Just after the Great War a regiment of British soldiers landed at a South Coast holiday resort. The veterans found the town in an uproar. A local strike was in progress, and the soldiers who sympathized with the strikers got out of hand and refused to carry out the instructions of their officers. Then the mayor, a kindly and generous man, talked to the war-weary men. He offered them refreshments, and invited them to be his guests at the local cinema. The soldiers eagerly responded to these advances, and a quarter of an hour later were laughing uproariously over Charlie Chaplin's delicious comedy in *Shoulder Arms.* Here was the little man going through some of the grueling experiences they had been suffering, but doing it in a way that made them rock with mirth. For the first time many of them realized, even amid the mud and blood of the trenches of Flanders, life had its humorous aspects. *Shoulder Arms* had done this.

"A true picture of a soldier's experience in France" was the verdict of one of the returned men, and his comrades emphatically endorsed it. When the show was over, thoughts of mutiny were forgotten and the soldiers went quietly back to barracks.

The author's naïve interpretation and approval of this incident does not prevent reflection on the use of entertainment as propaganda. The incident reminds one of a United States government bulletin issued when Russia was threatening defection from the Allies. It was announced that Chaplin comedies were to be sent to Russia to make Ivan more amenable to the economic mission that was to follow. The innocent films of Charlot!

THE NEW REPUBLIC,
October 21, 1931.

THE LIFE AND ADVENTURES OF CARL LAEMMLE

By John Drinkwater, Foreword by Will H. Hays.
[New York: G. P. Putnam's Sons, 1931.]

"Religion," says Will Hays, "is the world's greatest industry." And the movie is the world's greatest religion. The movie and its associates, radio and — soon to be — radiofilm, constitute the contemporary ritual whose holy city is Hollywood, and whose evangel is Will Hays. A theocracy dominates it, composed of high finance, producers — distributors — exhibitors, directors — scenarists *et al,* stars. The audience is laity.

In the routine of a theocratic ritual, it becomes increasingly necessary to repeat the divine origin of the priesthood. Fan magazines, ads, press-agent stunts merchandise the trade-marked stars to the layman. Books are written of (and by) the arch-priest, a Zukor or a Carl Laemmle. The movie being a democratic ritual wherein the priests get all and the laymen nothing, the former sell their personalities by means of nicknames and family titles. It is "Buddy" Rogers, and it is "Uncle" Carl Laemmle. "Say Uncle, you sucker, say Uncle!" In the earliest days, when Unk Laemmle was just beginning his movie antics, there were "Pop" Rock of the Vitagraph and "Papa" Lubin, pioneer buccaneer of the films.

Those were grand frontier days in the Americanned art. The aristocratic John Drinkwater, alias Horatio Alger, Jr., purchased at so much a wit to write the divinely inspired *Life and Adventures of Carl Laemmle,* tells of these days, but he tells very little. The picture he draws — from the biased data of Carl's agent, Dave Bader — is of a courageous "independent" champeening the "free settler" against the Trust. What's wrong with this picture? First of all, Laemmle was not alone. In the Universal the strong man was a Powers, whom Drinkwater mentions once off-handedly. Secondly, William Fox was the big shake of the "independents." Third, this was no victory of the weak over the strong. The "independents" won because they were a trust in themselves. The General Film, trustees of the Patent, were not implanted in the exhibition field of the movie. Fox was the owner of a movie chain. Laemmle started as an exhibitor, had a strong distribution unit. All he needed was a source, he had an outlet. In other words, these "independents" began with an audience: that's why they won. Actually, however, this was a victory for consolidation, as consequent events showed, and which Drinkwater doesn't mention. Nor does he mention how Laemmle and Powers squeezed out another partner, Mark Dintenfass.

When high finance entered the movie, trustification became fully crystallized. Laemmle did not establish independence. He speeded the three-in-one producer-distributor-exhibitor. By 1927, J. P. MacGowan, popular actor and director of railroad serials, could say in a highbrow magazine: ". . . the day is passed when small capital, coupled with boundless presumption is capable of creating a millionaire overnight. Daily it is becoming more substantially commercialized, which is but another way of saying the conservative element is coming into the ascendant."

This conservative element consolidated its interests both economic, and, in the Hays organization, ideologic. Mr. Drinkwater, whose nose is up in the air all through the book, isn't too hoity-toity to further the ideologic campaign of this crass element. He spends quite a few pages vindicating himself for having followed his biographies of Lincoln and Lee with this one of Laemmle. He needn't apologize for his subject – Laemmle is as much an instrument of a hypocratic [*sic*] society as the other two. But to make him the moving genius is a wanton hypocrisy itself, quite in keeping with the author's integrity. Making of this typically sentimental and malicious creature of circumstances – lucky Laemmle – a man of valor and idealism, has all the earmarks of potboiler priggishness. Drinkwater is no nearer to his subject than the distance of London to Hollywood. The idealism with which he credits Laemmle is the idealism of a Rockefeller – who establishes Chicago University on the corpses of Ludlow. The difference is but one of degree, of opportunity. We know what happens to food that doesn't leave the bowels. Bourgeois society is putrid with idealism.

Laemmle, Drinkwater says at the end of his well-paid hack job, was suggested for the Nobel Prize for producing *All Quiet on the Western Front*. A hardly noble fan magazine, *Photoplay*, reminded the public that no one was more venomous in his "idealistic" attacks on Germany than Uncle Carl. After the war, he used his ad. in the *Sat. Eve. Post,* "Watch this Column," to sob over the plight of his Vaterland — with no ulterior motive, of course. He stole a jump on the other producers to issue *All Quiet,* slapstick holiday. The star in this series is one of the erstwhile agonized Germans of *All Quiet.* Mr. Drinkwater says nil thereof.

The idealism of Laemmle — and he is a type — manifests itself in his penchant for youth. He is constantly "discovering" youthful talent, and as regularly dropping it. In his "Watch this Column," he puffed up the young comedian, Glenn Tryon — Glenn is having a precarious time of it now in two-reel farces not Universal in origin. Laemmle hired Paul Fejos, after the latter had made a spurious "art" film, gave him some work, dropped him. When Paramount imported Lubitsch, Universal imported Leni — and dropped him. Leni died. What did Universal have to do with it? As a suggestion, we might parallel this incident: Paramount imported the Swedish genius, Stiller — choked the spirit out of him — browbeat him — Stiller died. Greta Garbo, who came over with Stiller as a trivial incident, remains — as a golden trademark.

Laemmle's Universal, one of the most slovenly of companies, has been kept alive by "horse operas" — the tawdry westerns of a single stale formula; just as Tom Mix kept Fox in the saddle, and Rin-Tin-Tin kept Warner Brothers from going to the dogs. The movie ritual wants elegant unction now; therefore John Drinkwater rubs the banana oil. And his patent — gleaming with salvation — joins the evangel himself, Will Hays, to praise the movie — the gangster film — as a deterrent to crime. Well, the movie is no more a kibosh on racketeering than Drinkwater's blurb (mixture of contempt and padded praise) is a kibosh on the movie racket. Racketeering and movie are inseparable in the present pattern; and the first whisper in the movie business was racket. Its accents are thunderous now.

NEW MASSES,
July 19, 1931.

THE STORY OF FILMS

Edited by Joseph P. Kennedy. [Chicago: A. W. Shaw Co., 1927.]

The cinema was born in the laboratory and has been reared in the counting-house. It is this rearing which receives the attention of Messrs. Kennedy, Hays, Zukor, Giannini, Lasky, de Mille, Hammons, Sills, Kent, Cochrane, Katz, Loew, Fox and Warner. Since the contributions of these gentlemen were originally addresses before the Harvard School of Business Administration, it is, of course, the commerce of the films of which they treat. It is precisely this *commerce* which has thwarted the cinema as art. Mr. Lasky sanctimoniously calls the motion picture an "art industry." Certainly the association with the cinema of the mercantilists included in this course has produced very little art and been not very cordial to industry. Art and industry have at least one common purpose: economy. It is commerce that waxes on waste. It is not the way of an art or an industry to receive its dictations from the banker. Yet the spendthrift filming has led to this anomaly, as anyone may infer from Dr. Giannini's address on "Financial Aspects." Nor is it the way of an art to receive dictations from a political opportunist, as has occurred in Mr. Will Hays' "Supervision from Within" – observe the euphemism.

Not one of the contributors to this volume can be called a pioneer. A casual reading of Mr. Terry Ramsaye's documentary history of the motion picture is sufficient to prove that. Accident and opportunity made them magnates, and expedience and "luck" still exercise influences upon their methods. Training in cloth-sponging or fur-barter is no qualification for the development of an art form. Any data that the mercantilists can present only serve to indict them as intruders. The movie has been sullied with the numerous properties of commerce: world expansion, greed, bluster, sanctimony, waste, duplication of "successes," incompetence, evasion, expedience, accident, competitive practices leading to amalgamation, etc. The present volume is a sort of "pimple to this business of humbug," to paraphrase Hawthorne. But the curious student, the critic and the oppositionist, the diagnosticians and surgeons, will want to examine the fester. The lecturers are well-chosen representatives and they have their data down well. The juxtaposition of conceit and humility which informs their attitudes to the listeners is symptomatic of a pathetic insufficiency which is reflected in the products of their commercial zeal and enterprise.

It is significant that of the two persons chosen to represent the "art" of the film, Mr. Milton Sills — speaking on "The Actor's Part" — dwells upon the performer as merchandise; and Mr. Cecil de Mille, representing the director, is responsible for much of the vulgarism of concept and realization which constitutes the "technique" of the film *regisseur*. He, too, insists upon talking about money losses as major cinema errors. However, his dissertation is not without its value to the uninformed. At one point he stresses what seems to me a vicious mistake in direction: that the actor is his own determinant. That is, the actor needs no director to tell him how to perform. It is just this viewpoint which has thwarted the development of the unique cinema artist, the director. Until the director is completely the creator, and the actor — with the camera, the screen, the set, etc. — a submissive instrument, the movie will continue to be the hybrid it is. The supremest of directors, F. W. Murnau, demands complete but pliable submission to the central and initiating intelligence, himself.

There is one phase of the motion picture industry which is treated here quite well, as far as it goes, and that is the important division of "Short Reels and Education Subjects," on which Mr. Hammons speaks. The short film is a possible salvation for the film as art, but it is threatened with extinction by the development of the vaudefilm and presentation theatres. Moreover, as Mr. Hammons has remarked, the exhibitor is not friendly to the finely realized short film. So far as the educational film is concerned, it is still in its infancy.

THE ARTS,
April, 1928.

CINEMASTERS

Cinema, by C. A. Lejeune. [London: Alexander Maclehose & Co., 1931.]

The books on cinema in English are so poor and so few that any volume, written sincerely and with a degree of personal insight, is welcome. Of the books in English in the last few years the majority are British. And this is not surprising: it is only since 1926, when "the City" became interested in the film, that elite opinion has condescended to it. Previously it was a plebeian amusement, today it is the merchandise of empire and therefore "art." Once having become "art," the cinema entered into a category always respected in English publishing. However, the British books have been largely borrowed in their attitudes or vein. Of Mr. Lejeune,* a critic of the film before 1926, it must be said that his judgments are his own, as is his point-of-view, that of a polite and enlightened enthusiast. His "review of thirty years' achievement" is a follow-up of the expressions of personalities: in America, Chaplin, Griffith, Sennett, Fairbanks, Pickford, Lubitsch, von Stroheim, Nazimova, Disney; in Europe, Sjöstrom, Robert Wiene, Murnau, Pommer, Pabst, Feyder, Clair. He is not equipped for those inquiries that require a sense of social processes, although he does state correctly that the Soviet film, peak expression, is the articulation of a new social energy. In his section "Miscellany," where he considers categories like "Slapstick," "The Camera-Man," "The Experimental Film" (a mis-

* [Ed.]: An all-too-common error. The author is, of course, C(aroline) A(lice) Lejeune.

nomer), "The News-Theatre," "War Films," "Films of Travel," etc., he is often observant but rarely fundamental in the sense of stating beginning and conclusion. For Mr. Lejeune is essentially the highly-developed "fan" rather than the critic who does more than describe contours. Minutiae are lacking: this, of course, may make the book attractive to the one who is interested in opinions as conversations; it will be insufficient to one who asks for details and their operation. The method of writing criticism through single or singular personalities, even where general references are permitted to radiate from these personalities, is to obscure the currents of an art. This is all the more baneful to an art whose history is young, within our own experience, yet whose history is largely unknown, even mythical. Mr. Lejeune's own appended biblography indicates but two or three books before 1926, and of none before the war. His sole German references are to the two books by Balász and the one by Bagier, yet Germany in the last 25 years has contributed a wealth of film literature that would render much that is written today archaic and might have elucidated to Mr. Lejeune more precisely the evolutionary nature of the cinema. For instance, the author, in the pseudo-tradition of Gilbert Seldes, whom he respects, sees in Mack Sennett the originator of farcical humor in the film, rather than the timely instrument of a first, primitive expression. That Sennett really did not comprehend the rhetoric of this expression, as it might evolve, is to be found in his failure to exploit with understanding the volatile talents of Mabel Normand, as well as in his failure to grow beyond that early folk-utterance. Of course, the failure is only Sennett's to the extent that Sennett is representative of the Amercan cinema, the "movie," and as the latter is a response to the American society, as well as its agent. Lejeune, moreover, does not recognize that Sennett's own niceties are those he derived from Griffith, and that, perhaps unconsciously, the former is joshing the latter. Sennett's real talent was not creative but rather selective, he knew a good comique when he saw one, but they became most expressive when they left him. The tragedy in American film-comedy has been that there are great comic actors but no comic directors and no comic ideas. It must be said for Lejeune he is temperate and he recognizes that "Sennett is not a genius" and that when that director ventured beyond "fine craft," as he calls it, he is "indeterminate." The reason is simple: Sennett was the instrument of a first statement, he was an incident and not an "original."

Lejeune's good writing and his modesty, his appreciative taste, save his paper on Chaplin from the charge of "cultism." He writes without the necessary incredulity of one trying to evaluate an artist whose popular identity no longer coincides with his artistic. Lejeune avoids the "cutenesses" of the usual Chaplinades, but he does not accurately identify the artist. For him there is an equal development in Chaplin the artiste with Chaplin the director. This is not so. As long as the player was the *raconteur,* in those early films, there was his equality, even a complete coincidence. But since *The Kid* the player has transcended the director to the disadvantage of the entity, the picture. Nor does Chaplin derive chiefly from Sennett; Lejeune has omitted the sources in his own land, Fred Karno, and in France, Max Linder. Chaplin is not essentially an American artist; indeed his influence on the American film, as in the case of Langdon, has often been contrary to the organic development of the "movie." Lejeune has really consolidated, in a compact and polite form, the arguments that favor Chaplin without overstressing allegiance. Thus he can see that *City Lights* was not a victory for the mute film, but, though he does not phrase it so, a concession to the oral, for all its evasion of speech. When one peep of sound is added to a film, that picture must be considered as a "compound" rather than as a "simple" structure. But a larger compromise was Chaplin's when he forsook his major motif—the relation between himself and the millionaire—for a minor—the relation between the blind girl and himself. Chaplin's independence is mainly nominal.

Because this book is not, as it is called, a "review," but a collection of appreciations, the author had his rights in including Mary Pickford, though a consideration of her apart from the commercial history of the "movie" is an exaggeration of personality. It is, however, in writing on a Lubitsch as "poet laureate" that appreciation becomes overpraise. Indeed, Lubitsch is the case-in-point to prove the deficiency in film-impetus today to force affability expressed in Lejeune innuendoes and "touches" to incisive satire. Lubitsch is proof of the proposition, as is von Sternberg, that indulgence in frivolities and specious commentary can never lead to the creation of an important work: see the former's *The Man I Killed,* the latter's *An American Tragedy*.

Again, the appreciative method, the expression of personal gratitude, as it were, frequently overlooks the variability of a talent when it meets with another. Take the case of the German studio master, Pommer. It is true that he was one of the forces of the German "golden age." But first what was this "golden age"? It was the cinema responding to the War and the Inflation, when the middle class looked upon its plight pathetically and expressed its introspection rather than its objective situation, that is, shied from the situation to bemoan itself in simplism based on reality and in somnambulistic tales. In this period developed the German studio that has never been able to get out into the open both physically and mentally. At its height the German film was splendid, today it is formularized, save where a talent like Pabst, freeing himself from earlier preoccupations, now opposes the formula. Pommer belongs to that German studio of the past, and he is actually still with it in the nationalist U.F.F. Lejeune does not distinguish the rise and decline, he does not fully see the Pabst of yesterday and the Pabst of today, though he does recognize that the latter's *Die Dreigroschenoper*" is "the best earnest . . . of the future of the German cinema." And this earnest needs not, resists in fact, a Pommer, with whom Lejeune would join Pabst. Did Lejeune understand the social minds at work in the cinema, he would better understand the individual mind and know that when the American studio put the German Pommer to supervise over the Swedish lyricist Stiller, whom Lejeune does not fully appreciate, the studio was assuring a cleavage in the film *Hotel Imperial* and a poorer achievement than had Stiller been permitted his own expression.

(UNPUBLISHED MANUSCRIPT,
Circa 1931–32).

L. MOHOLY-NAGY AND HIS THEORIES OF PHOTOGRAPHY

Painting: Photography: Film, by Laszlo Moholy-Nagy.
[Boston: American Photographic Publishing Co., 1931.]

L. Moholy-Nagy, Hungarian resident in Berlin, is the spokesman of the advance guard of photography. He has expressed his viewpoint in these words: "Photography as a presentational art is not merely a copy of nature." But many will agree to that without going so far as Moholy-Nagy. He finds that among people "a new feeling is developing for the light-dark, the luminous white, the dark-grey transitions filled with liquid light, the exact charm of the finest textures: in the ribs of a steel construction as well as in the foam of the sea—and all this registered in the hundredth or thousandth part of a second."

Moholy-Nagy finds the indicator to his sphere in "the future of the photographic process," which will be the increased sensitivity in the control of "light phenomena." Therefore to him the film is the climax of the photographic processes, because "light phenomena generally produce higher possibilities for differentiation in motion than in a static state." There you have Moholy-Nagy's aesthetic of photography: "the differentiation of light-phenomena."

He lists the uses of photography, beginning with:

Registration of situations, of reality;

Objective portraits;

Advertising, political propaganda, posters; up to

Expressive portraits;

Interpenetration and organization of scenes, combining and projecting one upon the other and next to other, achieving what he calls a super-reality, a utopia of imagery, and jest or wit by means of juxtaposition;

Compositions of photo-pictures, *i.e.*, a narrative conveyed by the composition of photographs instead of verbal text;

Typofotos;

Absolute abstract light projections in planes or into space;

Simultaneous movies.

Before we consider what Moholy-Nagy means by these categories we might hear him upon the general scope of photography: "I myself, through my photographic work, have learned a great deal for my painting, and reversely, problematic positions of my pictures have very often given me suggestions for photographic experiments. It is true in general that imitative painting, rooted in the historic, will, through colored (and tonal) composition in the film, liberate itself with increasing certainty from the presentation of objective elements in favor of pure color relations; and the rôle of the real or the super-real or utopian presentation or reproduction of the object – which was the task of painting until recently – will be taken over by photography (or the film) which, in its methods, is organized with precision." Of course, he feels that this task of photography is a manifold one and will be performed into the future. He foresees the possibility "that the mechanical-optical color-composition – color photography, or film, will lead to entirely different results from today's light and other kind of exposures."

Among Moholy-Nagy's classifications of photography are: the photogram, typofoto, and polykino. The first is the camera-less photograph, the experiments by himself and Man Ray. The typofoto is a combination of typography and photograph, *e.g.*, Moholy-Nagy's project for a magazine cover in which printed letters and a numeral are photographed against a pictorial background. The polykino is the simultaneous movie, *i.e.*, a film in which different progressions are concurrently active. Upon the screen several sequences will cross each other.

Moholy-Nagy has a fourth class of photography, the photoplastic study, composed of a number of photographs, placed simultaneously. This is the static expression of what he means by polykino in the cinema. The typofoto is an experiment in the association of different kinds; photoplasticism is another experiment in composite and pre-arranged photography. Moholy-Nagy calls it a "compressed interpenetration of the visual and verbal jest; a weird linking with the imaginary of the most real, imitative means. But at the same time they may tell a story, and be of solid quality." By "jest" Moholy-Nagy means the use of photos so related as to produce a *humorous effect.* He continues: "The present method of cutting out, arrangement side by side, the fatiguing organization of photographic proofs, shows a superior form in contrast to the early pasting work of the Dadaists. But only through mechanical construction and development along big lines will photography and the film realize the marvelous possibilities for effect which are inherent in them." (The Dadaists were a French cult of artists who enjoyed dissociations and the illogical).

The *all* of photography, to Moholy-Nagy, is *light. "Light*: a Medium of Plastic Expression." And by that he means:

"Instead of having a plate which is sensitive to light react mechanically to its environment through the reflection or absorption of light, I have attempted to *control* its action by means of lenses and mirrors, by light passed through fluids like water, oil, acids, and crystal, metal, glass, tissue, etc. This means that filtered, reflected or refracted light is directed upon a screen and then photographed, or again, the light-effect can be thrown directly on the sensitive plate itself, instead of upon a screen. (Photography without apparatus)." I quote the conclusion of this portion as an emphatic reiteration.

"Since these light-effects almost always show themselves in motion, it is clear that the process reaches its highest development in the film."

Moholy-Nagy connects himself, because of his concern with the sensitivity and intensity of light and the *control* of these qualities in photography with the electro-magnetic ray, the x-ray and other *penetrations* through the eye-machine; in cinematography, with the first *absolutist,* Viking Eggeling, who filmed a moving point, and his followers, Hans Richter, Walter Ruttman, Man Ray, etc.; and with the color-organ as developed by the Russian composer Scriabin, the American Thomas Wilfred (the Clavilux), Alexander Laszlo the pianist; and with the reflector-light-and-shadow-play of the artists of the Bauhaus of Dessau, such as Schwerdtfeger, Hartwig and Hirschfeld-Mack . . . and others. Moholy-Nagy objects to the blending of the acoustic or musical with the optic-kinetic.

Moholy-Nagy's book, *Painting: Photography: Film,* concludes with a plan or typofoto scenario for his simultaneous film, his polykino: *Dynamics of a Metropolis.* By paralleling photographs, typography, abstract linear designs, indications of direction of movement and tempo, etc., Moholy-Nagy conveys the multiplicity and rhythmic construction of his film.

In final summary it may be said, in Moholy-Nagy's own words, that he believes, and upon this belief he bases his work, that "The world is learning to see things with new eyes."

AMERICAN PHOTOGRAPHY,
January, 1931.

9

OTHER WRITINGS

ALEXANDER BAKSHY

No American has captured in the written word the qualities of cinema so well as has Alexander Bakshy, a Russian-English critic. Mr. Bakshy's brief essay, "The Kinematograph as Art"—written in 1913, published in *The Drama* (Chicago) in 1916 and in his volume *The Path of the Russian Stage* in 1918—is an amazing statement of the cinema and an anticipation of its present and imminent problems. Bakshy almost 15 years ago recognized the movie as an art medium, but did not speak vaguely or too broadly. Bakshy more than a decade ago indicated the folly of the literary intrusion. He was not carried away by *Cabiria* as was Lindsay. Not even D'Annunzio belongs to cinema. Yet Mr. Bakshy kept his poise when he touched upon the intrusions. Unlike numerous other commentators, he was not shunted into an abuse of the inherent movie. He recognized that the usual attack is not the movie's peculiar concern, that it is really an attack upon evils not peculiarly the movie's. He understood that there is no quarrel between the mechanical and the non-mechanical, but between the artistic and the non-artistic. He remarks upon the necessity for independent film artists. The problem of commercial concentration was present ten years ago.

But the importance of Bakshy's contribution does not rest in these pointers to the negative aspects of cinema procedure. It consists of an immediate recognition of the character of cinema pantomime that is almost prophetic. Cinema pantomime, he said more than a decade ago, "is the most abstract form of pantomime," and should be left "to the dancing clowns and acrobats who do know something about the laws of movement."

This is a recognition manifested in the success of the greatest of the best pantomimists, the low comics. Bakshy saw in the ballet the rudiments of cinema rhythm. Quite a few years later the Léger-Murphy *Ballet Mécanique* appeared.

Bakshy resolved the optical problems of the film into simple terms of camera — a decade ago an amazing apprehension. What director today knows that the camera and not the picture is the medium? Bakshy anticipated by more than ten years the silhouette film; France produced a multiple reel movie of silhouette cutouts in 1926. He anticipated also a problem soon to threaten us, the natural vision film. Since its origins the movie has been abused by inventors and investors. The talking picture, the colored picture, the stereoscopic picture. Bakshy met the problem of the natural depth, three-dimensional film, not by opposing it, but by separating the cinema into two kinds of pictures: the one plane, flat film — which should be our present one — and the stereoscopic, depth film. A moving picture and a moving sculpture. This moving sculpture is quite different from Lindsay's sculpture-in-motion. Lindsay's is based on an analogy with sculpture; it is, in fact, only that sculpture in motion. Bakshy's conception is of three dimensions interrelated by motion, interrelated so as to create a rhythm, preconceived by the *regisseur* and sustained and exploited by the camera. The art training of a Lindsay is not such as would be very helpful to cinema, even were cinema only an extension of the graphic. And it is certainly evident that his understanding of art does not include a familiarity with its divisions and their circumscriptions and particular concerns. Bakshy is intimately cognizant of what belongs to each of the different plastics. He sees the confusion of plastics in futurism, which wanted to give kinematographic value to sculpture and painting. Time has been included as an element in painting by every important painter. But futurism wanted to *realize* time, not *visualize* it. To the movie the realization of time pictorially belongs — in other words, actual rhythmic motion. In his recognition of categories, Bakshy emphasized the fact that the movie is a medium, not of colors, but of tones or color-values. The French critics understand this, although French movies are full of color impurities. American journalistic critics, however, are unable to make the distinction. Mr. Quinn Martin waxes eloquent upon the adventurousness of Douglas Fairbanks in furthering Technicolor.

The work of Mr. Bakshy indicates what movie critics should be doing. Nor has Mr. Bakshy withdrawn. He has extended his consideration of the cinema. Last year he advocated the exploitation of the screen as the receptive medium. An elementary use of this in the enlarged film was made in

Chang and *Old Ironsides*. But Mr. Bakshy advocated a multiple screen for purposes of rhythm, relationship of minor to major actions, and climax. The unit could be separated into its elements and fused. Undoubtedly, someone will make use of this idea. And that is the point of Mr. Bakshy's importance. He is not a weathercock but a prophet. Criticism is altogether too redundant now. No one thinks it important to do anything else but repeat what has been said many times before. Criticism must have its wind. It must also have something to do with the generating of the wind. Its prophecy, however, must not be concerned with presentiments so as to appear miraculous, but subject itself to the discipline of its category. It must be a criticism in terms of the inherent qualities of the thing criticized. In this instance, the movie. From a scrutiny of the movie and what criticism of pertinence it has called form, certain tenets can be drawn. These tenets must be qualified, extended and applied, both by the practician in the cinema and the critic. In fact, the critic must be a practician as well. That is, his criticism must be such as to be immediately convertible into practice. Mr. Bakshy's criticism is of that kind.

NATIONAL BOARD OF REVIEW
MAGAZINE,
September, 1927.

THE MOVIE PALACE

A French writer, Alexander Arnoux, has said of the first movie houses of Paris, "they were ashamed of themselves and hid in the blackest bowels of the city." Yet these establishments, and similar ones in America — converted stores and stables — possessed at least one characteristic of the ideal cinema: the screen was flat against the wall. A decade ago Alexander Bakshy, a prophet among movie critics, remarked that the blank square on the wall is part of the picture house. It is, in fact, the distinctive essential which determines, or should determine, the interior plan.

Architects have recognized that the movie house does demand treatment differing from that of the theater, but have considered this difference "not sufficiently radical to submerge the traditional theater." To many of us, not architects, it seems that the interior arrangement of the ideal cinema must be radically different from that of the theater. Not alone is this difference produced by the problem of the projection angle, an engineering detail, but — and principally — by the receptive instrument, the screen. The proscenium frame determined the interior architecture of the theater. The screen determines the ideal pattern of the interior of the picture house. A young American critic, Seymour Stern, has from Mr. Bakshy's suggestive statement, promulgated a number of principles for interior cinema architecture. They are:

Provision for shadow silence, the abolition of the proscenium arch, the graduate convergence of all lines in the theater to the screen, marked elevation between rows of seats, and music to be hidden. This is an inclusive set of rules, all — with modifications — feasible, and many to some extent realized.

Mr. Stern's ideal cinema would eliminate chandeliers; many picture houses have substituted dimmed wall or alcove lighting, the Ufa-Palast-am-Zoo in Berlin is lighted thru squares cut into the ceiling — a severe, appropriate pattern of squares. This ideal cinema would eliminate the stage and the orchestral pit; in the little cinemas, particularly in their French parent, the cinema of Théâtre du Vieux Colombier, the orchestra of three or four pieces is hidden from the audience. This, of course, conflicts with the Roxy conception of the "presentation house," a conception which has snubbed the movie. It conflicts also with more polite conception of "Dr." Riesenfeld, wherein music is not subsidiary to the movie in the movie house. Mr. Stern's cinema would eliminate box seats, loges and balconies. This has been done in the intimate cinema and also in the larger stadium or bleacher-type house.

The essential principle of Mr. Stern's plan, the convergence of the lines to the screen, would form the inner hall into a sort of triangle with the screen as apex. This design is necessarily modified in execution by the line of vision. Similarly, his wish for marked elevation between rows must yield before the physical necessities which find expression in building regulations, providing for the amount of traffic the floor may carry and the omission of steps from the orchestra floor. Moreover, the projection of this film modifies the continual sweep of the auditorium from the screen to the projection booth. The stadium or bleacher type is the articulation of this necessary compromise, it maintains a convenient pitch.

The ideal cinema has, however, a greater foe than physical limitations with which to cope. It has, first, the traditional intruder into cinema practice, the theater, and, secondly, the investor or owner. The architect has been, of all artists, the most submissive to the investor. The owner can see no separation between cinema and theater; moreover, to quote an architect, "the vulgar tastes of the great majority of the owners, and their disinclination to pay the commission demanded by a competent architect," make "it not easy to find examples that rise above mediocrity." Yet money has been forthcoming for movie "temples," like the Roxy and the Paramount, but results are not beautiful nor relevant. The cause is to be found in the hybrid "presentation" program of a Mr. Rothafel — the ubiquitous Roxy.

In 1913, Roxy — still S. L. Rothafel — was tortured by "the monotony of the 'silent stage.'" To defeat this ennui he built the Regent Theater, 116th Street and Seventh Avenue, New York. He opened the theater with Kleine's production of *The Last Days of Pompeii*. For the first time an orchestra was introduced. An actor appeared reciting from Bulwer-Lytton. Singers emanated from charmed recesses. Soft lights played upon them.

Twelve years later Roxy proudly speaks of how he gave to a public Strauss' *Ein Heldenleben*. "The music," he says, "should interpret the action and lift it up and carry it over the flat dimensions of the screen."

Any artist of intelligence will tell you, that if an art is to transcend the medium, it must do so by virtue of the medium's characteristics. But Mr. Roxy wanted "atmosphere" — he found it in the military demeanor of the ushers, and he found it in the defeat of the movie house as a movie house. Dr. Riesenfeld has detected the anomaly in this situation. The movie house becomes a glorified vaudeville theater, and films are shown in legitimate theaters at steep rates. He says: "We build great palaces and call them motion picture theaters. They are misnamed.

"A motion picture theater, in my opinion, should be devoted to the best possible exploitation of pictures. The great houses make no pretense of doing this. They are half-breed institutions offering a polygot program that is a mixture of ballet, fashion shows, vaudeville acts — with a mere soupçon of film entertainment." But Dr. Riesenfeld, I believe, stresses music unduly. In his new Colony he has dignified and subdued the program of the "big house," the acts are less intrusive, the sequence less emphatic of display, the movie attains to a greater eminence: but it is still a long way from the ideal all-cinema, which should entertain almost solely with movies.

Dr. Riesenfeld suggests the exploitation of the short subject film. The animated cartoon, such as *Krazy Kat, Skating Whacks* or the Aesop Fable *Small Town Sheriff* are good cinema, and the Mintz moviezation of *The Elegy* contains the elements of the ideal motion picture. These belong in the movie house program, and they do appear in all but the "presentation house," or, if they do appeal there, they are sandwiched, with the main feature, between impertinent acts. This anomaly of a movie house inhospitable to the movie has been responsible for the thwarting of a distinctive movie house. The large orchestra has necessitated a pit which obstructs the natural convergence of the lines of the auditorium, or strictly, the spectatorium. The picture house emphasizes sight and all else is submissive to it.

The nature of the movie demands a movie house in which neither organs nor orchestras shall interfere with the requisitions made by the movie upon the eyes. This means, as Mr. Stern has said, a hidden orchestra, and, I add, a small one, and a submissive one. The requisitions upon the eyes urge the elimination of proscenium arches (the movie sequence does not occur within a frame) and all parallel lines above or about the screen. In the new Fox-Locust Theater in Philadelphia, a small house, a series of parallel lines running about the screen seriously impede the visual experience. As to music, let me remind you that Vachel Lindsay, America's first movie critic, wanted music absent from the movie house because it interfered with conversation.

America had the entire period of the war and the prosperous years after in which to arrive at a movie idiom and a movie architecture. She has arrived at neither. Her movie houses that found their art in "atmosphere" perpetrated such architectural atrocities as the make-believe outdoor theater wth a triumphal arch for the proscenium, Italian replicas, and walls and ceilings painted to fool us into the adulation of Mediterranean heavens. Far better the practical advice of the architect, that one should not worry about movie decorations, since the audience hasn't much time to look around between pictures. Germany began to think of movie architecture as early as 1911 when Lucien Bernhard designed the Princess Theater of some 400 seats.

By 1914 there were fine structures by Kaufmann, Poelzig and others. In that year appeared Schliepmann's inclusive book on the Lichtspielhaus, marking the first period of deliberate building. The war prevented the progress beyond this period, so that Paul Zucker's book on theaters and movie houses, published in 1926, adds nothing to the data. German "kinos" remain splendidly severe but not yet movie houses in their interiors. However, the German architect knows his categories, and is aware that in the "kino," at least, the "economy of necessity is the economy of beauty."

The American architect has been stopped at the engineering problems, not yet recognizing the architectural category of the movie house, which is an aesthetic problem. Hope lies in the statement of an American architect, that "the motion picture theater of today bears very little resemblance to the type which was developed soon after the movies became a popular form of entertainment, and the moving picture theater of today may possibly develop into as obsolete a type as the picture theater of 10 years ago is now."

This hope, I must admit, cannot be supported by current evidence. The large presentation house adds unto itself. The Mastbaum Theater to arise in Philadelphia's new theatrical district is to be a "stupendous" structure seating 5,000. The Carman – a neighborhood house in North Philadelphia – will be a presentation house. The associate editors of *The American Architect,* R. W. Sexton and B. F. Betts, have recently published a book on *American Theaters of Today,* which accepts the cinema as is without question. There is no concern over an "ideal" cinema. Roxy contributes the introduction. The volume is the most complete graphic statement of the architecture of the American theater. It is an extension beyond such volumes as *Theaters and Picture Houses* (1916), by Arthur S. Meloy, and *Modern Theater Construction* (1917), by Edward Bernard Kinsla.

Still, I find hope for my ideal of the movie house in the possibilities of the Little Cinema movement, which, if it is sincere, will need to determine for itself its own "sanctum sanctorum."

BILLBOARD,
December 24, 1927.

POP GOES THE MOVIE

It was in Breslau, Silesia, east Germany, 1851, the Lubins had a son, Sigmund, born to them. While young he was moved to Berlin. At 16 he had completed his schooling and a year later he was in Boston. After a few years in that astute city, Sigmund came to its sister town, Philadelphia. Here he saw a chance to open an optical shop. To get the capital, he returned to Germany. He could not, however, so the story goes, convince his friends or relatives of his prosperity virtual or prospective because he was wearing a topcoat in the winter. He stayed a year at home, then returned to Philadelphia and opened an optical shop on Arch Street, later transfering to Eighth Street, where today, opposite Gimbel's department store stands "Lubin's, the oldest optical establishment in Philadelphia." Enter this shop and find, although the business has long passed out of Lubin hands, a framed photograph of Sigmund and a mouldering volume of clippings about the Lubin films. For Lubin became eventually a pioneer buccaneer of the "machine-age" art, "the art of the self-respecting petty-bourgeois and the workingman."

Terry Ramsaye, reciting the story of Lubin's first days, relates a story of 1896. "Pop" Rock, later one of the founders of the dominant film company Vitagraph, had secured the rights to the Armat Vitascope for Louisiana. In New Orleans he attached to himself, or rather was attached unto by, the persistent admirer, Sigmund Lubin. The latter was peddling spectacles, a great variety not excluding smoked glasses, which he was trying to sell the Mardi Gras celebrants. An eclipse of the sun was impending. But Sigmund found his sun in "Pop" Rock of the massive gold chain and diamonds, the expansive Pop of the Vitascope. Lubin was attracted by the machine and that was his introduction to the movie.

In his optical shop Sigmund Lubin sold spectacles and ground lenses. He invented a number of machines, among them a multiple grinder that handled a large number of lenses of identical prescription simultaneously. His optical equipment was supplied by Charles Francis Jenkins, now active in television. Jenkins was manufacturing a new movie machine, the Phanatoscope. Sigmund Lubin had not forgot "Pop" Rock. He had kept on tampering with "taking" cameras and projectors. He began to handle the Phanatoscope. Quick to sense the possibilities of a mechanism, Lubin filmed *Horse Eating Hay,* an epoch-making film inauguration. Georges Méliès, a magician of the Robert Houdon troupe in Paris, was using the cinematograph for his magical illusion acts. Lubin began to produce legerdermain or trick photoplays, the beginnings of film cutting. A train would tear up a mountain, jump from peak to peak, and then go down the side. Later, Lubin's company was the first to show men jumping from skyscrapers, by using dummies. He very early photographed germs in movement by using a microscope. He anticipated the home movie with his small box for taking household pictures.

When the Lathams developed the Eidoloscope in 1895, they intended mainly to make records of important prize fights. These records did not get across. The shrewd Lubin saw a better way. Philly was a hot fight town and was replete with pretty good and fair fighters. The morning after a big battle, "Pop" Lubin, who seems to have come by the name early in the game, would take a couple of local boys. He had selected them for their supposed resemblance to the real principals of the bout. This was a primitive forerunner of casting to type. Lubin enacted the fight on the roof of his building where he had an open air prize-ring. The report of the fight would be read round by round. The fighters gave a condensed version of the rounds to make a complete fight. The film was rushed on the market as a "reproduction" of the big fight, with "reproduction" in small type. Lubin was an early exploiter of a favorite advertising trick, it seems. Two pugilistic stevedores were used for "The Great Corbett-Fitzsimmons Fight," in parentheses "(in counterpart)." Observe the use of the more or less unfamiliar word, "counterpart." The film made money. The method used may be considered to be an ancestor of the scenario, a film enacted to a plan. The Fitzsimmons-Ruhlin fight was counterparted similarly.

About that time Carrie Nation, the anti-saloon demon, was on the rampage with her little hatchet. Lubin tried to get her to pose. She said No! Lubin again was anticipating the current practice, this time the hiring of celebrities outside the movie. The refusal didn't daunt Lubin, and he went in for another traditional procedure, enacting the event. He got substitutes to raid a saloon. The people in the neighborhood thought it was the real McCoy. They joined in, and "Pop" had to pay $700 damages.

Lubin pioneered another practice. After Hollaman and Eaves had filmed the *Passion Play* successfully, Lubin did another in a Philadelphia backyard with frivolous actors from New York. Terry Ramsaye tells of Frank Tichenor, later important in the film business, who saw a Philadelphia girl he was fond of leaning out of a window, watching the actors in the film, and Lubin, who cared little for such intrusions, didn't notice her in the picture when it was projected. Or as Ramsaye says: "Lubin was broad-minded enough to overlook such inadvertences, and if he had known that he had an anachronism in the picture he would have charged more for it." Lubin could undersell his competitors because of his substitute methods. He was wise enough not to try as yet "duping," the making of a negative from a positive print. It was unsafe and would have meant a delay, an important consideration for the fight films especially.

At this time he was making short pictures which constituted a movie program in those days. But later when the technique of the film became improved and competition began to stiffen, he didn't hesitate to take part in the practice of "duping." He pirated the prints of practically every film made by Edison, Biograph, and Vitagraph companies. The pirating was mutual. In addition he took unto himself the films of the foreign producers, Gaumont, Pathé, Méliès, and Urban.

Between 1898 and 1900 Edison began the campaign to monopolize his patents against infringement. Biograph was the chief defendant, but Lubin too had to watch his step. Edison had patented his Kinetoscope in the United States only. Abroad the Warwick Trading Company and Pathé were the chief makers of cameras. Lubin used Warwick boxes.

Litigation drove him to Germany. He tried to make pictures there but the police restrictions were severer than the Edison lawyers. He came back to Philadelphia, after things had cleared a bit. His backyard was his studio and his cellar the darkroom for developing negatives. In 1906–7 the Motion Picture Patents Company was organized. The idea was to pool the Edison and Biograph patents, get Lubin to confess infringement, thereby establishing a needed legal precedent, and then join the leading producers into a combination. Lubin confessed guilt and became a member. The trust included Edison, Lubin, Biograph, Vitagraph, Essanay (Spoor and Anderson) and Kalem (*K* for Kleine who has recently died, *L* for Long and *M* for Marion). From Europe there were admitted Pathé, Gaumont and Urban. Gaston Méliès, brother of the Georges, who may be considered the real father of motion picture art, was given a single release each week as a supposed charity to Georges, but brother Georges never benefited from this.

Once admitted to the elect, "Pop" Lubin went full steam ahead and released two full reels each week, later adding another. He had two studios, his original one was in Arch Street on the roof of the old Dime Museum. It was a skylight affair and work had to be stopped in the afternoon when the shadow of the City Hall tower fell across the stage. This was on the south side of the street between Ninth and Tenth. He added to this major studio one on the second floor of 926 Market Street. The ground floor was a theater. This studio had a single stage in the rear. The business offices were in the front. On the third floor was the machine shop, with the processing departments on the fourth and fifth.

Lubin was the first producer to own a chain of theaters. It must be remembered that "independents" like Laemmle, Fox and the Warners edged into the producing business and fought the "trust" successfully because they had outlets before they had pictures. It was easy to turn to making films once there was one's own audience. Lubin kept turning stores into theaters in any good location he found. The wise fellows prophesied disaster. His six store properties became movie houses. He covered the stores with false fronts of stamped metal. From Philadelphia he went into Reading, Allentown, Wilkes-Barre, and out of Pennsylvania, into Wilmington, Delaware; Richmond, Virginia; and Cincinnati, Ohio. With the advance of the movie, Lubin built the first real theater for films, the Victoria, still standing on Market Street, across [?] the Post Office in Philadelphia. Farther west on the opposite side of the street he built another, the Palace, also still active. These houses were very profitable, and their overflow went into Lubin's three adjacent store-shows. For quite a time Lubin monopolized Market Street. Later others entered. He went off this main thoroughfare. Even today the Auditorium in Philadelphia's Tenderloin is known as Lubin's though none of the urchins who call it by that name knows why. For some reason Lubin became convinced in 1907 that the motion picture exhibition didn't pay and he unloaded his houses on Felix Isman, real estate operator. Isman sold the chain to Stanley Mastbaum. They formed the nucleus of the Stanley circuit, now owned by the Warner Brothers. Lubin, sad to say, sold his business about two years before movie exhibition moved into big money.

He stuck, however, to his film production. Continuing his follow-the-leader practice, he duplicated the first "big" picture, *The Great Train*

Robbery, with *The Bold Bank Robbery*. He saw the chance to do something new in cinema competition by running an advertisement in *The Billboard* offering the 600-foot picture for $66 and at the same time his Lubin's Exposition Model Cinegraph and accessories for $75, with 200 feet of film and 2 Monarch Records playing music for the films for $99, a $37.50 Victor Talking Machine gratis. This was an early introduction of synchronization. The movies in those days were "motion tableaux."

A "chase" picture had been very successful. It was called *Personal*, after the newspaper column. Lubin followed with *Meet Me at the Fountain*. On the success of the Broncho Billy "horse opera" series, Lubin inaugurated the Patsy Bolivar series and others. Ramsayye tells of a story of Lubin's duping of a film of Méliès. The Motion Picture Patents Company, formed from the Edison Licensees group, fined Lubin $1000. "I didn't dupe it," Lubin exclaimed. "Besides I didn't make any money on it and I won't pay any fine." No wonder Ramsaye calls him the humorist of the Patents Company.

Lubin was probably, with all his irascibility, a good-natured man. When Mark Dintenfass, associated with his father and brothers in the herring business and a member of a family that has given Philadelphia an eminent surgeon, turned to make films, Lubin rented him his roof studio. Mark was safe in the enemy's territory. The licensees could not think of hunting him in Lubin's quarters. Later "Pop" saved Jesse Lasky for Hollywood. Dintenfass became one of the Universal company that helped to break up the Patents Company. He himself was squeezed out of Universal and moved to the old eastern Hollywood on the Palisades of New Jersey. He is still a film producer.

In 1908 Lubin built his first real studio at Indiana Avenue and Twentieth Street. It didn't get done until 1914, when it was the largest producing center of its time, covering two city blocks. It took that long to complete it, because Lubin made a mistake by building first a single studio with a 60-foot height. It was later cut into two floors and divided into light and dark studios. Still everything was wrong. Lubin coaxed a Parisian who had come over to give him the layout and this man, Reigneau, gave it—and gave it all wrong. He built toning tanks of slate and the slate chilled the bath too rapidly. When an engineer ordered the slate replaced by soapstone, Reigneau defended himself by saying "it looked like slate."

In 1910 the General Film Company, organized by the Patents Company, bought Lubin's exchange in Philly, leaving "Pop" to concentrate entirely on production; and at the same time, since he was a member of the Patents Company, he shared in the profits of the exchange he had sold. Concentrating on production, he not only was active at Lubinville, his Philadelphia plant, but had bought property at Betzwood in the suburbs. His dream was to build an industrial village where he, Sigmund "Pop" Lubin, would be overlord, after the German pattern. He announced publicly that he would even make his own film stock. But when Eastman said "Let George do it!", threatening to withhold all supplies of raw film at once, "Pop" deflated his aspiration.

At the plant in Philadelphia Lubin finally had two fully-equipped studios able to handle five productions simultaneously. At Betzwood-on-the-Schuylkill, near Norristown, there was a 550-acre farm for productions, with a manor house, conservatory, guest house, fifty head of Texas horses, cows, deer, prize hogs, sheep, chickens, geese, swans, turkeys and "dogs of all nationalities." At least that was the boast. It was "THE UTOPIAN MOVING PICTURE PLANT OF THE WORLD," established at a cost of $2,000,000.

For production in Betzwood Lubin rigged up a dark studio, with electricity this time, rather than skylight. Now and then a company drove there from Lubinville to make a picture, but not very often, for the train service was wretched and the facilities poor. However, Lubin did make some big outdoor productions at Betzwood. He was the first to have the equipment of the Hollywood "back lot" or "ranch." On one occasion he made a Civil War film. The crowd of curiosity-seekers trampled down his truck garden and overran the place. They had brought no lunch and "Pop" Lubin had to feed them, because there was no restaurant in the vicinity. His publicity had overreached itself.

Betzwood was known as "the farm" and when he was asked how it was prospering, "Pop" replied in his brogue: "Well, my farmer tells me this morning I have 56 eggs. The cat has had chickens [*sic*] and the dog has had puppies – and one of the horses is dead. Where in hell is the profit?"

It was during the making of the Civil War picture that Lubin held up the work for two days while they persuaded him that Guy Oliver, now doing character bits in Hollywood for Paramount, would have to wear a crêpe-hair beard as General Grant. Lubin abhorred bald wigs and crêpe hair. There was a standing command that they were never to be used. It has been suggested he opposed them from financial bias, but it would seem he had an esthetic objection to them. One day he saw Willard Lewis, now dead, wearing a bald wig in a picture. Lubin yelled he could see the "join" on the forehead. Arthur Hotaling, who had directed the picture, called Bill Lewis in and showed "Pop" that Bill had shaved the top of his head because the hair was getting thin and he had been told shaving it would encourage growth. But "Pop" insisted he could still see the "join."

Epes Winthrop Sargent, now with *Variety,* joined the Lubin scenario staff in 1908, and describes "Pop" as a tall old man who was pretty hard to get along with. He tells me of an incident where Lubin was pinned down by him to the declaration that Bill Carr, scenario writer, had no scripts, Sargent knew better, that Carr had two prepared. He dared "Pop" to go face Bill with him. "Pop" was cornered. Instead of going down to the studio, he went upstairs to the drying room. Sargent followed him to the roof, down to the cellar and back to Lubin's office, where "Pop" clapped on his hat with "By God! I cannot have peace even in my own office." Twenty minutes later Sargent stopped into the saloon next door to get a cocktail on his way home. There was a yell from the other end of the bar, and there stood "Pop" all smiles. "He bought me three cocktails before he let me go," says Sargent. "I had him licked and he knew it and respected me for it." No hard feelings, but, just the same, "Pop" Lubin was a trying man to work for. Giles Warren used to say he lost thirty-five pounds in three months working for Lubin, and had to quit to save his health.

While Lubin has been called tight in his film making, there's a story which belies that legend. The hardy perennial *Uncle Tom's Cabin* had been made during his absence with Eliza escaping on sheets of paper for ice. The audience had to be told by a verbal call-boy, in original Elizabethan fashion, "this paper is ice." Lubin re-took the scene at an expense of $1,000. He himself was the brutal overseer, Simon Legree.

It was about 1910 that Lubin got his first stars. There was Florence Lawrence, actually the first "name" to be known by the fans. And the male star was Arthur Johnson from a Philadelphia stock company. Johnson was the loose, long-armed, tall hero of the Gary Cooper type, although a more gifted player. I cannot say, however, that he excited my juvenile interest, nor was the Lubin film my type in the days of Broncho Billy and the Keystone Kops. With the advent of these stars, whatever my reaction to them, Lubin's business boomed. From the two-reel film he passed into the five-reel. Before 1900, films ran from 25 to 75 feet. At Lubinville six regular releases appeared weekly. The total production was 6,000,000 feet a week. Until the five-reel film the Lubin company was pretty small and ordinary, although it witnessed the debut of Harry Myers (the *Connecticut Yankee* of the silent version and support of Chaplin in *City Lights*), Raymond McKee, and Mary Carr. The last was not a regular member of the troupe, but her husband was a director and now and then he would coax some writer like Sargent to write a part into the scenario to give her three or four days' work at $5 per. Occasionally her two sons got in too. Mrs. Carr was not too popular in the Lubin quarters. She was considered a trouble-maker.

Always worried by the fear of losing his business, Lubin declined to sell an interest in it. He made his son-in-law, Kingston Singhi, business-manager rather than hire a trained person. Singhi, whom he cherished, was divorced by Edith Lubin, and "Pop" built up the next son-in-law, Ira Lowery, who proved even less competent. Lubin, in the emergency, brought Singhi back to work with Lowery and the two almost crashed the business.

At one time Lubin had Tom Cochrane, brother of Bob of the Universal. Tom did such good work he had "Pop" scared. Lubin persuaded Cochrane to take a vacation. The latter went away for two weeks. When he got back "Pop" asked him how he was feeling. "Great, Mr. Lubin." "Then please you go over to New York and look for a job. You are through here."

Lubin could not keep up with one phase of the business, the growing salary. Sargent, scenarist and press agent, was drawing $100 a week. "Pop" saw him draw his salary one day and fired him. He substituted a woman for $25 but had to drop her. Then he called in Lawrence McCloskey, who built quite a formidable staff, including Clay M. Greene and John Ince. He paid a lot more than $100 a week to many of them.

To keep his actors away from the saloon across the street, a dump which in five years permitted three owners to sell out and retire on their incomes, "Pop" maintained a restaurant. The meal cost 25 cents and included soup, three or four choices of meats, fresh vegetables from the farm, dessert, coffee and milk, also fresh from the farm. It was a swell feed for the price, even in those days. But actors know how to kick even when they haven't anything to kick about. Lubin came upon a pair as they walked down the winding stairs. They were knocking the grub. "The restaurant is no good, hey?" he accosted them. Lamely they stalled; they had had beef, veal and mutton the day before and again today. Lubin listened. "I think myself it is rotten," he said, "I shut the damn thing up." And he did! After that he opened it only when the girls in the processing department were working overtime and the meals were free.

"Pop," if you believed him, was perpetually on the threshold of the poorhouse, and his books proved it, unless it paid him to show you an enormous profit with the same set of books. An old business custom. One day "Pop" lamented that one of his directors wanted to blow up a ship costing $20,000. Actually this was a fake vessel that some southern carnival had used and it was offered for $2,000, a reasonable enough price . . . It made "a great picture," reports go.

The *Passion Play* film he made early in his film career is remembered today for a gag. The crucifixion was deferred on Saturday morning because the act could not be staged before the City Hall shadow crossed the studio. Everyone was told to come 7 a.m. Monday and make up. Nemoyer, the Christ, went on a spree and Lubin was informed. It was a rule in those ancient days that when a player was told to make up, he was entitled to pay for the day, whether or not he worked. On Monday "Pop" was on the sidewalk in front of the studio by 6:30. As each player appeared, he was told by the producer, "Please you shall go home. We cannot crucify Christ today. He is too drunk." It was not meant flippantly, by any means, and "Pop" was forever unconscious of how his words sounded.

There was another incident when an actor, a "ticket" man, assured of four days work or tickets a week, was finally spotted by "Pop" after he had managed to avoid working by simply telling one director he was working for another. "Pop" asked him whether he was working. "Why yes, Mr. Lubin," he answered briskly, "I'm around here every day." "I know you are," said "Pop," "but do you *work* for me?" The "ticket" man was bounced.

George Rheem, a new member of the company, had his feelings ruffled when "Pop" told him he was rotten, after seeing him on the screen in the projection room. A few days later "Pop" was in a fierce distemper and he could not be soothed. The picture was — how bad! He must throw it away and betake himself to the poorhouse. There was only one good actor: George Rheem. Out of the dense darkness Rheem's voice issued: "Why Mr. Lubin, you said last week I was rotten." "You are," affirmed Lubin, "but you are better than those others."

The famous *Uncle Tom* film was Lubin's nemesis. He was the Legree of it and a lovely Legree he made, funny as Weber of Weber and Fields. Every time a friend came to Philly, he asked Lubin to show him the picture. Lubin was afraid to destroy it for fear of being guyed more than ever. It was a thorn in his ample flesh! Many years later the film vaults exploded. Lubin was in New York when he heard the news. He hurried back, and, met at the train, asked: "Is anyone hurt?" "No." "Thank God! Was *Uncle Tom* burned?" "Yes." "Thank God for that, too."

When the studios at Lubinville were active, the Lubin company was said to be worth some $10,000,000. Lubin was among the first to seek sunny and constant climes for movie production. He established studios at San Diego, Los Angeles, near Denver, and at Jacksonville, as well as at Newport, Rhode Island. When the Patents Company dissolved in

1915, the V.L.S.E. combine was made, Vitagraph-Lubin-Selig-Essanay, for joint distribution. In a couple of years, however, with the rise of the Famous Players and Selznick, Lubin the pioneer was out of the running. He tried to build on his stars: Harry Myers and Rosemary Theby, House Peters, June Daye, Orrin Hanley, Ethel Clayton and others. Numerous popular idols came under the Lubin Liberty Bell. There was, of course, Arthur Johnson, the first male idol of the screen, and his leading lady, Lottie Briscoe. Lubin rewarded his stars and writers with directorships and producerships. Among these were Barry O'Neill, Joseph Smiley, Arthur Johnson, who died prematurely, John Ince, Romaine Fielding, George Terwilliger, and Joseph Kaufman. Among the performers who became known to the public were: Earl Metcalfe, Bernard Siegel, Crane Wilbur and Billie Reeves, who came from Chaplin and Stan Laurel's old company, Karno's Komedy. Lubin brought Raymond Hitchcock and Rooney and Bent from the stage. In this and in the hiring of noted popular writers to prepare scenarios, Lubin, with Essanay and the other companies of the combine, was paving the way for the very thing that was later to depose him. He carried over famous plays and prepared the way for The Famous Players. Among the writers and their works that received the Lubin stamp were: Henry Arthur Jones (*Mrs. Dane's Defense*), Charles Klein (*The Third Degree, The Lion and The Mouse*), Clyde Fitch, Harrison Grey Fiske, Jules Eckert Goodman (*The Man Who Stood Still*), William Vaughn Moody (*The Great Divide*), Rupert Hughes (*Two Women*), J. Hartley Manners, George Ade (*The College Widow*), Winchell Smith (*The Fortune Hunter*), and Eugene Walter. Many of these have since contributed to the same authors and a number of these same works have been remade since Lubin. In addition to these outside writers, Lubin had his regular staff which included Shannon Fife, Terwilliger and Fielding, who also was starred and directed films. They prepared, with McCloskey, the shorts, the series and the comedies, which included the comic series with an all-Negro cast headed by John and Mattie Edwards.

Sargent has said to me that: "All in all 'Pop' was the most picturesque of that little handful of pioneers who stood still and watched the procession pass them." I can't say he stood still, but it must have seemed so to him as he saw the Laskys and Zukors and Selznicks fly by. And ironically enough he had helped one of these get started. It was in the Patents Company days that Lasky and Cecil De Mille and Dustin Farnum had made *The Squaw Man*—recently remade—in a west coast barn. They were amateurs and the film jumped terribly. They stood to lose everything, but came to Lubin, who, as a member of the trust, was not supposed to aid the "outlaws." But he did, he subdued the jumps, a matter of splicing simply, and saved Lasky for the Paramount.

The American movie invasion of Europe was anticipated by Lubin. He went in 1913 to "Americanize" the German capital in movie promotion. The German press hailed him as *"Der Kino König,"* the movie king. He was given every encouragement by the German press. Lubin said he would establish theatres in Berlin and spent $1,000,000 in exploiting the commercially virgin field. But the rush of the new film era had already begun in America.

Philadelphia too was grateful to Lubin, as a banquet in his honor by the Progress Club would indicate. Lubin did not die a rich man. It is said he had certain weaknesses, and of these weaknesses his wife took account. Wisely she did that, for it was their last funds after he went bankrupt. I am told his wife works in a hotel and the daughter runs a cigar stand in Atlantic City, the city where he built his magnificent home. The side street where the house stood was renamed, at Lubin's request, Kingston Avenue, for the son-in-law whom he loved most next to his pictures. It was in Atlantic City, in Ventnor, he died, on Monday, September 11, 1923, at the age of 72, after a year's illness. He who had been one of the first exhibitors of the movie when he showed it at the National Export Exhibition in Philly in 1899 died at midnight away from the lights — electric or calcium, as they had been in his early days — of the activity he had promoted. At his bedside were his two daughters, Mrs. Emil Lowery and Mrs. J. J. White of New York.

(UNPUBLISHED MANUSCRIPT,
probably written before 1930).

A DIET OF STARS

So universal is the appreciation of the movie, that the most erudite of spectators submits to every imposition, if it is suave enough, as "art." He has barely a viewpoint from which to appraise film performance as it refers to the medium in which it disports. The movie fan, whether popular or elite, can hardly be called gourmet, for the gourmet has his gastronomic creed, and the fan has only his promiscuous reaction. Take, for instance, the indulgence in George Arliss. What would a Brillat-Savarin of cinema say to this? He would say: "Messieurs, you are confusing the entree with a questionable entremet. Mr. Arliss is not indispensable!" Indeed, Mr. Arliss is to be dispensed with. He is not, like William Haines, of the category "tolerable but not indispensable"; but belongs rather to the class "too tolerable therefore treacherous." Yes, he is the perfect mechanism, the cynosure who thwarts the film. He is a mechanism effective only within a small range, a trivial range, of the film. He is ultimately overbearing in his futility, and reminds me of nothing so much as a desiccate but gentlemanly graduate seminar. Miss Ruth Chatterton's perfection is that of commencement day at the Academy of Dramatic Arts, whereas Ann Harding is cum laude at Miss Fishbone's Finishing School on the Hudson. Once classified they have neither terror nor charm. Though I think Miss Harding, aviatrix, would be handsomer if her hair were darker.

The scholastic tedium of this precious acting leaves a void in that part of the soul which is the empty stomach. It is not such fodder as builds stamina. Despite the fact that the guest or client takes each dish for its own taste, the à la carte service is not varied. It is really just a choice among tables d'hôtes, each one in spectacular dressing. There might be Sarah

Bernhardts on the half-shell. M-G-M specializes in these Duses running with Norma Shearer the starfish and Joan Crawford with her blue-plate eyes. Connie Bennett also concentrates her "personality" into her orbs, for which she is said to receive $30,000 weekly and Gloria Swanson's merchandised marquis.

We enter one of those cathedrals of the movie, where a great deal of bishoping goes on. I ask the head-waiter of the sanctum: "Is not the movie the dance of life?" He replies: "Sir, you will have solo dancing." "St. Denis or St. Vitus?" The dancing daughters of this modern age.

I protest the abundance of talent. I tell the host my tastes are for less spice and less sauce. *"Oui. Oui!"* he replies. "You shall have IT straight." Clara Bow! I object, I am a comparative herbivore; or at least I don't like raw meat. I want the ham smoked, cured, dressed and in omelets. I want it, preferably, at the butcher's and not in the temple of the film. But, sadly, almost all the acting in the movie — by young or old — is of the age before cold cream. Though I must admit, as one of the younger generation, that the old dogs have the better of it. Here's a list to warm the cuckolds of the heart: Ernest Torrence, Gibson Gowland, Jean Hersholt, George Fawcett (when not too coquettish), Alison Skipworth, James Kirkwood, Sam Hardy (much more acceptable than the mazola smoothness of William Powell or Paul Lukas), Eugenie Besserer (whose maternal instincts are less embarrassing than those of Mary Carr, Beryl Mercer and others who ought to be guillotined). Of course, there are veterans who don't deserve the respect due old age: such as H. B. Warner, Frances Starr, Tully Marshall, Hobart Bosworth (once a swell actor who has become heinous with the dramatic talkie of the preposterous Edmund H. Goulding school).

The good old acceptables are called "character" actors. An actor of the versatile order is called, casually, even contemptuously, a "character" actor. The "sweep up the kitchen" gamut type, with the speech of a dumb-waiter and the grace of a truncated parallelepiped Kay Francis to Carole Lombard to cold-in-her-smudged-nose Claudette Colbert — is star, featured player, artiste. Yet who was the veritable guiding star of *The Right to Love,* Irving Pichel, "character" actor, or Ruth Chatterton? In *Five-Star Final* the real spark of playing was kindled by Aline MacMahon, though Edward G. Robinson is hardly a flash-in-the-pan. In *Street Scene* it was David Landau who gave what little sense of permanent reality the film contained. But here again I must undersign the star. Sylvia Sidney is intrinsically a plum, although she has been handled like a dried prune by every director save Rouben Mamoulian.

What an actor is to be rests, in great measure, with the director: he is the chef. David Wark Griffith took this prerogative so literally and drastically, he made flat contours of his stars, who lacking spine and scope, eventuated into hams, minced hams. The tradition remains with Lillian Gish and is modernized by Dolores del Rio (griefs of the river!) and Farrell-Gaynor. In certain realms of film — the realm of the juvenile playboy, for instance — this cute acting may be made into something ingratiating. That was the case with Wallace Reid. They are still hunting a successor to him. Reginald Denny was too stolid and too grown-up. Yet, when Charles Farrell first appeared in *The Rough Riders,* his smile and manner suggested Reid. But it is too much to expect the arbitrary machinery of Hollywood — "camera test" and casting agent — to recognize what's what or who's who. Eddie Quillan, one of the few born *farceurs* among the younger men, is made into a juvenile. Glenn Tryon, juvenile, is procrusteanized into a *farceur*. Robert Williams, who died so prematurely, a lavish *farceur,* is filmed in a profile love scene in *Rebound* and the crowd roars at the flatulent scene which was meant to be dramatic. Ina Claire, one of the few genuine comediennes, is confused between comedy and pathos and her full intelligence thereby cheated. What will happen to that delectable mischief, Miriam Hopkins?

Cecil de Mille solves his problem simply. He believes in the self-responsibility of the well-paid actor. But imagine placing the burden of initiation on blond Bill Boyd or the obviously exotic Jetta Goudal or Victor Varconi, all of whom have come under the De Mille flag. The late F. W. Murnau had the true directorial rule. To him there were two poles of acting and no land between — the pliable player, the creative. Murnau handled both. His direction of the creative Emil Jannings in *The Last Laugh* remains his best job and Jannings' best role. It is now fashionable to laugh at Jannings. But there is a great difference between the hyperbole of the German actor and the diabolism of the Barrymore brothers or the hamfatuities of a Richard Dix — the advantage is all with Jannings, when he is under the reign and in the reins of a disciplining director. Of pliable players in the hands of an intelligent director the best instance is Murnau's control of George O'Brien and Janet Gaynor in *Sunrise.* Neither has been so good since. Given this relation of responsive pliability to perspicacious control we might expect good work from a host of young or quasi-young players, among whom I see: Madge Evans, James Dunn, — who knows? Russell Gleason, Sally Eilers, Sylvia Sidney, Judith Wood, Kay Johnson, Myrna Loy, Juliette Compton, June Sothern, Pola Negri, Mae Busch, Monte Blue (I include some relative old-timers whose whereabouts I do not know), Mae Clarke, Joel McCrea, Frankie Darro — whom I recall as the best child actor of the American screen, Ralph Graves (without Jack Holt), Bessie Love, Zasu Pitts (better than the rôles she has been given of late, but not the genius her loyalists would make of her), Fifi D'Orsay (if she'd drop her French façade), Renée Adorée (if she'd remain Gallic), Lars Hanson (one of the few imported actors worth the expense, now back in the old country), John Gilbert (superior to the legends about him and to the sort of thing he has been forced into; one of the few actors with a directorial sense), Greta Garbo (also superior to the myths about her and superior to the American director; needs one of sensibilities to appreciate her sensitivity — a Stiller, a Seastrom or even a Feyder); Marlene Dietrich (if she can be saved from von Sternberg). And there are others. Lois Wilson, by her performance in *Seed* — where she excelled the unleavened Conrad Nagel and the revue mannerisms of Genevieve Tobin — gave hints of what she might do in more inspired hands than those of John Stahl. There are occasionally novices of sufficient momentum to realize their rôles despite directorial inertia. Bette Davis is such a lass. My first meeting with her in *Bad Sister,* where she was much more commanding than Sidney Fox or the ubiquitous Nagel, shocked me. It was her eyes — she had *"The Wild Duck"* eyes! The mallard stigma seems to get all who play the child in that drama. Helen Chandler has the whole physiognomy. And that is one reason I object to Linda Watkins — she looks, talks and reminds me too much of Helen Chandler. But Bette Davis is potential material — she mustn't carry the "sins of her fathers" into the cinema; it might put her in the class with Joan Crawford and Constance Bennett. The sin is stodgy in *The Man Who Played God.*

If it isn't IT that precisely describes the elect, then it is S.A. — which stands for both Sex Appeal and Salvation Army. Indeed, recently the two have been made one through Joan Crawford. "Wash your cinema in the blood of the lamb!" Now, passion abhors promiscuity, and therefore Sex Appeal — like Sex — is not a fortuitous matter possessed by whomever the Press Agent serves. Of beautiful women there have been few in the films. I can think of but one sculptural entity or Greek classic in the whole American movie: Naomi Childers of Vitagraph. And Sex Appeal is as deliberately constructed for the idea of a particular film — rather than for the carnal prejudice of the audience — as the stylization demanded by the rôle. Such S.A. I can record in just two instances, neither American: Gina Manes as *Thérèse Raquin,* directed by Feyder (called *Shadows of Fear* in America), and Anna Sten in *Karamasov.*

Among the men there are certain divisions of magnetism: the he-man, the great lover, the boy friend. In the first list there are certain fellows like Walter Huston, the late Milton Sills, George Bancroft, Fred Kohler, Charles Bickford, the late Louis Wolheim, who has been presentable enough, but who too often failed to impress with their manliness because they asserted it too much, probably not their fault. Thomas Meighan has probably been the worst offender among them, although, recalling the era of Francis X. Bushman, I am grateful even for him. The great lover category must mention the cult of Rudolph Valentino. By the way, have you noticed how Elissa Landi resembles him? The Valentino succession has been one of the greatest drains on film endurance: Novarro, Cortez, La Rocque, Gilbert Roland (grr-r-r-r), and – though he escapes the final listing, Ronald Colman, who has been given plausibility by sound. The latest and least attractive addition is Ivan Lebedeff. Great lover par excellence has been John Gilbert, an actor who deserves a better recording than this category. The plot to disparage him seems official. Others await the accolade, drooling Robert Montgomery, trying to be perpendicular, and Clark Gable, already appalling with his "piquant cruelty" and dotty dimples. The most obnoxious category is that of the "boy friend" – woman's lone companion and the young sinner. Let these be in varying degree anathema: Buddy Rogers, Lew Ayres, Hardie Albright, Kent Douglass, Gene Raymond, Stanley Smith (whom the talkies blew in with the wings of song), Phillips Holmes (another sober Nagel), and the others you might mention.

The actor who wants to know what playing for an idea and in submission to a structure means should consult the comiques from Charles Chaplin (up to *The Kid*) to Harry Langdon, from the "Jack" Barrymore of *The Man from Mexico* whom the John of *The Man from Blankley's* did not revive, to Raymond Griffith; Chester Conklin and Andy Clyde; Ford Sterling and Mack Swain; Daphne Pollard, Polly Moran, Marie Dressler; Groucho Marx to whom his brothers are accessories and even impediments; to Edward Everett Horton, who has consistently shamed his "stars" like Douglas Fairbanks and Ann Harding; luscious Marjorie Beebe; W. C. Fields, the man in the brown derby; Bobby Clark, and – in memoriam – the superlative Mabel Normand, a gleaming lost star whom the American cinema never learned to use. That is the tragedy of the American comedy, the rhetorical American comedy – great players, but no themes, no directors. Langdon brought to the talkie a technique of speech-as-sound that was more significant than *Mickey Mouse* but no one realized it. Raymond Griffith of High (Hat) Comedy, was dim of voice. There was no intelligence of how to make this suit his comic talent; Griff is off the screen. Mack Sennett has not met the new medium, nor was he ever greater than the proportions of the first folk-statements of the Keystone pies. The farce directors come from other spheres. Marshall Neilan descends to the farcical film from the glamorous folk domains of Mary Pickford. Therefore the film that has been historically a pace-setter now lack impetus. But the players remain. Some of them become "character" actors. All in all, with the kinema kitchens what they are, the calories lost in the cans, there is one thing we may hope to derive from a diet of stars — pernicious anemia.

(UNPUBLISHED MANUSCRIPT,
Circa 1929–30).

FILM NOVITIATES, ETC.

In my Notes in the August *Close Up,* in my comment on the makers of *The Silent Enemy,* the reader will find the description, "novices with talent," which should read "novices without talent." I am glad the error occurred: it gives me a lead into some observations upon film novices.

Film criticism suffers from the presence of the perennial novice. He appears with a frenetic outcry of discovery and reiterates ephemeral platitudes. The novice is not always a minor, he may sometimes be mature of age, if not of judgement. Such one is Mr. Barnet G. Braver-Mann (né Braverman) of Detroit, Michigan. In the clarion of Hollywood, *Film Spectator,* Mr. Braver-Mann (then Braverman) recorded the tenets of the film structure. The omniscient *Literary Digest,* which presents both sides of unimportant questions, called Braverman "a challenging aesthetician." That noncommital, sphinxlike referee recognised in the dicta of the Detroit Aristotle "first principles of cinematic art." It should have read "principles of the first cinematic art." Ford's townsman (the townsman, i.e., of the Ford car), overcome by this acclaim from Funk and Wagnalls, the seat of American orthography, immediately restated his platitudes—a prerogative of youth—and put a hyphen into his name—signature of aristocracy—and published his restated platitudes in *Experimental Cinema,* Philadelphia—coast to coast. His tenets are emphatic as well as redundantly fallacious. Here they are in their spurious virginity:

"The medium of cinematic art is motion.

"Motion as an art medium is self-sufficient and has no affinity to such media as words (away with explanatory sub-titles), music (sound), speech (spoken titles), or painting (colour and static design).

"Motion applied to a succession of images can transmit thought, stimulate emotions, indicate time, place, character, sound, speech, atmosphere, physical sensation, and state of mind.

"Motion, when utilized as an art medium by artists, has proven the motion picture a major art form, logically independent, inevitably self-sufficient, and utterly free of intrusion by the mechanics of any other medium."

More than a dozen years ago, Dr. Hugo Münsterberg of Harvard University, at the behest of the film industry and by its subsidy, examined the movie to lend it scholastic sobriety and absolution as an art. He investigated it academically for its contemporaneous character, rather than for its nature as a medium in evolution. He approached the film in the capacity of a clinical psychologist drawing aesthetic conclusions from his analyses. His book, *The Photoplay,* is of importance in the history of film criticism. It gave the film the rights of an independent art and indicated its power over that of the theatre to objectify "in our world of perception our mental act of attention." Starting as a psychologist, he reasoned as psychologician, from recorded characteristics:

"Depth and movement alike come to us in the moving picture world, not as hard facts, but as a mixture of fact and symbol. They are present and yet they are not in the things. We invest the impressions with them.

"The close-up has objectified in our world of perception our mental act of attention and by it has furnished art with a means which far transcends the power of a theatric stage."

The psychologist is speaking here, and from his observations he comes to his statement of the art of the movie:

"Moving pictures are not and ought never to be imitation of the theater. They can never give the aesthetic values of the theater; but no more can the theater give the aesthetic values of the photoplay. The drama and the photoplay are two coördinated arts, each perfectly valuable in itself.

"The next step toward the emancipation of the photoplay decidedly must be the creation of plays which speak the language of pictures only.

"As soon as we have clearly understood that the photoplay is an art in itself, the conservation of the spoken word is as disturbing as colour would be on the clothing of a marble statue.

"The colours are almost as detrimental as the voices."

Fourteen years later novices repeat these criteria for the *initial* integrity of the movie. Indeed, the constant repetitions of this first-form attitude are wasteful and even effrontery, viewed in the light of the film's subsequent evolution. And yet they recur and recur with the dogmatic assertiveness of an original discovery. Or, Mr. Welford Beaton, editor and publisher of *Film Spectator,* the novice's godfather, stirred by the fundamentalness of the godson, re-discovers Münsterberg. Instead of seeing Münsterberg as the academic observer, Beaton—in true novitiate technique—accredits the scholar with having been a certain saviour of the cinema, had the moguls been attuned. This is nonsense: the moguls paid Münsterberg to vindicate the movie, and the latter did so.

Writing in *The New Republic,* July 23, on *In Darkest Hollywood,* Mr. Beaton says:

"No matter how far or in what direction screen art advances, Münsterberg's masterly analysis of its fundamentals will remain always the solid-rock foundation for all its literature. Only those who have read and mastered this work are entitled to boast that they have put their feet on the first rung of the ladder that leads to an understanding of the principles of the screen art." What Mr. Beaton has to say next is relevant to the preparations for an historical comprehension of the film, and especially of film criticism:

"In Hollywood there are twenty thousand people engaged in making for world-wide distribution examples of this art. Neither in the main Hollywood library nor in any of its branches can a copy of the book be found. It is not for sale in a Hollywood bookstore. I have not encountered a dozen people who have read it, or two dozen who ever heard of it. The film industry is one of tremendous proportions, yet this great contribution to its mentality is out of print. Hollywood talks in terms of the externals of motion pictures, but does not think in terms of their fundamentals."

Mr. Beaton might have told us just what Münsterberg has meant to the dozen people who have read him, including his own novices. The book is in the New York library but it has not prevented *Spectator's* young frenzied contributor, Seymour Stern, from blowing Münsterberg's "fundamental" precepts (concepts?) up to cosmic entities. This much can be said for Münsterberg: he was not an unqualified absolutist. He recognised a possible argument for colors, tolerated certain captions, and accepted harmonious musical accompaniment. The cart-before-the-horse logic informs Mr. Beaton's approach. He sees the individual as creating the environment. And believes that a devotion to Münsterberg would have saved the film—from the talkie. And harken to this absoluteness: "If Hollywood, which talks about nothing but motion pictures, had known what it was talking about, it never would have gone over so completely to the talkies. It would have known that they cannot permanently endure. It would have known that the silent screen art is fundamentally sound," (is his logomachy?) "and that if the order of their coming had been reversed, the silents, intelligently made, would have chased the talkies off the screen." This is the sort of hypothetical reasoning which is proof of the absence of the historical mind—the mind with a sense of sequence in evolution that would know of the movie's inherent development from the simple to the compound. Mr. Beaton's ignorance of aesthetics coincides with his ignorance of social manoeuvres. He terminates his articles with an attack: ". . . they selected Will H. Hays, who has had much experience in politics and none in business." Exactly. The movie industry, manipulated by Wall Street, selected Hays because, as a politician, he knew the "art" of subterfuge. He acts as camouflage, barrage, and decoy. Wall Street will take care of the business.

Novitiate is cult. In the September *Theatre Guild Magazine,* Braver-Mann discovers Charlie Chaplin. A long time ago I began to prick the cult of Chaplin. I know that others have questioned the absolute evaluation of him as (to quote Max Reinhardt) "the beginning and end of cinema." Bakshy in a brief note indicated Chaplin's inadequacy as a director of his comedies. Seldes—one of the inflaters of Charlot—like the weathercock he is, re-echoed faintly (in a vague mention) Bakshy's doubt. Silka in the *Filmliga tijdschrift* refused the sign to unqualified admiration of Chaplin. *Les Chroniques du Jour* devoted a special number to Chaplin, allowing some "Nos" from Carco *et al.* I am certainly not advocating muckraking—there is something of that suggested in Hugh Castle's article. Any full study or critique of Chaplin will not simply have to plough through the cultism of Delluc, Poulaille, Ivan Goll (*Chaplinade*), the effete poets and painters, Seldes, Stark Young, the Tribune Libre (which had a Gala Chaplin, not succeeded—for the first time in its history—by a discussion), etc.; but will estimate Chaplin socially, as I have indicated in the following:

"Chaplin brought into the comedy the English music hall, whose manner has been his stamp since. But his development, though it has been toward the more precise reference of satire, has not been without the influence of Sennett and Linder . . . Chaplin extended the comic type to a social center-of-reference and achieved therewith satire—the humour of society." In this article (*New World Monthly* February, 1930), I went on to indicate the failure to extend the uses of rhetoric in the movie comedy, and assigned as one cause of the failure "the cult of Chaplin."

"The emphasis upon Chaplin as the film's one full realisation has obscured the origins of American film comedy. It has also not considered

Chaplin's limitations as a director and the shortcomings of the artist as performer. He has not yet achieved a Don Quixote toward which his comedy tends but does not attain . . . ." In the August 20 issue of *The New Freeman,* I attributed the frustration to several causes: the cultist stress, Chaplin's own limitations and the suppression of the creative social energies.

A current instance of this cultism is a child's story written by Michael Gold, *Charlie Chaplin's Parade,* which never asks whether Charlie Chaplin is an experience of the child of today, if ever he were to the child for whom this book is meant—the pre-adolescent. In my work with children I have learned that Chaplin – subtilized and infrequent in his appearances – is considered "silly" by children in adolescence, whereas Lloyd – or even innocuous Bobby Vernon – would be preferred. (Date, as of 1928).

Braver-Mann goes typically into the Commedia dell' Arte for Chaplin's ancestry with a show of the knowledge of school books. Fred Karno is a more propinquitous forefather. B-M says "There is nothing stereotyped in the humour of any Chaplin comedy . . . ." Which is erroneous. Chaplin utilized English stereotype; that was his first achievement: the fitting into the movie progression of the intensive frame of English vaudeville. B-M vindicates Chaplin's "apparently unmethodical manner" by entrusting it to "feeling" (the quotes are Braver-Mann's). Murnau expressed it much more concisely and accurately when he spoke of the spontaneous film of a Chaplin as a *raconte.* But even the fact of Chaplin's being a *raconteur,* while it explains, does not excuse his directorial failure. As a matter-of-fact, Braver-Mann's attempt to validate the cult betrays Chaplin. His article is mainly of Chaplin the single personality. The brief space devoted to Chaplin the creator of the film and the rather quibbling criticism of Chaplin's "inability to think and work in terms of montage" reflect two things: Chaplin's directorial limitation, and Braver-Mann's shirking of a major problem. Chaplin's success in *A Woman of Paris* would seem to vindicate him as a director, but we must not forget the arbitrary limitations Chaplin set himself. The sustained interrelationship of characters was between two personages only, and the "visual continuity" did not comprise extensive reference. Ideologically and in treatment, the cinema will need to hold Chaplin (and Monta Bell?) responsible for an insidious influence, Chaplin's inspirational temperament could create entities in two reels; increasingly it has made what are but tableaux in his longer films. Every good director allows for the flexibility of the idea born "on the lot."

I too do not deny Chaplin's eminence. But at this late date it is cult-sycophancy to talk about such obvious Chaplin traits as "plasticity, imagination, and mastery of pantomime." By the way, had Mr. Braver-Mann read an article of mine — published several years ago in *The Billboard* — he might have added the choreographic value of Chaplin's two-reelers. The use of adjectives like Rabelaisian (an ignorant though popular use of that adjective incidentally) and Falstaffian do not concern the Chaplin of today — why have not his longer films been more than elongations of his shorter? And all of the numerous descriptions of his type have been anticipated in "the classic hobo," just as Harry Langdon has characterized himself as "a Christian innocent." Braver-Mann has not dwelt sufficiently upon Chaplin's fear of overacting and his penchant for good tastes: defects in a director . . . see D. W. Griffith. No Chaplin film beyond two reels can compare as a structure-in-comedy with *Hands Up!* No Chaplin film can equal in the enactment of the comic spirit such a work as Mark Twain's *A Connecticut Yankee in King Arthur's Court.* And Chaplin promised to give us a film of social quixoticism, where his pathos would render the humor poignant as a social indictment. He gave us *The Circus,* in which the pathos seeped out until it trailed after the conclusion of the film. America depressed him, and his own quasi-intellectuality hindered him. His book, *My Trip Abroad,* though prepared by Monta Bell, explains much of Chaplin's *impasse.* When he resists the sycophantic and ill-tutored Braver-Manns, the demi-aesthete of the Seldes ilk, the paternal metaphysic like Waldo Frank — trapped in controversies with the soul, the populists, the demagogues of letters, the specious enthusiasts, all who would inflict their cult upon him, and listens to demands which urge him to forgo spurious virtues, he may move beyond his present status. Though I doubt that he can do so, in the present mind of the movie.

The suggestion of muckraking in Castle's comments on Chaplin is induced by the typical London playboy tone. Yet Castle has put his finger on one of the ideological flaws in Chaplin's work: "the atmosphere of intellectual despair." It is this pathetic defeatism, this cynicism (which, by the way, in even more offensive forms is discoverable in Lubitsch) that attracts middle-class intellectuals. *Hands Up!* was much more heroic comedy. Castle, I believe, when his tone — as on page 135 — becomes direct, didactic even, says much more than Braver-Mann in a fraction of the space. The simultaneity of these considerations of Chaplin points to a crucial moment in Chaplin's career. Muckraking, especially in America, will corrupt the sincere criticism of the man, and equally unscrupulous defences will force a false issue. Chaplin, not ever a secure personality in the American scene, may be further confused. His enthusiasts have been unfair to him: their outcries have been forms of self-expression unmindful of the artist as a developing phenomenon. Add to these the journeyman of the Jim Tully and Konrad Bercovici type and you can have a sense of the sum of pressures upon the mind of Chaplin. Chaplin's severest critic (though this statement appear hypocritic) will be his best friend. Six years ago Gilbert Seldes (*The Seven Lively Arts*) said of Chaplin: "He is on the top of the world, an exposed position, and we are all sniping at him. . . . It is because Charlie has had all there ever was of acclaim that he is now surrounded by deserters." Muckraking began early, but it has not accumulated. The Seldeses of criticism will have been responsible for much that will ensue. In their zeal to disprove the effete Stark Youngs they are deflected from the intensive consideration of what is most assertive in Chaplin. True it is there is Sennett in Chaplin (I have said as much), and ironic it is that one who has been called too "literary" a film critic should urge against Chaplin's becoming too literary. Actually what I urge is that the Sennett presence should materialise in scope and the Chaplin in pointedness. "Irony and pity" comprise only a banal slogan: from Anatole France to Paul Eldridge. I disagree with Seldes that Chaplin has excelled in composition, or that the illusion of the impromptu is a dominant virtue. The arabesque of rhetoric articulating a conception of social experience is the end Chaplin should have sought — and would have — in a society where the Seldeses were muted and the critical perceptions active. The populists have done Charlie dirt. They have made their sentimental and wistful pleasure in his whimsicality stand for supremacy in appreciation. Certainly Stark Young was wrong in seeing Chaplin as too much theater — Chaplin re-converted his derivation — but that the latter has not extended his tendency far enough along the path toward fulfillment, was sadly perceivable in the fatuous and dissociated pity of *The Circus,* and in the foreshortened exposure of *The Pilgrim.*

CLOSE UP,
November, 1930

THE BOURGEOIS MOVIE CRITICS

Samuel Brody, for the John Reed Club, invited a number of film reviewers to take part in a symposium on "The Soviet versus the American Movies." Among the replies received was one from Creighton Peet, erstwhile of the *New York Post,* which canned him, it is said, for using the epithet "lousy." Mr. Peet, now with *The Outlook and Independent,* wrote: ". . . I am afraid I must refuse that interesting experience . . . I fail to see the least connection between the present Soviet films and our own. Russian films are made by the Government and are dished out to the population to teach them machinery, wash behind the ears and love the Soviet. American films are sent to a later-day population which understands these things and wants entertainment . . . fiction. As soon as the Russian people have attained that complete industrialization – that Fordization which they so worship – they will be quite classless. At this point a symposium on the differences, if any, between Russian and American movies will be in order, and I shall be glad to participate. Furthermore, in defense of the American movies it should be pointed out that they are not state-supported and must earn their way. Russian movies are in the position of a 'house organ' or 'company propaganda.'"

Mr. Peet has crudely expressed the troubled conscience of the bourgeois film critic. Bruce Bliven, qualified by prejudice, nostalgia for lost paradises and ignorance of the motion picture, is made film reviewer for *The New Republic,* and discovers in the Soviet masterpieces, *Old and New,* and *Turksib,* an apotheosis of the machine; whereas *The Silent Enemy,* a dreadful American picture is undersigned by him as Rousseau's reply to collectivism.

Peet, I happen to know, has enjoyed Soviet films. He chided Griffith for not including *The End of St. Petersburg* among the 50 best films. The last two sentences of his letter are a defense of the inferior movie against the superior Soviet kino. They admit the superiority of collectivist control over capitalist control. Peet has responded to the force of the propaganda of Soviet films, the propaganda which has *created* the values of these films as cinema; and now he feels guilty as a mouthpiece of his class. Therefore the perversity, the infantile prejudice which calls the Soviet ideal by the bourgeois concept of "Fordization."

Mr. Peet is among those who have supported "the cult of the Soviet film." The treachery of his peevish attack is duplicated even more insidiously in the exaggerated enthusiasm shown for the Soviet film, *Cain and Artem*. This picture, which belongs to the pre-dialectic period of the kino – the Teutonic period, was swallowed by such critics as Alexander Bakshy and by every newspaper commentator, in truth, the fervor exposed the will to disbelieve the persuasive message of the dialectic film. *Cain and Artem*, melancholic and pre-war, lacking positive conviction, served as a retreat for these bankrupt souls and permitted them the cry: "See, I am still a friend of the Russian film!" American public, says Peet, wants "fiction." This is not the only synonym for "entertainment." "Fiction" is what the American public gets: fake experiences!

NEW MASSES,
October, 1930.

THE FILM IN THE THEATER

The theater, even before the advent of the film, endeavored to compound itself with other media – perfumes, for instance, shadowgraphs, lantern slides, etc. The nineties in Paris produced at the Théâtre d'Art J. Napoleon Roinard's *Song of Songs* with an accompaniment of music and perfumes. This was the period of Rimbaud's sonnet on the colors of vowels and of Chardin Hardancourt's *Book of the Orchestration of Perfumes.* Such compounding however was within the original nature of the theater, which is an intensive medium. Succeeding compoundings coincide with the theater's attempt to cinematize itself. The theater is an intensive medium aspiring towards progressiveness, the cinema a progressive medium aspiring towards intensiveness. In the motion picture *The Passion of Joan of Arc* is the maximum of intensiveness; in the theater Meyerhold's *D.S.E.* is the maximum of progressiveness.

It is logical therefore that Meyerhold should be the pace-setter in cinematizing the theater. And equally logical is it that the cinema's pace-setter, Eisenstein, should issue from the Meyerhold stage. Meyerhold, in *D.S.E.*, has used bare fences on wheels to keep the scenes in constant and continuous shift and enacting several separate episodes simultaneously. In other words he has sought to achieve progressiveness within the intensive frame. Also he projects typographical commentary on screens to underline and elucidate the pantomime and conduct of the players. This is a cinematic compounding akin to the verbal legend – the caption – of the film.

But even before Meyerhold there was an attempt to use the movie in the play-in-flesh. At the Garrick Theater in New York August 23, 1897 there opened John J. McNally's *The Good Mister Best.* "The major interest of the piece," says Terry Ramsaye, "revolved about a bit of business by which the master of the household could press a button and see revealed on the wall what was taking place in any room of the establishment. He saw plenty. The revelation on the wall was a motion picture. The film work was done by J. Stuart Blackton and Albert E. Smith with their American Vitagraph." A duplication of this utilitarian exploitation of the movie is suggested, in reference to television, by the cartoonist Hayward in "Somebody's Stenog." The grandfather of the movie, Georges Méliès, employed the film in the '90s in his magical illusion acts in Paris.

It must be close to two decades since Hobart Bosworth presented his act from London's *The Sea Wolf* on the Keith circuit. Bosworth concentrated the story into one act by introducing the stage performance with an excerpt from his film of *The Sea Wolf*. The popular jazz orchestra, Horace Heidt and his Californians, has long enacted a clever vaudeville stunt, where a transparent grandeur screen on which a college boat race is projected is superimposed upon the musicians simulating oarsmen. The Paramount stage show has recently made use of an identical stunt. At the present moment, the film star, Edward G. Robinson, is presenting an integrated act of himself in film and person.

The dance has made its uses of the screen. The Russian Ballet, in its effort to modernize itself, has utilized a triptych screen as backdrop and wings, with the projection, an abstract film, changing to the dance movements. The dance director, Leon Soletti, and his colleague, the painter Fritz Goerz, long famous for their mechanistic ballets in Germany, have arranged with the Wiehr-Film of Dresden for a cinema dance-decor. Tests have been satisfactorily made in the Zentral Theater of Dresden, and Soletti is convinced that the painted set is finished. Three or more projectors are used simultaneously. The projections are unified in the pattern of the ballet, and this practice, Soletti believes, will become a part of the composition of the opera and operetta. The Soletti-Goerz system is patented in Germany.

The best-known and most integrated structural compounding of film and theater is that of the German left-wing director Erwin Piscator, who has recently gone to make talkies in Moscow. Piscator first used the film as a prologue, in which the persons of the drama appear, introduced by a speaker. He tried to tie up the sequence of scenes by inserting film-bits in the intervals. While not wholly successful, they educated Piscator in the coördination of screen and stage. He then placed two screens, one to the left and the other to the right of the scene. Instead of attempting the visual arabesque of his first efforts, he decided that the method he had considered least appropriate was the most fitting. He would project, in the Meyerhold manner, the text of the drama as an instruction to the audience. This would avoid any ambiguity in the propaganda of the play. As he perfected his method the didactic became an element of the drama, a reinforcement of the play's *tendenz.* The evolution follows from *Flags* through *Storm Over God's Country, Hoopla, We're Alive!* and *Rasputin.* In his "Red Revue" Piscator employed all possibilities of theatrical propaganda: music, satiric songs, acrobatics, sport, drawings, film. The last was projected in fragments between the spoken scenes. The effect proved tremendous. In 1925 the full integration of film with the dramatic action was realized in *In Spite of Everything,* where Piscator sought to represent for the first time "under a concise form the revolutionary summits of human history, from Spartacus to the Russian Revolution" and "to give a didactic image of historical materialism." Piscator had originally intended to present this gigantic enterprise in the open, but was forced to present it in the Grosses Schauspielhaus. The film served as the documentary base for the dramatic action. Piscator utilized authentic battle-scenes, demobilization records, photos of cadavers, etc., obtained from the national archives. Speeches in the Reichstag, extracts from the press, photos, war films, became incorporated in a dynamic drama, which involved the audience in its action. Just after the play had shown the Social Democrats voting the war credits, a silent film is projected showing a battle and the first victims. "This was not only the political stigmatization of the event, but it also agitated the human point of view, which is engendered by art." In *Storm* Piscator used film-portions specifically executed for the drama. In *Drunken Boat* the action took place within three screens on which the projections design the decor, create the atmosphere and locate the drama.

In *Hoopla, We're Alive!* Piscator intended the film as the dramatic pivot. The film being the major medium for the intensification of experience and the concentration of time, he used it, as a comment upon the action, to reveal the agonies of eight "infinite years" in seven minutes, and conveyed the "profound abysm" with a "maximum of violence." He employed the film abstractly as a "visual music" in which the sense of eight years is transmitted by a surface dividing itself rapidly into lines and squares of calculations – of days, minutes, seconds.

Piscator invented his "Global-Segment Theater" an armature of rigid metal, permitting simultaneous enactments in areas of different contours. This theater was used for the performance of *Rasputin.* At first the director projected the film upon plane surfaces, giving relief to the flat figures. The film was to him the enlargement of "the subject in time and space." It served to enhance the development of the action by reducing the details needed to explain the action and by its very ubiquity. Moreover, it served, like the antique chorus, as an accompaniment to comment on the action and also supplied a simple ironic contrast between pretenses (the spoken word) and facts (the data on the screen). Finally it served as a representation of future destiny. For example, as Rasputin speaks, a film is imposed showing the execution of the imperial family.

In comparison with Piscator's compoundings, the film-in-the-play of the Theater Guild's production of Chlumberg's *Miracle at Verdun* must appear naïve and literal indeed. The imitative Gate Theatre of London, directed by Peter Godfrey, has tried the film-commentary in its production of Greensfelder's *Six Stokers that Own the Bloomin' Earth,* where a 16-mm picture of morsels of white cut-outs moving resiliently in space (Man Ray's influence) and miniature edifices crumbling was projected. The Experimental Theater of Copenhagen, lacking the funds for film projection, used a lantern-slide. In *Marlborough s'en va t'en guerre,* as the soldier tells of his experiences, a slide, drawn by Hans Scherfig, was projected and revealed deliberately crude drawings of legs, arms, hands, barbed wires and descriptive words.

The talkie has been used in the stage production much as the mute film was employed in *The Good Mr. Best.* In an Earl Carroll revue talking-picture players and flesh-and-blood performers hold a conversation. This has been repeated since in revue and movie theater stage show. It is an elementary "stunt" use, a "gag."

(UNPUBLISHED MANUSCRIPT, *Circa 1928–29*).

A MOVIE CALL TO ACTION!

1.

How long will movie critics — embryonic or at land's end — especially those avowing a social conscience

> rehash broad generalities and serve them as dishes of first principles?
>
> confound first statements with first principles?
>
> wax anti-Hollywood without attempting to account for Hollywood in the socio-economy?
>
> talk about the Soviet film without investigating its history, understanding its social impetus or observing its direction?
>
> talk about the film at all without some application to research in the economic, political and aesthetic history on the film; in the accumulated criticism of the film; and
>
> ABOVE ALL, how long will these critics remain critics by frustration, egocentric, conspiratorial one with the other, inactive?

2.

We must unify our separate enterprises. Inter-criticism is essential, but not browbeating one of the other. Neither inflation nor contempt. Fewer effusions and more applied energies. Our mistakes of the past have been:

desultoriness; explosive letter-writing and not enough studious, constructive writing that attempts to create a basis for understanding and action; lack of discipline; uncritical enthusiasms and equally disproportionate dispraisals; envy; scurrility at large;

lack of organization;

sectarianism in two directions: the base — the worker, and the contact — the relatively congenial critic and film-lover.

3.

WE MUST ORGANIZE

with the worker;
to attract the contact for our uses.

Workers' units are already organized — not too excellently perhaps but as a nucleus — to view films, to listen upon films, to read upon films, and least, to make films.

Can we maintain any prospect of action in the non-worker groups that exist? Can we influence such an organization as the National Board of Review? Or the little cinema vestiges? The chances are not, and the question is: are they worth it?

Shall we organize a BROAD LEAGUE FOR FILM ACTION as contact and support for an immediate action, crystallized in the workers' clubs?

Shall we organize, in other words, on two fronts, in two directions for complete utilization of all possibilities?

The answer, I think, is YES!

4.

People who act make mistakes. People who do not act simply swear.

5.

We have nuclei. We have an organized group for initiation — the John Reed Club — and others. Federation is essential. We have periodicals: the labor press, *The New Masses, The Left,* etc.

We have international contacts. I guarantee that.

6.

What would a Federation do?

1) educate the workers and others in the part the movie plays as a weapon of reaction;
2) educate the workers and others in the part the movie plays as an instrument for social purposes — in the U.S.S.R.;
3) encourage, support and sustain the left critic and the left movie maker who is documenting dramatically and persuasively the disproportions in our present economy;
4) create a chain of film audiences who would morally and financially guarantee such films;
5) publish a periodical devoted to our purposes;
6) fight the class abuses of capitalist censorship;
7) attack the invidious portrayal in the popular film — of the foreign-born worker, the Negro, the Oriental, the worker generally;
8) oppose the interests of the institutions like the church as they participate in the shaping of the monopolized film;
9) make use of, when feasible, certain methods of direct action (I do not know that this is an immediate weapon, although the protest demonstration has been mobilized already. Large-scale boycott is something to look forward to);
10) distribute suppressed films of importance, and defend artists abused by reactionary elements (as in the Eisenstein case);
11) re-discover and present neglected films of significance;
12) educate the critic and worker by closer contact with the worker; THE SECOND PART OF NUMBER 3 IS EVENTUALLY OUR MOST IMPORTANT PURPOSE! THIS PURPOSE IS MADE MEANINGFUL BY NUMBER 12!

7.

It is most important that the critics seek to correlate a body of principles and unify a point of view. The most conscientious of French critics, Leon Moussinac, has not realized his full value to the social understanding of the cinema by neglecting to scrutinize his attitude for a set of values. When he wrote on the film from the aesthetic view, before he had resolved his stand into that of social attack, he approximated a body of principles. He has not done that in the higher level of social criticism. Is that possibly because he has not been impelled into action by the stimulation of immediate contact with the social stratum most concerned with the implications of his criticism—namely, the class-conscious worker?

The German critic, Béla Balázs,* has, on the other hand, shown a consistently increasing clarification, crystallization, activization. He is in immediate relation with the class-conscious worker of Germany who is already calling for PROLETARIAN FILM CRITICISM *from the proletarian!*

The difference between Moussinac and Balázs is the difference between the status of the revolutionary movement in France and in Germany.

The deduction is left to the reader.

* * * * *

Action without theory is aimless.
Theory without action is sterile.

WORKERS' THEATER,
July, 1931.

* [Ed.]: Balázs (1884–1949) was Hungarian.

A PROPOSAL FOR A SCHOOL OF THE MOTION PICTURE

This plan for a school of the film was drawn up by Harry Alan Potamkin in the winter of 1932–33, when it was considered possible that a large university was interested in establishing a separate college to be instructed by a faculty of specialists, similar to existing music, medical, architecture and business schools.

The School would provide a complete training in the arts and sciences of the cinema for students professionally interested in the films. A degree from the school would be an equivalent of a Bachelor of Science from any established college.

COURSE: The course would be for four years.
1st year: Elementary prescribed training;
2nd, 3rd and 4th years: Specialization on chosen subject.

CURRICULUM

I. *Prescribed Courses* (starred courses* are open to the general public)
  A. The Forms of the Cinema
    1. Industrial
    2. Ethnic
    3. Educational
    4. Abstract (absolute)
    5. News — film
    6. Dramatic

* B. The Cinema related to the Arts and Industry
* C. The history of the motion picture (continuous through four years) (a course for critics)
* D. Sociology of the Cinema
    1. Economic } aspects
    2. Political } aspects
    3. Problems of censorship
  E. Comparative literatures
    1. the drama
    2. the novel
    3. the short story
  F. Languages: — German, French, Russian
  G. Principles of the performance
    1. The actor's art
    2. Cinema acting technique
  H. History of Aesthetics
    1. Development of taste
    2. The sequence of styles
  I. Design
    1. painting
    2. sculpture
    3. architecture
    4. costume and decorative arts

II. *Specialized Courses* (2 or 3 year courses)
  A. Theory of Direction
    1. Direction
    2. Film Composition
      a. editing
      b. montage
    3. Studio methods
  B. Cinematography
    1. The chemistry of the film
    2. Applied optics
    3. Applied acoustics
    4. Camera techniques
    5. Lighting
  C. Acting
    1. History of the stage
    2. History of the dance
    3. Makeup

4. Laboratory
    a. improvisation
    b. mimetic
    c. stylization

D. Scenario
    1. Sources of film material
    2. Preparation of scenario
    3. Scenario laboratory
    4. Analysis of performances

NOTE: Optics – visual fatigue, etc. (see Society of Motion Picture Engineers) Acoustics – aural fatigue and limits, etc. (see the same)

E. Animation (cartoons)
    1. Color
    2. Sound
    3. Technique

III. *Seminar Courses*
    A. Studio methods
    B. Field work on actual productions
    C. Scenario laboratory
    D. Acting laboratory
    E. Design laboratory

IV. *Invited Lecturers,* on
    A. Financing
    B. Distribution

NOTE: *Equipment* would include a model studio for the study of supervision and management

Existing schools, similar to this proposal:
1. Moscow
2. Leningrad
3. Berlin (under the auspices of the magazine *Lichtbild Buhne*)
4. Great Britain. (See Government report: *Films in National Life*)

A LIBRARY OF THE MOTION PICTURE

Categories for a Catalogue

The two main categories:
1. Foreign Films
2. Domestic Films

I. *Films*

A.

1. Dramatic
2. Ethnological
3. Experimental
    a. abstract
    b. absolute
4. Educational
5. Industrial
6. Documentary (news-film)
7. Animation

B.

1. Popular success
2. Innovations in style and technique (principles of film-making)
3. Individual performances
4. Individual direction
5. National sequences — Swedish, Italian, etc.
6. Industrial sequences (Fox, Metro, etc.)
7. Subject-matter — folk films, gangster, prohibition
8. Serials
9. Shorts.
    a. travelogue
    b. vaudeville
    c. sport film
    d. dramatic
    e. private and experimental
10. Pivotal masterpieces

II. *Scenarios*

(By well-known or significant authors, or of worthy films)

III. *Designs*

A. Stage sets
B. Designs for costumes

IV. *Stills*

(see categories of I)

V. *Books, Magazines and Pamphlets*

A. History
B. Novels made into films
C. Legal aspects
D. Source material

POSSIBLE FACULTY

I. *Critics* for elementary lectures on the films and related arts (open to the public)

A. Richard Watts (*N. Y. Herald Tribune*)
B. Evelyn Gerstein (*Boston Transcript*)
C. Iris Barry (Founder: London Film Society)
D. Gilbert Seldes (*N. Y. American*)
E. Irene Thirer (*N. Y. Daily News*) – explanation of popular appeal
F. Terry Ramsaye (for Business History)
G. Harry Alan Potamkin (New School for Social Research)

II. *Scenario*

A. Elementary course
   1. Frances Taylor Patterson (Columbia)
   2. Karl Mayer (*Sunrise*)
   3. Frances Marion (for popular films)
   4. Carl Freund (*Metropolis*)

III. *Cinematography*

1. G. W. Bitzer
2. Alvin Wyckoff
3. James Howe
(D. W. Griffith)

} elementary

IV. *Theory of Direction*

1. Sergei Eisenstein
2. Pudovkin
3. Lewis Milestone (Dramatic)
4. Flaherty (Ethnic)
5. Pabst
6. Wm. K. Howard
7. René Clair
8. Anthony Asquith

V. *Animation*

1. Alex. Geiss
2. Fleischer
3. Walt Disney

VI. *History of the Films*

1. Alexander Bakshy
2. Harry Alan Potamkin

HOUND AND HORN,
October, 1933.

A BIBLIOGRAPHY OF THE FILM WRITINGS OF HARRY ALAN POTAMKIN, 1927–1933

Prepared and annotated by Jay Leyda, Irving Lerner, and Harold Leonard, with additions by Lewis Jacobs

American Cinematographer. "Tendencies in the cinema." 11 (June 1930) 14, 44.

"The woman as film director." 12 (January 1932) 10, 45. An appraisal of Germaine Dulac.

American Photography. "L. Moholy-Nagy and his theories of photography." (January 1931).

"Photographing the seasons. That old saw on the weather gets a new meaning." 26 (May 1932) 264–8. On phases of weather as filmic material, particularly for amateurs.

The Arts. "The story of films." 13 (April 1928) 268–70. Review of *The Story of Films*, edited by Joseph P. Kennedy.

Billboard (Cincinnati). "The movie palace." (December 24, 1927).

"The English music hall." 40 (September 8, 1928) 58. On the English music hall as the perfect training school for stage and film acting.

"The future of the film." 42 (June 14, 1930) 44–5.

Boston Advertiser. "Maid of Orleans in film." (March 30, 1930).

Boston Transcript. "Positives and negatives of French films." (January 20, 1930). Examines the work of early promising film makers.

"Of the man, his method and the maid." (March 29, 1930). Dreyer in theory and practice.
"German influences on the screen." (April 18, 1930).

Cinema. "The French film." illus. 1 (February 1930) 28–30, 56.
"The rise and fall of the German film." illus. 1 (April 1930) 24–5, 57, 59.
"The cinema in Great Britain." illus. 1 (May 1930) 24–5, 50.
"Film beginnings in Belgium and Holland." illus. 1 (June 1930) 26–7, 54.
"The golden age of the Scandinavian film." illus. 1 (September 1930) 26–7, 60.
"Cinema Italia." illus. 1 (October 1930) 20–21, 59–60.
"Cinema Iberia." The status of motion pictures over on the Spanish peninsula. illus. 1 (December 1930) 20–21, 60, 63.

Close Up (Territet, Switzerland/London). "The compound cinema." Part I: 4 (January 1929) 32–7. Part II: 4 (April 1929) 10–17. An essay on the aesthetic potentialities of a cinematic form compounded of many variants.
"The English cinema." 4 (March 1929) 17–28.
"Phases of cinema unity." Part I: 4 (May 1929) 27–38. Part II: 5 (September 1929) 171–84. Part III: 6 (June 1930) 463–74.
"The French cinema." 5 (July 1929) 11–24.
"The Aframerican cinema." 5 (August 1929) 107–17. On the depiction of the Negro in the American film.
"*Kino* and *Lichtspiel*." 5 (November 1929) 387–98. An analysis of the German film.
"Movie: New York Notes: I." 5 (December 1929) 493–505. An essay on the aesthetics of the sound film, with an analysis of the theories of Gilbert Seldes. Includes a review of Watson and Webber's *The Fall of the House of Usher*.
"In the land where images mutter." 6 (January 1930) 11–19. An analysis of sound, based on reviews of current films.
"Movie: New York Notes: II." 6 (February 1930) 98–113. A documented study of the portrayal of the Jew in films. Also contains notes on the philology of the sound film and reviews of *Applause* and Jo Gercon and Louis Hirshman's *The Story of a Nobody*.
"Movie: New York Notes: III." 6 (March 1930) 214–23. Interviews with Edgar Wallace, Rouben Mamoulian, and Karl Freund. Includes a review of John Gould Fletcher's *The Crisis in the Film*.
"The personality of the player: a phase of unity." 6 (April 1930) 290–97. An analysis of film acting.
"Playing with sound." 7 (August 1930) 112–15.
"Movie: New York Notes: IV." 7 (August 1930) 115–19. Reviews of *The*

Silent Enemy, With Byrd at the South Pole, and *The Man from Blankley's.*

"Movie: New York Notes: V." 7 (October 1930) 235–52. Reviews of current films. Includes a critique of *Scenario Writing and Producing for the Amateur* by Marion Norris Gleason and notes on American film critics.

"Film novitiates, etc." 7 (November 1930) 314–24. A polemic on contemporary film critics, with emphasis on the Chaplin cult.

"Reelife." 7 (December 1930) 386–92. A review of *Billy the Kid,* with comments on the "Realife" wide screen.

"The new kino." 8 (March 1931) 64–70. Reviews of *Perekop, Salt of Svanetia, Rubicon, Life in Full Swing,* and the animated cartoon *Mail.*

"Novel into film: a case study of current practice." 8 (December 1931) 267–79. A critique of *An American Tragedy,* with excerpts from Eisenstein's projected treatment.

"Dog days in the movie." 9 (December 1932) 268–72. A description of the current film season.

"The year of the eclipse." 10 (March 1933) 30–39. Reviews of *Cock o' the Air, Cabin in the Cotton,* and *I am a Fugitive from a Chain Gang.*

Creative Art. "The film until now." 8 (May 1931) 382. Review of Paul Rotha's *The Film Till Now.*

"Lost paradise: *Tabu.*" illus. 8 (June 1931) 462–3. Review of *Tabu.*

"Pabst." illus. 9 (July 1931) 74–5. Review of *Die Dreigroschenoper.*

"Celluloid: the film today." 10 (February 1932) 149, 151. Review of Paul Rotha's *Celluloid: the Film Today.*

"A history of the movies." 10 (June 1932) 490. Review of Benjamin B. Hampton's *A History of the Movies.*

"Cinematographic Annual." 11 (November 1932) 239. Review of volume two of *The Cinematographic Annual,* edited by Hal Hall.

Experimental Cinema. "Film problems of Soviet Russia." Part I: 1 (February 1930) 3–4. Part II: "Populism and dialectics." illus. 1 (June 1930) 16, 17. An interpretation of the Soviet film, stemming from a review of Winifred Bryher's *Film Problems of Soviet Russia.*

Films. "The cinematized child." (November 1939) 10–18. Analyzes the influence of the screen on children. Annotated by Edgar Dale. Published posthumously.

Film Weekly (London). "Camera work as an art factor." (December 31, 1928, January 7, 1929).

"France's Advance Guard in production." (December 17 and 24, 1928).

Front (The Hague). "The death of the bourgeois film." 1 (April 1931) 284–8. A survey of the current state of the cinema throughout the world.

Hound and Horn. "René Clair and film humor." illus. 6 (October 1932) 114–23.

"Pabst and the social film." 6 (January 1933) 293–305.

"Pudovkin and the revolutionary film." 6 (April 1933) 480–93.

"Eisenstein and the theory of cinema." 6 (July 1933) 678–89.

"A proposal for a school of the motion picture." 7 (October 1933) 140–3.

Liberator. "The white man's Negro." 3 (March 28, 1931) 7. On Hollywood's misrepresentation of the Negro.

Modern Thinker and Author's Review. "Film cults." 2 (November 1932) 547–50.

Movie Makers. "The closeup's the thing." illus. 4 (September 1929) 572, 597–8. An analysis of the use of the closeup as manifested in *The Passion of Joan of Arc.*

"The magic of machine films." illus. 4 (November 1929) 722–3, 744. Advice to amateurs on filmic dramatization of the machine.

"New ideas for animation: suggestions for amateur experiment." illus. 4 (December 1929) 800–01. Includes brief descriptions of the Japanese rice paper cut-out technique; Lotte Reiniger's silhouette films; Francis Bruguière's photo designs; and Ladislas Starevich's puppet films.

"The montage film." illus. 5 (February 1930) 88–9. Advice to amateurs on the use of montage.

"New backgrounds." illus. 12 (October 1937) 483, 502–4. Advice to amateurs on the use of light, prisms, screens, etc. in place of sets. Published posthumously.

Musical Quarterly. "Music and the movies." 15 (April 1929) 281–96.

The National Board of Review Magazine. "Alexander Bakshy." 2 (September 1927) 4, 6. An appreciation of one of the first film theoreticians.

"Cinéa-Ciné." 2 (October 1927) 4–5. An estimate of the French cinema.

"The plight of the European movie." 2 (December 1927) 4–6.

"*The Passion of Joan of Arc.*" illus. 4 (January 1929) 7–9.

"Comrades of 1918." (April 1931).

"*Road To Life.*" (February 1932).

"The ritual of the movies." Part I: 8 (May 1933) 3–6. Part II: "The child as part of the cinema audience." illus. 8 (June 1933) 3, 6, 8. An address delivered at the 9th annual conference of the National Board of Review, held February 9–11, 1933, New York. Discusses the interrelationship between the audience and the motion picture industry and the development of film clubs. In two parts.

New Freeman. "The mind of the movie." 1 (August 20, 1930) 538–41. A social analysis of the film.
"The film evangel." 2 (November 26, 1930) 254–6. A polemic on Will H. Hays.
"Motion picture criticism." 2 (March 4, 1931) 591–3.

New Masses. "Two Russian films." 5 (January 1930) 14.
" 'A' in the art of the movies and kino." 5 (December 1929) 14–15. Reviews of *Applause* and *Arsenal.* Reviews of *Love in the Caucasus* and *The New Babylon.*
"The old and the new." 5 (May 1930) 15. Review of *Old and New.*
"The film and the war." 5 (June 1930) 14–15. Reviews of *Journey's End, All Quiet on the Western Front,* and *Turksib.*
"Movies." 6 (July 1930) 17. Review of *The Silent Enemy.*
"Movies." 6 (August 1930) 13. Reviews of *The Big House* and *Numbered Men.*
"Movies." 6 (October 1930) 16. A comparative study of Pudovkin and Griffith based on analyses of *Storm Over Asia* and Griffith's *Abraham Lincoln.*
"The bourgeois movie critics." 6 (October 1930) 21. A letter criticizing Creighton Peet for his refusal to participate in a symposium on "The Soviet *vs.* the American Movies," held at the John Reed Club.
"What will Mr. Peet do about it?" 6 (November 1930) 23. A rebuttal of Creighton Peet's defense of his attitude on Soviet films, *vide supra.*
"The racketeer Paramount." 6 (November 1930) 15. A discussion of gangster films, based on reviews of Paramount's current cycle.
"Movies." 6 (December 1930) 19. Review of *Soil.*
"Movies, coupons and prunes." 6 (May 1931) 17. Reviews of current films in relation to the depression and the class struggle.
"Movies." 7 (June 1931) 19. Review of *A Son of the Land.*
"Movies." 7 (July 1931) 19. Review of John Drinkwater's *The Life and Adventures of Carl Laemmle.*
"Hollywood looks at war." 7 (August 1931) 19. Review of *The Spy.*
"Eucalyptus trees in Siberia." 7 (November 1931) 27. A polemic on Hollywood's interpretation of Communism and the Soviet Union.
"Cinema." 7 (May 1932) 28. Review of *Shanghai Express.* Article unsigned. Attributed to Harry Alan Potamkin on the basis of internal evidence.
"Tendencies in the Soviet film." 7 (June 1932) 18.
"Movies and revolution." 8 (December 1932) 21. Review of *Kameradschaft.*
"Gabriel over Roosevelt." 8 (May 1933) 24–5. Review of *Gabriel Over the White House.*

The New Republic. "The man nobody knows." 68 (October 21, 1931) 274. Review of *Charlie Chaplin, His Life and Art,* by W. Dodgson Bowman.

"The Mythical Art." (December 18, 1929). Review of *One Hour with the Movies and Talkies* by Gilbert Seldes.

New Theater. "Hollywood or Lenin Hills." 1 (April 1934) 9–10. On the Soviet Union as the refuge of exiled film artists. Published posthumously.

New World Monthly. "The motion picture comedy." 1 (February 1930) 117–21.

The New York Herald Tribune. "Cinematic Design." (July 9, 1932). Review of book by Leonard Hacker.

The New York Times. "Jean Painlevé's Movies." (June ?), Unsigned.

Pagany (Boston). "The future cinema: notes for a study." 1 (Spring 1930) 76–9.

Phonograph Monthly Review. "The phonograph and the sonal film." (July 1930).

Proletarskoye Kino (Moscow). *"Negr belovo cheloveka."* Trans. by P. Attasheva. illus. 1 (1931) No. 7; 52–4.

"'Movie' amerikanskoye kino." Trans. by B. Levchenko. 1 (1931) No. 10–11; 82–85.

Révue du Cinéma (Paris). *"Le cinéma americain et l'opinion française."* illus. 1 (October 1929) 55–9.
"Remarques sur D. W. Griffith." illus. 3 (February 1, 1931) 22–31.
"Films de guerre americains." Trans. from English. illus. 3 (May 1931) 38–43.

Theatre Guild Magazine. "Ladislas Starevich and his doll films." illus. 7 (December 1929) 34–5.
"Camera! Some unsung artists of the cinema." illus. 7 (July 1930) 19–22, 42. An evaluation of leading American and European cameramen. Reprinted under the title "Knights of the Camera" in *International Photographer* (Hollywood) 2 (September 1930) 14–16.
"Light and shade in the Soviet cinema." illus. 8 (May 1931) 20–23.

Transition (Paris). "Francis Bruguière." illus. 18 (November 1929) 81–2.

Vanity Fair. "Field generals of the film." 38 (March 1932) 52, 76. Brief appraisals of leading American film directors.

Workers' Theater. "A movie call to action." I (July 1931) 5–7. Describes the organization and function of the Workers' Film and Photo League.
"Who owns the movie?" Part I: 1 (February 1932) 27–9. Part II: 2 (April 1932) 18–21. On capitalist control of the American film industry and censorship.
"The new Soviet film." 1 (March 1932) 19–25. Review of *The Road to Life*.

Young Israel (Cincinnati). "The poet of the movie." illus. 24 (October 1931) 5–7. Biographical and critical notes on Jean Epstein. Written for children.

Book and Pamphlet. "Holy Hollywood." In Schmalhausen, Samuel D., ed., *Behold America!* New York: Farrar & Rinehart, 1931; p. 537–52. An essay on the spurious art and commercialism of Hollywood.

The Eyes of the Movie (International Pamphlets, No. 38). New York: International Publishers, 1934; 31 pp. An effort to sketch a Marxist interpretation of the American film, made up from scattered notes, ideas, and lecture material, together with portions of published and unpublished articles and reviews selected, edited, and arranged by Irving Lerner. Published posthumously.

Unpublished Manuscripts
"Pop goes the movie." A survey of the life and activities of the pioneer film producer, Sigmund "Pop" Lubin.
"The film in the theatre." Describes the use of cinema devices in theatrical productions.
"A diet of stars." Discusses the acting performances and personalities of movie stars.
"Cinemasters." A review of the book by C. A. Lejeune.
"First films." Notes the arrival of two directorial talents: Rowland Brown and Rouben Mamoulian.
"Maedchen in Uniform." A review of the film.
"Anti-Soviet Cinema." A brief history of anti-Communist films.

INDICES

General Editor's Note: Entries in the index are given with attention to standards of greatest possible accuracy or best acknowledged authority. In many cases, they correct, in effect, the forms as they appear in the text, where these have been left to follow, in the interests of fidelity, the disparate orthographics of the diverse periodicals for which Potamkin wrote, as well as his often vagarious and mischievously inventive usage.

GENERAL INDEX

NAME INDEX

FILM INDEX

(*continued from p. 453*)
nated: there are too many captions, well written though they are. Fewer captions jotted in the staccato brevity of many of the images that pass almost before one sees them—these would have better suited the film's attitude, and not served to weaken (even if in the minutest degree, as the captions do at present) the demanding simplicity and rigorousness of this beautiful work.

The Passion of Jeanne d'Arc is an historical film, but not a costume film; an historical film that is contemporaneous in its universal references. *The Passion of Jeanne d'Arc* is a religious film, but not a sanctimonious film. Life, it urges, is transcendent. It is a transcendent film.

NATIONAL BOARD OF REVIEW MAGAZINE,
January, 1929.

LEWIS JACOBS, author of the long-esteemed *The Rise of the American Film* (also published in this series), is a prize-winning film creator and distinguished film teacher, as well as a critic and scholar. Following early training as a painter, he became a film maker and critic, and worked as a screen writer in Hollywood for several leading film companies. His own films have won five medals at international festivals, as well as 22 citations of merit for direction and cinematography. Jacobs has taught film courses at the City College of New York, the New School for Social Research, and the Graduate School of the Arts of New York University. He is at present on the faculty of the Philadelphia College of Art and in 1976 was awarded that institution's distinguished Silver Star Award. For many years, he has served as American juror at the Venice Film Festival. He has published more than 50 critical articles, edited several collections — *Introduction to the Art of the Movies* (1960), *The Emergence of Film Art* (1968), *The Movies As Medium* (1968), and *The Documentary Tradition* (1971) — and was American Advisory Editor for *The International Encyclopedia of Film* (1972).